Mormons as Citizens of a Communist State

MORMONS AS CITIZENS OF A
COMMUNIST STATE

A Documentary History of the Church of Jesus Christ of Latter-day Saints in East Germany, 1945–1990

Raymond Kuehne

Foreword by Ronald Smelser

THE UNIVERSITY OF UTAH PRESS
Salt Lake City

First published as *Mormonen und Staatsbürger: Eine dokumentierte Geschichte der Kirche Jesu Christi der Heiligen der Letzten Tage in der DDR* by Raymond Kuehne (Hg.), Leipziger Universitätsverlag Press, 2007.

The Defiance House Man colophon is a registered trademark of the University of Utah Press. It is based upon a four-foot-tall, Ancient Puebloan pictograph (late PIII) near Glen Canyon, Utah.

14 13 12 11 10 1 2 3 4 5

LIBRARY OF CONGRESS CATALOGING-IN-PUBLICATION DATA

Mormonen und Staatsbürger. English.

Mormons as citizens of a communist state : a documentary history of the Church of Jesus Christ of Latter-day Saints in East Germany, 1945-1990 / Raymond Kuehne.

p. cm.

Includes bibliographical references.

ISBN 978-0-87480-993-0 (pbk. : alk. paper) 1. Church of Jesus Christ of Latter-day Saints—Germany (East)—History. 2. Germany (East)—Church history. I. Kuehne, Raymond M. II. Title.

BX8617.G4M6713 2010

289.3'43109045—dc22

2010007791

Cover illustration and design by Jessica A. Booth.

Printed and bound by Sheridan Books, Inc., Ann Arbor, Michigan.

Contents

Tables

Acknowledgments

I am pleased to acknowledge those who played a significant role in the preparation of this book. First and foremost, I am indebted to Henry Burkhardt for his seminar about the origins of the Freiberg Temple and his subsequent willingness to answer all my questions on numerous occasions. I also am indebted to the many members who supported and encouraged me, provided valuable materials, and participated in interviews that augment and complement the official records. My own interviews were carefully transcribed in Germany by volunteers: Karin Bauerfeind, Karla Liebscher, and Jessika Schlegel. I also thank the staff of the Church History and Archives Department in Salt Lake City, who provided access to numerous essential documents.

A special note of appreciation is due my wife, Genie, who encouraged and supported me throughout the various stages of this project. She will finally be able to read the full story that she had heard previously only in part, as I translated and read to her portions of the preceding German edition, which was published in January 2008 by the Leipzig University Press under the title *Mormonen und Staatsbürger: Eine dokumentierte Geschichte der Kirche Jesu Christi der Heiligen der Letzten Tage in der DDR.*

Foreword

Raymond Kuehne has written an intriguing history of the Church of Jesus Christ of Latter-day Saints in the former German Democratic Republic (GDR)—and much more besides. Starting with the initial goal of documenting the history of the Freiberg Temple in Saxony, the only Latter-day Saint temple ever built in a Communist country, he expanded his story to include the whole of East Germany. Moreover, he places his history of the LDS Church in a larger setting of social, cultural, and even political life in the former GDR.

The author raises some intriguing questions. How do we define religious freedom in an atheistic, totalitarian dictatorship? What were the boundaries between church and state in a Communist country? What activities did such a regime seek to ban as something dangerous to those in power? To what extent could the religiously inclined accept those limitations without abandoning the beliefs and practices their church expected of them? What conclusions should one draw from the fact that, while other denominations, especially the Evangelical (Lutheran) church, had begun a political opposition movement in the 1980s, the Mormons declined to join? Here we find a major division between the religiously inspired pacifist movement, Swords into Plowshares, and the "render unto Caesar" position of the LDS Church. How successful were the Mormons at practicing their faith, while remaining good "citizens" of a Communist state? These are the major themes of the book.

Kuehne's book is not primarily an interpretive study; the author eschews a critical stance on the LDS Church in East Germany. Rather, he tries to present his material in as neutral fashion as possible, largely in the form of primary sources (government and church documents, interviews, and private letters), thus allowing the reader to reach his or her own conclusions.

As he notes in his first chapter, the GDR was not the first totalitarian dictatorship in which Mormons were obliged to live. Rather it was preceded by the Nazi regime, a fascist state, which was more accepting of religion than the Communists later, but tried to bend the various denominations to its will and enlist them in its total war effort. Here again under Hitler, as later, most Mormons functioned as good citizens and, while they hated war, nevertheless fought for the Fatherland. And certainly the Relief Society must have had its hands full when the bombing campaign against Germany began in earnest in 1943.

What follows then, from the end of the war to the end of the GDR in 1990, is a history drawn in part from carefully selected (and, when necessary, translated) government and church documents, correspondence, and other sources. The historical context includes the time of the Soviet Military Administration, 1945–1949; life prior to the Berlin Wall, 1949–1961; life behind the Berlin Wall, 1961–1989; and, in several chapters, how the Church reached an understanding with the state and how that rapprochement enabled the Freiberg Temple to be built in 1985 along with new meeting houses. The last few years of the GDR were dramatically marked by the visit in October 1988 of President Thomas Monson with the GDR leader, Chairman Erich Honecker, which Kuehne describes in some detail, which led to the arrival of western missionaries in early March 1989, six months before the fall of the Berlin Wall.

Interspersed within the historical context are chapters that deal specifically with the challenges faced by the Church in its unique setting: how it functioned in a Communist dictatorship; the church-state conundrum; the legal status of the Church; the Church members' own definition of their citizenship; and much about youth, education, and missionary activities.

Moreover, the book is fascinating not just on an official level, but also on a personal one. Rich correspondence reveals much about private life in East Germany; about hard times and opportunities; about refugees and expellees, and how the Church reacted to these problems and opportunities; about food, housing, and travel; and about infrequent but treasured visits from Church dignitaries from the West. There follows a number of appendices, which contain, among other things, descriptions of trips taken by church groups over the years in East Germany.

Kuehne also raises at the end some themes that demand further research: Why, for instance, was there a dramatic increase in conversions between the time when the first missionaries arrived in March 1989 and the fall of the Berlin Wall in November 1989, when, according to some observers, certain impediments remained in place during those years?

Kuehne is in a good position to write and translate this book, which was originally published in German by Leipzig University Press in 2008. Son of a German immigrant family which came to the United States in 1929, Kuehne had his first experience in Germany as a missionary in the late 1950s. The author and his wife served a mission in the Freiberg Temple from 2002 to 2004, where he was inspired to write this history after meeting Henry Burkhardt, the first president of the Freiberg Temple. Burkhardt led the LDS Church in East Germany for thirty-eight years and will be the subject of Kuehne's next book—a biography.

The reader will discover much to learn and absorb in this study, which richly deserved translation. There is much to be gleaned here about religious life as it unfolded in a setting foreign to most American readers, one that posed risks and dangers, but also opportunities to practice a religious faith in an often hostile setting.

Ronald Smelser
Professor of History
University of Utah

Introduction

About 600 B.C., the prophet Jeremiah sent the following counsel to the former inhabitants of the Kingdom of Judah who had been taken captive into Babylon:

> Thus saith the Lord of hosts, the God of Israel, unto all... whom I have caused to be carried away from Jerusalem unto Babylon. Build ye houses, and dwell in them; plant gardens, and eat the fruit of them. Take ye wives, and beget sons and daughters; and take wives for your sons, and give your daughters to husbands, that they may bear sons and daughters, that ye may be increased there, and not diminished. *Seek the peace of the city whither I have caused you to be carried away captive, and pray unto the Lord for it: for in the peace thereof shall ye have peace....* After seventy years be accomplished at Babylon, I will visit you, and perform my good word toward you, in causing you to return to this place. (Jeremiah 29: 4–7, 10; italics added)

While Christians are urged to avoid spiritual Babylon, thousands of members of the Church of Jesus Christ of Latter-day Saints encountered a political version thereof when the Soviet army occupied the eastern part of Germany in 1945 and created the German Democratic Republic (GDR), better known as East Germany. While many members fled to the West, over six thousand remained in their homes. As in Jeremiah's time, they planted gardens, begat sons and daughters, and prayed unto the Lord. This book documents the experiences of those people during the following forty-five years.

Nowhere else in the world did six thousand members of the Church,[1] well organized in branches and districts, suddenly come under the control of an officially atheistic government. How did they interact with a government that attempted to suppress the religious activities of its citizens and their churches? How did they interpret the counsel of the Apostle Paul, to be subject to civil authorities? How did they react when President David O. McKay told them in Berlin in 1952 that if they were good citizens, if they honored and lived in accordance with God's commandments, they and their families would be protected from state-sponsored indoctrination?

This book confirms the obvious, that GDR citizens enjoyed less political, social, educational, and professional freedom than was available across the border in West Germany. However, religious freedom is more difficult to define, and the documents presented in this book challenge many of the traditional assumptions that circulate as fact outside the former GDR. For example, one member stated that "despite all our restrictions, we were able to live the principles of the gospel," and "what God expects of man, that we could do in the GDR." Another insisted, "Whether one wants to hear it or not, we could live in accordance with our convictions. I couldn't expect to have an extensive professional or business career, certainly not. But I must repeat, that we were able to carry out our church activities and live in accordance with our faith."

Do such comments accurately reflect religious life in the GDR? Before answering, readers may wish to consider a basic theological question. What does God expect from every person, regardless of where and when he lives on this earth, and can any government create conditions in which man is incapable of meeting those expectations? While the outward practice of religion can be restricted, can the exercise of God-given moral agency be prevented in any society, under any social or political conditions?

The policies and practices of the GDR's ruling Communist Party throughout most of that regime's existence assumed the eventual demise of organized religion. However, despite its considerable efforts, the regime could not extinguish all religious inclination. Eventually, it had to accept the fact that a segment of society would continue to practice religion and that churches could not be abolished without unacceptable political consequences, both domestic and foreign. The government's eventual acceptance of that fact led to internal debate regarding "acceptable" activities of churches. Similar questions are still asked today in most countries, even in western democracies: what boundaries should exist between church and state, what restrictions should be placed on religious activity, and when does a politically active church cease being primarily a church?

In the latter years of the GDR, the political opposition united under the banner of turning "Swords to Plowshares" and found support within many churches, especially the Evangelical (Lutheran) churches. That movement vigorously protested the worldwide arms race and the GDR's participation therein. However, LDS members did not participate in any political movement, at least not as an institution. Joseph Smith had stated, "We believe in being subject to kings, presidents, rulers, and magistrates, in obeying, honoring, and sustaining the law" (12th Article of Faith). However, did that principle apply to the political circumstances in the GDR?

In preparation for the GDR's twenty-fifth anniversary celebration in 1974, President Burkhardt was asked to submit "facts and materials to describe the relationship of your church to the state, to the GDR society and to issues of world peace." He responded:

> If the Church abandons the area of theology and turns to politics, it becomes, in our opinion, a political party. Of course, service on behalf of our neighbors and for peace is required by the gospel and one cannot be separated from the other. Both should not only be preached on Sunday, but must be practiced daily, not primarily within the church but rather in daily life, at the workplace and in society.... The practice and the form of engagement are left to individuals. In this manner, they become effective citizens, certainly Christian citizens, but with emphasis on the word "citizens."[2]

President Burkhardt's emphasis on the word "citizens," and the relationship between LDS citizens and their atheistic government, is the major theme of this book. Readers will have their personal opinion regarding many of the issues addressed herein, including the principle of separation of church and state, what constitutes freedom of religion and the duties of citizens toward a government that restricts religious activity and discriminates against people of faith in their social, educational, and professional pursuits. The LDS within the GDR held equally varying opinions on these same subjects. The goal of this project is to objectively document those opinions, not to critique or judge them. Therefore, the following chapters consist largely of source documents, reports, letters, and interviews that are presented directly to the reader. Short comments are added only as needed to introduce the relevant documentary evidence.

In November 2003, I interviewed many teenage members of the Church who had come to Dresden to listen to President Thomas S. Monson. I chose that age group intentionally, since most of them had been born after the collapse of the GDR. I asked each one individually, "When the history of the Church in the GDR is written, what topics should be included?" Following are their most frequent suggestions:

- The building of the temple
- Missionary and youth activities
- The difficulties members encountered in school and employment
- What members learned through their experiences
- Information regarding their meeting houses
- Whether they were satisfied with their circumstances
- How some of them managed to travel to the Swiss Temple
- How missionaries from the West arrived before the fall of communism

The following chapters address those questions and many more. While this book encourages readers to ponder the political, theological, or philosophical questions posed earlier, it also can be read simply to find answers to the questions asked by the young people interviewed in Dresden, i.e., "How did the Mormons live in the GDR, what experiences did they have in their education and professional pursuits, did they own their own meeting houses, what youth activities were allowed, why were they permitted to build a temple, how were missionary activities conducted, why did the government permit missionaries from the West to enter the GDR, and why were young men permitted to leave the GDR for missions abroad?"

In summary, this book presents a wide range of documents that show how the Church functioned in the GDR and how its members were able to live both as active Christians and as respected citizens in that country.

Some background concerning the author and the origins of this project may be useful. I was born in the United States of parents who left Germany in 1929. From 1958 until 1960, I served in the North German Mission, which coordinated activities in the northern part of West Germany and all of East Germany from its office in West Berlin. However, only GDR citizens served as missionaries in their own country. No wall separated East and West Berlin at that time, and the subway and elevated trains crossed from one part of the city to the other. East Berliners crossed daily to work in West Berlin or to attend church at the nearest West Berlin branch, and we crossed into East Berlin to attend performances at the Staatsoper and other theaters. Obviously, the open border within Berlin offered an escape path for GDR citizens who lived in East Berlin or elsewhere in East Germany, and we tried not to stare at obviously nervous people who were traveling westward with us, perhaps illegally. Often, they were taken off the trains before crossing into West Berlin, searched, and questioned about their reasons for being in East Berlin.

In 1982, the Church announced that a temple would be built in Freiberg-Saxony, the only temple ever built in a Communist country. I later served in that temple with my wife for eighteen months (2002–2004), where we became acquainted with Henry Burkhardt, who led the Church in the GDR for thirty-eight years. He also was the first president of the Freiberg Temple, following its dedication in 1985. One day, I asked him to discuss the origins of the temple with the temple missionaries. After a fascinating two-hour "seminar," we asked him where we could read more about the subject and were surprised when he said that the temple's history had never been written. The broader history of the Church in East Germany also had never been researched. A few weeks later, Burkhardt gave me eleven pages he had written shortly after the temple's groundbreaking ceremony in 1983. That manuscript became the start of my own research project. Within the limited opportunities available while serving in Freiberg at that time, I prepared a short article about the temple's origins, which was published in 2004.[3]

At the same time, I often spoke with the temple recorder, Karlheinz Leonhardt, who told me of his interest in compiling a history of the Church in the GDR. We discussed how such a challenging project could be undertaken, what documents and other source materials were available, and who could help with the project. Through contacts in the United States, I became aware of documents available in the Church archives in Salt Lake City, including government and mission records and oral interviews conducted by Church archivists shortly after the Wende.[4] Several members also indicated their willingness to provide their own documents. As a result, the project soon evolved from a study of the origins of the Freiberg Temple into a broader study of the relationship between the GDR and the Church and the effects of that relationship on the religious and secular life of Church members.

All German language sources cited in this book, including government documents, published articles and books, documents provided by members, and oral interviews have been translated by myself, and I am responsible for their accuracy. References to documents found in the LDS Church Archives are cited in the text by their Archive file number, beginning with LR, CR, or MS. East German government records not from the Church Archives are cited with a DO or DY abbreviation. In each case, the full citation is found in the Bibliography. Interviews are cited in the text by name and year. The years 1989 to 1991 are in the LDS Church Archives, 2003 to 2007 are in my possession.

Chronological History

Table 0.1. A Brief Chronology

Political History	Church History
Pre-1871 Germany consisted of independent states and principalities joined in loose confederations.	**1852** The first German Mission opened in Hamburg and closed in 1855; later the Swiss-Italian -German Mission included a few German members.
1871 The German Empire was established under Prussian leadership.	**1893** Most of the members of the Swiss-German Mission lived in northern and eastern Germany.
1914 World War I began.	
1918 The German Empire was replaced by the postwar Weimar Republic.	**1929** German members immigrated to America in large numbers until 1933.
1933 Hitler became chancellor of Germany.	**1938** Separate West German and East German missions were established.
1939 World War II began.	**1939** Americans left Germany. German members were appointed to lead the two missions.
1945 War ended; Soviet occupation in the East.	
1949 The Soviets created East Germany, or the German Democratic Republic (GDR).	**1946** Members in the Soviet Zone were supervised by mission presidents in West Berlin, via an East German counselor (Henry Burkhardt after 1952).
	1955 Swiss Temple dedicated.
1961 The Berlin Wall closed the last opening between West and East Germany.	**1968** Elder Monson's first visit to the GDR (in Görlitz).
	1969 Elder Monson created the Dresden Mission, led by President Henry Burkhardt.
1971 Erich Honecker replaced Walter Ulbricht as GDR head of state.	**1972** President Burkhardt allowed to attend General Conference in Salt Lake City for the first time.
1977 The GDR allowed the Evangelical Church to build new chapels.	**1978** The GDR suggested the Church build a temple.
	1982 Freiberg Stake established.
	1983 Groundbreaking for the Freiberg Temple.
	1984 Leipzig Stake established.
	1985 President Hinckley dedicated the temple.
1987 An Evangelical church in East Berlin was raided due to its political activities. Churches were warned about political activities.	**1988** President Monson met with Erich Honecker.
	1989 Church missionaries entered the GDR, seven months before the Berlin Wall fell.
1990 End of the German Democratic Republic.	

1 Germany before 1945

With the help of the Lord, it has been possible to maintain the East German Mission during [World War II] in the condition you knew it previously. (Acting Mission Presidency to President Thomas E. McKay, January 5, 1946, CR 271 40)

While this book focuses on the history of the Church of Jesus Christ of Latter-day Saints in the German Democratic Republic, every history requires an introduction that enables the reader to appreciate the story in its broader context. This chapter provides a short review of the history of the Church in Germany prior to the 1945 Soviet occupation of eastern Germany and the establishment of a separate East Germany.

It is well known that the Church's initial missionary activities and its greatest success in the nineteenth century took place in the northeastern region of the United States and in the British Isles. Less appreciated is the fact that in the first half of the twentieth century, more converts came from Germany than from any other non-English-speaking country. However, the twentieth-century success in Germany was not evident in the nineteenth century because the established "state" churches in Germany used their influence to prevent almost every form of missionary activity. Various forms of harassment by the police and even imprisonment were frequent and legal in those days.

The first German mission was organized in 1852. In the following year, 128 persons were baptized and 50 emigrated to Zion. At the end of 1854, the mission reported that its 69 remaining members were organized in four branches in northern Germany. One of the best known converts of that period, Karl Maeser, was baptized in the Elbe River near Dresden, in the Kingdom of Saxony. He presided over a new Dresden branch in 1855, but was forced to leave Germany the next year. Active missionary work in Germany ended shortly thereafter. Maeser later became the principal of the Brigham Young Academy. After 1861, Germany was included in the Swiss, Italian, and German Mission. In 1897, it again became a separate mission with 67 missionaries and 1,028 members in five districts—Berlin, Dresden, Frankfurt/Main, Hamburg, and Stuttgart. In 1904, Germany was under the supervision of the Swiss and German Mission.[1]

All American missionaries were withdrawn from Germany in 1914 prior to the start of World War I. This period in Church history has been well documented by Dr. Gilbert W. Scharffs. He wrote that membership increased, many Relief Societies were organized, and most meetings continued to be held during that war. Almost three hundred convert baptisms were performed annually, and that number almost doubled in 1919 after the war. He reported that this "progress was merely the beginning of a period of rapid LDS membership growth in Germany."[2]

The defeat of the German Empire in World War I and the democratic reforms associated with the new Weimar Republic removed the legal restrictions against proselyting activities, although some forms of discrimination and harassment continued. Daniel Ludlow wrote that "the rigors of war and defeat had produced a poverty and humility among the people that helped make them more receptive to the gospel message." Ludlow reported that there were more LDS in Germany in 1930 than in any other country outside the United States.[3]

The growth in membership after World War I is seen in the following statistics from the Swiss-German Mission in 1924 (see Table 1.1). These statistics have been arranged by region in order to highlight the faster growing eastern German districts, which would later constitute the East German Mission.

The faster growth of the Church in the eastern regions of Germany was accompanied by a similar rate of growth among other small religious organizations after World War I. Historians have recognized that the eastern German provinces, especially the area of Saxony, were more receptive to the socially conservative messages of these smaller churches, which were able to expand their proselyting activities during the Weimar Republic. The rapid growth of the Mormon Church in this region led to the division of the Swiss-German Mission in 1925. The western districts of Germany remained in the Swiss-German Mission, while the eastern districts, plus the Vienna district, became the German-Austrian Mission with a total of 6,125 members. By the end of 1930, the latter mission had grown to 7,431 members, with 138 missionaries from the United States and 13 local full-time missionaries.[4]

Membership growth slowed in the 1930s after Adolf Hitler and his National Socialist (Nazi) Party took control of the German government. Daniel Ludlow wrote:

> The coming of Hitler to power changed life for the Church and its members, not only in Germany but eventually in the rest of Europe as well. Soon, the omnipresent police state was making life in Germany more difficult for the Saints, especially the missionaries; many anticipated the Church would be closed down, but it never was. Both members and missionaries made every effort to get along with the regime while rejecting its excesses. What was important to them was to

Table 1.1. Swiss-German Mission Statistics at the End of 1924[1]

District	Baptisms	Membership
Berlin	145	914
Breslau	123	552
Chemnitz	126	1,337
Dresden	126	713
Königsberg	169	841
Leipzig	113	619
Stettin	192	772
SUBTOTAL	994	5,748
Cologne	114	601
Frankfurt/Main	71	517
Hamburg	187	1,239
Hannover	113	606
Stuttgart	218	995
SUBTOTAL	703	3,958
Basel	9	180
Bern	34	523
Zurich	38	507
SUBTOTAL	81	1,210
Vienna	14	186
TOTAL	1,792	11,102

1 Scharffs, 64.

be able to continue to preach the gospel, to stay in the country, and to keep the branches together and prospering after so many years of struggle. Moreover, their numbers were small and they had little leverage with the regime.[5]

The East German Mission

The German-speaking missions were realigned again on January 1, 1938, probably as a response to the emerging political situation and the threat of war. Switzerland and Austria were placed in a new Swiss-Austrian Mission, while the western districts of Germany became known as the West German Mission and the eastern districts became the East German Mission. The latter, headquartered in Berlin, was led by Alfred C. Rees and included almost eight thousand members in the provinces of Saxony, Brandenburg, Mecklenburg, Pomerania, Silesia, West Prussia, and East Prussia. It should be noted that the borders of the new East German Mission, by coincidence, closely matched the area of Germany that would come under Soviet control after World War II, except for the province of Thuringia, which was in the West German Mission until 1945.

With war threatening, President Rees was released on August 16, 1939, and Thomas E. McKay traveled from Basel to Berlin to familiarize himself with the situation in that mission. One week later, the Church instructed all American missionaries to leave Germany. President McKay returned to Basel after designating three German members to lead the mission in his absence. Herbert Klopfer became the "Mission Supervisor"[6] and Richard Ranglack and Paul Langheinrich were his counselors (LR 2428 2).

President McKay left Switzerland in April 1940, leaving all of the units of the Church on the European continent under local control. The acting leaders of the East German Mission ably directed the affairs of that mission for the next seven years, until November 1946, but their activities are rarely noted in published historical accounts. For example, a short article about the East German Mission by Preston Nibley, published in the August 1956 issue of the *Relief Society Magazine*,[7] made no mention of the local leadership whatsoever and implied that the mission was leaderless during those years. Richard Ranglack was living in Salt Lake City when the article appeared. Writing to Elder Ezra T. Benson on August 31, 1956, Ranglack summarized the extensive activities of the local leaders and expressed his hope that this information would "fill the gap" in Nibley's article. "I would also like to ask," he wrote, "how it was possible to have such a gap in our Church history" (LR 2428 2).

Although the East German Mission functioned effectively without direct American leadership during the war, acting President Klopfer was called to military duty in February 1940. Initially, he was stationed close to Berlin. His wife, Erna, explained in a December 1957 letter, "He came home every other weekend, and his counselors visited him on the other weekend to discuss mission problems and activities. He could also place telephone calls to the mission office as necessary" (LR 2428 2).

Letters from Berlin to Church Headquarters

Written communication between the mission and Church leaders in America continued during the first two years of the war. In February 1940, President Rees sent instructions to Brother Klopfer, together with a personal letter from Elder Joseph Fielding Smith and a second letter addressed to all members of the mission, in which he asked them to fully support Klopfer and his counselors. President Thomas E. McKay, who was assigned to oversee all missions in Europe, maintained a file of correspondence from the East German Mission that provides significant insight into conditions during those years. Most of the correspondence from Berlin was either written in English or translated by Sister Klopfer, who was fluent in that language. However, mail leaving Germany was subject to being read by government officials, which most likely influenced what was written. Nevertheless, the following excerpts from letters in McKay's file (CR 271 40) show that the mission continued to function under its acting leadership during this time:

> *April 16, 1940, Erna Klopfer to President Heber J. Grant:* Inasmuch as it is impossible for my husband, Elder Herbert Klopfer, for the time being to write to you, he has asked me to answer your letter of November 30, 1939, which arrived here just a few weeks ago.... Our districts and

branches are in good condition, meetings are being held regularly and are, as a rule, well attended.

April 16, 1940, Erna Klopfer to Thomas E. McKay: You may rest assured that all financial and other transactions of the East German Mission are taken care of in the best manner possible. My husband's counselors and the three lady missionaries in the office are working full time to "keep the ball rolling."... We are in constant touch with Brother Klopfer and he is informed in all matters, in fact so far he has been able in his spare moments to give directions and make decisions for the continuation of the work.

May 10, 1940, Erna Klopfer to Alfred C. Rees: In closing, permit me to say just a few words about the conditions in general. We sincerely hope that there are some [news]papers in the USA that are transmitting the truth about conditions in Europe. Germany is just as safe, no, much safer now than it has ever been before. All inhabitants of Berlin are continuing their daily jobs, the children go to school, the parks are filled with jolly people after the day's work, and the theaters and opera houses are filled to capacity every night. All Germans go to bed in the evening with full assurance that those keeping guard on the borders and in the air are protecting the country. We have plenty to eat. Everyone is conscious of the fact that war times of necessity require restrictions along certain lines, and every German is satisfied with the restrictions placed upon him because of lack of certain things, because he knows that he is safe. There is no need for the least worry.

September 9, 1940, Missionary Johanna Berger to Thomas E. McKay: In order to give you evidence of the fact that in spite of all efforts of Germany's enemies, normal life in all our cities and villages carries on as before, we submit the following facts to you.... Church activities have not changed in the least; regular services are held wherever our branches exist with at least the usual number of listeners or in quite a few instances an increased audience. Spring conferences have been held in all districts; every one of them was most successful. Prayers of gratitude are constantly uttered, for the Lord has protected us from harm and evil; the prayers in our services are also for those who stand far away protecting the nation and fighting for the rights of our country. Fall conferences started September 1st and will be as successful as ever before. Enthusiasm is felt everywhere; faith and confidence are evident throughout the country. Every German in his place performs his duty in loyalty and fidelity. The *Sonntagsgruß*[8] reaches every home of our members and friends; they are grateful for its messages. The Sunday Schools are well attended; the wives and mothers of our soldiers are lending their helping hands to the different institutions for the welfare of the needy, the bereaved and the wounded. We have contributed our share to the Red Cross; our families are all well taken care of by the institutions of our government. During the first eight months of 1940 the following statistical changes occurred: Members married members 36; baptized 55 [whether these were convert baptisms or baptisms of children of record is not stated]; children blessed 67; ordinations performed 77. Tithing increased 15 percent; Fast Offerings 2 percent; general donations doubled. So you see there is not the least cause for worry; all is well here, awaiting a speedy victory.

August 15, 1941, Acting Presidency to Alfred C. Rees: Although many of our leading officers, including our mission president, five of our proven district presidents and many of our branch officers, are far away from their homeland, fulfilling their duty as patriots in these perilous times of struggle of the German people, those elder brethren who have been called to fill the vacancies are satisfactorily taking care of their tasks everywhere. . . . As far as the war itself is concerned there are no differences between the thoughts and ideas of the entire German people and the Church of Jesus Christ of Latter-day Saints. The German people do not like war. This war has been forced upon us, and we are obligated to defend our country, as was also expressed by President Joseph F. Smith in his book *Gospel Doctrine,* page 419: "And while I think it is wrong, wickedly wrong, to force war upon any nation, or upon any people, I believe it is righteous and just for every people to defend their own lives and their own liberties, and their own homes, with the last drop of their blood. I believe it is right, and I believe that the Lord will sustain any people in defending their own liberty to worship God according to the dictates of their conscience, any people trying to preserve their wives and children from the ravages of the war." Thanks to the bravery of the German army, our land has been spared the ravages of war, with the exception of some damage done by the British Air Force. As long as this struggle of our nation at this time is for the protection of the German homeland and the German people, we believe that God will help us. This gives us peace at this difficult time. . . . We hope that the American people as such will turn their backs to the evil warmongers in the USA, and will not participate in a war against Germany. We know that you will use your influence in this respect. May you be understood correctly.

Herbert Klopfer's Instruction to Priesthood Leaders

Following the departure of the American leaders, Klopfer and his counselors took great care to maintain Church doctrine and practice as it should be and to correct the inevitable deviations that occur from time to time in Church units throughout the world, in the absence of effective communication. For example, on September 5, 1941, he sent the following guidance to branch and district leaders, which addressed specific issues and practices that he and his counselors encountered as they traveled through the mission:

> We consider it necessary to correct several false opinions within the mission.
>
> 1. Little children should be brought to the branch soon after their birth to receive from the authorized elder a blessing and a name chosen by their parents. . . . Neither the child nor the parents suffer any disadvantage if a child must leave this earth prior to receiving that priesthood blessing.
>
> 2. The opinion is heard at times, that greater blessings derive from holding a higher position in the priesthood. That is true only to the degree in which, for example, an elder faithfully carries out his assigned duties and responsibilities, but no greater blessings are received solely by advancing from priest to elder.
>
> 3. Relief Society meetings have not been held at times when no priesthood holder was present, although the sisters were present and prepared. The opinion that the sisters can meet only in the presence of a priesthood holder is incorrect. The branch president should be informed about the activity of the Relief Society, like every other auxiliary organization, but neither he nor his representative must necessarily be present when the sisters come together, although it is desirable that the priesthood holders support the sisters in their assignments.
>
> 4. Some branch presidents hold firmly to the false belief that only brothers may be asked to pray in sacrament meetings or that a priesthood holder must give the opening prayer in Sunday School. Although priesthood holders should be fully involved in giving prayers in the meetings of the Church, our sisters should not be excluded or restricted in such callings. They are just as worthy as the brothers to be the voice of the entire branch in prayers to the Lord.
>
> We wish to take this opportunity to draw the attention of our fellow workers to other aspects of Church work and request your due regard:
>
> The branch president administers the entire welfare activity of the branch, including fast offerings and the Relief Society. The Relief Society should not provide support to any family without the prior approval of the branch president. He, in turn, will insure that no needy members are ignored and that no duplication takes place, such as a family receiving fast offerings and Relief Society support in the same month.
>
> No one wishing to receive a blessing from an elder for health reasons should be denied. However, we do not want to reduce this holy ordinance to a meaningless, everyday occurrence by too frequent usage. It is suggested that the proper use of this ordinance be addressed

> from time to time in talks. There is no rule in the Church that would prevent non-members from receiving a blessing. However, an elder must be especially careful in this regard, and convince himself in advance, that such friends of the Church understand the purpose of this ordinance. (MS 8242)

Klopfer was transferred to France in late 1943 and then to Italy and Denmark. In March 1944, he was sent to the Russian front, where he was wounded and taken prisoner. He died in Russia the following spring. In anticipation of his absence, he had given his two counselors detailed written instructions for continued leadership of the mission. In that document, he told them that they had equal authority: "When you cannot reach agreement on fundamental matters, the issue should remain undecided until you reach a mutually agreeable decision" (CR 271 40). In his absence, Richard Ranglack assumed the overall leadership and Paul Langheinrich focused on the auxiliary organizations, welfare, and genealogy activities.

In Ranglack's letter of August 1956 to Elder Benson, he reviewed some of the activities conducted by himself and Langheinrich during the war:

> Brother Klopfer was called into military service February 20, 1940. Now the responsibility was placed on my shoulders, Brother Langheinrich and the other brethren.... From this time forth I, as the representative of the Church of Jesus Christ of Latter-day Saints in Berlin, had to go almost every month or two to the police headquarters in Berlin, department Geheime Staatspolizei [secret police], to answer questions on church matters. I was especially asked about our Tenth Article of Faith, our position concerning membership in the NSDAP [National Socialist German Workers Party], Hitler youth, bearers of the knight's cross, etc. The singing of songs that contained the word "Zion" was prohibited. I was also asked concerning our meeting halls, conference mottos, the gathering of Israel, the American church, and our views about the war. I had the responsibility that all the sermons given were of purely religious nature.
>
> Every printer in Germany was prohibited by order of the NSDAP to print books, pamphlets, etc., of a religious nature. Nevertheless I knew three printers who were willing to print for the East German Mission if they had the paper. At one time, three thousand hymn books, copies of The Pearl of Great Price and all kinds of forms were printed. We also printed part of *Jesus the Christ* by James E. Talmadge. Brother Martin Werner Hoope did the translation.
>
> We held district conferences twice a year since the spring of 1940 in the following districts: Königsberg, Danzig, Schneidemühl, Stettin, and Breslau. After the war, visits to these five districts had to be discontinued, since the Russians and the Poles would not give us per-

mission to do so. We also had district conferences in Dresden, Leipzig, Chemnitz, Zwickau, Erzgebirge, Spreewald, and Berlin.

At the office of the secret police in Berlin, I had to promise that we would only talk about religious subjects in our meetings and conferences. Keeping this in mind, we selected a motto for each conference, and we admonished the speakers to keep this motto in mind and not to talk about political matters.

In a few smaller towns, the local police went a little too far and prohibited our meetings; however, we were able, through personal contact or correspondence, to change the minds of these people and were again able to hold our meetings. (LR 2428 2)

Additional details about conditions in the mission were provided by Paul Langheinrich in a "Short Report on the Auxiliary Organizations from 1939 to July 1945," dated August 7, 1945, which was translated by Colonel John R. Barnes, an American army officer in Berlin, and sent to Thomas E. McKay:

Sunday School: The Sunday School was sustained in every respect throughout the mission, although the war did have some effect since many of the children were sent elsewhere for safety. Instruction manuals were on hand at all times until the first of 1945. The preparation of these manuals was done by the best members of the mission. In December 1944 we delivered Sunday School manuals covering the whole year of 1945 to each branch, since we anticipated chaos concerning future transportation and a period where communication with the branches would be impossible. We are now working toward the gathering of all dispersed members and anticipate returning to previous levels of attendance before the end of the year.

Relief Society: The true purpose for which the Relief Society was organized by the Lord was truly realized during the war. This organization also had its manuals, which, in the judgement of the sisters, were and still are very good. For the centennial celebration in 1942 [Orson Hyde's pamphlet, *Ein Ruf aus der Wüste—A Cry from the Wilderness,* was published in Frankfurt/Main in 1842], we distributed a jubilee manual jointly throughout the East and West German missions. Although we lost all books and materials in the fire of the mission office in 1943, we will, nevertheless, acquire as far as possible a copy of each manual that was printed and distributed during the war and send them to the General Authorities for inspection.

We began our real Relief Society assistance in 1943 when the greatest destruction began and many members lost all of their possessions. Members from every part of the mission contributed linen, clothes, household articles, furniture and almost anything that the needy members required. So much was contributed in two months that we asked the members to temporarily discontinue sending contributions to the mission, but to retain them in the separate branches. Demand for relief was very high. For example, thirty-five families of Königsberg were made destitute in one night. Thru the Relief Society, it was possible to care for the needy with almost every necessity in the shortest of time. As protection against destruction of gathered contributions, we established three storage buildings among members located in the countryside; and two of them are still stocked with necessities that we can use to help many destitute members who are still wandering about the country. One of the places fell into the hands of the Poles and has more than likely been pillaged and robbed. The members excelled and surpassed all expectations in making contributions. Of the goods received, over 80 percent was either new or in perfect condition. The members of the Relief Society were true to the church in every possible manner, both spiritual and practical. We brought members to Saxony who were in the most desperate circumstances, and many demonstrated that they were prepared to live the United Order. Only a very few needed to be removed from the refugee communities.

The Mutual Improvement Association: This organization could not function as intended because of many restrictions and prohibitions during the National Socialist period and during the war. As a substitute, an evening hour was organized, and the Beehive and Gleaner girls program continued at a reduced level. Boy Scout work was forbidden. An entertainment committee attempted to carry out several programs and some of the results were successful.

Primary Association: This organization was forbidden, but we held classes in some districts under the name of Primary Children. Manuals were distributed for junior and senior children, and under the circumstances, the classes were also very successful. Because of the forced dispersion of children and mothers in the last year, it has been almost impossible to continue most classes.

Genealogy: The big genealogy effort begun in 1938 was continued until 1942 without hindrance from the war, but difficulties arose later when the books and archives were secured for safekeeping. However, in Saxony the work has continued. Four young sisters were trained by us and are conducting genealogy research. We will have to do our utmost to locate the old records again in most localities, since a central government no longer exists in Germany, and no one is authorized or able to return those items. The government's bureau of genealogical research had made photostatic copies of over 50% of all German church books. The films must have been preserved somewhere in fireproof and bombproof vaults. We are trying with all our might to find out where

> these are hidden so that we can prevent their destruction by ignorant third parties and, if possible, to get them into the hands of the Church. Our own records were placed in several banks for safekeeping, but we don't yet know whether these have been destroyed by the Russian ransacking, since access to our strong boxes has been impossible to date.... Money for genealogy work is in several bank accounts, and it is our great desire that the Church won't forget about this money when other Church money, which also is frozen, is released.
>
> The slogan of the mission presidency during the entire war was: The war is not our affair, we didn't start it and cannot end it, but we can live and proclaim the gospel. None of our faithful members should suffer when it lies within our power to prevent it. We can say that God has truly helped us. He has inspired and blessed us so that we can truly say: "Many miracles have taken place in the East German Mission." With the Lord's help, we, His called servants, will work with all our might and strength as long as He leaves us in our callings, to focus on the welfare of the members in our mission, and help them as much as possible. (LR 2428 2)

Additional excerpts from Langheinrich's report regarding conditions in the mission after the war are found in the next chapter.

2 Soviet Military Administration 1945–1949

The Russians are apparently offering no objections to our religious activities. (Col. John R. Barnes to Thomas E. McKay, July 13, 1945, CR 271 40)

At no time had we thought that the Russians would help us in church matters, but we must say that at the present time we are having no trouble because of religious intolerance. (Acting mission presidency to Thomas E. McKay, January 5, 1946, CR 271 40)

Typical descriptions of the Church in Germany after the war begin with accounts of Elder Benson's arrival in March 1946. However, the war ended in May 1945, and the acting presidency that led the East German Mission during the war continued to do so through 1946. This chapter describes their relationship with officials of the Soviet Military Administration in Germany (SMAD), efforts to provide food and lodging for members, especially for the refugees from the former eastern provinces, their imprisonment by German officials for two weeks in October 1945, and other events prior to the arrival of the new mission president, Walter Stover, in late November 1946.

The first postwar communication between Church headquarters and the mission leadership was established by LDS army officers assigned to the American occupation forces. Two of them, Colonel John R. Barnes and Major Donald C. Corbett, are quoted frequently in this chapter. Barnes had served in the West German Mission until the evacuation of American missionaries in 1939. He arrived in Berlin in early July 1945 and began to send reports, his own and those written by the mission leaders, to Thomas E. McKay in Salt Lake City. Corbett arrived in Berlin in August 1945, and became the LDS servicemen's group leader. He had served as mission secretary and district president in Berlin prior to the war. These and other LDS servicemen provided valuable assistance to mission leaders, within the restrictions established by their American commanders. Fraternization with the local population was officially prohibited, but the duties of these two men enabled them to maintain significant and effective contact with the German leadership, who often sought their assistance and advice.

Reports from Berlin

Excerpts from reports written by Colonel Barnes and sent to President McKay describe the condition of the mission in 1945. They are taken from McKay's file in the Church Archives (CR 271 40):

> *July 13, 1945:* The presidency as it now stands is Richard Ranglack, Mission President, Paul Langheinrich and Max Jeske, counselors. In addition, there are four lady missionaries active. They are Angela Patermann, Renate Berger, Helga Birth, and Ingrid Bendler. They are running things in the mission office and in and around Berlin. The presidency is devoting its time to taking care of the outlying districts and branches. They are now on their second tour of the mission since the fall of Berlin. The first was two or three weeks ago. They started out on their bicycles, but had them taken from them and continued on foot and by hitchhiking on wagons or whatever they could use. It was really traveling without purse or scrip. They made a preliminary survey and started things rolling to care for our displaced members. They are now making a tour of Saxony, Chemnitz, Leipzig, Zwickau, Cottbus, Annaberg and Berlin. It is quite interesting to note that they have had almost continuous contact between districts here, though practically none with the West German Mission, nor has the West German Mission had very good communications within itself.
>
> *August 10, 1945:* In spite of their need, the members are not disheartened, but are looking forward to further growth of the Church and increase in related activities. They are not afraid of the future. Their spirit is perhaps better than ever before, particularly the spirit of cooperation. During the last months of the war, the members started collecting excess clothing and necessities into safe places. Now camps or colonies are being formed on a cooperative basis. Displaced members are gathering at Cottbus, Chemnitz, and other places and there they are finding help from other members. Buildings have been obtained. The stock of stored clothing and food is being used to take care of those who have nothing. In one house you may find a dozen families living cooperatively. In many ways it is a carry back to the early days of the Church when the Saints suffered so much and were driven closer together by the suffering.
>
> The mission presidency is due back soon from its second tour of the mission.... They helped in the organization of relief centers for the members and obtained buildings and necessities for the bombed out and displaced persons. On their present journey, they are traveling by rail. Cooperation on the part of the Russians who occupy almost the

whole of the East German Mission is all that is to be asked. There is no hindrance, but to the contrary, there is cooperation. The outlook is definitely good. There are at present 12 districts, 65 branches, 221 elders, and 410 members of the Aaronic Priesthood. The total membership is 7,610.

August 19, 1945: From the Russians we have obtained permission to buy food from the farms, procure a truck, purchase cattle, purchase cloth for clothing, and enter the lock boxes of the Church at the banks as soon as it can be arranged.

August 30, 1945: Three of the local brethren are on the road again. They have word that all of the refugees in the Saxony area are being refused ration cards for the next month, and so they are going there to organize assistance.... The brethren left yesterday morning armed with plenty of letters of authority and identification from the Russians. They are going to set up refugee camps for the members in the area of Cottbus. It is planned to set up installations for 50 members each in some small hotels and the like, which some of the members and friends there own. With the authority obtained from the Russians, purchases will be made from farmers to lay in a stock of food in each camp to last for 40 weeks.... We also have authority to buy material to make clothing for the needy.... Here in Berlin we are getting a quarter -ton of soup bones from a Russian Army sausage factory every day. These are distributed among the members to aid in their nourishment problems. It is not costing us anything.

Paul Langheinrich's report of August 7, 1945, cited in the previous chapter, includes the following summary of the mission's efforts to feed Church members after the war:

Since the end of the war, the nutrition and feeding of the members in most sections of the East German Mission has been a catastrophe. The members in Saxony in the Erzgebirge lived for days on end only on potato peelings. The brethren of the mission presidency visited this locality in spite of many difficulties, and it was possible with the help of the Lord to assist these members and relieve many of their needs. In the worst places—Annaberg/Buchholz and Schwarzenberg in the Erzgebirge—with permission granted after a visit to the Russian commanding officer in Annaberg, we slaughtered a 16 ½ Zentner ox [Zentner = 112 U.S. lbs.], a pig and a calf. We divided them among the members according to their needs. Also, oatmeal, grain and potatoes were located and now are on their way to this locality. A kettle was provided for a common kitchen in the meeting house and good meals will now be distributed to all tithe payers of Annaberg/Buchholz.

> A small farm that belongs to a member was declared church property for the present time of emergency, and all products, except for a little that must be given to the government, are divided among the members of the branch. The mission leaders will do all they can to help the members.
>
> About 150 members are now gathered in a refugee facility in the meeting house in Cottbus, because they are not able to return to their homes and they cannot obtain ration cards elsewhere. The local brethren, especially Brother Wagner in Annaberg, with the help of the branch president, Brother Schramm, are working untiringly for the members. In Cottbus, it is the district president, Brother Lehnig, who is caring for the members. It is our desire to arrange one or two more camps, since some necessities of life are in very short supply in Cottbus. Fats, milk and sugar are mostly needed.

Despite the mission's considerable efforts and the cooperation of the Russians, finding enough food for the refugees was a constant and serious problem. On September 14, 1945, Langheinrich wrote to Barnes:

> Tomorrow, about two hundred members, who no longer have a home or a homeland and who are not receiving ration cards, are moving to Wolfsgrün, where I have leased a nice home.... While the Soviet officials have given me permission to buy food anywhere within their Zone, it is difficult to obtain anything since all goods are being kept off the market. It would be different if we could offer a secure currency. That is the purpose of my letter. Would it be possible for the Church Presidency to provide a large sum, perhaps $30,000 to $40,000 in cash? (CR 271 40)

Barnes sent Langheinrich's letter to Thomas McKay on the same day. In his own accompanying letter, he said that Langheinrich is looked upon as another Brigham Young by the members, and "it is well deserved." Regarding the facility in Wolfsgrün, Barnes wrote, "It will be a wonderful refugee camp, but food is the problem. Full authority is available from the Russians to buy food on the open market and from the farms, but credit is no good, only cash speaks.... If [the refugees] have no established residence, they are not entitled to ration cards, and they will not accept new residents in any of the towns. They will, however, permit us to organize these refugee centers and get the food on the open market." A response to Langheinrich's request for American funds is not known. While Barnes also repeated Langheinrich's reference to two hundred refugees being sent to Wolfsgrün, other contemporary sources indicate that the number of members residing in the Wolfsgrün villa never exceeded one hundred at a time.

From June 16 to August 3, 1945, and again between September 11 and 16, the mission leaders traveled constantly throughout the Soviet occupation zone to locate, assist, and organize the members. A day-by-day report of their activities, found in Appendix A, graphically describes the condition of the mission and the members in the first months after the war.

The Mission's Relationship with the Soviet Military Administration

Most Church members had very negative and tragic experiences with the Soviet Army, especially when combat soldiers came in contact with the civilian population, mostly women and young girls. That history is well known and will not be repeated here. However, another perspective is seen in accounts of the relationship between the Soviet officers and Church leaders at the end of the war. The Russians and the Americans were allies in the war, and the mission took advantage of that relationship and openly identified itself as a church headquartered in America. Paul Langheinrich, for example, was prepared from the outset to develop and build upon this relationship. He wrote:

> On April 23 [1945], I looked from our balcony as Russian soldiers came down our street. I had placed on our house door [the temporary mission office] the following sign: "American Mission. Entrance only with permission of the commanding officer in the Wilsmakerstraße." I had arranged that with a Russian officer. (MS 5382 1)

The mission's letterhead stationery said it was a branch of an American church, and the identification papers it issued also emphasized the Church's ties to America. Walter Kindt, who served as a missionary for five years, provided copies of two identification documents issued by the mission under that letterhead:

> *February 14, 1946:* Herr Walter Kindt, Dresden, Gutschmidstraße 1, is authorized to carry out the duties of a missionary for the above church in Germany. In this capacity, he has been assigned to conduct and oversee religious instruction. He is particularly assigned to care for the oppressed, bombed out, and refugee members of the above church. Herr Kindt is engaged in the service of U.S. America and may not be hindered in his work. All agencies and offices are requested to provide him with the necessary protection and support.

> *March 20, 1946:* In accordance with Allied agreements and with the permission of Herr Marshall Shukov and his deputy, Herr General of the Army Sokolovsky, the above church is authorized to conduct religious services and religious instruction in the entire Russian occupied zone of Germany in their own meeting houses. The missionary, Herr Walter Kindt, is stationed for this assignment in Dresden, and we request that he be given a permit to reside in Dresden. The missionaries are classified under paragraph III/16/, Minister, for the issuance of ration cards by the SMAD. According to direction of the SMAD in Pots-

dam, all commanding officers and agencies are requested to provide necessary protection and assistance to these missionaries.

Excerpts from reports concerning welfare work, the rescue of genealogical records, and the leadership's travels provide additional evidence of the mission's relationship with the Soviets:

Paul Langheinrich: The Russian officers in Karlshorst [headquarters of the SMAD] promised me a railroad car [to transport genealogical records]. I want to emphasize that I was never disappointed by a higher Russian officer. Their word was always honored. No one received railroad cars at that time, but they always gave them to me. (MS 5382 1)

Major Donald Corbett: Karlshorst was the final authority for matters under appeal. Paul early had established good rapport with the Russian commanding officer, and he felt free to go to him in person with his needs and desires. He enjoyed friendly entry to the Russian headquarters. His ingratiating smile undoubtedly had much to do with it. He would go to Karlshorst and walk right past the Russian guards and their Tommy guns. One time Arthur Gaeth, former president of the Czechoslovakia Mission, who was visiting with me in Berlin after broadcasting the Nuremberg trial of top Nazi leaders, was taken by Paul to see General Sokolovsky. After the experience, Arthur said to me, "Paul nearly scared me to death today. He would go charging past those Russian guards so fast I couldn't keep up with him. I hung back, not sure it was safe. Paul, way ahead, would stop, turn around and motion me to hurry up."[1]

Alfred Paul Schulz: Less than two weeks before the conference [March 1946 in Leipzig], I went to the office of the commandant. At the press office I was treated politely by the Russian officer. He explained that I could not hold a meeting without previously obtaining a permit. Because Captain Braun was not there at that time he made an exception and gave me a permit. I also received permission to have our posters and handbills printed. Everything happened in a miraculous manner. Many were surprised because the Russian officer stood up several times to help me. He just signed the paper, leaving it up to us to write the permit. (MS 2002)

Paul Schmidt: When we were ready to announce the dedication of our meeting house [in Gera, December 1946], we needed permission from the Soviet authorities. We had our request translated into Russian and took it to the office. There we read the name of the officer on his door: Major Dickenstein. He was a Jew. Sitting behind his desk, he asked us what we wanted. I gave him our written request, which he read with interest and said, "You don't need permission to use the building, but I will approve it anyhow. Now I will also approve the five hundred invitations." He went into another room, returned with a large stamp that he used on our request, signed it, and the matter was settled.[2]

Walter Kindt: We decided to hold a large meeting [in Halberstadt] about the restoration of the gospel and invited the residents of the city to attend. We prepared placards and handouts to be printed with the challenging title, "Is there a God?" Brother Pöcker and I went to the local office of the Communist Party to present our request. We were introduced to the Russian commanding officer who listened to our request and carefully read the text. To our surprise, he asked a few polite questions, left the room and returned with the necessary approval documents. He then said, "I am a professor of astronomy at the university in Moscow. Would you please explain God to me?" I proceeded to teach about the creation, how everything was organized out of existing matter, with existing energy, by a being, an eternal God and creator. The commanding officer responded with great interest, thanked us and asked, "Can I do anything else for you?" I said, "Yes, we need a better place for our religious services." He responded, "What a coincidence. We are moving our headquarters out of a church building. You can have it." It was a small chapel in the center of town that had been used previously by the Evangelical church, connected to a larger, destroyed cathedral. The chapel had suffered only minor damage and included classrooms and even a kitchen. We were amazed. It was a miracle. (2003)

Walter Fassmann: [The Russian Major asked,] "Where did you go recently in Berlin? We know exactly which train you took, which train you returned on and many other details." I spent quite a bit of time with him discussing the Church. We spent over two hours talking before he allowed me to leave. Before I was out the door, he had one last question for me, "Have any of the Russians given you much trouble?" "Not yet," I responded. "Well," he said, "If anyone bothers you because of the Church, just let me know."[3]

Wolfgang Kelm: In regard to our September 1950 district conference in Leipzig, it was much more difficult to negotiate with the Germans than with their Russian colleagues. (2005)

Herbert Schreiter: The Russians controlled [the Prellerstraße meetinghouse in Leipzig] during the time we met there. But the house was returned to the city in 1952, and they didn't allow us to continue to use it. We lived there because I was the building caretaker. I didn't have other employment. Where should we go? The Russian Colonel came by and saw that we had packed our hand wagon for the move, but didn't know where to go. He went crazy and said, "That's impossible! You move back into the house and stay there until you receive a proper apartment." That is what the Russian said, and that is what happened. (1991)

In 1995, Frédéric Hartweg, Joachim Heise, and Horst Dohle published a valuable two-volume compilation of church-related policy deliberations and documents of the GDR's ruling political party, which will be quoted extensively in the next chapter on church-state relations. The following comments by Hartweg and Heise regarding the relationship between churches and the Soviet occupation forces in the immediate postwar years are relevant here:

> *Hartweg:* It is generally acknowledged that the Soviet occupation forces were, in most cases, kindly disposed toward the churches. They often viewed church officials as neutral discussion partners and potential trustworthy officeholders. They considered the re-establishment of organized church life as a component of good public order. The SMAD, and especially its local representatives, often constituted a type of "appeal board" against the restrictive actions of the German [Communist]-dominated administrative offices.[4]

> *Heise:* In accordance with the Allied agreements, [the political officers of the SMAD] gave the churches wide latitude to operate immediately after the war. [They] sought contact with church representatives, tried to develop harmonious relationships, demonstrated an obliging attitude toward churches, and tried to reduce conflicts between churches and German officials. The SMAD considered the churches to be an influential force for good order, and they did not want to do without their experience and cooperation in postwar Germany. The SMAD restrained German officials here and there when their restrictive actions regarding churches and their social activities stood in the way of the SMAD's political goals.[5]

As noted earlier by Paul Langheinrich, the wartime collaboration between the United States and the Soviet Union provided an additional reason for good relations between representatives of the mission and the SMAD. However, with the onset of the cold war, the location of the Church's headquarters in America no longer provided any advantage. On the contrary, it was disadvantageous. Kurt Löffler, the state secretary for Religious Affairs after 1988, said:

> The SMAD did everything possible to gain the support of the people and rarely operated via prohibitions. The initial approval of the Church of Jesus Christ of Latter-day Saints originated with the Soviet Union, i.e., with its occupation forces. They had determined that all those that

> had been persecuted under Fascism would again be free to operate, but only on our territory and only with our personnel, i.e., only with GDR citizens. Thereby, of course, the Church was robbed of its most important instrument, its external missionary activity. But that had nothing to do with the Mormon Church itself, but with world politics. If the Church had been headquartered in Leningrad, no problem. Unfortunately, its headquarters was in Utah. (2003)

Food for the Refugees and Imprisonment of the Mission Leadership

Prior to the end of the war, the Allied powers had agreed that the eastern border of Germany would be moved westward to the Oder and Neiße rivers. Polish and other nationalities were to be settled in the former German territories. The result was a massive evacuation of millions of Germans, including many Church members, from Germany's former eastern provinces. While the mission hoped to retain these refugees within its territory, the Allies had agreed that refugees from the eastern provinces should be settled in the British and American zones. To encourage or force these refugees to move westward, German officials in Saxony refused to provide them with ration cards. Ranglack explained the problem to Richard Barnes on August 24, 1945:

> We are receiving cries for help from members and district presidents in Saxony because evacuees from all parts of Germany must leave Saxony by August 31st, and no ration cards will be issued for them beginning in September. Included in that category are many of our members from Königsberg, Tilsit, Elbing, Schneidemühl, Danzig, Breslau, Schlesien, etc. The cries of the members for help are sounding in our ears so loudly that we must provide help immediately. (CR 271 40)

With or without ration cards, the mission leaders took action to feed the refugees. On August 9, 1945, they sent a letter written by Langheinrich to Field Marshall Shukov:

> The above church is a division of the Church of Jesus Christ of Latter-day Saints in Salt Lake City, U.S. America. The members of our East German Mission are found in seventy-three branches spread over the entire area occupied by the Red Army. They have been forced to suffer harassment and persecution because of their known international orientation and their genuine Christian opposition to Hitler's actions. . . . To avoid further harm to the health of our members, we would be very appreciative if you would permit us the following:
>
> 1) We request permission to freely purchase food supplies in the various regions under your control when such items are available.
>
> 2) We need a truck to transport these goods. Alternately, when it is not possible to provide an allotment of gasoline, a good Holzgenerator-Lastwagen [a truck that ran on wood smoke] would be acceptable. We

> request written documentation of your permission to obtain the same and to use it without limitation.
>
> 3) We request permission to occasionally purchase cows, pigs, or calves, etc., in the various regions and to slaughter them for distribution to our members. We assure you that we would make only sparing use of this permission in order to provide a small supplement for our suffering members, especially the sick and the children, but especially for all those who have not received any ration cards because they cannot presently return to their former homeland.
>
> None of us were ever members of the NSDAP or any part thereof. We are convinced that only with your help can we receive the necessary assistance. Just as we rejoiced over the victory and the freedom we obtained through the Red Army, we rejoice that we will find protection and help today. We send our friendliest greetings and best wishes. [Signed] The President of the East German Mission of the Church of Jesus Christ of Latter-day Saints, with headquarters in Salt Lake City in the USA. (MS 5382 1)

The SMAD responded on August 16, 1945, in a letter signed by General of the Army Sokolovsky:

> In answer to your letter of August 9, 1945,
>
> 1) Free trade is allowed in the Soviet zone of occupation. Therefore, you can purchase the food you need. You need no permission for that from the Soviet occupation offices.
>
> 2) You can obtain the vehicle in the same manner, either through purchase or from the municipal authorities of the city of Berlin or in any other location.
>
> 3) You can obtain cattle and other goods, because, as I said, free trade is allowed in Germany. (CR 271 40)

Armed with the SMAD's letter, Paul Langheinrich and two companions sought lodging for the refugees in the southern part of the mission, specifically in a villa in Wolfsgrün, a remote area in the Erzgebirge, not far from the Czech border:

> *Arnold Schmidt:* Brothers Langheinrich and Jeske and I traveled together [August 1945] to Wolfsgrün to see the mayor in order to obtain the villa, which was empty. The mayor was not opposed to the plan, as long as the Russian commanding officer in Eibenstock gave his written permission. . . . As we went through the forest, we united in prayer to request the blessing of the Lord. The Lord was merciful and heard our prayer. When we came to Eibenstock, Brother Langheinrich went to the commanding officer and soon had the written permission in his hands. (MS 14466)

> *Paul Langheinrich:* I had prepared a request and the officer wrote on it, "You can have the requested house." We met with the community council and signed an agreement. We would not have to pay rent, but were responsible for repairs. The Germans did not provide ration cards for our 99 refugees, who lived there almost a year, but with the help of the Russian officers, we were able to bring in that which we needed. (MS 5382 1)

The lease agreement, dated September 3, 1945, and signed by Paul Langheinrich, Max Jeske, and six representatives of the Blauenthal council is shown here in full:

> The following agreement between the community of Blauenthal and Herr Paul Langheinrich and Herr Max Jeske, Berlin NW 21, Rathenaustraße Nr. 52, was agreed to today:
>
> The former NSV [National Socialist welfare program] home for mothers will be leased to the above-named persons until December 31, 1946. In the event that the home is put up for sale, and Herr Wolf Bretschneider does not exercise his purchase option, Herr Langheinrich and Herr Jeske will have the right to purchase it. In either event, occupancy may take place on September 3, 1945. Herr Langheinrich agrees to make the existing feather beds available to poor residents of the community. A lease price is not anticipated for the above lease period.
>
> The former house custodian, Erich Mehlhorn, who lives in a building on the grounds, must vacant that building and leave the property by September 30, 1945. Erich Mehlhorn is relieved of his duties as of this day. In case notification of the termination of the lease is not made three months in advance, it is automatically renewed for another year. In that eventuality, a lease price will be determined by the above parties. (CR 271 40)

The mission now had an excellent facility for the refugees. However, the SMAD's permission for the slaughtering of animals was not welcomed by the local German officials who wanted to move the refugees westward, instead of feeding them. The resulting conflict with those officials led to the imprisonment of six mission leaders on Saturday, October 6, 1945. Six days later, Colonel Barnes described the problem in a letter to Thomas E. McKay. "The mission leadership had traveled to Zwickau on the weekend to make preparations for the refugee camp where the members from Breslau will be lodged. Everything went well. They slaughtered two pigs and were making sausage when the criminal police came and arrested them. The police did not want to accept their explanation or the letter from the Russians" (LR 2428 2).

Paul Langheinrich explained the imprisonment in a 1968 letter to Justus Ernst, who was compiling documents for the Church archives:

> The district president in Zwickau illicitly conducted a slaughter on the basis of the written authorization I had received from the Russians. The criminal police came to me and asked if I had been aware of the slaughter, and I answered yes, so that nothing would happen to him. . . . In the evening before the closing prayer [at the district conference], I said, "Brothers and Sisters, have no fear. When Amen is said, the police will come and take me." (LR 2428 2)

The arrest was appealed to the provincial magistrate for Saxony, with a copy of Langheinrich's letter from the Russians. The magistrate responded on October 8, 1945, in a letter addressed to Richard Ranglack:

> Representatives of your East German Mission delivered to me a letter, signed by the deputy to the commander of the SMAD, General of the Army Sokolovsky, and requested my opinion on the matter. . . . Regarding paragraph 3, according to the current laws and regulations of the Soviet occupation officials, live cattle may not be sold in the county of Zwickau. However, it is permitted to sell any remaining meat after the required consignment [to the government] has been met. No facility is permitted to sell food or meat before it receives written confirmation that it has fulfilled its required consignment. (MS 7648)

Following the intervention of the Russian commanding officer in Zwickau, the six men were released from prison on October 19, 1945. Five days later, Langheinrich provided a detailed account of the incident in a letter to the Russian commanding officer in Dresden:

> The Soviet headquarters in Germany gave [the Church] written permission to make unlimited purchases for the care of our needy members. Since July, our activities in this regard have been constantly hindered by German officials. We now respectfully request, Herr provincial commanding officer, that you accept this plea for help, so that we can continue, without restriction, the welfare work that was authorized by officers of the Red Army.
>
> We will now explain the reasons for this letter. We returned in early July of this year from a trip, which we undertook with Soviet permission from Berlin, through the occupation zone to Annaberg in the Erzgebirge. We learned there that the need was very great, that their diet actually consisted of potato peelings. With the written permission of the local military commander, we bought an ox as well as other food items, which we intended to distribute to our members. Although we had the written permission of the Soviet military commander in Annaberg for each individual purchase, the district magistrate confiscated the meat. He also instigated the mayor of Geyersdorf to do the same a second time. They were ordered by the military commander to

immediately return the meat. Since that time, we have had to endure continual harassment and persecution, which reached its peak on October 6, 1945, in Zwickau.

With permission of the military commander in Eibenstock, we took possession of the former NSV home for mothers in Wolfsgrün in the Erzgebirge. In order not to ignore the German officials, we also concluded a unanimously worded and signed lease agreement with the town council of Blauenthal, in whose jurisdiction the above home is located. Now that we have partially organized the home, and would have already completed that task, if we had not been constantly harassed, the district magistrate in Schwarzenberg, influenced by magistrate Schmidt in Zwickau, tried to take the home from us, despite the Soviet authorization.

Our greatest concern in bringing the anticipated 150 members into the home, was to lay up adequate food stores, since it is almost impossible to reach Wolfsgrün in the winter. For this reason, we slaughtered two pigs in the vicinity, with a total live weight of 200 kilo and also in Zwickau two pigs and a calf, together about 260 kilo. It was to be made into sausage, or used for ongoing needs. For each purchase, we had the written permission of the responsible Soviet office or the district magistrate and the written permission for free trade in a letter from the highest Soviet office in Germany, signed by General of the Army Sokolovsky.

On October 6 of this year, the criminal police in Zwickau confiscated all the meat, fat, and sausage, except for seven pounds, as well as sixty bottles of fruit juice, which were intended for the sick and the weak. Our appeal, that we were only acting with permission of the Soviet office, was turned down with the words, "Yes, you indeed have the permission of the Russians, but we don't agree with it, we won't accept it, and we will oppose it!"

In the following days, magistrate Schmidt allowed our supply of hard sausage from earlier slaughters to be confiscated.... To prevent us from taking countermeasures, they placed me and five of my colleagues in the Osterstein prison in Zwickau for two weeks, because I had said, "I will appeal to the county commander." We were released on October 19 through the intervention of the county commander in Zwickau.... In the course of the investigation, not the least charge of misconduct was made against any of my companions.

I will now provide my own opinion concerning this arrest. In the course of my constant travels, often day and night, I had lost sixty pounds. Our Father in Heaven knew I needed a vacation. However, he also knew that I would never sit still if I were free. So he gave me a two-week vacation in prison. My cell mate was a stranger from East Prussia who was on a hunger strike, so I had a double ration. When released, I had regained five pounds. (MS 7648)

The Russians almost always supported the Church in its refugee activities. On December 13, 1945, for example, the military headquarters in Berlin wrote to the civil magistrate in Schwarzenberg regarding the refugees in the villa, "You are hereby informed that this office clearly forbids the evacuation of the 85 persons who are being supported by the Church of Jesus Christ of Latter-day Saints in the Wolfsgrün facility. It is further ordered that those persons who are carrying out work for a company be given the corresponding ration cards" (MS 5382 1).

The district government later claimed that Langheinrich had ignored government agencies when he entered into the lease agreement for the villa. Langheinrich answered that accusation on January 17, 1946:

> A lease arrangement was concluded with the Wolfsgrün town council on September 3, 1945. At that time, the anti-fascist town council did not inform us that a district government had assumed responsibility for Saxony. Therefore, if someone has the opinion today that we avoided the district government, that does not represent the facts. (MS 5382 1)

The response from the district government on January 29, 1946, shows that the main issue was not the villa itself, but rather the feeding of the refugees, specifically the SMAD's permission for the mission to slaughter cattle. In fact, the letter was titled, "The feeding of refugees" and stated:

> You must certainly have been aware via the public postings, newspaper notices, and radio announcements that refugees assigned to the American zone were to have registered at the designated places so that transportation to their assigned areas could be facilitated. Provision for the feeding of these refugees would be done by the district governments in the designated camps. Under these arrangements, refugees would remain in the resettlement camps for only a short time before being quickly transported to their future places of abode. No resettlement camps existed in the vicinity of Wolfsgrün/Erzgebirge, in which the 90 persons of concern could have been fed.... Moreover, we are interested in knowing how these ninety refugees were fed in the meantime. We request your report on this subject. (MS 5382 1)

Paul Langheinrich responded by writing to General Dratwin on February 5, 1946:

> The only order of the SMAD that was followed [by the German officials] was that our refugees were allowed to remain in the home under discussion. The other orders of the SMAD were not implemented, with the justification, "We make the decisions in Saxony." Today we were again informed by telegram, that these refugees were to be evacuated

> from this home on February 6.... I now respectfully request that the Herr General issue an order to Saxony that allows our suffering members to remain in the home and be issued ration cards. (MS 5382 1)

The SMAD responded quickly. On February 13, Arnold Schmidt informed the mission office by telegram, "The order has been issued. We will receive ration cards" (MS 5382 1). Most of the refugees left Wolfsgrün in the course of 1946 and were settled in the American and British sectors. The home was finally closed at the beginning of 1947. Additional details about life in Wolfsgrün are found in Appendix B.

In a biography about her husband, Walter Krause, Edith Krause wrote: "Some brothers were imprisoned because they were accused of dishonestly taking over the villa in Wolfsgrün."[6] However, the documents presented above show that the imprisonment was occasioned by the slaughtering of animals for food. Occupancy of the villa was only an ancillary issue that angered some local officials because it hindered their efforts to move the refugees westward.

Locating and Securing Genealogical Records, 1945–1946

In his previously cited letter of August 9, 1945, to Field Marshall Shukov, Langheinrich requested permission to locate and secure parish church records that the Nazi government had placed in mines and old castles for protection during the war. Upon receipt of written approval, Langheinrich assigned two missionaries, Erich Sellner and Rudolf Pöcker, to locate the records. After they reported their first discoveries in February 1946, Langheinrich and Ranglack visited Major Corbett to obtain his advice. They specifically asked if it would be okay to use mission funds to secure and transport the documents. Corbett described that encounter in an account he wrote later in collaboration with Langheinrich:

> I had no official designation that authorized me to speak for the Church, but as group leader of the LDS servicemen in Berlin, I was frequently contacted by the German brethren for assistance with the more serious problems.... When the two German friends called on me that afternoon, Brother Langheinrich said, "Brother Corbett, we have found a large store of German church records in the province of Thuringia. There are many books and a large quantity of microfilms. We want to secure them for the Church for genealogical purposes." I asked, "How did you find them?" "Brother Sellner, at my request, went in search for them. We had learned that they had been deposited during the final months of the war in Central Germany."... I asked, "How many books do you estimate there are?" Brother Ranglack replied, "Several thousand volumes and several thousand microfilms. We cannot tell exactly as they are not all in one place." I asked, "What is involved in getting them?" "It will take several workmen to assist in carrying and loading the books, or we could take our sixteen mission-

> aries," answered Brother Langheinrich. He went on to explain that it would not be difficult to find workers but the big problem was feeding them. Also, he thought that it would require three railroad cars to transport all of the records to Berlin. "How much will that cost?" "About 1,500 Marks a car," Paul answered. They were hesitant about paying out money for such a purpose from mission funds, and there was some doubt about their authority in money matters.
>
> Further discussion with the brethren was resolved on the basis that we were acting in an emergency to take advantage of a priceless opportunity presented by the Lord. If what the brethren said was true, and there was no reason to doubt them, the cost involved to transport the records was infinitesimal. I suggested that they go ahead and get the job done and pay what it cost them.

Corbett said that the two men returned three days later and asked him to accompany them to the new mission office in West Berlin.

> I was not in the least prepared for the sight that met my eyes. Before me was a bank of heavy books, five thousand of them, stacked one on the other, three to four feet high, covering half of the large floor. I was astounded at the sight. It was fantastic and unbelievable. The brethren showed me other interesting things, including thousands of microfilms spread out on a clean basement floor to dry thoroughly. The time I spent there with the brethren remains one of my most cherished memories.[7]

An article in the newspaper *Neue Zeit* on June 9, 1946, entitled "Verschleppte Kirchenbücher aufgefunden" (Hidden church books found), described the recovery of these records:

> At the spring conference of the Church of Jesus Christ of Latter-day Saints (Mormons) in Leipzig, participants were shown wondrous, ancient, parchment church books. We inquired about the reason for the display and received the answer from the mission's president for genealogy in the east branch of the Mormons. The pigskin volumes with the yellowed pages are a small part of a huge collection of genealogical documents, which were discovered and brought to light in recent months by Mormon missionaries. Most of these valuable church books had been hidden by the National Socialists in bombproof mines and old castles, whose locations were known by only a few people. Voluntarily and with good support from Marshall Sokolovsky, two train cars full of those church books have already been transported to Berlin. The castles Rothenburg and Rathsfeld in the Kyffhäuser region, a mountain range in Thuringia on the southern edge of the Harz, were particularly rich sources of documents. For example, a

> large Jewish card file and Jewish church books were discovered, which had been hidden there in 1941. Large quantities of church books from East Prussia, which had been stored in a salt mine in Schönebeck (on the Elbe River southeast of Magdeburg), also were found. The searchers found 32,000 films nearby, each a photographic copy of a church book, and additional thousand of photocopies of valuable files, including civil registers of births and marriages. At least six more carloads of records will soon be brought to Berlin. Planning is underway to travel in the Polish-occupied regions, to rescue other documents left behind in that area.
>
> When all these treasures have been assembled, voluntary workers from all Christian confessions will establish a genealogical archive in the Museum of Ethnology in Berlin-Dahlem, that will serve everyone. New wood for the bookcases is already available in the courtyard of the building. The work can begin! It is a true labor of peace for everyone, for many Germans and foreigners, since the collection includes many church books from countries that we once occupied, whose documents were lost in the chaos of recent years. This archive will be an unending treasure chest for genealogy researchers, historians, and biographers. (MS 7648)

Further details about the recovery of these records, from reports written by Paul Langheinrich and two of his missionaries, can be found in Appendix C.

The Arrival of Elder Ezra Taft Benson

On January 14, 1946, the First Presidency of the Church announced the appointment of Elder Benson as president of the European Mission, with the special assignment to determine the needs of the members and to coordinate the distribution of food, clothing, and other necessities. He arrived in London on February 4 and visited western European countries and Scandinavia before arriving in Berlin on March 20 with his secretary, Frederick W. Babbel, and Max Zimmer, the new president of the West German Mission. Major Corbett said that "they made my office in the U.S. military compound their first point of call." He found lodging for them and coordinated their other logistical needs with the American military. The accounts of Benson's activities in Berlin were recorded in the journal of the European Mission and copies were added to the manuscript history of the East German Mission a few years later. The following excerpts from Benson's first visit to Berlin were written either by Benson or his secretary:

> We have had several conferences with the acting mission presidency regarding many emergency and long-time mission problems. Too much cannot be said for the splendid work which has been performed by our local leaders here under the most adverse conditions. The Lord has blessed their faithful efforts in a most remarkable manner.... Pos-

> sibly the most remarkable activity of these brethren during the entire war period, and which should not be made public at this time, pertains to genealogical records which have come into our hands.
>
> A very vigorous missionary program has been undertaken by this mission. They now have twenty-one full-time missionaries working in all parts of the Russian military zone, four lady missionaries working full-time in the mission office, and six more brethren also being called to work as full-time missionaries. Present conditions in this mission make it impossible to send missionaries from Zion, inasmuch as the entire mission is in the Russian zone of occupation. Local missionaries, however, have been well received and are able to pursue their missionary activities almost unhindered. All of our branches and districts in the areas now occupied by Poland are closed to any missionary work and all Germans in those areas are being deported as refugees, primarily to the British zone of occupation.
>
> In recent months two homes for refugees have been established to take care of their temporary needs. In Cottbus, the branch meeting house has been remodeled to care for between 100 and 150 members and another beautiful home, a former castle [villa] at Wolfsgrün in Saxony, has been placed at the disposal of our church by the Russian government. Here they have been caring for about 100 families [actually 100 members]. In spite of receiving no rations as refugees for nearly five months and arriving without bedding or clothing beyond that which they were wearing, the members organized local welfare groups and were not only successful in caring for their immediate clothing and subsistence needs, but were also able to work cooperatively to secure work and homes for the able-bodied families so they might move out and become self-supporting. Those remaining in the temporary quarters were required to work among the members in the branches and districts, and they received work receipts, which served as the basis for receiving needed assistance. The future is very critical however, inasmuch as all the members have shared every available item and they are now faced with very urgent needs. (LR 2428 2)

Benson held long meetings with the acting mission leaders on March 22 and 23. Detailed minutes of the meetings were included in a report by Major Corbett, entitled "Visit of Elder Ezra Taft Benson to Berlin, Germany, 1946," which was placed in the European Mission journal under the date of Sunday, March 24, 1946, and later added to the East German Mission history. Benson informed the acting mission leaders at that time that Walter Stover had been called to preside over the East German Mission. However, since it was not known when Stover would be allowed to enter Germany, his calling was not made public. Instead, Benson appointed Richard Ranglack as "President of the East German Mission of the Church of Jesus Christ of Latter-day Saints with full authority to direct the affairs of the mission, both spiritually and temporally" and issued a statement to that effect. Benson also informed the mission leaders of plans to provide welfare assistance, encouraged them to print their own books when possible, stated that efforts were underway to have the Church officially recognized in Germany, and noted that a special missionary fund for the support of local, full-time missionaries had been established. He also provided advice on the following topics:

> *Genealogical records:* Continue to find and preserve all available records in accordance with the permission granted by the Soviet military forces. The records, books, films, and photostatic copies belong to the individual parishes and/or the state and are not to be regarded as property of our Church. Our chief interest in gathering and preserving these records and returning them to their rightful owners should be to gain the friendship and confidence of the groups concerned so that we as a Church might be permitted to have free access to all such records and also receive permission to microfilm them at a later date.
>
> *Mission finances:* All tithes and surplus fast offerings are to be remitted to the mission each month. Each branch should submit a proposed budget for the current year based on its estimated monthly needs. No additional expenses should be paid from tithing funds except upon authorization of the mission presidency.
>
> *Refugees from the former eastern provinces:* The government has assured housing and employment in the western sectors of Germany. The project at Wolfsgrün was being discontinued due to pressure from German authorities. Large refugee projects were not to be encouraged. The members do not understand the United Order. The Church does not sponsor communal living, and the United Order does not provide for mutual ownership. Instead, welfare programs should be organized to help members become independent and self-sustaining. (LR 2428 2)

On Sunday morning, March 24, members of Elder Benson's group split up to visit each of the five branch Sunday Schools in Berlin. In spite of the inadequate facilities, seventy to ninety members, nearly half of whom were children, were in attendance at each branch. Corbett wrote, "During all this time, Brother Langheinrich was busy searching for a place large enough to accommodate the Berlin members of the Church in a large conference." He found an auditorium in a bomb-scarred school in the Russian sector of Berlin, where nearly five hundred members assembled to hear Elder Benson in the afternoon. Excerpts from his talk follow:

> I support none, nor condemn any for what has happened. God will be the judge. The fruits of disobedience are everywhere in evidence.

> No nation can escape the horrors of war unless it lives according to God's word. As a Church, we always have been and will continue to be against war. The Lord makes it plain in His revelations to us that we should denounce war and proclaim peace.... Peace comes from within; it cannot be imposed; it must come from the hearts of men. The application of the Gospel message in the lives of men and women will bring peace. There is no other way. Christ said that no man should rule unjustly over his brethren. When the wicked rule, the righteous mourn. God has also said that we must be loyal to those who have power over us. But when a nation follows unrighteous leaders, the righteous will suffer with the wicked. I recognize that the Lord has predicted wars, but God would much rather have us live in peace by living the Gospel.... We recognize that those who have suffered wars may not always have been personally responsible, for the Lord has said that the good and true must suffer difficulties, even with the possibility of giving up their lives. However, I know that God will recompense the losses of the righteous in His own way. (LR 2428 2)

Elder Benson returned to Berlin for three days in June to make arrangements with the International Red Cross for the receipt and distribution of welfare supplies for the East German Mission. No welfare items had yet arrived in Berlin. On July 26, he returned again and remained there for a few days while awaiting a visa to enter Poland. His next visit to Berlin took place during September 16–19, 1946. As always, he met with the acting mission president, Richard Ranglack, and together they visited a warehouse to view the first welfare supplies that had recently arrived in Berlin. The next shipment of supplies arrived shortly before his next visit on October 21. At that time, he reported that the first shipment was still being sorted by the responsible relief agency and nothing had yet been distributed to the Church members. Benson's last visit to Berlin took place on December 4. This time, he was met by the newly arrived Walter Stover, who had been allowed to come to Berlin from Switzerland a few days earlier. In a meeting attended by 774 members of the Berlin District on that day, the acting mission presidency of Richard Ranglack, Paul Langheinrich, and Max Jeske was released and Walter Stover was sustained as the president of the East German Mission.

The following day, Benson spoke at a missionary meeting attended by all thirty-one local, full-time, German missionaries. Walter Kindt, one of the attendees, provided the following account of Benson's talk in which he addressed the status of members in the refugee home in Wolfsgrün:

> I feel for these people, who have been driven from their homeland into a new land. Their family ties have been broken, and it is possible that they will never be reestablished. I have never been forced to live through such a situation, and they should receive our help and our love. However, the Church has had similar experiences in the past. There was

a time when all members of the Church were refugees. We had experiences then where the people also wanted to work together, but it didn't go well. Today, some people have had to come together, to live together. When that happens, you just have to do the best you can.

When I went to Langen [a refugee camp established by Church members in West Germany], twenty-two people were living in one room, families and people of all ages. They slept, lived, and ate together, all in one room. We know that this is not good for the welfare of the people. But they did what they could. I was pleased to hear that these people prayed together every morning and evening. They said that there was no quarreling. Such arrangements are possible, when it is necessary, and when the Lord permits it. But such arrangements should not be preferred or advised, unless we are forced to do so. Communism is not the United Order. The United Order says that every family should live and work by itself, to support that family. They should also contribute items that are set aside, so that those who have nothing can receive something. The welfare plan is designed for this purpose.

In the United Order, every family should have its own possessions, have control over its possessions, and be free to manage the same. The surpluses, which the family does not need, are contributed to the storehouse. And that is how we should work with the refugees. We should find living quarters as soon as possible so they can live together in families. Perhaps it is necessary for many families to live together. Should that be the case, then we must be careful and do everything to support these families. (Copy from Walter Kindt)

President Walter Stover

Walter Stover did not obtain permission from the American military forces to travel from Switzerland to Berlin until the end of November 1946. His initial authorization was valid only for thirty days and was renewed through February 25, 1947, at which time he returned to Switzerland and left the affairs of the mission in the hands of Richard Ranglack. In the meantime, Elder Alma Sonne had been appointed president of the European Mission as successor to Elder Benson and had arrived in England on November 16, 1946, together with Walter Stover. Sonne explained Stover's status in a letter to the First Presidency on February 16, 1947:

> It should be stated, perhaps, that President Stover has not been very successful in his contacts with military officials in Berlin. This is probably due to his German background, which naturally places him under some suspicion, and also because he has been investigated and is being watched by the . . . U.S. Army because of the unusually large quantity of goods and supplies brought with him from America. This

> information has come to us in confidence from our American brethren stationed in Berlin. (CR 271 5)

Stover received permission to return to West Berlin on March 20, 1947, and he also was authorized by the SMAD to attend five district conferences in the Soviet zone. Francis R. Gasser, a civilian employee of the American army and later the vice consul in the American consulate in West Berlin, traveled with Stover to these conferences and wrote reports from which the following excerpts were taken:

> In the Russian zone of occupation there are 49 branches of the church with a membership of 5,513 members; in Berlin there are five branches with 1,252 members.
>
> The Erzgebirge District is the smallest district with 390 members in three branches: Annaberg-Buchholz, Schwarzenberg, and Wolfsgrün. Attendance at the Sunday afternoon session in Annaberg on March 23rd was 328, including 124 friends.
>
> The next weekend the group drove to Zwickau. That district consists of eight branches: Zwickau, Plauen, Auerbach, Meerane, Planitz, Werdau, Wilkau, and Hohenstein-Enstthal, with 762 members. Total attendance at the Sunday afternoon session was 540, including friends.
>
> President Stover held a district conference in Berlin-Wilmersdorf on April 5–6. During his stay in Berlin, he has been able to secure the release of LDS Welfare clothing and food supplies which had been stored in the warehouse of the International Red Cross in Berlin since last year. Under his direction some 72 tons of food and clothing have been transported to the mission home, unpacked, shipments made up and repacked and dispatched under very difficult transport conditions.
>
> On April 12 Stover traveled to Erfurt via Naumburg an der Salle and Weimar. The Erfurt District is composed of five branches: Erfurt, Gera, Weimar, Gotha, and Nordhausen. It was strange to see so many women present and so few men. Many of the former male members of this district are still prisoners of war, whereas a greater number of them still remain "missing in action"; 331 of 441 enrolled members attended the final Sunday session.
>
> The Dresden District is composed of six branches: Cottbus, Forst, Görlitz, Bischofswerda, Rammenau, and Dresden, with 855 members. Attendance at the final session in Dresden on April 20 was 610.
>
> The Leipzig District is composed of branches in Halle, Magdeburg, Halberstadt, Dessau, Aschersleben, Bernburg, und Leipzig, with 669 members. Attendance at the final session on April 27 was 644. (LR 2428 2)

Spring district conferences in the northern part of the mission were conducted by Heinz Hinkel, the mission secretary, since President Stover did not receive further travel permission from the SMAD. He also was not permitted to attend the one-hundredth anniversary Pioneer celebration in Dresden in July 1947.

Welfare Assistance from America

The efforts of the acting mission leadership to provide food and lodging for members of the East German Mission immediately after the war were described earlier. The later and better known welfare activities initiated by Elder Benson have been described by Frederick Babbel in his book *On Wings of Faith*, published in 1972. Only a few additional documents directly relevant to the East German Mission will be noted here. On July 8, 1946, Elder Benson sent a report to the First Presidency, which included a summary of assistance to date:

> We have now established two refugee camps, one at Langen near Frankfurt, and the other at Wolfsgrün. [He did not mention the refugee center in Cottbus]. . . . At Wolfsgrün, our members occupy a large castle [villa] in cooperation with the Russian military authorities. We are sending food to both camps, both purchased on the market in Switzerland and being supplied . . . from the Church welfare stocks. Facilities at both camps are badly taxed and our members continue to arrive from branches in what was formerly Germany but which is now Poland. . . . We have authorized the brethren in Berlin to proceed immediately to negotiate with the Russian military authorities for the rental or purchase of lands formerly used as a military training camp. Much of this land can be used for agricultural purposes but some of it will have to be cleared first. It is intended that the land be divided up into small farming plots where the people can become largely self-supporting and self-sustaining. We hope to be able to purchase some finished barracks and necessary additional lumber and materials for the construction of new buildings. We also anticipate the purchase of horses, cows, pigs, and chickens, and possibly the importation of small gardening tools and implements. . . .
>
> The general policy seems to be that these people [in Wolfsgrün] should move into the British zone. However, the Russians have shown no disposition to force them to leave their zone, provided they can be properly taken care of. To date we are receiving very satisfactory cooperation from the Russian authorities. (CR 271 5)

One month later, on August 7, 1946, Benson wrote again to the First Presidency and reported changed conditions in Wolfsgrün and the fact that no shipments had yet reached the members in the East German Mission:

> The refugee camp at Wolfsgrün has been taken from us by the Russians, allegedly due to the pressure of other German citizens who objected to the special consideration being given to our people. I do not know to what extent the press publicity on this matter may have affected the action taken. However, I am not greatly disappointed because there was developing a feeling, which was being encouraged by some, that the group was approaching communal living, which they had mistakenly understood to be the United Order. I have discussed this entire matter with the acting mission presidency and have found them in full sympathy with the counsel given them. The other proposed camp will likely not be considered further due to the fact that the Polish and zonal authorities are insisting that refugees from Poland go to the British zone in accordance with the policy adopted some time ago by the four occupying military forces.
>
> The last of the shipment of supplies which we purchased in Switzerland will be distributed next Friday, August 9. No church welfare products have reached the districts of the East German Mission. However, in checking with the International Red Cross office here today, . . . I learned that a Red Cross train is just leaving Geneva for Berlin and points en route. It is expected that this train will carry some of our welfare supplies. (CR 271 5)

On October 22, 1946, Benson reported to the First Presidency that the second shipment of Church welfare supplies, consisting of thirty-five tons of food products, had recently arrived in Berlin. The first shipment, received previously, was stored in the mission home, from which point it was being distributed throughout the various districts. Regarding these supplies, he quoted Richard Ranglack, who was still serving as the acting mission president, "The amount and condition of the clothing and food supplies far exceeded even our fondest expectations. . . . We have been able to supply the most urgent needs of the Berlin area and are preparing cases for shipment to the various districts throughout the mission." (CR 271 5)

Shipments into the Russian Zone, however, continued to be a problem. Elder Alma Sonne wrote to his daughter on February 5, 1947:

> The Germans are starving and freezing and relief distribution is difficult, almost impossible, under the military restrictions. We have a couple of carloads of welfare supplies in a warehouse in Berlin, which the Russians have not yet permitted us to distribute among the people. The four [allied powers] are suspicious and jealous of each other and apparently will not even cooperate on relief matters. It is disheartening in view of the dire need for relief among the people. (MS 16395)

In April 1948, Walter Stover gave a more positive report to the First Presidency on the status of the welfare assistance:

I am happy to say that last year every member of record in this mission received a total of eighty-five pounds of supplies through the welfare plan, exclusive of clothing. This made the members very happy and was a material help. But food is still very scarce and difficult, and even the above quantity was not enough to banish hunger.

Except for all types of underwear, for clothes for the ages of four to sixteen, women's shoes, men's suits and pants, we have been abundantly supplied with clothing. Except in the articles mentioned, each member is sufficiently supplied with two years at least. We have a number of supplies in clothing left which can, perhaps, be reworked into underwear and children's clothing.

We had no appreciable difficulty in bringing all these supplies into the Russian zone. As late as yesterday I received word that a truck and trailer with several tons of supplies went safely through the Russian checkpoints into one of our districts in Thuringia. (LR 2428 2)

The Church was required to give a portion of each shipment to local agencies for distribution to nonmembers. The following government document, "Mormon Contribution and the People's Solidarity," shows how a 1948 shipment was shared:

Zentralausschuss der Volkssolidarität—Auslandsspenden
Berlin, October 1, 1948
Circular #39/48

An agreement was reached between the East German Mission of the Church of Jesus Christ of Latter-day Saints (Mormons), represented by President Walter Stover, and representatives of the Secretariat of the Central Committee for the People's Solidarity and the Commission for the Distribution of Foreign Contributions for a joint distribution of a foreign gift of food, which was provided by the Church of Jesus Christ of Latter-day Saints (Mormons).

The distribution is based on a total of fourteen thousand needy persons, of which eight thousand are to be identified by the Mormons and six thousand by the People's Solidarity. Those chosen by the People's Solidarity will be needy persons over sixty years of age in the same localities in which the needy Mormons are assisted.

Each needy person identified by the Mormons will receive eight cans of fruit or vegetables, two cans of milk, three kilograms of wheat bran, and one kilogram of corn or wheat flour. Each needy person identified by the People's Solidarity will receive eight cans of fruit or vegetables, two cans of milk, one-half kilogram of wheat bran, and one-half kilogram of wheat flour. The difference in the distribution results from the fact that eighteen thousand kilograms of food have already been allocated to the feeding of children through the People's Solidarity of Leipzig. (LR 2428 48)

A portion of the above shipment was sent to the city of Forst on the German-Polish border. A document dated October 22, 1948, stated that 182 needy nonmembers in Forst were to receive food, of which 82 would be chosen by the branch president of the Mormons and 100 chosen by the People's Solidarity of Forst. The following items were shipped to Forst for distribution to the nonmembers: 296 kg of wheat bran, 50 kg of flour, 82 kg of beans, 364 cans of milk, and 1,456 cans of fruit and vegetables, including peas, corn, beets, tomatoes, apricots, apples, plums, and peaches (copy from Eberhard Gäbler).

Church members later commented about the Church's welfare assistance:

Joachim Meyer: We received clothing and various canned goods and as a result had more than many of our friends and acquaintances who did not belong to the Church. Of course, some of the welfare assistance was given to the state and only a portion reached the members. Nevertheless, it went very well until 1949, and we constantly received something from the Church during those three or four years. It helped us to survive. We didn't have a government until 1949, but were governed by the SMAD.... There existed a fairly good relationship between President Stover and the Soviet offices. There was a degree of cooperation. That is why it was possible for the Church's welfare to reach the members. (1989)

Alfred Bastian: I had a very good relationship with the school director, and there was an empty room in the school. When we received food from America, I stored it there for the branches in Schwarzenberg, Blauenthal, and partially also for Zwickau until it was distributed. We received clothing shipments, which were also stored there. We ate very well in the Church, the members received a warm meal several times during the week. They had a bowl of stew, a very good warm meal, following the Sunday meetings. (1991)

Hans Schult: In my opinion, that was a great event. There were packages with canned goods, mostly peaches. Also cracked wheat in small packages and fat in large cans. It doesn't sound very proper, but we always called it "monkey fat" since it was made in a different manner. In Germany, fat is obtained by cooking the meat, but the Americans, I believe, lay the bacon in a type of press and extract it cold. That's why my father called it "monkey fat." But it tasted excellent to us. We also received shoes. I received, for example, a pair of military boots and a leather jacket, perhaps such as pilots used, and many other items of clothing. We received very much.

One-third of all these welfare shipments, as I recall, were given to other churches, one-third went to the People's Solidarity, and one-third was for our Church. So we were told. We didn't really understand that at the time, since our Church had contributed it, but in the meantime we came to understand that one needs to help others who also are hungry. If in the future, in times of need, we have food and we could help others who are not members of our Church, then it is our responsibility to do that. At least that is what we've been taught recently. Therefore, I now understand the principle that was applied at that time, even though it was conducted within different political circumstances. Otherwise, nothing would have been allowed to enter the Soviet zone. (1991)

Conferences and Special Meetings, 1945–1949

District and mission conferences were a particular source of spiritual strength for the members in the immediate postwar period. Despite the extremely difficult conditions that existed at that time, the mission leaders organized outstanding conferences and special events. Reports of the following typical activities can be found in Appendix D:

District conference in Leipzig, March 1946
District conference in Dresden, May 1946
Mission conference in Leipzig, June 1946
Mission conference in Dresden (one-hundredth Pioneer anniversary), July 1947
Freud-Echo (Echo of Joy) conference in Berlin, June 1948 Mission Choir Tour, July 1949

3 The Church-State Relationship in the GDR

As long as the church remains church and the state remains state, I'm convinced that these two institutions can live together peacefully. (Prime Minister Otto Grotewohl, 1949)

In twenty-five years no one will even speak about churches anymore. (Walter Ulbricht, chairman of the State Council, 1960)

Many opportunities are opening now and in the future for churches, as churches within socialism, to work cooperatively toward the deepest humanistic goals. (Erich Honecker, chairman of the State Council, 1978)

We assume that churches and religious organizations will continue to exist for a long time and that it is therefore necessary to consider what role they should be accorded in a socialistic society. (Paul Verner, Politburo member responsible for church policy, 1980)

Christians are very typical citizens of the GDR. . . . We are not an atheistic state, rather a state of workers and farmers. Religion and church are a normal part of life in socialism, in fact they are a "standard" of everyday life. (Klaus Gysi, secretary for Church Affairs, 1987)

I realized that it would not be easy for the churches to get used to us, but I didn't realize that it would be so difficult for us to accept churches as a normal part of life. (Klaus Gysi, former secretary for Church Affairs, 1990)

As indicated by the above statements, the GDR's policy toward churches changed significantly during its forty-year history, and the relationship of the LDS Church to the government underwent similar changes, as described in the following chapters. An understanding of the relationship between the state and the LDS Church requires a short introduction to the generic church-state relationship within the GDR. For example, the government's suggestion in May of 1978, that the Church build a temple in that country, took place shortly after the Politburo's decision to permit the Evangelical churches to construct new meeting houses and was consistent with the GDR's stated principle regarding the equality of all churches. The 1988 meeting between Chairman Erich Honecker and President Thomas S. Monson, which opened the GDR's borders to missionaries, also was closely linked to broader state-church events of that time.

Historical Church-State Relationships

The historical development of Europe had always included a special relationship between the ruling monarchs of each country and a dominant church, either the Catholic or one of the Protestant churches. These "state" churches exercised varying degrees of political influence. Each of the independent German states and principalities that were combined into the new German Empire of the late nineteenth century had already developed a special relationship with either the Catholic or an evangelical church. Therefore, the German Empire contained several recognized "state" churches. While small "free" churches, including the LDS Church, had gained a foothold in Germany, their activities in the nineteenth century were frequently restricted by the government at the instigation of the state churches. However, the defeat of the German Empire and the establishment of the Weimar Republic in 1918 resulted in major social and legal changes that included the constitutional separation of church and state and the official equality of all churches. While the former state churches still exercised considerable influence in political affairs, the smaller "free" churches experienced significant growth after 1918, especially in Saxony and other eastern provinces that would later become East Germany. While the Nazi government that followed the Weimar Republic restricted all churches to some degree, its defeat in World War II once more provided new freedom for religious organizations, even under the Soviet Military Administration. However, the formal establishment of the communist-dominated German Democratic Republic in 1949 presented all religious organizations with the necessity of working with a socialist government whose goal was the eventual disappearance of churches, but whose constitution proclaimed freedom of religion and the equality of churches.

A theological encyclopedia published in the GDR in 1981 described the options available to churches within that socialist system:

> The liberation from fascism brought to churches in the GDR complete self-determination in the regulation of their affairs, but also of course an end to their former privileges. The Soviet military government initiated the first steps in this regard, in that it cancelled the antichurch rules and regulations of the Nazis and restored religious freedom. . . . The separation of church and state and the freedom of churches from meddling by the state were not just proclaimed in the 1949 constitution of the GDR, but were principles that guided its ac-

> tions. Of course, it was necessary that churches accept the existence of the state and adapt themselves to new social conditions. The socialist constitution of 1974 contains, in Article 20, paragraph 1, the principle that every citizen is guaranteed the same rights and responsibilities, regardless of philosophy of life or religious orientation. Freedom of religion is further defined in Article 39: "Every citizen of the German Democratic Republic has the right to declare his religious faith and to engage in religious activity. Churches and other religious organizations organize their affairs and conduct their own activities in conformity with the constitution and the regulations of the German Democratic Republic." These regulations provide the churches with a good, but also the only, basis for the further development of their relationship to the socialist state.[1]

Another entry in the same encyclopedia described the relationship of individual Christians to the state:

> The relationship of individual Christians to society and the state is, of necessity, different than that of the churches. They are one with all citizens, whereas the status of churches, as institutions, is characterized by the principle of the separation of church and state, although they are not, of course, outside the legal sovereignty of the state. The position of the church and of Christians is defined by the socialist constitution. Particularly noteworthy is the guarantee of equal rights for all citizens (Article 19). That exists regardless of nationality, race, philosophy of life, or religious persuasion and is expressly based on the statement, "Freedom of conscience and religion is guaranteed."
>
> Christians, who have proven themselves to be antifascist, or who have undergone a reorientation because of their historical experiences with imperialism and fascism, are working with Marxists on an equal footing to create an antifascist society. All democratic mass organizations offer Christians the opportunity for unlimited and equal participation in the creation of the socialist society.... Christians are given manifold opportunities to be involved in social affairs and to exercise all rights and responsibilities of citizens, which are guaranteed in the constitution of the GDR via the principle of equality.[2]

Prior to the official establishment of the GDR in 1949, the East German Mission received a copy of the country's proposed constitution for review and comment. The mission's response, dated April 28, 1947, was written by Paul Langheinrich:

> We received your letter of April 15, including the brochure "Otto Grotewohl, Deutsche Verfassungspläne." We have read it with great interest and wish to share with you our perspective regarding this draft.

It is about time that state and church are separated. Our 11th Article of Faith states, "We claim the privilege of worshiping Almighty God according to the dictates of our own conscience, and allow all men the same privilege, let them worship how, where, or what they may."

Religion is a personal matter, and the man or woman who is chosen to guide and direct the affairs of our country must be nonpartisan and not influenced by any church ties. Neither money nor position, but ability alone should be the deciding factor for anyone. It would be good when a way could be found to bring the highest possible degree of education to all segments of society, so they are able to think clearly and make decisions in the future. No Pied Piper should have the opportunity again, as in 1933, to take advantage of hard times to lead the people into disaster. If it had been openly known before 1933, that the crisis had been intentionally created by a small circle of people, events would have taken a different course.

We teach that all mankind is one large family and that every dispute and war is madness. Our members are always instructed to maintain order within their own families and to help the poor. According to the teachings of our Church, freedom is obedience to just principles, and these can only exist when a true government of the people acts for the welfare of all people. You may be assured that you will find full support from the members of our Church for everything that contributes to the welfare and security of our people and all mankind.

I would be pleased to discuss these matters with you, and remain respectfully, on behalf of the Church, Paul Langheinrich (MS 13216)

Political Organization of the GDR

With the backing of the Soviet occupation forces, the previously existing Communist Party of Germany (KPD) and the Social Democratic Party of Germany (SPD) were merged on April 21, 1946, into the Socialist Unity Party (Sozialistische Einheitspartei Deutschlands) or SED,[3] which became the official state party of the GDR when that country was established and formally recognized by the Soviet Union in 1949. Several other political parties, such as the Christian Democratic Party (CDU), continued to function in the GDR but had no significant influence on national policy.

The Central Committee of the SED was responsible for implementation of decisions made at the party's periodic conventions. The Central Committee, in turn, chose the members of the Politburo, the most powerful operating institution in the GDR. The Politburo made all important decisions concerning church policy and instructed the prime minister (chairman of the State Council) regarding his interactions with church representatives. The Central Committee also established its own secretariat, whose members functioned as intermediaries between the Politburo and the operating ministries and agencies. However, the historian Joachim Heise emphasized that "it would be an unacceptable simplification to imply that the religious policies conceived and stipulated by the Politburo were also implemented as such within the GDR. Rather, there were significant differences in the individual districts, counties, and municipalities."[4]

During the first decade of the GDR, an office known as Liaison to the Churches, which reported to the deputy prime minister, Otto Nuschke, was officially responsible for the implementation of the government's state-church policies. That office, however, did not have a rank equal to the government's operating ministries, such as the Interior Ministry and the Ministry for State Security (Stasi). Offices within those two ministries competed for influence in setting church-state policy, which resulted in different interpretations of the country's constitution and the Politburo's directives. Although each competing office endorsed the principle of separation of church and state, Nuschke's office interpreted the rights of religious organizations more liberally than did the other offices. However, Nuschke was a member of the CDU Party, and his influence gradually declined. Joachim Heise explained:

> The SED leadership began to exercise ever greater power in church-state matters even prior to the official establishment of the GDR. Step by step, it sought to reduce the influence of the churches and to restrict the activities that the SMAD had previously permitted. The SED considered these restrictions as essential for the creation of the foundation of socialism in the GDR, and party officials devised a series of administrative actions, including a public education program based on popular science, that kept its antireligious goals in the public's eye. This approach did not succeed immediately, since the SED leadership did not wish to openly challenge the SMAD's agreements with the churches or confront officials who sought compromises with the churches.[5]

A proposal presented to the secretariat on April 6, 1949, emphasized the need to be circumspect regarding antichurch activities. Entitled "Measures to Reduce the Influence of the Churches," it stated:

> Numerous incidents in recent times have proven that the churches and sects have considerably expanded their activities and have greatly increased their influence, especially among women, youth, and [refugees from the former eastern provinces]. Therefore, a series of actions are necessary to restrain the influence of the church. [However] we must avoid any appearance of antireligious propaganda and any action openly directed against religion and church, in order not to give cause for political opposition against the SMAD or the SED.[6]

On July 26, 1952, the Politburo reviewed and approved a position paper entitled, "Analysis of the Politics of the Churches," which stated in part:

> The forces of imperialism no longer have any legal home within the GDR. Therefore, they are increasing their efforts to use the reactionary leadership of the churches as tools for the implementation of their political goals.... The leadership of the churches is conducting comprehensive ideological efforts that are intended, under the cover of church teachings, to turn the largest possible part of the population against the GDR. The Marxist-Leninist philosophy, which will bring freedom and peace to nations, is being [negatively] contrasted with Christianity. [Dialectical] materialism is presented as an ideology of hate, because it clearly and unambiguously reveals to oppressed people their true enemies. Instead of encouraging the fighting spirit of people to oppose oppression, exploitation, and the terrorist actions of imperialist powers, people are taught the ideology of patience, the ideology of "Love your Enemies."[7]

The SED's economic and religious policies led to widespread unrest, which culminated in the civilian uprising of June 1953. After its suppression, the Politburo issued several new directives, including "Party Policy Regarding Church Affairs," which was approved on March 14, 1954. Its basic principles were sent to local party officials via a circular signed by the Central Committee. It was the first time that the SED leadership had composed such a comprehensive and detailed statement of church policy and formally shared it with district- and county-level officials in this manner. The text began with the claim that the Evangelical and the Catholic churches were the strongest legal institutions in the GDR that "support the forces of imperialism." Joachim Heise said that the Politburo's goal was to gain a broad base of support among the adherents of all religious organizations. The Christian population was to be enticed to "participate in the resolution of the vital issues facing the German people" and to isolate the "reactionary forces" in the churches.[8]

Simultaneously, the SED increased its pressure on church leaders to make public statements in support of the government. In December 1955, Deputy Prime Minister Otto Nuschke addressed the CDU leadership and said:

> The foundation of church life in the GDR is the "Staat der Arbeiter und Bauern" [Workers and Farmers State]. Only when that fact is recognized, only when the churches accept the fact that their development must take place upon that foundation, can a resolution of all existing church-state problems be achieved. The churches can no longer ignore this fact. Church leaders can no longer assume that the GDR is an interregnum, which sooner or later will cease to exist.... Our state expects nothing less than loyalty from the church. That is a correct and justifiable expectation.[9]

To win popular support for the government's antichurch initiatives, party officials were told to avoid any public criticism of religion per se. Church leaders and their ties to "reactionary" churches in the West could be criticized but the religious feelings of Christian people must not be violated. The Politburo emphasized that initiatives to implement a "progressive" church-state relationship must be shown to be in the interest of Christian people. "It must be conducted in a manner that in no way harms the religious feelings and sensitivities of people."[10]

The Jugendweihe

To facilitate the atheistic upbringing of its youth, the Politburo, against the opposition of the established churches, ordered the implementation of the Jugendweihe, a youth instruction and initiation program. The Jugendweihe had been developed in the nineteenth century by the smaller reformed churches in Germany as an alternative to the traditional confirmation or communion ceremonies of the state churches. It consisted of culturally based moral instruction and culminated in a ceremony that took place upon completion of basic or elementary school at age twelve or fourteen. The Jugendweihe did not have a large following in Germany, and it was initially prohibited in the GDR. However, the Politburo turned to it at this time as an instrument of ideological indoctrination of young people. The purpose of the Jugendweihe was evident in this excerpt from the Politburo's March 14, 1954, statement on the program:

> Currently, children are being sent to confirmation and communion classes by parents who do not have close religious ties to the churches, because there is no alternative ceremonial introduction for children into the next phase of their life after graduation from school. It is in the interest of a stronger civic upbringing to resolve this problem by planning now to implement the Jugendweihe in 1955.[11]

Students who did not participate in the Jugendweihe faced considerable discrimination. They were usually not allowed to continue their education to the higher grades that prepared them for the Abitur, an examination required for admission to a university or technical high school. The Politburo also initiated new restrictions on church-sponsored youth organizations and increased their efforts to entice young people into the state-sponsored Free German Youth (Freie Deutsche Jugend or FDJ).

The State Secretariat for Church Affairs

In March 1957, Nuschke's office of Liaison to the Churches was replaced with a State Secretariat for Church Affairs. Its primary function was to convey to the churches and religious organizations the "rights and interests of the state" and to see that they conduct their activities "within the bounds of relevant laws and ordinances." Werner Eggerath, the first state secretary for Church Affairs, was followed by Hans Seigewasser in 1960, who served until his death in 1979. Thereafter, Klaus Gysi led the office until replaced by Kurt Löffler in July 1988.

In a 1991 interview, Secretary Löffler gave his perspective on the church-state relationship and his role as state secretary:

> There was a strict separation between state and church in the former GDR. The churches had absolutely no right or opportunity to address state matters, e.g., issues concerning economic development, education policy, cultural programs, military service, etc. The constitution included specific provisions regarding religious freedom—the freedom to join religious organizations and churches—and it gave the churches the ability to conduct their activities without state interference.
>
> The GDR had a State Council composed of ministers similar to cabinet members in the U.S. government. Each minister had a corresponding state secretary, who was the ministry's operating officer. However the state secretary for Church Affairs had no operating authority. His exclusive function was to bring the wishes of the churches to the state and to convey the wishes and expectations of the state to the churches. The relationship between the secretary and the individual churches was more or less friendly according to the personality and orientation of the discussion partners.
>
> I have presented the ideal concept and the ideal relationship. However, with the steadily declining economic status of the GDR, the clearly growing restrictions on personal freedoms, the growing involvement of the state in decisions of daily life, from schooling to professional development to job assignments, etc., the churches increasingly came to be the [unofficial] representative of the people whose interests were no longer guaranteed by the politics of the state.

Günther Behncke led the legal division of the Secretariat for Church Affairs from 1981 to 1990 and contributed significantly to the success of the Church in that last decade of the German Democratic Republic. He also offered his perspective regarding the church-state relationship in the GDR in a 1991 interview:

> I was responsible for all questions that arose regarding the constitutional rights of the churches and religious organizations in the GDR and the principle of separation of state and church. In other words, I was responsible for the preservation of the constitutional rights of the churches and religious organizations with regard to the state, but also, of course, for the preservation of the state's interests in regard to the churches. Here in the GDR, constitutional rights and constitutional reality were often far apart. We had an excellent socialistic constitution, which basically defined all democratic civic freedoms: religious freedom, freedom to assemble, freedom to associate with others, etc. But it was often quite different in practice.
>
> We had a system of laws, rules, and regulations in our country, and many government offices were theoretically responsible for their ap-

> plication. There were many ultra-leftists in the districts and counties (we called them "concrete heads") who, when in doubt, ruled against the churches. In those instances, we in the secretariat had to intervene. Where possible, most of the decisions from our office were in favor of the churches. Of course, Herr Behncke could not high-handedly make decisions, but Herr Behncke was able to influence and facilitate to some degree.
>
> When the party and government leaders announced or wrote that there was room in the GDR for all people, independent of their religion and faith, then we had to be fair and just to all people and all churches and religious organizations in our practice. That was my basic conviction and my starting point in discussions with government functionaries at all levels, including with the conservative orthodox Communists. I always made it clear that for me, as a representative of this state, there was no difference between constitutional law and constitutional reality.

Over the years, the Church developed a good working relationship with officials within the State Secretariat for Church Affairs. When President Henry Burkhardt sent birthday greetings to Secretary Kurt Löffler on August 25, 1989, shortly before the Berlin Wall fell, he referred to the building of the temple and the opening of the country to missionary activity and said: "All these things are an indication of the good atmosphere and mutual respect that has always been evident in the discussions and negotiations with the staff of the secretariat, which you lead" (Dresden Mission Office Files, hereafter abbreviated as DMO).

Jürgen Warnke was legal counsel to the Church's Frankfurt regional office for many years and worked closely with Secretary Löffler and Herr Behncke. After the fall of the GDR government (the Wende), he wrote to Behncke on March 15, 1990, and said that it had been especially important for religious minorities to have a responsive contact person within the government and that the secretariat had been particularly helpful in facilitating discussion between the state and the Church. (DMO)

The Erich Honecker Era and New Church Buildings

A far-reaching change in the leadership of the GDR took place in May 1971 when Erich Honecker replaced Walter Ulbricht as first secretary of the Central Committee of the SED. Four years later, he also replaced Ulbricht as chairman of the State Council. This change in leadership coincided with a significant organizational change among the major churches of the GDR. When Germany was separated at the end of World War II, eight Evangelical state churches within East Germany continued their membership in the Evangelischen Kirchen in Deutschland (EKD), an association based in West Germany. In 1969, those eight Evangelical churches separated from the EKD and created a new association, known as the Bund der Evangelischen Kirchen (BEK). The

GDR welcomed their separation from the EKD but did not welcome and did not initially recognize the new BEK association because the state preferred to negotiate separately with each church.

During the transition period between Honecker and Ulbricht, the BEK had submitted a request for construction of new church buildings, a request that would come to have a significant impact on the LDS Church. For economic and political reasons, the GDR had already approved the rebuilding of a few historic churches destroyed in the war. This "Sonderbau" or special construction program had been limited to selected historic structures, and all building costs had to be paid with Western money provided by churches and foundations outside the GDR. However, the BEK now proposed a significant expansion of that program by requesting a number of construction projects for meeting facilities in new urban areas where no church building previously existed. After most of their requests had been refused by local authorities, the BEK appealed its proposal to higher authorities. Subsequent discussions with officials responsible for church policy led to a decision in June 1976 to expand the Sonderbau program. The government's new policy is described and justified in excerpts from a policy paper entitled, "Information about the Efforts of the Churches to Build Centers in New Settlements in the GDR":

> The churches have requested, especially for new urban areas, the building of so-called parish centers or multipurpose buildings for traditional religious services and seminars, with ancillary facilities for social gatherings of men, women, youth, and children and occasional overnight lodging. The installation of larger kitchen facilities is anticipated in some instances. Declining membership and the fact that church programs are attended only by a small number of members, have led to a desire for erection of smaller buildings instead of spacious facilities for worship services.
>
> The fact that the churches are making special efforts to attract the youth has influenced the proposed type of buildings. The churches intend to use these multipurpose buildings to create youth-oriented facilities for programs such as dances, amateur plays, musical activities, and social gatherings.
>
> We must recognize that the churches are already conducting such activities in new urban areas despite the absence of appropriate facilities. They are establishing, for example, home-based programs for small circles of members, especially in areas where they do not have access to other facilities. The activities in these smaller circles, conducted outside of regularly used church facilities, are less transparent and more difficult to observe than in official church facilities.[12]

Paul Verner, a Politburo member responsible for church policy, briefed district party officials about the BEK's proposal on July 22, 1976, and justified the Politburo's approval:

> We have invited you to this meeting at the request of the [Central Committee's] secretariat to clarify several issues about our policy toward the churches.... We approach all church policy issues according to our main political goal, which is the overall development of our society, and we resolve them primarily by involving the religious-oriented segment of the population in the formation of the emerging socialistic society in the GDR. We have approached the issue of the church's buildings from the same perspective. At our suggestion, a discussion was held with the chairman of the Conference of Evangelical Church Leaders, Bishop Schönherr... concerning this matter. Bishop Schönherr was informed that our party leaders are prepared to set aside land on which to build churches in new cities and in new residential areas.
>
> The problem results mainly from the efforts of the churches to adjust their building status to changed social circumstances. Their declining membership requires smaller buildings and rooms.... Our party's youth policy, effective education and training in our schools and teaching facilities, and the growing influence of our socialist youth organizations are leading the churches to greater effort to attract the youth to church activity. The churches, therefore, have requested the building of so-called community centers or multipurpose buildings, especially in new residential areas.
>
> Undoubtedly, the requested church buildings will make their church work easier. That is one view. On the other hand, it is clear to us that the churches are able to function in the new urban areas even without the appropriate facilities. We know, for example, that they have organized so-called family circles and meet in private apartments. You know from your own experience, dear comrades, how complicated it is to control such activity or to prevent it through administrative measures, and you know what unfavorable effects such measures can have on our effort to recruit church officers and church-oriented citizens to an open-minded and loyal participation in our socialist society. In addition, small group activities, especially outside regular church facilities, are less transparent and more difficult to observe. On the basis of these considerations, we intend to have you individually review each of the churches' requests for construction in new communities and submit your recommendation (for or against) to our secretariat.[13]

Six months later, on February 1, 1977, the Politburo formally approved a document entitled, "Construction of Church Buildings in New Areas," which was not made public until one year later. It contained the following four points: (1) the ten projects requested by the BEK for new residential areas are approved; (2) if church-owned land is not available in the desired area, construction can occur on land leased (not purchased) from the government, or church-owned land elsewhere can be traded for land in the desired location;

(3) each proposed project shall be reviewed in advance by the responsible district council for conformity to local building guidelines and "church-state policy"; and (4) building costs shall be calculated on a "Valuta" basis, i.e., expenses shall be paid with money from the West.[14]

On March 6, 1978, Chairman Erich Honecker met with the BEK leadership in an historic summit meeting, frequently referred to in subsequent GDR documents as the "Spitzengespräch." The meeting took place at a time of increasing ideological dispute between the government and the major churches, which had adversely affected the government's domestic and foreign reputation and initiatives. It was in the government's interest to establish a more effective working relationship with the churches.

During the meeting, which was conducted without public notice, Chairman Honecker informed the BEK leadership of the government's decision to expand the previous special building program to permit construction of new church buildings. He also stated that the government would organize a nationwide five-hundredth anniversary celebration of Martin Luther's birth, allow the BEK to use state-run television for periodic programs, and liberalize the regulations regarding the importation of church newspapers and literature. More significantly, Honecker told the BEK leaders that all GDR citizens would be treated equally, that a qualified citizen, for example, would not be prevented from being a chief physician just because he was a Christian.[15]

The following day, *Neues Deutschland,* the SED's official newspaper, reported that the leadership of the evangelical churches had met with Erich Honecker in an open, relaxed, and friendly atmosphere. The historian Horst Dohle, a former official of the Secretariat for Church Affairs, described the March 6, 1978, summit meeting as the most significant event in the church-state history of the GDR. He said the meeting and its outcome came as a total surprise to church members and SED Party members alike:

> The SED members thought: "Everyone in Berlin must have gone mad, because we are supposed to be opposed to the church!" Members of the churches accepted the news with great suspicion, as if church leaders had betrayed the interests of the common Christian, had capitulated to the SED, and had allowed themselves to be misused in a spectacular show of supposed harmony.[16]

It is noteworthy that this public reaction was similar to the reaction of some LDS Church members ten years later upon hearing about the 1988 meeting between Erich Honecker and Thomas Monson (see Chapter 17).

Two weeks later, on March 22 1978, Paul Verner summarized the results of the "Spitzengespräch" in a meeting with district leaders. However, his description of the summit did not fully match either the tone or the specifics that the BEK leaders had heard directly from Honecker, thus revealing that at least some Politburo members were not in total agreement with Honecker's new church policy. Horst Dohle described Verner's speech in this manner:

Verner stated that this meeting was unique in the history of the GDR and would significantly influence church policy in the future. It proved that the churches in the GDR have accepted the inevitable development of socialism in the GDR and adjusted to it. That was certainly a correct conclusion by Verner, since the churches did not anticipate the end of the GDR, nor was its end at all evident. . . . Verner then expressed the hope that the meeting would greatly increase the willingness of Christians to work for the good of the society. While critics of the BEK within the churches would increase their criticism of their leaders, acceptance of March 6th would be the dominant attitude within the church.

Verner said that March 6 was an extension of previous church policies and did not constitute a new church policy or any revision thereof. At this point in his talk, if not earlier, it became clear that Verner was not willing to consider a new formulation of the rigid orthodox-ideological view of religion and churches despite previous social-political experience. The ideological core of his historical view remained unchanged.

The last point in Verner's talk, where he addressed the future implications of the March 6 meeting, deserves special attention. He indicated that it would be impossible after this meeting for the GDR to be weakened from within "through the development of opposition from the church." He then added a few additional comments, which clearly revealed the helplessly arrogant and contradictory nature of the GDR's church policy. On the one hand, he pointed out "that religious convictions and institutions will continue to exist for a long time." . . . On the other hand, he endorsed the current church policy and rejected any illusions of a creative revision thereof. For example there would be no possibility of an equal partnership between state and church, no "critical critique" of the state from the church and no role for the church in discussion of issues related to public education, youth policy, and legal issues. Whereas Honecker, according to church notes, said at the end of the meeting that "the issues voiced here will motivate the representatives of the state to consider these issues," no evidence of that was visible two weeks later with Verner.

This meeting had a relaxing effect on the relationship between state and church into the 1980s and enabled a vastly superior and pragmatic style of interaction and of discussions worthy of that name. . . . It was a process of critical solidarity, of critique accompanying established power, a sensitive early warning system of social conflicts. But since the SED leadership lacked the necessary confidence to allow its own power to be critiqued, to say nothing of an ability to critically analyze itself, it labeled the church's way as inappropriate "meddling in state affairs." The reference to the "Spirit and Letter of March 6, 1978" degenerated in the church policy of the SED to ritual, static incantations.

> With the violence associated with the events of November 1987 in the Zionskirche in Berlin [see Chapter 17]...nothing remained of the innovative opportunities associated with March 6, 1978.[17]

Two years later, on May 16, 1980, Paul Verner again addressed the status of church-state policies during a seminar for responsible officials. The following excerpts reveal an outward optimism as well as signs that the summit of March 6, 1978, had not resolved the conflicts between church and state:

> The development of the churches...after the significant discussion of the chairman of the State Council, Erich Honecker, with the leaders of the BEK in March 1978 confirms that we are making good progress toward the achievement of our church-state goals [the gradual establishment of communism]....The majority of the clergy, even those with definite reservations about socialism, now accept the socialistic society as the place in which God wishes the church to function....Some see the opportunity to be a Christian without the formalism of a church.
>
> These developments received a strong impulse from the discussions of March 6, 1978....It had a relaxing effect on state-church relations and allowed a more open atmosphere and greater willingness for dialogue in many localities. It is not a matter of making concessions to the churches, rather it is the logical consequence of our political strategy...in which the evolving socialism is being developed with and for all citizens.
>
> Naturally, the discussions of March 6, 1978, and their outcomes have initiated or strengthened a number of ancillary effects and tendencies in the churches, which are not in our best interests, especially regarding exaggerated demands on the socialist state [and] the efforts by church people to get involved in our education efforts and to oppose the communistic upbringing of the children. Education is the responsibility of the state, not of the church.
>
> In that regard, there are certain illusions about the social status of religion and church. We hear, for example, the idea that state and church, scientific philosophy and religion have equal legitimacy and equal value, and that our Marxist Party should cease advocating our atheistic philosophy. I wish to draw attention to several items that are in direct opposition to the spirit and goal of the discussions of March 6, 1978:
>
> 1. The intent to develop the church into a forum for dissenters or a place for propagation of political and social theories that contradict socialism.
>
> 2. The right to make the church into a home for or representative of such citizens, who have, for various reasons, a distorted relationship to the state.

3. Statements which contain a clearly false characterization of the relationship of Christian citizens to their country and its politics.

4. Nonfactual descriptions of the status of working people in the GDR, which include claims of fear, suspicion, and resignation.

We assume that the churches and religious organizations will continue to exist over a long period of time. It is therefore necessary to consider how churches can be integrated into the socialist society.... A church in socialism must meet the following basic requirements:

1. It accepts the socialist social system and the socialist state and carries out its function in the socialist society in such a manner that its actions are in agreement with the basic interests of the socialist state and its citizens and operates in accordance with the laws and the norms of socialism.

2. It contributes to the strengthening of the GDR and to an increase in its reputation abroad. In accordance with its calling to serve people and society, it encourages its members to greater achievements and to work for the benefit of society and for every single person.

3. It supports the peace policies of the socialistic states....

6. It respects the basic principle of the separation of state and church, which enables it to preserve its independence in the socialistic environment and simultaneously prevents it from meddling in the exclusive interests and areas of competence of the state.[18]

The State-Church Relationship in Conflict

Seven years later, the November 1987 raid on the Zionskirche in Berlin fully exposed the church-state conflict. In response to the political activity of some churches, Werner Jarowinsky, a Politburo member responsible for church-state affairs, was instructed to prepare a statement regarding the proper relationship between the state and church for presentation to Bishop Leich, the chairman of the Conference of Evangelical Church Leaders in the GDR. Following approval by the Politburo, it was formally, though not cordially, read by Jarowinsky to Bishop Leich on February 19, 1988. Following are excerpts:

> Events and activities in the sphere of the evangelical churches have been increasing in recent times, which cannot remain unchallenged.... They are in direct opposition to the long-proven form of communication, cooperation, and respect that is due the state, parties, and social organizations and which are required from the churches under our constitution. It must be stated: There can be no law-free zone even within the church. There is a tendency toward injury and disrespect of the socialist legitimacy and government order, including clear misuse of church buildings.... The preconditions for state-church relations has always been... the acceptance by the church of full responsibility for everything that takes place in church facilities, and especially strict conformity to the principle of separation between state and

church. That is and remains the basic principle of our church politic—to the church, that which belongs to the church, to the state, that which belongs to the state. Just as we guarantee religious freedom and do not meddle in the religious affairs of the churches, the church cannot and may not concern itself with functions belonging to the state or meddle in state affairs.

Among the events which raise justifiable concerns, are activities in some Berlin churches, which have become an unacceptable, dangerous burden. Purely political, inflammatory activities are organized, antigovernmental proposals and calls for confrontation and riots are allowed. . . . It is now time, without delay, to take action and to guarantee that all churches again become churches.[19]

The Church of Jesus Christ of Latter-day Saints

In the midst of this growing clash between the evangelical churches and the state, President Burkhardt met with Günther Behncke on February 11, 1988, in the offices of the Secretariat for Church Affairs. Burkhardt told Behncke that the Church believed in the separation of church and state and expected its members to act accordingly. Behncke encouraged him to share the Church's position with government officials. Two months later, Burkhardt wrote to Erich Honecker and requested an opportunity for general authorities of the Church to meet with him in October. The stated purpose of the meeting was to convey personal thanks for the freedom of religion in the GDR and for the building program that had permitted the Church to build the temple and several meeting houses. The letter also indicated an interest in discussing "problems of our time" with the chairman. Chapter 17 details the background to this request, its acceptance by Honecker, and the preparation by the Church and the state for the meeting.

Prior to meeting, Burkhardt sent Honecker a declaration that detailed the Church's philosophy and practice regarding church-state relationships. The text of the declaration (see Chapter 17) shows that its authors were fully aware of the problems and the principles expressed by Paul Verner and Werner Jarowinsky regarding the conflict between the evangelical churches and the state.

Horst Dohle said that the meeting between Erich Honecker and representatives of the LDS Church signaled to other churches "the readiness of the government for discussion and negotiation about legitimate issues," which the government had refused to hold at that time with the Conference of Evangelical Church Leaders.[20]

4 The Legal Status of the LDS Church

> *It is recommended that the following sect be prohibited—Church of Jesus Christ of Latter-day Saints—Mormon. (Interior Ministry, November 1950)*

> *It is hereby certified that the Church of Jesus Christ of Latter-day Saints in the GDR is a recognized religious organization, which possesses legal status under §15.2 of the ordinance of November 6, 1975, concerning the establishment and activity of associations. (Günther Behncke, Secretariat for Church Affairs, May 2, 1985)*

The path to full legal authority for the Church in the GDR was long, difficult, and complicated. That path began in 1945, when Paul Langheinrich registered the Church with the SMAD in Berlin-Karlshorst. However, after the new GDR government was established in 1949, the Church's name was not found on the SMAD's list of registered churches. Therefore, many branches were informed by the police in June 1950 that they were illegal. Fortunately, the reason for this first legal challenge to the Church was soon discovered. The SMAD had recorded the "Mormon Church," not the "Church of Jesus Christ of Latter-day Saints." President Walter Stover explained the problem in a letter to the Interior Ministry on July 12, 1950:

> After receiving notices from county police offices in Chemnitz, Freiberg, and Brandenburg, we ... now submit the official registration of our church for your information. We emphasize that our church has been named the Church of Jesus Christ of Latter-day Saints since its establishment in 1830 and is only known popularly as the "Mormon Church." ... Our church was officially registered in 1945 with the SMAD as well as in various locations where we have branches in the present GDR—earlier the Soviet Occupation Zone. (MS 13918)

The problem was resolved within a few weeks, and church meetings were resumed. However, the Church had to remove the name "East German Mission" from all of its correspondence, apparently out of concern that the name might indicate some official tie to the state. Walter Kindt, the district president in Leipzig, received the following instruction from the police office in Leipzig:

> This is to inform you that according to Leipzig district police directive #174, dated August 2, 1950, the name "East German Mission" is prohibited and may not be used in written correspondence. You are to immediately remove that name from all written material and forms. Any branch that continues to use that name, even in correspondence, must immediately cease any further activity. (DMO)

In Zwickau, Walter Fassmann decided that the branch could continue to function under the name "Mormon Church" until the formal name had been registered. All signs with the full name of the church, as well as the name "East German Mission," were removed. However, several members did not agree with his decision, and one of the local brethren expressed his disapproval in a talk on Sunday, July 16. On the following day, Fassmann received a letter from the police that said, "Inasmuch as it was discovered that members of your groups are not willing to accept the decision between you and us, we feel that it is our duty to prohibit any further meetings until a final decision in this matter has been made." (LR 2428 2)

President Burkhardt commented later concerning this episode:

> The Church's activities were prohibited simply because the name East German Mission was politically unacceptable to the government. We could not hold religious services for fourteen days. The brethren reacted quickly, and as soon as we ceased to use that name, we again received permission to hold our meetings. Actually, it was the only instance where we were officially prohibited from assembling. (1991)

The mission's name was not officially changed until 1957. After Elder Spencer W. Kimball visited the mission in 1955, he wrote to President Harold Gregory:

> It was my understanding that the term "East German Mission" is not permitted on stationery or letterheads or otherwise.... North German Mission and South German Mission might be more appropriate, and this would still leave room for another German mission, the East German Mission, when the curtain is lifted.... I am bringing this matter to the attention of the First Presidency and the Twelve. (LR 2428 39)

While the problem of the SMAD's registration of the Church under the wrong name was resolved at that time, the new GDR government was still intent on reducing the number of small religious organizations. Various options were discussed, beginning with the following proposal of the Interior Ministry, dated November 1, 1950:

> In accordance with Article 43 [of the GDR's Constitution], the activities of the twelve organizations recognized as legal public corporations [Körperschaft des öffentlichen Rechts] should be authorized. All other religious organizations and sects, regardless of whether or not their activities were previously permitted by the SMAD or by German offices after the creation of the GDR, should be placed in one group and treated as follows: . . . religious organizations that operate only within the GDR and which can be shown to have no connections to the West, especially to Switzerland, England, and the USA, may be authorized. The following is recommended for individual sects that were previously authorized:
>
> Christian Scientists: prohibit
> New Apostolic Community: prohibit
> Christian Community: prohibit
> Seventh-Day Adventists: prohibit
> Church of Jesus Christ of Latter-day Saints (Mormon): prohibit
>
> Members of this sect recently prepared group sheets for genealogical research, which were sent to town mayors for confirmation and revision. Its headquarters is in the USA and its German leadership is in Berlin-Dahlem. (MS 13918)

The Interior Ministry's proposal was not implemented, but the ministry prepared a second proposal on August 15, 1951, which stated: "All entities in the Register of Organizations are to be reviewed [and] only those religious organizations without legal corporate status, whose primary office is within the GDR, should be authorized." At that time, the headquarters of the East German Mission was in West Berlin, and the mission did not even have an office in the GDR.

Although this second proposal also was not implemented, its provisions were likely known to district and county councils, which would affect relationships between the mission and local government officials. Therefore, Henry Burkhardt, who became a counselor to the mission president in 1952, asked Paul Langheinrich to inquire about the legal status of the mission. Langheinrich responded on June 9, 1953:

> In response to your request of yesterday regarding the registration of the Church, I can inform you of the following: In 1945 I personally had the Church registered with the SMAD at its headquarters in Berlin-Karlshorst. Today I went to the Secretariat for Internal Affairs in the Interior Ministry of the GDR regarding your request. The representative, Herr Schwarzer, authorized me to inform you that the Church of Jesus Christ of Latter-day Saints is authorized within the territory of

> the GDR. Local police offices have this information. If anyone is not aware of this fact, ask them to check with the nearest police office, or if in doubt, at the county office. (DMO)

However, President Burkhardt wanted to have written confirmation of the Church's legal status and authorization.

> We didn't have anything in our own hand. Officials at that time were hesitant to provide us with written statements, so we went directly to the office of Otto Nuschke, who was responsible for Church Affairs. He was a very reasonable person and a member of the CDU Party. You could talk rationally with him. He gave us a written statement, that the Church was authorized to function as a religious organization in the GDR, of course on the condition that we do so only within our own circle of members, without any proselyting. With this written statement we could always successfully say, in subsequent years, that the government had authorized us. That prevented many officials from causing major problems for the Church. Some individuals still attempted to make trouble for us, and occasionally they succeeded to a lesser degree, but in general the Church could function. (1991)

The statement from Otto Nuschke's office, dated August 26, 1955, said, "Regarding the visit of your two representatives, Henry Burkhardt and Eberhardt Sommer, I confirmed to them that in accordance with the guidance of the Interior Ministry, dated April 3, 1951, your religious organization is authorized to operate within the territory of the GDR and the democratic sector of greater Berlin" (DO 4/722).

In the meantime, Burkhardt had established a mission office in Leipzig in the summer of 1952, which he moved to Dresden the next year. He wrote, "That decision subsequently proved to be of benefit to the Church, since the government always wanted organizations to have an independent administration in this country" (DMO).

Although the mission had an administrative office in the GDR since 1952, that office did not meet the test of being the mission's "primary" office. Until 1969, the official headquarters of the mission was in West Berlin, or later in Hamburg. A document from the Secretariat for Church Affairs, written about 1954, listed two categories of approved religious organizations. The Church was described as a religious organization headquartered in West Berlin:

> *Legal Corporate Organizations:* Twelve churches were named, including the Evangelical, Catholic, Old Catholic, Old Lutheran, Methodist, Baptist, Jewish, and Russian Orthodox churches.

> *Other Religious Organizations:* Twenty-one were named, including "the Church of Jesus Christ of Latter-day Saints (Mormon), Berlin-Dahlem" with about four thousand members in the GDR. (MS 13798)

Although the mission now had written confirmation that it was an approved religious organization, it did not have the legal corporate authority required to purchase property in its own name. This problem was noted in a memorandum by a government official, dated November 3, 1952:

> A representative of the Church of Jesus Christ of Latter-day Saints (Mormon) came to me today concerning the following matter: The leadership of that religious organization wishes to purchase property in Leipzig. Although it is a legally registered entity, the purchase of property by persons or entities headquartered in West Berlin or West Germany is not permitted at the present time. The fact that they recently opened an office in Leipzig does not change this fact. In response to his question of whether his religious organization should cancel its present registration in order to establish a new entity in Leipzig, I declined an answer, but suggested he take up that matter directly with the Interior Ministry. The goal of purchasing a house did not appear to me to be an adequate justification for such an action. I asked him whether he considered it worthwhile to abolish a legal entity that is recognized in all of Germany, just to accomplish this minor goal. In my opinion, and in light of the present political situation in Germany, it would seem to be enough to just establish a separate administrative organization within the GDR. The visitor left to consider these issues in greater detail. (DO 4/722)

The above reference that the Church was an organization "recognized in all of Germany" refers to the official registration of the East German Mission and the West German Mission, after their creation in 1938, as a joint "Verein" (e.V.), namely the "Verein der Deutschen Mission der Kirche Jesu Christi der Heiligen der Letzten Tage." A "Verein" is a broad term that includes social, sporting, and religious organizations. In the Church's case, the 1938 Verein registration, which covered both missions, was modified in 1943 to designate Herbert Klopfer as its legal representative. Klopfer was later replaced by Paul Langheinrich. When Langheinrich later registered the East German Mission as a religious organization with the SMAD in 1945, that action did not affect the existing civil registration of the two missions as a joint Verein. However, when the headquarters of the East German Mission was moved to the American sector of Berlin in 1945, the mission no longer had a primary office in the GDR. Therefore, the government ruled that the mission did not have legal standing to purchase property in the GDR. The official who met with Burkhardt in 1952 did not encourage him to terminate the Verein, since such an action would adversely affect the West German Mission without any guarantee that the GDR would allow the East German Mission to register itself separately as a new Verein.

However, one year later, the Church was granted full legal corporate status in one of the states of West Germany, which meant it was legal in all of West Germany. Since the existing Verein registration was no longer required in West Germany, it was terminated, without consideration of the impact of that action on the East German Mission. Only later was the effect of that action understood. Elder Kimball made the following notation during his visit to Berlin on August 25, 1955:

> When we incorporated in West Germany we had to relinquish our association status and did not realize what that would do to our status in East Germany, but it seems to have had the effect of disfranchising us there and losing for us our recognition.... Cannot buy buildings. Difficulty in getting land. (Copy from Edward Kimball)

The East German Mission attempted to reinstate its Verein status the following year. Excerpts from related correspondence follow:

> *Internal memorandum of the Interior Ministry, March 20, 1956:*
> The [Mormon] church is an America religious organization. The leader of the group in Germany and the leader of the East German Mission are American citizens. The organization was, until recently, registered as a Verein in Berlin-Charlottenburg. After it was accorded legal corporate authority in West Germany, the Verein registration was terminated. As a result, the branches in the GDR no longer have legal status. (DO 4/722)
>
> *Letter from the Dresden Police to the Mission, April 11, 1956:*
> The submitted application of the above-named church for registration in the Register of Organizations was rejected. There is no possibility for registration as a religious organization in that Register. Religious organizations can obtain legal authority only through the bestowal of corporate status by the state. (DMO)
>
> *Letter from the Mission to the Interior Ministry, April 18, 1956:*
> We were informed via a letter of April 11, 1956, that our application regarding registration in the Register of Organizations was rejected. We were instructed to contact you directly. Since we are urgently dependent on corporate status, we would greatly appreciate a rapid response. (DMO)
>
> *Letter from the Interior Ministry to President Burkhardt, May 14, 1956:*
> We wish to inform you, that this issue requires a thorough clarification. We ask that you wait for the ruling being presently considered. (DMO)

Apparently, no decision was forthcoming. Five years later, on March 1, 1961, a five-page report entitled "Mormons" was prepared by the main office of the national police. It also stated that the mission's registration had been terminated after the Church was granted legal corporate status in West Germany. "Therefore, the branches in the GDR no longer have legal authority" (DO 1/11 HVDVP/865).

The next reference to the Church's legal status in the GDR is found in a letter from Stanley D. Rees, president of the Hamburg Mission, to Elder Thomas S. Monson on October 17, 1969, in which Rees wrote, "I have just received the report, 'Legal Recognition of the Church in East Germany,' dated October 15, 1969, from Brother Dean Larsen in Frankfurt.... My question is: If we apply for legal recognition in East Germany and receive such, are we, as a church, in essence recognizing the East German government, even though our own United States government does not do so? Could this in any way cause us difficulty or embarrassment?" (LR 2428 25)

Neither Larsen's report nor an answer to President Rees's question has been found. However Rees's letter indicates that the Church did not have legal corporate authority in the GDR at that time. No further correspondence regarding this issue is known, until the 1985 letter cited at the beginning of this chapter. Günther Behncke stated that he did not know when the Church was given full legal authority, but assumed it was granted shortly after the Church established the independent Dresden Mission in 1969. Behncke said that his 1985 letter was only a written confirmation of an already existing legal status (2006).

Since most members believed that the Church did not have legal corporate authority before 1985, it has been generally assumed that title to all buildings purchased by the Church prior to that year were recorded in the name of a trustee, typically a member of the local branch. However, as shown in Chapter 11, some buildings (including Forst and Werdau in 1981) were officially recorded in the Church's name, without a trustee, before 1985. Why that was permitted in some circumstances and not in others is just one more example of why descriptions of the Church's status and activities in East Germany cannot be accurately described on the basis of one or two anecdotal reports.

5 Life Prior to the Berlin Wall 1949–1961

> *The Church played an important role in the members' lives in those years. We were enthusiastic, and many social programs were conducted simply to provide members with an alternative to the problems of daily life. (Joachim Meyer, 1989)*
>
> *The members often felt they had no alternative but to leave the country. Of course, that set back the Church numerically, but we couldn't prevent them from leaving. (Henry Burkhardt, 1991)*
>
> *A brother from the West said to me, "You didn't accomplish more in the GDR than to just maintain the existing branches. You didn't make any progress." I, of course, had a different opinion and said, "Only to maintain something is certainly no great virtue, but it was an accomplishment in those days, and it required significant effort." The Church can grow on that foundation today. (Gottfried Richter, 1993)*

While the East German Mission had established a good relationship with the Soviet Military Administration immediately after the war, foreign policy differences eventually led to growing tension between the Soviet Union and the United States. The resultant Cold War had a negative impact upon the mission. For example, the June 1948 monetary reforms in the western occupation zones were immediately followed by commensurate changes in the Soviet zone, which severely hindered travel, communication, and the shipment of supplies. The transfer of operating authority from Soviet officers to the new GDR government led to additional restrictions on the Church, as shown in the mission's quarterly report in December 1949:

> As 1949 ended, our mission activities in the Russian occupation zone were greatly handicapped.... We had forty-five local missionaries serving full-time missions there. An order issued recently by the Russian-

> controlled government indicated that unpaid missionaries would not be recognized as professionals, and that our missionaries would, therefore, have to register with the employment office. They would then be required to accept any work assignment given them, which in most cases would be work in the uranium mines or with the police. So far, we have been successful in transferring our missionaries from those locations where their presence is no longer desirable, in order to protect them from such work assignments. (MS 1359)

How did the Church cope with these conditions? This chapter describes the East German Mission in the 1950s, the effort of members to travel to the new temple in Switzerland, problems associated with the emigration of members from the GDR, and reports of members who were imprisoned while conducting Church-related activities. It ends with the attitude of the government toward the Church in the 1950s. Missionary work, youth activities, meeting houses, and the members' experiences in educational activities and professional careers are addressed separately in later chapters.

Contacts between the West and the East

Personal contact and communication between mission presidents who lived in West Berlin and the members in the GDR was difficult but adequate. While transit between West Germany and West Berlin was possible only by air or via three closely controlled highways, the border between West Berlin and East Berlin remained open until the erection of the Berlin Wall in August 1961. Many East Berlin residents worked in West Berlin and crossed the border daily. Tourists also crossed the border at will, on foot or via the city's subway and elevated trains, as did the author when he was a missionary in West Berlin in 1959. The mission president always had a counselor in the GDR (Henry Burkhardt after June 1952), who came regularly to West Berlin for consultation, as did district and branch presidents and other members. The mission presidents often went to East Berlin but were only infrequently allowed to enter the GDR proper, except for visits to Leipzig during that city's biannual fair. The mission journal (LR 2428 2) recorded the ability or inability of mission presidents to visit the GDR beyond East Berlin in the 1950s:

> *March 1950:* President Stover and his secretary, Herold L. Gregory, visited the branches in Leipzig, Delitzsch, and Dessau during visits to the Leipzig Fair.
>
> *May 1951:* Conferences of the Dresden, Leipzig, and Mecklenburg districts were held during the month, but the mission president was not permitted to attend.

August 1953: President Glaus was in Leipzig for three days during the fair and met with district and branch presidents, missionaries, and the members.

September 1954: President Gregory visited the district conference in Leipzig during the Fair.

October 1955: President Gregory received permission to attend the celebration of the Dresden branch's one-hundredth anniversary.

December 1955: President Gregory attended the Sunday evening service in Leipzig. On Monday, he attended a meeting of all missionaries, which had begun on Saturday under President Burkhardt's leadership.

February 1956: President Gregory visited the Zwickau district conference.

May 1956: President Gregory attended the Karl-Marx-Stadt district conference. This was the first visit of an American leader to that city in the past decade.

July 1956: The mission president visited district conferences in Zwickau and Karl-Marx-Stadt.

December 1957: Many travel restrictions were initiated, and it was almost impossible to obtain a Soviet visa. In an effort to force acceptance of the GDR government, travel was permitted only with a GDR visa, which was discouraged by the American consulate.

March 1958: The government encouraged visitors, including Americans, to travel to the Leipzig Fair. However, control points were established on all highways to prevent visitors from traveling beyond Leipzig.

The mission journal also recorded the following visits of general authorities to Leipzig and West Berlin in the 1950s. Since travel between East and West Berlin was still possible at that time, these visits allowed members in the GDR to see their American leaders more often than did most members elsewhere in the world:

June 1952: President David O. McKay spoke to 1,200 members in West Berlin.

Feb. 1954: Elder Henry D. Moyle met with GDR's district leaders and nine hundred members during a conference in West Berlin.

Aug. 1955: Elder Spencer W. Kimball interviewed all GDR missionaries and met with district and branch leaders during a visit to West Berlin.

July 1956: Elder Adam S. Bennion met with GDR missionaries in West Berlin.

Sept. 1958: Elder Henry D. Moyle attended a conference in Leipzig.

Sept. 1959: Elder Marion G. Romney attended a conference in Leipzig.

In March 1960, Henry Burkhardt and his wife flew from West Berlin to Hamburg with President Percy Fetzer to attend a district conference. Such access to the West ended with the Berlin Wall in August 1961.

The 1950s was described by members in the following interview excerpts:

Joachim Meyer: Church attendance was high during the war and in the immediate postwar years. Even those who had been inactive for years attended often because it was the only positive activity for most people. Of course, the welfare program also enticed many to attend. The meetings were full or overfilled during those years. Many activities were conducted throughout the week. We had priesthood and Relief Society meetings on Monday, Tuesday was usually filled with activities in members' homes or elsewhere in the vicinity, Wednesday was Mutual, on Thursday the youth came together for sports and other activities, on Friday we often held gatherings in members' homes, Saturday was usually filled with activities for all members, and on Sunday we were together from early until late. The Church played an important role in the members' lives in those years. We were enthusiastic, and many social programs were conducted simply to provide members with an alternative to the problems of daily life. It was a wonderful time. (1989)

Joachim Albrecht: As branch president, I had to register our meetings every week with the police. By the end of 1955, that was relaxed, and we described our activities for an entire month—what day, what time, etc. In 1957, we were told only to report meetings that fell outside of our normal meeting times, which were registered annually. (2004)

Gottfried Richter: I submitted a request for a meeting at which we intended to speak about misuse of alcohol, tobacco and other stimulants. That topic was rejected. They said, "That is not a responsibility of the Church, it is a matter for the Association for Dissemination of Scientific Knowledge. Do something else on that day." So I said, "Okay. We will speak about the Word of Wisdom." They approved that. (1993)

> *Eva-Maria Bartsch:* Everything that took place in the Church needed to be made known. Every youth activity had to be cleared with the police. My father said: "Well, if they want to know, why not. We aren't doing anything improper." (1993)

> *Henry Burkhardt:* When we submitted a program, we generally did not go into detail as much as the police often required. They wanted to know specific times in various cities, who the speaker would be, and what he would say. It took a while before we were able to convince those people that we couldn't provide details of a talk to be given by a speaker in a branch. The result was that someone would be present in almost every Sunday service, to see if we were speaking against the state or were encouraging our members to oppose the government. But we considered it our responsibility to teach the gospel and not to make political statements. The result was that we didn't have any trouble. Over the years we were able to report monthly, and later we just reported our meeting times annually. (1991)

> *Frank Apel:* Earlier, it was hard for our leaders. Every meeting had to be submitted and approved. The government assumed that when people met together, it could lead to opposition. Our church had a reputation. They thought, "That is an American church. Maybe they will all become spies." When I became a branch president in 1968, we only had to report our meetings every quarter. By 1974, we didn't have to report regular meetings anymore. (1991)

President Arthur Glaus met with the GDR's district presidents on May 24, 1953, in West Berlin. The minutes of the meeting, taken from the mission history, provide another perspective of conditions within the mission at that time:

> *Brother Schramm, Erzgebirge:* The work in the Erzgebirge District is progressing well. We don't have any major restrictions or problems with the police or government officials. We were prohibited from conducting a proposed concert, which we could have held in our own facility but not in other places. We do have problems in Auerbach, because of the distance to that branch. When you travel there, you cannot return until Monday. And we cannot adequately care for the members in the restricted zone [in the Erzgebirge, where the Russians were mining uranium].
>
> Bicycles should be purchased to reduce our travel expenses. Brother Schmidt travels every other week to Auerbach because they have no priesthood members. We have many poor members in our district, about forty-eight widows in Buchholz alone. On the average, they receive only forty-five marks monthly. The branch does all it can

to help them. There is a particular shortage of fat, sugar, and meat. We cannot store significant amounts of food without coming into conflict with the police. These are our major problems. We have appointed district missionaries, since we are not allowed to have other missionaries.

President Glaus: He suggested that we try to bring our average meeting attendance to 40 percent. The care of the poor was discussed yesterday in the Relief Society meeting. We must work together on this matter to avoid mistakes. The food packages we sent were received. Brother Krause said that one package a month, which contains only a little of everything, will certainly be allowed. As to the question posed by President Glaus regarding what can be purchased in Annaberg, Brother Schramm said that practically nothing can be bought, especially fat and sugar. It is better in Dresden, where those who have ration cards can obtain a little butter now and then, but elsewhere nothing. President Glaus requested comments and suggestions regarding how the distribution can be better handled than in the past. The previous method, whereby sisters traveled [from West Berlin] into the Russian Zone and personally distributed food supplies can no longer be carried out.

Brother Auerswald, Chemnitz: The sending of packages at Christmas (sent as gifts from the West German Mission) didn't work because the return address was listed as the Church. The Customs office confiscated everything. It would have been better if the district president had been informed of such action in advance.

Brother Birth, Dresden: Brothers Eggert and Lehnig received a fine of over 150 marks or thirty days in jail regarding an alleged illegal meeting. In fact, that meeting had been registered. The brothers have decided to pay the fine. They have to go twice a week to register the meetings. They are asked questions such as, "What are you doing, why do you have a piano?" The tension is especially severe in Cottbus. The cooperation among the members is good. It is especially advantageous for us that the [mission] office now is in Dresden. The work among our youth has improved. Package shipments are not received, except in Bischofswerda. President Glaus emphasized the low attendance figures (20 percent among a membership of four hundred). Many members live outside the cities. When Sunday School is held at noon, and they have to return again at three o'clock for the worship service, most of them can't do that. If the second meeting were held later, then that would be bad for the members who have to remain between meetings. At the request of the mission, we have initiated welfare programs in which food supplies are distributed. Many items have been collected in Görlitz, but they must be distributed before they spoil. Also, it is dangerous to store food, since it could be viewed as hoarding.

Brother Auerswald, Chemnitz: To increase attendance in the meetings, all families received a written invitation from the visiting teachers. That has had some success, but we must see if it continues over time. Five hundred persons attended a special meeting called by the missionaries, but the following meeting was again poorly attended. Many members attend only now and then. In one meeting of the visiting teachers, it was learned that many families live with very serious problems. With the money that we receive from the mission, we buy fat and lard (when it is available). Retired persons were especially appreciative of the supplemental assistance.

We recommend that the Nössige branch be moved from our district to Dresden. The same applies to Marienberg. They have thirteen members, but no leadership. Brother Ulbrig still helps out there, but we can't service them out of Chemnitz. The police have recently been hounding us and have prohibited table tennis, boxing, etc. Instead of Mutual, we have a Bible hour. Some of the youth feel neglected. The older youth are poorly instructed in the gospel. We had a meeting with the parents, but they said they can't do it. It would be better if someone worked with the youth who understands them and can lead them.

President Glaus: What can be done so that the members can purchase fat and lard when it is available at the market? Suggestion: put the money into our bank accounts and quickly purchase and distribute food when it is available. It was also suggested that the branch president or the Relief Society President have cash on hand and then be reimbursed. The problem is that a businessman can only have seventy-five marks on his person. Otherwise he must have proof as to the source of that money. However, a private person (an employed person) has no such restriction. He can save money. In any event, it would be advisable to establish bank accounts for the church, to which the mission can send money. That is the only way.

Brother Langheinrich, Genealogy: Research can be done in the East, but many members haven't pursued it rationally. They shouldn't attempt to first convert the pastor. The members in Mecklenburg have been successful. You just have to go about it properly. It now is progressing in Dresden. We will discuss genealogy at a later time.

Brother Otto: We must find ways to support the youth. I am aware of instances in which the youth are not being well served in the branches. The youth need to be spoken to personally. The goal of youth work is to give them a personal testimony. When dance evenings are forbidden, we shouldn't attempt them. It would be good to hold discussion groups on Sunday or during the week. It shouldn't be too difficult to plan such programs.

Brother Nitz, Berlin: We struggle with some problems, but certainly not to the degree as in the East Zone. Both of the East branches have been evicted from the schools in which they used to meet. The West Berlin branches are well taken care of, although they suffer from shortages of personnel. We had to close the branch in Eberswalde, since none of the brothers there hold the priesthood.

Brother Krause, Mecklenburg: Everything we do is punishable. Economically, we are worse off than at the end of the war in 1945. The security forces still collect material to be used against us, and that adversely affects the members. When someone goes away [over the border], that is their personal decision, but unfortunately, some members then send letters and write that they buried a watch or something in a garden. I've been shown such letters by the police, who say that they have nothing against the Church, but such things shouldn't happen, since it adversely affects us. They forbid us to play tennis, to organize discussion evenings, etc. The police chief in Wolgast said that we could conduct Mutual if we report everything properly, even the songs, etc.

They monitor my bank account every month. I keep twenty-five marks of Fast Offerings in cash. We have an account for the branch at the Post Office. We suggest the Relief Society do the same. Regarding assistance for the poor, I often distribute fish at night. When packages are sent, it must be done carefully. The packaging and the handwriting must be varied. They should contain only a little of everything that the members can eat and feel full. Every member should lay aside enough food from which they can live for a month. We cannot store food in our meeting houses. The branch president must have a list that shows what a sister received each time, so that she can receive something different next time. Many receive only forty-five to sixty marks as a pension, from which they must pay fifteen marks for rent, so many have no money with which to travel to the meetings. No printed material may be sent here, not even the Book of Mormon and the Doctrine and Covenants any longer.

No invitations should be mailed any longer, as was recently done by the Relief Society. In Warnemünde, many active members lost their jobs and their children were removed from school. We are very satisfied with our youth. They cause us no problems. There are even some officials who treat the Church kindly. Many of those who oppose us are acting upon orders of the party. It has taken seven years to lay the foundation for genealogy activities, and our application for an archives pass has been approved. We receive all information that we request. But it has happened that a page has been torn out of the church books, etc. Such instances, of course, ruin what has carefully been accomplished. We have access to Greifswald, Rostock, and Berlin. It would be better if the members write to us when they need something, instead of coming personally. We must have a document from the government that the Church is recognized. Every district president should have such a document in his possession.

Brother Auerswald: When the Church was prohibited, we were not allowed to hold any meetings, since they said we were not registered. We then appealed that and went there every day. After four weeks, we were notified that it was approved. We had to register the meeting every month. Other churches had the same problem. In any event, we must make it clear that our mission office is in Dresden and that Brother Burkhardt is the responsible person.

Brother Neumärker, Zwickau: All the branches are operating adequately. There are 150 members in Plauen, but the activity level is very weak. No visiting teacher work is being done. We had to assign the missionaries. We held our conference in the Werdau branch. We are told that we can only teach religion. Games and discussion sessions are prohibited. It is not advisable to designate the Mutual hour as "Bible Hour." Better would be "Evening Hour," since that would accommodate everything. Regarding finances, all our branches have their own bank accounts. That avoids the need to keep money at home. The account must be called: Church of Jesus Christ, followed by the branch name. The name "Bezirkskonferenz" also causes problems. [The GDR called its own administrative subdivisions "Bezirks."] "Distriktskonferenz" would be better. Otherwise, the level of cooperation is good. Zwickau and Plauen do not have good attendance. Brother Starke, from Plauen, personally wrote to the members and invited them to the meetings.

Brother Roscher, Thuringia: We have 572 members in six branches, of whom 200 live far away from the meeting house. They are visited by the missionaries. We held a special conference and distributed invitations. The youth are in good hands with the missionaries. We will attempt to achieve better attendance in the worship services. Twenty members in the Gotha branch live outside the city and have little or no money to travel to the meetings. If we could help them with travel money, they would certain attend.

Brother Hegewald, Leipzig: In general, the Leipzig district is moving forward. We wanted to hold a youth worship service in Leipzig, but it was not approved. When we talk with the youth, they view it as a sermon. You have to spend an entire day with them, so they recognize that we sympathize with them and hold them in esteem. The branch president in Leipzig said that we should support our members with money instead of food. Many live far from each other, and when we support them with money, the attendance will certainly rise. In Leipzig itself, the attendance is already improving, especially since the meeting house has an attractive and friendly appearance. In Naumburg, we have problems when young brothers speak. One elder laughs at and distracts them and also bring a bad spirit into the meeting.

Brother Sommer, MIA: We have attempted to rename the program. [The government claimed that MIA was a separate, unregistered "association."] However, "Bible Hour" would be more dangerous than Mutual, since they would then ask what that is. We have welcomed the suggestion to call it an "Evening Hour." According to Brother Burkhardt, several districts are using the name "Improvement Hour." The following name was finally decided: "Mutual Improvement Classes." When we are asked about the new name, we must all be agreed on the answer.

The youth in Thuringia are exemplary. Since we have been restricted in the conduct of sporting activities, we have to emphasize religious subjects. The manual we received has been revised in that manner. We suggest that when you engage in sports, that you do so far away from your meeting houses, even outside the city. But the youth must be led by someone who serves as a central point around whom they can gather.

The mission has printed a manual, modified from the Anderson Plan, that contains nothing dangerous. Suggestion: Provide the addresses of the full-time and district missionaries to the mission office and copies will be sent to them individually.

Brother Krause: Regarding the missionaries, I wish to say that they should not be called before we are entirely confident about them. We should review their background, from what families they come, etc. The missionaries must have the respect of the district and branch presidents. Fortunately, there are few troublemakers. Otherwise they are all hard workers. The format of our religious services leaves much to be desired. Instead of sermons, many useless things are said. Most likely, the fault lies with poor preparation. There aren't enough workers. Most branches are in the hands of the missionaries.

President Glaus: We must try to place more branches in the hands of local brothers who have a good family life and keep the commandments.

Brother Krause: Regarding the Hohenstein branch, it is impossible for the brothers to purchase bicycles themselves, so perhaps we can assist them. Primary classes have been prohibited and our table tennis has been confiscated for use by the FDJ. We need missionaries in Plauen.

Brother Schramm: We have asked all priesthood holders to visit a member every Sunday prior to the meetings. We've had success with that.

After Herold Gregory became the mission president, he wrote to the First Presidency on April 1, 1954, regarding a problem with the sustaining of general authorities at district conferences. "These conferences are often visited by local police. If during the meeting a long list of American names are sustained as leaders of the Church, this obviously casts a great deal of suspicion on the membership.... It would seem that without any fear in any quarter, the name of the president of the Church could be mentioned and voted upon.... As to local brethren in district or branch offices, I am sure those names would be available to the police at any time anyway, whereas there is some justification for the fear of mentioning all general authorities by name." The First Presidency responded on May 10, 1954: "We are sympathetic with your views, and regard it as wise to limit the sustaining of general authorities to the president of the Church whenever there is apprehension as to consequences" (LR 2428 39).

On July 31, 1956, President Herold Gregory wrote a long report to Elder Adam S. Bennion on the status of the mission. Excerpts follow and other portions will be quoted later in this chapter:

Conferences: District conferences are being held quarterly in nine of our twelve districts as suggested by Elder Henry D. Moyle during his visit in Feb. 1954. However, in the Mecklenburg, Thuringia, and Leipzig districts, the distances are so great and the members so poor that we have not tried to hold these conferences quarterly. The conferences in East Germany are under the direction of the counselor in East Germany, inasmuch as the mission president generally cannot travel there. The mission president was successful in obtaining permission to attend district conferences in Zwickau and Karl-Marx-Stadt during the past six months. At the moment, however, the situation seems to have been somewhat tightened, and it is doubtful if any visas will be obtained for future trips into East Germany.

Literature: It is almost impossible for us to get manuals and other important literature into East Germany because of stringent controls. We have been moderately successful in smuggling some items into East Germany, but we try to hold this to a bare minimum. During the past six months, we have presented every branch with an assortment of standard manuals and church books that they are to maintain in their branch libraries, so we may not have to worry so much about this in the future. Our present policy calls for furnishing each branch with one copy of each acceptable manual. We consider it unnecessary under the circumstances to offer manuals for sale to the general membership, inasmuch as the shipping thereof into East Germany is so hazardous. An acceptable manual is one which does not contain any anticommunism statements.

Missionaries: Conferences for full-time missionaries are held on the Saturday preceding the quarterly district conferences, in accordance with the recommendation of Elder Spencer W. Kimball. [In the East], the counselor meets with them, but they do not regard his opinions the same as those coming from the mission president. Once each five or six months we have tried to call all the East Zone missionaries together for instruction, but this usually involves a great deal of lost motion and fooling around. It also disrupts the operation of the mission home and office, since these members from East Germany are very inconsiderate in their attitude and just drop in, expecting to be waited on and fed, not realizing the tremendous load it throws on the mission president, his wife, and staff. Fortunately it was possible to meet with all the missionaries in East Germany in Leipzig, thus avoiding most of the unpleasant byproducts of the conference.

Administration: The Iron Curtain is naturally our biggest problem. Free, uninhibited intercourse with East Germany is unheard of. Practically all of the administration must be done through the counselor in East Germany, who is only able to come out to West Berlin about once a month. He brings all branch and district reports with him. If they are sent through the mails, in all likelihood they would be intercepted. Not only is this a great inconvenience, but the information thus intercepted is compiled and used subsequently as evidence of irregular activities by our members, even though we are only carrying out purely administrative functions. As a result of this iron curtain situation, we have to call our district presidents together once or twice a year to discuss procedures and practices. Whenever possible we have also called all branch presidents together for one day a year.

The counselor in East Germany is a local brother, who, with his wife, is on a long-term missionary status, being supported entirely by funds donated for this purpose by members of the church. He has an automobile and can move about freely within East Germany to take care of the affairs of the church there. He cannot get a job because of his affiliation with the Church and his missionary activities over the past five years. No firm would consider him a good risk. He cannot drive his car to West Berlin. (LR 2428 2)

The Mission Counselor Responsible for the GDR

After serving two years as a missionary, Henry Burkhardt was called to be a counselor to President Glaus in 1952. He continued to serve subsequent mission presidents in that capacity until 1969, when he was called to lead the new Dresden Mission. Despite significant obstacles, he maintained adequate communication between himself and the mission presidents in West Berlin during those years. Examples of his long service to the Church are found in Chapter 20. Two descriptions of President Burkhardt were written by Elder Spencer W. Kimball. The first was contained in notes that Kimball typed on August 25, 1955, during his visit to Berlin:

> I had a conference with the presidency, including President Henry Burkhardt, first counselor, a twenty-five-year-old unmarried (soon hopes to be) tall young man from Dresden. He is the mission headquarters behind the curtain. He has a mission car, office, two missionaries in the office, and much freedom and discretion. Standard works are recognized but manuals and literature otherwise are suspect. Telephone calls and letters are censored and photographed. Too-frequent movement across the curtain brings suspicion. President Gregory may not safely make regular trips, only rarely and occasionally may he go through without much hazard. Brother Burkhardt is a virtual mission president without title but with much authority of necessity. If he comes to the other sectors [West Berlin], suspicion is leveled at him, yet he comes occasionally. Today when he came from the East, he was given a notice to appear tomorrow at a certain office.... It could mean anything—Siberia, death, prison, discipline, reduction of liberties, or it could mean nothing. He wishes to take another of our brothers from that sector to go as far as he can to the very door of the office to which he must go. I fear and shall worry until he is back safe and sound. (Copy from Edward Kimball)

Following his visit to Berlin, Elder Kimball wrote to President Gregory on October 21, 1955, regarding Burkhardt:

> We were pleased indeed with President Burkhardt, who in spite of his youngness seems to have judgment and wisdom beyond his years. He has such a sweet spirit and a splendid attitude, and I am sure he has done a great service and will be able in the future to do even a greater one.... It seemed to me that [he] should continue to confer with the entire mission presidency as often as wisdom would dictate. (We must protect this good man against harm to himself.) So long as occasional irregular visits are safe, he can keep up to date and get your counsel frequently enough that no serious problem would need develop. Should emergencies arise so that he could not contact you, perhaps the best thing to do would be for him to call into council with

> him some of the district presidents who are mature and wise. This is an emergency program. I suppose for the present the mission car should continue to be at his disposal and his expenses paid. You will be wise in all these matters and follow the conventional procedures so far as it can be. We realize that east of the curtain are many different situations, and you will meet them wisely as you have done in the past. I understand that Brother Burkhardt would like to be married and settle down to regular living. I assume that he has finished his regular mission and that he is just continuing to serve until released. If he remained in Dresden or moved to Leipzig or any other community and secured employment and got married, he could likely still continue as your counselor and handle the work quite effectively under your direction and he could do a considerable amount of visiting branches and districts on weekends and much work by correspondence. (LR 2428 39)

President Burkhardt did marry shortly after Elder Kimball's visit, but he was not able to "settle down to regular living." The special circumstances and problems associated with operating the mission within the GDR required the full-time work of a resident authority, especially since the mission president could not enter the GDR very often.

Leadership of the Auxiliary Organizations

The fact that the mission was composed of four districts in West Germany and six or seven districts in the GDR posed unique administrative problems. For example, the mission's Relief Society and Primary and Mutual organizations in the 1950s were each led by one presidency, composed of members from each side of the border, despite the restrictions on travel and communication across that border. Käte Würscher, a GDR citizen, served as the Relief Society president for a few years before she left for the West. In a memoir written in 1975, she commented on her travel on both sides of the border:

> I was called in February 1953 to serve in the mission's Relief Society after Sister Berger, the former president, left the GDR. I began my work under the direction of Sister Glaus, the wife of the then mission president. My first trip lasted four weeks, and I attended the conferences in Erfurt, Karl-Marx-Stadt, Leipzig, Zwickau, and Annaberg. During the intervening weekdays, I and the leaders of the various branches visited the members and the sick. It was very difficult to reach the branches in the Erzgebirge. The government feared espionage, and it was necessary to obtain permission from officials in Karl-Marx-Stadt. Until the borders were closed [August 1961], I also was able to visit the western districts, Hannover, Hamburg, Flensburg, Berlin, and Bremen. It was two different worlds but one spirit. (MS 14071)

The Mutual program in the 1950s, as well as its problems regarding the coordination of activities on both sides of the border, is described in greater detail in Chapter 9.

Travel to the Swiss Temple, 1955–1957

Despite restrictions on their travel, many GDR citizens managed to reach the Swiss Temple after it was dedicated in 1955. In a report dated July 31, 1956, President Gregory summarized how this was accomplished:

> A resident of East Germany is not permitted to visit any country other than West Germany. Still our members risk their security to visit West Germany, and once there they apply for permission to visit Switzerland and go through the temple. A great number have already done this, and thus far there have been no repercussions. Elder Bennion was agreeable to presenting this problem to the First Presidency for their recommendation. It should be remembered, however, that the members in East Germany feel their isolation very much, and if they were asked not to go to the temple in Bern, it would certainly be a matter of grave disappointment to them. Already, those who have had their endowments have shown a greater degree of cooperation, enthusiasm, and complete understanding of the Gospel and its workings. We hope it will not be necessary to ask them not to go to the temple at the present time. (LR 2428 2)

Many of the temple-bound members traveled to West Germany in large groups in order to obtain a 50 percent reduction in rail rates. The mission president encouraged group trips to take advantage of the reduced fares. For example, thirty-four members from Leipzig traveled together to the temple in May 1957. Several members described their temple trips and why it ended in 1957:

> *Henry Burkhardt:* My wife and I were sealed in the Swiss Temple in 1955. We had permission to travel to West Germany, but not to Switzerland. We obtained the documents for Switzerland in West Germany. That was not to be made known to officials in the East. We couldn't speak about it. (2003)

> *Lothar Ebisch:* My wife and I and our two children went to the temple in 1956. In those days we could request an "Interzonenpass." No one asked where we were going, and we didn't have to identify specific relatives we were visiting. The West German government also helped us. We gave their police our Interzonenpass and received a temporary West German passport, with which we traveled to Switzerland. Whoever was fortunate to receive an Interzonenpass traveled. We were issued a Temple Recommend in the GDR. (2003)

Eve Dzierzon: My parents went to the temple when I was three years old. My other two siblings did not go. They were older and remained behind. (2003)

Herbert Heidler: I went to Switzerland for the first time in 1956. It was not legal, but many members wanted to go to the temple. I said, "We'll try it," and issued twenty-nine Temple Recommends. We traveled together to Frankfurt, gave the police there our cross-border permits, and received West German documents. Later, the Church said we shouldn't go to the temple in this manner. But we did it and didn't regret it. I am sure that the Stasi knew about it, because they monitored everyone. (1993)

Joachim Meyer: My wife and I traveled with my parents in 1957. After that, only retired people could do so, and even they could not go beyond West Germany. If they did, and it became known, they no longer received permission. (1989)

Henry Burkhardt: The last time was in 1957. Apparently, the government was not pleased that members went to Switzerland, and the opportunity ended. (2003)

Inge Burkhardt: There was an elderly retired sister in Halle who was permitted to travel to West Germany. She continued on to the temple in Switzerland and wrote a postcard from there to members. As a result, her pension was terminated. She didn't receive any money after that. (2003)

Gottfried Richter: Many retired members traveled to West Germany and then to Switzerland. That was easy to do, but it was not legal. The GDR threatened to jail violators for two years. Then the Church said: "If we issue members a Temple Recommend, we are supporting an illegal border crossing." So we were not allowed to issue temple recommends, unless the people had a visa for Switzerland. That was very wise. (1993)

Walter Schiele: Since that time, we tried to negotiate with the government. But they, of course, were fearful that if many members were allowed to travel to the temple, some of them might not return. We kept trying to find a legal way until Herr Honecker finally said, "Build a temple right here in the GDR." (1991)

President David O. McKay's personal journal contains the following story about the travel of GDR members to the temple:

> President and Mrs. Samuel E. Bringhurst met with the Presidency and gave a very interesting account of their work at the Swiss Temple. One incident they related pertained to the visit of one hundred German members in the Russian zone to the Swiss Temple. They came at a great sacrifice. Their money devaluates four times as they cross the border, and by the time they reached the Temple they were almost penniless. They were housed and fed by the members of the Church in the Swiss Mission. They were served breakfast at six a.m. before the Temple session, and the first morning it was something to see them ask for more milk, cup after cup. One old sister said she wished there was some way she could take some of it back with her. [Milk was available in the GDR, but it was often just skim milk.] They were ever so humble and appreciative of all that was done for them, and especially for the privilege of going through the temple for their endowments.[1]

The opening of the Swiss Temple led to questions about the availability of temple clothing throughout Europe. On November 2, 1955, the First Presidency sent the following instructions to President Gregory:

> We are now suggesting to you and all other mission presidents in the European area that when requests come to the branch presidents and to the mission presidents for temple garments…that members be counseled to obtain through commercial channels one-piece underwear which conforms to the approved pattern of the temple garment, and that when such articles…have been so secured that members be authorized [to make appropriate changes to them].(LR 2428 39)

The mission history contains two additional references to temple clothing:

> *July 31, 1956:* Our welfare program in East Germany is producing garments for our members. It will, however, be some time before the production and sales can offset the capital investment advanced for knitting machines. The opportunity may present itself whereby the church can purchase a knitting factory at a very reasonable price. Already several members are employed full time in the production of garments and other knitted goods. This looks to be our best welfare project in the mission. (DMO)

> *September 2, 1956:* It was also brought to the attention of the brethren that garments which are being made in the East can now be obtained at eighteen East marks per pair. The quality is inferior, however, [and most members] still buy those being sent from Salt Lake City, although the cost is much higher. (DMO)

Käte Würscher, the Relief Society president in the GDR, described related activities concerning temple clothing within the GDR:

> A sewing room for all temple clothing was created in the mission office in Berlin-Dahlem. Five sisters came together weekly to do the work.... These sisters later worked in Karl-Marx-Stadt to assist everyone who had been to the temple.... Weaving looms were also available in Cottbus, and related items were woven there using available material. We were fortunate and proud to have resolved some problems in this manner. Later, we received garments in larger quantities through the assistance of President Stover. (MS 14071)

In 1964, President David O. McKay offered to send temple clothing to members in the GDR. Elder Ezra T. Benson suggested that they not be sent directly, in order to protect the privacy of the members and because the government imposed high custom fees on such imports. Instead, the clothing was sent to West Berlin and carried into the GDR individually (LR 691 25).

Rudi Lehmann stated that "garments were sent from England and brought into the country through various means, often by visiting church leaders.... They also could be obtained from the weaving facility in Cottbus. But those were mostly for winter. They were made with thick yarn. We purchased them occasionally, and then said that we preferred to wait until others came from America" (2004).

Local Welfare Projects

In 1955, President Gregory asked all of the branches to establish local welfare projects. The following excerpts from the history of the Görlitz branch were provided by Ulf-Michael Lehmann. They show how one branch responded vigorously to that request:

> The project began on May 1, 1955, on a 70-square-meter garden plot on Nieskyer Straße. Beans, tomatoes, radishes, cucumbers, carrots, kohlrabi, celeriac [root celery], and pumpkins were planted. Three sisters each attempted to raise five chickens. The harvest was a success. The first produce was sold and the enthusiasm grew. By September 1955, another 330 square meters were added. More garden tools had to be purchased, including a sprinkling can, despite the frequent rain. The history recorded an unfortunate loss, the theft of the largest pumpkins. More work assignments for the entire branch membership were required to utilize the entire 400 square meters. Some of the produce was used for various branch activities.
>
> Since the lease costs were too high, a better garden plot was located in Görlitz-Weinhübel on the Karlstraße. Work began on the new 1,000-square-meter garden on March 30, 1956. The following were built there: a chicken house, a shed, a restroom, a garden gate, etc. It

was difficult to obtain the necessary cement and wood, since both were in short supply. Since various tools and supplies had to be obtained and a watering system had to be built, financial assistance was requested from the mission, which provided 1,140 East marks. With this assistance, thirty-one families were provided with food items for winter storage. The project included fifteen chicks that didn't need to be fed too long before they were brought to use! In August, an area was planted in grass, so that the small children of the members working there could have a play area with a sandbox. The welfare project was productive. Only a plague of caterpillars had to be conquered. The welfare project included a hand-knitting machine purchased for 290 marks that could be borrowed by the sisters for 50 pfennig a day. Postage stamps were also collected.

The project survived the flood of 1958. Fruit, vegetables, shrubs, and flowers grew despite the many intensive downpours. The flowers from the welfare garden were used for Mothers Day and other worship services, fruit and vegetables for a youth gathering at Pentecost, for Thanksgiving or Christmas celebrations, and for meals during district conferences. The sick and needy received bottled fruit. On September 6, 1959, the cost of a bus that took members to a conference in Leipzig was partially subsidized by the welfare project. Sister Karin Weinhold, who served a full-time mission, received support from the welfare fund in November 1959.

In the spring of 1961, the branch took over a new garden in the Sonnenland area of Görlitz-Weinhübel. The old garden in the Karlstraße remained simultaneously in production until March 1962. Again, the new area needed to be prepared, paths built, and bushes planted. The garden had ten fruit trees and one Hazelnut tree. In 1962, an old street car was moved to the garden as a summer house. In 1963, hundreds of carnations were sold at the weekly market. The garden provided all branch activities with flowers, fruit, and vegetables—the latter fresh or bottled. The branch history identified the following garden produce in 1966: apples, pears, cherries, plums, nuts, various types of flowers, strawberries, currants, gooseberries, onions, carrots, tomatoes, cucumbers, salsify, lettuce, red beets, brussel sprouts, beans, and always new weeds.

All financial obligations were repaid by 1966. Rudolf Baier had obtained an interest-free loan to purchase the Sonnenland garden, and the Relief Society had also loaned money. Everything was now repaid. In February 1967, the question was raised whether to continue the welfare garden, and in October of that year, Erich Hein leased the garden for thirteen years. The land was later sold to a private homebuilder. The secretary of the welfare project, Liesbeth Alzog, who had served in that capacity and as a worker for sixteen years, closed her re-

> port in September 1971 and noted that the project had been a blessing for all members.

Only one other report regarding welfare projects has been found. Details about the project in Leipzig, which was organized by Karl Pabst, are not available. Whether it involved multiple gardens or one common garden is not known. However, his daughter-in-law, Petra Pabst, provided an interesting perspective to this project:

> Karl Pabst was an excellent gardener, and he tried to inspire all members to establish gardens, which, for example, my father, Walter Schiele did. Sister Gerda Fischer does remember that when the harvest had been stored in bottles in the meeting house, the men would not allow the fruit to be used, not even as a contribution to a Relief Society bazaar. Today, Gerda laughs at the stinginess of the brothers, but the sisters at that time did not find it so funny. (2006)

The Church from the Government's Perspective

The mission did not have a public relations program in the 1950s, so the government's understanding of the Church was based largely on typical negative and erroneous accounts of its history and theology, which were written by opponents of the Church and augmented by local reports from police and SED officials who tried with limited success to describe the Church activities they observed. Excerpts from one report by an unnamed SED functionary in 1954 are typical of that time:

> The founder of the group was the American Joseph Smith, born in 1805. His parents were superstitious and earned their bread as peddlers. Their son grew up without any education. He supposedly became aware, in a vision, of golden plates that were invisible to other people.... When the practice of polygamy became known, he was arrested and murdered by an angry mob.... It is assumed that the requirement to practice polygamy grew when many men were killed by natives as the group traveled to Utah. The followers of this sect also attempted to entice young girls and women to emigrate to Utah, in order to have cheap labor. (MS 13798)

The above report ended with a positive sentence about the Church: "The members are encouraged to energetically support government initiatives."

In Eberswalde, a party member prepared an undated report about the local branch. The author described the members' religious convictions and activities and noted that their district president, Erwin Rathke, visited from Berlin every three weeks. Concerning Rathke he wrote: "Since he knew that I am a party member, he tried to tell me that his sect and communism have the same goal, namely the preservation of world peace." The report did not contain any negative comments about the Church and ended by stating, "This sect conforms to the social structure and laws of the countries in which it functions" (DY 30/iv 2/14/250).

Another example of the government's attitude toward the Church is seen in a 1956 report regarding a complaint by the branch president in Rathenow, that government officials had impeded his efforts to obtain an appropriate meeting house (see Chapter 11 for details). At the end of his report, a police official wrote the following to the Interior Ministry's religious affairs department:

> The branch has sixty-three members, the majority of whom are workers. The group is supported via voluntary contributions from its members, who meet every Sunday, Monday, and Thursday to conduct religious instruction or worship services. They seldom conduct public activities, and no negative events have been recorded. (DO 1/11 HVDVP/865)

Another police report, dated March 1, 1961, included a description of the mission and its leadership plus a few statistics:

> There are currently sixty-four units and about 4,710 members in the GDR, including nineteen units and about 1,380 members in the district of Karl-Marx-Stadt alone. Other groups include: Leipzig, six units with 517 members; Dresden, four units with 747 members; Erfurt, four units with 341 members; Halle, seven units with 264 members; and Berlin, one unit with 390 members. A few additional groups are found in other districts. Its followers come mostly from the petty bourgeois. The current thirty-year-old leader in the GDR, Henry Burkhardt, was given the leadership of this group at the age of twenty-two.
>
> Although Burkhardt has always claimed that a close connection with West Germany does not exist, it has been determined that he often travels to West Berlin to see [mission president] Gregory. It was evident in an August 26, 1955, report from our church affairs department, that Burkhardt was completely under the influence of the West Berlin leadership, from whom he receives his assignments.
>
> The basis of their doctrine is the Bible and Book of Mormon from Joseph Smith. They want to preach the gospel worldwide, and they believe in a life after death. Their genealogical activities are related to that belief. . . . Their earlier practice of polygamy was prohibited in 1890, and there is no indication that it was practiced thereafter.
>
> An instance of illegal transport of eggs into West Berlin in 1956 led to a closer examination of this religious organization. The following was determined: The leadership of the Mormons in the GDR comes from America via West Berlin. It was found that a West German church publication [*Der Stern*] has been distributed at meetings in the Karl-Marx-Stadt district since 1956. The branch leaders also fre-

quently received packages with food from America, which they distributed to the members. However, these shipments have been greatly reduced in recent years. The members are required to attend religious services that are held at least every Sunday, and every member must give the "Presidency" of their religious organization one-tenth of their income each month. The American leadership in West Berlin also requires the members to constantly carry out "good works." These "good works" frequently take the form of sneaking food into West Berlin, as happened in the 1956 instance.

It has been determined that Mormons have been guilty of illegally leaving the country for years ["Republikflucht"]. Apparently, they are going from West Germany to their main center in the state of Utah in the USA. The leader of the organization in the GDR is supposedly unaware of this, as he stated on February 17, 1956, during a meeting in the office of the Secretariat for Church Affairs. The following escapees are known:

Potsdam, 1955: Two persons (mother and son)

Karl-Marx-Stadt, 1952 to January 1961: Ninety-six persons left illegally for West Germany and the USA, mostly from Plauen, Hainichen, Freiberg, Zwickau, Aue, and Hohenstein-Ernstthal.

Cottbus, 1955: Six persons (a preacher couple with four children) plus another member. One illegal refugee returned voluntarily for the third time.

1956: The daughter of the district president with her husband and two children. It was also determined that applications for travel to Switzerland have been submitted, supposedly to visit relatives. Actual reason was to visit the Mormon temple in Switzerland. Applications to visit relatives in West Germany have also been submitted frequently in other districts during past years. It was later determined that these persons participated in Mormon meetings.

Dresden, 1956: The mission president Burkhardt from Dresden was warned about transporting Western proselyting materials.

1960: Other members were also found to have such materials while they were engaged in door-to-door proselyting. That also happened in the districts of Potsdam, Magdeburg, and Gera.

It should be noted that during the Leipzig Fair, meetings are held in the Mormons' building in which West Germans and Americans participate. During one such meeting with about four hundred persons, Fetzer from Berlin-Dahlem was present. At the end of the meeting, Fetzer retired to another room to hold consultations with church officials.

In another matter in 1955, a progressive member of the Mormons in [one] branch was relieved of his position as branch leader because he attended a training session of the Freedom Council and was otherwise active in the Freedom Council. (DO 1/11 HVDVP/865)

The Emigration Problem

Shortly before the erection of the Berlin Wall, the central office of the national police sent the following document, dated June 6, 1961, to all district police offices:

> It has been learned that the opinion has been expressed in one of the Mormon branches, that their God has instructed the members to leave the GDR. Based on that opinion, four members of the branch recently left the GDR illegally. It is therefore necessary to intensify the observation of the Mormon branches to determine where similar opinions are being discussed and whether Mormons have recently left illegally. Such information and the names of illegal departures among the Mormons are to be immediately provided to the office of the national police. (DO 1/11 HVDVP/865)

The unending stream of members fleeing the GDR was also a concern of the mission leaders. The minutes of a meeting between President Gregory and the district presidents, held in Leipzig on September 2, 1956, included this statement:

> The meeting closed with the greatest problem to these brethren—that of having their members flee to the West. It was pointed out that much of the cause could be laid to the fact that relatives in Zion write to these good people, telling them how nice it is and how they wished they could be there, too. The children are also the cause of many people leaving the East Zone. They want their children to have freedom rather than stay under communistic rule. President Gregory...encouraged the brethren to have their members stay where they are. They will surely be blessed for following the advice of the authorities. (LR 2428 2)

Members described the effects of the emigration upon the functioning of the Church and the morale of the members:

> *Alfred Bastian:* The prophet had said that we should remain in our country. District officials said: "Zion is in the home, Zion is in every branch, and Zion is not in Salt Lake City." But throughout the mission, five, ten, fifteen, or twenty members left every week, out of every branch. Those who left from Annaberg are too numerous to count, but at least 120 to 150 left, half the branch. It severely damaged the public image of the Church. (1991)

> *Joachim Meyer:* Many already left prior to the war, and the emigration continued until 1960. Most went to America and some to West Germany. Many large families resulted from those who left. If they had all

remained, we might have had two or three wards today in Annaberg-Buchholz. (1989)

Sieglinde Müller: We had a district president. Every time he visited, he preached, "Stay where you now live." Then suddenly we heard the next Sunday that he took off for the West. Can you imagine that? It naturally shocked us. It's impossible to understand. (1993)

Manfred Schütze: All district presidents before me left. Some had to, some didn't have to. When the Berlin Wall was built, we were visiting in the West. I spoke with my wife and said, "You know that so many have gone, but we are going back." When we returned, people were already thinking of taking over our apartment. They were all amazed. However, I said, "I have a calling and we are staying here." (1991)

Henry Burkhardt: The members often felt they had no alternative but to leave the country. Of course, that set back the Church numerically, but we couldn't prevent them from leaving. Everyone knew about the announcement that President McKay had made, that members should remain in their homeland and strengthen the Church there. But the members who wanted to leave often said: "Germany exists also in the West, so we are not violating this guidance from the First Presidency." This excessive emigration continued until 1961, until the Berlin Wall was built. Then it essentially ended. (1991)

Hans Schult: I now see that it wasn't very helpful for the development of the Church in our country, that so many members left. The First Presidency under President McKay had published statements in 1953, in which the members were asked to remain in their home countries. But many said at that time, "That applies to all countries of the world except to the Communist countries." It was a very critical time because not only did many members decide to leave, but also priesthood leaders, including branch and district presidents, and entire families. Brother Krause often quoted from the scriptures in that regard concerning the shepherd and the flock. That means that when someone has been called, for example, as a branch president, he cannot leave, he must stay with the flock. He also said encouragingly, "We live in the best country, at the best time and under the best circumstances, and one day we will recognize and see that to stay was a good decision."

We remembered the promise of President Monson in Görlitz, that the members in this country would receive every blessing that they received in other parts of the world. That was a good message for us. The mission president at that time, Brother Burkhardt, also was a great example. He and many other leaders in the Church didn't leave. He lived under significantly worse conditions than we encountered. We

> thought of an example in the Book of Mormon. Ammon went into the land of the Lamanites. He was immediately thrown into prison. Then he became a servant to King Lamoni and earned his confidence. Only then was Ammon able to preach the gospel to the king, to his father, and to the entire country. He accepted his difficult circumstances and problems. We haven't experienced such situations. Many left to avoid those difficulties, or for a better temporal life. Who knows which it was? We were not imprisoned because of our faith. We were not persecuted. We could hold our meetings. We certainly were presented with problems, but we attempted to resolve them. Naturally we all looked to the West, since people had it easier there. But the material life is only one side of the coin, and the purpose of this life is the other side. There were also uncertainties in the West that would have to be considered, and the care of our parents kept many people from leaving. We don't consider ourselves as heroes. The situations were varied and often not simple. Today, I have begun to reconsider and to have understanding for those who left. Not everyone had the spiritual strength to set and pursue goals, or they were not supported by people they could trust, or did not recognize that some things were more important than an easy life on this earth. We certainly had problems and difficulties, but we also tried to overcome them. (1991)

The above statements represent the opinions expressed in interviews conducted by Church archivists shortly after the Wende and by the author a decade later. However, those interviews were conducted among members who remained in the GDR, who were the focus of this research project. Many of those who left the GDR have different opinions. One member who escaped in 1961 read an early draft of this chapter and responded to the author. His perspective deserves to be included here:

> *Manfred Henkel:* In my opinion, the book's description of the members who remained in the GDR as the "good" and those who left as the "less good" or even as traitors to the cause is too simplistic. Many of those who left played significant supporting and leadership roles in the branches of the Church in West Germany. It took courage to leave father and mother, homeland, jobs, and friends and to start over economically again in order to obtain freedom for themselves and their children. Perhaps some who remained in the GDR didn't have this courage or had come to terms with the regime or had fallen away from the Church. While those who remained for worthy reasons deserve unlimited respect, it is also possible that those who voted with their feet caused the Communist leadership to make positive changes that benefited the members who stayed behind. After fleeing in 1961, I met Brother Stover again. During our conversation, I told him that I had left the GDR. He responded: "Why didn't you do that long ago?" (2006)

6 Living with the Wall 1961–1989

> *I would like to report that the Church is at the present time enjoying a good amount of religious freedom, being permitted to hold regular meetings and carry on the Church programs.... The spirit among our people is excellent. As a whole, suppression seems to unite. (President Joel A. Tate, January 1966)*
>
> *We had precisely the same Church program as in the West, and we conducted it earnestly. Sometimes we didn't have the same capacity, since too many people had left, but the program as such was at least as good as in the West. (Hans Schult, 1991)*
>
> *Our teaching material was usually one year late. We first had to obtain it and then copy it. However, the proper order of the Church was always maintained. We were the only Communist country in which the regular Church organization existed.... The Church was conducted properly here. (Walter Schiele, 1991)*

For political reasons, the East German Mission was renamed the North German Mission in 1957. In July 1961, the mission's headquarters was moved to Hamburg, and a new Berlin Mission became responsible for Berlin and the GDR region. Percy Fetzer remained in Berlin as mission president, with Henry Burkhardt as a counselor for the GDR. Six weeks later, on August 13, 1961, the Berlin Mission itself was divided, this time by a wall erected between West and East Berlin. The building of the Wall did not come as a total surprise. Rumors had circulated for years that the GDR would have to do something to prevent its citizens from exiting through the only opening in the border between East and West Germany. The two options were to create a barrier between East and West Berlin or to establish a barrier between East Berlin and the rest of the GDR, which would be much more difficult. These rumors were reported in the mission's 1958 quarterly report:

> *December 31, 1958:* Brother Burkhardt reported that the communist regime plans to deny residents of East Germany entrance into Berlin. The purpose of the maneuver is to cut the flow of refugees who come to East Berlin, cross the border into West Berlin, and fly to West Germany. Since Berlin is under four-power control, passage between the two sectors [of Berlin] cannot be prohibited. However, if the East German government succeeds in prohibiting entrance to East Berlin from the surrounding areas, communication [with members in the GDR] will be almost impossible.
>
> Two weeks before Christmas, the Russian representative to East Germany put forth a proposal to shut down all connection between East and West Berlin. In this way he hoped to make the "Iron Curtain" completely foolproof. Many East Germans have to pass through West Berlin to get to their work in East Berlin. The East Germans protested and the action was never put into effect. (LR 2428 2)

A few days before the construction of the Wall on August 13, 1961, President Fetzer began to receive reports of increased border patrols on roads leading into East Berlin. He wrote about the event in the Berlin Mission journal and described its immediate impact upon the Church and its members:

> *August 10/12:* No one seems to understand the significance of the commotion and restrictions.
>
> *August 13:* We have received reports from all sides that Berlin is surrounded by tanks and armed guards, that the travel between the East and the West has been sealed off, that pickets have been set up during the night, and that tanks have been placed at street border crossings to seal off all physical communication. Telephone and telegraph are all shut down. Machine guns have been set up in buildings flanking the routes into West Berlin. Some of the Saints who are visiting in West Berlin had a premonition and remained in West Berlin over the weekend.... Some are returning to their homes in the East with a heavy heart for they have a feeling they will never see their loved ones in West Berlin again.... The branches in Neukölln and Berlin-Nord are without branch presidents. The Berlin District is without leadership because Erwin Rathke and his second counselor are locked out.... Immediate temporary leadership was installed to take care of the meetings for the day and for the following week. Thousands of people are gathering at the street crossings into East Berlin, where they hastily erected barricades and barbed wire to deny the right to enter. Rifle squads and tanks are patrolling.... Consensus of opinion is that if the U.S. does not step in to verify the four-power treaty arrangement, that it will be necessary for many to leave Berlin. (LR 691 2)

The impact of the Wall on the organization of the Church in Berlin was well described in a brochure published by the Berlin Stake upon its twenty-fifth anniversary in 1986:

> The Berlin District's branches in Friedrichshain, Potsdam-Leest, Neubrandenburg, and Rathenow...were cut off on that day from the West Berlin branches in Charlottenburg, Dahlem, Neukölln, North, Spandau, and Tempelhof. The district president lived in East Berlin and could no longer care for the branches on the other side of the Wall. Three branch presidents, almost all counselors in the branches, three-quarters of the district council, the Elders Quorum leadership, all auxiliary leadership, and more than one-half of all elders lived in East Berlin or the GDR and were now separated from West Berlin. (LR 694 23)

President Fetzer recorded his first efforts to reestablish contact with the branches in East Berlin and throughout the GDR:

> *August 24:* Walked across the line to inquire what the restrictions would be [to enter East Berlin] and were told that we could come through at any time.
>
> *August 27:* Elder Owens and I stripped the car and our pockets and drove to the Friedrichstraße entrance into East Berlin. Our car had to be preceded by soldiers with guns with bayonets to part the crowd so that we could drive through the West Berlin area to reach the checkpoint of East Berlin police border guards. We were held up momentarily at the "S" maze obstruction, our passports examined, and we were allowed to proceed without further examination. The brethren we met in the Friedrichshain Branch were President Henry Burkhardt, President Fischer of the North Branch, and many of the Saints who are restricted to East Berlin....The Friedrichshain Branch has been substantially strengthened in leadership and in numbers by the blockade. (LR 691 2)

The history of the Berlin District noted that Sister Fetzer accompanied her husband on the August 27 visit to the branch in Friedrichshain and recorded the following visits by general authorities of the Church during the next month:

> On Friday, September 8, 1961, we had a second, even greater experience in the Friedrichshain Branch. Elder Delbert L. Stapley, assistant to the Quorum of the Twelve, Elder Alvin R. Dyer, and President Fetzer visited. Only the district president, Elder Erwin Rathke, had the privilege to discuss the new problems with these brethren. However, on the following day, Saturday, Elder Nathan Eldon Tanner, assistant

to the Twelve, and Walter Stover visited us. President Burkhardt had asked all district presidents to come to this meeting in East Berlin. We discussed the growth of the Church in general as well as in our mission. We also discussed the problems that have arisen through this separation. (LR 691 2)

The Berlin Stake

The Church had already begun to plan a reorganization of the branches in Berlin before the Wall was built. President Fetzer had written on July 27, 1961:

> Prepared plan of contemplated master Berlin district organization which should be a forerunner to the eventual organization of a stake in Berlin. Prepared lists of officers of the various organizations, district presidency, and district high council. . . . Estimated possible stake organization to be a year or more in the future. (LR 691 2)

The erection of the Wall moved this plan forward in time. On August 24, 1961, President David O. McKay wrote in his journal:

> I presented to the Council the recommendation of the First Presidency that a stake be organized in Berlin, Germany, where there are at present about 1,600 members of the Church. I stated that it is felt that the situation there could be handled better as a stake than as a mission under present conditions, and that through a stake organization, the local people in that area could be trained to take over the leadership of the stake under present conditions, and particularly if the situation should develop that our missionaries would have to leave there. I explained that the mission would continue in Berlin, in addition to the stake.[1]

On September 6, 1961, President McKay wrote again in his journal about conditions in Berlin and noted: "I mentioned the decision to organize a stake there, and it was agreed that East Berlin should be brought into that organization."[2] McKay's comment shows that the ramifications of the Berlin Wall were not fully comprehended in Salt Lake City. With the new travel and communication barriers between West and East Berlin, it would have been impractical, if not impossible, to administer a stake split in that manner. President Fetzer described the eventual organization of the stake:

> September 5, 1961: President Dyer called from Frankfurt stating that President McKay had directed that the Berlin Mission should be organized into a stake and he further stated that Elder Delbert L. Stapley and he were designated to proceed immediately to lay the groundwork for the organization of the stake and then to organize it. . . . It is evident that this people in an island surrounded by an anti-Christ government

> should be made substantially capable of providing their own leadership and administering the affairs of the Kingdom independently.

> September 8, 1961: We drove to the East zone with Elders Stapley and Dyer and . . . met briefly with Brother Erwin Rathke in the Friedrichshain Branch. Elder Stapley personally authorized Rathke to retain his presidency, but to preside from this date on over the remainder of the one-time Berlin District [i.e.,] the cut-off branches of Friedrichshain, Rathenow, Potsdam, Brandenburg, and Leest. (LR 691 2)

The Berlin Stake was organized on September 10 and included the following six units in West Berlin: wards: Spandau, North, and Dahlem; branches: Tempelhof, Neukölln, and Charlottenburg.

On September 21, 1961, President McKay made a final journal entry regarding the political situation in Berlin. His comments reflect the uncertainty and concern about the Berlin crisis that existed among the Church leaders at that time:

> During the meeting today Elder Delbert L. Stapley gave a report on his recent trip to Germany. Speaking of the Berlin crisis, he said that the present action of the East German Communists in Russia [GDR leaders were visiting in Russia] indicates that all of Berlin is going to be taken within the Communist camp. We have only 6,500 soldiers [in West Berlin]. The British and French are represented, but we are not in force sufficient to resist any offensive action on the part of the Communists. They have built up this wall that separates East from West Berlin. The Communists have put up two lines of barbed-wire fence about eight feet high, separated ten or twelve feet with heavy barbed-wire entanglements laced in between. They have uprooted the trees with bulldozers from this line of fencing about 150 feet, so that it is clear and open. This is patrolled by the East German or Russian soldiers. They are entrenched and moving their people back, and it seemed to be just a maneuver to take over West Berlin.
>
> Elder Stapley said it would be very difficult to defend Berlin as he sees it. . . . He asked our new stake presidency what would happen if the Communists took over, and they did not seem to have too much concern. In other words, we have more concern here than the West Germans have. Elder Stapley felt it was because they have lived under domination so many years they do not know anything else, but if they had the privilege of getting into East Berlin and seeing the conditions under which the people live it might change their minds. He said that if the Communists were to close the corridors they could starve Berlin and it would not take too long. He did not see how Berlin could be maintained without being completely destroyed. He felt the situation requires rather careful watching from our standpoint and was

> very apprehensive about it. He thought it would only take a few hours to bring the entire city of Berlin into the Communist camp.[3]

Elder Stapley's comments about the attitude of the West Berliners toward the events of August 1961 are difficult to understand. Certainly, the residents of West Berlin were fully aware of the social, economic, and political conditions that existed on the other side of the border. It would seem more likely that they simply saw the Berlin Wall as a desperate measure by the GDR to halt the flood of escapees, rather than a prelude to an invasion of West Berlin by Soviet forces.

Communication Maintained Despite the Wall

The wall between East and West Berlin certainly made communication more difficult, but contrary to widespread belief, the members in the East were not cut off from Church leaders in the West. Before the Wall was erected, President Burkhardt came to the mission office at least monthly, and district leaders and missionaries came for occasional instruction. Although travel from east to west was no longer possible, the number of leaders who went from west to east actually increased. President Fetzer and subsequent mission presidents frequently crossed from West Berlin to East Berlin to meet with President Burkhardt in Friedrichshain, and the GDR allowed westerners to attend the Leipzig Fair. Church leaders took advantage of this opening to attend mission conferences in Leipzig that were planned to coincide with the biannual fair.

On January 14, 1962, Elder Kimball and his wife accompanied President Fetzer and his wife when they met with district leaders and members in East Berlin. Excerpts from Elder Kimball's personal notes follow:

> We fearfully and quietly drove to the Wall where the East German soldiers stopped us and looked at our passports. We were asked to get out of the car, and we went into a building while they searched our car. We opened our wallets to show what we had therein. They looked us over carefully, asked a few questions and seemed to determine we were only more of the many American tourists just going over to look around. . . . Once in the [meeting house], it was light and warm and what a greeting! They did not know we were coming, at least not that we the Kimballs were! It could not be publicized. Only the top people knew and they were not sure, as there is no telephone service and letters would be indiscrete. The door opened, and they caught sight of us. In their loneliness they said it "was like angels from heaven," not that we could ever make such pretense, but they feel so deserted, so lonely. As one sister put it, "We are in prison." They seemed overjoyed.
>
> The Priesthood meeting, Relief Society, and the meeting of the district presidents were in session. Camilla [Kimball] and Thelma [Fetzer] went into the women's meeting and we went in with the district presidents. We found in attendance:

Pres. BURKHARDT, counselor to President Fetzer overseeing East Germany
Pres. ERWIN RATHKE, of the East Berlin District
Pres. ZAADER, counselor in the East Berlin District
Pres. HERBERT GULLA, of the Zwickau District
Pres. WALTER KRAUSE, of the Mecklenburg District
Pres. EBERHARD GÄBLER, of the Dresden District
Pres. GOTTFRIED RICHTER, of the Karl-Marx-Stadt District
Pres. WALTER SCHIELE, of the Leipzig District

I write these names in capital letters, for I think the Lord will do that through his recorders. I think the BOOK OF LIFE will so record such courageous devoted men who carry on under such adverse circumstances. My heart went out to them. My soul and my emotions were touched. I felt I was in the presence of great and good and noble men.

The presidents sat around the table with grim faces. Once in a while their faces broke into a smile or a short laugh but they were stolid. One president said, "We ought to get a wagon and bust a hole in the wall." . . . Some talked of WHEN the Wall comes down, and some said IT WOULD GET WORSE instead of better.

We went into the regular meeting and the room was filled. . . . There must have been about eighty people and nearly every seat was full. We sat on the stand and after the song and prayer and song and the sacrament, President Fetzer and I spoke. The first song was sung with gusto though some sang through their tears. Our presence and their limitations seemed to touch their hearts and stir their memories and thoughts. One distinguished woman on the front seat fought hard to control her tears but they continued to come. She would dry them and sing a few words but then a fresh flood would come. Their prayer was one of faith and thankfulness. Then they sang "I Need Thee Every Hour," and I had much difficulty with my own emotions as I realized how much they needed the Lord now. Many handkerchiefs came into evidence, and several wiped their eyes and sang through their tears, "Ich brauch dich, O ich brauch dich!" I thought of our liberty and blessings and prosperity and thought of so many of us who do not seem to evidence by our works that we need the Lord. I spoke on the Lord's experiences and sufferings and spoke of Joseph Smith's jail experiences and of their courage.

These people are made of steel. I wonder what I would do in their shoes. After the meeting concluded, the sisters continued, and we went back to the district presidents' meeting to give them help. I found them orthodox and eager to carry on the program of the Church as it should be done. They asked many questions as to procedure, then asked for news of the Church. . . . I told them of the great missionary movement and its progress and the numerous converts and that the new converts of 1961 would fill their little hall a thousand

> times. They gasped. I told them of new stakes in Europe, the South Seas, Alaska, and Mexico City, and their eyes beamed.... They were hungry for news and seemed fed and comforted in knowing that the Church was moving forward even though they were imprisoned and limited.
>
> Our duty done, we bid a fond and affectionate farewell to the Saints. Some embraced us as they said goodbye, some shed tears, and the farewells were tender and a bit sad. How grateful they were that we had come. They said now they could stand it longer and their courage was bolstered, though I think I was lifted by them far more than they could possibly be helped by us.
>
> I folded up my notes into a very tiny pack and held it tightly in my hand. I did not want the names of any of these brethren to fall into their hands. I pushed it back into the folds of the front seat as we were asked to get out of the car and go into the building to be checked and while they checked the car.... To my great relief my names and notes were still hidden well in the fold of the leather seat.
>
> Now we are in the streets of West Berlin and we breathe easily again but are pensive and thoughtful and sad. We are still seeing those iron-folks in their fond farewell—in their perplexity—in their near hopelessness. Oh! If we could help them! O how our hearts ached for them in their loneliness and isolation and fetters! And our determinations were that we would always remember them in our prayers. Please, Heavenly Father, release them from their incarceration and pressures and indoctrinations, if it please Thee! (Copy from Edward Kimball)

Two months after Elder Kimball's visit to East Berlin, Elder Theodore M. Burton, president of the European Mission, traveled to Leipzig with President Fetzer in conjunction with the Leipzig Fair. They met with all of the district and branch presidents in the GDR on Saturday and attended two sessions of a mission conference on Sunday, March 11, 1962. Since the meeting house in the Gerberstraße could only accommodate 375 persons, members were given entrance tickets to one of the two sessions. Everyone attending the conference was photographed by government agents from a second floor window of a building across the street from the meeting house. (LR 691 2)

> *Walter Schiele:* We always had two conference sessions in Leipzig. While the first members were in the building, the next lined up outside. When the meeting was finished, the first left and the rooms were aired out before the second group entered. That, of course, attracted the attention of the police, who parked their car nearby and observed everything. Since everything was peaceful and well organized, they soon left. The visiting Church authorities said that they had also attended the Fair while in Leipzig. They certainly must have done so,

> since they had to be honest, but the main purpose of their visit was, of course, to support the members here, and to reestablish and maintain communication with us. (1991)

The Berlin Mission history reported three subsequent visits:

> *September 8–9, 1962:* President Fetzer met with district and branch leaders in Leipzig. Two Sunday meetings were held as before. The youth chorus of seventy-five voices sang beautifully under the direction of Joachim Lehnig and Gerwin Baasch.
>
> *October 14, 1962:* President Fetzer attended a district conference in Friedrichshain. Two "earnest investigators" were present at the meeting. One had a tape recorder in his lap and another was taking pictures of everyone who participated in the meeting with a telephoto lens–equipped camera. During the meeting, a statement was read that the Church of Jesus Christ of Latter-Day Saints was the only "Volkskirche" in existence, which means the only church of the people, by the people, and for the people. This declaration was made so that when the transcript of the meeting was made, the East German Communists would know that we were the type of church that met the specifications of a church according to the Communist doctrine, except for the belief in God, which they omit.
>
> *March 8–10, 1963:* Presidents Burton and Fetzer, their wives and two American missionaries attended the conference in Leipzig. Three Sunday sessions were held, "early", 11:30, and 2:00, each with the same speakers but attended by different members with different choirs. (LR 691 2)

The visits by Church authorities from the West did not always proceed without problems. Following the March 1963 meeting, Presidents Fetzer and Burton returned to Berlin in separate cars. President Fetzer carried the mission's six-month reports. His car was not thoroughly searched, but President Burton's car was detained for nine hours and thoroughly searched. All of the genealogical records he was transporting were confiscated.

President Fetzer was released shortly after that conference. The manuscript history of the Leipzig Branch contains the following 1963 entry regarding his tenure and that of his successor, President Tate:

> Never before had a mission president [Percy K. Fetzer] devoted so much time to visit the GDR. He personified for the members here the connection to the Church. The problems and concerns that had been magnified by the construction of the Berlin Wall, which many had seen as the final and complete separation from the headquarters of

> the Church, was very well offset by the courage and dedication of this brother.... President Joel A. Tate was a successor in the best meaning of that word. Through his contacts with members in the GDR, which he not only carried out via mission conferences, he soon became well known. He conveyed feelings of safety, peace, und unquestioned unity. (MS 17716)

President Tate visited the Friedrichshain branch on August 4, 1963, and noted that the meeting room was filled with young people who bore their testimonies:

> It made one assured that the future of the church would be in good hands as these young people grow up to assume leadership responsibilities. We were thankful to know we had such fine youth in the East Zone. Later we learned that these young people had ridden from different areas in East Germany on their bicycles to a camp about thirty miles outside of Berlin. The camp was located on an island, which required transportation by ferry to get there. Because the ferry did not run early enough for them to be on time for church, they put their clothes in a small rubber boat and swam to shore. Such love and devotion is hard to find any place except among those who have testimonies of the truthfulness of the gospel. (LR 691 2)

President Tate took his first trip to Leipzig on September 6, 1963, where a baptism was held early on Sunday morning in a nearby bathhouse. The first session of conference was reserved for the youth, and 308 (mostly youth) were present. Another 368 members attended the second session at 11:30, and 318 attended the 2:30 session. Tate was again in Leipzig on March 7, 1964. Six members from Czechoslovakia also were present at that conference (LR 691 2).

Further West-East contacts took place during October 1964. Donna H. Sorenson, member of the General Board of the Sunday School, Clark N. Stohl, member of the General Board of the YM-MIA, and Dorothy P. Holt, second counselor in the presidency of the YW-MIA, attended a special meeting in the Friedrichshain Branch, to which all district and auxiliary leaders from the GDR were invited. The leaders from America had planned only to attend a stake conference in West Berlin, but President Tate obtained permission from the First Presidency to take them into East Berlin to instruct the GDR leaders as well.

Reports in the Berlin Mission history from 1964 to 1966 show that President Tate continued to travel frequently to the GDR. In November 1964, he attended a district conference in Dresden on Saturday: "It was the first time in about eight years that a mission president was able to go to Dresden or any of the cities in that part of the mission. We went into the East Zone as tourists and spent some time going through the Zwinger Art Galleries." On the next day he attended Sunday School in Freiberg and then traveled to Karl-Marx-Stadt to attend the fast and testimony meeting.

In February 1965, Tate attended the district conference in Erfurt, and in April he attended the Mecklenburg District conference in Wolgast, the first time since the start of the war that a mission president was present. He attended the district conference in Annaberg in May and a special genealogy conference in Dresden in June. In July he traveled to a district conference in Werdau, spoke at a sacrament meeting in Prenzlau in August, and later attended the conference of the Dresden District in Cottbus. During the fall, he attended district conferences in Neubrandenburg, Leipzig, and Erfurt. In November he accompanied Elder S. Dilworth Young of the Seventy to Annaberg for a conference of the Karl-Marx-Stadt District. Following those activities, President Tate wrote to President David O. McKay on January 10, 1966:

> We are grateful to the Lord for opening the way for us to travel as tourists into East Germany, to be with our people, partake of their spirit, and in a small way help them. In the fall of 1964, we first learned of the possibility of making such trips. We were still unsure but determined to try and were fortunate in making one trip in November of that year. Everything went so well that we immediately made plans for 1965.
>
> In the East we have seven districts, forty-seven branches, and 4,800 members. We also have six Elders Quorums. Out of twenty-four scheduled district conferences, we attended thirteen, visiting each district at least once, some twice, and the Berlin East District conferences four times. In addition, we attended a genealogical convention in Dresden, attended a youth outing and conference, and visited six branches where we were able to hold special meetings.
>
> I would like to report that the Church is at the present time enjoying a good amount of religious freedom, being permitted to hold regular meetings and carry on the Church programs. Of course we have not been permitted to supply them with all of the latest Church publications.... The spirit among our people is excellent. As a whole, suppression seems to unite.... I have two wonderful counselors in the East. They are truly dedicated. The Church is their whole life. Our district presidents are tremendous. (LR 691 25)

Was the Wall a Hidden Blessing?

The negative consequences of the emigration of members from the GDR in the 1950s were addressed in the preceding chapter. Although a few members obtained permission to emigrate legally after the construction of the Berlin Wall, the flood of departures ceased. The Wall did complicate Church administration and made daily life in the GDR more difficult in many ways, but the following excerpts from interviews present another perspective to the impact of the Wall:

> *Manfred Schütze:* I recognize today, that the Wall was the best thing that could have happened to us. We had lost so many members prior

to that time. They all went to West Germany and America, simply because they believed, and rightfully so, that conducting their lives in accordance with the principles of the Church was not always possible. They left by the dozens, yes, by the hundreds. It appeared as if all the branches would die. But then it ended. That was a blessing, as bad as it sounds. We now had to focus on ourselves. Consider what happened during the following years in the GDR, how strong the Church has become, how strong the members have become. We later had a patriarch, our leaders could travel to America, we had stakes, even a temple. All that is a miracle to me and not an accidental miracle. The stakes that we have and the many opportunities to develop as a Church, the strong members, everything that took place, were only possible because of the Wall. But one often doesn't see it when one is enmeshed in the problems. So, I didn't understand that in 1961, not at all. Today, looking backwards, I understand it much better. (1991)

Henry Burkhardt: Many of our active members left the country, with the result that a series of branches had to be closed. We did not have the leadership. The branches were small and had to be combined. We were very concerned about how to maintain them. Missionary activities were severely curtailed in the 1960s. We could only meet with friends or through the referral program. That, of course, had its positive aspects, although limited. They certainly were not at all comparable to our present-day successes, but for us at that time, we were successful. We found new members, trained new leaders, and actually had an increase in branches. That was a great testimony for us, how the Lord continued his work in the East.

We were not able to officially bring manuals, teaching materials, etc., into the country. We had to more or less smuggle items, and then only in very limited numbers, one or two copies. We began then to copy those materials with typewriters, with numerous volunteers. In that way we were able to hold our heads above water. Mostly we used the scriptures during those years. But I didn't find that to be a deficit for the members. Their faith was greatly strengthened through that necessity. (1991)

Dieter Lehm: I actually didn't see any disadvantage. One had to live the Gospel at home, since we couldn't do much in public. We could think and live it, we could speak about the Church with our friends and acquaintances. But it was forbidden to do that publicly. (1991)

Jürgen Pabst: In 1985, my wife and I were in the United States for four weeks. We experienced freedom at that time. No one asked us to identify ourselves. No one required anything of us, no registration where we stayed overnight, etc. As we returned, crossed over the border, and

> met our regional representative, he said: "There is no turning around now." That was actually upsetting, as I realized, "Now I'm here and if the people who run the government don't want me to leave again, I won't get out of here for the rest of my life." At that moment it was clear to me that my freedom was entirely dependent on the will of someone else. (1993)

> *Lothar Hubert:* We lost personal freedom because of the Wall. We always had felt a little slavery or pressure from the government, and we were more or less used to that. But now it was perhaps more intense. They could do more to us than earlier, and no one could escape. Many members had left prior to the Wall, and our branches became smaller and smaller. It was a catastrophe when someone left. So in that regard it was a blessing that few members could leave. The Church was an island on which we lived, where members unconsciously became closer to each other and where all of your friends lived. It was often difficult to administer the Church, but when I now look back, it was also beautiful, because we had been welded together. (1993)

> *Joachim Lehnig:* That which we wanted to do in the Church and in accordance with our beliefs, that we could do. We could not travel to Switzerland to go to the temple, certainly not. But we couldn't do that earlier [before a temple existed], and the members grew and became stronger anyhow. (2003)

Organizational Changes after the Wall

The mission had to be reorganized after the Wall was built. President Burkhardt met with the district presidents and the district leaders of the MIA in Leipzig on November 26, 1961. That was followed by a conference in Dresden on December 9 and 10, 1961, at which time the existing auxiliary oversight boards were revised and new ones established. The Wall was not mentioned in the minutes of that meeting, but President Burkhardt did make a joke related to the new travel restrictions when he said:

> I greet you on behalf of President Fetzer. He sends his personal greetings and best wishes, and hopes to be able to meet with you again soon. He would very much like to be here, but he can't afford the travel costs! I suggested that the Elders Quorum in Annaberg would support him, but he didn't accept the offer. (LR 2428 57)

Burkhardt's next comment shows, however, that he did view the construction of the Wall as a serious problem at that time. He could not have foreseen how well communications with the mission president would be maintained in the future or how often the mission presidents and other Church authorities would be able to enter the GDR. Therefore, he explained to the assembled Church leaders:

> We all recognize the circumstances under which the members in this country are living, and they are not, from our perspective, ideal circumstances. However, the work of the Lord cannot suffer as a result of conditions imposed by man. It will more or less depend on us, and how we carry out our callings, whether the work of God will continue to go forward with success in this country.
>
> Previously, we were strengthened anew by each district conference. That will change in the future, since from today on you will need to go to district conferences to bring that strength to others, which you earlier expected to receive there. We are certain that such sources of strength can only flow when they have been fed, so you, as new sources, will be fed in the future, but in different ways than before.

President Burkhardt then announced that the mission's six districts in the GDR would be combined for certain functions. For example, the administration of the auxiliary organizations would be led by three larger geographical units he called "bezirks," which he also referred to as minimissions. However, the existing districts would remain as before. The bezirks were:

- Berlin – Mecklenburg
- Dresden – Karl-Marx-Stadt
- Leipzig – Zwickau/Erfurt

He also established or revised boards or committees to oversee activities within the bezirks and districts. In the past, such committees had been responsible for activities throughout the mission, including the Western districts. The new committees applied only to the GDR:

- Genealogy (existent already for two years)
- Aaronic Priesthood under age twenty-one
- Aaronic Priesthood over age twenty-one
- Mutual Improvement Association, Young Men
- Mutual Improvement Association, Young Women
- Relief Society
- Sunday School
- Primary Association

Burkhardt stated that each committee would have three members, one from each of the three bezirks. The present district leaders for auxiliary organizations would continue to oversee activities within their districts, but now under the supervision of the bezirk committees.

With these changes, the Berlin Mission essentially became two missions under one president, one for the GDR and one for West Berlin. Obviously, President Burkhardt's responsibility for oversight of the Berlin Mission's activities in the GDR increased with these changes.

The new committee structure continued with only minor changes when a new Dresden Mission was established eight years later, in 1969. At that time, he described the work of the committees in more detail at the beginning of the journal that he maintained for the new mission.

> The main assignment of these committees was to oversee the spiritual and administrative matters relevant to their area of responsibility. A special task for most of these committees was the preparation of the teaching material for the various classes. When the original material was not available, they had to develop their own, but whenever possible, they attempted to follow the subject matter and the material set forth by the Church's boards. Typically, when a copy of the relevant manual was available, it had to be duplicated by retyping it. This difficult and time-consuming task was undertaken by members of the committees personally, or some of the work was done in the mission office in Dresden. We are thankful that we have matched the current program for almost every organization of the Church and only infrequently have had to use material taken from previous manuals.
>
> The twenty-eight members of our various committees are performing their duties well, and we are thankful for them, since it is through their good work that we are able to speak of success in all areas of the mission. We admire how these members develop the activities of their organizations, without guidance from the Church's main boards, in order to help individuals better understand the Gospel and align themselves with the basic principles of the Church. We appreciate these programs of the Church and are thankful that they are available to us, even though occasional difficulties need to be overcome. (DMO)

Overview of the Church in the 1960s

The Dresden Mission file includes a report on the status of the Church in the GDR that was written by President Burkhardt about 1969. Those portions regarding missionary work, youth activities, the youth choir, and meeting houses can be found in later chapters that address those topics. The other sections are quoted here:

> *Elders Quorums:* Six Elders Quorums, comprised of 418 elders, contribute to the support of our branches. The Karl-Marx-Stadt District alone has two quorums with 142 elders. Our elders perform a good work and are almost 100 percent active. Unfortunately, many of our brothers are elderly and not always physically able to undertake all assignments. If

we were able to fully count on every brother, then we could accomplish much more in certain priesthood activities. Then one elder would be responsible for eleven members, and the goals of the home teaching program would be met. We do have some concerns regarding our priesthood programs, and the missionary activity has problems that we have not yet been able to resolve.

Home Teaching Program: This program of the Church has also been initiated in our mission. We have the *Handbook for Home Teachers* as well as various instructions that are available in all other missions of the Church. Significant effort has been made in the individual districts to prepare our brothers for home teaching activities. The program has been enthusiastically accepted. Since some problems still remain, it is essential that we constantly instruct our home teachers about the importance of this work and not let this new program revert to the earlier form of priesthood visits.

Priesthood Genealogy: Many members of our mission have always been engaged in this work. However, the enthusiasm has increased ever since this genealogy work became a special program of the priesthood. We cannot say that we are completely satisfied with what has been accomplished to date, but we are thankful for the considerable work that has been submitted in the past. We expect another increase in the number of group sheets submitted this year, since instruction has been conducted in all districts in which our members have been specifically told to not neglect this work for our dead. With opportunities made available to us, we have established a small archive, whose beginnings are certainly modest, but which nevertheless have a financial value of about 25,000 marks. After all available material has been catalogued—and new genealogical material is constantly being added—we will be able to begin to help all our members with their genealogical research. About six hundred family group sheets have already been compiled from this material. We have great expectations for this work and are satisfied with what has already been accomplished.

Training: Beginning this year, the mission's committees will institute training for all auxiliary organizations in every district, to bring the program of the Church closer to every officer. In this way we achieve a closer contact with our members, cooperation is improved, and the underlying goals of the individual programs become more evident. The committees for genealogy and the Primary initiated this instruction last year and have already achieved success.

MIA and Achievement Programs: The achievement programs of the MIA and the young priesthood members has been well received. Our young brothers and sisters are pleased when they meet the requirements of the individual achievement awards, which encourage them to new heights, and very few fail to meet the requirements in the following year. We have been especially pleased that some of our young members have met the requirements to become Master M-Men and Golden Gleaners. We appreciate the programs of the Church and are thankful that they are available to us, even when challenges must be overcome.

Vacation Activities: Even our children in the Sunday School and Primary ages are cared for. Since 1962, they have been brought together for two or three weeks in homes of good members or in small camps during vacation time. The largest camp for Sunday School and Primary children was held in 1965 in Radebeul, by Dresden. Participants numbered fifty-two children and nine adults. Since 1963, the Relief Society has endeavored to include its sisters in vacation activities. Needy sisters have had the opportunity to rest and recover for two weeks, mostly during the summer in Mecklenburg and in Wolgast. Our sisters have appreciated this opportunity, and they are thankful for the efforts that the Relief Society committee has made to carry out this activity.

Family Home Evening Program: The Family Home Evening program has been well received after it was reinstituted. Although our families have no manual to guide their planning of Home Evenings, they are trying to conduct the program weekly. Some branches give occasional tips for organizing these evenings, and the members are reminded via talks at district conferences, that the Home Evenings should serve to unify the family and establish better relationships among its members.

District Conferences: Six of our seven districts hold four conferences each year. Only the Mecklenburg District continues with a spring and a fall conference, because of the long distances. All conferences are held in accordance with the *Handbook for District and Branch Presidents*. Although some problems emerged when the Priesthood and Relief Society meetings were moved from Sunday morning to Saturday, these guidelines have now been successfully instituted.

Importing Church Literature: There has been a shortage of written materials and Church scriptures throughout all past years. In 1966, we received permission from the government to import two thousand songbooks and five hundred Triple Combinations. These imports gave members a spiritual uplift, and we hope to receive permission for additional material. We recently submitted a request to import one thousand copies of *Jesus the Christ* and hope that this book will soon be in the possession of our members. [See Chapter 12 for more details about literature.]

As compensation, we tried to have special worship services for all members of the mission twice a year in connection with the Leipzig spring and fall fairs. However, after President Tate found ways to enter the GDR more often, we scheduled his visits primarily to coincide with the several district conferences. It is amazing how much strength and encouragement our members received from those visits. President Loscher is attempting to continue those visits when possible, and we believe they will assist our members to remain close to the Church.

Welfare Program: We are concerned about the problems of our older members who are no longer able to hold a job, most of whom must get by with a pension of only 110 to 120 marks a month. Since the cost of living for clothing, food, and coal is quite high, these members are often not able to afford these necessities. Of course, each branch tries to assist the needy through its Fast Offerings, but the available funds are usually not sufficient. We have been thankful that in most years, the mission presidents have given permission to assist these needy members with an annual supplement to purchase potatoes and coal. We think that it will be necessary to provide a one-time support action again this year.

Temple: About 250 of our members were able to visit the temple in the time when it was possible. Two elderly sisters, among those able to attend the temple, were called to sew temple clothing. These two sisters fulfilled their assignment for about ten years and produced a small supply of temple clothing. So far, garments have been provided by the mission president. The needs of most have been met, and we appreciate the support we receive in this regard.

Czechoslovakia and Poland: We have maintained a connection with our brothers and sisters in Czechoslovakia and Poland since 1955. We attempt to give these members—especially those from Czechoslovakia—opportunities to participate in our worship services. We have invited their youth to our youth activities. When material needs existed, we attempted—in Poland as well as in Czechoslovakia—to be of assistance. We have been able to develop a good relationship between our members and those in these two countries and hope to have continued opportunities to remain in contact. We are especially thankful in this mission, that we have relatively good opportunities to develop the program of the Church. We remember often, that we are still the only mission that exists in the socialist camp, and certainly have the obligation to help those who must cope with far greater problems. (DMO)

The Work of a District President

Church leaders in the GDR generally retained their assignments far longer than in America. Walter Schiele served as a district president in Leipzig from 1955 until 1978. He described some of his experiences in an interview:

> I was the district president for twenty-three years. Jürgen Pawelke has been the branch president in Halberstadt for forty-three years, since his mission. We did have alternatives. The Church's preference is to make more frequent changes, but we thought that when someone is doing a good job, then let him continue. Maybe that was wrong, but that was how it was. I had thirteen branches in my district, later fourteen. Most of them were small, except for Leipzig. We were ambitious and visited every one each month, and we could do that by arranging the meeting times so we could visit two or three branches on Sunday. We left home at 6:00 a.m. and returned at 10:00 p.m. or later when we traveled by train. Later, we advanced to a motorcycle with a sidecar, which allowed all three of us to travel together. Then we were not tied to the train schedule. Even later, we had cars, which was a great improvement. However, the farthest branches, Magdeburg, Halberstadt, and Nordhausen, were 130 kilometers away. We didn't have autobahns, just regular roads with bad surfaces, which shook up the riders. We had quarterly district conferences. During the week we had MIA on Tuesdays, Priesthood and Relief Society on Thursdays, Sunday School on Sunday morning, and the worship service in the evening. In between we could do a little missionary work. Our time was well occupied. (1991)

Young members also provided considerable service at an early age, especially in the smaller branches. Two examples follow:

> *Manfred Schütze:* I was a teacher in the Gospel Doctrine class in Sunday School at age fourteen. That was normal. We had a very small branch, and the branch president had to wait a long time until I became a priest and could bless the Sacrament. We gave a talk every Sunday or every other Sunday and also taught a class every Sunday. That gave us so much strength, because we had to study the gospel. We had twenty members, maybe thirty or forty, but never more. We also had what you call a speaker exchange, so that the members didn't always hear the same speakers. That was an even bigger challenge. The district president said, "When we pay for your travel expenses, then we also expect that you give a good talk." That was a huge challenge, and we really grew as a result.
>
> We had many single sisters, many children. You must imagine the conditions in 1961, for example. Many members had gone. Who remained? My generation, we were about twenty or younger. The thirty-

and forty-year-olds were gone; the fifty-year-olds probably also. But the sixty- and seventy-year-olds remained. So we had a very low number of members in middle age, who normally are the strength of the Church. So we youngsters had our responsibilities, and we knew it. We few had to carry the load at a younger age, but it really was not a burden for us, it was an opportunity. (1991)

Carmen Schlegel: We were a very small branch with only two young women. When we had activities, we went to our teacher in the neighboring village. One week we traveled to her home on our bicycles and the next week she came to us on her moped. I received callings when I was very young. I was the secretary in the Primary before I was twelve years of age. After I completed Primary, I was called as a teacher. Later I was in the Primary leadership while still young. (2004)

A Proposed Stake for the GDR

After he visited the mission in August 1955, Elder Spencer W. Kimball wrote to President Gregory about future stake organizations:

> There are several places in Europe where provisional or embryo stakes are almost ready to go to work. This is the ideal. The mission has as one of its responsibilities the creation of stakes. So I hope it will not be long until all the missionary district presidencies are called by some other name and that districts are organized in several areas in East Germany, which will approximate this small stake with a presidency, a high council, auxiliary executives and boards, and a program limited only by the size of the groups. Again, I realize this is a dream of the future, but that future can be made the present before too long. (LR 2428 39)

The first stake in Europe was organized in England in 1960. The first German stakes followed one year later in Stuttgart, Hamburg, and West Berlin. The reasons for the West Berlin Stake were described previously. After the Berlin Mission was closed in July 1966 and the GDR was placed under the North German Mission, its president, J. Peter Loscher, and his successor, Stanley D. Rees, began to lay the groundwork for stakes in the GDR.

President Loscher administered the GDR as if it were a separate mission. He had two counselors for the western portion of his mission and two counselors, Henry Burkhardt and Walter Krause, for the GDR. Loscher visited Burkhardt in Dresden in December 1966 and wrote in the mission journal, "The membership of the mission is 7,112, of whom 4,756 are in the East Zone.... The forty-seven branches are well organized and follow the program of the church as much as it is possible without any printed material" (LR 2428 2).

Shortly thereafter, Loscher wrote to John E. Carr, the representative of the Church's Presiding Bishop, in Frankfurt on February 4, 1967:

> An observation that I want to share with you, Brother Carr, is that I feel definite that the stronger part of our priesthood and the branches with less problems, better organizations, and greater devotion and dedication to the work are found in East Germany, and not in the western free world where our German-speaking people assemble. It is indeed a wonderful experience to be in touch with these people. Instead of us giving them strength, anyone ever getting in touch with these people returns a better man, strengthened and encouraged that the gospel of Jesus Christ is really a power unto salvation. (LR 2428 25)

Loscher continued to travel frequently to the GDR in early 1967. He visited Annaberg in February and wrote thereafter in the mission journal:

> It is so remarkable what these people are doing every place in the whole of East Germany with the limited means and materials at their disposal to make some wonderful meetinghouses and places available for the Saints. This one in Annaberg is a wonderful example. It seats over six hundred people and it was a sight to behold, to look in the faces of these wonderful Saints, hear their singing, and feel their wonderful united spirit. (LR 2428 2)

Following his visit to Dresden on March 12, 1967, he again praised the GDR members in his journal:

> It is marvelous how well these people are organized and how seriously they take their callings, everyone being well informed. Because of the lack of written material, they have to work out their own lessons, instructions, and programs for years ahead. One is amazed with how well this work is handled. In the evening, the Dresden branch was visited and some excellent talks were given, especially by the younger generation. I left the East Zone and the association with the Saints deeply impressed with their loyalty and devotion. In spite of having several dozen building projects going, for which they pay their share, the tithing is steadily on the increase, and there are at the present time three-quarters of a million East German marks in the bank. Not only is this part of the mission self-sustaining, but in every respect it also has a tremendous surplus. Not enough can be said about the loyalty of Henry Burkhardt and the fine work that he's doing in the office, supported by Sisters Beck and Vogel as his helpers. One also has to admire the untiring efforts of Walter Krause in taking care of the buildings to make them truly houses of worship, especially considering that he has to do that under almost impossible conditions and strict government regulations, not being able to get materials, etc. (LR 2428 2)

During a visit to Werdau in May 1967, Loscher visited the Grabbaum family and wrote in the mission journal:

> She showed us how they have to make fifty to one hundred copies of each lesson manual that is smuggled in from the outside, and it is commendable, how these people work day and night to make this material available. It is admirable, inasmuch as they are not allowed to print anything. (LR 2428 2)

President Loscher was replaced by Stanley D. Rees in July 1967. Later that year, President Rees was asked by Elder Harold B. Lee to consider the organization of stakes in the GDR. Rees responded on February 23, 1968, in a letter to Elder Lee:

> During your visit here in Berlin, you will recall that through Brother Fetzer, you asked me to look into the possibility or advisability of creating a stake in East Germany. During my first visit after this request, I discussed the matter with my two counselors in East Germany and asked them to thoroughly investigate and consider the matter, and that I would discuss it with them again on my next visit. I have just returned from a conference in East Germany and discussed the matter with them again. We considered the possibility of a single stake for the whole of East Germany. Because of the distance that people would have to come to attend stake meetings, this was not considered to be practical. It is only practical to hold meetings in various strategic areas, because of the large size of the East German area.
>
> Then the matter was considered of organizing a stake in a particular area. It was felt that this might have a tendency to divide the Church operation, rather than unify it in their particular case. As you know, they are more or less cut off from regular contact with the Church and it is their fear always that they might slip away from the true order of the Church. They felt that with one stake within the Mission, that there would be a tendency to be a division of unity, not only in doctrinal matters, but also in operational matters. They also expressed the fear, in which I concur, of too much contact with the Church through its various organizations if they were to be organized as a stake. I mean by this, that things would be coming through the mail and so on, which may be injurious to their cause because of the tight security regulations and restrictions.
>
> Our united opinion in the matter, Brother Lee, after discussing it thoroughly, was that under the present circumstances there would be more disadvantages than advantages in organizing a stake in East Germany at this time.
>
> These, in general, were the thoughts that were expressed and the conclusion that we reached. I hope this will be of assistance to you in

> determining the course which you feel should be followed regarding these good people. (LR 2428 25)

Two GDR leaders later explained why it wasn't possible to establish one or more stakes in 1968. Frank Apel, who became the president of the Freiberg Stake four years later, said:

> I know that the leaders of the Church in Salt Lake City had wanted to establish a stake here in the GDR. The brethren in the mission presidency, however, simply could not imagine such an undertaking. They didn't have a full understanding of stakes in general. I don't want to cast any blame there, not at all. But when the Church leaders, especially Elder Monson, asked: "Brethren, how about a stake?" they answered, "Oh, that wouldn't work," and they had a hundred reasons why it would not work. (1991)

Gottfried Richter, a counselor in the Dresden Mission presidency from 1969 until 1984, had a different opinion:

> We had a well-organized operation. We had outstanding conferences, wonderful conferences. But when Church leaders came to us, they always said, "Why aren't you a stake? You have such a wonderful spirit, wonderful singing, wonderful talks, etc." It was difficult then to explain to the brethren, in a few words, why it wouldn't necessarily work to have a stake. I always told them, "When you come to our conferences, you hear our enthusiastic singing and you hear the loud amens. But you don't know what every single person experiences during the week, what he has to live with, and how hard life is for many." There were many problems, also problems of a political nature. The State Secretary for Church Affairs knew us, they knew the leaders here in this country, President Burkhardt, the district presidents. Those people became unsettled with every organizational change. Who is that new official? There was a great amount of insecurity among those people. They were extremely sensitive, insecure. So a stake just wouldn't work. Everything takes time and requires preparation. (1991)

At the end of his February 1968 letter to Elder Lee, President Rees added this final suggestion, which appears to have had an immediate effect in Salt Lake City: "One thing I am sure would be appreciated by the Saints in the East would be a visit from one of the general authorities. This, of course, would have to be done without fanfare and without announcement, but it would be a wonderful thing for them to be able to meet with one of you brethren" (LR 2428 25).

The Assignment of Elder Thomas S. Monson 1968

No general authority had visited the members in the GDR for five years since Elder Burton's visit in March 1963, even though Elder Benson resided in Frankfurt between January 1964 and September 1965. Elder Lee responded immediately to President Rees's suggestion with a question concerning the current political conditions that would be encountered in arranging a visit to the GDR. President Rees answered on March 14, 1968:

> It is true that the East German government does not allow West Berlin residents to come into East Germany at all; however, they do allow those from the remainder of West Germany to come as tourists. In my own case, I go in as an American citizen and tourist and doubt that it makes any difference to them as to how I come in or from what entrance.... The main point is that we do not leave the impression that someone from the outside is directing the affairs of the Church there.
>
> I just recently received a letter from Brother Percy Fetzer, asking whether or not I felt it would be good judgment for five members of the General Board to go as a body into East Germany for a conference. My own opinion is that it would definitely not be advisable to have such a large group of obvious leadership going in at one time. It would also be very advisable before any of the representatives go into East Germany, that they be carefully instructed as to the problems there, so that nothing would be said or done which might hurt the work.
>
> I agree with you, that it would be a wonderful thing if a way could be opened for these wonderful people to be able to more completely work in the programs of the Church. They do enjoy much freedom and perhaps our greatest temptation might be to overwork the present freedoms to the point where further restrictions might be put upon our operation there.
>
> P.S. It would be a wonderful thing if a general authority could arrange to go into East Germany with the mission president periodically. (LR 2428 25)

Shortly after this exchange of letters between President Rees and Elder Lee, the First Presidency announced that Elder Thomas S. Monson would represent the Quorum of the Twelve in Europe. President Rees wrote to Elder Monson on May 29, 1968:

> I must say that I was highly pleased to learn of your assignment to preside over the Germanic missions of the church.... I hope that it would be possible for you on some occasion soon to go with me into East Germany to attend a conference there. This would necessitate some advanced notice so that arrangements could be made. The only way we can make connections there is to visit regularly scheduled meetings. It would also not be possible to announce your arrival other than

> by verbal announcement to the brethren, during one of my visits. No fanfare could be given to the visit; however, they would appreciate such a visit from you immensely. It has been a long time since a General Authority has visited these wonderful Saints and they are very devoted and faithful people. (LR 2428 25)

On July 31, 1968, Elder Monson flew to Berlin to meet with President Rees. He asked for a list of the future district conferences and chose the Dresden District conference that would be held in Görlitz on November 9 and 10, 1968. Monson later described that historic meeting in his personal journal:

> A marvelous spirit prevailed. My, how the German Saints can sing the hymns of Zion! One of the songs was especially beautiful and so meaningful when one considers the humble circumstances of these wonderful people. Following are the words:
>
> If the way be full of trial, Weary not!
> If it's one of sore denial, Weary not!
> If it now be one of weeping, there will come a joyous greeting,
> When the harvest we are reaping, Weary not!
>
> (Chorus) Do not weary by the way, whatever be thy lot;
> There awaits a brighter day, to all, to all who weary not!
>
> If the way be one of sorrow, Weary not!
> Happier will be the morrow, Weary not!
> Here we suffer tribulation, here we must endure temptation;
> But there'll come a great salvation, Weary not!
>
> If misfortune overtake us, Weary not!
> Jesus never will forsake us, Weary not!
> He will leave us never, never, from His love there's naught can sever;
> Glory to the Lamb forever! Weary not!
>
> These members love the scriptures. I learned that they have almost no written manuals or materials, just the standard works. Yet they are so well informed.... I was touched by the sincerity of these wonderful Saints. I was humbled by their poverty. They have so little. My heart filled with sorrow because they have no patriarch, they have no wards or stakes—just branches, they have few teaching materials. They cannot receive temple blessings, neither endowments nor sealings.
>
> I stood at the pulpit with tear-filled eyes and a voice choked with emotion and made a promise to the people, "If you will remain true and faithful to the commandments of God, every blessing any member of the Church enjoys in any other country will be yours."

> This evening in my hotel room, as I realized the full impact of the promise I had made at Görlitz earlier today, I dropped to my knees and said to my Heavenly Father, "Father, I am on Thy errand; this is Thy Church. I have spoken words that came not from me, but from Thee and Thy Son. Wilt Thou, therefore, fulfill the promise in the lives of this noble people?" (*Faith Rewarded*)

The promises made by Elder Monson in Görlitz were a source of great spiritual strength for the members. Manfred Heller's recollection of that meeting during a 1991 interview is typical of many others:

> I will never forget the experience in Görlitz because I felt such a wonderful spirit there and knew that Elder Monson was really a prophet of God, an Apostle of the Lord, and that he had spoken prophetic words that in these last days have been fulfilled and that are still being fulfilled. At that point in time, we could not actually believe that we would ever enjoy the full blessings of the gospel. We always asked ourselves, "How will we ever reach the temple? How will that ever happen?" And yet it has all been accomplished in a wonderful manner. There was such a spirit in that meeting that no eye remained dry. That impacted our hearts so strongly that we can still testify of it today. I will never in my entire life forget that.

Following his visit to Görlitz, Elder Monson wrote to President Rees on November 21, 1968:

> I don't know when I have been so impressed with the spirit of the Saints as when in attendance at the Dresden District conference. I shall ever remember the spirit and singing which made the conference a day not to be forgotten. I am happy that you are going to visit the Saints on a regular basis for I know how much they mean to you and how much the Gospel means to them. If there is anything I can do to be of assistance in this regard, please let me know. (LR 2428 25)

Monson wrote to Rees again on February 28, 1969, "My next visit will be to attend the branch and district presidents' meetings in Dresden on June 14 and 15. I feel this series of meetings with branch and district presidents will be of great importance. Have you been able to place a *General Handbook of Instructions* in the hands of either of your East German counselors? A good portion of our agenda could well be constructed around the *Handbook*." Rees answered: "I have placed a copy of the *General Handbook of Instructions* in the hands of my first counselor so that by then they should be thoroughly familiar with its contents" (LR 2428 25).

In the meantime, President Rees had become concerned about a report on Elder Monson's visit to Görlitz in the Church's West German magazine, the

Stern. An excerpt from a letter of an unnamed GDR member had been printed, which said, "We experienced on Sunday morning a very special surprise. President Rees attended with his wife, and Apostle Thomas S. Monson appeared with him." Because Monson had traveled to the GDR as a tourist, Rees was concerned and wrote:

> In the March issue of the *Stern* on the last page just inside the cover was a report of our visit with you in Görlitz for the district conference. I caught my breath when I read this since such an announcement definitely indicates our purposes in visiting the conference. Such a thing could very easily result in our being denied admission into the East Zone, and, if not even worse, a curtailment of activities for the Saints.
>
> I have no idea how this information got to the *Stern* or who approved its printing. My purpose in writing this letter is to ask whether or not any steps can be taken to prevent future publication of any activities in the East. I am sure this would be a safeguard for continued operations over there. (LR 2428 25)

A second similar incident in West Germany one year later led to action taken by the Church to protect members in the GDR from potentially damaging news reports. Rolf Maichel recounted this incident from his own experience and subsequent conversation with President Burkhardt:

> About 1970, a very active group of youth in the Hamburg stake published its own newsletter, which was distributed to about two hundred members. It contained trivial reports from its members. One member, who had recently visited in the GDR, wrote a report about the status of the members in that country, with emphasis on youth activities. The report described problems that the youth had with the government and was, of course, not particularly complimentary. Several weeks after the article was published, President Burkhardt was asked to meet with the Secretary for Church Affairs, Herr Seigewasser, who threw the newsletter on the table and angrily asked how such "false" information came into the hand of "hostile foreigners." The Church subsequently prohibited the publication of our newsletter, and the *Stern* was instructed again not to print anything about the members in the GDR. I later visited President Burkhardt, who told me how important it was to handle all information very carefully, because the ears of the secret police were everywhere, and we did not want to endanger the members. (2006)

Elder Monson traveled frequently to the GDR in the following years to discuss the activities of the Church with President Burkhardt. These meetings often took place in Burkhardt's car, where they could talk without fear of the listening devices that had probably been installed in the Church's meeting rooms. Burkhardt said:

> We remained often in my car and held our discussions there. He wanted to be informed about our activities and problems with the government. It was important for him to really understand the conditions in the East and which of the many stories that circulated were true. He was a man who wanted to be informed, and whatever he learned, he never forgot. He had a good memory and also could interpret and evaluate information very well. It was important for him to become personally knowledgeable of circumstances in the East. He came relatively often to our country. I believe that no American stake saw him as often as we did in the GDR. And that, of course, strengthened our members, to feel how they were being watched over by the brethren. We had a good relationship with President Monson. (1991)

A New Dresden Mission, 1969

Elder Monson returned in June 1969 to organize a new mission for the GDR. That change coincided with a requirement by the government that religious organizations had to be led by a citizen of the country if they wished to be officially recognized. The political circumstances also led the Church to make special arrangements for the oversight of the mission, as described in the mission journal:

> Henry J. Burkhardt was called as the mission president with Walter Krause and Gottfried Richter as his counselors. President Burkhardt was also ordained a high priest. President Fetzer, the regional representative, will provide ongoing support to the mission and will visit at least twice a year. This support is unusual within the Church, since regional representatives are only responsible for stakes. President Stanley D. Rees will serve temporarily as a facilitator to insure even better communication with the mission. (DMO)

Gottfried Richter emphasized the significance of this mission for the government. "They were always suspicious because of our ties to an American mission president. Elder Monson understood that. Now the Dresden Mission was responsible for the GDR region, and it was an independent mission" (1991).

However, some government officials were still suspicious and sought to determine the Church's "real" motives for this change. The following undated and unsigned memorandum from the files of the Secretariat for Church Affairs was probably written by an official within the Interior Ministry. It shows how closely the government observed this administrative change:

> Apostle Monson announced that the church of the "Mormons" in the GDR would hereafter constitute a separate mission, that would be directly responsible to the church's leadership in the USA.... Despite the creation of its own mission in the GDR, which was previously discussed between Apostle Monson and the district leaders in the spring of 1969 in Berlin, it is clear that separation from the Hamburg Mission doesn't change anything regarding reporting relationships. In fact, the GDR mission will now come under the direct control of the leadership in the USA. This is evident in the fact that the American functionary Apostle Monson and President Fetzer are responsible for the control and guidance of the mission in the GDR. As both of them mentioned, they will come frequently to the GDR to discuss with Burkhardt and his deputies all matters regarding the church in the GDR.... This control and guidance from functionaries of the main office of the Mormons in the USA shows the danger that American influence within the Mormons in the GDR will be strengthened. It increases the chance that attempts will be undertaken to draw the Mormons within the GDR into the political aggression of U.S. imperialism. These conclusions are supported by the fact that various functionaries of the Mormons in the USA occupy influential positions in the American government and in its armed forces. For example, two functionaries within the leadership of the Mormons are members of the cabinet of the American President Nixon. For this reason, the state should consider actions that could be undertaken to restrict American control and guidance of the mission. (MS 13918)

A Patriarch for the GDR

Normally, patriarchs are found only within a stake organization, but the GDR had no stakes and therefore no patriarchs. After Elder Monson organized the Dresden Mission, he wrote in his journal on July 23, 1969:

> Following my visit last month to East Germany, as I reported to the First Presidency and Twelve, I expressed my sorrow at the inability of so many of our Saints living there to receive their patriarchal blessings. I mentioned that although Brother Karl Ringger, an ordained patriarch from Switzerland, had been able to journey behind the Iron Curtain to provide some blessings, the vast majority who desire patriarchal blessings have as yet been unable to receive them. President David O. McKay said to me, "Brother Monson, whom did you say accompanied you on this visit?" [Monson replied, Brother Percy K. Fetzer.] Then President McKay said, "Why don't you ordain him a patriarch, and then each time he goes into that area, he can give patriarchal blessings to the worthy Saints there." (*Faith Rewarded*)

President Fetzer was ordained, but the number of members who desired a patriarchal blessing greatly exceeded the opportunities Fetzer had to give blessings during his visits. President Rees wrote to Elder Monson on October 14, 1969:

> I might also report that things seems to be going well throughout the Dresden Mission. [The members] were particularly happy with the possibility of receiving patriarchal blessings from Brother Fetzer. President Burkhardt, however, reported that since the beginning of the patriarchal blessings, the demand has become so great for these blessings that he is wondering if there might be a possibility of further opportunity being given to them for such blessings. In other words, the possibility of all those who desire blessings to receive them becomes an almost arithmetical impossibility. (LR 2428 25)

The problem was eventually resolved when Walter Krause was ordained a patriarch on April 3, 1973. He continued to serve simultaneously as President Burkhardt's counselor in the mission presidency for several years thereafter.

Further Visits from the West

Although leaders within the GDR did not consider the conditions for establishment of stakes in the GDR to be favorable in 1969, it remained a goal of Church leaders in Salt Lake City. After Elder Monson organized the Dresden Mission, he continued to build a foundation for eventual stakes and wrote in his journal on July 1, 1969:

> Today I met with Brother Percy K. Fetzer relative to matters in East Germany. Invited to the meeting were the [officers] of the auxiliary organizations and Elder Hartman Rector. We made preliminary arrangements for the auxiliary officers in turn to accompany Brother Fetzer to East Germany. It will be a glorious thing for the Saints behind the Iron Curtain to have a greater portion of the full program of the Church. (*Faith Rewarded*)

The visits of mission presidents and other Church leaders immediately after the building of the Berlin Wall were previously described. Those visits increased again after the establishment of the Dresden Mission. In addition to frequent visits by Elder Monson, assistants to the Twelve, members of the First Quorum of Seventy, and presidents of the North German (Hamburg) Mission appeared regularly in the GDR. These men often were accompanied by their wives and officers of the auxiliary organizations of the Church, and they conducted training sessions for district presidencies and auxiliary leaders in the GDR. President Fetzer was especially determined to find ways to increase the number of visitors from the West. On December 8, 1971, he wrote to President Bryson of the North German Mission:

> As you are aware, we go into Dresden twice each year. It would now seem very important that with a format of two additional interim meetings with the stake presidencies [in the West], some effort should be made to go into the East Zone two times more or a total of four times a year. When next you meet with Henry Burkhardt, would you pose the following questions:
>
> 1. Would it be unwise to go to Dresden four times a year?
>
> 2. If we go to Dresden twice a year, what other cities would prove feasible other than Dresden?
>
> 3. Would East Berlin offer sufficient security where we would not excite the authorities and cause some repercussion against the Church by meeting in Berlin?
>
> The last experience in Berlin leads me to the conclusion that the place is under constant observation and that it is electronically bugged so as to preclude any privacy. If so, we would then be asking for trouble. (LR 2428 25)

President Bryson answered on January 18, 1972:

> I visited with Henry Burkhardt in Berlin on January 9th and discussed all of the points that you mentioned in your letter relative to your coming into the Dresden Mission four times a year. Henry saw no particular problem in this, and thinks everything would go fine. Henry listed Mecklenburg, Berlin, Dresden, Annaberg-Buchholz, Karl-Marx-Stadt, and Erfurt. He listed Dresden, Erfurt, and Berlin as places that might be visited more than once a year.

The visits of Church leaders from America not only served as opportunities to train the leadership within the GDR. They brought hope and encouragement to all members:

> *Hans Schult:* President Monson always made sure that general authorities were present at every mission conference. Initially, they attended meetings when they came in connection with the Leipzig Fair. That was bold on their part. President Monson also came to Leipzig at the time when members endured freezing temperatures in their meetings. They bundled themselves in their coats and sat close together in the smallest room. He had similar experiences in Görlitz. These were tremendous accomplishments on the part of the leadership of the Church, and the members recognized it as such. We are very thankful and will never forget those times. (1991)

> *Walter Schiele:* It served the members very well, that these brethren came here to help us. They often brought their wives, which was especially positive. (1991)

> *Dieter Lehm:* Bishop Peterson attended a two-day conference in Dresden, and I sat fairly close to the front. The spirit that I felt at that time was powerful. I considered these brothers truly as general authorities, and what they said was absolutely important for me. I took notes, and we often discussed them later in the branch. It was something unusually special for me, because the spirit that came from these brothers was very strong. I knew that they were servants of the Lord, who were chosen to teach us. They didn't just give talks. It was also important for the development of the Church, because we felt we were no longer alone. We were a part of the broader Church, a fully valued part of the Church. (1991)

President Burkhardt was the only mission president who had never attended a General Conference of the Church. In his 1983 manuscript about the origin of the Freiberg Temple, he described a meeting with Elder Monson in Erfurt on October 24, 1970, when they met in Burkhardt's car, because the danger of being overheard in the meeting house was too great. "Suddenly, Elder Monson asked if I could imagine attending the General Conference in Salt Lake City. On the basis of my experiences in the GDR, I told him that there was no chance of that happening. But Elder Monson responded with a prophetic statement, 'When the Lord considers the time to be right, you will attend a conference in Salt Lake City!'"[4]

In July 1971, President Burkhardt received a personal invitation from the First Presidency to attend the General Conference in April 1972. His first application for a travel visa was turned down by local government officials, but seven months later, with the help of the Secretariat for Church Affairs, and after traveling more than three thousand kilometers between Berlin and Prague (the closest American embassy), he finally received permission to attend the conference.

The GDR government, through its informants, certainly followed his activities in Utah closely, and President Fetzer was equally watchful about anything that could adversely affect political relations with the government. Elder Benson, not unexpectedly, made some negative comments about communism during his talk. When Fetzer wrote to President Bryson on April 18, 1972, he mentioned a newspaper article that quoted Elder Benson's talk and said:

> This item was the only situation that caused Henry some anxiety, but the brethren toned it down so that there could be no complication. I asked Henry to let me know or let you know if there were any spin-off reactions because of his visit. This will be extremely important. The brethren have indicated their desire to have Krause and Richter come. It will interest you to know that the Dresden Mission has been put on the general authorities' visiting schedule which will directly affect you and me as occasion arises; therefore, it would be well to keep

> close contact relative to any attendant problems that might develop. (LR 2428 25)

Following the conference, Bryson met with Burkhardt and wrote to Fetzer on July 6, 1972, concerning opportunities for future meetings in East Germany:

> Henry thinks that would be just wonderful. Since his return, things seem much easier and freer, but he says not to be misled, since they are still Communists and haven't really changed. However, they treat him with a great deal of deference. There comes again the question, as to whether it would be advisable, now that some of the restrictions are lifted, that these visits, at least the visits made by the general board members and the visiting authorities, and perhaps even including yourself, be made as official visits. I don't think we had better do anything until he talks further, but he thought he might discuss this with some people he has become acquainted with since his permission to travel was granted. (LR 2428 25)

President Burkhardt's counselors were subsequently allowed to attend General Conference. Walter Krause went first, in April 1973, during which visit he was ordained a patriarch. District presidents eventually were given an opportunity to travel to Salt Lake City, and in many instances, their wives were allowed to accompany them.

A further opportunity to train GDR leaders was a regional conference held in Munich, West Germany, August 24–26, 1973. Elder Monson asked President Fetzer to determine if GDR members could attend that conference, and if yes, what steps should be taken to insure that the interests of the Church would not be damaged if any of them failed to return to their country. Fetzer wrote to Bryson on May 29, 1973:

> Elder Monson called me to ascertain the procedure President Burkhardt will take to avoid defection by those who expect to attend the Area General Conference in Munich. Will he undertake to interview all who have expressed a desire to attend? If a personal interview is undertaken, will each person that is interviewed be asked to sign a form that could be devised expressing a definite statement that would refer to defection? As you may surmise, the brethren are concerned. It is implied by this questioning that appropriate measures should be taken to safeguard the position of the Church in relation to the government. (LR 2428 25)

President Bryson responded on May 29, 1973:

> I can appreciate the concern that Brother Monson and the other brethren have relative to the responsibility of the people from the

> GDR traveling to Munich and being sure they came back. President Burkhardt has met with the officials in Berlin. It seems now that he will be able to formulate a letter of responsibility to be signed by each person who travels, and that the East German government will accept this in place of President Burkhardt being liable for each individual person traveling. This would also, we are sure, relieve the Church itself of responsibility should there be a defection. President Burkhardt has already interviewed all of those who may go and tells me he will do so again and do everything possible to fix the responsibility on them to be sure they return.
>
> The women over sixty and the men over sixty-five classify as retired or "Rentner" and may come and go to West Germany without special permission of the government. Those that we seek permission for, and for whom there would be responsibility, are those of the branch, district, and mission presidencies with their wives who are invited, making up approximately 250 people.
>
> It is very likely, in fact it seems practically assured now, that permission will be granted for the administering priesthood leaders and their wives to attend the conference. There seems to be no restriction in the number. (LR 2428 25)

Bryson's optimism, however, was premature. Instead of hundreds, only seven members received official approval. Frau Janott, an official within the Secretariat for Church Affairs, explained the decision in her summary of a meeting with Church leaders:

> The mission president Burkhardt and his deputy Krause appeared at a meeting on August 7, 1973.... After comrade Weise said that we could not support the attendance of about three hundred GDR citizens at the regional general conference in Munich, because it was not necessary for church policy, and after he explained the options available to them, they expressed understanding for our decision. Since the regional general conference does have the characteristics of an international meeting,... it could have unfavorable foreign policy consequences if a religious organization in the GDR, which has been independent since 1952, was not represented. Therefore, we suggested that the organization's leadership form a new delegation, consisting of the mission president, the two deputies, and an additional four district leaders. This suggestion was accepted. (DO 4/1534)

Although only seven Church leaders officially attended the conference, many additional members of retirement age traveled independently to Munich, which displeased the government. President Burkhardt was once more called to the office of the Secretary for Church Affairs, where an official told him that over one hundred retired members had attended the conference. According to that official's notes, Burkhardt was asked if he had organized their travel. He denied being responsible for it, and added that he had only seen about fifty such persons in Munich, and they had already been in West Germany for other reasons. Burkhardt also was quoted as saying that the official delegates had noticed more moral filth, drug users, drug trafficking, and pornographic establishments and newspapers in Munich than they had ever thought possible. These observations had occupied their discussions during their return to the GDR, and they were twice as happy to return again to the peace and moral cleanliness of our country. (DO 4/1534)

The Dedication of East Germany, 1975

The authorized travel of Church leaders described above are examples of an improving relationship with the government in the 1970s. The Church also received permission to print and/or import some books and other printed materials. However, travel to the temple in Switzerland, despite considerable diplomatic efforts, continued to be refused. Access to the ordinances and blessings of the temple was emphasized by Elder Monson when he rededicated the country on April 25, 1975. He wrote in his journal:

> I mentioned to the brethren [the mission presidency] that while I was dedicating the land of Portugal earlier this week, I felt impressed that I should offer a similar prayer to invoke our Heavenly Father's blessings upon the German Democratic Republic. President Burkhardt was assigned to suggest a place where the dedicatory prayer could be offered, perhaps on Sunday morning. (*Faith Rewarded*)

President Burkhardt asked his counselors to find an appropriate place. Gottfried Richter described the setting:

> I had recently taken a walk to a beautiful place between Dresden and Meissen, a beautiful place on a hill. The Elbe flowed below, above was a rock outcrop, behind was a forest. The group, including Elder Monson, President Schwendiman and his wife, and the mission presidency with their wives, went there the next morning. The weather was threatening. (1991)

Elder Monson described the event in his journal that evening, April 27, 1975:

> The setting was as beautiful a spot as could be imagined. We walked through the woods for about twenty minutes into a clearing overlooking the Elbe River, with Meissen on the right and Dresden on the left.... During the prayer, I said, "May today mark the dawning of a new beginning of thy work in this land." As I spoke these words, we heard the unmistakable sound of a rooster crowing, followed by

> the pealing of a cathedral bell in the distance. The day had been overcast, but during the prayer the sun shone brilliantly upon us, warming our bodies and giving us the assurance that our Heavenly Father was pleased with the prayer which was being offered. (*Faith Rewarded*)

The complete text of Elder Monson's prayer is found in Appendix G. Many members kept a copy of it in their scriptures, and the reading of the text or the playing of its tape recording became a spiritual highlight of many outings of members to the location. At the time, they could not imagine that a temple would actually be dedicated in their own country just ten years later, but they had faith that a way would be found, whereby they could reach the temple in Switzerland. The subsequent events, beginning in 1977, that led to the dedication of the Freiberg Temple in 1985, are detailed in a later chapter.

Two Stakes in the GDR

On August 29, 1982, Elder Monson wrote in his journal:

> Elders Harold B. Lee and Spencer W. Kimball, as members of the Council of the Twelve, each made the comment at the time the Dresden Mission was created, "I hope the day will come when we can have a stake in that part of the world." That day is today.... Today I created the Freiberg German Democratic Republic Stake. Approximately eighteen hundred members in the Karl-Marx-Stadt and Dresden districts came together to form the stake.... This was a day never to be forgotten, for today prophecy was fulfilled. At my second visit to the Dresden Mission, I stood at the pulpit [1968 in Görlitz] and told the people I had never seen greater faith and that surely the Lord would reward such faith by providing every blessing that other members of the Church would receive. I have seen the step-by-step unfolding of this prophecy and know it came from the Lord. (*Faith Rewarded*)

Frank Apel was called as stake president with Heinz Koschnicke and Reimund Dörlitz as his counselors. President Apel was quoted previously as to why a stake had not been created a decade earlier. He also explained why it was created at this time:

> Then came President Hans B. Ringger. He was the regional representative and a man of powerful resolve and the ability to achieve. He had traveled throughout the GDR, looked over the situation and said, "Now we will establish a stake." Then he developed a plan. The creation of a stake came out of his vision. He presented his plan to the First Presidency, and the preparations began thereafter.
>
> President Burkhardt was instructed, but I didn't know that at the time, to combine branches. For example, we had a branch here in Freiberg, another small branch with fifteen to twenty members five

> kilometers away in Brand-Erbisdorf, and another small branch ten kilometers further in Großhartmannsdorf. They were all combined in Freiberg, so it could become large enough to be a ward. Similar actions were taken elsewhere, in preparation for creation of a stake that stretched from Görlitz to Plauen. (1991)

The Dresden Mission continued to function for another two years until a second stake was organized in Leipzig. Gottfried Richter said:

> When the Freiberg Stake was organized, the rest of the GDR remained within the mission. Elder Monson said to us, the mission presidency, "Brothers, your assignment now is to work on your demise." That meant to strengthen and build up the remaining portion of the mission, the remaining branches, so that the next stake can be created. (1991)

Elder Monson described the organization of the second stake on June 2 and 3, 1984:

> When we entered the Leipzig chapel, I was amazed that all of the priesthood brethren who had assembled for our interviews were singing. These brethren love to sing. It is almost as though there has been a time warp take place in their lives. They are unpolluted by the softness and degeneracy which one sees in many countries, including our own. There is no pornography or drug use, and while freedoms are restricted, our Church members seem to draw closer together in unity and combined faith. They are as pure a group of priesthood brethren as I have ever met. The only equal happens to be the priesthood brethren whom I interviewed prior to the creation of the Freiberg Stake.
>
> We made our selection of a stake presidency. Brother Manfred Schütze is the president, Brother Gerhard Müller is the first counselor, and Brother Jürgen Pabst is the second counselor. (*Faith Rewarded*)

The Dresden and Karl-Marx-Stadt Districts had been combined in 1982 to form the Freiberg Stake. The remaining four districts in the GDR were combined to form the Leipzig Stake. Although each stake contained about one-half of the GDR members, the Leipzig Stake covered a much larger territory. Since the Berlin Stake was restricted to West Berlin, none of the nearby branches could be added to it, and the Church did not want to leave any part of the GDR outside of the two stakes. Therefore the Leipzig Stake stretched from the Baltic Sea in the north to Thuringia in the southwest. President Schütze described some of the challenges associated with such a large stake:

> The stake extended five hundred kilometers from north to south and about three hundred kilometers from west to east. We had twenty-

one units. That is a very large number. I and my counselors were always traveling, and we could not travel together. Often, we left Leipzig on Saturday and stayed overnight somewhere in order to visit our branches on the Baltic Sea the next day. If you know what a Trabant is, then you know how difficult it is to travel three hundred kilometers in a car. No autobahns, just narrow and bad streets.

On certain Saturdays we held all of our consultations in Leipzig, a type of "Super Saturday." Often, the members left home at two or four in the morning, to travel three hundred kilometers. The High Council began at eight a.m., followed by leadership meetings and then further board and committee meetings until five p.m. But then we had to stop, since the people had to travel four hours home and prepare for their Sunday morning meetings. It was a very spiritual time when you work with such good people as we did. Yes, there are good members throughout the world, but the willingness and dedication of our members to carry out their assignments was always greater in the East and was really amazing. Also the leaders of the auxiliary organizations had to work very independently and responsibly, and that they did, so that we were able to overcome many problems. (1991)

Governmental Reaction to Organizational Changes

Since all members now belonged to one of the two stakes, the Dresden Mission was closed in 1984. For the previous thirty-two years, ever since the East German Mission opened an office in the GDR in 1952, Henry Burkhardt had been the government's contact person. Now the Church's official leadership consisted of two stake presidents, while Burkhardt became the president of the Freiberg Temple, then under construction. These changes caused some concern within the government, just as had happened in 1969 when the Dresden Mission replaced the North German Mission. Four weeks after the release of the Dresden Mission presidency, Elder Monson happened to meet Dr. Dieter Hantzsche, the GDR's lead architect for the Freiberg Temple, during a visit in Frankfurt, in West Germany. Monson summarized their conversation in his July 5, 1984, journal entry:

> Dr. Hantzsche inferred that things were not going well at the moment, which prompted me to invite him to speak to me privately and candidly relative to the work of our church in the German Democratic Republic. We learned that there had been too many Church visitors to that country and that the government was confused with respect to stake organizations and the new role of Henry Burkhardt. Further, with the construction of the temple, the stake center at Freiberg, the projected stake center at Leipzig, and a building at Dresden, they knew that the influence of the Church was more visible than it had heretofore been. We were able to make plans for the necessary orientation meetings and the drawing up of a set of governing procedures,

> such as the Articles of Faith, which will give the government a general view of the objectives and purposes of the Church. I think it was a wonderful coincidence that we should meet Dr. Hantzsche during his visit to Frankfurt. (*Faith Rewarded*)

An undated government document, "Recommendation for Further Work of the Office of the Secretary for Church Affairs with Functionaries of the Church of Jesus Christ of Latter-day Saints (Mormons)," shows that Dr. Hantzsche was aware of the concerns of government leaders at this time. The document stated:

> It is recommended that Burkhardt, the president of the Mormons in the GDR, be asked to provide the Secretariat with the following information regarding the church he represents:
>
> 1. The revised statutes of the religious organization that reflect the recent creation of the Freiberg and Leipzig stakes and the inauguration of the temple;
>
> 2. Identification of the functionaries of the stakes (stake president, counselors, patriarch, etc.) and of the temple presidency (including foreign members), as well as the headquarters of the present leadership;
>
> 3. Identification of the responsible member of the Mormon leadership within the GDR, who has been assigned responsibility for direct liaison to the Secretariat for Church Affairs or to relevant governmental bodies (district councils, county councils);
>
> 4. What activities are conducted by the religious organization? (For example, temple activities, genealogy, mission activities, women's activities, choir activities, etc.).
>
> It also should be explained whether the Mormons in the GDR are responsible to the regional office in Frankfurt or whether the GDR members constitute an independent regional authority that might be extended to specific areas outside the GDR. In addition, the use of the temple must be explained, e.g., whether its cult activities will only be carried out for GDR citizens or whether travel to the temple from either socialist or capitalist countries is anticipated. (DO 4/921)

These questions were transmitted to the Church, and a response, "Description of the Current Status of Our Church within the GDR," was prepared by Jürgen Warnke, the legal counsel to the Church in Frankfurt, in consultation with Manfred Wünsche, the East German lawyer who assisted the Church within the GDR. The document was approved by the Church's area presidency and President Gordon B. Hinckley and was given to Klaus Gysi, the Secretary for Church Affairs, on September 27, 1984. The four-page document covered the following themes: Purpose of the Church, Structure of the Church in the GDR, Meetings, Administration of the Church in the GDR, Buildings within the scope of the Special Building Program, Temple, Scriptures and Printed Materials. In the section regarding the Structure of the Church, it was stated that "the Presidency of the Church in the GDR represents the Church in the GDR both internally and externally. The Presidency consists of the President of the Church in the GDR [Henry Burkhardt] and the [two] stake presidents as his deputies" (MS 13918).

On January 23, 1985, Elder Monson wrote in his journal:

> This morning Hans Ringger, Joseph Wirthlin, and I crossed the border into East Berlin, where we met Henry Burkhardt. We then paid a visit to the state secretary, Minister Gysi. I was impressed by this civil servant. He knew a great deal about our church and spoke fluent English.... After a leisurely period of time, he complimented us on our statement of purpose document which had been previously submitted, and he offered whatever help he could to make our temple dedication the success we anticipate it will be. I felt pleased with Minister Gysi's attitude. (*Faith Rewarded*)

The Church recognized the government's need for a single point of contact and created the "Presidency of the Church of Jesus Christ of Latter-day Saints in the German Democratic Republic," which met regularly until 1990. President Burkhardt described its purpose:

> Two stakes were created out of the mission. That was our goal, and my calling as mission president was thus ended. However, the government needed someone whom they could contact when there were problems to solve. That was not a Church calling, but rather a political one, essential to continuation of the Church, and I was asked to continue to be that person for the following years. (1991)

Günther Behncke, head of the legal division of the Secretariat for Church Affairs since 1981, said that he personally had not been concerned about the organizational changes of 1984:

> I knew, of course, that the structure of the Church had been revised, since Henry Burkhardt had become the temple president, and that the position of our contact person was officially vacant. But that did not affect our evaluation of the Church. Officially, nothing had changed, and there was no fear among the government leaders. We took notice thereof and considered it to be an internal matter of the Church that didn't concern the state. We also had determined that these three men worked harmoniously together, and they had a good relationship with us, that is, with the Secretariat. I wish to describe it as a mutually trusting, one could almost say, a friendly relationship, that had evolved. There were no taboo issues. Everything was placed openly on the table,

even if at times there were differences. Tactical differences didn't play a role in our relationship. (2005)

With his assumption of the new temple-related activities, President Burkhardt's responsibility for the Church's daily administrative functions, which he had conducted since 1952, had to be transferred to another person. Manfred Heller became the new office manager for the GDR region. However the most critical correspondence continued to go out under the letterhead of the president or the entire presidency of the Church in the GDR. In fact, the extent of that correspondence increased considerably after 1984. For example, in December 1985, the regional representative, Dieter Berndt, recommended "that the Presidency of the GDR increase its contact with the responsible ministries and respond publicly to events such as anniversary celebrations or birthdays and retirements of public officials." (DMO) Examples are found in Chapter 14.

The GDR's View of the Church's Influence

Documents from the 1970s and 1980s show that the government increasingly came to believe that the Church exercised significant influence in the world and especially within the U.S. government. For example, a newspaper article about the Church in 1974 noted Elder Benson's earlier position in Eisenhower's cabinet and said, "A tiny sect has grown to become one of the richest and strongest churches in the United States... and its influence reaches into the highest levels of government in Washington."[5]

The Church's opposition to President Reagan's 1981 proposed MX-Missile program (see Chapter 14) was also frequently cited by the government as an example of the Church's influence in America.

This perception of the Church's influence apparently contributed to the government's decision to allow President Burkhardt to travel to Utah to attend the April 1972 General Conference. It also influenced the decision to allow Burkhardt and other representatives to attend the August 1973 regional conference in Munich. It is interesting that the previously cited memorandum regarding travel to the Munich conference stated that the Church in the GDR "has been independent since 1952." President Burkhardt did establish an office of the East German Mission in Leipzig that year, which he moved shortly thereafter to Dresden. However, the government had earlier rejected his claim that this branch office in the GDR was proof of "independence" from the Church's headquarters in West Berlin. Therefore, while the later reference to the mission's independence is important, it is not clear why 1952 was cited, rather than 1969, the date when the Dresden Mission was established.

Other documents of the 1970s and 1980s show an evolution in the government's attitude toward the Church. For example, a July 27, 1978, memorandum from the Secretariat for Church Affairs concerning temples (see Chapter 15), contains only neutral comments about their purpose, as opposed to previous typical comments about strange "cult" practices. Another example is a memorandum from May 18, 1979, concerning the Church's interest in buying German genealogical records that had been microfilmed prior to World War II. The document focuses primarily on the opportunity to obtain needed Western currency, but it also contains several positive statements about the Church's genealogical research facilities, without any of the previous negative comments about genealogical research and its uses. The Interior Ministry and the Secret Service approved the sale (MS 13798).

The following excerpts from the Stasi file on Gottfried Richter, which Richter provided to the author and the LDS Archives, show a typical evolution in the government's view of the Church:

> July 28, 1983, Introductory Report:
>
> Burkhardt and Gottfried Richter, owner of the business Bürobedarf Rabus and honorary first counselor of the mission president, are placed under operative control in the "Perle" OPK [Operative Control of a Person]. Both persons are longtime leading members of the Mormons in the GDR. . . . With the construction of the "endowment house" or temple of the Mormons in Freiberg, this church and its leaders have taken on greater political-operative significance.
>
> A "prophet" and his counselors have developed strict guidelines for their members throughout the world. These guidelines are conveyed to "stake" leaders and mission presidents through so-called "traveling apostles." It is an operative certainty that every U.S. government from the past to the present has exercised influence on this church. One former full-time member of the CIA is even now active full-time as a "traveling apostle."
>
> The greatest current efforts of these functionaries and their members to strengthen their branches are of political-operative significance. That includes the building of a "stake" of the Mormons in Freiberg and the planned building of a "temple," also in Freiberg.

The second Stasi report from Richter's file is not dated, but was written after 1984:

> It has become clear, especially with the construction of an "endowment house" or temple in Freiberg, that the religious organization of the "Mormons" has obtained a firm foothold in the GDR, which has been further hardened by the creation of two stakes, 1982 in Freiberg and 1984 in Leipzig. According to their doctrine, all members of this religious organization are required to recognize state authority and to comply with its laws. The members of this religious organization perform their military service in the NVA [National People's Army] with weapons and they participate in elections. In general, they give the impression of being loyal persons, that is, progressive, regarding socialist

state authority. They do not engage in discussion of current political issues in their religious meetings. The entire religious meetings of the "Mormons" are focused on an ever-closer feeling of unity within the family as well as in the broader religious community.

The religious community does not join with other churches, religious organizations, or sects. They especially do not have any connection with or contribute to Evangelical-Lutheran initiated activities regarding the "independent peace and environmentalist movement."

Since the religious organizations of the "Mormons" have no paid ministry and operate primarily with the support of part-time workers, they have at their disposal significant financial resources. Every member must contribute the so-called "tithing" monthly, to which are added further requests for contributions. In that regard, several functionaries in the Freiberg Stake have decided to contribute their year-end bonus to the building of the "temple" and have simultaneously called upon all members of the Freiberg Stake to follow this example. Further significant financial resources will be provided by the headquarters in the USA. Travel to conferences in the USA are also paid by the central church.

The so-called genealogy research, together with other activities, is related to their effort to increase membership. All related information is documented and sent to the central church in the USA. To what degree this work of the "Mormons" is used for intelligence gathering has not been determined to date.

The last example from Richter's Stasi file is the January 11, 1989, final report:

It was the goal of the OPK to determine to what degree the leading powers of the "Church of Jesus Christ of Latter-day Saints" (Mormons) use their position for hostile-negative activities. Richter is responsible for the Public Affairs work of the Mormons. He was, for example, responsible for all publicity in regard to the dedication of the Mormon temple in Freiberg, which was opened to visitors on June 30, 1985. In all his activities, Richter has kept to the official position of his church, which was presented in the Declaration of the Mormons at the time of the meeting with the Chairman of the State Council of the GDR, Erich Honecker, on October 28, 1988. In the course of the "who is who" investigation of Richter, no evidence was found that he ever participated in any way in a hostile-negative manner. It is recommended that the OPK "Perle" be ended. (MS 16594)

7 How Mormons Defined Citizenship

> *Many West German members asked us, "How could you even live in the GDR?" I said, "Good," even if I would have preferred a different government. (Rolf-Thomas Lehmann, 2003)*

> *The laws are such today, that it is not necessary for us to violate them. We have freedom to assemble and to honor our God. We have the right to own property, although perhaps not to the extent in other countries. But we are prepared to recognize and support our country's laws. (Joachim Meyer, 1989. Interviewed in Salt Lake City before the Wende)*

This chapter presents the personal opinions of members regarding their relationship to the state and the experiences they encountered living in a state that often did not respect their religious beliefs and activities.

> *Jürgen Schiebold:* We read in Romans, "Be subject unto the higher powers." That is confirmed in the Articles of Faith, and when we read the Doctrine and Covenants, it is confirmed again, how we should live. Whoever lived accordingly could live in the GDR. He could live his religion and be a Christian. He could help his neighbor. There was no obstacle to that. What God expects from man, that he could do. He could be a diligent worker. Of course he couldn't travel far or do other things. Okay, that was perhaps a restriction of freedom. As a child, that wasn't even noticed. Youngsters certainly had broader desires. That is natural in man, who always yearns for what he doesn't have. Church leaders always taught us to be thankful for this land and for the gospel. The Church was here in its purity, and it provided many activities. (1993)

> *Jürgen Pabst:* We were taught in the Church, "When you are obedient, you will be able to practice your religion. You will not come into confrontation when you obey the state, unless it requires something

that contradicts the gospel." If the head of state commanded me to kill someone, that would not agree with my conscience, and I would not do that. But otherwise, I personally had no problems. I'm aware of others who could not live with the existent circumstances. Acceptance of the state was a problem that did arise now and then among the members. (1993)

Klaus-Peter Kretzschmar: The 12th Article of Faith was a motto for me throughout my entire life. I knew it as a young man in the MIA. It showed me what characteristics I required, not only within my family but also outside. I also accepted the principle stated in the Doctrine and Covenants, section 134, that we must be subject to governments. That doesn't mean that I must accept everything, but that I must do what is required. However, I also tried to express my opinion openly and honestly, and it went well with me. We were invited to meet with the mayor [in Schwerin] regularly and with the head of the local Interior representatives, who wanted to talk with us to ascertain what we thought about specific things. They didn't question us like the Stasi, but invited us and said, "What can we do to make things better? Tell me what you think." We had good relations with the city throughout the years and accomplished much that we otherwise would have not accomplished if we had remained remote. Our branch regularly received congratulatory messages from the city leaders at Christmas, Easter, on the anniversary date of our branch, on GDR anniversaries, etc. That doesn't happen today. (1993)

Hans-Jürgen Bartsch: I don't think that the 12th Article of Faith played any particular role; in fact, everyone tried to interpret its meaning for themselves. It was mentioned in the branch and was perhaps also quoted, but rarely was anything preached about it. Personally, it meant that I should support a just government. I didn't work against our government, but I also didn't do anything to support it. I wasn't politically active in any way. And that is how most of the members responded. (1991)

Walter Schiele: We often said that the Jehovah Witnesses were very strict. They said, "We will not take up weapons, we won't go into the army." The result was that they were imprisoned during the Nazi period and again here by the Communists. We accepted military service, as I often said, out of cowardice. I could have refused it, too, and then I would go to prison. So I thought, "Well, perhaps you will be lucky and not have to shoot anyone and will avoid war." I and many others achieved that. We attempted to be submissive but also wise, to avoid problems. We wanted to preserve the Church. To do that, some compromises were necessary. If we had been prohibited here, that wouldn't have benefitted anyone. (1991)

Klaus Peter Bartsch: The 12th Article of Faith was taught here. It actually gave us strength to respect this government and to show obedience. We were not able to identify with the government in every instance, but we practiced obedience. Through that obedience, it was possible for the blessings that President Monson requested for us to bear so fruitfully. It was simply a requirement that we not openly oppose the state. It is not the role of the Church of Jesus Christ to embroil itself in politics. Later, people criticized us a little, because we did not get involved as did the Evangelical and the Catholic churches, and others that openly made their buildings available for political meetings and propaganda. We lived our gospel and conducted our Church as always. These worldly political things don't belong in God's church. (1993)

Günter Schulze: As members, we honored this Article of Faith despite intrigue and humiliation. We respected laws, country, and even government, and it certainly led to the blessing of being able to build a temple. (1993)

Hans Schult: I believe that this Article of Faith was written for the entire world, and it makes no exceptions for Communist countries. When I gave talks or presented lessons, I always said that we must distinguish between the laws of the land and political directives. I didn't respect political directives. I never attended May 1st demonstrations on a Sunday. I told my boss, "Sundays I attend church." I went when May 1st fell on a work day, because I belonged to the labor union. We had wonderful family legislation, protection for children, protection for women. We had laws about employment. It was extraordinarily difficult for a boss to throw out a worker. The law was there for the worker and even more against the bosses, even if they were comrades (party members). I must say that from my perspective, we were not persecuted. We were not heroes. We could hold our meetings. We had enough freedom to pray at home, to hold family home evenings. We had enough freedom to carry out home teaching visits and to attend all meetings and district conferences. But many of our freedoms were not used, because we were too lazy. In my opinion, we had no restrictions in the Church and could have been more diligent. (1991)

Siegfried Schmidt: When I became a bishop, I had the responsibility of coordinating with the state. Perhaps those who never lived here cannot imagine that it was possible to have good experiences in that regard, when you live in accordance with the principles of the gospel.

> We lived in a system that had specific playing rules. When you followed those rules, then you could exist here. It wasn't necessary to deny your faith and you also didn't have to make compromises between the gospel and the way you lived. Whenever I held responsible callings, I always attempted to apply the principles of the gospel in my association with these people. I dealt with them politely. I explained what the Church needed, but always in a polite manner, as expected of Saints. I dealt with these people as if they were my brothers and sisters in the Church. I never treated them as my enemy. And that actually helped us, in that the Church had a very good reputation with the government, and they listened to us. That meant that when we had problems, we were at least listened to.
>
> That is something that our next generation and all people who may experience similar conditions in other countries can learn from us. When we really follow God's plan and live according to Christ's example, then we can do well despite any situations we may encounter. Those members who really lived the principles of the gospel were able to feel comfortable in this country. I actually had all that I needed to conduct my life in such a manner that I could work for the Lord. (1991)

The Ministry for State Security

The Ministry for State Security was usually designated by its German initials, MfS, or simply as the Stasi. The MfS was officially responsible for preventing, uncovering, and defending against actions by foreign sources, especially "imperialistic" secret services and agents and other hostile powers that opposed the GDR. Long after other agencies had designated members of the Church in general as "loyal" and had developed good relationships with Church officials, the MfS was still active in trying to identify potential or actual "enemies" within the Church. Gottfried Richter, whose personal Stasi file was summarized earlier, said:

> The State Security Service was one thing, the lead officials of the GDR another, and they were not always in agreement. It was the duty of one to be suspicious and to seek information. The other looked forward a little, beyond minor differences. At the time when the Church was generally viewed with suspicion, one activity that especially contributed to that suspicion was our genealogical work. It was assumed for many years that our genealogical documents were nothing more than a sophisticated system for transmitting coded intelligence via numbers and dates. That was stupid, of course, but they believed it for many years. (1993)

In addition to its army of official agents, the MfS recruited vast numbers of GDR citizens as "informal" workers, known as IM, informants who secretly observed and reported on their friends and relatives at home, on the job, and in their personal activities. It is known from Stasi files, for example, that at least twenty-one IM informants were assigned to observe and report on the daily activities of local Church officials during 1985 for the Freiberg Temple open house. Each IM assignment had to be justified in writing. The following statement was a typical part of those justifications:

> It has been determined that the Mormons in America are political and ideological advocates of the right wing of American conservatism. Their church leaders have close ties to American government circles, and close ties also exist between their church and secret service agencies within the USA. Moreover, it has been determined that because of the institutional structure of the Mormons, favorable conditions exist for the development of information collection or even broader negative, hostile activities.[1]

Stasi informants occasionally attended church meetings, and it was generally assumed that listening devices had been hidden in many of the meeting houses. The Stasi considered President Burkhardt to be an actual or potential "enemy of the state," and informants were assigned to observe and reported on his every movement. Although the Church and its members developed effective and friendly working relationships with most government agencies, it was very difficult to avoid the reach of the MfS. The following examples provide insights into the challenges that members faced on a regular basis in the GDR.

> *Henry Burkhardt:* We had a number of informants among our own members. I knew, for example, that in the larger branches, more than one member had to work for these people, and that they observed and reported on each other without being aware that they themselves were being watched. It was a very terrible time, but fortunately most of those people were known to me. In one branch, I knew it was the branch president. He never revealed it to me, but I knew that he worked for these people and that he had been assigned to observe a sister who had also been assigned to observe him. The system that existed in our country was unimaginable. Therefore, we had no possibility of doing anything in our church life that we had not already made known to the government, because we were certain that the government would know the next day if we did not do what we had told them.
>
> When foreign visitors came, we had to inform the county council in advance and ask if that person could present a message. Once, we received word that a General Authority would visit, but something prevented him from coming. I was called the next day and told, "Herr Burkhardt, Elder Packer was present at a meeting yesterday and you didn't inform us." I could calmly reply, "We had no visitor." An infor-

mant among us had reported the anticipated visitor. We always tried to make the most of these instances.

For me personally, it was an advantage when I knew who the informants were. And if the MfS had not recruited that person, they would have recruited others, and then I couldn't be sure what they would report. In the case of the branch president who was an informant, the brothers in the district presidency came to said and said, "You must release him." I said, "Brethren, he can provide better information than anyone else. He knows exactly what takes place in our church, what is in accordance with the principles of the Gospel, and also what is not in accordance with the laws of the land. If I replace him with another who is not so well informed, he could provide false information." That man was both branch president and informant for many years. Later, he was very surprised when I told him that I had known for years that he worked for the MfS. He is still very active in the Church, and I have absolutely no hard feelings toward him. However, he still does not know who was assigned to watch him, to spy on him.

People ask how such a thing was possible. It was a devilish system, and we simply had to live with it, adjust to it, survive with it. The government would have had false ideas about us if inactive members had carried out that activity. They picked up my closest associate, Brother Schulze, and questioned him several times. He was told not to tell his wife, but he naturally refused, telling them, "How can you expect that I not tell my wife where I was this afternoon. She must know that I was with you." Whoever talked openly and frankly with these people was released.

But I'm aware of other instances in the 1950s, where, for example, a brother was taken by the police and told to sign a report. He was asked to state in that report that I worked for the American secret service. The brother said, "I cannot sign that." They beat and imprisoned him. After he was released, he first informed me of what had taken place and then immediately left for West Germany. There were such members, who were true to their principles. I was also taken by the police frequently, but they had no evidence against me and had to release me. (1991)

Hans Schult: I once told the mission president, "Brother Burkhardt, I believe there are people in our meetings who work for the company." We always called the MfS the "company." He said, "Well, and? Preach the gospel to them, maybe you can convert them." We had no other choice. Would you want to constantly beat your head against the wall? There were brothers who did that. But they were also the ones who then submitted applications to emigrate. But my calling was here. If I and my wife had not returned from America, my children would have lost faith in me. They had been raised with the motto, "We are living in the best of times, in the best country, under the best conditions." We felt we had been given our assignments, our callings, here.

While traveling, I often felt that a car was following me. It was an unpleasant feeling. All members had that impression, but especially those who had leadership positions. You had to assume that there were informants in the branch. Many of the brethren shared amongst themselves the frequent attempts that had been made, with varying degrees of pressure, to recruit them as informers. (1991)

Lothar Hubert: A man once contacted me on the telephone and attempted to recruit me for the Stasi. I said, "I don't want to do that." He continued to try, although I remained firm. I was supposed to provide reports about what took place in the Church, how many members we had, etc. He then went to the place where my wife worked and greeting her in a friendly manner, "Guten Tag, Frau Hubert." A colleague asked, "Do you know that person?" He then would visit my wife's boss and upon leaving would say, "Auf Wiedersehen, Frau Hubert, and give my regards to your husband." That was an example of the methods used by the secret service. Once, two young girls came to our meeting. They knew all the church songs and said they were members, but they had been sent by the secret service. (1993)

Jürgen Pabst: After I received church callings that required me to interact with government offices, I had the constant feeling that I was being watched and that my conversations were being monitored. I was not really concerned, since we never did anything in church or outside of church that was hostile toward the government. But I always had the feeling that someone was standing behind me. It would be incorrect to say that I felt a fear of persecution or repression. But when I now consider those experiences more deeply, there were times when I did feel more apprehensive. When I considered that every bird could fly over the Wall, over the border, but a person, an intelligent being, would be shot if he tried to do likewise, that was something that I could never understand. But I never dealt with that so intensively that it caused me any internal turmoil. (1993)

Herbert Heidler: I was never afraid when the Stasi came to our meetings. To the contrary, I said, "A person can never know too much." If they learn something about the gospel, then they can come to better conclusions. One time I had the courage to approach the person and said, "If you want to know more about the Church, I would be pleased to invite you to my home." But he said, "No, no, no." We had no problems because of our response to them. Once in a while members would say, "I saw so and so once at a certain place." I replied, "Well, perhaps you have also seen me there." We were often asked to go to such places to answer questions. (1993)

Manfred Heller: There once was a young man who exhibited great interest in the Church. He participated in our religious services and other meetings and appeared to desire baptism and membership in the Church. He had a zest for learning. One day I was asked to appear before the traffic police on the charge that I had parked my motor bike illegally. I went as instructed, although I was not aware of any such violation, and was directed to a room where two men introduced themselves as members of the secret service. They questioned me about President Burkhardt, about Church activities, etc. In the course of the questioning, the phrase "North German Division" was mentioned. At that time, we belonged to the North German Mission. This young man had apparently not understood the name correctly and had considered the "North German Division" as a type of underground movement. And so he passed that along to the secret service.

Because Brother Burkhardt had contact with and connection to the First Presidency, and had been able to travel to General Conference sessions, they frequently attempted to dirty him somehow. They wanted to find reasons to discredit the Church through him. They tried to do that through cunning devices, but it never worked. I always dealt with them in a consistent manner, stated my principles and told them that if they had any problem with President Burkhardt, they should please discuss it with him personally. Since they didn't know how to proceed further with me, I didn't have any further problems with them.

The encounter produced a strange feeling, but I cannot say that I was actually fearful, for I knew with certainty that the Church would not engage in anything illegal that would violate the laws of the land or the government. That was always our position, as far as I knew. So we basically had nothing to fear. (1991)

Lothar Ebisch: I personally had at least five or six unpleasant encounters with these people. They came in a friendly and polite manner to the factory in which I worked and inquired about the operations of the business and my responsibilities therein. But they soon began to ask about the Church. As a rule, they wanted to know something about Brother Burkhardt. I said, when you want to know something about that man, you should go to him directly. Later, I was asked to come to one of their offices where they showed me an issue of the *Stern*, which supposedly had been brought into the country illegally. I asked, "Where did you find it?" They said, "That's our business." I responded, "Then you'll have to resolve it yourself." One time, they asked me about a "General a. D." [außer Dienst, i.e., retired] and why we had expressed appreciation for him. Sometimes they were so uninformed. It concerned an emeritus General Authority, not a military general.

Later I attended this large area conference in Munich. We submitted, through our mission president, names of members whom we wanted to send there and whom we trusted. The list included the serial numbers of their passports. That was judged to be a violation of law. I said, "Wouldn't you prefer that we select people whom we know are loyal citizens who will return?" After that they left me alone. (2003)

Walter Schiele: It was always difficult to obtain a private telephone. Some physicians lived next to us, and they had waited ten years for a telephone. When I became a district president, I received a telephone in eight weeks, because they wanted to listen in on our conversations. You could hear the crackling when they did so, and then we said to each other, "They are listening again." More than once, I received letters in a plain envelope with a West German return address. Upon opening them, I found material from a group of lawyers in West Berlin that described violations of civil rights in the GDR. It was very dangerous to possess such material. A policeman lived next to me. I immediately rang his doorbell and delivered the letters to him, so they wouldn't have a reason to conduct a search of my house. Their people always came into our meeting house, posed as investigators, bought a songbook, and sang along with us. (1991)

Alfred Bastian: A functionary came to me and said, "Since you do so much good in the church and in society, we will give you a free vacation." We traveled to Tabarz in the Thuringian forest. In this hotel were twenty people from the Hungarian and Czechoslovakian governments and a church leader who supervised all the pastors in the county. The meals and other services were like in heaven. When we returned home, I reported to the people who had sent me there and thanked them for the lovely vacation opportunity. They said, "Next year you can travel to an oceanfront facility where it is even nicer." Then they said, "Could you also do something for us, by providing some information about this or that person?" I said, "Now I understand what you want. I'm supposed to be an informant and report on activities in the branch. That I can't do." They then tried the same thing with another brother, a school teacher. When they couldn't convince him, he was transferred to another school twenty-two kilometers away, just because he wouldn't agree. We had those kinds of problems in our country. They were always seeking people who would report on church activities and members. (1991)

Herbert Heidler: They recruited many people simply by accusing them of breaking some law. When someone made a political comment or did anything that was not permitted, he was picked up by the Stasi. Then they told him, "We'll forget your violation if you work for us." (1993)

Anonymous: They sent a young man to me, a well-known local man with a good reputation. He was supposed to spy on me. I was a bit naive and trusted him. I taught him the Gospel. He was often in our home, he became a member, became an elder, and went to the temple. He was active in the Church for four or five years until the Wende. He is still a member today. But after the Wende he became very, very sick, mentally disturbed. He reproached himself and apologized. He doesn't attend meetings anymore, but never rejected the gospel. I've spoken with him but didn't want to pursue the circumstances in detail. I told him, "Whatever happens, I still love you, you are my brother." There was no reason to excommunicate him. Regarding his motives, why he did that, it certainly was not voluntary. Since it happened in other instances, I assume that he had come into conflict with the law. Perhaps nothing serious, but they took advantage of it, and he submitted to them out of fear. (2003)

Imprisonment of Members

In some cases, harassment of Church members went beyond the use of informants. Imprisonment and/or harsh physical treatment of members for church related activities was not common, but it did occur. The jailing of the mission presidency in Zwickau in October 1945 was described previously in Chapter 2, and two instances regarding the administration of Church funds by Walter Fassmann in 1951 and Henry Burkhardt in 1952 are addressed in Chapter 13. Walter Kindt's report of the jailing of Rudolf Pöcker, the branch president of Halberstadt, taken from the mission history, is excerpted below:

> On September 2, 1950, I went to visit the branch president of the Halberstadt Branch, Rudolf Pöcker. When his wife came to the door to let me in, I was told that there were three criminal policemen in the living room with him.... After a stay of about one hour, the three officers concluded that they should take the tithing book, a large file containing several letters, a small file containing the financial report, the triple combination, a book from a local book dealer which he had received as a gift, an issue of *Das Beste* [*Readers' Digest*], and two newspapers from West Berlin.... On Thursday, Otto Klietz (the man from whom Brother Pöcker had received the newspaper) was also arrested. (LR 2428 2)

Kindt assumed that the arrest was part of an attempt to close the branch in Halberstadt. Pöcker remained in jail for three and a half months until released at the instigation of the Russian commander, General Schukow, following a personal request by Paul Langheinrich. Immediately after his release, Brother Pöcker went to West Berlin. His wife followed shortly thereafter, and they immigrated to America.

Heinz Kulke, a member of the Görlitz Branch, was taken by the Stasi for questioning in October 1954 and again the following February. Following the second episode, he left for West Berlin, where he made the following statement, dated February 7, 1955:

> I, Heinz Kulke, born November 24, 1918, in Görlitz, resident of Görlitz... make the following sworn statement for the record: On October 17, 1954, I was taken for questioning at 6:45 a.m. From 7:00 a.m. until noon, I was accused of spying for America, engaging in currency manipulation related to genealogy work, and conducting neofascist activities. The agents of the State Security Service changed their tactics at noon and attempted to recruit me to work for their agency, for which they said I would be well paid. I supposedly would earn more money than I have ever earned in my life. In answer to my question, whether I was supposed to spy or report on the church to which I belonged, I was told in these exact words: "Our activities are not directed against the church, but the church is composed of people who make mistakes, and that is what you should report to us in detail." I was informed that I may not talk about my assignment, otherwise I could expect to be sentenced to twenty-five years of forced labor. I responded: "I cannot work in secret, all my activities must be in the open."... After additional sessions of questioning and imprisonment in a dark, windowless cell, I was allowed to go home at 5:00 p.m.
>
> On February 5, 1955, I was again taken for questioning.... I was given a typed, page-long statement, in which it was said that Henry Burkhardt, counselor in the East German Mission, had conducted spying activities for the American espionage service. Brother Burkhardt's name had also been mentioned often during my first questioning on October 17. Money had been placed next to the statement that I was asked to sign.... I tore up the statement. One of the three men present at that time struck me in the head, such that my glasses were thrown across the room into a corner. The glasses were severely damaged. Another man approached me and struck me so forcefully between my legs, that I become ill. Then I was again taken into a dark cell. I was permitted to go home about noon. (LR 2428 2)

Werner Mehnert, a full-time missionary, was arrested and imprisoned in the fall of 1958. The mission history noted his status on March 31, 1959: "We are happy to report that Elder Werner Mehnert, our missionary in prison, is to be released on May 8th. At the prison, it is known that he is innocent of any wrongdoing. Between his industry and cheerful acceptance of his lot, he has found favor with those in charge and may be released ahead of the date set at first" (LR 2428 2). Gottfried Richter explained why he was imprisoned. "A copy of the *Stern*, which was not an approved publication, was found in his possession. It contained a quote from J. Edgar Hoover, 'I would rather go forward with Jesus Christ than backwards with Karl Marx.' Brother Mehnert was accused of teaching that, which was a crime. He had a trial, which the public could not attend, and was in jail for three-quarters of a year" (1993).

Members were also subject to arrest for offenses not related to Church activities, but which the government tried to use to attack the Church's credibility. In one instance, an article appeared in the *Berliner Zeitung* on June 8, 1958, which stated that a member had been caught crossing the border from East Berlin into West Berlin "with thirty-seven eggs packed individually between Bible verses." She was quoted as saying that the eggs were to be made into noodles for members in the West as part of the "good works" required by her Church leaders, and that she had been required previously to bring thirty and fifty jars of fruit to the mission office. She was sentenced to four months in jail. The article said that the Church's headquarters were in New York City and that its long arm was in Berlin-Dahlem, from where its fingers reached into the GDR. The claim that the eggs were packed between Bible verses and the reference to New York City as the Church's headquarters are indications that the true details of the incident were not as claimed.

Military Service

While Church members were happy if they could somehow avoid military service, they accepted the call to serve when it came to them. Rolf-Thomas Lehmann and Frank Fuchs describe their army experiences in Chapter 9, during an interview about their experiences as youth in the GDR. Two additional interviews are quoted here. Jens Schlegel's experiences were similar to those described by Lehmann and Fuchs, while Andreas Ortlieb's unique experiences stand in stark contrast to those of members who were drafted for the typical eighteen months of military service.

> *Jens Schlegel:* I had my Bible and my Book of Mormon with me while I was in the army, and no one said anything. It was tolerated. They knew that I attended church. When I think back on that time, I realize I was always treated a little like a privileged person. It was easier for me to obtain leave, or to choose the day of the week when I could leave. I could also go home, which was otherwise rarely granted. In fact, an officer once drove me home on his way elsewhere. I had absolutely no complaints. I didn't experience anything negative in my army time. (2004)

> *Andreas Ortlieb:* In 1984, I was not drafted into the National People's Army, but into the riot police [Bereitschaftspolizei], special police units under the control of the Interior Ministry. That was a very difficult experience. These police units operated under more severe political guidelines, so I was questioned, naturally, about my religion and my philosophy of life. I was asked if I was a Christian and if I believed in God. I stated that I was a member of the Church of Jesus Christ of Latter-day Saints. The interview was conducted by a Stasi officer, who knew from my file that I belonged to an American church. He told me, "We have no place in this country for such people. We will make that very clear to you during your training over the next two years." (2003)

Ortlieb's encounter with the Stasi officer took place in Schwerin several years after he had declined the government's offer to attend medical school in return for a three-year military obligation as an army officer, described later in Chapter 10 about the advanced educational opportunities for Church members. His refusal to accept the offer, and his subsequent study of music for four years, was recorded in his personnel file and known to the interviewer. The officer also questioned him about possible contacts with Americans. At that time, he had none. He was asked how he would spend his free time, for example on Sunday when given leave. He said that he would attend church at the local branch. The officer responded, "Then there will be no leave for you outside the barracks," and he was not allowed to leave for the next six months. In a 1993 interview, Ortlieb provided other examples of the attitude of the riot police toward Christians. On one occasion, he and fellow inductees were told, "All Christians may go one floor higher and shoot themselves with a pistol. Such people are completely superfluous here." Ortlieb said that one Christian inductee did take his own life because he could not live with the conditions in the barracks.

Successful Appeals of Local Government Restrictions

The 12th Article of Faith did not require the Church or its members to accept actions of the government that they consider to be unconstitutional or discriminatory. The following examples show how members appealed the decisions of local officials to the highest levels of government.

> *Allocation of Gasoline:* In 1955, Werner Leichsenring was the branch president in Auerbach/Vogtland. He had purchased a motor bike to carry out his church responsibilities, but the local officials refused to grant him a permit to buy gasoline. His initial efforts to appeal that decision are not known, but he eventually took his case all the way to the president of the GDR, Wilhelm Pieck, who referred his letter to the Deputy Prime Minister, Dr. Otto Nuschke. An official in Nuschke's office then wrote to the traffic department of Karl-Marx-Stadt and asked them to reconsider its earlier decision. Shortly thereafter, Brother Leichsenring received an allocation of ten liters of gasoline per month. (DO 4/722)

Importation of Songbooks: In March 1965, President Burkhardt asked permission of the secretary for Church Affairs to import two thousand songbooks, as a present from the Church in West Germany. After his initial and two subsequent requests were ignored, Burkhardt wrote directly to the GDR's top official, Walter Ulbricht, Chairman of the State Council. Two weeks later he received a response from Ulbricht's office informing him that the request was being considered. Shortly thereafter, the secretary for Church Affairs asked Burkhardt to submit his request again, which was promptly approved. Further details are found in Chapter 12.

Purchase of a meeting house in Annaberg: Gerhard Krämer had leased a large factory building in Annaberg for his personal business, and the branch had renovated a portion of it as a meeting house, which was also used for district conferences. They had even constructed a baptismal font in the basement. A state-owned company used another part of the building and paid rent to Brother Krämer. The branch later wanted to buy the entire building from the willing owner, but the state-owned business protested the sale because it did not want to pay rent to a church. With the active support of the CDU party, to which a few members belonged, the branch appealed the case to the county council and eventually to the secretary for Church Affairs. The sale was approved, and the state-owned business paid rent to the Church. Further details are found in Chapter 11.

A meeting house in Leipzig: The branch in Leipzig had been allowed to lease several ruined buildings over a number of years, which members turned into respectable meeting rooms, only to be subsequently evicted for various "civic" purposes. In 1968, they were sent to a vacant building that had earlier been a movie theater and then a warehouse. After several months of intense labor, and on the eve of holding their first meeting in the renovated building, local officials withdrew the occupancy permit. It was obvious that the city was determined to restrict the activities of all churches in that city. After fourteen additional months of appeals and lobbying activities, which involved the highest levels of government, the branch was finally given access to the building. It would serve as their meeting house until a new facility, a stake center, was built in 1986. Details are found in Chapter 11.

8 Missionary Opportunities

We had full-time missionaries in East Germany. It was possible, just as before, to call young men as missionaries, but of course they couldn't serve abroad. (Henry Burkhardt, 1991)

It is said that we didn't have missionaries here until 1989. That is true only in regard to missionaries from abroad. We served as full-time missionaries, in complete accordance with missionary rules. We were separated from our families for two years [or longer]. When our first daughter was born in 1953, Henry Burkhardt asked me if I was ready to fulfill a full-time mission. We might see our wives during a conference somewhere, but we had no vacation from the work. (Gottfried Richter, 1993)

The growing and later declining number of full-time missionaries who served in the GDR between 1945 and 1961 is shown in a variety of documents:

August 1945: There are at present four active missionaries, all in Berlin. (Col. Barnes to Thomas E. McKay)

January 1946: Twelve missionaries are presently serving, and we hope to be able to call others soon. (Acting mission presidency to Thomas E. McKay)

February 1946: I took sixteen missionaries. (Paul Langheinrich, describing the recovery of genealogical records hidden by the Nazi government during the war)

March 1946: A very vigorous missionary program has been undertaken by this mission. They now have twenty-one full-time missionaries working in all parts of the Russian military zone, four lady missionaries working full-time in the mission office, and six more brethren being called to work as full-time missionaries. (Elder Ezra T. Benson)

April 1947: Movements of our thirty-three local missionaries are watched carefully. Everyone is watched. (President Walter Stover to the First Presidency)

July 1947: The forty missionaries trekked to Dresden from their various fields of labor. (Pioneer celebration)

August 1955: We went to a meeting [in West Berlin] of the thirty-four full-time missionaries from the Russian Sector—twelve young women missionaries and twenty-two elders. Eight were over twenty-five years old, including one who was fifty-two, one forty-one, one thirty-three, and one twenty-nine. None of the thirty-four speak any English. (Elder Spencer W. Kimball)

March 1960: The seventeen full-time missionaries had a meeting here with the mission president, Percy Fetzer. (MS 17716)

Excerpts from mission reports and interviews provide a variety of insights into the circumstances associated with full-time missionary service in the GDR:

Herbert Schreiter: There were few members in Bernburg in 1946. I told myself, "Something must be done here." I had some posters printed and organized a special church service in a school. Fifty-nine people attended the meeting. (1991)

Manfred Schütze: On our return from the cemetery, my family saw a large poster on the wall of a factory building [in Bernburg]. It read, "Does life continue after death?" Grandfather said, "That is exactly the question we have." That church service, organized by the missionaries, was the turning point in the life of my entire family. (1991)

Wolfgang Kelm: Tracting from house to house was not permitted during my mission from April 1949 until August 1951. We could only teach those people to whom we had been referred by members. (2005)

Frank Apel: We did traditional missionary tracting in Stendal in 1959. We didn't ask, but just went from door to door in one street after the other. Suddenly a man on a bike stopped next to us, showed us his badge and told us to follow him. We went to the police station where we identified ourselves and said what we were doing. We were told not to continue that activity because people had complained that they were being bothered by us. That was just a pretext. So we went into another area and did as before, giving out the Book of Mormon. When we returned two weeks later, the people warned us, "The police were here. Don't go any further." So we stopped tracting. (1991)

Erich Ortlieb: I was on a mission from 1958 until 1960. Tracting was forbidden in many cities. I wasn't afraid because it was not forbidden by the constitution or the law. The Communists here called it "house agitation." They told us that the people were complaining and they didn't want us to bother them. I always told them, "Give us a written statement that our activities are illegal." They didn't want to do that. We stopped tracting there but simply went to another town. As we gave out copies of the Book of Mormon, the police came along behind us, to every house and apartment, and collected the books. But they didn't forbid us to tract. In Naumburg, the criminal police visited us in the morning in our apartment. They reviewed all our books and pamphlets. All were approved except a few pamphlets. (1993)

Herbert Heidler: We went door to door until 1961. It varied by location. But it was forbidden throughout the entire country two or three years later. We used the Anderson Plan with flannel board figures. Later, we had a new plan with pictures. We obtained them partially from West Germany, but we also created some ourselves with a typewriter. We had only a few copies of the Book of Mormon and almost no pamphlets. Once we were able to print a few about the plan of salvation or the Joseph Smith story. It took considerable effort to obtain permission, and then it was only for a few copies, maybe fifty or so. But we loaned out the Book of Mormon. When people no longer wanted it, we gave it to another family. I had three baptisms during my mission. (1991)

Günter Schulze: We distributed tracts despite the obstacles. We took advantage of opportunities and addressed people while sitting on a bench in a park or at a cemetery. We spoke to people on buses and trains. Missionaries had to wear a hat, and a nineteen-year-old with a hat, especially in the summer, attracted attention. People always responded to us politely. (1993)

Joachim Meyer: Of course, you can't compare the missionary work that we conducted at that time with the work of today's missionaries. But we had our missionary plan that called for us to arise at six a.m., followed by an hour of personal preparation and two hours of gospel study. Then we visited friends or members. We also had responsibilities for branch activities. That continued until nine or often until ten at night. Our days were busy. (1989)

> *Joachim Albrecht*: We worked closely with the members, who led us to friends with whom we could meet. We had two sister missionaries in one branch. They led the Primary and worked with children they met on the street or at playgrounds. They built up a strong Primary, which led to additional contacts with the children's parents and several baptisms. (2004)

In 1955, President Burkhardt met with officials of the Interior Ministry responsible for church affairs to complain about police harassment of the missionaries. To document his complaint, he provided those officials with the following excerpts from a letter he had received from sister missionaries in Rathenow:

> When we submitted our meetings for the coming month, the police commissioner told us, "You are not supposed to solicit door to door for the church! You know that is prohibited." We were actually not doing that in Rathenow, and we said so. He responded, "Don't lie to me. You were seen in the Forststraße." We said, "We live there." "No, not where you live. You were soliciting house to house for your church." "No, that is not true," we said. He said, "The people wouldn't tell me things that are not true." We said, "Then let us face those people who made that accusation." He didn't respond to that but said, "Well, you'll be in trouble when I catch you doing that! Moreover, you also solicited outside of Rathenow! You were caught in the act in Schönhausen." We said, "That is not true. We only visited a member of our Church in Klietz by Schönhausen." "So you were soliciting there!" "What do you mean by soliciting? Aren't we permitted to visit our members?" "You are not permitted to conduct any solicitation!" "But can we or can we not visit our members?" After we posed that last question three times, he said, "Well, first it must be determined who are and who are not members." We said, "Well, those who have been baptized by us are members." At that point, another policeman joined in the discussion and said, "Yes, you are permitted to visit them." Whereupon we finally received the same answer from the police commissioner. (DO 4/722)

Missionaries Served as Branch Leaders

> *Gottfried Richter*: Many hundreds of members left, including branch and district presidents. Then missionaries were called who not only served as missionaries, but very often led the branches. (1993)

> *Frank Apel*: It was our assignment as missionaries to lead these small branches. My missionary companion was simultaneously the branch

president. We took care of everything that needed to be done, prepared lessons, gave talks, and blessed the sacrament. (1991)

Marianne Ortlieb: We also worked to bring the youth back to the Church. I was a counselor in the Mutual program, and we were successful in activating the youth. We taught lessons and also led the Primary organization. (1993)

Wolfgang Kelm: Of course, we were also responsible for finding and training future leaders and to prepare the branch to become independent. (2005)

Joachim Albrecht: It is evident that the missionaries accomplished a major work in the period from 1946 through 1960, because most of the branches did become independent. (2004)

Elder Kimball met with the missionaries from the GDR during his visit to West Berlin on August 26 and 27, 1955. In his subsequent twenty-three-page report to President Gregory, Kimball made the following comments concerning the missionaries' involvement in branch leadership responsibilities in the GDR:

> May I reaffirm the things which I mentioned many times while in the mission, that local leadership should replace the missionary leadership. I realize that this is not always possible and certainly not possible overnight, [however] the missionaries should be proselyting. . . . We are aware of the emigration influence; also of the jealousies and the weaknesses, but I am sure that a well-organized program, with special help to certain individuals, will gradually reverse this process. I think some missionaries feel honored with the positions and find branch work easier to do than proselyting. . . . I am not blind to the difficulties. I know it will be a superhuman task to turn the train around and start it in the other direction, but I am sure that you brethren can do it.
>
> If I interpreted your figures right, the thirty-four full-time missionaries in the East Zone baptized only twelve people in the year or an average of 1.7 per month. . . . I realize the difficulties with the Curtain, the restrictions, the limitations, but I hope there will be some way through Brother Burkhardt or otherwise to stimulate these missionaries. There cannot be conversions without hours, devotion, and cottage meetings. (LR 2428 39)

Financing of Full-Time Missions

Wolfgang Kelm: We paid the rent for our rooms and provided for our own breakfast. We were invited by members for our noon and evening meals. The Relief Society took care of our laundry needs. Our travel expenses were reimbursed by the mission. Therefore, I only needed fifty East marks each month. (2005)

Joachim Meyer: We were supported by our parents. Of course, we also received twenty marks from the Missionary Fund now and then. But we were often invited out to eat, so we usually made do on seventy marks a month. We paid our rent, but meals were inexpensive at that time since we had ration cards. If we needed additional clothing, our parents took care of that. (1989)

Frank Apel: My mother was alone and we didn't have much money, so I could not have financed a mission by myself. President Burkhardt took care of that. I was supported by a brother in Idaho and regularly received funds from his Elders Quorum. (1991)

Elder Kimball to President Gregory: I have already sent to you $100 for the East Zone and written you to the effect that we have about $2,400 pledged for East German missionaries. Surely we could greatly increase the number of full-time missionaries from the East. (LR 2428 39)

Eberhardt Sommer: My father was not a member of the Church, and my parents didn't have much money for a missionary. The district president knew that I didn't have any money. He said, "The district and I will support you." (2005)

Joachim Albrecht: Our district president said they would like to send me on a mission. My father was not a member of the Church, so the district president came to our house and asked my parents if they would support me. My father presented his reasons, his arguments, why that was not an easy thing to do. But then he agreed to do it anyhow. (2004)

Initially, the missionaries were ordained as elders by the mission president. However, for a variety of reasons, including the difficulty of travel to West Berlin and a tradition of not ordaining young men quickly to that office, missionaries often departed on their missions as holders only of the Aaronic Priesthood. Heinz Hinkel began his mission in December 1945 as a priest at age twenty-three. He was ordained an elder by President Walter Stover in February 1947. Wolfgang Kelm was ordained a priest on his seventeenth birthday in 1949 in Berlin and left the next day for his first field of labor in Halberstadt. Joachim Albrecht was eighteen years old and a teacher when he left for his mission in November 1953. Two months later, he traveled to Berlin, was officially set apart as a missionary, and ordained an elder. Henry Burkhardt began his mission in May 1950 as a teacher. He was ordained as a priest in July of that year and as an elder in October 1951. He became a counselor to the mission president in June 1952. Shortly thereafter, he began to conduct some of the ordinations himself, with permission of the mission president.

Because advancement within the priesthood traditionally did not take place as rapidly in Germany as in America, Elder Kimball addressed that subject in his previously cited letter of October 21, 1955, to President Gregory:

> Greater care should be exercised to see that worthy boys are ordained deacons at twelve, teachers at fourteen, and priests at sixteen. This has been neglected many times. There seems to have been a feeling that there should be a long time elapse between baptism and quorum work and a greater degree of maturity of boys than the ages stipulated by the Church would show.

Further examples of the activities of full-time missionaries in the 1950s and 1960s can be found in a collection of their personal experiences, entitled *In Ostdeutschland auf Mission: Erinnerungen, Tagebuchaufzeichnungen und Zeugnisse ehemaliger Missionare*, compiled by Melani Schiele in Leipzig.

The End of the Full-Time Missionary Program

The number of full-time missionaries in the GDR declined toward the end of the 1950s. A mission report dated March 31, 1959, described the status of the program at that time:

> During the afternoon we held a conference [in Leipzig] for the East missionaries, giving them ideas, material, and testimony to aid in their work. There were seventeen present. Their missionary activity is very much hampered as proselyting in most of the cities is forbidden. They are denied the use of all tracts and literature published in West Germany. The missionaries do the best they can by visiting members and friends through appointment. Nevertheless, the records show twenty-nine convert baptisms and twenty-four children of record baptisms for the East. (LR 2428 2)

President Burkhardt invited the remaining full-time missionaries to a conference in Dresden during the Christmas holiday period. The program was phased out shortly thereafter. President Fetzer wrote on April 25, 1961, "Brother and Sister Burkhardt visited Berlin and reported that missionaries have been ordered to leave three of the cities. The district missionaries are doing an excellent work and will soon take the place of the long-term missionaries" (LR 2428 2). Following the erection of the Berlin Wall, Fetzer wrote again on October 1, 1961:

> As of this date, the work of the long-term missionaries in the east part of Germany will have been suspended. The police authorities will not countenance proselyting nor any aggressive missionary activity. The

> word has come to us that all we are expected to do is to sing and pray and listen to the minister preach. No other activity is necessary nor will be acceptable. The missionaries are unable to register in compliance with the law for any type of living quarters in an area where the Church is not already established. (LR 691 2)

While the impediments to missionary work were obvious and substantial, no official reason for the demise of the full-time program was given. Therefore, members gave their own reasons, and the difficulty in finding suitable employment after serving a mission was most often cited:

> *Joachim Meyer*: There was a law that all adults were required to work. Missionary work was not an acceptable substitute for employment. (1989)

> *Joachim Albrecht*: The state required young people to work, and missionaries were not engaged in activities that benefited the economy. We heard that often, and therefore it became continually more difficult to call missionaries. Missionary callings did not end because of direct government demands, but the problems associated with issuing such callings became more serious. (2004)

> *Günter Schulze*: I couldn't find work and was unemployed for six months because I had served a mission. I wanted to study engineering in Leipzig, but that was not approved because I had served for two years without pay. It was recorded in my personal file. Every time when I applied for employment, I had to do so in writing, including the jobs I had held from my youth, and there was that gap in employment. I had to write, "Worked for the Church." (1993)

> *Erich Ortlieb*: When I went on a mission, I had to obtain signatures from several people at my place of employment on a form that stated why I was leaving. My division leader said, "How could you write 'mission' on that document?" He wouldn't give me a referral but said, "When you are finished with your mission, come back here." I did that, but then he said he didn't have an opening for me. At another place of employment, the party secretary asked me many questions about the Church and the mission. He was very polite but said at the end, "The next time you change jobs, you should expect to have difficulties because you were on a mission." (1993)

> *Herbert Heidler*: Men obtained work after their mission, but the options were limited. I was not able to obtain work in the profession that I had learned. I found work through an entrepreneur who had many connections. (2005)

The conflict between employment and missionary work had existed for many years. The government had said in 1949 that unpaid missionary work was not a recognized profession and that such persons had to register with the employment office. A mission report in 1956 stated that Henry Burkhardt could not get a job because of his affiliation with the Church and his missionary activities over the past five years. No firm would consider him a good risk. Therefore, he was supported entirely by funds donated by members of the Church. Interestingly, President Burkhardt did not personally attribute the termination of the missionary program to conflicts with the government, severe as they were. Instead, he said it was a decision of the First Presidency:

> Alvin R. Dyer, as a representative of the First Presidency, immediately released the missionaries at a meeting in 1961.... Some missionaries could not finance their own missions and were supported by Elders Quorums, individual members, and the branches. That was considered to be a paid ministry, which the Church didn't practice. The brethren didn't understand the circumstances and conditions in the GDR. Since President Dyer came here as a General Authority, I had to accept it, although I didn't agree with the decision. (2005)

President Burkhardt's statement appears to be confirmed by a notation that Elder Kimball made following his visit to Berlin in 1962. He wrote, "Missionaries are being released as their terms expire and none others appointed, this subject to the instructions of the First Presidency" (Copy from Edward Kimball).

The end of the full-time missionary program impacted some of the smaller branches rather severely:

> *Frank Apel*: The small branches especially missed the missionaries and the support they had provided. Some of those branches were closed since they consisted mostly of just one or two families. Those members were assigned to other branches, which were often far away. (1991)

> *Joachim Meyer*: The young members were especially impacted. The missionaries had devoted considerable time to youth activities on weekdays, which was essential. Some branches had large numbers of youth. In one, the average total attendance was forty, of whom twenty-eight were young people. But when the missionaries were withdrawn, some of the youth came less often to church. (1989)

District Missionaries and the Referral Program

While the traditional full-time mission assignments ended in 1961, the mission did not cease its missionary efforts. President Burkhardt gave the following description of the district missionary and referral programs in his introduction to the journal history of the Dresden Mission:

We had full-time missionaries until 1961. Since then, we have attempted to carry out proselyting activities without them and to assume those other duties that had been previously placed on their shoulders. When the Referral Program was introduced to us, we felt it was an inspired program and were convinced that it had been created especially for our country. At district conferences, we made our members acquainted with the wish of the prophet, "Every Member a Missionary."

Our best result occurred in 1960–1961 as a result of intensive work by our district missionaries. Entire families were converted at that time, who continue to be our best members today. The following statistics clearly show that more people accepted the gospel during those years of intensive proselyting work than in the following years.

Table 8.1. Baptisms

	Convert Baptisms	Children Blessed
1959	15	51
1960	50	42
1961	43	29
1962	23	33
1963	17	23
1964	18	25
1965	10	18
1966	6	30

After the first district missionaries completed their assignments, few members were willing to undertake this activity. Despite considerable efforts by our district leaders, we did not experience the success we had anticipated in calling additional missionaries. No district conference passed in which we did not speak about this subject or challenge our members to dedicate themselves to this work. We continually attempted to reinvigorate our missionary activity. Otherwise, sooner or later, our membership would decline as older members passed away. (DMO)

The reports of district conferences in 1961 show the emphasis that was placed on missionary activities. The summary of the Karl-Marx-Stadt conference, held in Annaberg-Buchholz on May 6 and 7, 1961, is typical:

Conference Theme: Every Family a Missionary Family

The question was posed, how our missionary activity could be developed and strengthened. Three successful district missionaries spoke, as well as a brother who, with his five-member family, was converted through the missionaries a few months earlier. He now holds the priesthood, and his family is a support for the branch. Members were emphatically told that our district missionaries need more referrals. It was explained again how referrals should be made, for example, that based on our experience, we do not want anonymous referrals, referrals that request a specific missionary or referrals on the condition that the gospel be presented in any manner other than that provided for in our program. (LR 2428 40)

Herbert Heidler, who served on and/or led the mission's missionary committee from 1964 until 1984, gave the following example of how some members conducted missionary activities in those years:

> We had an elderly sister in the branch who went to the park every day in the summer, sat on a bench, and initiated conversation with those she encountered there. We received most of our referrals from her. During the two years of the district missionary period, we had nineteen baptisms, mostly as the result of her referrals. We did not have such members everywhere, but that was an interesting experience for us, which we attempted to instill in other members. It was our best opportunity to conduct missionary work. (1993)

As elsewhere in the world, many convert baptisms resulted from friendships initiated and fostered by members:

> *Elder Dieter Uchtdorf*: Some days after World War II, my grandmother was standing in line for food when an elderly single sister with no family of her own invited her to sacrament meeting in Zwickau. My grandmother and my parents accepted the invitation. They went to church, felt the Spirit, were uplifted by the kindness of the members, and were edified by the hymns of the Restoration. My grandmother, my parents, and my three siblings were all baptized. (October 2004 General Conference)

> *Gottfried Richter*: I met a young girl in a business establishment. We agreed to meet on Sunday following her church service. Then she said, "Isn't that foolish, that you wait outside for me instead of going to church with me?" So I went with her. This young sister sang in the choir. The songs greatly impressed me. Then two brothers spoke. I immediately heard the claim of the Church, the lofty claim that it was the restored Church. Then the young lady said, "If you want to learn about the gospel, you should attend Sunday School." I also attended Mutual. They had a problem and needed someone who could give a lesson the next week. I believed them and gave a lesson, but they didn't really have a problem. Then they said, "We have choir practice for an hour. You have a good tenor voice. Wouldn't you like to sing in the choir?" I did that, and soon I was fully integrated into the Church. (1993)

It was often a challenge to fellowship strangers when visitors at meetings might be Stasi informants. President Burkhardt addressed that challenge during a meeting of the mission's committees on September 8 and 9, 1973:

> We must cultivate the spirit of missionary work more intensely within ourselves. Some branches had invited friends to attend our recent youth activity. Naturally, we welcomed that, but there was a problem. These young people came here and didn't know anyone. It would have been wonderful if our youth had paid attention to them. But the youth thought, "We don't know you, so we can't get involved with you." These young people had to stand on the side and watch while others amused themselves. I felt badly about that. We must take advantage of the opportunity to make contact and to welcome each stranger in our midst. When strangers come into our branches, we maintain a certain distance. Of course, we must be careful what we say, but that is no reason not to warmly welcome that person.... It is not easy to preach the gospel in other parts of the world. The members elsewhere don't have it any easier or more difficult than we do here. (DMO)

Other Missionary Activities

Although the district missionary program was successful for only a short period, Church leaders constantly sought other opportunities for members to become involved in missionary activities, despite the existent restrictions.

> *Herbert Heidler*: Members in the Dresden Mission were once more called as full-time missionaries in 1978. This time it involved retired couples and single sisters, a total of twenty members, who fulfilled eighteen-month missions. An additional three couples were called later. But when they had completed their time, we couldn't find more who were prepared to fulfill such a mission.... These elderly members remained in their home towns, primarily visited inactive members, and tried to bring them back to activity. Now and then, they also identified friends of members to teach, and some baptisms resulted. It was an interesting time for these members.
>
> We also had young people who wanted to serve a mission. In January 1982, we called youth on missions, who served under unusual circumstances. They gave up their jobs and moved to cities where they were needed, where they also sought and found new employment. They were employed full-time and still managed to devote twenty hours a week to missionary work. They also supported these small branches to which they had been sent. A total of seven young brothers from Dresden, Leipzig, Bernburg, and Zwickau accepted this assignment. But that was only done once. The burdens were too great for these brothers. It was a test, and the test showed that it wasn't the

> ideal program. But we did it, and we also gave the youth the opportunity to say, "Good, I was a missionary." (1993)
>
> *Hans Schult*: A young man terminated his employment and sought another in the town to which he had been sent as a missionary. But the strains in that program were too great. The young people had to work all day, often at hard manual labor, and then do missionary work in the evening. They couldn't handle that physically and perhaps also not spiritually. (1991)

Statistics on the number of convert baptisms in the GDR are available for most years. They were most frequent in the immediate postwar period and again between 1959 and 1964, as shown earlier. The latter increase is attributed to the work of the district missionaries. The number of convert baptisms declined sharply after 1964. Between 1975 and 1984, an average of seven baptisms took place each year. The baptisms that followed the arrival of full-time missionaries from the West in early 1989 are addressed in a later chapter.

9 Church Youth Programs

The youth of the GDR are today's Church leaders in our region. (Frank Fuchs, 2003)

It was difficult to carry out youth activities. We were not permitted to dance in our meeting houses. We had trouble even renting a steamship or organizing any activities outside our meeting houses. But I believe, as is often the case, that when a person experiences pressure, he develops resistance to that pressure, and that actually made us quite strong. It is similar to a tiny chick in an egg. It must fight its own way through the shell. (Manfred Schütze, 1991)

The Constitution of the GDR guaranteed religious freedom, but the government's definition of religion excluded many of the Church's traditional youth activities. Dancing, sports, social games, nature hikes, group vacations, and scouting activities were, at various times and locations, declared to be outside the accepted definition of church functions. According to the state, such activities were the sole responsibility of official state-sponsored youth organizations, such as the Young Pioneers and especially the Free German Youth (FDJ). All young people were expected to join these organizations. While membership was no guarantee that active Christians would be treated equally in their educational and professional activities, failure to join almost always had negative consequences.

An article in the GDR's 1981 *Theologisches Lexikon* described the goals of FDJ and the role of young Christians within it:

> The FDJ embodies the political unity of the GDR's young generation. As a socialistic mass organization, it voluntarily unites young people, who together with all workers, form the developing socialistic society and thereby create the prerequisites for the gradual transition to Communism. The FDJ relates to all young people, irrespective of their

> social background and philosophical conviction. It pays attention to every young person, is concerned about their personal development, and helps them to reconcile their personal interests with those of the greater society. From its beginning, young Christians have worked responsibly within the FDJ and have made significant contributions to the achievement of its mission. They have the same rights and responsibilities as all other members. Variations in philosophy of life and motivation for political activity are respected. The respect that young Christians enjoy within the FDJ is determined by the degree of their participation.[1]

Fortunately, the official restrictions upon church-sponsored programs were not uniformly applied, and Church leaders usually found ways to carry out excellent youth activities, either with or without government permission. Despite significant handicaps, the Church's activities in the GDR were comparable to and sometimes better than those conducted in other countries.

This chapter begins with the Church's program for its youth above age twelve, the Mutual Improvement Association (MIA). That organization's activities in the first years after the war have been described by its then current leaders, beginning with reports provided by Elfriede Falkner Gäbler:

> We began MIA activities in the branches immediately after the war. Since we were dependent upon the occupation forces and their administrative personnel in each city, the implementation of the program was not always uniform. However, the activities of the Beehive Girls, the Gleaners, and the M-Men were resumed, and we had special activities for members and friends over age twenty-five. We had very good manuals such as "Love, Marriage and You," as well as others that addressed life's goals. Once a month we had an evening where we discussed interesting and worthwhile topics of general knowledge.
>
> Due to losses during the war, we didn't have enough priesthood leaders in our branches, so the missionaries were branch presidents and auxiliary leaders. At first, overall leadership for the MIA Young Women and Young Men programs came from the mission presidency in Berlin. As missionaries, Wolfgang Kelm and I were the MIA leaders in the Leipzig district. We also had the assignment to re-establish the branches. We couldn't tract door to door, but held meetings in the homes of members and friends. Many were refugees from the eastern provinces, or lived in temporary housing because their homes had been destroyed.
>
> We considered ways to bring friends and investigators into the branches and came up with the idea of MIA-sponsored "Ballad Evenings." Ballads speak to the spirit of the German people. We looked through ballad books and sought out relevant scriptures and appropriate music to add variety to the ballad presentations. With approval

> of our district president, Walter Kindt, we traveled to the different branches of our district and presented these programs. They were well received, and our meeting houses were always filled to capacity. We often didn't have enough chairs. Many later converts were visitors to such evenings. We adapted the program to the needs of each branch and successfully involved friends in the presentations.
>
> We had a lot of fun. Once, Wolfgang Kelm had a bad cold. During the morning practice, he had to constantly reach for his handkerchief. We said, "What will you do tonight when your nose runs?" He thought he would just let it run. Because he was presenting the ballad, "Das Elend" [The Misery], we suggested that he say, "I have an 'Elend' in my nose." That evening his nose did run, and he let it run! We laughed so hard! Afterward, I had to present a ballad. My voice was strained from laughing, and the listeners said, "Sister Falkner was very emotional about the ballad." (2005)

The ballads were accompanied by short, relevant, scripture-based talks. Program summaries provided by Sister Gäbler show that in 1951, Ballad Evenings were held throughout the Leipzig district in Delitzsch, Dessau, Gotha, Weimar, and Erfurt. The Leipzig MIA also traveled to Chemnitz in 1949 to present scenes from Goethe's *Faust,* and in 1950 a drama evening was held in Leipzig with introductions to *Faust,* Schiller's *Räuber,* and Lessing's *Nathan der Weise.* Similar activities were conducted in some of the larger branches.

After the GDR was established in 1949, the new government tried to force these activities to be conducted through the FDJ. However, the members successfully resisted. Sister Gäbler provided further descriptions of the MIA in later years:

> Beginning in 1956, Brother Joachim Lehnig became the leader of the mission's MIA-Young Men program. A youth conference was held on Easter weekend of 1961, attended by youth from the mission's western districts as well as from the entire GDR. During that conference, Brother Lehnig stated that this might be the last time the entire mission could join together in such an activity. No one anticipated the Berlin Wall at that time, but it was built on August 13th.
>
> I was the Young Women leader for the Dresden district at that time, and our MIA activities continued as before. We had youth conferences with volleyball, table tennis, dance evenings, and much more. I don't think that our young people were denied anything. We had an annual summer camp in Trassenheide on the Baltic Sea and held large youth conferences in our meeting house in Dresden.
>
> After the consolidated program was introduced in 1980, our gospel lessons were moved to Sunday, and the youth gathered on Wednesday afternoon for activities. However, we missed the previous combined activities with the older members, so we held a monthly activity for

everyone. We felt that both young and old belong together, and that prevented generational problems. We still come together at specific times: Fasching celebrations, Easter egg hunts, and for Christmas and New Year's celebrations. Looking back, we are very thankful for the MIA activities in those years. They greatly enriched our lives. (2005)

Three of the MIA-Young Men leaders added their recollection of the program:

Wolfgang Kelm: At the conclusion of my mission in August 1951, I was called to be the mission MIA leader. I continued in that assignment until July 1952, when I left the GDR. I lived in East Berlin, and Ursula Hübner, who was responsible for the Young Women, lived in West Berlin. We reported to a counselor in the mission presidency. At least once a week, I traveled to the mission office in Berlin-Dahlem to work with Sister Hübner. We organized a district youth conference for East and West Berlin, which was carried out without any government restriction. I traveled frequently to district conferences in the East Zone to represent the mission presidency. We prepared instructions that went to all branch and district leaders in the East and in the West. (2005)

Eberhardt Sommer: I was called to lead the Young Men in 1952, while serving a mission in the GDR. It was difficult to be responsible for an area in the West that I could not visit. Often, we were not able to ask the mission president for guidance and direction. He said, "I give you free rein, and we'll discuss later what you did." He trusted us. We visited all the branch and district conferences, since the mission president could not enter the GDR. We were not supposed to have a youth organization in the East. Boy Scouts were prohibited, so we called them Brigham Young Youth and did the same things as the Scouts. We had over six hundred young people. Many branches were composed of 50 percent young people. Most of our baptisms came via the youth organization. (2004)

Joachim Lehnig: I returned from my mission in 1955 and was called to be the mission's MIA leader in 1956. Technically, we reported to the mission president's counselor, but we considered ourselves to be the MIA leaders because we didn't have good communication with him. We had to work independently, but met with him from time to time in Berlin. I did that for several years. We also had to type out all of our manuals. I cannot explain what a huge task that was [see Chapter 12]. (2004)

It is noteworthy that the above descriptions and examples of MIA activities in the 1950s, as described by MIA leaders some fifty years after the fact, present an entirely different image of conditions in the GDR than seen in the very negative and pessimistic comments of district leaders that were recorded during their meeting on May 24, 1953, and quoted previously in Chapter 5. The difference may be due to the passage of time, during which perspectives and memories can change, or it may simply reflect basic differences between people who have common experiences. Following are a few examples of the statements made in 1953 and reported in Chapter 5:

> We can only teach religion. Games and discussion sessions are prohibited. . . . They forbid us to play tennis or to organize discussion evenings. Primary classes have been prohibited and our table tennis has been confiscated for the FDJ. . . . When you engage in sports, do so far away from your meeting houses, even outside the city. . . . The police have recently been hounding us and have prohibited table tennis, boxing, etc. Instead of MIA, we have a Bible hour.

Government documents provide another perspective of MIA activities. A February 1952 report by the local police in Erfurt was entitled, "Regarding Wednesday Meetings Known as the Mutual Improvement Association":

> It has been determined that the above-named religious organization has recently begun to hold a special weekly activity, which has led to a higher attendance than earlier. This is because a leader of the sect is currently presenting a lecture series consisting of eleven successive lectures that address the moral relationships between people. The first two lectures were entitled, "May I kiss?" and "How should I love?"
>
> These evenings were publicly announced and guests were invited. . . . The topics were addressed partially in lecture and partially in seminar format. Intensive discussions have already taken place during the first two sessions, in which people criticized the preacher's presentation. Some said that the type of people expected by the preacher do not even exist. . . . The preacher, for example, described the American youth as kindhearted and devout, who mostly live without any corrupting passions. To the subject of "May I kiss?" he said that the "cold kiss" is practiced in West Germany, which he said would certainly be desirable, but which unfortunately doesn't exist here.
>
> In addition, a youth group within the sect consists of ten girls that have the name of "Gleaners." Some of these girls wear a yellow blouse and a black skirt embroidered with wild flowers. These "Gleaners" are involved in choirs, amateur plays, and cultural activities. The children of members of this sect are organized in a special group called "Beehives." (DO 1/11 HVDVP/865)

President Burkhardt summarized the mission's youth activities during the 1950s and 1960s in the introduction to the journal history of the Dresden Mission:

> We attempt to give special attention to our youth, to help them with their problems and to have them join with us in completing specific assignments. We can say that we have been successful in this area, especially when we consider the many problems that assail our youth from the outside. We attempt to bring the youth together through mission youth conferences, which however, are usually associated with a series of problems. Our last successful activity was in 1965, when we brought the youth together in a tent camp for two weeks. Unfortunately, we were unable to arrange a similar activity last year and this year, because we couldn't reserve the necessary space or obtain permission for the activity. Actually, no youth gathering takes place that isn't accompanied by significant problems. Earlier, it was primarily the problem of finding the necessary food, while now the challenge is to obtain permission for the activity.
>
> For example, in 1954, we had a gathering of about five hundred youth in Dresden, who were together for ten days. The youth were well fed, but we often didn't know in the morning where we would find the ingredients for lunch. But the youth were always enthusiastic, which continues to be the case today. (DMO)

Members later described their experiences and impressions of MIA activities:

> *Walter Schiele:* The MIA [in Leipzig] was excellent. Of course, that was a large branch. We organized wonderful programs, including music and talent evenings. We staged theater plays. Leipzig was especially known for its scenes from Goethe's "Faust." We even performed at conferences. In those days, conferences ended with a special activity on Monday. We also performed in various branches. But it was more difficult for smaller branches to do what Leipzig did. (1991)

> *Joachim Meyer:* There were many branches with few youth, often just two or three. The result was that the Church couldn't offer those few youth enough activities. Most of them joined the FDJ, the only official youth organization in our country, which had many facilities where the youth could dance. That naturally attracted some of our youth. They simply sought conversation and sociability that the small branches could not always offer. (1989)

> *Jürgen Pabst:* I was once a teacher in the Primary. Then I had the same youth later in MIA. We were always together somewhere in our free

time, the youth and I. We shared our problems with one another and helped each other. (1993)

Manfred Schütze: Thirty youth went once to the Baltic Sea, where we had a youth camp. But not officially. The Church wasn't permitted to organize one. Everyone arrived individually with his tent. Officially, everyone cooked for himself and lived by himself, but we were always together. Our youth leader was Walter Krause. On Friday evening we had a dance in the small Wolgast meeting house. That also was not official. We could not play the music so loudly that it was easily heard outside. We had to pull all the curtains. But it was very nice, and Brother Krause had just obtained new records from West Berlin, the newest hits of that time. It was a very great evening. That was on Friday, and on Saturday we were on the beach. (1991)

Joachim Lehnig: There was a large tenting place in Karlshagen that was not in great demand, and we had many tents in the mission. We didn't reserve a place. That was not officially possible. We managed anyhow. But we had to be disciplined, don't do anything dumb, don't attract attention, so that no one would notice what we were doing. (2003)

Manfred Heller: In Karlshagen, everyone had to register separately. Of course, someone always organized it so that the youth had a corner for themselves, but we couldn't register as a church. (2004)

Joachim Lehnig: Brother Burkhardt was the person who made it all possible. One cannot imagine all that he dragged to these camps with his car and trailer. The Church supported these youth gatherings, otherwise we could not have financed them. It was important for the youth, they were the future of our Church. Father Krause was the one who cooked, when that was possible, and he was the father of the youth. Everyone called him Father Krause. He was someone to whom you could go and discuss your problems. He could listen. But then he also could say, my dear friend, get a grip on yourself. He could do that in a fatherly way. (2003)

Hans Schult: There were a series of youth gatherings at the mission and at the district level, and later between the stakes. The direction, the experience, and the examples often came from Brother Krause, who organized youth activities in a way that no one can match today. He went to a forester and asked if he could rent a barn for a week. Then he built a shack in the forest for a kitchen and invited all the youth, whoever wanted to participate. Or we packed a can of peaches or wheat from the welfare shipment into our backpacks and traveled to the Baltic Sea, where we went into a local restaurant and asked the owner if he could cook up something for us. In those days, the restaurants had little with which to cook something, so he also received a portion of what we had. (1991)

Herbert Heidler: We were told that our youth should go to the FDJ, if they felt the need to dance. But people smoked there and alcohol was available, and we didn't want to do that to our youth. We simply organized dance evenings without permission. We often covered the windows and kept the music low. I mean, we did not obey the government in everything. We said, "We owe it to the Church to do something for the youth," whatever the consequences. And we were always lucky. We didn't have any bad consequences. I believe that God was on our side. (1993)

Karla Liebscher: A tent camp was set up in Seehof by the Schwerin Lake in 1960. Many youth from all of the GDR assembled there, I think for two weeks. Every branch sent their youth and each group had to bring their own tents. The weather was very bad and it rained very hard for at least a week, so that the camping place was in deplorable condition, partially under water. A nearby farmer took pity on us and allowed us to overnight in his hayloft. A few weeks after this camp, someone knocked at the door of my student room. A member of the Stasi introduced himself and asked me about the camp and the Church in general, about missionaries and how the Church was financed, etc. (2005)

Mission-wide Youth Conferences

Restrictions on church-sponsored youth activities intensified soon after the GDR was established in 1949, when local officials began to require prior approval for any large youth gathering. Some of the mission's youth conferences were held on long holiday weekends, such as Easter, Pfingsten (Pentecost), or New Year's, while others ran for an entire week in the summer. Since local officials generally had a narrow definition of acceptable church-sponsored activities, the mission eventually began to designate some of the longer mission-wide gatherings as "Jugendgottesdienste" (youth worship services). While the program included regular church services on Sunday, and most mornings began with brief religious services, each request submitted to local officials was carefully formulated to highlight the religious components of the program and to downplay or avoid mention of the more extensive social activities. Government officials were certainly aware of these discrepancies, but they usually looked the other way, especially when the activities took place within the Church's meeting houses or otherwise didn't attract public attention. Members often said, "We operated at the fringes of legality, and we did it again and again." Most of the later large mission-wide conferences were held in Dresden, where the Church had renovated a former German officers' casino in the Dr. Kurt Fischer Allee into a large meeting house. An example of an early youth gathering over a long weekend took place in 1949 in Chemnitz:

> *Elfriede Gäbler:* All youth, whether from Chemnitz or elsewhere, gathered on Saturday at six p.m. in the meeting house in Chemnitz. During the morning service on Pfingsten Sunday, the following main question was addressed: Can a person maintain his status in the Church without a true testimony of the gospel? On Pfingsten Monday, all the youth participated in various competitive sports. An evening dance concluded the event. (2006)

A two-week mission-wide tent camp was held in the Grunewald forest in West Berlin on August 24 to July 7, 1950. The youth from two western districts of the mission, Kiel and Hannover, joined with the youth from the GDR.

> *Wolfgang Kelm:* It was possible then to cross into West Berlin. President Stover obtained tents from the American army, which were set up by the American missionaries serving in West Berlin. The first order of the day was to wash with cold water! The days were filled with various sporting events, followed by an evening discussion hour led by interesting people, including President Stover. (2005)

A youth activity in Dresden, at Easter 1956, provides an example of how requests were worded in order to obtain permission. The request submitted to the police is presented first, followed by the government's approval statement and then the mission's description of the actual event.

> We intend to conduct a series of Easter religious services between March 30 and April 2, 1956, in our Dresden meeting house, at Dr. Kurt Fischer Allee 12. An estimated 350 persons from our various branches in the GDR will attend. The following gatherings are planned:
>
> Friday: 10:00 a.m. Opening service, 3:00 p.m. Banquet
>
> Saturday: 9:00 a.m. Morning service, 3:00 p.m. Social gathering, 7:00 p.m. Religious instruction
>
> Sunday: 9:00 a.m. Morning service, 11:00 a.m. Testimony meeting, 5:00 p.m. Sacrament meeting
>
> Monday: 9:00 a.m. Morning service, 10:00 a.m. Religious instruction, 2:00 p.m. Small concert
>
> In addition to the above religious services, individual small groups will visit places of interest in Dresden on Saturday and Monday, to occupy the time between the individual activities. (DMO)

The request was reviewed by the police, which sent the following note to Dresden city officials:

> We are of the opinion that a prohibition of the activities planned in Dresden is not required. We request, however, that you contact other responsible offices to determine the extent to which an observation of these activities is possible, and inform us of any decisions that are made. (MS 13918)

The activities actually conducted during that Easter weekend were described in the mission journal. They varied considerably from the submitted request and included sporting events, a dance, and discussion groups. About 250 youth attended:

> Friday: 10:00 a.m., Opening service. President Burkhardt counseled the youth to live within the existing order and show the world that we are children of our Heavenly Father and members of His Church. 2:30 p.m., Afternoon program with the theme: "In the Realm of Flowers," poetry, prose and music show the wonders of the creation. 5:30 p.m., Members from the Cottbus branch performed the theatrical piece "The Way to Truth" and also gave a reading of "The Prize."
>
> Saturday: 8:00 a.m., Morning service. Later, the sports enthusiasts gathered for competition (soccer and table tennis), and the more peaceful attended a presentation of "The People Who Knew No Sickness" (or "The People of Hunsa"). In the afternoon, the youth gathered under the theme "German Humor," which brought them to laughter for three hours. Items were presented by various branches.
>
> Sunday: 9.00 a.m., Morning service. 11:00 a.m., Testimony meeting. 4:00 p.m., Sacrament meeting. The message from Henry Burkhardt: "It is easy to give away what doesn't belong to us. But it is expected of us to give from that which we have. When we sing about wonderful Zion, we should realize that we can only have it when we have contributed to it by our willingness to sacrifice. We must build it through our personal efforts."
>
> Monday: Morning sports. Then the orchestra from the Cottbus branch played to the theme "Dance in the Spring" from 3:00 until 9:00 p.m. (DMO)

Not all requests for youth programs were approved. Numerous activities had been planned in connection with a 1968 Pioneer trek, which would take place at various localities from July 20 to August 3, 1968. These activities could not easily be described as "religious services," and they clearly exceeded government guidelines for church youth activities. A memorandum from the State Secretariat for Church Affairs in Berlin, dated July 22, 1968, stated why they were not approved:

> On the basis of information we received, the following actions were taken: Discussions were held in Potsdam, Halle, and Dresden with

the responsible leaders of this organization, and they were informed that it cannot be the responsibility of religious organizations to conduct tourism and vacation activities for the youth. The state cannot approve the so-called Pioneer Trek.

These discussions caused the deputy leader of the organization, Herr Krause, and the youth representative, Herr Sommer, to come to the office of the State Secretary on July 17, 1968, to present a request for permission to conduct their activity. They were given the same explanation, that a government office cannot approve such developments, because they go beyond the practice of religion and are not the function of a religious organization.

On the basis of this information, a meeting of leaders of the Mormons took place in Dresden on July 18, 1968, and thereafter the chairman of that organization, Herr Burkhardt, and the previously mentioned Herr Krause, informed the [Dresden] Bezirk Council, that the planned gatherings in Dresden, Karl-Marx-Stadt, Annaberg, and Freiberg would be cancelled. They accepted the government's opinion and recommended to their branches, by telegram, that the vacations be conducted in their own localities.

The planned mission week in Schwarzenberg from July 29 to August 3, 1968, which anticipated a significant expansion of religious activity through nature walks, dances, camping events, sport tournaments and other social activities, also cannot be approved. The local offices have informed the responsible representatives of the religious organization that such activities may not be conducted.

The planned series of activities of the Mormons for 1968 have been officially cancelled by their leaders. However, during discussions with the Dresden Bezirk Council, it was requested that the office of the State Secretary be advised that the leadership of the Mormons will want to meet with us in October 1968. They had requested such a meeting ten years ago and have not yet received an answer, although their members are good citizens (most of them are in fact activists) [positively involved in professional or social organizations]. They do not wish to present demands, but wish to describe their situation and enable state offices to understand that they guide their members to be good citizens and workers of the GDR. (MS 13798)

Additional descriptions of typical youth outings and other activities of the 1970s are taken from the journal history of the Dresden Mission:

Year-end Event in Dresden, 1970–1971:

December 31: Since it should be an event for all who are young or still feel young, we began immediately after the evening meal with a dance evening. The bands from Karl-Marx-Stadt and Berlin-Friedrichshain played enthusiastic and lively rhythms, so that all dance lovers could have a good time. During the dance, several members added to the evening with funny stories. Shortly after 11:30 p.m., we sang the song, "Now the Day Is Over." Then Brother Burkhardt gave us words of good counsel appropriate to the ending of a year and the beginning of another. After everyone was wished a "Happy New Year," the dance continued until 1:15 a.m. About 240 attended the event.

January 1: Breakfast was eaten at 9:30 a.m., followed by the youth choir practice at 10:00 and the youth religious service. Discussion groups and a walk followed in the afternoon. The discussion groups were divided into three subjects: Courtesy; Engagement and Marriage; and Saving and Recalling Technical Information. Everyone assembled again at 4:00 p.m. for an introduction to the opera "The Magic Flute," and we went to the Opera House that evening to see the performance. Present, about 160 people.

January 2: All the youth assembled at 8:00 a.m. for the morning service. Later that morning the sisters received good instruction about doing professional quality handwork, while the sport-minded engaged in table tennis, bowling, chess, and target shooting. In the afternoon we visited the historical museum and the art gallery. In the evening we had a hobby show, with many interesting presentations of individual hobbies.

January 3: All the youth participated in Sunday School. The subjects were "The Word of Wisdom" and "The Greater Probability of the Existence of God." A highpoint was the testimony meeting.

Year-end Event in Dresden, 1971–1972:

December 31: The theme was "Poets and Singers Gather at Hans Sachs' Place." Decorations included a market place, well, beer barrel, and store. Brother Wolfgang took the lead as Hans Sachs. The youth came dressed in self-made middle ages costumes and enriched the evening with twenty presentations that they had composed themselves—a song, a poem, a rhyme, or a street ballad.

January 1: A table tennis competition was conducted; also the best chess players were determined. Several handicrafts were pursued. In the afternoon, a quiz activity was held, in which several areas of knowledge were addressed: sports, literature, theology, geography, etc. A music evening was presented in the evening by members from Cottbus.

Youth Religious Service in Dresden, Pfingsten 1972:

Although the weather was not friendly (it rained), everyone arrived in good spirits. Because the planned dance evening was cancelled, a competition in "Free Speech" was conducted. On Saturday morning, everyone met at the train station and traveled toward Wehlen. It rained heavily, but all were optimistic that the sun would shine. However, it rained even more as we arrived at the Bastei. The planned outdoor theater visit in Rathen literally fell in the water. So we took the ferry across the Elbe and returned to Dresden on the next train. When we arrived at the meeting house, we found all rooms had been heated, so we could quickly dry out; 198 participated in this trek in the rain. After the evening meal came the highpoint of the outing. President Burkhardt reported on his trip to Salt Lake City, with a slide show that greatly impressed all who were present.

The next day, Sunday, was a spiritual feast for all. It began at 8:00 a.m. with a choir practice. After breakfast came Sunday School and a choir concert. Under the worthy baton of Brother Gerwin Baasch, the youth choir sang inspired and enthusiastically. Later we had a question and answer session. All of the youth had the opportunity to write down their questions, which were answered as well as possible during that meeting.

On Monday, after the morning service, everyone enjoyed the wonderful sunshine during a substantial walk through the well-known Prießnitzgrund. A little sport and play was enjoyed during the walk. (DMO)

Members' Recollections of Youth Conferences in Dresden

Eveline Dzierzon: Each youth conference was filled with imaginative activities. Every branch had to bring something to enhance the evening dance, either sing an amusing song, read a funny story, or present a sketch. We always had time to see interesting sights or go on long walks. And a testimony meeting was held. (2004)

Manfred Schütze: We had a large meeting house in Dresden where we could put up 100 to 120 youth overnight. It was a former officers' casino, and units of the Russian and GDR army and the special police responsible for security on the trains were based in surrounding buildings. The Stasi occupied the floors above us. We were right in the middle of everything. The young people brought air mattresses and blankets, and youth leaders stayed with them the entire week to oversee the activities. It was always the best spiritual experience that the young people had, and they all looked forward to those occasions. (1991)

Joachim Lehnig: We did wonderful things at the youth conferences in Dresden. There is a picture of a dance at the court of the pharaoh. The Dresden youth had built columns for the court, and we selected a young man to play the pharaoh. He had an impressive crown. Every branch had to bring tribute to give to the pharaoh. I'll never forget one group. They carried what looked like large grape vines, but the grapes were actually apples. It was so well done, and everyone cheered the tribute bearers. You can't imagine the spirit it brought to the dance. (2003)

Eva Kretzschmar: Before going to the youth conference, we brewed onion skins like tea and put that in the bath water. After an hour in the bath, our entire body was brown as Romans, so that our appearance matched the theme. On other occasions, we danced in our meeting house, using a small radio that received a weak signal from a West German station that played modern dance music. What I found so appealing was that most of the youth came to these events with the intent just to be together and have a nice time, regardless of the circumstances. (2004)

Günter Schulze: We decided at one time that we could no longer have dances in the meeting house, because it was officially forbidden. We found a place outside of Dresden, a restaurant with a nice dance floor and stage, and made arrangements with the owner to meet there. The youth traveled in small groups, using public transportation. That was done unofficially, and we were very thankful to the owner. He knew that he was incurring some risk in accommodating us, but he said he wanted to help the youth of our Church have a fine evening. (2005)

Andreas Kretzschmar: The youth conferences were high points in life for us. It was never the question of whether we would travel to them, but how to travel, whether by train, bus, or maybe with a moped. For me and for all of us, it was a "must" to be there. What was offered, what our own members organized, was simply gigantic. First, simply the food. There were things to eat that were otherwise never seen, for example, Nuss-Nougat-Aufstrich [almond-nougat spread, like peanut butter] on bread or something else special. And there was always a rich variety of activities. We were often out in nature and went for long walks. One time we took the train from Dresden to Bischofswerda, where we had a pioneer dance in stocking feet to protect the new wood floor. Later in the evening, when it was already dark, we walked back to Dresden, which was at least twenty kilometers. We had many sport activities. In Dresden, we could play volleyball in the courtyard. And we had to contribute our own efforts to the activities. For example, for social and discussion sessions, we presented stories, sketches, music, etc. Focused discussions on specific topics were always enjoyable for the youth. For example, "What am I seeking in a partner?" Health topics were addressed. Then, of course, dance evenings, where the themes included a Roman ball, with the appropriate scenery and dress. (2004)

> *Jens Schlegel:* One day always was reserved for a walk somewhere, for example through the Sächsische Schweiz, long walks of the kind that no one does today, that few youth would be willing to do now. We had very long nature walks, where we left early and returned late in the evening. Once we took the train from Dresden to Rathen, to the open-air theater, and back to Dresden on foot. Or we took the narrow-gauge train to Frauenstein, walked from there to Freiberg, and then took the train back to Dresden. Those were walks that required an entire day. (2004)

> *Lothar Ebisch:* Once we went to Friedensburg, where Elder Monson had dedicated the country. Along the way, we noticed we were being closely observed by the police, who drove by on their motorcycles or watched us from various locations. Then we wandered over the hill toward Moritzburg, where we swam in a lake. Later, as we approached the narrow-gauge railroad that ran between Moritzburg and Radebeul, we saw more people at the train station who observed us. They traveled with us to Radebeul, where we intended to transfer to the regular train to Dresden. Suddenly we were surrounded by the Transport Police and directed to wait in the tunnel under the train tracks. When we asked why, they gave no answer, except to wait patiently. After a long wait, we were finally allowed to assemble in front of the train station, where we were again surrounded by the police. After two hours, we were allowed to go onto the train platform. After my repeated requests for an explanation, the police said they had determined that some youth had acted in an undisciplined manner on the small train. That was, of course, not true, just an excuse to hold us. In any event, we were finally allowed to proceed, under their watch, to the Dresden train station. We walked from the train station to our meeting house, this time accompanied by plainclothes police.
>
> We think the reason was that a large meeting of Young Pioneers was being held at the same time in Dresden. Apparently, their overseers felt somehow threatened when another youth group, in fact a Christian group, was traveling in the same vicinity at the same time. After that experience, we felt somewhat restrained for the rest of the week. We were careful, but still did all that we had planned to do. (2003)

The youth conferences resolved or at least reduced some of the concerns of the young people. One such concern was the desire to find a partner within the Church, when so many lived in small branches with few other youth:

> *Andreas Kretzschmar:* We took the Church very seriously in the GDR because it was a place of peace for us. We were always a group unto ourselves, and we had been taught that we should marry within the

Church. So the youth conferences were our best opportunity to meet others. Many marriages resulted, because it was the only time that we were together long enough to become well acquainted. Of course, that could have the appearance of a marriage mart, but what other alternatives existed? It was normal that many found their partners there. The purpose of these conferences was to grow spiritually, and friendships resulted naturally in that process. (2004)

Carmen Schlegel: We never considered these conferences as marriages marts. We went to be with youth from other branches, to experience a few beautiful days together. Of course, friendships developed at those times; that is only normal. (2004)

Eveline Dzierzon: I went to the youth conferences as soon as I was old enough. It was important to me to always be there. My Patriarchal Blessing said that I should pray to find the right partner, and I did that especially whenever I went to a youth activity. The way I found my husband was very strange. I became acquainted with two young men at a youth conference. Both wanted to write to me. But then, as if someone spoke to me directly, I knew who the right one was. I didn't have to make the choice myself. (2004)

Reiner Dzierzon: Perhaps it was a marriage mart in some ways, but how else was it to happen? How else could we get to know others in the Church? (2004)

Eva Kretzschmar: At one time, there were few singles left in our marriageable age group. Two of them said to each other, "We are still single. Each of us would like to marry and have a family." So they married, not out of love, but out of reason, because they wanted to be married and have a family. And they are still married. Love grew within the marriage, and they are still happily married today. (2004)

Food was another feature of the youth gatherings. Members often said in interviews, "The food was simply fantastic. The sisters created wonderful meals. It was like a regular buffet. Beautiful fruit was available. Where did they find that?" Two Church leaders answered that question:

Manfred Heller: The food was secured through appropriate connections. For example, we had a sister in Dresden who worked in a meat market. Someone else had connections to a grocery store, where they could obtain drinks and other things that otherwise were seldom available. Close to our old meeting house in Dresden was a private wholesale operation where you could buy, for example, fifty jars of pickles or two hundred bananas. The Church had a good reputation with the owner. The items could have been sold to other organizations, but he preferred to make it available to the Church. The Church was an independent institution that stood somewhat outside the dominant circle of organizations in that state-run society, so it was given preference by those who wanted to give the state a little jab. And Brother Burkhardt had a good relationship with these people. He was a real gentleman, a polite person, considerate of and helpful to others, as a member of the Church should be. I mean, it was a pleasure for people to interact with him and to support him. (2004)

Günter Schulze: About 1970 to 1971, I was asked if I would help find food for the youth conferences. We had a small delivery truck in the mission, which I used for this purpose, not only for the youth, but also for the genealogy sessions that lasted one or two weeks, and for other events where food was needed. And why were we so successful, despite the difficult conditions, to have plenty of food for 100 to 250 youth or for 50 or more genealogists? When I received this assignment, I prayed at home that Heavenly Father would help us, that we could obtain all that was necessary. We could buy sausage and bread, but so much fruit, cheese or meat, etc., seemed impossible. We had a dear sister who had connections to a butcher, but everything else needed to be researched and sought for. I went to the stores and vegetable wholesalers and told the appropriate people, "I'm from the Church of Jesus Christ of Latter-day Saints. We are located in the Dr. Kurt Fischer Allee. We have a large conference with so and so many attendees, who stay with us several days or up to two weeks. We need this and that in terms of fruit, vegetables, and other items such as cheese, meat, etc." To my great amazement, every one of those dealers always said that if it was for the Church, then they will gladly help us. I must say that these people who operated stores in those days (they were not their own stores, but state-owned businesses) were inspired. They guaranteed us that we would obtain the fruit and vegetables that we needed. Of course, it was dependent on the harvest time. When it was peach season, we received peaches, or melons in the melon season, but we used whatever was available. It continued in that manner until shortly before the Wende. (2005)

The Pioneer Trek and the Mission Youth Choir

In 1962, the youth and many of their leaders used their vacation to conduct a "Pioneer Trek" on bicycles through the southern part of the mission, during which they presented choir concerts in the branches along their way. That event led to the organization of a Mission Youth Choir, which presented numerous musical programs throughout the mission each year until it was disbanded in 1973. President Burkhardt wrote in the mission journal in 1969, "We have determined that many friends attend these performances. In fact, the attendance at performances in Leipzig often exceeds that of the district conferences. We are thankful for the Youth Choir, which is one of our best missionary activities." (DMO) The origin of the choir, examples of its performances, and the reason for its unfortunate termination are presented below:

> *Joachim Lehnig:* Following our 1961 youth conference in West Berlin, we decided to offer another, even larger conference next year for youth from the West and the GDR. Then in August came the Berlin Wall. We were all depressed. We asked ourselves, "What should we do for the youth next year?" I traveled once with Bernd Schröder and asked him, "How would it be if the youth met somewhere and traveled together on bicycles to the various branches, and fashioned a choir out of the participants to present special performances composed of choir music?" "That would be great," he said. "It would be a stimulating substitute for what we had planned." I recommended the activity to Brother Burkhardt, and he thought it wasn't a bad idea. Then I approached Gerwin Baasch and said, "Gerwin, we need a choir director. Can you participate?" (2003)

> *Gerwin Baasch:* We met in Leipzig and rode our bicycles to the various branches, a kind of round trip through the GDR, including Leipzig, Erfurt, Annaberg, Freiberg, and Dresden. A few brothers sent their sleeping bags and other baggage ahead with a car. But we had a large group of youth that went on their bicycles. Choir practices were held in each branch, followed by concerts in the evening. The youth also gave talks. Everyone was very enthusiastic. After we gave our last concert in Dresden, President Burkhardt said, "Actually, it is a shame to let this choir disband." So we decided we would come together again now and then. (1991)

The "Pioneer Trek" took place between July 7 and 21, 1962. Shortly thereafter, one participant, Herbert Goliasch, wrote a detailed account of the group's daily experiences, which is found in its entirety in Appendix F. An excerpt from the first page follows:

> It is difficult to find rational words to express a great joy, which one's own feelings can hardly contain. But the "Pioneer Trek" of the youth of the Berlin Mission was nothing less than a great joy for everyone who followed the call of the two MIA missionary committees to travel to the branches and proclaim the gospel through music. To be truthful, long and wide discussions took place in advance of the trek. Not everyone was excited about sacrificing their vacation for such a "strenuous, unpeaceful, and hardly relaxing endeavor." A few youth preferred their comfort over a Church activity, and some "experienced" brothers and sisters also doubted the feasibility of the plan. But the

truthfulness of the testimony of Nephi was proven once more, who, standing before an apparent hopeless situation, said with certainty that the Lord gives man no commandment without preparing a way to accomplish it. Despite all prophecies of doom, the trek was a great thing.

In a 1991 interview, Gerwin Baasch explained how the choir functioned in years following the Pioneer Trek:

> In each branch where members of the choir lived, one member was responsible for coordinating the practice of the choir's songs. We then selected days on which the choir would assemble in various branches for a combined choir practice, which usually began on Saturday at ten a.m. and continued into the evening, often until ten p.m., with short breaks for meals and relaxation. The choir's concerts followed on Sunday.
>
> I believe the quality of those meetings was very high. We didn't just sing, but also gave short talks that matched the theme of each program. The theme might be the Apostasy, the Restoration, or the Book of Mormon, themes that met the Church's most important missionary goals. Most of the talks were given by choir members, which strengthened their testimonies and added to their enjoyment. The choir had additional positive influences far beyond its performances. For example, when choir members returned to their home branches, the easier songs that we sang were taught to other members.
>
> I have a letter from a member of the mission youth choir that read, "I joyfully recall that beautiful and spiritual time. I think about the long and difficult practices that were generally carried out by the singers with dedication and joy, without complaint, and the happy hours when we laughed together. The very beautiful concert in Leipzig, where we sang "Give us peace," remains with me today. Also that concert in Neubrandenburg! Oh yes, those were beautiful hours that I would have paid any price not to miss, hours in which I learned so very much. That time bore rich fruit, more than you probably realize."
>
> I have found that when we go into other branches today and meet former members of the youth choir, that we soon say something like, "Do you still remember those wonderful times when…" When we now come together in the evening, we often take out a folder of our choir music, sit at a piano, and sing.
>
> I believe that we helped to give many branches the opportunity to hold special meetings to which they could invite their friends. Often, there were more friends than members at the concerts. It was a time when most people were fearful of joining a church, since it led to problems on the job or with one's professional advancement. But it was a great opportunity for the youth to be active in the Church, to

> be enthusiastic, which, of course, had positive effects on their personal development and their progress within the Church. (1991)

Performances were held frequently. For example, between October 1971 and June 1972, the choir performed in Bischofswerda, Dessau, Dresden, Aschersleben, Karl-Marx-Stadt, Leipzig, Weimar, Zwickau, Görlitz, Erfurt, Halle, Mittweida, Bernburg, Halberstadt, Werdau, and Forst.

Detailed descriptions of each concert, including the choir practices, the titles of each selection, and the accompanying talks, were preserved by Marion Kirchert of Leipzig and added to the mission history. Following are excerpts from a presentation in Halle, a choir practice in Dresden, and the choir's tenth anniversary program in Dresden:

> Halle, Sunday, October 24, 1971:
>
> After Sunday School, we were served lunch, which the sisters in Halle had lovingly prepared. Strengthened thereby, we were able to begin at about 12:45 p.m. with several activities to strengthen our voices and our singing, under the direction of Brother Gerwin Baasch. We then sang with fine voices, "Der lohnendste Dienst," "Selig ist's, dem Herrn vertrauen," "Glaube der Väter," "Gib doch das Beste dem Meister," and "Ich will den Herren loben." The youth choir practice ended at 3:15.
>
> The theme of the evening performance was, "Surely the Lord God will do nothing, but he revealeth his secret unto his servants the prophets." The program included:
>
> Choir: "Ich will den Herren loben"
>
> Message: Bro. Helmut Fischer, "9th Article of Faith."
>
> Choir: "Der lohnendste Dienst"
>
> Message: Bro. Alfred Weilert, "Prophets are called by God."
>
> Choir: "Gib doch das Beste dem Meister"
>
> Message: Bro. Gerhard Müller, "Some claim that prophets don't exist today."
>
> Solo: Sis. Barbara Dittrich, "Die Heilige Stadt"
>
> Message: Bro. Walter Schiele, "We are the salt of the earth."
>
> Choir: "Glaube der Väter"

> Dresden, Saturday, November 6, 1971:
>
> The youth choir practice began at 10:15 a.m. under the direction of Bro. Lehnig. Gerwin Baasch was in Japan with the Leipzig Orchestra. The songs were practiced separately with the brothers and the sisters. First, we sang "Vorwärts, ihr Menschen" (Jean Sibelius), "Freiheitschor" (Georg Friedrich Händel), "Preis der Liebe" (Helmut Richter), and "Hebe deine Augen auf." After practicing these songs, we began to practice "Vater unser" with full strength. That was a completely new song for us. Although it often didn't sound quite right in

practice, we still sang it undauntedly, with our entire countenances beaming. We paused at about 1:30 p.m. to be strengthened by lunch. We resumed at 2:30 p.m., this time singing all together. The practice ended at 6:10 p.m. We had practiced eleven songs in about six and a half hours.

Tenth Anniversary Celebration, Dresden, September 16–17, 1972:

This gathering of the choir was very special. Not only because it is especially good when the entire choir comes together, and not only because it is wonderful to honor God with music and song and to bring joy to the members. This time we had an additional reason to come together. Such an event doesn't happen often!

We began on Saturday at 10:30 a.m. with our practice. Then we sang the song, "Ein armer Wandrer," followed by: "Wie groß ist dein Werk," "Jauchzet Berge voller Freud," "Calvary," "Vorwärts, ihr Menschen," "Die auf den Herrn hoffen," "Der lohnendste Dienst," and "Selig ist's, dem Herrn vertrauen."

After a tasty midday meal, we began to practice again: "Führ uns, mächtiger Jehova," "Glaube der Väter," "Preis der Liebe," "Wacht auf, ihr Völker," "Hosianna," "Die Himmel erzählen die Ehre Gottes," "Glaube nur," and what was absolutely essential, we also sang the song that had accompanied us throughout the ten years, "Glory, Halleluja."

After we were strengthened with coffee and cake, we returned again to practice. Gerwin Baasch led us through a very lengthy but thorough "Sitzprobe" [to determine the best seating order]. After Bro. Baasch was satisfied with the seating order, he had us practice several songs again: "Calvary," "Preis der Liebe," and "Die auf den Herrn hoffen." Our practice finally ended at 5:15 p.m. Today's was the longest and most comprehensive practice since last year.

The choir's concert followed at 6:00 p.m. After two hours, we had our evening meal. Afterward, all the choir members remained together. We wanted this day, which we had experienced in such a wonderful, spiritual manner, to be concluded in a lighter manner. We danced.

On Sunday morning the choir assembled again. We practiced the songs that we wanted to present in the sacrament meeting.

Recollections from Choir Members

Eveline Dzierzon: I sang with the youth choir. Sometimes it was every week, but usually less frequently. It was wonderful, and just as with missionary work, it was always recorded how many friends attended. Wherever we went to give a concert, it was advertised in advance, and the members also invited their friends. We were not allowed to openly proselyte, so that was our missionary contribution, and it was fun.

There were always at least twenty choir members at each performance, but usually forty, fifty, or sixty. It was a matter of who could come that day. At first, I was still too young and waited longingly, because my older sister was already a member. I think we had to be sixteen. The boys wore a white shirt and the girls wore beautiful, identical blouses, which we received from West Germany or West Berlin.

Over the years, Gerwin Baasch received numerous letters from former choir members regarding their choir experiences. Anonymous excerpts follow:

> I actually learned about the gospel through the youth choir, its enthusiasm, and the strength of the music. I remember how the strong spirit that we felt at that time greatly helped me in my daily life, then and thereafter.
>
> A special highpoint for me was singing in the Freiberg Cathedral. It gave me self-confidence. I knew that we are members of the true church of God, that Christ lives, that we are never alone, and that we need not hide, even when many of our classmates and our teachers argued against the existence of a God. "The Lord Is My Shepherd" is one of my favorite songs. The conviction that grew out of that helped me to successfully complete my studies in Weimar and to master so many other challenges.
>
> I never pictured myself as a great singer, yet I enjoyed singing. It was tremendous to sing our wonderful church hymns under your direction. We came together as young people, became acquainted with other branches, and could present our testimony of the truthfulness of the gospel of Jesus Christ through song. It was simply super to be involved, and it was especially a welcome relief to the events of every day, a time to be recharged. That time helped me greatly to strengthen and build my testimony. It was never a burden, always a joy and a reward.
>
> The time devoted to the mission youth choir was never a sacrifice. I was always happy when I could travel on the weekend and come together with members of other branches. Once, I was asked on a Saturday afternoon if I could travel to Freiberg with the youth choir. I immediately packed my things and left. It was one of the most beautiful weekends.
>
> I remember the togetherness and the teachings. The themes, quotations, and the talks were presented with boldness and spirit.
>
> The most special for me was to be together with the youth of the Church, something that I rarely had experienced earlier. It was spe-

> cial for me to sing together with them. Those gatherings brought me closer to the gospel and helped me to become acquainted with young members of other branches, because I had almost never been to a youth conference. It was like finding a new family, where I was accepted, where I found friends and experienced so much enthusiasm.
>
> It was a beautiful, spiritual time, and the camaraderie was outstanding. The practices were very strenuous, but that joyful feeling after a successful concert was a rich reward.
>
> In the choir we were "many" and not so alone as in a classroom or on the job.
>
> For me, it wasn't only a singing of songs but rather a source of strength, which I did not experience at home.
>
> I remember especially the dedication of the meeting house in Leipzig, the former movie house. That blue sign over the door served as a magnet for the curious and the investigator. It was amazing, how people doing their shopping nearby would come in, sit down, and listen to our choir practice. I will never forget the spirit I felt at that concert.

Eveline Dzierzon had mentioned earlier the beautiful blouses that the girls in the choir wore. She went on to say, "Unfortunately, we couldn't wear them very long. It happened suddenly. The choir was disbanded. I don't know why, but we were all very sad" (2004). The last concert took place on December 9, 1973, in Werdau. Thirty-two years later, President Burkhardt told the author the reason for that decision:

> I personally was not pleased that the choir was disbanded, but I was told to do so. Earlier, I had been asked by a visiting Church authority to explain the reason for the mission youth choir. I said that the choir carries out missionary work through concerts in the branches, in order to bring friends into our meeting houses. After some passage of time, I was suddenly informed by the area presidency in Frankfurt that I had to disband the choir because such a program didn't exist elsewhere in the Church. We had danced a little out of order, but with success. I don't know who was actually most influential in the process, or how information about the choir reached the First Presidency, the Council of Twelve, or the area office in Frankfurt.
>
> It was not possible at that time to go from door to door. But what could be nicer than missionary work through music? Under the direction of Brothers Baasch, Lehnig, and Schulze, the choir actually conducted missionary work. It presented special sacrament meetings and concerts to which members easily could bring friends. The choir was

well known. However, that also meant that some of the youth were often not in their home branches, which upset some people. It is understandable that when the youth were missing, some branches were almost dead. I understand both sides. But the choir was disbanded because such a thing didn't exist elsewhere in the Church. I didn't have the right to oppose what these brothers told me, although I knew the work of the choir, valued it, supported it, and personally traveled with it at times. I received instructions to disband the choir, and I informed its leaders of my instructions. They were sour, rightfully so. I also didn't feel it was the right thing to do. (2005)

Gerwin Baasch: I was informed in December 1973 that the choir had to be disbanded. We all greatly regretted it since it was for us in the GDR an opportunity to openly present the Church to the public. In a country like the USA, where everyone could listen to the Tabernacle Choir every Sunday on the radio, it might be hard to understand what a wonderful opportunity we had to do missionary work through the choir in the GDR. Very unfortunate. (2005)

Joachim Lehnig: Brother Burkhardt said we had to stop with the choir. The youth should all work actively in their branches and do missionary work there. We were all very sad, but obedience is better than sacrifice. Brother Burkhardt gave the instruction and we couldn't continue it on our own. We were obedient. (2004)

Eva Kretzschmar: We had to be sixteen to sing in the choir. I wanted to begin in the very year it was disbanded. Branch choirs were okay, even later at the stake level, but in our case, the choir involved the entire mission, the entire GDR. Those were things, guidelines, that we always implemented precisely as written. Whether they were always meant as they came to us, that is questionable. There are things that were sometimes so finicky, but perhaps it was also right. (2004)

Joachim Albrecht: We had many programs in the Church that came about through personal initiative, where we did something to attract attention. I think that the mission youth choir was a great idea in that spirit. It held the youth together and strengthened the branches, enabling them to do missionary work. Each year we planned a special meeting with appropriate themes for the talks, but especially surrounded by music. Branch conferences were also done in that manner, but the music that a small branch could offer wasn't much. So the mission youth choir was there to help us. Members from neighboring branches joined with us on those occasions. We had beautiful meetings organized with the help of the choir. (2004)

Seminary and Institute

The Church's seminary program was introduced in the GDR in 1980 at the request of Church leaders in Frankfurt. Members described how they became acquainted with the program and how it functioned in their country.

Carmen Schlegel: The seminary program was introduced to us during an interesting youth conference in Dresden in the summer of 1980. It was a very special youth conference, a spiritual time when we had seminary classes every day. Beginning in September, it was held regularly once a week, and later, as I recall, we had a Super Saturday every other month when the seminary students from the entire district came together. (2004)

Manfred Schütze: We actually didn't have enough teachers, since everyone was already busy with three or four callings. But we said, "Okay, seminary is important," and the program was instantly received with great enthusiasm by the youth. As district president, I also taught seminary in our home or in meeting houses. We brought the youth together by car, just as it was done around the world. Our weekly lesson consisted of one page, copied by typewriter, from the manual. The seminary manual had thirty-four lessons for each year, and only the teacher had the written material. The students just had their scriptures.

The youth were enthusiastic, and we lost very few of them in those years. In fact, the spirituality increased. Previously, our youth conferences consisted mostly of social activities. Now, seminary was added to each conference. We had a high standard, and that led to greater spirituality. During those years, more than 90 percent of the students completed seminary. Later, we had similar experiences with the institute program.

We also discussed many issues related to atheism, especially issues that the youth were confronted with in school or at universities. Since I had experienced that in my youth and during my own university experience, I knew as a youth leader how to help them, because the Church had the answers. For example, the materialists always posed the question in the advanced education classes, "What came first, spirit or matter?" We read in section 93 of Doctrine and Covenants that spirit and matter are eternal. Eternal means always. Then we read from the teaching of Joseph Smith, where he commented on those scriptures. That helped the youth, and there were other similar examples. (1991)

Klaus Peter Bartsch: I was fortunate that my mother was a seminary teacher, so I had the opportunity to read directly in the manual. I regularly soaked up that material. I studied it for hours, because I found there the explanations that helped us understand the gospel better. The seminary and institute programs were really a source of strength. (1993)

Our Experiences as Youth in the GDR

Four members, born between 1954 and 1960, met in Görlitz on October 12, 2003, in a joint interview about their experiences as youth in the GDR. The interview began with just one question, "What in your opinion is the most important subject that should be addressed when compiling a history of the Church in the GDR?" The immediate and unanimous answer: "The youth conferences!" The discussion proceeded from that topic without further questions, driven solely by the interests of the interviewees. The four participants were Michael Lehmann (ML), Rolf-Thomas Lehmann (RL), Ingrid Przybylla (IP), and Frank Fuchs (FF):

> *FF:* I recall the youth conferences very well. We had one in Dresden every summer. The effort that was required to plan and provide for a group of eighty to a hundred youth was enormous—food, travel, lodging. It was a special experience for me, to leave my home and bed and sleep on air mattresses with my friends.
>
> *RL:* It was something exceptional, which we did not take for granted, as is sometimes the case today with our children. It was a taste of Zion, finally an opportunity to be together with 20, 40, 60, or 120 youth of similar age and principles. We usually met in August, initially with the wide age span of twelve to thirty. Then the minimum age was raised to fourteen. Later, we met separately on successive weeks, ages fourteen to eighteen and eighteen to thirty. My first youth conference in 1973 was still for everyone from twelve to thirty. I was quite small, the others rather big. But I looked up to them, and it was wonderful. The idea, that we could openly sing with a guitar was something that I had never experienced, it was forbidden or at least discouraged at that time. That fascinated me. The Church had to call these gatherings "Youth Religious Services." We were counseled not to say "Youth Conferences."
>
> *FF:* When we had dances, the windows had to be covered and the music couldn't be too loud, because units of the Soviet army and special police were lodged close by.
>
> *ML:* What especially impressed me was the dedication of the sisters and brothers in the mission presidency and the MIA leadership, who prepared these activities weeks in advance. The feeding and lodging of 120 people couldn't be left to chance. Everything was done professionally. It was amazing, what was actually possible in the GDR! Food items were available in large quantities that otherwise were rarely seen. While it was advantageous to buy in large quantities, it was evident that the Church also had good connections. Some of the

youth who attended were not members of the Church, including investigators who were later baptized or who married members of the Church.

FF: But it was always a relatively closed group, and very few nonmembers attended. The number of attendees who were not known to us from previous gatherings was small. Therefore, wherever I travel today, for example, to Neubrandenburg, in another district, I know all the members. We knew each other by name, street and house number.

RL: When I was in the army in a huge regiment, I assumed that I was the only Mormon there. Once, I wanted to at least attend an Evangelical church service on Sunday, but I didn't know where to find one. Someone told me that another soldier attended church services somewhere. I assumed he was Evangelical. I went to him and said I wasn't Evangelical, but rather a Mormon, a member of the Church of Jesus Christ of Latter-day Saints. He said he was also a member. At first, I thought he was kidding me. Certainly, he must have heard that I was a Mormon and wanted to make fun of me. After all, I knew every Mormon of my age in the entire GDR. He had to struggle to prove to me that he really was a member of our Church. He had only recently been baptized in Erfurt, one of very few converts, and hadn't yet attended a youth conference. I had not thought that I would ever find another member in the army, especially one who had never attended a youth conference.

ML: When we visited a cultural site in Dresden, our 120-member group would always attract attention. Even if we went in four groups, we were still four times 30 youth in a museum. I can imagine that our large numbers caused the police to be worried, since any large assembly of people caused that reaction on their part. When we were in a museum once, a supervisor asked if we were an FDJ group. We said we were not, and named our church. The lady was astounded and said, "I have never seen such a disciplined group!" Our public outings were always disciplined. Disciplined behavior was simply an unwritten law. We were always aware that negative behavior of an individual could damage the reputation of the group, our mission president, and even the Church. Not that we behaved out of fear, but we all had the feeling, "I never want my behavior to bring our church leaders into dispute or endanger them!"

RL: During one youth conference, we were all lodged in the huge Dresden meeting house. The mission president was also sleeping there. There were other occupants in that house, above us, who felt disturbed by our level of noise during the night. They phoned President Burkhardt and complained to him. Suddenly he was standing in front of us in his pajamas! We felt ashamed that we had disturbed him and the other occupants and tried to be more quiet. Brother

Burkhardt was for us at that time what we would consider an area president today. For us, he had the character of a general authority.

FF: My experiences at youth conference were a major foundation of my testimony today. Someone else might have had other experiences at home or in their home branches, but I gained my testimony through the youth conferences. Once, a much older dear brother came to us in the night and requested that we should sleep, and talk less. I had the feeling, "Dear Brother, we could do anything right now except that. What we are doing is important for me right now and for the next decade!" We sat on our air mattresses next to each other and talked about everything that concerned us. For me, it was the most important thing. Someone said, "There are nights in which you must talk about your testimony, when you cannot sleep." It was difficult to explain that feeling to that dear brother, but I am happy today to have had those experiences. My friends on the air mattresses then are today the branch presidents, bishops, or members of stake presidencies. The GDR youth are today the Church leaders in our region.

RL: Another result of the youth conferences was the high percentage of marriages. Not all, but very many marriages come to pass because of those events. Otherwise I would have had few chances to marry within the Church. When one of my work associates asks me today, "Why did you marry a wife from Leipzig?" I answer, "Because I wanted to marry a Mormon." They don't understand that we lived like people in the Diaspora. As a result, members throughout the former East Germany are frequently related to one another.

ML: The strong middle-aged group of members was missing during our youth, not only as a result of the war, but through inactivity. There were the elderly and then us. So my age group was pulled into responsible positions at an early age. For example, in 1972, at age eighteen, I was a counselor in a branch presidency. Incidentally, there weren't many alternate attractions in those days. The youth were often reminded that they were the future leadership. We believed that and earnestly tried to turn the vision of our leaders into reality. We used the strength gained from the youth conferences to prepare ourselves for service in the Church, to be able and worthy so the Lord could use us.

In the 1970s and 1980s, we were challenged to prepare and conduct youth conferences for the next generation. We were only twenty or twenty-five years old and ventured rather far ahead in that work. Sometimes our leaders had to tell us, "Please don't plan to hold religious services outside." Out of the safety of our previous experiences at youth conferences, we asked, "And why not?" Maybe we didn't have the wider perspective, which the mission presidency had learned in the past through their problems and experiences with the government. However, we also had our own experiences and had learned to work, study, and serve within the existing GDR society, in the army, etc. We were brave enough to take a further step forward, were sometimes held back a little by our leaders, but were always ready to put to use the freedom that we felt existed at that time.

RL: We perceived our service in the Church as an opportunity, not a burden. Nevertheless, we did far more than would be normal for members of our age. Said in a positive sense, we were a bit precocious in carrying out our spiritual responsibilities. However, that didn't damage us. I was a Sunday School president as a seventeen-year-old priest. That was a large responsibility, but also a tremendous training opportunity, which we treasured.

FF: I grew up in a branch with an average attendance of 150. I served as a counselor in the Sunday School. When I moved to a smaller branch, I received many other assignments, one after another, but often simultaneously. I found that I was able to learn much that today would be called "management" through those assignments. We were told, in effect, "Now you are the Sunday School or Quorum president. Do it, and then consider how to do it better."

IP: As we began to assume more responsibility, we still didn't have original copies of the Church's teaching materials for the auxiliary organizations. Everything had to be typed with multiple copies. Sometimes we also had to prepare our own material. The scriptures were our only foundation. For that reason, we used them intensively and came to know them. That helps us today when we want to share our testimony.

RL: Before the Wende, we didn't have many opportunities for leisure activities, so you could say that after our jobs, the Church became our entire life. There wasn't much else for us. Many members were happy when after working hours, after the political chaos of the day, we could become involved in church activities and experience or create something that functioned well, which brought satisfaction. The Church was a refuge for many, where you could breathe again. Therefore, activity levels in the branch were high. We could not understand it, when we heard that few people in the West were willing to go on a mission. We thought that we would have gone immediately if our social circumstances had been different. Today, we can better understand that situation.

ML: In the GDR, we clearly did not have the ability to travel far. Our family spent its annual vacation within our own borders: Thuringia's forest, Zittauer mountains, Elbsandstein mountains, Baltic Sea, or short trips to Poland and Czechoslovakia. Nevertheless, I don't think that we were actually "imprisoned," as is so often claimed. I was always free to live according to my beliefs. After the Wende, there were many more types of temptation. We didn't have many opportunities to do bad things because they never appeared in our vision. The party had already forbidden it, so we didn't have as many opportunities to make decisions. It was basically a dictatorship. Only today do I realize how free I actually am. Our country was flooded with a market economy that can divert us from our good intentions.

Many GDR politicians also thought that everyone would willingly work to strengthen the state from the time they woke up in the morning. Indirectly, we did strengthen the state, not because we were great fans of socialism, but because we lived and worked here. We tried to perform our work honestly, just like citizens of any country. That tended to benefit the system under which we lived. In my first class in 1974, at the engineering technical high school in Cottbus, we were greeted by the instructor with the words, "Dear comrades and independent Communists!" I knew who the comrades were, but who were the independent Communists? He meant that all students who didn't belong to the SED Party were nonetheless Communists since they lived and studied here. We [Mormons] were often accused of being too friendly to everyone rather than fighting against the government. We were also criticized when our mission presidency met and talked with our government's leaders. However, that was the assignment given us by our prophet, whom Brother Richter often quoted, "Soften their hearts!" We preferred to communicate peacefully and calmly with our fellow men, not to gain favors from the state, but because we placed God as our highest priority, and we just wanted to be able to live our religion according to the dictates of our conscience, which we were granted. Through our actions, we were recognized as loyal, hardworking, and honest people.

FF: Everyone had to come to terms with or compromise in some way, but that didn't require a person to violate his principles. In school, people were amazed at my knowledge of the political economics of socialism or scientific communism. I had already learned in Church how to handle philosophical arguments.

ML: We were recognized in our school years for our dedication to principles. I was scheduled, for example, for a competitive sport activity that took place on a Sunday. My sport instructor was convinced that he needed me for a relay race, but I didn't want to participate on Sunday. His response was, "How can parents deny their children the sporting spirit? That is not fair or comradely." Suddenly, I heard myself as a second or third grader say in front of the entire sports group, "It has nothing to do with my parents. It is my decision. I don't wish to participate in competition on Sunday." To which he responded, "Everyone listen. He does have a sporting spirit. In fact, he has his own conviction, and I'll accept that." That might have been the start of my own testimony, as I expressed my own convictions for the first time. That was an example from school sports. Whenever we said, "No thank you, I don't do that for religious reasons," or "That doesn't conform to my religious beliefs," it was accepted. Of course, that also meant that someone could answer, "I accept your convictions, but I nevertheless cannot allow it." Your confession was both a protection and a target.

Dedication to principle can also affect other aspects of life. During my studies from 1974 to 1978 in Cottbus, the security person at the school, who also reported to the Stasi, asked me one day to report any disturbances among the students. I was able to avoid that burden with a quote from the Book of Mormon, that all secret workings were evil in God's eyes. Of course, I was observed more closely after that.

IP: There was a Stasi informer in my office. When he began to talk with me, the other colleagues warned me about him. The party leader in that office wanted to recruit me for the SED. I declined, for Christian reasons, but he didn't give up. When he later left that office, he asked me about the Bible. I gave him one as a present.

RL: An active Marxist I knew in the army had a political perspective that he honestly represented and which we frankly discussed. He spoke up for me when I requested leave to attend a Church conference, which was granted. Committed Communists and Christians often had a good relationship, because each honestly lived their convictions. We were also taught to practice the 12th Article of Faith, and the leaders of the state recognized that. We tried to call good that which was good. Even when the GDR's system was irritating, we tried to be loyal to the state.

FF: We were prepared to support the government when it also supported us, when it allowed us to live our religion. I would not place the chairman of the State Council above Jesus Christ. So the question of recognizing the government was always a matter of making personal discretionary decisions on specific issues. The Lord's principles were, for me, the deciding measure. One of those principles says something about the relationship to my country. Everyone must constantly evaluate and decide on each situation. Someone can misjudge another's decision from outside, because he hasn't experienced that situation. But that is how I acted.

ML: In summary, it can be said that we loved our country but not the government!

FF: There was no explanation, no commentary about the 12th Article of Faith. Just some manuals and the scriptures.

RL: A copy of the book *Articles of Faith* by James E. Talmage was in every branch and in every home. The 12th Article of Faith was applied as written. Regardless if someone lived in a kingdom like the Swedish members, or in a presidential democracy like the American members or in a socialist state, there were no extra guidelines or instructions.

ML: Of course, we wished for printed manuals or temple visits, which were denied us. But we knew that we were not responsible before God for those restrictions. I often heard these words in prayers,

"Please bless those who lead this state, that they will permit us to serve thee." Such phraseology taught people not to be negative, but rather to nurture love of neighbor and loyalty to all fellow men, regardless of their personal religious beliefs, or even when they had none. Such attitudes also made us acceptable in the society in which we lived. Wherever we worked, whether in a factory or an office, people gladly worked together with a Christian, even with a confessing Mormon. When we were brought into responsible positions, we brought with us honesty, trust, and reliability, without opposition to the state. That we were not Communists and represented a different philosophy was well known and didn't have to be additionally emphasized.

RL: Members of the Church were accepted in factories and offices as equals. We were given responsibility as deputy leaders of a group or area, but rarely as the leader. That was reserved for SED members.

When I, as a school boy, was given an award for academic achievement, the document carried a socialist emblem or slogan. I still have those awards. I received them for my zeal for learning. To retain them didn't make me a fellow traveler of the ideology of the system. He who lived in the Stone Age and participated in the hunt for mammoths, brought something home for his fellow men and was appropriately rewarded. But his participation did not automatically make him into a committed mammoth hunter, just because he was born in the Stone Age.

A student with very good Russian language skills, who was also a member of the German-Soviet-Friendship (DSF) group, was eligible for the Johann-Gottlieb-Herder silver medal. My Russian skills were very good, but I was not a member of DSF. The school wanted to award me with the medal, but I didn't want to join the organization. My mother, who also was not a DSF member, encouraged me to reconsider my decision. I did, joined the DSF, and received the medal.

FF: The philosophy of socialism said that external conditions were to be changed by force, if necessary, and that people would then develop into socialistic beings. It was clear to us, however, that the opposite was true. We had learned in the Church that Jesus Christ and his teachings would change the hearts of people and then they would change their external environment.

RL: We were not allowed to teach our beliefs publicly, but we could engage with other religions. State agencies, schools, and parties didn't want to hear from us, but religious organizations invited us to talk with them. In fact, we had those opportunities more often then than now. We had good discussions in the 1980s. The Church's public affairs activities in the GDR included visiting churches and talking with their members. With the building of the Freiberg Temple came curiosity and interest. The Temple's open house led to an invitation to make a presentation to a church group in Görlitz.

FF: We were invited by a Catholic youth group. In his introduction, the leader that evening began with ugly comments about the Mormons, the temple, etc. We sat quietly in the second row, when suddenly another youth leader stood up and said, "I'm amazed that our guests are still here. If someone had spoken about my faith in that manner, I would have left. We should let them speak, for that was the purpose of this evening." Then we were allowed to make our presentation about the Church. Those in attendance knew that the opening remarks were wrong.

RL: At the end of the evening, everyone turned toward the cross in prayer and we heard these words, "Please forgive us, that we injured brothers of another faith." That was a true ecumenical act of faith, not of an organization. Four or five of the members then invited us to their home for further discussion, where we spoke about the temple until one in the morning. Those are examples of encounters with people of other faiths. Today, there is less interest in the teachings of our Church. We were discovered in those days as a religious group on the periphery, which was not meant negatively. People just didn't know much about us and wanted to know more.

FF: I'd like to add something about army service. The question that I faced was not whether I would serve, but what to make of that time. I allowed myself to be led by the Lord then as before. I didn't abandon the training that I had received from childhood, whether I went to school, into the army, or during my later studies. I went my way and soon realized that people accepted me for what I was.

RL: I don't know of any member who refused military service. Most of them served the basic period of eighteen months. During my time, I had experiences similar to those a missionary has today: leave home, stand on your own two feet, do something worthwhile, declare your beliefs, and always teach others about your faith. That was my experience, even if my son, a full-time missionary, would say, "Father, that was no full-time mission." It was for me. I went into the army with a little New Testament and with a father's written blessing. That's all I took, because I didn't know what was permitted. My triple combination, which was printed in Frankfurt/Main, stayed home. Later, I took it and even the Church's publication, the *Stern*. The *Stern* was legally imported in Poland, and came via them to us. It circulated through the company. As I noticed what was permitted and what was not, I became more and more open.

ML: I was impressed when I heard that President Monson visited with Chairman Erich Honecker in 1988. Somehow, I was not shocked or surprised. For me, it was the next logical step. We had watched the efforts of our mission presidency since our youth as they guided and trained us. They always had to justify the development of the Church to government leaders. We wanted more progress, were ready to stand up for the Church, and were inspired with the thought: The Lord is with us!

RL: In 1988, I was allowed to go to West Germany at the death of an uncle. At the train station, I bought a newspaper, *Neues Deutschland,* with the report of President Monson's visit with the leaders of the state. I felt that I had finally been recognized as a Christian and no longer limited to worshiping God in a backyard church building or in a former factory building. But acquaintances and work associates criticized us. "Why should you as such a small church have such a large article on one entire page of *Neues Deutschland*?" But the GDR had finally acted in accordance with its theory that all churches were equal, whether a large or a small church! No discrimination!

A BYU television station also came to our country at that time, and a reporter asked me what I thought of President Monson's visit. I tried to say that it was wonderful that we now had a temple, a patriarch, new meeting houses, the *Stern,* the seminary and institute program, but we still needed full-time missionaries! We didn't know that missionaries had just been approved in that meeting, and that they would arrive soon. The reporter also asked, "Are you happy here?" My happiness could only be complete after the missionaries arrived. We couldn't do enough as part-time missionaries after our work day.

FF: We read in the scriptures of miracles thousands of years ago. Now we have experienced our own miracles. I was not present when Elder Monson gave his dedicatory prayer, but I have a copy of it. I lived with it and saw the promises fulfilled. It impressed me to know that God is predictable. He knows me and cares for me. That knowledge sustained me then and now. But I cannot give my testimony of modern miracles to my children. The youth of today must gain their testimony under even more severe conditions and circumstances. It is harder today. While the freedom to choose correctly is greater now, so are temptations like pornography, which are just one click away. It is harder because so much brutality confronts us today, brutality that can lead to feelings of hopelessness.

RL: West German members asked us, "How can you live as a Mormon in the GDR?" We said, "Well," even when we would have preferred a different government. With few exceptions, we didn't have pornography in the GDR. Prostitution was prohibited, and few people had weapons. There were few political extremists. I didn't know of these things and was not enticed by any of them. Therefore, I could answer the West German questioner and say, "Well." Of course, in return, we had this "state religion" of Marxism-Leninism, and that irritated us tremendously.

FF: Whether it was easier or harder then is a big question. I was taught to ask the Lord to help us find solutions to problems. Everyone who takes drugs loses some of his decision-making ability. He is

> no longer himself. Those are problems we didn't know in our youth. We had other problems. In my opinion, they were not as extreme as those with which we presently live.

When Michael Lehmann transcribed the above interview for the author, he added this final thought:

> This interview should convey to the attentive reader something about our experiences as youth in the GDR. Regardless of what ideology ruled then or rules now, this is our homeland, in which we were born. To be actively involved in the affairs of our country does not mean that one was necessarily a supporter of the existing dominant philosophy. It is possible under any condition to be a life-confirming, sincere, and honest Christian, who is earnestly engaged in applying tolerance and freedom of choice in a meaningful manner.

10 Education and Employment

Every citizen has the right to employment, and to free choice thereof, according to society's requirements.... The state guarantees the opportunity to advance from one educational level to another... based on performance, society's requirements, and the social structure of the population. (Articles 24 and 26, GDR Constitution)

*He is a master craftsman of the old school, whom you would no longer expect to find in a country of state-owned companies. He is a specialist in automobile electronics who has established his own business with three employees, one apprentice, and an office clerk.... Within the niches of the GDR, within the limits of its small freedoms, his example shows that more is possible than we think. (*Münchner Abendzeitung*, a West German newspaper, October 25, 1986, in an article about Frank Apel)*

Challenged by the Church to give their best effort in all things, the members in the GDR have been successful in daily life as skilled workers, engineers, doctors, and independent craftsmen. (Presidency of the Church in the GDR, 1988)

Experiences in Elementary School

Joachim Meyer: We had no trouble in school or elsewhere until the government was formed in 1949. However, beginning in the 1950s, there was significant discrimination if you were active in a church. Restrictions were placed on those who said, "I'm a member of the Church." (1989)

Eva Kretzschmar: My school years were not very pleasant. You could not talk about religion, since the state was officially atheistic. We were subjected to nasty remarks, were laughed at. The teachers discriminated against us. They let us know that our beliefs and activities were nonsense, that we were engaged in baseless fantasies. That wasn't universal. Many accepted us. But others constantly made verbal jabs that hurt children when they were embarrassed in front of the class. (2004)

Andreas Kretzschmar: There was a difference between city and village schools. I attended a village school where many religious people lived. There were three Mormons in my class of thirty children, and a total of five in the school, out of about two hundred students. There were also many Protestant students. The state was atheistic, and the education was oriented toward atheism, but I actually had few problems because the classes in the village were filled with more Christians than in the city. (2004)

Lothar Hubert: As a schoolchild, I had to stand up and let the entire class laugh at me. Their goal was to embarrass me so I would give up my beliefs. When I was about twelve, I had to learn to defend my religion. I stood up, and I was embarrassed, but not because of the gospel. Thereafter I was proud that I had stood firm. Later, as an adult, I always asked the teacher to come to my house and said, "I'm a Mormon and I do not want my children to experience what I experienced, being laughed at. We should be tolerated and respected." I also referred to the laws of the land that prohibited discrimination. (1993)

Klaus Peter Bartsch: We were constantly taught Marxism-Leninism. You could not fail that subject, and you had to take a position in regard to it. We often approached the subject by writing, "Dialectical materialism teaches that..." In that way, we weren't saying what our opinion was. But that wasn't acceptable to many teachers. They wanted us to take a personal position. But we continued to write, "Marxism-Leninism teaches..." That way, I didn't violate my own conscience. We discussed this problem often with our children. In family home evenings and at church, they learned correct teachings and how to cope in school. We taught them how to approach philosophical challenges, so they wouldn't succumb to what they heard. (1993)

Manfred Heller: Marxism, Leninism, and political economics of socialism were required subjects. It was called "citizenship" in elementary school. While everyone had to deal with it, you didn't have to agree with it, i.e., you had to be able to discuss it orally or in written school assignments, without necessarily endorsing it. Personally, I didn't have any problem in school because I made it clear from the outset that I belonged to the Church and had a different philosophy. When our children entered school, I sometimes invited the teacher and the school principal to our home and explained the position of our Church, that we strongly support family life, work diligently and honestly, respect our physical and social environment, and care for others in society. Most people accepted that. (1991)

Herbert Heidler: The evolution of man was taught as fact. We often used our family home evenings to compare and contrast those teaching with the gospel and to assist our children to know how to handle these issues in school. The problem wasn't so great that it overwhelmed us. We didn't fear those teachings; in fact, they caused us to consider, compare, and discuss these things, so that our children could develop their own strong principles and perspectives. (1993)

Klaus-Peter Kretzschmar: Our children had to live with conflict. They were taught things in school that were opposed to the teachings they received at home. It began with the story of creation. "Pure nonsense," they were told. They were taught for eight hours in school, then they came home where the parents explained it differently. But we were successful in raising our children to know what was right. Our teachers in Primary and Sunday School also were a great help. The children learned that not everything they were taught in school was correct. So they had to learn to adjust. That wasn't always easy, but they managed it from the start. (1993)

Michael Schult: Actually, these differences never bothered me because I learned early on to distinguish between facts and philosophies. Facts can be taught and learned. A philosophy of life cannot be taught. A person develops that himself, over time. (1993)

Jürgen Pabst: We grew up with these differences. That was our life. Certainly, there were confrontations. On the one hand, we were taught in church that God created man, and we have a testimony of that. The school taught that man evolved from lower forms of life. Naturally, our children asked us about that, and we explained that God is our father and that he created these things. In their school assignments, some of our youth wrote what they had been taught in school and added at the end, "That is what we are taught. I have a different opinion." In that way, the teacher could judge their knowledge and not their opinion. I learned what was taught in school, and when required, repeated it. But I let it be known that it was not my personal opinion. (1993)

Jürgen Schiebold: We had to stand up for our principles, and that helped us become stronger in those principles. That was especially important in school. The teachers tried to convince us that the path we were pursuing as Christians was not correct. They tried to show us that Marxism-Leninism was the better philosophy and that we should go that way. As a child, I didn't have the necessary arguments to confront the teacher. As a youth of seventeen or eighteen, it was much easier to talk about it, to discuss those differences. But despite all the criticism and teasing that went along with the school experience, I never felt that my freedom had been restricted. (1993)

Participation in the Young Pioneers and Free German Youth Programs

Frank Apel: All four of my children were in the Young Pioneers and none of them fell away from the Church. The children were always enthusiastic at the beginning because they received a blue scarf and a pin. Later, they had to search the house for the scarf. I didn't have any concerns about their participation, and the Church didn't take a stand on it. We said, "Everyone must make their own decision, it is up to the parents." It was our duty to plant the gospel in the hearts of our children, and when they had a testimony of the gospel, the Pioneers didn't harm them. (1991)

Jens Schlegel: I was a Young Pioneer. That went until the fourth grade, when it was called Thälmann-Pioneers. At first we wore a blue scarf and later a red scarf. Then starting with the seventh or eighth grade, I became a member of FDJ. That was just a natural thing to do, to join. In both organizations, you learned and did things similar to what we did with the Boy Scouts or the Young Women's program in our Church. We sometimes helped older people. We had a slogan, "Improve our cities and towns," and we had related work assignments, called "Subbotnik," where we cleaned the streets or the sides of roads. Nothing much was said whether you participated or not, but it was always better to participate now and then in such an activity. (2004)

Carmen Schlegel: I didn't participate in either organization because my parents said we had the Church. They taught many things similar to the Church's programs, respect for older people, etc. There were members of other churches in our area who also didn't join either organization. I didn't have any problems. Once, the teacher said something to my father, but he said "no" and that was it. Once, May 1st fell on a Sunday. We were supposed to go marching on May 1st, but I attended church instead. At the end of the year, it was noted in my school report card that I had missed one day without an excuse, because I didn't march and attended church instead. My father objected, and the notation was removed. (2004)

Eveline Dzierzon: The Pioneers met in the afternoon, always in conflict with our Primary, so we chose to attend Primary. I never met with the

Pioneers. When I started an apprenticeship, I told my instructor what church I attended and she never asked me to join the FDJ. But there was another girl, an Evangelical, who also didn't want to join. The instructor insisted that she join. Apparently, that girl was just a "normal" Christian, but I was different and the teacher accepted that and never made any effort to change my mind. I had two sisters, who also did not join the Pioneers. We went to a village school, and they gave us a little more freedom. I took the same approach with my children. I explained to the responsible people in advance that we had our religion and wanted to live in accordance with it, and we didn't have any problem with our children. (2004)

Reiner Dzierzon: I didn't join the Pioneers or the FDJ and had no problem. Our family was well known in the city and we were accepted as such. They knew what church we attended. (2004)

Lothar Ebisch: I let my children choose. We had raised them in the principles of the gospel. They had to go to school, but I never forced them to join those organizations. As a result one of my boys and our youngest daughter did not join. Nothing was said to me, perhaps because I was also a person of some status in the community. No one would have dared to challenge our decision. (2003)

Andreas Kretzschmar: I joined the FDJ because they had interesting programs and activities. After I had completed my studies, I worked in a large company, where I was asked to join the party. I declined, saying that I had a different philosophy of life and that I engage with society in other ways. That decision did not necessarily contribute to my professional advancement, but I also did not notice any direct negative impact. I learned that a person could be successful while remaining true to his principles, without being confrontational. I would have had problems if I had always stood in opposition. Being engaged in good causes doesn't necessarily mean that we should always support the existing system, but it does pay to stand up for the good. (2004)

Beate Werner Hall: I did not join the Pioneers. When it came time to choose a profession, however, I could have had problems if I wasn't a member of FDJ. I joined late, in the ninth grade. It gave me more options. (1993)

Manfred Heller: During my school years, from 1948 to 1960, I was able to complete my Abitur without joining the FDJ. Later, it was different for my children, and we left that decision to them, whether to join or not. All of them chose not to join the FDJ. That was a difficult decision, because most of their schoolmates did join. (1991)

Jürgen Pabst: I must say that I had absolutely no problems in school. I was a member of the Young Pioneers. That was common with us. It was difficult to avoid it. However, I never joined the FDJ. I was able to avoid that, without having any negative consequences. (1993)

Hans Schult: When our children entered school, my wife went to the teacher and said, "Our children are raised religiously at home. If you have any problems, please invite us in. We will talk with you, but we do not want our children to be burdened by these issues." Our children didn't have any problems, but our son was the only Mormon in his class, and he came home one day and said that he wanted to attend the Young Pioneers. The next day he said, "The Pioneers meet on Wednesday afternoon and I've been invited to attend." My wife went to the school, talked with the teacher, and told her, "We are not opposed to our son meeting with the Pioneers, but we have religious instruction in our Church on Wednesday afternoon, and he attends those classes." Two weeks later our son came home again and said, "I can meet with the Pioneers after all. Their meetings have been changed to Tuesday." (1991)

Henry Burkhardt: When children entered school, they were automatically enrolled in the Young Pioneers, of course with the permission of the parents. Since it was my personal conviction that our children should not participate, we didn't approve. That was not well received, because the teachers were judged by whether 100 percent of their class was enrolled. Our daughter began school in September, and her teacher made an appointment to visit with us later that year. She spent an hour in our home, but didn't say a word about enrollment in the Pioneers. As she prepared to leave, I asked, "Have you forgotten to discuss something with us?" She said, "Do you mean the Young Pioneers? Oh, forget about that. I will accept your decision." With that, the issue was resolved for us. Many other members thought they must participate, and they immediately enrolled their children.

I recall my son's experiences. Because they valued his attendance and opinion, they combined the FDJ meeting with a school class so that he could attend. The FDJ held a roll call ceremony every Monday, where the students assembled in the school's court in uniform. He was always the only one who appeared without an FDJ shirt. That was noticed, but as the result of personal discussions with the school director and teachers, together with his academic performance, we didn't have any problems. (1991)

A related youth program of the state, the Jugendweihe, was described previously in Chapter 3. The Church did not take a stand on members' participation.

Joachim Meyer: The Jugendweihe, when considered as an oath or vow, is a promise to be loyal to the state. It was not expected that the youth thereby join the party. The vow was just a pure formality. We didn't take it so seriously, so most of the youth participated, just to get it out of the way. A few members said, "No, we will not participate," but then there were consequences. All of my children participated, and they didn't turn out any better or any worse as a result. (1989)

Lothar Ebisch: Three of my children attended the Jugendweihe. That was not a problem. It did not entail any political obligation. It was a pleasant celebration, and the youth received a certificate and some flowers. That was it.

Herbert Heidler: The decision to participate in the Jugendweihe was left to the parents and the children. The Church didn't make a recommendation. Personally, I let my children participate. The Nazi regime had a similar mandatory program when I was a young person. I went, experienced it, and returned home, exactly as if I had gone to see a movie. For that reason, I also allowed my children to go to the Jugendweihe. It had no significant influence on the nature of man. One of our Articles of Faith says that we should be subject to those who have authority over us. That was also my opinion. But some members said, "No, they want you to swear to be loyal to the state," and they didn't want to do that. Often there were consequences when the young people tried to obtain a good apprenticeship or attend school of higher education. (1993)

Discrimination in Higher Education

Manfred Heller: Yes, there were problems regarding admission to higher education, universities, etc. Priority was given to people who complied with the regime or the dominant society. Naturally, they were advanced faster, because it was in the state's interest to bring people who believed in and were adhering to the system into responsible positions. (1991)

Günter Schulze: I wanted to study and become an engineer in foundry technics. That was not approved, because I had worked for the Church without pay for two years as a missionary. Each time I applied, my missionary service was noted. I had to show my work history, and there was a gap during my missionary time. I had to enter, "Active for the Church." Our son couldn't follow the profession he wanted. He wanted to be a trainer, and that meant educator, and a Christian couldn't do that because he couldn't support Marxism-Leninism. Many of our youth couldn't pursue their desired profession. That was sad. My children understood and didn't complain. They said, "We are Christians, we will remain Christians and we'll act as Christians. We will do what is necessary." That was the end of the problem. (1993)

Henry Burkhardt: We had a girl in one branch who did join the FDJ. She also stood by the teachings of the Church. She was dismissed from the FDJ because she wasn't in conformity with the basic principles of the FDJ and because of her religious orientation. The FDJ separated itself from her. Naturally, she couldn't pursue a higher education. But that was common at that time, and the youth didn't dwell on it very much. (1991)

Herbert Heidler: I was not allowed to pursue a higher education. Actually, I wanted to become a teacher in 1961, but I was not selected because I had fulfilled a mission for the Church, and my philosophy of life was not considered appropriate for the profession of a teacher. To educate children, one had to follow the socialistic philosophy. I was told that very directly. That same thing happened to my daughter, who did very well in school and wanted to attend the advanced high school. She was turned down, because I [her father] did not exhibit the proper philosophy. When that happens, it hurts. But we were not sorry that we had chosen a different path. (1993)

Hans Schult: My son came home one day and said, "I can attend the advanced high school. You just have to complete the application." But it was then discovered that he was not in the FDJ, and the application was denied. The denial did not mention the FDJ. Instead, we were told: "There were four applicants from his class, and only two could be selected. So your son fell out." We went to the principal and asked, "Was the denial based on his church membership?" He said, "No, of course not!" When the party secretary at my place of employment learned that my son had been turned down, and that he had not been in the FDJ, he said, "I'm sorry, but I can't help you. Your son had to be in the FDJ." He was allowed to pursue an apprenticeship and earned his Abitur on the side. After three years, he was permitted to study at a technical high school. He had to take that little detour. You had to be sly. (1991)

Joachim Meyer: I wanted to study to become an engineer, and I tried often to qualify myself for professional advancement. I was told that if I wasn't in the party, not in the FDJ, and not in the military auxiliary unit at work, then it wouldn't be possible. That is how it went at that time. Party members were given priority, so many people joined the party, not out of conviction, but just to further their careers. (1989)

> *Gerwin Baasch:* It was not quite so troublesome in my time, but we experienced it later within our own family. Our oldest daughter didn't join the Young Pioneers. We didn't think it was necessary. Christ would soon come. But our daughter suffered greatly from those decisions. In the ninth grade, her performance evaluations were 1.2 on average [1.0 being the highest]. Then she was told that she could not pursue the Abitur for various reasons related to the society's workforce needs, etc. However, her teacher told us that the only reason was her Church membership. She said, however, that we could not quote her in our appeal of their decision, for she would deny she had said such a thing, to protect herself. We were told that our daughter could pursue an apprenticeship and the Abitur simultaneously, if she could raise her grades even higher. She accomplished that, but later her new instructor said, "I understand you are attending a church. I suggest that you pursue a different profession. You won't advance far in this one." Church members often raised red flags within the government. They wanted politically dedicated workers. (1991)

While discrimination against active Christians was widespread, many members found ways to obtain the advanced education they desired. The Leipzig Branch History named several members who had pursued advanced studies there over the years: "Manfred Schütze from Bernburg, at the Institute for Teacher Training; Heinz-Jürgen Sickel from Naumburg, at the Medical Faculty of the Karl Marx Universität; and Frigga and Sigrun Bauerfeind, at the Medical Technical High School." Gottfried Richter said, "It is a fact, that even in those years we had physicians, engineers, and other professionals in our ranks. Many young people studied at universities and at other institutions of higher education. They often did not arrive there on a direct path" (1993).

The historian Joachim Heise said that discrimination not only varied by region, but also from school principal to school principal and from teacher to teacher. The following experiences of members who were able to complete their studies at institutions of higher learning reflect those variations within the GDR.

> *Charlotte Jentzsch:* One son wanted to attend an advanced school, but he was not admitted to do so because he had not attended the Jugendweihe, neither had he been a Young Pioneer. My husband then spoke with the county school council, and he was admitted to the school. Sometimes those exceptions were made. Another son was able to pursue an engineering degree after he had apprenticed. Our third son wanted to be a teacher. He had been an FDJ member and had completed an apprenticeship with an Abitur. He was allowed to study and became a teacher. Members often had serious problems and couldn't study. But my husband always talked with the officials and quoted our constitution regarding freedom of religion. You could also threaten to

take up an unfavorable decision with the next highest level. That made them a little fearful. (2004)

Andreas Kretzschmar: After completing the eighth grade in my village school, I attended the gymnasium [the academic high school] through the twelfth grade. I completed the Abitur and went directly to Freiberg to study at the Bergakademie [Mining Academy]. There were two factors: first, a high level of academic achievement, and second, whether a person was true to the system. But being true to the system didn't necessarily mean being engaged on behalf of the system. I didn't create any friction or contention within the system, so the system had no complaint with me. In school, I learned and repeated back the atheistic lessons, but I never internalized it.

Before I moved into student housing in Freiberg, I prayed to my Heavenly Father, that he would grant me a roommate who accepted my philosophy. There were fifteen students in our seminar group, including two Christians—one Evangelical and one Mormon. We two were assigned to the same room. However, I also got along well with Communists and other party members, who were true to their philosophy. They recognized that there were errors in the party's platform, but nevertheless supported its goals. Perhaps that was a reason why I didn't have problems during my school and advanced study years. (2004)

Bernd Kleinert: It was relatively simple for me, and I didn't experience any degree of discrimination. The first hurdle was to be recommended for advancement from elementary school to the gymnasium, and teachers had the most influence in that matter. A positive political attitude was required, but no one raised an issue in my case. I was a member of the FDJ, although everyone knew I was a Mormon. My parents submitted the application for the gymnasium and the teacher signed it. My father was a medical orderly [first aid attendant] in a large factory. He was a salaried employee ["Angestellter"], whose children were not typically favored for educational advancement. But he was also a brick mason by profession, i.e., a "worker," so I was a worker's child. I entered the gymnasium in the ninth grade and completed the Abitur in the twelfth grade. Simultaneously, I also completed an apprenticeship as an orderly. Thereafter, I would normally be expected to serve one year as a nursing assistant in a hospital before being permitted to enter medical school. However, in some years, the military drafted many nursing assistants, which greatly reduced the number of medical school applicants. That apparently happened in my case, because I was allowed to enter medical school without first serving as a nurse. To my knowledge, most members of the Church who became physicians followed similar, relatively smooth paths to medical school.

But many colleagues, who were not members of the Church, had to wait two, three, or four years before they were admitted to medical school. I believe the Lord played a role here, because so many of my colleagues encountered more difficulty than we did. (2004)

Gerhard Müller: I completed the Abitur after four years in a gymnasium, and then applied to study medicine. I was not initially accepted for political reasons. My father wasn't in the Communist Party, I didn't have a political recommendation from school and I had not participated in a youth organization. I had to work for one year before I could apply again, this time successfully. I first studied chemistry, then moved into a clinical position and simultaneously began to study medicine. (1993)

Andreas Ortlieb: I was a Young Pioneer and also a member of FDJ. When I was sixteen, I decided I wanted to study medicine. I had the necessary school grades, and I met another requirement for advancement to higher education: my father was considered to be a worker. So I went to the school director and he gave me a contract to study medicine at the Martin Luther University in Halle, a very good institution where Brother Müller works. I was told, "We will sign the contract immediately, but there is one condition. You must agree to serve three years in the National Army and become an officer." I couldn't do that. So they said, "Forget we had this discussion." It was the first significant discrimination I had experienced as a member of the Church and as a Christian.

Since I also enjoyed music very much, I applied for advanced music study. The entry tests and discussions were successful, and I was told, "You are so talented, that you can study any of the instruments in an orchestra. Choose what you wish." That compensated for much that had happened earlier, and I studied music for four years in Leipzig. (1993)

Antje Ritter: I was raised as an atheist by my parents. I was even an SED Party member, because I knew it would help me achieve my professional goals. I wanted to study medicine and become a physician. Since I had no ideological differences with the party, I chose the "secure" path and joined at the age of eighteen. I completed the Abitur with honors, and received the highest recommendation, "Especially Suited for Study," which guaranteed that I would be accepted at the university of my choice.

I became acquainted with my future husband, Lothar Ritter, in the first months at the university. His path had been different than mine. He had also completed his Abitur with honors at another school, but probably due to his membership in the Church, he received the lesser recommendation, "Suited for Study," although his grades were the same as mine. When challenged, his teacher said that she was only permitted to award the highest recommendation to a very few students. However, she had given the higher designation to weaker students in his class. She justified her actions by saying that Lothar's school grades would enable him to gain entry to a university without her help. However, he was not accepted the first time he applied to study medicine. Instead, he worked for one year as a nursing assistant in a university clinic and applied again, this time successfully.

With hindsight, one can say that Heavenly Father allowed members of the university's admissions committee to use their agency in a manner that allowed Lothar and me to begin our studies in the same year. In addition to our common interest in medicine, we had many opportunities for discussion about our religious and philosophical principles. Of course, as a result of my upbringing, I didn't share his perspective. But our parents had taught us respect and tolerance, so our friendship continued despite those differences. However, our religious discussions became more frequent. I also became acquainted with other youth of the Church, and I noticed that they were all people who appealed to me. I was also able to tolerate or even support most of their perspectives and opinions. I became friends with many of them through repeated activities, including youth conferences.

As an atheist, my greatest challenge was to develop faith in a higher being for whom mankind was his highest priority. As a student of medicine, the atheistic theory of evolution no longer was sufficient for my growing understanding of the wonder of human life. The existence of a higher being that was involved in the creation of human life seemed more logical and correct. This internal process of new understanding developed over more than two years. During those two years, I saw instances where medical students left the party for ideological reasons and were not allowed to continue their studies, although their skills often exceeded those of their fellow students. The leading professors were true party followers, who most likely were told to lay snares for such students, which led to their departure from the university. Those cases had an impact upon me. While I was coming to new understandings regarding God and Jesus Christ, I was not able or willing to express them openly because I wanted to complete my studies. The moral conflict within me grew. While the teachings of the Church became clearer and more understandable, the conflict with my professional goal also grew and appeared to be unresolvable.

In the meantime, the relationship between Lothar and me developed beyond that of just fellow students. That led to new problems, for I knew precisely that his goal was to have a wife for all time and eternity, even though there did not appear to be any possibility of reaching a temple in the foreseeable future. Fortunately, I had a discussion with

Patriarch Walter Krause. I shared with him my conflicts and thoughts concerning membership in the Church. It was no longer a lack of faith, but rather a fear that it would require my exit from the party, which could result in an exit from the university. I was surprised to hear that it was not necessary to leave the party right away. Instead, I was told to pursue my professional goals energetically, until a future time of relative independence from such parties and organizations, when I could resolve the problem and clear my conscience. I was baptized shortly thereafter, and Lothar and I were married in 1980. In April 1989, in the week in which I successfully completed my specialty doctoral training, I submitted my application to leave the party for religious reasons. There was absolutely no problem, nor did it result in any discussion with party officials. Rather, I had the impression that my membership in the Church had been known for years and that the subsequent steps were anticipated. (2004)

Elfriede Gäbler: Our son [Wolfgang] was ready to move from the elementary school to the advanced high school in 1967. We submitted the application, which was denied. We appealed. My husband's place of employment submitted a good recommendation about his own work accomplishments, and in his letter to the county school official, my husband emphasized that he, a worker, never imagined that his son would be denied entry to a high school in a "Workers and Farmers State." We subsequently received word that he would be accepted, and he was able to complete the Abitur during the twelfth grade. (2006)

While the Abitur opened the door to attending a university, Wolfgang Gäbler was not accorded the additional "with honors" designation that would normally be given to someone with his academic accomplishments. The school director justified that decision on the grounds that Wolfgang had not been a member of FDJ. Whereupon his father wrote the following letter to the local education department on June 22, 1971:

The academic achievements of students in the twelfth grade of the advanced high school "Rudolf-Rothkegel" in Forst were announced on June 18, 1971. My son, Wolfgang, was accorded the designation "very good." However, according to existing standards, the designation "with honors" could have been applied. At a subsequent meeting with responsible officials, including the school director, which I attended at my son's request, we were informed that the designation "with honors" could not be awarded because he had received a 2 in general citizenship.

My son did not join the FDJ because of his philosophical orientation. However, he has been acknowledged by school officials to have made more contributions to society than many FDJ members. In response to our question as to what was missing in his social behavior, we

> received the following answer: "Wolfgang did not achieve a sufficiently positive influence upon his school comrades, which would have more likely been achieved as a member of FDJ. Moreover, by not joining the FDJ, he did not adequately express his support for the state."
>
> Now I must ask you, can support for the state be shown only through FDJ membership? Is membership in the FDJ more important than actions, which reveal a person's true orientation? Can't an honest Christian also be a valuable citizen of the state, without membership in the FDJ? I have the impression that my son Wolfgang has been falsely judged by his philosophy of life, and I politely request a review of the decision of the school's evaluation committee.

Wolfgang Gäbler was subsequently admitted to the Technical University in Dresden, where attempts were made by the FDJ to recruit him, but he encountered no further obstacles to his academic studies.

Career Development and Worksite Relationships

> *Manfred Heller:* The leading positions in all businesses and public institutions were filled by members of the party. You could advance to a certain degree, but not to the top. (1991)

> *Rolf-Thomas Lehmann:* Members of the Church were accepted in factories and offices as equals. We were given responsibility as deputy leaders of a group or area, but rarely as the leader. That was reserved for SED members. (2003)

> *Klaus-Peter Kretzschmar:* Eighty percent of the people in the Erzgebirge were religious. Mormons were still a small minority, but it was not difficult for us to attend Church. From my first days at school and thereafter as an apprentice, on the job or in advanced education, people knew what church I attended, and it was not a problem. The disadvantages appeared later in life. When my boss took his own life, I was told, "You have seniority and you are the most qualified in this field, but you cannot be the department leader because you are a Christian." Six months later, I became the deputy chief (the chief was a party member), because they realized that the operation didn't function well without me. (1993)

> *Joachim Lehnig:* We were taught in the Church to be reliable and honest and not to make trouble. We tried to live accordingly and to apply those standards on the job. That was noticed. There was one task in our department that no one liked to do, and that was to purchase or otherwise obtain the necessary materials for our operations. It was always troublesome. My boss went to the district leadership of the

party and asked if I could be assigned that job. I became the department leader. At times I attended meetings of the company's leadership, at the highest level of the conglomerate. The first time I attended that meeting, I was told by the party's leaders, "We know that you are a church member, and that it is common in your church to proselyte or otherwise to make your beliefs known. We request that you not do that on the job, i.e., don't speak about your church." I said, "Fine. If that is what you ask, then I will comply, but you should know, that if someone asks me a question, he'll receive an answer." I could have become a general director. That is stated in my Stasi file, but I was not a comrade. (2003)

Lothar Ebisch: I was the technical leader in what was initially a private and later a state-owned company. Then I became the factory leader. I was open and frank from the beginning. I said I am an active Christian, a Mormon, a member of the Church of Jesus Christ. How you wish to use me is up to you. When you don't want me to do something, just say so. I traveled to leadership meetings every week. Something nonalcoholic was always placed at my seat at the table. I was respected in every way. The director was a Communist. He knew what my philosophy was, and he respected it. I was never provoked politically or otherwise misused, never. In 1984, when I left the company to accept a paid Church position [regional building representative], I was told I would be welcomed back, since they assumed that the Church employment would be a temporary matter. I was always dealt with very, very fairly. (2003)

Siegfried Schmidt: I first became aware of the pure political nature of things after I completed my apprenticeship and began to work in a state-owned company. Things happened whereby I had to declare and stand up for my religious principles. I was encouraged to join the FDJ. Then the leading people of the company wanted me to join the party. I declared frankly, "I am not opposed to certain party practices, but we have different philosophies of life. I have my perspectives and will not depart from them. I will gladly do the work assigned to me and will try to be an influence for good among others, but in accordance with my philosophy." That was the only time that anyone seriously tried to recruit me. When you were open, frank, and honest, then you were left alone. (1991)

Karla Liebscher: Personally, I didn't experience any noticeable disadvantage or problem because of the Church during either my apprentice time or in my studies, perhaps because I never spoke with anyone about my Church membership. My problems began first on the job. I was a trainer of metallurgical laboratory workers and later a supervisory instructor in the professional development department. It was the desire of the leadership of the company's education department that all persons engaged in professional training be members of the SED. To avoid the constant pressure to join the SED, I became a member of the CDU [Christian Democratic Party]. According to the deputy director, that was the dumbest thing I could have done. I was told that I no longer had the ability to work effectively in my profession. I was not capable of developing "socialistic characteristics" in people. I was subjected to various harassments, but fortunately was supported fairly well by the CDU's leadership. However, the company employed other methods to reduce my responsibilities. After a ten-year effort, they succeeded in placing me under another supervisory instructor who was a member of the SED. (2005)

Eveline Laube: We had a teacher in our branch who had joined the Church. That led to big problems at her school. She was required to attend all possible meetings and was asked to prepare reports that were rarely discussed. Finally, a friend at school suggested that she join the CDU to gain some peace. She did that, and it worked. She had become political, she had joined a party, regardless of which one. It made a difference. (2004)

Manfred Schütze: When my future wife and I finished our university studies, we wanted to return to my home city where we were needed by the branch. Near the end of our studies, we had served a practical training period there and must have done a good job, because the school directors had asked us, "Wouldn't you like to work at our school?" We said, "Gladly, with pleasure, but we probably won't be permitted." They said, "Leave it to us." A few months later, we came to the university interviews that would determine the schools to which everyone would be sent. They asked, "What would you like?" I said, "I would like to go to Bernburg." "Oh," they said, "everything has already been arranged for you. We have a request from the Halle District. You are going to Bernburg." The same happened with my wife.

So we went to Bernburg, and it was, naturally, difficult. When you are a member of the Church and work in an atheistic school, many problems arise. Officially, no one could do anything to us, since the constitution said that we could be religious. Of course, we had no opportunity for advancement. We could never become a director of a school or hold any other leading position.... We had to be prepared to lose our job at any time. We were often told, "People who go to church every day, preach there, where the wife plays the organ on Sunday, and are supposed to be socialistic teachers in our schools from Monday through Friday, that isn't possible. In the future, we will no longer work with such people." (1991)

Hans Schult: When I applied for my first job as an academically trained engineer, I had to fill out an eight-page form. Question: "Do you belong to any organization or religion?" I answered: "Member of the Church of Jesus Christ of Latter-day Saints." When I came to the oral interview, I thought I was certain to be hired. Then three days later I was told, "We are very sorry, but the position has been filled by another person." Later, I had no problem with my bosses, because I always said from the beginning who I was. I was a known entity. Once, I was supposed to become chief of development in a factory. I told my boss, "I'm a Mormon." He said, "If you are not opposed to the GDR and not opposed to peace, then that makes no difference." But he also said, "Whether my successor will think as I do, that I don't know." (1991)

Dieter Lehm: I once had my Church books at my place of employment and was warned that I shouldn't do that. I shouldn't bring such things to work. Otherwise, I didn't have any problems. (1991)

Marianne Ortlieb: I entered an apprenticeship and had to fill out a personnel form. I wrote that I had been in the FDJ for two years. I had joined so they wouldn't continue to put pressure on my father. I never left the organization officially, but just didn't attend any longer. So I was asked by the FDJ secretary at work why I didn't attend meetings. I said, "I no longer attend because I go to the Church of Jesus Christ." Then people from the county leadership came and tried to force me to participate. I told them about all the things I do in the Church. They stopped arguing with me and said, "You are really a multi-functionary." They left me in peace thereafter. (1993)

Gottfried Schmidt: I worked in Freiberg for the electric company, and April 14, 1982, was one of the most beautiful days of my life. I was sitting next to my supervisor on a bench in front of my work station during our lunch break, when he said, "Gottfried, I want to share with you something that I've been instructed not to tell anyone. Promise me, on your honor, that you will not speak of it to anyone?" Then he said, "We will go into my office, and you have only ten minutes to look around." My anticipation was very great.

He had a ten-foot-long conference table, on which I saw several drawings. As I glanced quickly over the papers, I was overcome with feelings that I can hardly describe. My entire being responded and I felt like I was standing outside my body. Was I dreaming or would there really be a temple within the GDR? He then gathered up all the drawings and said, "I must return everything to the county council." Before he left, he added, "I was certain that you, being a Mormon, already knew about this project, but I can tell from your reaction that it was a surprise. I'm pleased that I could share this with you. And I will

> see that you, as a Mormon and a good colleague, have the honor of being the first to bring the electric cable to the temple lot." That took place on December 1, 1982, whereby I became the first elder of the Church to work at the construction site. (2004)

In 1986, a West German newspaper reporter was permitted to travel through the GDR for the purpose of describing the conditions of daily life in that country. One of his articles, entitled "A Mormon Has the Party's Blessing," addressed the professional and religious activities of Frank Apel, president of the Freiberg Stake:

> Frank Apel is a sturdy, easygoing, and friendly man, whom you would be pleased to introduce to your friends at the local pub. Although he doesn't drink any alcohol, he gladly celebrates, but with apple juice. Born in 1940, he lives in Freiberg/Saxony, a city with fifty thousand inhabitants. He is a master craftsman of the old school, whom you would no longer expect to find in a country of state-owned companies. He is a specialist in automobile electronics who has established his own business in the rear of Ziegelgasse 13 with three employees, one apprentice, and an office clerk. He repairs the electrical components of the "Trabbis," the Trabant cars that people bring to him. "No one needs to wait longer than two or three days at my shop."
>
> Can a private enterprise even exist in the GDR? "Of course," says Apel. "My business nets two thousand marks every month." That is a lot of money in the GDR. A man like Apel, a business like his, is actually urgently needed.
>
> To accommodate this visit from the West, Apel left the "Trabbis" to his employees for an entire morning and showed me what else he has accomplished, including things that people with our perspective would not expect to find in the GDR.
>
> Born and raised in the GDR, Apel is the president of a religious group, the Mormons, which are headquartered in America and officially call themselves the Church of Jesus Christ of Latter-day Saints. He even built a huge temple for his church, in fact the first one that the Mormons have built on German soil, whether in the Federal Republic or in the GDR. And all that with the blessing of the atheistic SED Party. Apel was also able to prevent outsiders, including the police, from entering the temple, their most sacred building.
>
> A local meeting house, the size of a large, well-furnished schoolhouse, also was built next to the temple, all financed with contributions from abroad and with local money. Every Mormon, about five thousand in the GDR, contributes one-tenth of their income to the church.
>
> Apel is not even a member of the SED, and his four children somehow avoided membership in the Free German Youth. Is that possible?

"It is possible, with conditions. We are not opposed to the state," says Apel. "We do not oppose it and can, therefore, live in peace." That is clearly the secret of peaceful life in the GDR. Those who don't aggravate the state manage quite well there. As Günter Gaus, former permanent representative of the Federal Republic in East Berlin, wrote that a person can withdraw into a niche of private life, but those who wish to pursue a career have to join the party. However, a man without a party badge is allowed to repair the broken headlights of a Trabant. Even if he is a Mormon.

We traveled a few streets farther with Apel. He was able—it is actually possible—to buy and renovate a single-family home. Patience and good connections are essential, since nothing functions in the GDR without them. But Apel, born in Freiberg, certainly has friends in his own city. The needed bathroom tiles—rare commodities—arrived on time. Purchase price and renovation costs were about 100,000 marks. He will soon be able to move into the house.

Apel will be permitted to travel again to America, to the Mormon gathering in Salt Lake City. Within the niches of the GDR, within the limits of its small freedoms, his example shows that more is possible than we think. (*Münchner Abendzeitung*, October 25, 1986)

Mission leadership and priesthood in Berlin, 1940. First row, left to right: Hans Böttcher, Martin Werner Hoppe, Walter Fassmann, Arthur Böhme, Frederich Wernick, Friedrich Fischer, Richard Ranglack, Herbert Klopfer, Paul Langheinrich, Arno Dzierzon, Willy Bobry, Hanskarl Schade. *Courtesy Armin Langheinrich.*

Refugees Living in Wolfsgrün Villa, 1946. *Courtesy Karlheinz Leonhardt.*

Wolfsgrün Villa, 1991. *Courtesy Karlheinz Leonhardt.*

Mission Choir in Dresden, 1949. Henry Burkhardt, last row, far left. *Courtesy Karlheinz Leonhardt.*

Walter Stover and East German missionaries, 1949. First row, left to right: Heinz Hinkel, Walter Stover, Walter Fassmann, Richard Ranglack. *Courtesy Wolfgang Kelm.*

Walter Stover and mission leaders, 1950. First row, left to right: Fritz Lehnig, Walter Fassmann, Walter Stover, Heinz Hinkel, Anton Larisch. Second row, left to right: Arnold Schmidt, Erich Sellner, Walter Kindt, Hans Böttcher, Walter Krause. *Courtesy Walter Kindt.*

Leipzig meeting house, 1950. *Courtesy Wolfgang Kelm.*

Inside Leipzig meeting house, 1950. *Courtesy Wolfgang Kelm.*

Mother's Day in Dresden, 1951. *Courtesy Karlheinz Leonhardt.*

The last full-time East German missionaries, 1959. *Courtesy Karlheinz Leonhardt.*

Henry Burkhardt, 1954.
Courtesy Henry Burkhardt.

Former movie house in Leipzig converted into an LDS chapel, 1968. *Courtesy Eberhardt Werner.*

Creation of the Dresden Mission, 1969. Front row, left to right: Helen Rees, Inge Burkhardt, Thelma Fetzer, Edith Krause. Back row, left to right: Thomas S. Monson, Stanley Rees, Henry Burkhardt, Percy K. Fetzer, Gottfried Richter, Walter Krause. *Courtesy Henry Burkhardt.*

Neubrandenburg meeting house before and after renovation, 1970. *Courtesy Karlheinz Leonhardt.*

Freiberg Temple open house, 1985. *Courtesy Holger Bellmann and Karlheinz Leonhardt.*

Freiberg Temple open house, 1985. *Courtesy Holger Bellmann and Karlheinz Leonhardt.*

Aerial view of Freiberg Temple and Chapel, 1985. *Courtesy Holger Bellmann and Karlheinz Leonhardt.*

The first full-time Western missionaries, 1989. *Courtesy Karlheinz Leonhardt.*

11 The Old Meeting Houses

The external appearance of our meeting houses was quite different than today. They were old factory buildings at the rear of other buildings, or you could smell that they had served as restaurants for many years. Their external appearance also reflected the absence of many other desirable features. But they were clean and functional, simple and humble. (Gottfried Richter, 1993)

Yes, we will have towers, a tower for the city hall and a tower for the cultural center. We won't need other towers in a socialist city. (Walter Ulbricht, May 7, 1953, at the inauguration of Stalinstadt, the first new city to be built without a church)

The Church's old meeting houses in the GDR provide valuable insight into, and documentation of, the relationship between church and state. Finding, renovating, and maintaining appropriate meeting houses was a constant problem well into the 1980s. The war had destroyed uncounted numbers of buildings in Germany, and the GDR was not willing to allocate scarce building material to the construction or renovation of buildings for religious purposes. Therefore, most branches of the Church were directed to severely damaged buildings, which the members partially or fully restored with great personal sacrifice and tremendous ingenuity and skill, and from which they were often subsequently evicted, only to begin again at a new location.

Günter Schulze: I still marvel today, how we were able to maintain our meeting houses or meeting rooms with such primitive and limited materials! Everything was accomplished with our own imagination and initiative. For example, when cement was available, five or ten sacks were purchased. If wash basins were available, several were purchased and used later where needed. All renovations and repairs were to be included in the government's five-year plans, but our needs were never considered. So we used cars and trailers to haul material during the night, so the brothers could build and renovate on Saturdays, since they had to work for their own support during the week. It didn't always look beautiful, and it was not always done in accordance with code, but it appeared orderly and clean. Initially, there was rarely a piano or other musical instrument available for purchase, to say nothing of an electric organ, but we always received help from dear people who said, "It is available for the Church." Employees of the State Secretariat for Church Affairs said, "Miracles must exist, for the Church always finds what it needs." (1993)

Manfred Heller: You had to have good connections—hand worker X, who knew hand worker Y—to obtain wood, cement, bricks, or whatever was needed. Many projects were carried out by Walter Krause. With his ingenuity and connections, he found wood, glass, roofing paper, and other materials needed to renovate and maintain meeting rooms throughout the GDR, and many members voluntarily sacrificed their time and resources to maintain those facilities. Everything had to be done by the members, and they did it gladly. (1991)

The words "Walter Krause" and "meeting houses" almost became synonymous. He was a carpenter by profession and was frequently asked to plan a project, obtain government approvals, find building materials, and provide his own skilled labor. Although building materials were usually in short supply, almost everything could be found somewhere in the country. The challenge was to know when, where, and how to obtain it. Krause described conditions in the GDR with the following story:

A brother came from the Frankfurt area office to review Dresden's financial records. He asked Brother Burkhardt, "Tell me, why does Brother Krause buy roofing paper in Werdau for a project in Görlitz?" I met him later in Leipzig, and he said to me, "So, you are the man who submitted the building charges." I answered, "Here are twenty marks. Go to a store here and buy a pair of pliers and four pounds of nails." He said, "That shouldn't be difficult." I said, "He who has faith can do everything." In the store, he was asked, "You want to have nails? Where do you come from? You can't buy nails here." He couldn't comprehend that. There were no pliers. There were no nails. A brother in Steinpleis, who is a roofer, said, "Walter, I'll give you the roofing paper. But if you are stopped along the way, don't say that you got it from me." There are many such examples. (1991)

As a branch and district president, and as a factory manager, Lothar Ebisch had extensive experience relevant to the renovation of buildings:

> When we rebuilt or renovated buildings, we generally had to obtain materials through connections and acquaintances. For example, cement was sold to private citizens by the sack at state-owned companies, two sacks per person. So we sent in four or six members. But the supply was usually exhausted after one day, and then you had to wait several days. So we gathered and saved together. When you held certain positions, you usually knew someone who knew someone else, and that person might be able to buy six or eight sacks, or even an entire car load. I once ordered three wagons of lime from Berlin-Rüdersdorf. One car went to a factory in Zwönitz, one went to the local building department in return for tiles, and another was for me and my neighbors. The lime was officially paid for and distributed to others. But you needed to proceed with much skill and diplomacy and have good connections.
>
> We were proud of our meeting houses, with their warm-water heating and wooden parquet floors. We made a tour with Presidents Hales, Ringger, and Burkhardt to visit these buildings. Perhaps outsiders couldn't really judge what we had accomplished. Some might have been taken it for granted. But for us, it was a tremendous, self-sacrificing achievement. (2004)

A report at the beginning of the journal history of the Dresden Mission, written about 1969, mentioned fourteen meeting houses. Eight were described as Church-owned: Bischofswerda, Cottbus, Freiberg, Neubrandenburg, Prenzlau, Schwerin, Wolgast, and Erfurt. The term "Church-owned" must, however, be further defined, because the Church did not initially possess the legal right to purchase buildings or property in its own name. Therefore, most of these buildings were actually owned by members, acting as trustees for the Church. Which of them were in legal possession of a trustee is noted below, when known. The other six facilities were described as "not owned": Blauenthal, Groitzsch, Hohenstein-Ernstthal, Schwarzenberg, Staaken, and Annaberg. Why more facilities were not included in that second group is not known. However, this chapter includes additional reports on buildings in five more typical cities: Rathenow, Werdau, Forst, Dresden, and Leipzig. Information about the temple and the new meeting houses built in the late 1980s can be found in Chapters 15 and 16.

Church-owned Meeting Houses, 1969

> *Erfurt:* This is the first Church-owned property obtained after the war. [Walter Stover bought it with his own money.] A handsome building was changed into a meeting house with much effort and love. Classrooms are presently being added from a former commercial building.

Cottbus: Because of specially favorable circumstances, we were able to assume ownership of this meeting house in 1959 for the price of 22,000 marks. The inside of the building was previously renovated and modernized. [Fritz Lehnig leased the property, and the Cottbus branch began to use the upper floor in 1937. Use of the building as a refugee center after 1945 is described in Appendix B.]

Freiberg: We had the opportunity to purchase this property [via a trustee] in 1962 for 15,000 marks. The entire building had to be renovated, which was a problem because of a shortage of building material. The renovations continued until 1965, but we were able to hold our services there throughout most of the reconstruction period. The cost of the renovations and the furnishings was about 64,000 marks.

Neubrandenburg: An old house that had to be substantially rebuilt was purchased [through a trustee] for 9,660 marks. The total cost of the renovation is estimated at 90,000 marks.

Bischofswerda: We bought the property in 1963 for 28,460 marks. An old building at the rear of the property is to be converted into a meeting house. It has taken four years to obtain the necessary approvals for that conversion. The old building has now been torn down and the new building should soon be constructed.

Joachim Albrecht: Brother Koschnicke bought the property [in Bischofswerda] for the Church. It included a residence and an old commercial building in the back. The latter was rebuilt. Actually, "rebuilt" is too generous. The entire building was torn down since the walls were not stable. Only the foundation was left. The bricks were cleaned and reused. The building was dedicated in December 1969. (2004)

Prenzlau: We own a small meeting house in Prenzlau, but not the ground itself. It was built in 1961 at a cost of 5,637 marks and fully meets the needs of the small branch.

Schwerin: We bought a small property [via a trustee], which included an old building that was converted into a meeting house.

Blitz newspaper, May 7, 1995: Who hasn't already taken a relaxing walk along Schwerin's Schlossgartenallee and passed by this building? Until 1956, it was the home of the Schwerin branch of the Church of Jesus Christ of Latter-day Saints. The half-timbered house was originally built in 1846 as a stable, part of an estate. In 1944, the stable was converted into an emergency apartment. Then the Church bought and transformed the building, which was almost a ruin. The "Old Stable" was converted into a functional, more useable church building.

Wolgast: A small lot was bought in 1953 [without a trustee], and a barracks is to be built on it as a meeting house.

Hans Schult: We initially held meetings in Sister Skibbe's home. At that time, old munitions of the former German army were buried in the Baltic Sea, but the wooden containers were brought back to the shore by the workers. We were allowed to take the containers, and Brother Krause made benches out of them for use in the Skibbe family's meeting house. We later met in various buildings, including a wood factory, a mill, and a store. Each eviction required more renovations in the next building. Wherever we moved, Brother Krause used the wood from the old containers. Mormons never give up. We received no help from abroad. We did it all ourselves. (1991)

Meeting Facilities Not Owned, 1969

Blauenthal: Our little branch in Blauenthal had probably the worst meeting room. Our members met for years in a shed that previously was a break room for workers in an old quarry. Neither electricity nor running water was available. Since the building was in a remote location, it was often vandalized. In 1964, a state-run company reopened the quarry and wanted the shed. Negotiations over two years resulted in our being assigned to rooms in a former manor house, which we, of course, had to first renovate. But with the help of the state-run company, which strongly supported our interests, we managed to create a proper meeting home.

Hohenstein-Ernstthal: At the moment, our meeting house for the Hohenstein-Ernstthal branch is being repaired at a cost of 15,000 to 20,000 marks. Invasive moisture threatens the building's collapse and necessitates immediate action. We hope to resume meetings in the building this year.

Staaken: With the closing of the borders around Berlin, many of our members who had attended the branch in Berlin-Spandau were forced to create their own meeting place. At first, they attempted to travel to the branch in Potsdam, but the distance and poor train connections made it difficult to attend services there. A lease agreement was reached on March 1, 1964, for a garden plot that included a small house, which was converted into a meeting place at a cost of about 1,500 marks. The new branch in Staaken was opened on June 14, 1965.

Schwarzenberg: Our branch in Schwarzenberg was assigned to new rooms by the city in 1965. The members worked diligently to renovate the facility and create an appropriate meeting home in six months. Our cost estimate was 14,000 marks, but when we finished in early 1966, the total cost had reached 30,265 marks, due to unanticipated expenses and higher prices.

Groitzsch: Our goal for the past two years was to build our own meeting facility on property we had leased. Recently, the branch was informed that construction would not be permitted. Despite new appeals, we must accept the fact that the building of a meeting house is not likely very soon.

Manfred Schütze: Sunday church services in Groitzsch involved the utilization of most of the rooms in the Böhme family home. That had been the case for many years, because local authorities constantly denied efforts to build or lease another facility. After much fasting and prayer, Sister Renate (Böhme) Ritter had an idea. She applied for a permit to build a small weekend cottage for her father-in-law in the large garden directly behind the house. At the same time, she had been operating a "doll clinic," to which individuals and organizations brought damaged dolls for repair. Since she didn't have a separate facility for that business, dolls in various stages of repair, or awaiting repair, were stored in every conceivable corner of the house. The arrival of the state building director happened to coincide with a particularly high number of repair requests. The entire house was filled with dolls. The director said, "You have a doll house here and no living quarters. You must build a doll clinic." While the clinic was being built, the government issued a ruling that prohibited the use of private living quarters for religious meetings. When the branch leaders asked the city where they should meet, it was natural that they were referred to the doll clinic under construction. With extra labor from the members, the clinic was modified to accommodate the branch's needs. Church services were held there for the first time in May 1977.[1]

Annaberg: The branch in Annaberg was initially located in a room in a former restaurant. It was in very poor condition. Through the efforts of the branch president, we obtained a new home in 1960, in a factory building, part of which was converted by the members into a wonderful meeting house.

Lothar Ebisch: Annaberg had a very large branch and needed a relatively large facility. The branch had rented various locations until Brother Gerhard Krämer leased a large factory building in the Bahnhofstraße. He didn't need all the rooms, only some on the top floor

> and in the basement, and he rented the remaining rooms to the Church. With very intensive and often difficult work, the brothers tore out the old machinery, removed the flooring, took out walls, and repaired the roof. A machinery room was converted to a baptismal font, the first one in the GDR. It included changing rooms. Through connections, the brothers obtained and installed new parquet flooring. They also fashioned a simple but effective system to heat the rooms and installed a folding wall to expand the main meeting room. Brother Gulla, in Gotha, had a private carpenter shop, and he built coat closets for the first floor, which were installed by the members. Brother Gulla also made wood veneer sheets used elsewhere in the building. Classrooms were built on an upper floor, and the outside appearance of the building was improved. We then had adequate facilities to easily accommodate over four hundred to five hundred members for our district conferences, which were usually held in Annaberg. I kept the county council informed of all these improvements. Now and then they provided us with official authorization to purchase materials.
>
> We later attempted to purchase the entire building from its owner. A state-owned business was housed in the basement, and it objected to the sale because it did not want to pay rent to a church. Members in Annaberg who belonged to the CDU brought the matter to the attention of the CDU in Karl-Marx-Stadt, which in turn made contact with responsible officials within the SED. The matter then proceeded from the district council to the State Secretariat for Church Affairs, which finally approved the sale. The Church took ownership of the building [without a trustee] in the 1970s, and the state-owned business paid rent to the Church. We were amazed, but that is how it went when you had such people supporting you. (2003)

Descriptions of other typical meeting facilities in Rathenow, Werdau, Forst, Leipzig, and Dresden follow:

Rathenow

A memorandum from the national police to the Department of Cult Affairs in the Interior Ministry, dated July 21, 1956, described the meeting house problems in the city of Rathenow:

> When the meeting room of the above religious organization in Rathenow, Forststraße, was torn down in 1955, incident to the city's redevelopment program, the preacher Gierke came to the county police office and requested assignment to a new meeting room. The county police referred him to the responsible housing department in Rathenow. Shortly thereafter, the preacher Gierke returned and stated that he had been assigned a meeting room at the Duchrow Company, which, however, had been taken from him after the fire department

> inspected the room and judged it to be inappropriate. Following that denial, the housing department assigned the religious organization another facility, a barracks. However, the religious organization refused to accept that facility, and they subsequently conducted their cult activities in private homes.
>
> Since the religious organization numbers sixty-three members, and since private homes do not generally meet the safety requirements for meeting facilities, the fire department evaluated these rooms, found them to be inadequate for the same safety reasons, and prohibited their use. The police then suggested to the religious organization that it contact the restaurant Rosendiele in Rathenow, to rent a room there for their cult activities. The county police office has not heard from the religious organization since that time, and it is not yet known where they conduct their cult activities. (DO 1/11 HVDVP/865)

Werdau

It was not unusual for a branch to lease and extensively renovate a facility with the approval of the building's owner and then attempt to purchase the building from a willing owner, only to have a government office prohibit the sale to the Church or to a trustee. Klaus Schreiber provided the following report about such an incident in Werdau:

> In July 1946, members of the branch viewed the restaurant Schillerschlösschen in Werdau. The dance hall was full of furniture and junk, the window glass was broken, and the windows were nailed shut. The roof was leaking and the floor was beginning to rot. Arrangements were made with the owner, Herr Kolditz, to rent part of the building. Members repaired the roof, cleaned and painted rooms, installed heating equipment, and performed many other repairs. The building was dedicated on August 26, 1946, and renovated frequently thereafter. After the owner died in the 1970s, efforts were made to buy the building, with one of the members serving as trustee. He submitted an application to the responsible office, which was denied. He then tried to purchase it privately, i.e., not as a trustee for the Church. In that instance, he wanted to buy the entire property, which included a house and ancillary buildings. He intended to rent the dance hall to the Church and use the other facilities for various business purposes. He was known to be a member of the Church with little income. When asked why he wanted the property, he explained that he wished to establish a private business as a roofer, with his son. Again, the purchase was not approved. (2004)

The Church subsequently tried to buy the building directly. Negotiations with various agencies continued for several years. On February 20, 1979, Walter

Krause met with an official of the Secretariat for Church Affairs in Berlin, who summarized their discussion in the following file memorandum:

> Herr Krause informed me of the following: In Werdau, by Zwickau, District Karl-Marx-Stadt, his church has used a former restaurant property for many years. This property is the private possession of Frau Kolditz from Werdau.... His church wishes to purchase this house, and Frau Kolditz is prepared to sell it. The local offices, however, are not willing to permit the sale, because, in their opinion, the church does not have legal standing to buy property.
>
> Herr Krause said that the church has acted as an owner, and has invested a considerable amount of money in the building. On my recommendation, Herr Krause will once more request approval from the local offices in Werdau. Should they continue to oppose the sale, he will contact the representatives of the Interior Ministry and the representative for Church Affairs in the Karl-Marx-Stadt district. I informed Herr Krause that we in this office will only become directly involved if the comrades at the Karl-Marx-Stadt district council request our opinion. (MS 13918)

Two years later, on October 12, 1981, the property in Werdau was finally sold to the Church, directly, without a trustee.

Forst

The branch in Forst had an experience similar to Werdau's, and was eventually able to obtain title to a building, without a trustee, despite significant opposition from local officials. The following information was provided by Eberhard and Elfriede Gäbler:

> Our meeting rooms in Forst were destroyed during the war, and the members met in their homes for one year after May 1945. Later, we rented space in an Evangelical building until they began to use part of the building for a kindergarten. Since our own children had increased in number as members moved in from outlying areas, we sought new quarters. In 1951, we rented space in a former gas station and car repair shop at Spremberger Straße 52, a very favorable location with a bus stop almost at the door. The building was subsequently renovated several times with mission funds. The owners, Emma and Marie Schneider, attended all of our religious and social activities until their death, even though they were not members.
>
> In the early 1960s, the city council began to show considerable interest in our meeting rooms and exercised a degree of pressure on us. We expressed our willingness to move if given rooms of equal value, which was impossible in a city severely damaged during the war. It was

> obvious that if the city could provide us with comparable rooms, then they didn't need ours.
>
> When the elder sister, Emma, died, Marie Schneider became the sole owner of the building. She attempted to transfer title to us, at no cost, in 1972, 1973, and 1975. Each time, the city council was equally determined to take the rooms from us and would not approve her requests. Once, we were threatened with eviction by eminent domain. Eberhard Gäbler responded, "We respect the power of the state, but we don't fear it!" In early 1981, Marie Schneider went to the offices of the chairman of the county council and demanded to speak with him, although it was after office hours. She was finally allowed to speak with the deputy chairman, to whom she presented her demand, that the building be transferred to the Church. (2005)

Marie Schneider's insistent visits to county officials were finally successful. A notarized document, dated June 25, 1981, signed by Marie Schneider and Henry Burkhardt, "Mission President of the Church of Jesus Christ of Latter-day Saints," designated the Church as "purchaser in sole possession" of the building. The Church was recorded as the property's sole owner (Staatliches Notariat, Forst, 20-171-81, 4371) on September 1, 1981 (copy). The original building was considerably renovated and enlarged after the Wende and continues to serve the members in Forst.

Leipzig

The following descriptions of meeting houses in Leipzig after 1945 include the dramatic 1968–1969 conflict with the city over the use of a renovated former movie house. The information is taken from the manuscript history of the Leipzig branch (MS 17716), augmented with contemporary correspondence, interviews, and copies of letters in the author's possession:

> The Leipzig members managed to find and rent meeting rooms soon after the end of the war, despite the terrible destruction of the city. The branch first met at Tauchaer Straße 19-21 (presently called Rosa Luxemburg Straße), where members had to make numerous repairs, including damage from a large bomb that had fallen through the building without exploding.
>
> *Alfred Schulz:* A bomb had smashed through the roof so that we could see the sky. I asked the members to help, and almost all did. Then I asked two of the brethren to come from Annaberg to do some masonry work. After these brethren had worked for ten days, this part was done. The roof had been fixed, although it still leaked. (MS 8242)

Three years later, in September 1949, the branch rented a villa in the Prellerstraße.

Arno Niepraschk: The villa, which was in good condition, had been confiscated by the Russian commander and offered for rent to the Church. An inner wall was removed in order to accommodate up to two hundred members for worship services. (Copy from Melani Schiele)

Our joy [in the Prellerstraße] lasted only until the fall of 1951, when the house changed ownership, and our rental contract was not renewed. Instead, we were given rooms in the basement of an apartment house at Humboldtstraße 15. Once again, the new quarters had to be renovated. However, the facility was too small for the branch. Instead, a burned-out warehouse and factory building, known as "Wichenbergs Hof," was found nearby at Gerberstraße 19–27. We were allowed by the administrator of the property to restore the rooms. It was hard work and required all of our strength. The work began in November 1951 and was finished the following spring. The branch met there for the next sixteen years, and mission conferences also were held in the building during the biannual Leipzig Fair from 1957 to 1964.

Because of the expansion of Gerberstraße into a main thoroughfare, that building was demolished, and the branch faced another move. In 1968, the city council authorized the branch to occupy a former movie theater, the Lichtschauspielhaus, at Ernst Thälmann Straße 74. The building was located behind a row of apartment houses. It had been built about 1880 as an indoor market and was later used as a movie theater until 1950. Since then, it had been a warehouse.

With the assistance of contractors, the branch installed a new electrical system and heating and sanitary facilities, repaired the roof, ceiling, and walls, and painted the inside of the building. The main room had a high, curved ceiling without supporting or dividing walls. We created classrooms by installing wood-glass dividing walls saved from the former meeting house. The front of the building received new stucco and paint. A small sign with the Church's name was placed at the entrance of the passageway from the street to the building, and the name also was painted in large white letters on a blue background over the main entrance to the building.

The renovations were finished on September 6, 1968, after more than four months of work. The mission youth choir was scheduled to give a concert! Many curious people passing along the street came into the building to hear the choir practice. We were enthusiastic about the great missionary work we could accomplish.

Walter Schiele: The concert generated a bit of traffic, and people reported it to the city officials. Someone said, "People are marching

> around the city." A councilman told us, "You must come to the city hall!" (1991)

> On Saturday, September 7, 1968, with little advance warning, Brothers Schiele and Schreiter went to the city hall, where they were met by councilman Ritter with the following words: "We have been kept informed in detail about your work on the building and have not hindered you. But the posting of your name on the street and over the main door is too much! You are ordered to remove the name on the street, and the name over the door is to be painted over with the same color as the building by midnight tonight, otherwise we will close the building." It was further alleged that we had made structural changes to the building. (MS 17716)

> *Walter Schiele:* They wanted to close the house immediately. I asked, "For what reason?" "Well, we have received a complaint that young people are marching around in the city and inviting people to attend." I said, "That is absolutely not true. The youth choir, which is here, sings inside, not outside." Of course, we had laid out a red carpet toward the street, and many people who knew the old movie house wanted to see what we had done. In any case, we were allowed to hold the Sunday activities. A few days later, I went to the building with the city councilman and four or five men. They also brought someone from the building inspection department, who knew he had to find something wrong. (1991)

On September 18, 1968, the city's building inspection office sent a letter to Walter Schiele, which stated that renovations had been carried out without prior authorization. Further use of the building for meetings was prohibited pending the submission and approval of a project plan that described work already performed or anticipated.

> *Walter Schiele:* All gears were set in motion to meet the city's requirements as soon as possible, and to avoid future excuses for keeping the building closed. All required architectural work and related documentation was completed by December 16, 1968, and submitted to the building department. It was our hope to hold services in the building again at Christmas. (1991)

On December 24, 1968, Walter Schiele and Herbert Schreiter were asked again to come to the city hall. According to the Leipzig branch history, city councilman Wieczorek informed them, "The building is urgently needed as a location for political mass meetings. You will, naturally, be compensated for your work." The brothers responded by indicating that two cultural centers and other facilities already existed in the neighborhood. They were told that their suggestions would be considered, but they had only been invited to city hall to receive the city's decision in a friendly, personal manner, rather than by letter. Then Councilman Ritter cynically wished them a "Merry Christmas."

> *Walter Schiele:* They told us, "We must take the building from you." I told them, "You are worse than the Nazis." Councilman Ritter wanted to know what I meant by that. I told him, "The Nazis prohibited our scouting program and the singing of songs that mentioned Zion or Israel, but then they left us alone. But you have thrown us out, after directing us to occupy this building. Here is your letter." They wanted to take the letter from me, but I said, "It is a photocopy. You can have it, because we have many more. We have sent copies to America and elsewhere." They said, "Do you want to take us to court?" I said, "I would gladly, but we aren't allowed to do that. However, we will fight for our meeting house." (1991)

A vigorous fight was initiated. Many members complained directly and in writing to local officials, the Secretariat for Church Affairs, and even the head of state, Walter Ulbricht. The following excerpts from letters written at that time are taken from the Leipzig branch history:

> *February 20, 1969, Herbert Heidler to Councilman Ritter:* Even if you intend to take this home away from us, which would indeed shake the trust of the members in our socialist state, that is no reason to prohibit our use of the building at present.

> *March 3, 1969, Richard Jahn to Chairman Walter Ulbricht:* I am an energetic champion of socialism in our German Fatherland and a former member of the Task Force against Fascism, as well as a member of this Christian church. The action taken by the city adversely affects a large number of our members. The closure of our meeting house has prevented our members from assembling for several months. Our predominantly middle-aged fathers of families are an important constituency of our democratic socialist society and embody the ideal of responsible family life and loyalty to the constitution. Personally, I am an eighty-two-year-old fighter of the First World War, and I also participated in the second war. So allow me, on behalf of myself and my fellow members, to present to you, who have been placed by providence at the head of our democratic Germany, a request that is consistent with your lifelong political work. Confirm the confidence I have in you, and use your power to restore our meeting house to us.

> *March 6, 1969, Walter Schiele and Herbert Schreiter to Chairman Walter Ulbricht:* Since we have been unable to conduct regular religious

services for almost a year, we must consider our congregation as having been liquidated. We, therefore, appeal to you.

March 19, 1969, Gerhard Krieger to Chairman Walter Ulbricht: I must interpret this closing of our building as an indication that we are not allowed to exist, just because we are a church. Yes, we are the Church of Jesus Christ of Latter-day Saints! We have been authorized in accordance with the constitution of our government. Therefore, we have the right to engage in the spiritual welfare of our members. In his presentation to Christians at a conference of the CDU's leadership, Hans Seigewasser, the state secretary for Church Affairs, emphasized that a firm basis would be created for the unhindered exercise of spiritual care, according to the humanistic principles of equality among members of society. Our Church has followed that path, and now we have been severely hindered. I wish to briefly note, that you personally have often spoken in favor of the existence of churches in the GDR. Therefore, local offices cannot be allowed to inhibit these activities!

February 21, 1969, Gerwin Baasch to Prof. Dr. F. K. Kaul, Editor of the GDR Radio Program, "Prof. Dr. Kaul answers": Please allow me to request your advice. We view [this meeting house issue] as a violation of our rights, a form of liquidation. We consider it as interference in the exercise of our religion, which was guaranteed in the constitution we approved. I respectfully request your advice and ask whether our interpretation of this action is in accordance with existing law.

Professor Kaul answered on March 11, 1969, "I have discussed your matter with the chairman of the Leipzig city council and await his response." After receiving the response of the city council, Kaul wrote again to Gerwin Baasch on April 23, 1969:

I was informed by the Leipzig city council, that the necessity of using the facility for other state purposes was explained to you, and that you will be offered a substitute building. If that is not satisfactory, then it would be appropriate for you to pursue the path you had suggested, namely to contact the State Council and the Secretariat for Church Affairs to seek a satisfactory resolution.

In anticipation that Professor Kaul's inquiry to the city council would not produce a satisfactory response, Baasch had already done exactly what Kaul suggested. He wrote the following letter, dated April 7, 1969, to the chairman of the State Council, Walter Ulbricht, and to the secretary for Church Affairs:

I have the impression that the basic reason for these actions is an illegal liquidation of the Church of Jesus Christ of Latter-day Saints. I base this impression on several facts known to me: (1) We were told to remove the sign with our name from the street entrance and to paint over our name above the main door. We were told it constitutes "advertisement." We were also told, "We have been kept informed in detail about your work on the building and have not hindered you. But the posting of your name on the street and over the main door is too much!" (2) When the building was closed, our representative was told, "When you have fulfilled all requirements, you will no longer be allowed to enter from Ernst Thälmann Straße 74, but rather must use the back entrance to the building." (3) When our leaders were informed on December 24 that we could no longer use the building, we were told it was because of "political-cultural reasons." Over time, we have been given so many different reasons, explanations, and justifications, all quite contradictory, that I must assume that the only reason must be an intent to liquidate the Church. However, since the constitution allows the exercise of our religion, a liquidation could only be accomplished with such underhanded means.

We teach correct principles, follow the laws of the land, teach clean morals, pursue continued education and professional development, are good workers (a survey among our male members shows that about 75 percent are holders of state honors), teach members to follow principles of good health, and teach avoidance of all harmful substances. So what could be the reason for imposing such actions upon our Church? I assume that these actions are not in accordance with our country's leaders, but rather that some functionaries have misused or exceeded their authority.

You see, honorable Chairman of the State Council, that we as Christians have applied our strength for the welfare of the state. We are not shirkers. In consideration of our positive orientation to the first Workers and Farmers State on German land, the trouble that we have received from several state functionaries causes us great concern. The members of our Church breathed easier after the defeat of Hitler's fascism, when their persecution of us ended. Everyone is pleased with the success and the accomplishments of the GDR, which you recently emphasized during your tour of the Leipzig Fair. Should now this Workers State, in the twentieth year of its existence, carry out arbitrary measures against active workers, only because they worship a God?

Very honorable Herr Chairman of the State Council, I most respectfully ask that you help us, help our Church regain our legally assigned meeting house, which we renovated with difficult and voluntary labor.

On April 8, 1969, Gerwin Baasch and other members of the Leipzig branch took the above letter directly to the office of the State Council in Berlin and to the Secretariat for Church Affairs. At the latter office, a representative of the state secretary requested a copy of the city's letter of April 30, 1968, which had directed the branch to move to the former movie house. Herbert Heidler explained what happened that day:

> I personally accompanied Gerwin Baasch and the Hachbergers when they traveled to the State Council in Berlin. We were received by a certain Herr Bachmann, but he told us he couldn't help us. We were directed to meet with the state secretary, which we did immediately. Herr Seigewasser was not present, but his deputy was. He listened to us and said, "We will see what can be done." He telephoned to Leipzig and told us, "Go to the district councilman on Tuesday and you will receive your house." All four of us went to the district councilman on the next Tuesday. He didn't say a word about the state secretary. He just said, "We have considered the matter once more and have decided that you may retain that building and hold religious services." (1993)

> *June 6, 1969, memorandum from Walter Schiele:* On Wednesday, June 4, 1969, I met with a worker in the building department and was received with this comment: "Well, the matter has been resolved, you are again in the building." In response to my comment, that we have not yet received word of that permission, he looked at me in disbelief. I then called the city councilman for building affairs, Herr Wieczorek, on June 5, 1969, and received from him the answer that he could not decide the matter.

> *June 17, 1969, memorandum from Walter Schiele:* The mayor informed us that the building will be returned to us.

The Leipzig branch met in that facility from 1969 until a new meeting house and stake center was completed in May 1986 (see Chapter 16).

Dresden

In early 1946, the Church received permission to renovate a portion of a three-story building in the Dr. Kurt Fischer Allee for a meeting house that served the branch for the next forty-two years, until a stake center was built in that city in 1988. Work on the building, which had been a German Army officers' casino, began six weeks prior to a district conference planned for the first week of May 1946 [see conference report in Appendix D]. Walter Krause and Walter Kindt, two full-time missionaries, were assigned to oversee the renovation and assist the local members. The following excerpts are taken from their personal accounts, written in the 1990s and provided by Walter Kindt:

> *Walter Krause:* The place was in ruins, but the brothers and sisters, together with the missionaries, began with a prayer in their hearts. They had eight weeks in which to complete the renovations and had em-

ployed professional construction workers to oversee the project and to provide additional labor. When those men arrived at the building, they realized they were supposed to help this little band of women and old people renovate the building. The hired workers soon left because the task appeared insurmountable and the members didn't seem likely to have the money to pay for the work. But it was clear to us that, with God on our side, we could do it ourselves. Mountains of rubble had to be removed, and we had to create much out of nothing. We installed windows and doors. The walls were repaired and painted. But the most difficult task was to break through a thick wall of sandstone [between two rooms].

We spent many hours standing in front of that wall, deciding what we should do. We finally decided that we had to remove it by ourselves. The first day went well. But one of the brothers was worried. Something wasn't right with that wall. Why did the professional workers leave? What were they afraid of it? One night, during our evening devotional, a brother said, "This is the room in which we are to hold the conference. What if the wall were to collapse?" Three days later it did collapse.

There was a double door at the location where we wanted to break through the wall. We removed it carefully, placed supports all around and conscientiously removed one rock after the other. Between the wall on the meeting room side and a parallel wall in the next room, was a dark, empty space. We were surprised to find another wall inside that space, also made of sandstone blocks. We asked everyone to stand back from the wall and to be careful as we removed the supports. That was done by Walter Kindt with the help of a younger brother, who pulled the last rock with all his strength while Walter applied his crowbar. The supports fell with a huge crash and a thick cloud of dust. Everyone, except Walter Kindt, was on the meeting room side and they stood as if paralyzed as sandstone block after sandstone block emerged from the opening. I cried out, "Walter!" From the other side came a voice, "I'm here!" He was not injured. What had happened? The middle wall was just a partial wall over which sandstone blocks had been stacked without any mortar. It had been held up only by our supports.

Walter Kindt: Still more difficult was another task that our little group had to master. We had to install four steel beams to support the walls. Each beam weighed 400 kilograms [880 pounds], which we had to move with our own inexperience and strength. The task appeared impossible, but we began, as always, with a prayer. Before we went home exhausted each evening, we met to sing a song. We felt that the songs of Zion never had been sung before with such feeling. The spirit of the Lord helped the sisters and brothers to prepare themselves to move those heavy beams. With the efforts of eight women, two deacons, and two older brothers, the beams were brought into the building (by rolling them forward on logs), where they were lifted onto pillars.

> *Walter Krause:* A young deacon was supposed to move one of the logs forward. As he grasped it, the sisters and brothers let loose of the beam and its full weight rolled over his hand. He screamed and we quickly lifted the beam so he could retract his hand. A missionary [Brother Krause, himself] said, "Come with me, brother, it will be okay." They went into a room and looked at the hand. It was bleeding, but the missionary promised him that he wouldn't lose even a fingernail, and that his hand would be healed. That promise was fulfilled. Within a short time, the brother was able to resume his work and even shake hands.

> *Walter Kindt:* With God's help, work that appeared impossible was completed. It was accomplished with joy and in harmony, something only possible by children of God. The spirit of unity and harmony during those weeks was proof that we worked with the Lord. Often, our daily ration for that heavy work consisted of only one hundred grams of bread and a few potatoes. When the work was completed, we fasted for a successful conference. We felt it was a great blessing to be able to obtain and use this wonderful facility in a destroyed city.

Later, the heating system in the Dresden meeting house was condemned because of an unsafe chimney. Günter Schulze described how the members repaired it:

> In 1974, the branch president gave me the assignment to repair the chimney. Where could I find the necessary bricks and tiles, the cement, the scaffolding, and the professionals who knew how to build a chimney? I went to a man who was experienced in that field. He had additional friends, and they said, "When you bring us the bricks, tiles, cement, etc., and also the scaffolding, we will help you build a new chimney."
>
> I said to Joachim Lehnig, "Bricks are fabricated in the Spreewald." "Yes," he said, "but they won't sell you any. None are available." Several weeks went by. Toward the end of the year, Lehnig called me and said he knew of a factory that had an excess of bricks. We had a planned economy under socialism, and their plan had been filled, and then some. He managed to ship a freight car load to Dresden. But how was I to unload them in Dresden and transport them to the meeting house? I thought and prayed about that until I drove by a gardening store in the Reickerstraße one day and thought, "Maybe they have a vehicle I could rent." I went to the fleet manager and explained my sit-

uation. He reserved a tractor and two trailers for me, and we emptied the entire freight car on January 1st.

Now, where would I find cement? There was none available. Suddenly, some appeared, but it was limited to one sack—twenty kilograms—per person. I went around and gathered up my retired members. They all purchased one sack of cement. Then I went to a large construction company and asked if I could borrow scaffolding. They said that they had some old scaffolding, which was not in good condition, but they could loan it to me. But how could I transport it to the meeting house? I was driving by the gardening store again when I heard, as if someone was sitting next to me, "Stop! Don't drive any further!" I heard that three times. I was in a hurry, but at the third instance I stopped and wrote down what I was doing and what I had heard. As I was writing, I heard, "Okay, now you can drive further." Really! I arrived at the garden shop and told them what I needed. The secretary said, "If you want a vehicle, you came too late. The boss just left." Then she looked at me for a while and said, "But be happy that you didn't arrive earlier. There was a big argument here. People were screaming at each other. If you had come at that time and asked for help, the boss would have lost his temper with you." So I waited thirty minutes until he returned, and I could calmly explain my needs. I obtained a vehicle to transport the scaffolding. That was the story of the chimney. If you hadn't experienced it, you probably wouldn't believe it. (1991)

12 Importing Church Literature

We had a saying, "You can leave your wallet or other valuables in the meeting house and will certainly find it again the next Sunday. But if you have a copy of the Stern *and forget to take it with you, chances are that you won't find it again." This little joke accurately described the hunger for current information about the status and teachings of the Church. We had no literature, just the scriptures. Today, I know that was good, because we read the scriptures and had few manuals. There are two sides to everything. (Manfred Schütze, 1991)*

The American as well as the Soviet occupation forces implemented import restrictions immediately after the war. The following excerpts from a letter sent by the acting mission presidency to Thomas E. McKay on January 8, 1946, describe efforts to overcome those import restrictions and the relatively liberal attitude of the Soviet military forces regarding church issues in the immediate postwar period:

> Despite our overall material distress, the members have expressed their urgent wish to achieve closer ties with the Church through its publications.... We have the opportunity to take over the print shop of a former member of the Nazi Party at a relatively low cost because the owner no longer has permission to pursue his profession. It is a modern print shop with photo offset equipment that can print musical notations. In fact, our most recent songbooks, printed before the start of the war, were produced in a quality edition at an inexpensive price in that shop.
>
> The purchase has the full support of the American military government, the Russian occupation forces, and the local German officials. With the approval of the military and local government officials, we have registered our printing company at the license office under the name Fortschritt-Verlag-Berlin. The license will enable us to print and

> distribute newspapers, books, and forms in accordance with local laws and ordinances. (CR 271 40)

No response to the proposal is known. However, the Soviet occupation forces continued to be generally supportive of the mission's printing requests. They were particularly helpful regarding advertisements for the mission's conferences and other activities (see further examples in Appendix D). For instance, a mission conference was held in Leipzig in June 1946, which was announced on the radio three times each day for two weeks preceding the conference. Alfred Paul Schulz, who organized the conference's logistical arrangements, described the printed materials:

> I found a shop that printed the following items for me: A large placard for every advertisement pillar in the city, a smaller placard for every street car, six thousand handouts, one thousand formal invitations, three thousand conference programs, and two thousand meal coupons. The city officials posted the large placards on the pillars, and the transportation agency placed the signs in the street cars. The radio station was also directed to assist us. (MS 8242)

In June 1948, the mission organized a large week-long conference, Freud-Echo, held in Berlin-Grunewald. A detailed report written by Heinz Hinkel can be found in Appendix D. It includes this comment related to the printed advertisements. "In those days, one could see the exalted image of Angel Moroni, who invited everyone to listen to messages from the servants of God. An impressive placard, a good advertisement for our work!"

Church Manuals, Missionary Tracts, and Other Church Material

Since new manuals could not be imported, the following prewar instructional materials were used in Halberstadt, and probably elsewhere, in 1946–1947:

> M-Men and Gleaners Classes:
>
> Pioneers in science
> Appreciating the *Book of Mormon*
> Marriage and family life
> Establishing personal standards
> Letter writing, books of remembrance, and etiquette
>
> Adult Classes:
>
> The development of opera and the dramatic arts
> *A Rational Theology* by Professor John A. Widtsoe
> The Prophets of the Old Testament (LR 2428 54)

Paper was in short supply in the 1950s, and the requirements of churches did not have a high priority with the government. Moreover, the new GDR government was not as liberal about printing church materials as the Soviets had been. On February 8, 1952, Waldemar Nitz, president of the Berlin District, wrote to the government's Office of Church Affairs and described his unsuccessful efforts to print new songbooks:

> Our members in the GDR urgently need approximately four thousand copies of a songbook, whose copyright is held by our Church. Since the printer, Konrad Paris, with whom we are familiar, expressed his willingness to print our books, we gave him a contract on July 12, 1951, and asked him to obtain the necessary clearances. We were subsequently informed by the advisory council for printing affairs on August 15, 1951, that our request must be submitted through a print shop licensed by the GDR. It recommended the Evangelical Church Press.
>
> We submitted the appropriate request to the Evangelical Church Press on September 10, 1951. It declined the job. The advisory council then referred us to the Evangelical Printing Press, which accepted the job and promised to complete the printing in early 1952. In early January, that shop suddenly returned the book to us with the explanation that the printing could not be accomplished because the Church of Jesus Christ of Latter-day Saints did not belong to any of the Evangelical church associations.
>
> We were subsequently directed to the Union Press and submitted our request to that company on January 17, 1952. They declared their willingness to undertake the work, but said it could not be accomplished before the end of the year, because paper for this job had not been included in the current plan.
>
> Negotiations with various companies have been conducted without success for six months. These books are essential for the conduct of our church services. We would be very appreciative if an early allocation of paper could be achieved with your help. (DO 4/722)

A response to Nitz's request was not received until 1956, when the mission was told to await an announcement regarding relevant government guidelines. New songbooks were finally imported from West Germany ten years later, in 1966. Other Church literature was in equally short supply, and missionaries from the GDR often picked up a few tracts when they came to the mission office in West Berlin. The mission journal and member interviews describe other means whereby literature in limited quantities was transported across the border:

> *September 4, 1954:* President and Sister Gregory left in the Pontiac for Leipzig to attend the fair and also the district conference.... It was possible for the Gregorys to take into the zone and deliver to our authorities there a large number of MIA manuals and materials, as well as forty-eight song books, and some welfare cheese and butter for general distribution. (LR 2428 2)

April 12, 1956: Three missionaries and President Gregory left by car for a conference in Hamburg. Leaving Berlin in the late evening hours, they delivered six packages of lesson manuals and other church literature to some of the brethren from behind the Iron Curtain along the dark road. There was practically no other way to get lesson material into the hands of the members in East Germany. It was not that there were objectionable things in the manuals, it was just the policy of the Communist regime not to permit any literature of any type from the West to be circulated in East Germany. Through this action it was now possible to supply each branch with a fine assortment of standard lesson manuals in the event of any political eventuality. (LR 2428 2)

Henry Burkhardt: We had a missionary conference in West Berlin. Each of the [GDR] missionaries pocketed books and traveled via the city train from Grunewald to Potsdam. I waited there at the station and loaded copies of the Book of Mormon, songbooks, or whatever else arrived into my car. Once, I noticed that we were being observed, so I drove on the ring highway toward Nauen, exited in Leest, and drove into the Kolbins' yard. I did a lot of dumb things. (2003)

Joachim Albrecht: We didn't have many tracts with which to do missionary work. We did take a few tracts from the mission office, maybe four or five copies of the Joseph Smith story. After we presented the first lesson and had an appointment for the second, we would give the people that tract and would take it back after they had read it, because we were not allowed to sell anything. We did the same with the Book of Mormon. We did have permission to carry the standard works, but it was very confusing in the 1950s. In my own church books, I used a black pen to obliterate any reference to the West German Mission or to publication in West Germany. (2004)

June 30, 1955: A brother from Rathenow came to the office of the mission president. He had reason to believe that a plan was under way to abolish the Church entirely in the East. He complained about anti-communism references in certain manuals and books that had found their way into the Russian Zone. Elder Burkhardt reported that the mission counselor for the MIA, Eberhardt Sommer, had been picked up several times and questioned with regard to the Church. At one time they presented Elder Sommer with some manuals of the Church that had been confiscated by the East Zone police. In view of this situation a letter was mimeographed and mailed to each branch president in East Germany stating that until further notice no literature would be mailed into the East. (LR 2428 2)

Eberhardt Sommer: I received all of the mail for the MIA from Church headquarters in Utah, including the teaching material for our young people. Some of it was not acceptable as far as the Communists were concerned. Elder Benson's speeches against the Communists were not very helpful. They seized various items. (2005)

President Harold Gregory summarized the problem in a report to Elder Adam S. Bennion in 1956:

> It is almost impossible for us to get manuals and other important literature because of stringent controls. We have been moderately successful in smuggling some items into East Germany, but we try to hold this to a bare minimum. During the past six months we have presented every branch with an assortment of standard manuals and church books, which they are to maintain in their branch libraries. In the future we may not have to worry so much about this element. Our present policy calls for our furnishing each branch with one copy of each acceptable manual. We consider it unnecessary under the circumstances to offer manuals for sale to the membership, since bringing them into East Germany is so hazardous. An acceptable manual is one which does not contain any anticommunist statements.(LR 2428 2)

Since manuals could not be imported or printed, the Church had to find other ways to provide necessary teaching materials:

Henry Burkhardt: We could not officially import manuals, teaching material, etc., so we more or less had to obtain them illegally, but only in very limited quantities, i.e., one or two copies. We then organized many volunteers, who used typewriters to copy these manuals for our approximately fifty-two branches. It was a very primitive process, but the teachings provided by the Church at that time were made available to and used in our branches, always one year later than in the West. We needed one year to copy these manuals. Although we were certainly skirting the law, use of typewriters was not technically prohibited. It was an approach that I could personally justify. However, it required an enormous amount of work. (1991)

Manfred Heller: We were totally cut off from teaching and study materials. We only had the standard works of the Church and some old items that members had saved, for example, *The Articles of Faith* by Talmage, *A Marvelous Work and a Wonder* by LeGrand Richards, *Gospel Doctrine* by Joseph F. Smith, and *Church History* by Joseph Fielding Smith. Otherwise, we didn't have any manuals. Occasionally, a manual or an outline was carried over the border by visitors, which were copied here by sisters using ancient typewriters, with up to eight carbon copies. Often, these were sisters in need of financial assistance, who performed the work at home, coordinated by the mission office. The completed manuals, which were barely readable if you had the seventh or eighth copy, were provided to each branch. Additional manuals and teaching outlines were initiated and organized by the relevant mission committees for genealogy, Primary, MIA, etc., based on known Church principles. (1991)

Günter Schulze: Brother Richter from Chemnitz had a wholesale business that provided the paper. Only thin airmail paper would work, and even then the sisters had to hit the keys very hard so that the seventh copy would be readable. Seven times seven was forty-nine, and that was enough to provide each branch with one copy. We were also able to copy entire handbooks with thermal copy machines and chemical paper. Every page had to be pulled individually through the machine. Then the thirty or forty pages were given to Brother Dzierzon in Freiberg, and he attached cardboard covers and adhesive backs. Copying with thermal machines was half-and-half legal. We avoided being punishable. (1993)

Gottfried Richter: We needed paper for hundreds of thousands of pages, which was not normally available. But I had it. My business was a blessing for the Church. Paper and office supplies may have been common in the West, but they were a huge problem for us. That was resolved by my business. Connections and contacts were most important in the GDR. Not money, but connections. (1991)

Michael Lehmann: I dictated page after page for my mother. She always made nine carbon copies! We were allowed to use them at home to prepare our lessons, but not during the lesson. (2003)

Hans Schult: We received the manuals two years late, first in the U.S., followed by the German-speaking areas. Then they had to be copied and bound for us. The mission presidency really accomplished a great service. It involved multiple manuals for the priesthood, Sunday School, Primary, Relief Society, etc. (1991)

Eveline Laube: Sometimes the copies were in poor condition, difficult to read. Some letters consisted only of holes. And our manuals were not used just once, so you could not underline the text or make marginal notes. The lessons and visiting teaching topics that the sisters used were typed out for us. Every branch received one copy, but we were not permitted to bring them to meetings. To be safe, we taught from notes we made for ourselves at home. (2004)

> *Helga Schaarschmidt:* Only the teacher had a manual. The students had nothing. Teachers prepared at home and went to meetings without the manual. The mission leaders always reminded us not to bring the manuals. We didn't have any visual aids, no pictures, nothing. (1991)

In 1964, President Burkhardt suddenly decided to destroy as many of the copied manuals as possible. Two members described how they assisted him:

> *Walter Schiele:* We were allowed to have the four standard works. They were adequate, but the manuals had wonderful supplementary material. However, when their use became dangerous, the instruction came from President Burkhardt, "Destroy the manuals." We had a large iron stove at that time in the Gerberstraße in Leipzig, and we burned manuals the entire night, everything. We had to be strict. I even burned *A Marvelous Work and a Wonder*. (1991)

> *Walter Krause:* After President Burkhardt told me what had happened, I began to collect the manuals that we had copied. I filled an entire trailer and drove my old Mercedes at sixty kilometers per hour at night on the autobahn. I took Helaman, my young son, with me and always placed my work tools on top of the manuals. When I arrived home, I said, "We must dig a big hole here in the garden so that we can destroy everything." As I threw the last of them in, a local official came by and said, "What are you doing there?" I said, "I'm burning my garbage." If he had looked in the hole, we would have been finished. (1991)

President Burkhardt recognized that he was not able to collect all the manuals. He said that some branches refused to part with them, and many members hid their own copies. "Members said that the mission couldn't have them. I didn't pursue the matter any further. We collected those that were voluntarily given to us" (2005).

Since no one was told why the manuals had to be destroyed, some members came up with their own reasons. In her book about Walter Krause, his wife Edith wrote that "Brother Gottfried Richter had to be protected, since his company had provided the paper."[1] Her statement, while plausible, is not factual. According to the two people most knowledgeable on this subject, the destruction of the manuals had nothing to do with Gottfried Richter or his company. Richter often said that he sold paper legally to the Church, just as he had done with other churches and government organizations. When the question was posed directly to Henry Burkhardt, he told me, "Printing was not allowed, but what we were doing with typewriters did not constitute printing. It was natural that members would ask why, since the manuals were not printed, just retyped. But I could not reveal the actual reason" (2005). He then explained the true facts and circumstances, which will not, however, be repeated here.

As noted earlier, the restrictions on importing church literature even affected songbooks. Following are excerpts from correspondence in 1965 between President Burkhardt and government leaders in Berlin, including an appeal to the head of state, Walter Ulbricht, which finally resulted in permission to import new songbooks in 1966:

> *March 17, 1965, to the State Secretary for Church Affairs:* We request your advice and support regarding the following inquiry. For more than twenty years, it has not been possible for our members to obtain songbooks. Our current books are old and unusable, and it has become urgently necessary to find replacements. Church leaders in West Germany are ready to send us two thousand new songbooks as a gift. Would you please be so kind and show us how we can take possession of these two thousand songbooks?
>
> *April 28, 1965, to the State Secretary for Church Affairs:* Since we have not yet received an answer, we wish to kindly inquire whether our letter arrived in your office.
>
> *June 29, 1965, to the State Secretary for Church Affairs:* We find it incomprehensible that we have not received an answer to our original letter or to our subsequent inquiry. Therefore, we are sending this third letter, in the hope of hearing from you.
>
> *August 31, 1965, to Walter Ulbricht, Chairman of the State Council:* We kindly request your assistance because we have not received an answer to our three previous letters.... We assume that longer patience on our part will not result in an answer from the state secretary and do not see any other way to obtain help. We, therefore, turn to you with a request for assistance. Earlier, we had relied on a May 14, 1956, message from the Interior Ministry, which told us to await an eminent ruling. Again, we received no subsequent information concerning this matter.
>
> *September 11, 1965, from the Office of the State Council:* We hereby inform you that your petition to the Chairman of the State Council of the GDR is being considered. Please be patient and await further information.
>
> *September 28, 1965, from the State Secretary for Church Affairs:* Your petition to the Chairman of the State Council concerning the above matter was forwarded to us. Please submit an appropriate application in triplicate with the donor's information and precise address. In addition, we request that you enclose a copy of the proposed item to be imported.

January 13, 1966, from the Ministry for Foreign and Inner-German Trade: The import permission is attached. (Copies in the author's possession.)

Beginning in 1966, after the successful import of the songbooks, requests to import other Church literature encountered fewer restrictions. The following examples of successful and unsuccessful requests are taken from the files of the North German Mission (LR 2428 25):

July 13, 1966, President Burkhardt to Henry G. Tempest, Frankfurt/Main: I just received permission to import five hundred Triple Combinations. I am very pleased. Many of our members have asked for years if we could obtain the Triple Combinations. Now that an official way has been opened, there will be great joy here.

July 25, 1966, Henry Tempest to President Garrett L. Myers, North German Mission: I am enclosing a copy of the permit issued by the GDR giving permission to send five hundred leather-bound copies of the Triple Combination to President Burkhardt.... I think it would be well to discuss with President Burkhardt and President Krause what they will need next. Perhaps a printed book or copies of the missionary edition of the Book of Mormon or something else that would assist them in the promotion of the Church programs. I am sure that as you discuss it with them, some book will come to mind that will serve a great purpose. What about *Jesus the Christ*?

October 18, 1966, President Myron Bangerter, North German Mission, to John E. Carr, Frankfurt/Main: I am sure you are familiar with the attempts which have been made in the past to secure permission from the government to send certain Church books to the Saints within East Germany. Explicit permission must be granted by the state before they are allowed to have such books for use. The process is usually long and drawn out, but the results have been gratifying. With the last year, permission was obtained to send two thousand songbooks and five hundred Triple Combinations. These books were received with great joy and are treasured and used lovingly by all who have received them. It is now thought feasible that an attempt be made to secure permission to send one thousand copies of *Jesus the Christ* into the country.

February 4, 1967, President J. Peter Loscher, North German Mission, to John E. Carr: A few days ago I returned from a conference trip to East Germany, and I was successful in delivering to Brother Burkhardt, my counselor, a copy of *Jesus the Christ* in German. This book is to be used for approval of the East German government to let us send about a thousand copies.

Manfred Heller, who managed the administrative office in Dresden after Henry Burkhardt became president of the Freiberg Temple, said that it became easier to import or print materials in the 1970s:

> Through the Helsinki Accords [Conference for Security and Cooperation in Europe of 1975], the GDR was politically obligated to relax some of its social restrictions on its citizens. The accords had a noticeable effect, especially on our efforts to obtain Church literature. Not only did it become easier to import the standard works of the Church, but we were able to receive the *Stern* and manuals from West Germany. Our requests also were processed more quickly. (2004)

Excerpts from the files of the Dresden Mission support Manfred Heller's statement that conditions improved after the Helsinki Accords:

> *March 7, 1979, Triple Combination:* The Dresden District Council informed us that the import of the Triple Combination has been approved.
>
> *December 8, 1980:* Received permission to import one thousand copies of *Jesus the Christ.*
>
> *February 19, 1981:* The Dresden District Council granted permission to import three copies of the *Stern.*
>
> *September 22, 1981:* Our request to import *The Miracle of Forgiveness* has not been addressed. It was decided that we should wait until spring. [Several members stated that the book was not approved because it said that the wife should remain at home with the children and that mothers, not the state, are responsible for raising of children. However, no official reason for disapproval has been found.]
>
> *December 20, 1985:* It is anticipated that fifty copies of the *Stern* will be approved effective February 1986.
>
> *September 22, 1987:* The State Secretariat agreed to review and process our request for six hundred copies of the Priesthood study guide, *Come to Christ,* and seven hundred copies of the Relief Society study guide, *Come to Me.* We hope to import those two items in December 1987. (DMO)

Even as the importation of literature increased in the 1980s, President Burkhardt reminded local leaders that some of the approved items, especially the *Stern,* were to be used with great discretion:

> *March 5, 1987:* President Burkhardt repeated the continuing rule that [the *Stern*] not be used openly during church services, because the government has approved it only for Church leaders' personal use. He asked stake presidents to remind the members to act accordingly.

The ongoing sensitivity related to Church literature is evident in the following guidance sent by Manfred Heller to all stake and ward leaders in the GDR:

> *September 23, 1987:* Dear Brethren: With the support of the state secretary for Church Affairs, it has become possible for you to receive the *Stern*. Your receipt of this literature is based on your calling as a member of a stake presidency, high council, or as a bishop or branch president, to enable you to receive the messages of the general authorities of the Church, which you should then bring to the attention of the members of your assigned wards and branches in an inspired and appropriate manner. To avoid unnecessary problems, it is recommended that you not bring attention to the magazine itself or make use of it in a manner that makes it visible in Church meetings. After a certain period of time, older copies may be placed in the ward libraries. (LR 2428 54)

Less than two years later, in January 1989, all members were permitted to order the *Stern* and receive it through the regular mail. Interestingly, this concession, which was a significant liberalization of the GDR's import policy, was not mentioned in any historical record of the Church in the GDR, perhaps because of the longstanding tradition of not bringing undue official attention to the magazine, which was printed in West Germany.

A major purpose of the GDR's restrictive import regulations regarding church literature was to control the content of religious material. However, even when the content was acceptable, the volume of the Church's requests created occasional problems for the state. In one instance, when the Church offered to provide paper and ink and pay all printing costs so that more of its literature could be printed in the GDR, the state cited the principle of equality as the reason for its rejection of a request:

> *September 22, 1987:* The State Secretariat supports the principle that all churches in the GDR are equal and that the LDS Church cannot be favored just because it may be able to cover the material and financial costs, if other churches do not have that possibility.

However, in other instances, the Church was allowed to import paper and book covers, ink and glue so that books and manuals could be printed in the GDR. The government also relaxed its import restrictions in the late 1980s, especially following President Monson's October 1988 meeting with Erich Honecker. Jürgen Warnke, a West German lawyer who provided legal services to the Church in Frankfurt/Main, summarized the status of imports at the end of the GDR period:

> We were able to bring carloads of books and magazines over the border every other week. However, we had to be sure that the manuals didn't contain any objectionable material. I had to read every manual in advance. For the first time in my life, I read the Relief Society magazines and actually found passages that would have caused us considerable trouble. I had to say, "Here is something, there is a passage. They must be taken out." I found, for example, a sentence in a seminary manual that said, "Communism comes from the Devil." A Primary manual had a picture of soldiers from the former German Empire together with Russian soldiers. We had to cut such things out. (1991)

Requests to import Church literature continued up to the collapse of the GDR. In August 1989, after the arrival of missionaries from the West, Burkhardt wrote to the secretary for Church Affairs, Kurt Löffler, to request literature needed by the converts:

> With the generous support of the government of the GDR and with your valuable assistance, the Church's Dresden Mission has been organized, missionaries have undertaken their activities in our country, and people have begun to join the Church. The new members have the understandable wish to possess the holy scriptures and other complementary literature that has been legally imported into the GDR, but which is currently not available. For this reason, I respectfully ask that you favorably review and support the import of
>
> 1,500 copies of the Triple Combination (in leather)
> 1,000 copies of our Church songbook
> 500 copies of *Jesus the Christ*, by Talmage
> 500 copies of *Doctrines of Salvation*, vol. 1, by Joseph F. Smith
> 500 copies of *Gospel Doctrine*, by Joseph F. Smith
> 2,200 copies of a supplement for teachers of religion classes.
>
> These items contribute to the members' personal study of the scriptures, while the supplement for teachers supports the Sunday religious teaching in the thirty-two wards and branches of the Church of Jesus Christ of Latter-day Saints in the GDR. (DMO)

The regime collapsed in November 1989 before any decision regarding this request was made.

13 Financial Administration

If I have made proper calculations [regarding tithing and fast offerings], the members in the East Zone are more faithful, devout, and devoted than the ones in the West. (Elder Spencer W. Kimball, 1955)

Members in the East German Mission were known for their faithfulness regarding the payment of tithes and offerings prior to the war. One year after the start of the war, a September 9, 1940, letter from Johanna Berger, a secretary in the mission office, to President Thomas E. McKay stated that during the first eight months of 1940, tithing had increased by 15 percent, fast offerings by 2 percent, and contributions in general had doubled (CR 271 40).

At the end of the war, the mission had more than one million reichsmarks in bank accounts and in cash. Although the bank accounts in the Soviet Zone were frozen, some of the cash was used to obtain a lease on a new mission home in the American sector of Berlin and to pay for the railroad cars used by Paul Langheinrich to transport government and church records that had been located in salt mines and castles where the Nazi government had stored them for safekeeping during the war (see Chapter 2).

On March 22, 1946, Elder Benson discussed administrative matters with the acting mission presidency in Berlin and provided the following guidance for management of the mission's finances: All tithes and surplus fast offerings should be remitted to the mission each month, each branch should submit a budget for the year based on its estimated needs, and no tithing funds should be used for additional expenses unless authorized by the mission presidency (LR 2428 2).

A Separate Bank Account for the GDR

In June 1948, lack of agreement on economic policy among the occupying forces led to the replacement of the reichsmark, which was still being used on both sides of the border, with new currencies in the West and in the East. The new East mark had no official exchange value in the West, and both the SMAD and the subsequent GDR government officially prohibited its transfer outside the Soviet Zone. Initially, mission leaders, in accordance with Elder Benson's guidance, continued to bring excess funds from the GDR to West Berlin, where they were kept in the mission office for future needs within the GDR. Walter Fassmann, a counselor to President Walter Stover, explained that this practice was changed sometime in 1951:

> President Stover asked me to be responsible for all the [GDR] money in the mission. He asked me to open a bank account in Zwickau so the districts could send me the tithing and other contributions. Until that time, each district president hand-carried the money to the mission office in West Berlin. That was illegal and quite risky. I went to the bank and opened an account for the Church of Jesus Christ of Latter-day Saints.[1]

The new bank account in Zwickau did not immediately end the financial problems associated with operating one mission that covered two countries with different currencies, which could not legally be taken across their borders. One example is documented in the account of Fassmann's arrest in 1951:

> *Walter Fassmann:* President Stover said that they were planning on buying a branch meeting house in Leipzig and there was not enough money in the bank [in the GDR]. He asked me to take 25,000 East German marks [from West Berlin] to the bank and deposit them for the purchase of the property. He gave me a certificate stating where the money came from and the purpose of the money. The money was placed in my pockets. [Fassmann was searched at the border and the money was found. The police did not initially believe the documentation, and he was taken to the police station in Leipzig.] There they told me everything looked in order and let me go. [However, a soldier] began to shout, "You can't simply allow a man with twenty-five thousand marks in his pockets to walk free." The soldier put up quite a fuss, and the police officers asked me to return. The money was confiscated, and I was thrown into prison [where he remained from May 24 to May 30, 1951, until his story was confirmed]. I asked them about the money, and they told me, "Don't worry, it is in good hands." Then they released me.[2]

> *Herbert Schreiter:* President Stover intended to buy the villa in the Prellerstraße and wanted to smuggle the money into the GDR to pay for it. . . . Eight days later, the doorbell rang at our room in the Prellerstraße, and Brother Fassmann was standing there. His face was very white. They had released him, but the entire money had been lost. (1991)

Walter Fassmann: [Late one night a member of the secret police came to me and said,] "Herr Fassmann, the trouble you had with the money will soon be coming before the court in Zwickau. The prosecutor is a woman and she is a Communist sympathizer. They will prove that you changed West German marks with great profit into East German marks and you were caught smuggling the twenty-five thousand East German marks back into East Germany." He advised me to get out of East Germany if possible.[3]

Fassmann left the GDR in 1952, and Henry Burkhardt replaced him as mission counselor in June. However, earlier that year, Burkhardt had his own encounter with the police regarding Church funds, as recorded in the mission history:

March 31, 1952: Elder Henry Burkhardt, president of the Thuringia District, while bringing in yearly reports to the mission headquarters in Berlin, was stopped in the Russian Zone for questioning. The fact that he was carrying tithing lists caused him to be held for three days. It is illegal to send or carry money from the Russian Zone into Berlin or the Allied Zones. It was believed that he had previously sent the tithing money into Berlin and was now bringing in the lists. However, when it was proved that he had legally deposited the money in Russian Zone banks, he was released. (LR 2428 2)

Six years later, Burkhardt was detained once more. "On May 24, 1958, we learned that Brother Burkhardt, upon leaving Berlin and returning to the [Russian] Zone was held and questioned overnight. He was released but all of his forms, reports, etc., were held. They were later returned to him. At this time it was decided that no more reports would be sent from the East" (LR 2428 2).

Several former GDR missionaries have stated that they continued to take money into West Berlin at times after a bank account had been established in their country. For example:

Günter Schulze: Although all of the money should have remained in the GDR, many of us missionaries often smuggled money. We can admit that today. We hid money in the fingers of our gloves, traveled to a missionary conference in West Berlin, and turned in the money, simply to help Brother Burkhardt. (1991)

However, Burkhardt said that no money was smuggled into West Berlin after 1952, i.e., after the accounts were established in the GDR:

After I was called to be a counselor to President Glaus in 1952, we established our own office here in the GDR, first in Leipzig and later in Dresden. At that time, I met the former counselor, Brother Fassmann,

> at the train station in Leipzig. He was headed to the West and gave me thirty thousand East marks as the foundation for our mission. I deposited it in Leipzig. Officially, we were independent, and I informed the government of that fact. Therefore, it would have been wrong, it would have ruined the Church, if we had still smuggled to West Berlin. That did not happen. Even the East Berliners did not bring their money to West Berlin, which was still possible until 1961. Instead, they deposited it into our bank account. (2005)

Every branch had a bank account, and expenditures from those accounts were controlled by Burkhardt, under guidelines provided by Church leaders. Joachim Albrecht said, "We went to the bank every week and deposited the tithing money into our account. The mission office had control over each branch account and authorized expenditures from them" (2003).

Elder Spencer W. Kimball visited the mission in 1955 and afterward sent a report to President Harold Gregory. Under the heading, "Problems peculiar to the East German Mission," he wrote:

> It is our understanding that tithes were formerly collected by branch presidents, and it was left to their discretion what they thought the branch needed. They would send in the surplus, if any, to the mission. It is my understanding that you are trying to get this matter in line in the Russian Zone so that there will be a report of all tithes received and sent to the mission office at Dresden, and a careful budget worked out so that the branch will have a definite amount to count on. It is my understanding that funds are sent from the branches to the district presidents who send them to President Burkhardt, and that all funds are at the disposal of and according to the judgment of Brother Burkhardt. Would it be better if the funds and reports went directly to President Burkhardt rather than through the district presidencies? (LR 2428 39)

On Sunday, October 13, 1957, the GDR issued a new East mark, and every citizen was permitted to exchange only three hundred marks into the new currency. Quick-thinking citizens in the East who held more than three hundred marks avoided a loss by dividing the balance with friends, although such measures were illegal and violators were subject to punishment of up to one year in jail. The mission history reported that members in Schwerin saved six thousand marks, and Burkhardt saved a similar amount. Although it was illegal to take East marks out of the country, some banks, smaller currency exchange offices, and individuals in the West had held large amounts of East marks. They became worthless. The mission office in West Berlin had over eight thousand East marks that had been accumulated over time from various sources. Those funds were lost. (LR 2428 2)

Financial Administration in the Dresden Mission

As noted earlier, a separate Dresden Mission was established in 1969. Günter Schulze was a counselor in the mission presidency and explained how he managed the mission's financial accounts in the later years of that mission:

> We had a bank account, whose number was on our letterhead. Everything was completely official. The state knew exactly how much money we had, although bank accounts were supposedly confidential. The branches transferred tithing and fast offerings, as well as contributions for missionary, building, and maintenance activities, to Dresden. When the branches occasionally needed additional amounts for fast offering expenditures, those funds were transferred back from Dresden. When, for example, funds were required to renovate meeting rooms, the branch would submit a proposal with an estimated cost, which was reviewed by the mission presidency. If approved, we could transfer funds to that branch as needed, up to the approved amount, without further review by President Burkhardt. The entire bookkeeping, the transfer of moneys, the related oversight of branch and district reports, a total of fifty-three monthly reports, was a big job. In the second half of the 1980s, Church officials responsible for finance came from Frankfurt/Main to audit our books, every tithing receipt, every expenditure. No instance of improper accounting was found. (2003)

The members in the GDR were not only true to the principle of tithing. They paid a generous fast offering and contributed to building, missionary, and branch accounts. Mission reports show that tithing receipts increased 128 percent from 1966 to 1984 despite a decline in membership, while fast offerings increased by 168 percent during the same period. Member contributions fully covered all Church activities in the GDR, including typical operating costs of the mission, districts, branches, youth activities, official travel, and the preparation and copying of instructional material. Significant expenditures also were made for renovation, maintenance, rental, and purchase of meeting houses. Although the building of new meeting houses in the middle and late 1980s had to be financed with Western currency, a condition imposed by the GDR government, the land for those buildings, as well as typical equipment and supplies for the operation of those buildings, was purchased with East marks from the mission's account (DMO).

After the First Presidency announced the Freiberg Temple project in October 1982, local members were encouraged to make financial sacrifices for its construction. It is widely known that the temple had to be built with western currency. However, the funds contributed by the members were used to purchase the temple lot, some of the construction material, and the furnishings within the building. The operational costs of the temple also were financed with the members' temple contributions until the collapse of the GDR government. A few months after the October announcement, President Burkhardt reported on the status of the local contributions in a July 6, 1983, letter to Church leaders in the GDR:

> We are very thankful for our sisters and brothers, who, in the absence of any specific request, have allowed themselves to be led by the spirit. The majority of our wards, branches, and individual members have truly demonstrated their loyalty and submission to our Heavenly Father, so that the goal given us by the leaders of the Church has been reached and oversubscribed. The needs of the temple, therefore, have been met by our members, and we wish to hereby express our most heartfelt thanks for the willingness to sacrifice, which has been demonstrated in the past seven months. We will end this action on September 30, 1983. (DMO)

Manfred Heller, who directed the administrative office from 1984 forward, addressed the broader implications of financial management within the GDR:

> It was not possible to transfer the members' tithing and other contributions to the headquarters of the Church, since that would have violated the country's currency regulations. The funds had to be administered within the GDR and were used to maintain the Church's entire operation in the GDR. President Monson frequently mentioned the fact that the Church in this region was able to independently maintain and support itself, even financially. Naturally, we could not have built the new buildings that we now have with our own resources. That was not possible. But the ongoing upkeep and technical maintenance requirements of our buildings was covered solely by the contributions of the members. In fact, we were able to establish and maintain a reserve so that we did have to live on a hand-to-mouth basis. (1991)

14 Improved Relations in the 1970s and 1980s

> *We believe that all men are bound to sustain and uphold the respective governments in which they reside, while protected in their inherent and inalienable rights by the laws of such governments.... We do not believe it just to mingle religious influence with civil government.* (Doctrine and Covenants 134: 5, 9)

During the first two decades of the GDR, the Church's relations with the government focused on efforts to clarify or improve its legal status. Beginning in the 1970s, greater effort was made to establish personal friendly relations with government officials, to educate those officials about the Church's position on the separation of church and state, its noninvolvement in political issues, and the duty of members to be responsible citizens. The Church also exhibited an increasing willingness to state its principles in words that would be recognized and accepted by government officials.

For example, when the First Presidency invited President Burkhardt to attend the April 1972 General Conference in Salt Lake City, the text of the invitation letter appears to have been worded to appeal to the government. The original letter has not been located, but President Burkhardt quoted portions thereof in his February 24, 1972, request for a travel visa as follows:

> The President of the Church, Joseph Fielding Smith, hereby invites you to participate in this world conference.... It appears to us that this is a critical time for an assembly of leaders of the world to proclaim and promote world peace, to strengthen attitudes and beliefs, and to emphasize the brotherhood of man. You can make a considerable contribution to this worldwide leadership meeting. (DMO)

The phrases "promote world peace" and "brotherhood of man" were frequently used by the GDR in its own public relations campaigns, and their use by the Church in this instance was certainly intentional. Perhaps they were a factor in the government's eventual approval, although it took seven months to obtain that approval.

President Burkhart did attend the April 1972 General Conference, returning again in 1975 and almost annually thereafter. During a meeting with President Spencer W. Kimball in 1975, he was surprised by Kimball's counsel to "develop a good relationship with the GDR's leaders." Kimball also added his personal philosophy, that the world only changes when people change themselves. He told Burkhardt:

> If you want to see a change of things in East Germany, it must begin with you personally. It must begin with you because you are the leader there, and you must have a change of heart, which means you must force yourself to befriend the Communists. You cannot hold any grudges against them. You must change your whole outlook and attitude. (Personal communication from Edward Kimball, confirmed by Burkhardt)

Burkhardt initially resisted that advice. His unspoken response was, "You don't know the Communists. You cannot develop a good relationship with them. They are against religion, often threaten to throw me into prison, and constantly make trouble for me." He said later that "it took a long time before I came to realize that Communists were also children of our Heavenly Father, and that I should deal with them accordingly, in a friendly manner. And from that time forth, miracle after miracle occurred in the history of the Church in this country. They became friendlier and more receptive to me, as a representative of the Church" (2003).

President Kimball gave the same advice to Burkhardt's counselors when they came to General Conference:

> *Gottfried Richter:* While preparing to attend General Conference, members told me, "We will no longer accept such treatment from the government. We must hire a lawyer. We must resist." Since it was my turn to attend General Conference, Brother Burkhardt told me to discuss it with Elder Monson. I did tell Elder Monson, and he said, "Come with me." He took me to see President Kimball, who listened carefully. Then he stood up, came to me, and said with his deep, sonorous voice, "Brother Richter, soften the hearts of these people. Don't harden them." He repeated that once more. This was the calm advice of a prophet. While the other churches hardened the hearts of those people, we softened them over time. I now repeat that advice so casually, but Brother Burkhardt absolutely could not abide the entire Communist society. He didn't like it at all, and it was not easy for him. He didn't want to curry favor with them, but he began to do what President Kimball had counseled, "soften their hearts," and it worked. (2003)

In preparation for the twenty-fifth anniversary of the GDR, Dr. Helmut Obst, assistant professor for ecumenical theology at the Martin Luther University at Halle-Wittenberg, asked President Burkhardt for a summary of "facts and material that would illuminate the relationship of your church to the issue of peace, to the state, and to the society of the GDR." President Burkhardt responded on February 28, 1974:

> There are no statements of our Church on political and social issues, and we do not have an archive or statistics concerning activities, statements, or explanations of Church members on this subject. Since our founding or restoration, the Church has operated in all countries on the principle that state and church are strictly separate in all matters. We are of the opinion that the only purpose of a church should be to preach the gospel of Jesus Christ and encourage its members to practice its principles in daily life. It is our opinion that a church has no right to deliver political statements. That is the function and the privilege of the state or political parties. If a church abandons the area of theology and turns to politics, it becomes, in our opinion, a political party.
>
> Of course, service on behalf of our neighbors and for peace is required by the gospel and one cannot be separated from the other. Both should not only be preached on Sunday, but must be practiced daily, not primarily within the church but rather in daily life, at the workplace, and in society. That is what the Church teaches its members, and it is grounded in our Articles of Faith. All are challenged to do their best for their neighbors and to be an example for the welfare of society. The practice and the form of engagement are left to individuals. In this manner, they become effective citizens, certainly Christian citizens, but with emphasis on the word "citizens."
>
> Members of our Church are active as representatives in the GDR. They participate in social organizations, National Front committees, "Christian Circle" workgroups, as jurors, etc. Some are members of block parties, and many hold state and local awards. A high percentage of our brothers have been honored as "activists." However, they do not act in that regard as representatives of the Church, but rather in the exercise of their rights and responsibilities as citizens. (DMO)

President Kimball not only asked Burkhardt and his counselors to develop friendly relations with Communist leaders, but exercised his own diplomacy in this regard. In August 1977, he traveled to Poland on a trip that signaled his intent to improve relations with all countries, instead of pursuing the strong anticommunist rhetoric of the postwar years. During his return, he also stopped briefly in East Germany. On short notice, every branch was informed that he would be in Dresden on August 24, and 1,400 members traveled there in the middle of the week to hear him. Burkhardt described the visit:

I invited officials from the Dresden district council, and a representative of the local office responsible for church affairs, Frau Fischer, was present. She was seated in the front row. We didn't know in advance what President Kimball intended to say, and surprisingly, he spoke about the 12th Article of Faith. Frau Fischer was very impressed. At the close of the meeting she came to me and said, "Herr Burkhardt, did your president speak about that Article for my benefit?" I replied, "Absolutely not. That is a message that we all needed to hear at this time, and that is why he spoke about it." It was a unique experience for us, to receive that message from President Kimball.

The officials realized that when we said something, we did so honestly and sincerely, and that we didn't try to get around the laws of the land. We had to obey them. We did avoid some to a certain extent, for example, when we copied teaching material with typewriters. In that regard, we did try to get around the laws, but it was something that I could absolutely reconcile with my conscience. So we always tried to act correctly. Those people noticed that, and since they could believe what we said, they became more and more obliging toward us. That happened very seldom with Communists, but they slowly understood that we really meant what we said. (1991)

The Church and the Stationing of the MX Missiles

On May 5, 1981, the First Presidency published its opposition to the proposal of the U.S. government to station MX Missiles in Utah and Nevada. Shortly thereafter, Gottfried Richter and Günter Schulze attended a meeting of GDR church leaders with the secretary for Church Affairs. Richter described what took place at that time:

> State Secretary Gysi held a lecture about specific instances in which churches had become involved in political issues. Then he spoke about the peace issue. That was a very popular theme in the GDR. He said: "There is an American church that has recently taken the position that America should not build these special missiles." I spoke up and said: "Herr State Secretary, that wasn't an American church. It was the Church of Jesus Christ of Latter-day Saints. They took a position on the MX Missile System, and as a result, the program collapsed. I will quote some passages from it." When I finished, Frau Janott came to me and said: "Herr Richter, the state secretary would very much like to have the text. Can you send it to us?" I told her that I had two copies and gave her one. She thanked me profusely. (1993)

On July 16, 1981, an article entitled "Our fathers proclaimed peace: Mormons protest against building the US-Intercontinental MX Missile," appeared in the newspaper *Neue Zeit*. It began with the statement that Richter had quoted:

> Our fathers came to this western area to establish a base from which to carry the gospel of peace to the peoples of the earth. It is ironic, and a denial of the very essence of that gospel, that in this same general area there should be constructed a mammoth weapons system potentially capable of destroying much of civilization.

Günther Behncke said that Erich Honecker was aware of and very impressed by the First Presidency's position regarding the MX Missile and other statements of that period regarding peaceful resolution of international conflicts. These statements were repeated in several internal government documents, including the following excerpt from a report that Secretary Gysi received in January 1988, entitled, "Regarding the Structure of Churches in the USA":

> Regarding the Mormons: Until the end of the 1970s, the Mormon church emphatically supported every weapon system proposed for the defense of the USA. However, with its statement of May 1981, it not only opposed the stationing of missiles in Utah and Nevada, but also resolutely criticized all atomic weapons. . . . Those two states are part of the stronghold of USA conservatism. Senators Laxalt (Nevada) and Garn (Utah), both of whom belong to the Reagan wing of the Republican Party, refused to support President Reagan's proposal to station the MX Missile on the territory of those two states, with the result that he had to distance himself from the project. (MS 13918)

After the construction of the Freiberg temple had been approved, President Burkhardt wrote to Secretary Gysi and requested an opportunity for Elder Robert D. Hales to meet with and personally thank Gysi for his support of the project. Shortly thereafter, and at the request of Elder Hales, Burkhardt wrote to the GDR's ambassador in the United States, Dr. Grunert, to schedule a meeting in Washington, D.C., during his return from the April 1983 General Conference. Dr. Grunert had spent three days in Utah earlier that year as a guest of the Church (DMO).

The following year, David M. Kennedy, former secretary of the treasury and ambassador to NATO, also visited the GDR embassy in Washington, D.C. A short report said that "Ambassador Kennedy from Salt Lake City met with comrade Dr. Herder for thirty minutes on September 25, 1984." It did not mention any specific issues, but noted that he was a special representative of the First Presidency (MS 13918).

David Kennedy's activities on behalf of the unsuccessful effort to allow members to travel to the temple in Switzerland are addressed in the following chapter. These diplomatic activities coincided with President Kimball's personal advice to President Burkhardt to "soften their hearts."

Another example of diplomatic outreach can be seen in the friendly letters sent to GDR leaders at this time. It was tradition in the GDR for organizations to send formal greetings and best wishes to government leaders on birthdays and other special occasions. The letters subsequently appeared in newspapers. President Burkhardt was encouraged by Church leaders to participate in this tradition and wrote the following to Erich Honecker in 1986:

> On the occasion of your re-election as Chairman of the State Council of the German Democratic Republic, I wish to convey sincere and hearty greetings from the members of the Church of Jesus Christ of Latter-day Saints as well as from myself. Permit me to thank you for your untiring efforts on behalf of the citizens of our country, including the members of the Church of Jesus Christ of Latter-day Saints, and to wish you health and creativity as you work responsibly for the well-being of the German Democratic Republic.[1]

A Public Relations Campaign

Public interest in the Church, its teachings, and its relationship with the government grew considerably after the official announcement of the Freiberg Temple in October 1982, and Gottfried Richter was asked to coordinate the mission's public relations activities. In October 1985, he published a short introduction to the Church, entitled, "Man nennt sie Mormonen…" [They are called Mormons…], which appeared in a monthly Catholic magazine.[2] His article concluded with this statement:

> The Church has always stood for a separation between church and state, and it is thankful that this principle has become reality in the GDR. It is also thankful for the guaranteed and practiced equality of all religious convictions. At the end of June 1985, a temple was dedicated in Freiberg. Over ninety thousand visitors saw it during the preceding two-week open house, after listening to an introductory presentation in the newly completed meeting house of the Freiberg Ward. Additional church buildings are in various stages of planning and construction in the GDR.
>
> All these activities can only be accomplished in peace. Through the First Presidency and the Council of the Twelve, the Church effected a cancellation of the proposed huge project…to station the MX Missile in the federal states of Utah and Nevada. It also took a distinct stand against all similar plans. The Mormon pioneers settled this territory and, with sacrifice, caused it to bloom, so that the message of peace, instead of death and destruction for countless people, could be taken from that location into all the world.
>
> The Latter-day Saints in the German Democratic Republic know that they live in a good place. In their daily work and in their public activities, they attempt to do their very best. Mormons have always considered honest, hard work to be the source of blessings. They look to both the near and distant future with faith and confidence.

The challenge given President Burkhardt by President Kimball, "Establish a good relationship with the government," also was practiced by President Monson and Elder Russell M. Nelson, when they spoke at a conference attended by 1,500 members on August 24, 1986, on the grounds of the Leipzig Fair. Several GDR authorities, including members of the local district and city councils, were present. Five days later, the deputy chairman of the district council for interior affairs described the meeting to his superior:

> A number of general authorities and church leaders from the USA, Switzerland, West Germany, and West Berlin traveled to this conference.... In their opening remarks, which were marked by strong emotion and spirituality, the offices of the GDR were thanked for their decades of understanding and extensive support. The faithful were challenged to serve the state continually and to be good citizens. The attending representatives for church affairs within the district and city councils were asked to convey the most heartfelt greetings and thanks to their superiors. (MS 13918)

American Indian and Cultural Programs

Germans have a great interest in and curiosity about American Indians, due in part to the many books written by Karl May. Elder George P. Lee, a member of the Seventy and an Indian by birth, visited the Karl May Museum in Radebeul, in the vicinity of Dresden, in late April 1987. While there, he responded to questions from a newspaper reporter with his personal comments about war and peace, which were printed shortly thereafter in the *Sächsische Zeitung*:

> What happened to Dresden, the cultural center of Europe, during the war is a continuing and serious admonition for peace, for the preservation of human life. Allow me to mention something about my father. He gave me the conviction, which has deep roots among Indians, that the power of man over nature includes the obligation to care for it, for its own survival and for the welfare of mankind. To meet that responsibility, there is nothing more important today than peace.[3]

One year later, in May 1988, the Lamanite Generation, a musical group sponsored by Brigham Young University, toured the GDR and performed in major theaters throughout the country. The group featured American Indian, Polynesian, Mexican American, and native Latin American students in both traditional and contemporary productions. Kurt Löffler, who was state secretary in the Ministry of Culture prior to becoming state secretary for church affairs, commented on the impact of the performances:

> It was an overwhelming success, a glimpse into cultural arts that captivated the audience.... I should add that this tour greatly increased the social authority of your church and contributed significantly and

> directly to its greater freedom in the GDR. You can debate theistic or atheistic beliefs and philosophies of life. You can argue over interpretations of fact. However, when one is exposed to life through artistic testimonies that affect one's emotions rather than one's rational thinking, it can provide openings to consideration of different philosophical and religious positions. The approach of that ensemble, its clear and simple presentation of different cultures in a manner that is a prototype or example of tolerance, left a deep impression on the manner of thinking of many decision makers in the GDR. (1991)

After the 1988 tour of the Lamanite Generation, the briefing document prepared for Chairman Honecker's October meeting with President Monson stated that the Church had proposed another tour of the group in 1989, and both the Ministry of Culture and the Secretariat for Church Affairs supported the proposal (MS 13918). The group returned in May 1989 and gave eleven performances in eight GDR cities.

The Church Introduces Itself

In 1988, the Church published a twenty-six-page brochure, *Die Kirche Jesu Christi der Heiligen der Letzten Tage stellt sich vor* [An Introduction to the Church], written by Gottfried Richter. Its first twenty-three pages are a summary of the Church's history, an introduction to its doctrine, and a description of its organization and worldwide activities. However, the last three pages are particularly relevant and important. They were added as plans to arrange a meeting between President Monson and Chairman Honecker were being developed (see Chapter 17). The three pages summarize the Church's view of its place in the GDR society and the rights and responsibilities of its members as citizens. Much of the text was incorporated into the official declaration given to Honecker later that year (see Chapter 17). These three pages, together with the declaration, constitute the most complete public statement of the church-state relationship in the last years of the GDR regime:

> *How do Mormons live in the GDR?*
>
> That question, often asked by visitors to the temple grounds in Freiberg, will be answered here. Many visitors are interested in the Church's role in, and attitude toward, our society and in its relationship to governmental entities. We also are asked about the social status of individual Mormons in our society, our position regarding women, marriage, family, and professions, and where the Church stands on the major question of the day—peace and the search for it. We have clear answers to all these and many other questions, because Latter-day Saints rely on revealed truth, not "opinions."
>
> In the GDR, all citizens are protected in the free exercise of their religion. The equality of all religious beliefs also is a fundamental com-

ponent of the state's policy regarding religion. This equality of religions not only is declared, but is practiced. The extensive building program of the Church throughout our country is a visible example, and the members are thankful for it, especially when they consider the history of the Church in the former [German] empire and under fascism. Persecution, suppression, slander, inexplicable hate, and "false witness" were permitted by the state in those days and were thus the constant companion of the Church.

The separation of church and state, which has been implemented in the GDR, has been a longstanding goal of the Church since its earliest days. This has not gone unnoticed in the world, and foreign visitors to the temple grounds and to our meetings often mention it. Indeed, members of the Church in the GDR continue to attract the attention of our entire membership in over 130 countries. However, that attention has never caused the members here to feel that they are "unusual" Mormons. They have and have had their own problems, just like members anywhere else in the world. That is entirely normal. However, they appreciate and respect the exceptionally high social conditions and the general security of this socialist state.

The prohibition against the manufacture, distribution, and importation of pornographic materials is greatly appreciated. The support for large families and young married couples, as well as the care of the sick and aged, which are accepted norms within the GDR, are especially appreciated by the Church, because they are not so common in most parts of the world. People have learned more about the GDR in all countries where the Church is established, and this true picture has been furthered by our leaders, who, like other Church leaders from around the world, have been able to attend the General Conferences in Salt Lake City for many years.

Latter-day Saints have never been "dropouts," but rather are positive and forward-looking in thought and action. The doors of the Church are wide open for all people of good will who come to learn about the gospel, are seeking solutions to personal problems, or are simply seeking information. However, and this must be emphasized, the Church is absolutely not open to those who seek to use it as a platform for opposition or for the pursuit of "special interests" that are not consistent with the revealed mission of the Church and its authorized activities. This Church is not a church whose program is determined by its members. It is not, and will never be, such a church. Rather, it is a "church from above," which follows its revealed purposes. No one has the right to alter the Church's doctrines or programs to accommodate their own unrighteous desires. Peter and his associates found fish of all types in their nets, and it is so with those who join the Church today. They are quite varied, but they are united in one wish and desire, to improve themselves and become perfected through the gospel.

All Latter-day Saints are working toward that goal. An attitude that says "That's how I am and you have to accept me as I am" is not acceptable. Mormons believe in the eternal, unlimited progress of man. It is from that perspective that we interact with others in society.

"He that is idle shall not eat the bread nor wear the garments of the laborer," is a very old and common expression among the Mormons. Honest and dedicated effort is considered the source of blessings. To crave much, but not be willing to work for it, is becoming a frequent description of our time. That attitude is not found among true Latter-day Saints. Diligence, thrift, soberness, and joy in learning characterize most members. The phrase "It is impossible to be saved in ignorance" gives direction to members' lives, and they strive to improve their own abilities and those of their children. Challenged by the Church to always do their best, the members in the GDR have been successful in daily life as skilled workers, engineers, doctors, and independent craftsmen, in agriculture, trade, and other professions. Many of them have received high state honors. Their positive approach to life, their healthy lifestyle (avoidance of alcohol, tobacco, drugs, and other stimulants) enables them to pursue their professional careers and their responsibilities in society, church, and family in a responsible manner.

The Church, the kingdom of God on the earth, is not an end in itself. Through its priesthood programs and auxiliary organizations, it energetically devotes itself to the temporal and spiritual welfare of the individual, to the human spirit and its progress. Building upon its Christian philosophy of life, the Church makes use of its extended international relationships to constructively contribute to improved relations among nations. In that regard, it also supports our government in its pursuit of peace, coexistence, and good neighbors.

The young men of the Church accept their obligation for military service. Mormons are absolutely not "draft dodgers." "We believe in being honest, true, chaste, benevolent, virtuous, and in doing good to all men; . . . If there is anything virtuous, lovely, or of good report or praiseworthy, we seek after these things" (13th Article of Faith). The Latter-day Saints in the German Democratic Republic know that they are in a good place. They have no other program and no other goals than are held by members of the Church elsewhere in the world.

A Doctrinal View of Government

One year after the above brochure, the Church published another significant statement regarding its role in GDR society. Simply entitled "Die Gemeinde in Leipzig," it began with a summary of the development of the Church in general followed by a short history of the Leipzig branch/ward. However, as with the preceding brochure, the last few pages are the most important, as they present a scriptural explanation of the Church's attitude toward government in general and specifically toward the GDR. The last paragraphs regarding the Church's mission to proclaim peace and renounce war are particularly noteworthy, since they incorporated contemporary statements of President Spencer W. Kimball, in which he labeled excessive reliance on military armaments as an extreme form of idol worship that leads to destruction, not peace and safety:

> In 1835, the Church adopted a "Declaration of Belief Regarding Governments and Laws." This declaration became Section 134 of the Doctrine and Covenants, one of the Church's standard works. It remains valid today for members in every country and includes the following:
>
> "We believe that governments were instituted of God for the benefit of man; and that he holds men accountable for their acts in relation to them.... We believe that no government can exist in peace, except such laws are framed and held inviolate as will secure to each individual the free exercise of conscience, the right and control of property, and the protection of life.... We believe that all men are bound to sustain and uphold the respective governments in which they reside, while protected in their inherent and inalienable rights by the laws of such governments... and that all men should show respect and deference to the laws, as without them peace and harmony would be supplanted by anarchy and terror; human laws being instituted for the express purpose of regulating our interests as individuals and nations, between man and man; and divine laws given of heaven, prescribing rules on spiritual concerns, for faith and worship, both to be answered by man to his Maker.... We do not believe it just to mingle religious influence with civil government, whereby one religious society is fostered and another proscribed in its spiritual privileges, and the individual rights of its members, as citizens, denied."
>
> We thankfully recognize that the principle of separation of church and state is a fact in our country. A quick review of the history of our branch shows that the Latter-day Saints have never before been able to practice the basic principles of their faith as completely and undisturbed as today. With the dedication of the Freiberg Temple, all ordinances of the gospel are available to the members in the GDR. We consider the privilege of attending the temple and the convenience and comfort of the new meeting houses as a blessing and as an expression of a good relationship with government offices.
>
> Since 1989, and after a break of fifty years, foreign missionaries have again been allowed to proclaim the gospel in our midst. Young members from the GDR have simultaneously received the same opportunity to serve as full-time missionaries in other countries for two years.
>
> The Church in the GDR intends to continue on this path of growing trust and mutual respect between church and state. It encourages its members to devote their best efforts to serve society. Each individual can do that by practicing the ideals of Christian living. A prophet

of the Book of Mormon summarized the consequences of such a life, that "when ye are in the service of your fellow beings ye are only in the service of your God."

The members of the Church consider personal freedom of choice to be a sacred gift from God. This God-given right, which allows mankind to choose their own path between good and evil, between life and destruction, provides, however, that men must accept the consequences of their actions. When men live in accordance with godly principles, the blessings of the Lord follow them. When they disregard God's advice, he does not protect them from the consequences of their mistakes.

Conflict and war, according to this religious view, are not caused by God and therefore not fatefully unavoidable. Rather, they are much more likely to be the consequence of godless behavior, i.e., improper use of choices available to mankind. Since the consequences of war are not limited to its instigators, everyone has not only the right, but also the responsibility, to do everything possible to preserve peace, in order to protect themselves and their personal freedom. The Church recognizes that its members may serve in the armed forces of their countries within limits determined by their personal conscience. The Lord allows his children to defend themselves, their families, and their homeland under specific and very narrowly defined circumstances. The same teaching, however, says with great emphasis that we are blessed when we forgive those who trespass against us. Gospel teachings do not say that armaments are unnecessary. However, to rely only on weapons demonstrates a lack of faith in God. In our present day, an increase in weapons doesn't increase security, but brings more danger. Mankind has amassed so many means of mass destruction, that the destruction of the entire earth is, unfortunately, within the range of possibility. We are, however, not the owners but rather the stewards of this world, given the assignment from God to protect and care for all life on this planet. We are stewards of our air and water, our culture and our science.

The Lord will at some time require us to give an accounting of our stewardship, as described in the parable of the Last Judgment. Strictly considered, excessive armaments are the most extreme form of idol worship. Those that rely on weapons technology are building upon a false God that cannot save us, but rather leads to destruction. Not military strength but righteousness brings peace and security to nations. The Lord said in an 1833 revelation, "Therefore, renounce war and proclaim peace." That instruction includes not only the preaching of the word but also the application of that principle of the gospel in daily life.

The varied history of the Leipzig branch teaches us respect for our forefathers' faithfulness, steadfastness, and willingness to sacrifice, which they proved again and again in difficult situations. They teach

> us to be thankful for the many opportunities we have today to live our faith in peace and prosperity. The promises of God and the desire to always be true to the Lord, permit us to look forward to the near and distant future with full confidence.

A final statement regarding the Church's relationship with the state in the last months of the GDR's existence is found in the birthday greeting that President Burkhardt and his counselors sent to State Secretary Kurt Löffler on August 25, 1989. It began with the traditional best wishes for "health, creativity, and personal well-being" and referred to "the improvements in the relationship between the state and the Church," the "building program, the liberal arrangements for importing Church literature and teaching materials," the approval for missionaries to enter and leave the GDR, and the permission "for fifty-seven young men and priesthood leaders from our branches to participate in the Church's youth camp in Koblenz, in West Germany." At the end, Burkhardt stated that "all these things are expressions of the good atmosphere and mutual respect that is always evident in discussions and negotiations with your associates in the State Secretariat. Be assured that we will continue to work in the future so that this improved relationship is not only maintained but continually furthered. It is our wish to continue on the path of growing trust and mutual respect for different philosophies of life" (DMO).

15 The Origins of the Freiberg Temple[1]

On April 23, 1983, a groundbreaking ceremony for the only temple of the Church built behind the Iron Curtain was held in the city of Freiberg. Twenty years later, President Burkhardt provided his perspective of that ceremony:

> We had invited a long list of government representatives, Communists who did not believe in God, who did not pray. President Monson told them that before we have the groundbreaking ceremony, we will dedicate the land. We will bow our heads, fold our hands, and pray to our Heavenly Father. Well, I sat there across from these people and thought, I must work with them. How will they react? I prayed with only one eye, and with the other I looked upon that miracle. All the Communists sat there with bowed heads and folded hands. . . . At the conclusion, they came to me and said, "We've never experienced anything so beautiful as this." They were deeply impressed. The deputy chairman of the county council told me, "If we can do anything to help, let us know." (2003)

Two years later, in June 1985, ninety thousand visitors (in a city of fifty thousand) toured the completed temple and adjacent meeting house during a two-week open house. Visitors wanted to see what a small American-based church had been allowed to build in the officially atheistic GDR. Many stood in line for as long as seven hours. One evening, many visitors were still waiting outside at the normal closing time of 8:00 p.m. The doors remained open until the last visitors exited at 1:15 a.m.

How did this unusual event come to pass? And why was the government so willing to help? Was it a matter of economics, since the GDR needed the Western money that the Church paid for its construction? Was it perhaps a miracle, wrought by the faith of devoted members? This chapter analyses these and other theories about the origin of the Freiberg Temple by presenting documentary information not previously considered.

Following the temple dedication, Elder Monson wrote in his journal on June 29, 1985:

> Frequently people will ask, "How has it been possible for the Church to obtain permission to build a temple behind the Iron Curtain?" My feeling is simply that the faith and devotion of our Latter-day Saints in that area brought forth the help of Almighty God and provided for them the eternal blessings which they so richly deserve.... All honor and glory belong to our Heavenly Father, for it is only through His divine intervention that these events have taken place. (*Faith Rewarded*)

Ten years earlier, on April 27, 1975, Elder Monson had requested divine intervention when he rededicated the country from a hill overlooking the Elbe River near Dresden:

> Heavenly Father, wilt Thou open up the way that the faithful may be accorded the privilege of going to Thy holy temple, there to receive their holy endowments and to be sealed as families for time and all eternity?... [W]ilt Thou intervene in the governmental affairs? Cause that Thy Holy Spirit may dwell with those who preside, that their hearts may be touched and that they may make those decisions which would help in the advancement of Thy work. (*Faith Rewarded*)

Those who heard Elder Monson's prayer did not imagine that a temple would be built in their country in their lifetime. They simply hoped for permission to leave their homes long enough to visit the existing temple in Switzerland.

The Influence of the Swiss Temple

The 1955 dedication of the Swiss Temple, the first one in Europe, changed the course of history for the Church in the GDR. President Burkhardt explained the impact of that temple:

> The commandment to attend the temple... remained an important but unfulfilled part of the gospel plan for everyone in Europe and other parts of the world where no temple existed. Hardly anyone had the expectation of attending a temple during their lifetime, despite their faithfulness to the commandments of God.... [However] after the temple in Zollikofen was dedicated in 1955, the wish burned within many members to go there.... Nothing was more important to the priesthood leaders of our country than to find opportunities to fulfill this wish of our members. The temple in Zollikofen—so near and yet so far away for the members of the GDR—was the most sought-after goal.[2]

The announcement of the Swiss Temple brought hope to East German members and a new incentive to reach the West. Members immediately began to make the necessary spiritual preparations. Temple-related topics dominated Sunday School, Relief Society, priesthood, and sacrament meetings throughout East Germany in 1955 and 1956.

As described earlier in Chapter 5, many GDR members actually managed to reach the Swiss Temple in its first two or three years of operation. Of course, the government soon learned of the illegal travel to Switzerland and made travel to West Germany more difficult. To protect itself from the charge of supporting lawbreakers, the Church also stopped issuing temple recommends except in those few instances where the members could show they had permission to travel to Switzerland. Thus, travel to the Swiss temple effectively ended after 1957, except for a few older pensioned members who were given greater freedom to travel.

After 1957, Burkhardt continued to seek ways to bring members to the Swiss Temple, but without success. Once, in the early 1970s, he asked all of the district presidents to assemble lists of members who were worthy and desirous of going to the temple. He hoped such information might soften the hearts of GDR officials. He took a list with the names of three hundred members to Berlin but was fortunate to be allowed to return home that night. He was threatened with imprisonment because he had violated a law against collecting personal information for religious purposes.

"Why Not Create an Endowment House?"

In May 1978, Elder H. Burke Peterson, a counselor to the Presiding Bishop of the Church, visited the Dresden Mission. Accompanied by Burkhardt, he visited several branches where the members, at considerable personal sacrifice, had created modest meeting rooms in old buildings. While traveling, they spoke of the faithfulness of the members and their desire to go to the Swiss Temple. On May 10, the two men were in Groitzsch, not far from Leipzig, where Elder Peterson admired the small meeting rooms that members had built. (See Groitzsch meeting house in Chapter 11.) What took place there was described by Burkhardt in his account of the origin of the Freiberg Temple:

> While visiting the building in Groitzsch, Bishop Peterson initiated a subject that I had never before considered. He said, "Why wouldn't it be possible to dedicate one or more newly renovated rooms in such a building in which members could receive their personal endowment?" He was remembering the former Endowment House in Salt Lake City, which was used before the temple was built. Bishop Peterson returned and gave this report to the First Presidency. Although I never saw that report myself, he certainly reported that the possibility existed to create an endowment room in a selected meeting house.[3]

On May 31, 1978, just three weeks after Elder Peterson's comments in Groitzsch, Burkhardt and Gottfried Richter met with officials of the Secretariat for Church Affairs in Berlin on other business. Burkhardt's entry in the journal history of the Dresden Mission that day is the earliest account of the government's suggestion regarding a temple:

> We had a pleasant discussion about the visit of Brother and Sister Richter to the General Conference in Salt Lake City. Temple visits for the members [to Switzerland] were also discussed. When asked about the prerequisites for a temple [in the GDR], Brother Richter stated that it was necessary to have a certain number of members. President Burkhardt added that an ability to maintain the building's inviolability ["unantastbarkeit," or sanctity] was an essential prerequisite. However, [the officials] suggested that the Church consider the construction of a temple, because the travel of large numbers of members to capitalistic countries was not possible. (DMO)

President Burkhardt elaborated on the May 31 meeting in his later account of the temple's origin, which was written in 1983:

> During a May 1978 meeting at the Secretariat for Church Affairs in Berlin, at which time I again raised the topic of our members traveling to the temple, I was given a different suggestion, namely, to build a temple in the GDR. That suggestion was entirely unexpected, and I tried to present all possible reasons why it would not be possible. I mentioned that we did not have the required number of members for a temple district. I especially mentioned the sanctity of such a building once it has been dedicated. Also, that only the First Presidency could decide such a question. Despite all my reasons for declining the suggestion, I was politely asked to discuss the idea with the First Presidency, and I brought the subject to their attention through our regional representative, Dan C. Jorgensen.[4]

Elder Monson's published journal makes no mention of the government's suggestion or of Elder Peterson's idea about creating a room or rooms for endowment ordinances in an existing meeting house. However, on May 25, 1978, Monson did mention a different approach to the challenge of providing temple ordinances. He wrote that President Kimball asked him to meet with the First Presidency relative to a discussion pertaining to the members in East Germany and their inability to receive temple ordinances. His journal gives no further details, but subsequent events indicate that instead of pursuing Elder Peterson's endowment room idea, the Church leaders had developed a new plan to bring members to the Swiss Temple. Monson reviewed that plan with Burkhardt and his counselor, Günter Schulze, during a meeting in East Berlin on August 25, 1978, and wrote thereafter:

> We discussed a plan whereby six specified couples' names would be provided to David Kennedy, and he in turn would make an effort with the government to emphasize the importance of a one-time visit to the temple by every Latter-day Saint. The theory was that if we could establish a record of credibility, with about six couples going to the temple for their own endowments and sealing and returning to their homes in the German Democratic Republic, and then having perhaps six other couples go, the approximately eight hundred worthy but nonendowed persons in the German Democratic Republic could receive these blessings. (*Faith Rewarded*)

Four days later, on August 29, David Kennedy presented the plan to the Foreign Ministry in East Berlin. The mission file shows that a long-distance call from West Berlin was received in the mission office in Dresden the following day:

> Brother Dan Jorgensen informed the mission president that David Kennedy had visited the Foreign Ministry of the GDR and discussed temple visits. He suggested that five of our district presidents travel there with their families. The mission president should submit relevant applications to the state secretary for Church Affairs. (DMO)

On September 5, 1978, Burkhardt and Schulze went to the State Secretariat to pursue Kennedy's plan. What they were told sent history in a different direction:

> We were told very distinctly that the visit of Brother Kennedy was not appreciated, that no approval for temple visits could be made, and that all related discussions should be carried out only through the mission president. It was indicated once more that the Church should be informed of the suggestion of the Secretariat, to create opportunities for temple ordinances here in this country, so that the members do not need to leave this country. Upon leaving, we were told that President Schulze should discuss this matter with the First Presidency during his conference visit in Salt Lake City. We were asked, however, to handle these matters with utmost confidentiality, so that no information reaches the public. (DMO)

This news apparently reached Elder Monson immediately, before President Schulze traveled to General Conference, and he wrote in his journal on September 8, 1978:

> Held a meeting with the First Presidency relative to East Germany and the visit of David Kennedy to that country. Our desire is to open up a way for faithful members of the Church in that land to gain exit

> visas to have their sacred ordinances performed in the Swiss Temple, after which they would return to their homeland. Our hopes are high, but realistically, we feel our prospects for gaining the necessary approval are rather dim. (*Faith Rewarded*)

The Church's plan was unacceptable to the government because it would have required significant exceptions to the existing travel restrictions and would have opened the door to similar requests from every other religious organization. The Kennedy initiative was not mentioned again by Elder Monson in his journal. Instead, he seems to have discussed alternatives with President Burkhardt while attending the next district conference in Dresden on October 21 and 22, 1978. His first journal entry regarding the government's suggestion appears on November 22, 1978:

> This morning I had the privilege to meet with the First Presidency, there to discuss with the brethren how we might provide the blessings of the temple to our worthy Saints in East Germany. I mentioned to the presidency that the East German government has asked why we do not build a temple in their country for all of the socialist countries of Europe.... It appears as though the government will not permit its citizens to have visas to go to the Swiss Temple; hence, the only possible way we can provide endowment and sealing blessings for the Saints would be through providing a facility of our own in that country. (*Faith Rewarded*)

Monson's next journal entry regarding temple ordinances for members in the GDR appears on January 24, 1979:

> This morning I again met with the First Presidency to discuss the Dresden Mission and how our people might best receive their temple blessings. Due to their inability to leave East Germany, it may be necessary to provide some facilities there for such ordinance work. (*Faith Rewarded*)

The January 24 meeting with the First Presidency certainly was more detailed than implied by Monson's brief journal entry, because one week later, on February 2, the First Presidency wrote a letter to President Burkhardt that included a preliminary sketch of a building. The letter said:

> We were pleased to learn from you that the authorities of your government had suggested that we build a sacred edifice in the German Democratic Republic, that our members there may receive these ordinances which mean so very much to them. Enclosed is a preliminary sketch of the exterior of such an edifice, as well as a floor plan. After you have had an opportunity to meet with the appropriate officials,

> you could so advise us of their response, after which more formalized drawings would be prepared. Please convey our sincere gratitude to your government's officials for their kind understanding and cooperative attitude. (Copy in author's possession)

The various terms used to describe the proposed building in these earliest sources are noteworthy. In his initial journal entries, Elder Monson usually called it a "facility," the First Presidency used the term "edifice," and the government called it a "temple." It also would be called an "endowment house" before it evolved into and became universally designated as a temple. Monson carried the First Presidency's letter and the sketch to Burkhardt in East Berlin on February 10, 1979, and wrote that day:

> Took the plane to Berlin, Germany, where I had the opportunity to join Dan Jorgensen and Elder Theodore M. Burton. We had a special prayer at our hotel room, where I revealed to these brethren some tentative plans for a small facility to be erected in the German Democratic Republic for the purpose of temple work. We then placed the temple drawings as inconspicuously as we could within Brother Jorgensen's briefcase and drove across the border.... Henry Burkhardt had tears come to his eyes when he saw the beautiful drawings of the projected building. He felt very good about the proposal and will respond to his government's invitation now, in that they had previously suggested that perhaps a temple could be built in that country, rather than our requesting permission for citizens of the German Democratic Republic to go to Switzerland. (*Faith Rewarded*)

Burkhardt described his first response to these events in a 1991 interview:

> Personally, I had never believed that we would have a temple, but the brethren said, "We will consider it." I understand that they needed time, since it was the first time that a temple would be built in a Communist country. I was deeply impressed that the brethren didn't immediately say "no." ... The police or other government officials had the right to come into our meeting houses at any time, to observe what we did there. So it seemed almost impossible, that they would permit closed-door temple activities without observing them personally.... But they told me, "Absolutely no problem. We don't need to go inside. If that helps you, it can be arranged." Of course, the General Authorities had to seriously consider that. Almost none of these brethren could really believe that the government would keep its promise. So that is how the preparatory work for the temple started. (1991)

Why Did the GDR Suggest a Temple?

Subsequent developments regarding the planning and construction of the temple will be addressed after consideration of why the government suggested that it be built. Günther Behncke offered perhaps the most fundamental and succinct reason:

> What took place in the 1980s—the opportunity to build a temple and other meeting houses—would not have happened if the summit meeting of March 6, 1978, had not taken place. It was a matter of equal entitlement. (2006)

The summit meeting of March 6, 1978, between Erich Honecker and the chairman of the Conference of Evangelical Churches, was previously described in Chapter 3. It had followed the decision of the Politburo on February 1, 1977, to allow construction of new church buildings in localities where none had previously existed. Behncke explained the effects of the summit meeting on the temple and later Church buildings:

> Until 1978, it was not permitted to build churches in new residential areas, i.e., in new towns or new subdivisions that were "socialistically" organized. The idea was that socialist areas didn't require a church. Suddenly in 1978, a change of mind took place. Honecker declared that he was prepared to permit churches to be built even within new developments.... You can see in that decision that the leadership of the SED had made significant concessions, that the anticipated demise of churches was not imminent. Anyone who permitted new churches to be built in new developments conceded that, at least for the next hundred years, churches would continue to survive.
>
> The results of the summit meeting affected relationships with other religious organizations, for example, the building program of the Mormons. It was a matter of equal entitlement. The state could not say that only the Evangelical churches, due to their size, could build. No, the state had to follow its own principle, that all churches and religious organizations in the GDR had equal rights. When, therefore, the Evangelical and Catholic churches had the right to build, that same right had to be granted to the small organizations, assuming, of course, they had money. (2006)

The suggestion made to Burkhardt in the offices of the State Secretariat for Church Affairs on May 31, 1978, took place less than three months after the summit of March 6, 1978. At that time, Burkhardt was told that further discussions with the state secretary would be required before the suggestion could be finalized. Shortly thereafter, the Secretariat prepared a proposal entitled "Long-range Plan to Exert Political Influence on Churches and Religious Organizations in the GDR Apart from the Evangelical and Catholic Churches," which was discussed and approved by the Workgroup on Church Affairs of the Central Committee of the SED on July 27, 1978. One part of the proposal addressed the specific role of temples in the LDS religion:

> There also is a religious issue with the Mormons, which constantly causes problems. Their faith requires them to engage in so-called temple work, which can only take place in a temple. However, the only temples in Europe are in capitalistic countries, which means that they cannot accomplish their most important religious obligation.... These examples underline the conclusion that in these churches, the conflict between acceptance of socialistic-oriented citizenship and an exaggerated religious belief is heightened. (MS 13798)

Obviously, the temple and the subsequent new meeting houses could only be built within the conditions set forth by the GDR's special building program, which required that all expenses be paid with Western currency. However, the earliest internal documents regarding the government's rationale for building a temple do not mention money. Instead, they reflect an effort to resolve the conflict between socialism and religion. A similar description and justification of the temple is seen in a letter sent by State Secretary Gysi in 1985 to colleagues who occupied comparable positions in other socialist countries, in which he informed them of an opportunity to visit the temple during the open house:

> The state's approval to build this place of worship resulted from the weighing of various church-state considerations, including: that the members of the Church of Jesus Christ can only carry out their religious marriages (sealing) in an exclusive-for-that-purpose temple; the leadership and the members of that church conduct themselves as loyal citizens; the relationship between the church leadership and the state's offices are open and trustworthy; and the presence of the temple removes the need to request travel to the USA to perform marriages. (DO 4/921)

Other justifications for the temple are given in the following unsigned document, which was probably written in 1985 as a briefing paper for officials who had to respond to criticism from other churches of the government's approval of the temple. Although many statements therein are contrary to the historical facts presented in this chapter, the document does provide insight into the government's need to justify its decision to its critics. It also is a reminder that written documents should not always be accepted at face value:

> 1. Reasons for the decision to approve the building of the temple:
> The Mormons are one of more than forty active religious organizations in the GDR. While they are very small, all churches and religious

> organizations in the GDR have equal rights according to the constitution of the GDR. And as people can see for themselves, new churches and religious centers are being built in many localities.... In this case, the government of the GDR simply made the decision because the Mormons submitted such a request. That is a normal occurrence, and it could be approved because the financial means had, in the meantime, been assured. However, I should also note, that in addition to the Mormon temple in Freiberg, typical Mormon religious centers will be built in other cities of the GDR by 1990, for example in the capital city Berlin, Leipzig, Dresden, and Karl-Marx-Stadt.
>
> 2. Why was Freiberg chosen as the location?
> Freiberg was chosen following constructive and mutual negotiations because favorable property was found there, which met all requirements for construction of a temple. Freiberg is located between the two large Mormon branches in Karl-Marx-Stadt and Dresden. Finding an appropriate building site in large cities is not a problem in the GDR. The Freiberg location was a mutual decision. The appearance of the temple, as proposed by the Mormon architects and in agreement with the state's office, fits harmoniously into the historic landscape and in an historic city. (DO 4/987)

As already shown, the Church did not initiate the proposal, and as will be shown, the statement that the Freiberg location was chosen by the Church ignores its earlier unsuccessful effort to build the facility in Karl-Marx-Stadt. Moreover, Freiberg was designated by the government before a specific building lot was even considered. And despite the beauty of the temple, no one familiar with the city and the temple would say that it was built there because it fit harmoniously into the historic city. In fact, it was built outside the historic city center because the city fathers, who heartily welcomed the temple, correctly said that its proposed design would clash with and therefore violate the historic view of the city's inner core, which the city had previously agreed to maintain. Finally, despite the claim that the building of the temple was a "normal occurrence" in the GDR, the ninety thousand visitors who came to the open house testified that this was not business as usual.

The distortions of fact in the above explanation of the origin and location of the temple were matched by later well-meaning efforts by members to explain the temple on the basis of unsupported claims and false assumptions. For example, in April 1995, the *Stern* published an article by LaRene Gaunt concerning some of Elder Robert D. Hales's work in Europe.[5] The author claimed that the Church made repeated requests to build a temple in the GDR, which were denied due to a scarcity of building materials, and that the project was only approved when the necessary materials were found in Freiberg. None of those statements are supported by the facts presented in this chapter. The suggestion to build the temple came from the government, not from the Church, and the location of building materials had nothing to do with the decision to build in Freiberg.

Günther Behncke was the Church's main contact person within the State Secretariat for Church Affairs since 1981. In a 1991 interview, he provided interesting insights into the attitude of some government officials regarding the Church and the temple, both before it was built and during the open house:

> None of the senior officials understood what was meant by a temple. Questions emerged among those in the top echelons, "What takes place therein, surrounded by secrecy? Is morality threatened?" I had to write a new justification at least ten times, to explain why the temple was so important for the Mormons that they couldn't do without it. I obtained information from America about temples and focused on the sealing act, which is performed there, as the central issue. That was appealing, since the divorce rate in the GDR had reached a high point at that time. Some of the men high up in the government and also in the party said, "If the Mormons have such a good character, that they stand for the continuation of marriage throughout their entire life and beyond, why shouldn't we permit a temple to be built?"
>
> Later, of course, there were some problems. The temple was completed, and as was their tradition, the Mormons were hospitable people. They held an open house for two weeks, and you can imagine what happened in Freiberg! Freiberg was in the atheistic GDR, and the atheistic GDR citizens stood in line for up to six hours, for fourteen days, to tour the temple. Sometimes the line was a thousand meters long. Then the local "orthodox" Communists turned to the government, to Honecker, and asked, "What is going on? So many people are going to the temple."
>
> Here is a funny anecdote. Klaus Gysi, the state secretary, had to officially inform the Politburo about what was happening. Thousands of people were standing there, and our citizens didn't believe in God. Gysi told me, "Write a page to explain what is happening, what the Mormons do, what their religion is, etc." It required two pages, although it was just an overview. However, Gysi said, "It is too long. We have old men in the government and they can't read so much. Reduce it to three sentences, three sentences that will convince the old men in the leadership that everything is okay down there."
>
> That was normally impossible to do, but I did it and wrote, "(1) The Mormons work hard and honestly and are loyal to the state, which is consistent with their Articles of Faith. (2) The Mormons pursue their daily life with the view that the family has the highest priority and that a marriage is entered into for life and shouldn't be dissolved. (3) Their religion forbids Mormons to use alcohol, nicotine, and other addictive drinks." Those were all things that didn't otherwise happen in our country. The work ethic was terrible, people divorced very often, the

> GDR had the highest divorce rate in the world, the people were turning more and more to alcohol, and coffee consumption was constantly climbing.
>
> I gave that to my state secretary, who said, "Very good. The old gentlemen will understand that, but I will add one sentence," and he wrote something like, "Points 1 and 3 are fully atypical of citizens in the GDR. Therefore, this church has no chance of ever having a large following." (1991)

Not every part of the government was inclined to be as friendly. As shown earlier, numerous Stasi informants were assigned to monitor the daily activities of Church leaders. However, such monitoring also was a positive factor in the decision to build the temple. Kurt Löffler said that the government had observed the members over many years and had determined that they were good workers, sincere and reliable family-oriented citizens, who did not participate in antigovernment activities. However, in Löffler's opinion, an equally essential factor was the arrival of a new generation of leaders within the GDR, including the replacement of Walter Ulbricht with Erich Honecker as first secretary of the Central Committee in 1971. Löffler characterized the new generation as more pragmatic and less doctrinaire than their predecessors. He said they were more "socialist" than "communist," and were therefore prepared to accept the religious interests of their citizens, as long as those interests did not threaten the government (2003).

Although many members may not share Löffler's opinion, he presented as evidence Honecker's initiative in the 1970s to create a new and more open relationship between the state and the churches, a relationship in which the churches would be officially recognized and accepted, as long as they did not threaten the authority and sovereignty of the state. This interpretation is supported by the documents of the time. It is also consistent with the council given to President Burkhardt by President Kimball, who said that "the world changes when people change."

The First Temple Plan

As stated earlier, Burkhardt received the first external drawing of the proposed temple from Monson on February 10, 1979. The plan showed one building with two separate functions, a branch meeting house on one side and an endowment house on the other. The endowment house did not include a font for proxy baptisms, since it was intended to be used only for sacred ordinances required by living members. Burkhardt presented the plan to the government in March 1979. He was asked to inform the First Presidency that the project could only be undertaken in conformity with the special building program, i.e., the funds for construction must be provided in convertible currency. That was foreseen and posed no problem. Elder Monson wrote on March 28, 1979:

> Brother Burkhardt indicated that the government authorities liked the building plans we have submitted and, after indicating that Western money would be required to purchase materials, seemed to give the green light for us to proceed in our steps to have a suitable building in Karl-Marx-Stadt. (*Faith Rewarded*)

This is the first reference to Karl-Marx-Stadt as the intended site for the proposed facility. President Burkhardt's 1983 account also states that the First Presidency authorized him to obtain a building permit for an endowment house in Karl-Marx-Stadt.

That city had been chosen primarily for two important reasons. First, its large branch could easily provide the staff for the endowment house. Of course, the members didn't know that the planned building included such a facility. Second, the branch had been assigned to one ruined building after another by the city's Communist leaders, who were determined to reduce religious influence in that city. Among all needy branches in the GDR, the situation in Karl-Marx-Stadt was especially urgent. Therefore, the offer to build a temple provided a way to simultaneously achieve two goals by combining the endowment house and a new meeting house under one roof.

Burkhardt returned to Berlin on April 25, 1979. He was asked to submit a written application, which he did in the form of a letter, dated May 17, 1979. It provides considerable information about the project, and is shown here in its entirety from his 1983 manuscript:

> Ever since the Church of Jesus Christ of Latter-day Saints was restored and organized again on the earth in 1830, it has been known as a "temple-building church." Ordinances, which are conducted in the temples of the Church today as in ancient times, cannot be performed in any other place. It is the goal of every member of the church to be joined there as couples and families for eternity.
>
> Our discussions over many years with the Secretariat have repeatedly been concerned with the possibility for members of the Church of Jesus Christ of Latter-day Saints in the GDR to visit one of the sixteen temples located throughout the world, in order to receive the ordinances that are the goal of every true member. The nearest opportunity for members in the GDR to visit such a temple would be either in Zollikofen, near Bern, Switzerland, or the temple near London, Great Britain.
>
> During our May 1978 discussion, you asked if the First Presidency of the Church would be prepared to construct such a building in the GDR. Since our present membership of about five thousand in the GDR is not enough to justify construction of a temple, I personally met with the First Presidency of the Church during my General Conference visit in March/April of this year. Following intensive deliberations, we came jointly to the decision to construct a so-called

endowment house in our country, which also would be available to members of the Church in other socialistic countries. An endowment house, as existed once at the beginning of the Church's history when it was not feasible to build a temple, is in its functions decidedly less than a temple, but achieves almost the same purpose. We have decided to erect this house at an appropriate location that would simultaneously resolve the longstanding need of our branch in Karl-Marx-Stadt for a proper place in which to conduct its regular worship services.

The plans prepared by the Church architects, which you have already received, is a project unique in the entire world. It provides for a building to be used first as an endowment house, exclusively in the east wing, and as a meeting house for the Karl-Marx-Stadt branch in the remaining part.

The Church, however, insists on the sanctity of the east wing of the building. In further explanation, permit me to perhaps mention that a temple (endowment house) can be visited by the public before its dedication, but afterward can be entered only by members of the Church who possess a valid temple recommend from their branch president. For this reason, I wish to emphasize once again the "Unantastbarkeit," as mentioned in our discussion of May 1978.

Overnight lodging opportunities with all sanitary facilities could be arranged for out-of-town visitors in the middle and western portions of this project.

The First Presidency of the Church has declared its readiness, after an appropriate building lot for this purpose has been found and acquired, to finance the building of the endowment/meeting house in the full amount of the estimated cost of about seven hundred thousand dollars, through a lawful method. We are thinking in that regard of the LIMEX building contractor, regarding which, however, further discussions with you would be necessary.

Since the First Presidency of the Church, and I as mission president in the GDR, have carried this decades-long need of our members close to our hearts, we wish to quickly complete the project. I would be very thankful if this great religious need of our members could have your support and assistance. Our members would then no longer search for ways to travel to one of our temples.

Since only the First Presidency and I are aware of this project at this time, the First Presidency requests that further negotiations be conducted only with me.[6]

The Struggle in Karl-Marx-Stadt

The two years following the submission of the application on May 17, 1979, were a critical period in the history of the temple, and we are solely dependent on Burkhardt's 1983 manuscript for an account of that time. The only entry in Monson's published journal was a brief notation on December 2, 1979, when he wrote, "The only problem seems to be the insufferable delays of government red tape." His journal doesn't have another entry concerning the project until June 1981.

Actually, the plan to build in the city of Karl-Marx-Stadt had run into much more than red tape. It had encountered strong Communist opposition in a city that had been a stronghold of leftist ideology long before the creation of the GDR. The 1953 renaming of Chemnitz as Karl-Marx-Stadt reflected that determined ideology. No church building of any denomination had been built there since World War II, and local officials saw no need to make an exception in this instance. Moreover, the Politburo's decision of February 1, 1977, regarding new church buildings stated, "The building projects will be evaluated by the relevant district councils in view of local building rules and church policy considerations."

After he presented his proposal on May 17, 1979, Burkhardt was asked to meet in August with Frau Dr. Schumann-Fitzner, the State Secretariat's legal counsel. He did so and answered questions about the organization of the Church, the purpose of temple ordinances, and the use of both parts of the proposed building. At the conclusion of their discussion, she promised to support the proposal and to make the necessary contacts with other government offices, including the Karl-Marx-Stadt district council. She indicated that the entire review process could take up to one year.

President Burkhardt contacted Dr. Schumann-Fitzner again almost one year later, on March 7, 1980, while making preparations for his trip to General Conference. She promised to give him a response within a week. When that didn't happen, he called her again. She told him she would be traveling to Karl-Marx-Stadt at the end of March to meet with the local officials and to negotiate an appropriate building site. Burkhardt left for the conference without a definite answer.

Upon his return, he was invited again to Berlin where he was informed that the district council had agreed to find a building site by June 30. However, the site would not be within the city or the county (both called Karl-Marx-Stadt), but rather elsewhere within the much larger district, also called Karl-Marx-Stadt. (A district encompassed several counties.) He knew that a building lot outside the city and the county would not meet the needs of the local branch for its own meeting house. Therefore, he immediately went to Karl-Marx-Stadt to speak directly with the district council and restate the Church's needs. He was emphatically told that no site within the city would be approved, because it already had more than enough church buildings. Burkhardt persisted and repeated his reasons for a location within the city. After considerable discussion, the council agreed to reconsider its decision. He informed officials in the State Secretariat of his activities, and they agreed to support his position, although they could not overrule the district council.

In the course of these negotiations, Gottfried Richter learned that the Evangelical church in the city wished to sell property where a large building had stood until 1945. On September 5, 1980, Burkhardt returned to the district council and informed them of this option. He was told again that no permission for a church within the city's boundaries would be approved. Moreover, he was informed that the district had decided to allow the endowment house to be built in Freiberg, about thirty-four kilometers (twenty-one miles) east of the city of Karl-Marx-Stadt. When asked about a meeting house for the branch in Karl-Marx-Stadt, he was told that the council would attempt to find another building that could be renovated for that purpose. He wrote later, "Karl-Marx-Stadt was a major socialist city, whose leaders thought that atheism was marching triumphantly forward. It would have been a blow against the ruling ideology of the day, if they had permitted a single new church building."[7] The State Secretariat in Berlin was unable (or unwilling) to overcome the firm position of the district council.

From an Endowment House to a Temple

President Burkhardt and his counselors knew that if they refused the Freiberg location, they could be assigned to an even less favorable location. Therefore they began to weigh the advantages and disadvantages of Freiberg. The better they became acquainted with the facts, the less inclined they were to reject Freiberg. He wrote:

> This city lies in the middle between Karl-Marx-Stadt and Dresden, an autobahn was recently completed between Leipzig and Dresden, which passes close to Freiberg, the Annaberg-Buchholz branch is also only fifty-six kilometers from Freiberg, [and] there are other small branches in the neighborhood of Freiberg. So we could not ignore the feeling that we shouldn't reject Freiberg. Further days of fasting strengthened this impression, which I shared in writing with the area president [Elder Robert D. Hales] and the First Presidency.[8]

In the meantime, the district council had asked the Freiberg county council to accommodate the Church, and on January 15, 1981, the latter asked Burkhardt to send a floor plan and an external sketch of the proposed building to them. He sent the same plan that had been prepared for Karl-Marx-Stadt, i.e., one building with two separate functions. The Freiberg county council and the city mayor, Dr. Werner Runge, then invited Burkhardt to meet with them on March 24. At that meeting, which was conducted in a very friendly and open manner, Runge said that the city welcomed the opportunity to build something for the Church, especially since Freiberg would be celebrating its eight-hundredth anniversary in 1986 and wanted to upgrade its appearance. The temple would be a welcome addition. However, the inner city was a cultural/historical site subject to relevant guidelines of the United Nations. It would not be possible to accommodate the type of building the Church had proposed within the inner city. The officials requested additional details about the Church's needs so they could suggest appropriate building sites. They also suggested that the Church include lodging and car parking facilities since they understood that the building would be used by members from other socialistic countries. Burkhardt left with the feeling that the city and county were proud to be able to undertake this project.[9] Before leaving to attend the General Conference the next day, he wrote in the mission journal:

> We indicated it would be at least three weeks before we could inform the county council of our decision and provide the requested clarifications. Among decisions to be made, we must consider whether:
>
> (a) the size of the required property should be increased
> (b) an apartment building for coworkers and guests should be added
> (c) the combined meeting house and endowment house should be changed to an endowment house without a meeting house (eventually a temple in miniature)
> (d) Freiberg should be accepted as the final site, or whether to continue to seek a meeting house and endowment house within the city borders of Karl-Marx-Stadt.
>
> My personal impressions: I was very pleasantly impressed by the correct and clear discussion at this meeting. President Richter and I had a definite feeling that the city fathers of Freiberg are proud of the expected building. The chairman of the county council noted his assumption that this building was not just for the use of our members in the GDR, but rather for members from other socialist and Scandinavian countries. They are counting on many foreign visitors coming to Freiberg and for that reason, suggest we consider planning at the outset for vehicle parking, overnight lodging, and living quarters for the workers.
>
> Since the Freiberg branch has its own meeting house, there would be no need to add another one, so we could use the entire building as an endowment house. Since the city fathers are comparing it with our nearest temple in Zollikofen, I have had the strong feeling that perhaps under these circumstances, the possibility for proxy baptisms should be added to the present plan of the endowment house.
>
> Although a decision in favor of Freiberg would not solve the need for a meeting house in Karl-Marx-Stadt, the entire mission presidency is in agreement that an endowment house in Freiberg would bring great blessings to all members in the affected area. (DMO)

Burkhardt briefed Elders Monson and Hales on April 2, 1981. On April 5, he met with Elder Hans B. Ringger, the regional representative, Emil Fetzer, the Church architect, and Marvin R. VanDam and Bishop H. Burke Peterson from the presiding bishopric's office in Frankfurt. At the conclusion of these meetings, the plan for an endowment house had become a plan for a temple. In a letter to the meeting participants, dated April 6, 1981, Bishop Peterson wrote:

> 1. The facility, hopefully to be constructed in Freiberg, East Germany, can probably serve and be referred to as a temple.
>
> 2. The temple building should include an ordinance room large enough to hold a busload of Saints plus a few, a sealing room, a baptismal font, an area for initiatory ordinances, clothing/dressing facilities, a small entrance foyer, an interview-instruction-office room for the president, and a records office for the recorder.
>
> 3. The proposal should include a separate small meeting house and mission office facilities on the same property, which can also serve as a sleeping and eating facility for temple patrons.
>
> 4. The currently owned meeting facility might be converted to apartments that may be used in conjunction with the temple. It is not expected, however, that there will be a need for a full-time temple president at the outset.
>
> 5. Patron attendance at the temple will be scheduled—by appointment, in effect.
>
> 6. Architectural planning and design will be under the direction of Emil Fetzer in Salt Lake City. Konrad Nagele, the Building Division manager for Europe/Europe West will serve as project construction manager. Hans Ringger, as regional representative, will be the ecclesiastical contact for the project.
>
> 7. Communications and planning between Salt Lake City and Europe will flow through and be coordinated by Brother VanDam.
>
> 8. Emil Fetzer will, as quickly as possible, send preliminary sizing and utility use specifications to Brother VanDam, who will promptly forward them to President Burkhardt. (Copy in author's possession)

After returning from Salt Lake City, Burkhardt wrote to the Freiberg county council on April 29, 1981: "We have definitely agreed upon Freiberg as the location for our temple, and our architects have begun to prepare the detailed project plans in accordance with the suggestions and thoughts of the mayor and city architect." He received new building plans from Salt Lake City on June 21, 1981, which included two buildings, and wrote later, "Regarding the temple (and no one speaks now about an endowment house), a meeting house for the branch in Freiberg was added, which would serve simultaneously as a hostel for the temple visitors."[10]

Elder Monson did not attend the April 5 meeting, and his published journal does not mention it or the apparent agreement regarding the Freiberg location. His next entry was on June 3: "Met with Burke Peterson and Emil Fetzer relative to schematic plans for a new temple in the German Democratic Republic." Two days later, he again did not mention Freiberg as the location when he wrote:

> I met with the First Presidency and with Burke Peterson, there to discuss the matter of the proposed temple in the German Democratic Republic. I asked the brethren of the presidency if they felt it was time to share with any of the other General Authorities the confidential work we are doing with regard to this building. The presidency felt that such sharing could be deferred until we are more certain of our location and the approval of the plans of construction. (*Faith Rewarded*)

The project did not move forward during that summer, probably because the legal counsel, Frau Dr. Schumann-Fitzner, had retired. Burkhardt returned to Berlin on September 22, 1981, to meet with her successor, Günther Behncke, and wrote thereafter:

> It appears that this office now wishes to push the project forward as fast as possible. Herr Behncke immediately arranged for a meeting with Herr Seidel, general director of the Ministry for Foreign Trade, on October 1, 1981, to discuss the opening of an account for the Freiberg project. Herr Behncke said, "The state has given a green light for its construction." (DMO)

Despite Bishop Peterson's letter of April 6, neither of Elder Monson's June entries refers to Freiberg, and Burkhardt began to hear through his contacts that Monson was not yet convinced it was an ideal location. On October 2, 1981, Konrad Nagele sent a letter to Marvin VanDam, on behalf of Elder Ringger, Burkhardt, and himself, in which he summarized the meeting between these three men and Herr Seidel the previous day. He then addressed "the question of whether the building should be in Freiberg or in Karl-Marx-Stadt" and noted that the consensus reached at the April 5 meeting in Salt Lake City was to accept the Freiberg offer, Burkhardt had conveyed that decision to Freiberg officials on April 29, the government in turn had conveyed its approval to Burkhardt on September 22, and failure to continue with the Freiberg location would mean starting all over again, which was out of the question. He concluded with a warning that to suggest the temple be built elsewhere ran "the risk that the project could be delayed for years, with the eventual risk of losing all that we have accomplished so far" (copy in author's possession).

On November 5, 1981, President Burkhardt sent a personal letter directly to Elder Monson, in which he presented his own reasons for choosing Freiberg:

Much time has passed since our discussions in the spring and the submission of our plans for Freiberg. Since then, I have prayed often for clarity regarding this project, and am now very certain that the decision in favor of Freiberg is the best and most correct decision that could be made. During the intervening time, I tried again and again to evaluate other options, to determine if there were other places better suited for the establishment of this building. But every time I came back to Freiberg.

At first, the decisive factor for me was that our government had given its approval for this city. Because the Freiberg city fathers were very friendly and receptive to this project, understood its purpose, and considered it important that we build there, a very good relationship developed between both parties. I came to understand that to reject the approval we had obtained from the government would delay for many years the opportunity to make all of the ordinances of the gospel available to our members. From my perspective, it would be irresponsible to intentionally cause such a delay.

Moreover, when I viewed the situation from the perspective of the entire mission, Freiberg is a much more favorable decision than Karl-Marx-Stadt or Leipzig. If Karl-Marx-Stadt were the choice, we would have had, in addition to that branch, only the branch in Annaberg-Buchholz as a nearby support. If we were in Leipzig, we would have had only the Leipzig branch to handle the work. In the case of Freiberg, we have the nearby branches of Annaberg-Buchholz, Dresden, and Karl-Marx-Stadt, plus five smaller and middle-sized branches in the immediate vicinity, all between five and fifty kilometers from Freiberg.

The travel situation is very favorable. You can reach Freiberg very well via the autobahn. Whether you come from Thuringia in the west, Mecklenburg or Berlin in the north, or from the eastern regions of our country, the autobahn passes within seventeen kilometers of Freiberg. Since most of the members will come by train, Freiberg has very favorable connections from the district capitals of Dresden and Karl-Marx-Stadt. From Leipzig or from the Erfurt area, you can reach Freiberg via Karl-Marx-Stadt. From the north, Mecklenburg, Berlin, Cottbus, or from east Saxony, you can reach Freiberg via Dresden. Favorable bus connections exist from Annaberg-Buchholz. After consideration of all these factors, I find the prospect of locating in Freiberg to be a great blessing.

I only want to let you know, dear Elder Monson, that I personally feel very good about Freiberg as the location and stand fully and entirely behind that decision. My counselors have the same feelings and share my opinion. It is my great wish to soon be able to report further progress in this area. (Copy in author's possession)

After reassuring Elder Monson about the Freiberg location, Burkhardt's next task was to locate a specific building site. Although cars and buses became the predominant means of travel to the temple, few members had cars in 1981 and Burkhardt assumed that most would come by train. Therefore, he wanted a location with good access to the train station. On January 19, 1982, he met with Freiberg officials, who had identified two potential sites, and he visited those sites with Frank Apel, the mission's executive secretary. One site was immediately adjacent to the old town, just outside the city wall. While it had good connections to the train station, it was rather small, was next to a heavily traveled road, and was so far below the level of the adjacent road that travelers would look down upon the temple. Moreover, the site was over a former mine shaft, with indications that the ground might sink. The second site was on the extreme northwest edge of the city near the top of a small hill. It was farmland without nearby public transportation at that time. Utilities would have to be extended to the site at additional cost, but it offered excellent expansion possibilities. Burkhardt wrote, "At that time, we received a very definite revelation in our heart that this was the place where a worthy house should be built to the Lord."[11]

During the next week, President Burkhardt's two counselors and Elder Ringger, Konrad Nagele, and Marvin VanDam visited the site. Elder Hales visited on February 9. They all preferred the second site. Elder Monson arrived on February 28 and wrote a long account of that day's events, which is noteworthy by its absence of any direct comment regarding the lot itself. Instead, he briefly described the city. "This morning we drove to Freiberg and saw the site selected for a temple there. All of the buildings in Freiberg are ancient and dilapidated. This is a university city where Henry D. Moyle studied following his mission in Germany. New apartment buildings, though stereotyped and somewhat drab in appearance, are planned to be constructed across the street from our site" (*Faith Rewarded*).

The last two words, "our site," may reveal Elder Monson's acceptance of Burkhardt's recommendation to build the temple in Freiberg. His otherwise unenthusiastic journal entry might be explained by Burkhardt's recollection of their conversation that day, when Monson asked him, "Have you thoroughly considered this choice? Freiberg? Is that really the right place? How will the people come here without adequate public transportation?" Burkhardt said that Monson "wanted to create doubts in our mind, that is, to challenge our conclusions." Burkhardt did his best to answer Monson's questions but felt that his best answer was to communicate the strong positive feeling he and his counselors had received following their prayers and fasts. They felt deeply that this was the place the Lord wanted, despite all the reasons they had presented earlier while trying to build in Karl-Marx-Stadt (2003).

After Elder Hales visited the site on February 8, 1982, he organized a temple committee with the following members: Henry Burkhardt, Gottfried Richter, Günter Schulze, Frank Apel, and Karlheinz Leonhardt, with Gottfried Teubner as secretary. The last two men were members of the city council, and Elder

Hales decided that they should be fully aware of coming events in order to represent the Church's interests, if necessary. The committee's tasks were described in the minutes of the first meeting:

> 1. Planning of the groundbreaking, cornerstone, and keystone ceremonies and the physical and financial contributions of the members.
>
> 2. Organization of all public relations activities.
>
> 3. Responsibility for placing the temple into operation.
>
> The committee members were emphatically instructed that no information about the project may be released until the groundbreaking ceremony, and that only three members of the Quorum of Twelve Apostles and the First Quorum of Seventy had been informed of the project. (Copy in author's possession)

Although the negotiations between the Church and the government were supposed to be confidential, information about the project eventually began to leak out. For example, Gottfried Schmidt, a member of the Freiberg branch, was informed by his supervisor at the company that would provide electricity to the worksite (see Schmidt's account in Chapter 10). The problem of premature disclosure was discussed at the second meeting of the temple committee on April 24, 1982. The protocol stated:

> The question is being increasingly raised among members and nonmembers whether a temple will be built by the Church in Freiberg. The committee members asked what they should do if they encounter this question. Elder Ringger said that the president of the Church is the only person authorized to inform people when and where temples of the Lord will be built. If we encounter the question, we should answer that it could happen, but it is a matter only for the Prophet. (Copy in author's possession)

The plan to build a temple in Freiberg was officially announced in Salt Lake City on October 9, 1982. At Elder Monson's request, the groundbreaking ceremony, held on April 23, 1983, was witnessed only by a small group. He wrote that "we had not made any public announcement, since there was a feeling this was in the best interests of the work." The invited guests included Robert D. Hales, Enzio F. Busche, Hans B. Ringger, Konrad Nagele, Emil B. Fetzer, local and regional priesthood leaders, the mayor of Freiberg, and representatives of the city and county councils and the Building Academy of Dresden, whose architects prepared the final plan under guidance from Emil Fetzer.

The Property Is Purchased with East Marks

After his first visit to the building site on February 28, 1982, Elder Monson wrote that "the government is willing to make the temple site available on a very long-term lease, that we might construct a building." President Burkhardt, however, had a different idea and told county and district officials that ownership of the land was essential. They told him that would not be a problem.

GDR law prohibited any reduction in the amount of state-owned land. After 1978, the Evangelical and the Catholic churches were allowed to build new facilities in areas where they didn't own land because the new program allowed churches to exchange their existing land for new building sites. However, the Church did not own any property that could be traded. Elder Monson might have accepted a long-term lease, but President Burkhardt wanted to buy the land. Therefore, the good will that had been developed between the state and the Church led government officials to find ways to help the Church. "It was a question of fairness," said Kurt Löffler. "Other churches had their land. The LDS did not. Without land, the temple couldn't be built" (2003).

As it turned out, the proposed temple site was not state land. While it was being used as a state cooperative farm, the government had confiscated the land from two elderly couples who had never received compensation. Since it was technically private land, its sale did not reduce the amount of state-owned land.

Although the temple's construction costs were reimbursed with Western currency, the land was purchased with the mission's East marks. The official value of the farmland was 17 East German cents per square meter, a minuscule portion of its potential value as a building lot. Since the money would be paid to the official owners, President Burkhardt said that he could not accept the land at that price and received permission to pay a total of fifty cents per square meter in 1982 (2003).

As was the custom at that time, the owners first received the official purchase price, and the additional money was given to them unofficially. They were, of course, thrilled to be paid. In 1987, the Church purchased an adjacent small tract from the same owners for the construction of ancillary buildings. A final piece of land along the road was purchased from the city in 1990 to expand and protect the view of the temple when approaching it from the city.[12]

Additional property, on which a single family house was built for the temple president, was also purchased later with East marks. While Bishop Peterson had stated in his letter of April 6, 1981, that a full-time temple president was not anticipated in the near future, Elder Monson asked Burkhardt after the groundbreaking ceremony, where the temple president would live. "He cannot live here on the temple grounds, and he cannot live more than ten minutes away. Find a lot, where you can build a house for the temple president." Burkhardt said that Dr. Vetter, the deputy chairman of the county council, who had been impressed by the ceremony, approached him and offered his assistance. "I gave him the necessary information and he found the property on which the president now lives.

And he did that at a time when it was very difficult to build private homes. They did everything possible for us" (2003).

Apparently, Elder Monson's question about the temple president's home was not a total surprise. One month earlier, Burkhardt had already submitted to the State Secretariat "an application for the expansion of the temple property and for the building of a house for the temple president." However, actually finding and purchasing the property was facilitated by Dr. Vetter. In the GDR, connections were very important.

But why did the government accept East marks for these property transactions? Why didn't they use this opportunity to obtain additional Western currency? When asked that question, Kurt Löffler explained that land in the GDR was simply not for sale to outside interests. Although Western money "was needed to compensate the state for the loss of its material and manpower resources, that applied only to building expenses. If we had sold our land for Western money, it would have opened doors to other buyers. We didn't want that kind of precedent" (2003).

Löffler's statement is not presented here as the official government reason why the Church was able to purchase land with East marks, for no official documents on that subject have been found, but it is compatible with the statement of Lothar Ebisch in the following chapter that land for the Church's new meeting houses was always purchased with East marks. In summary, the sale of land for the temple as well as for the new meeting houses in East marks challenges a common assumption that these projects were initiated by the GDR primarily as a means to obtain Western currency.

A final example regarding the use of East marks concerns the temple's heating plant. The initial plan developed by the GDR's architects anticipated a heating plant that would burn the soft brown coal widely used throughout East Germany, which left its cities blackened and its air polluted. A tall chimney would have risen above the temple. Burkhardt declared that plan unacceptable, and Dr. Hantzsche promised to search for an alternative. He later informed Burkhardt that a pipeline carrying natural gas from Russia to West Germany passed by Freiberg. It was a major source of Western money for the Soviet Union. The GDR had only limited access to the pipeline, and while a few private homes in the Freiberg area were connected to it, larger facilities, such as the nearby university, were not given an allotment. Burkhardt discussed the issue with the Ministry for Foreign Trade, and the Church was granted an allotment. The cost of the gas was paid with East marks until the Wende (2003).

A Temple with a Limited Life Expectancy

Although President Burkhardt was frequently encouraged by President Kimball to establish friendly relations with the GDR's representatives, the leadership of the Church clearly was opposed to Communism. President Benson, who succeeded Kimball in 1985, was particularly well known for his frank comments on that subject. Perhaps Benson's strong opposition to Communism was the reason for an unusual promise by President Kimball. When Elder

Hales organized the local temple committee in early 1982, he conveyed to its members Kimball's personal greetings and a promise that he would remain on the earth until the temple was dedicated, despite his well-known health problems. He passed away a few months after the temple dedication.

The First Presidency's decision to build a temple was a recognition that other options did not exist for members in the GDR to receive the blessings of a temple. The decision, however, was accompanied by a concern that the building could be violated at some time in the future by the state. Therefore, the first plan had provided for an endowment house under the same roof with meeting facilities for the local branch in Karl-Marx-Stadt. That approach would have helped the branch to retain and use the entire building if the endowment house were subsequently violated.

The concern about possible government intrusion continued after the project received a friendly welcome in Freiberg. For example, the temple's schedule for the first weeks following its dedication in 1985 focused entirely on members who had not yet been able to personally attend a temple. Each ward and branch was assigned a specific day, and members received all of their temple ordinances during that day. If the temple had been subsequently desecrated, it would have fulfilled its main purpose. Proxy ordinances could be sent to other temples if necessary, as had been done in the past.

The fear of possible desecration appears to have been more pronounced among Church leaders in America than in the GDR. The former were clearly concerned that government officials might insist on personally monitoring temple activities, despite their earlier promises to the contrary. However, based on their more frequent interactions with the government in recent years, Church leaders in the GDR generally did not share that concern. While Stasi informants continued to monitor the Church's activities, and were certainly present among the many visitors during the open house, available government documents do not give any indication of plans or activities that could lead to a violation of the temple. Construction workers were even informed of the Church's teachings regarding the Word of Wisdom, and when asked by project supervisors not to smoke while working on the building, they willingly complied.

Given the concern about possible desecration, President Burkhardt was not surprised when President Hinckley quietly expressed his hope, following the dedication ceremony, that the temple would not soon become a museum. However, Burkhardt also noted that Hinckley appeared to be more relaxed about the temple's future after he lunched with Hermann Kalb, a representative of the state secretary for Church Affairs (2003).

In light of the uncertainty regarding the temple's future, it is not surprising that the Church attempted to limit its financial loss should the building be desecrated. Several examples of cost avoidance can be seen in the temple's initial size, facilities, and materials. Members frequently described the quality of the materials as "mittelmäßig," or mediocre, and after the temple's expansion in 2004, the Church's website stated that "quality construction materials were not available during the original construction of the temple."[13] However, availability of better material was not the real problem. President Burkhardt, Dr. Hantzsche, and Lothar Ebisch, the regional building supervisor, have said that better quality items were available within East Germany or could have been imported if requested. Hantzsche said that the temple was built exactly as specified in instructions from Emil Fetzer, and that his own recommendations for better materials and facilities were turned down. Lothar Ebisch confirmed that and said he heard Fetzer express concerns about the temple's life expectancy:

> Brother Fetzer was constantly driven by his perception of our Communist situation. He believed that sooner or later, the house would be desecrated, and he was not the only person who had that fear. Perhaps their fear was justifiable to some degree, but we didn't see it that way. Yes, they continued to spy on our members, but once they promised us something, said "yes" to us, then we could count on that. That was our view of the situation. If they had tried to enter the temple, it would have been over our dead bodies. . . . However, we didn't focus on the material deficiencies. The temple was something special for us. We were happy that we had a temple. (2003)

An example of "mittelmäßig" materials was the temple's water pipes. Hantzsche warned that local water conditions would lead to corrosion of the galvanized iron pipes that had been specified. More expensive alternatives, such as copper piping, were available but not authorized. Ebisch said, "We had better quality in the GDR, or we could have imported it. Imports were not restricted." As feared, the pipes corroded and had to be replaced within a few years.

Hantzsche considered the temple to be a "closed building," i.e., none of the windows could be opened. He knew that the specified air circulation system could not provide a comfortable temperature on hot and humid summer days because it neither cooled the air nor reduced the humidity. He recommended the installation of an air conditioning system (2003). These systems were available in East Germany, especially when manufacturing projects required "clean rooms" in windowless buildings, and such a system was already functioning in a building in Freiberg. However, Hantzsche's recommendation was rejected. As a result, President Burkhardt reported in 1990 that "since the opening of the temple, about 250 to 300 visitors have fainted due to inadequate air circulation and high temperatures, especially in the sealing rooms."[14]

Two other European temples built at the same time, one completed in Stockholm in 1985 and one near Frankfurt/Main, which was announced before Freiberg but not completed until 1987, had air conditioning. Frankfurt's weather is similar to Freiberg's, while Stockholm is somewhat cooler. But there was no concern about the expected life of those temples. An air conditioning system was finally installed in the Freiberg Temple in 1994, after the reunification of Germany.

Hantzsche recommended that the deep excavation specified for the foundation of the temple be used to create basement space for future expansion or for functions that could not be accommodated within the small floor plan. Basements are normal practice in Germany. However, he was told to push the dirt back around the foundation (2003). Without a basement or other options, the temple's laundry facilities were located in an interior room of ninety square feet that did not allow adequate venting for the washers and dryers.[15] Temperatures in that room often reached ninety degrees, with very high humidity, which created difficult conditions for the temple workers. The lack of air conditioning also contributed to the laundry room problem. Lothar Ebisch said:

> They often saved money in the wrong places. For example, the foundation was so deep that they certainly could have had a cellar. But the space was filled in again. The utilities and technical equipment, laundry facilities, space for the temple workers, etc., could have been placed there. The baptism font was most primitive. Everything had to be squeezed in on one floor. (2003)

Hantzsche also recommended that the space under the adjacent meeting house be used to provide for overnight lodging of patrons who had to travel long distances, or for other future needs. Again, he was told to push the dirt back around the foundation walls. Patrons requiring overnight lodging had to be accommodated in makeshift sleeping, eating, and washing facilities in the meeting house or in a former meeting house eight miles to the south. Finally, in 1994, two additional buildings for overnight lodging, laundry facilities, workrooms for the temple engineer and maintenance staff, changing rooms for temple workers, and the sale of temple clothing were added.

The Temple Open House

An open house was held June 1–16, 1985. June 3 was reserved for VIPs, who received personal invitations printed in West Germany and imported with permission. Among the VIPs were representatives of the state, other churches, and political parties. None of the church representatives attended on VIP day, but many were seen there on following days. Further details concerning the open house are found in Appendix I. Below are recollections of members who assisted visitors during the open house:

> *Cornelia Ortlieb:* Masses of people came to see the temple. It was the first time that most of them had heard anything at all about the Church of Jesus Christ of Latter-day Saints. (1993)

> *Dieter Lehm:* More than ninety thousand people came in those twelve days. They stood for four hours and even longer. It was cold, it rained, and the people stood and stood. When we arrived [from Annaberg], we asked ourselves, "What is going on here?" The streets were totally

packed. We never imagined it was just because of the temple. The police stood along the streets and closed some of them to avoid chaos. We never imagined seeing so many people there.... The television station carried a program about the dedication. It only lasted one or two minutes, but it was on television. Also in those days, positive articles about the Church appeared in the newspapers, and people tried to write accurate accounts. That was different than twenty years earlier, when lies and negative things were written. They made an effort to report accurately and objectively. That was real progress. (1991)

Marianne Ortlieb: We also had trouble with the public. I gave a woman an invitation to the open house and thought she would eat me alive. She said, "You can build your temple because you've joined with the state. I want nothing to do with you." We also had trouble on the job. One person told me, "Honecker wants to go to the USA, and that's why he approved everything for you." (1993)

Gottfried Richter: Some just came out of curiosity. But I could read their faces. Even though they didn't know it themselves, many came out of a longing for something better, something more beautiful, something more noble than they had. Each of us who worked at the temple at that time had many wonderful experiences. One evening I was standing a little away from the temple and looked toward the entrance. A young woman came out. Her face showed that she was inwardly very deeply stirred. She looked around and saw me standing with a badge and approached me, along with her husband, a tall strong man, and a young boy, perhaps eight or nine years old. Without any introduction, she asked, "What is eternity?" One cannot respond to such a question with a quick answer. I said, "You are a beautiful family. How long do you wish to remain together?" She looked at her husband and at her boy. The boy looked up at his parents. You could see they loved each other very much. Then I tried, with simple words, to explain what eternity is and what it has to do with the temple. They walked away in deep thought. (1993)

The temple dedication took place on June 29 and 30, with four sessions on Friday and three on Saturday. In the first session, President Hinckley spoke the dedicatory prayer in English, after which it was read in German. The full text can be found in Appendix J. A total of about 2,400 members attended the seven sessions.

President Burkhardt often said, "The Lord held this temple project securely in his hand and inspired the participants so that all decisions were favorable to his intent." Given the difficulties associated with this project, one could ask whether the "hand of the Lord" was also present in the failed attempt to build an endowment house in Karl-Marx-Stadt? Without the resistance of dedicated

Communists in that city, a very small endowment house would have been built there that would have been of limited usefulness after the collapse of the GDR less than five years later. In that case, and given the existence of a temple near Frankfurt/Main, it is unlikely that the Church would have built a second temple in a unified Germany. That would have been a significant loss not only for the members in the former GDR, but also for the growing number of members from the former Soviet block countries east and south of the GDR who now come to the Freiberg temple. Due to the fact that the temple was forced (or led) from Karl-Marx-Stadt to Freiberg, enough land was obtained for a complete temple, for its later expansion, and for lodging facilities for members and temple workers that enable patrons to come from distant countries and stay for a week at a time.

Readers will have their own opinions concerning the importance of the various factors that made the Freiberg temple possible. They include, on one hand, Elder Monson's dedicatory prayer of 1975, the faith, sacrifice, and dedication of the members, their reputation as honest and valuable citizens, and their acceptance of President Kimball's challenge to develop good relationships with government officials. On the other hand, changes in the leadership of the GDR, Honecker's summit meeting of March 6, 1978, the expanded special building program, the application of the GDR's constitutional principle that all churches and religious organizations have equal rights, the goal of some members of the Secretariat for Church Affairs to reduce the conflict between a socialistic-oriented government and the religious beliefs of its citizens, and the country's need for Western currency are all relevant factors that deserve serious consideration.

It is not possible to turn back the clock and eliminate those factors one at a time to determine which of them would have had the largest influence. But the events and documents show that the need for convertible Western currency was a necessary but not a sufficient factor by itself. It also may be difficult for some people to accept that some government officials had an understanding or sympathy for the religious concerns of its citizens. But in his 1975 prayer on the Friedensburg outside Dresden, Elder Monson asked God to "intervene in the governmental affairs" that the hearts of those who preside "may be touched and that they may make those decisions which would help in the advancement of Thy work." Whether hearts were touched can only be known by those officials who three years later suggested that a temple be built.

President Burkhardt offered his personal perspective about the origin of the temple when he commented on the effects of Elder Monson's 1975 prayer:

> On that morning, a prophet of God prayed that the members in this country would receive the blessings of the temple. He did not specify how that was to happen, but just that worthy members would come into possession of those blessings. At that time, we were prohibited by law from traveling to the Swiss temple, and no one had ever thought that there could be a temple in the GDR. There had never been a temple

> in a Communist country, in a country that attempted to eliminate or reduce churches. However, the first steps toward a temple began just three years later.[16]

A final comment regarding the decision to build the temple in the city of Freiberg should be added here. In contrast to the long and unsuccessful effort to build in Karl-Marx-Stadt, President Burkhardt emphasized the friendly reception that he and his associates received from officials and citizens of Freiberg, which continued throughout the construction period, during the open house, and thereafter. One example of that friendly reception was visible on postcards sold in Freiberg during the last years of the officially atheistic GDR regime. The temple was featured on postcards of Freiberg, next to views of the city's historic old town square and medieval building facades.[17] Those images stood in stark contrast to the 1953 claim of Walter Ulbricht, quoted at the start of Chapter 11, "We won't need [church] towers in a socialist city."

16 New Meeting Houses in the 1980s

> *In the 1980s we said, "Our best missionaries are our meeting houses." At each open house we had several thousand visitors, who simply came because the architecture of the chapels was so beautiful. Therefore, we could do missionary work within our buildings. They were magnets, especially in an environment where houses were in ruins or uncared for. (Manfred Schütze, 1991)*

The expansion of the GDR's special building program, which permitted Evangelical churches to be built in new residential areas, led directly to the temple in Freiberg. That program also enabled the Church to construct new meeting houses, beginning with the stake center in Leipzig and extending to smaller chapels throughout the GDR.

The Leipzig Stake Center, 1980–1984

When the Karl-Marx-Stadt district council refused to allow the endowment house to be built in that city, and before Freiberg was chosen as the new site, President Burkhardt met with representatives of the Secretariat for Church Affairs to inquire about other options. Excerpts from the Dresden Mission's journal describe those discussions:

> *October 15, 1980:* While searching for a solution, President Burkhardt said that the temple then should be built in the city of Leipzig. Frau Dr. Schumann-Fitzner said that it would be even more difficult to have a building of that type in Leipzig. President Burkhardt then took the opportunity to state that preparatory work should be started now for construction of a meeting house under the special building program. Frau Janott asked if a building for Leipzig would be paid for with hard currency. He said it would. (DMO)

The Leipzig project proceeded slowly because the temple took priority with the Church and the government as that project moved toward Freiberg in early 1981. References to Leipzig appear again in the mission journal history in late 1981:

> *December 3, 1981:* The president of the Leipzig branch was invited to a meeting with the city council, regarding the building of a meeting house. Since he had not been informed about it, he asked the mission president to be present. Herr Güntherberg said that the state secretary for Church Affairs had informed the Leipzig district council of the receipt of a petition from the mission president regarding the building of a meeting house within the Leipzig city boundaries. The city will support us, since the district council considers the project to be a government request.
>
> *August 25, 1982:* Two building sites were suggested to us. We went first to the Oeserstraße and then to the Stieglitzstraße.
>
> *August 28, 1982:* President Burkhardt met in the morning with Elders Monson, Hales, and Ringger in Leipzig. Everyone was quite pleased with the property in the Stieglitzstraße, although the Oeserstraße also looked very good.

The eventual choice of the Oeserstraße site was influenced by emerging plans for a stake in Leipzig. The property in the Stieglitzstraße consisted of two pieces of land narrowly connected, neither of which was large enough for construction of a large building. On January 20, 1983, President Burkhardt wrote to Secretary Gysi:

> The construction of our temple in Freiberg and the organization of our stake in Freiberg . . . resulted in an enlarged Leipzig district. While our original building plan for Leipzig assumed a chapel capacity of 250, this organizational change requires us to expand the chapel to 400 seats. . . . The Oeserstraße property will enable this expansion. (MS 13918)

The Oeserstraße property was owned by the state. Memoranda from the files of the secretary for Church Affairs show how that problem was solved with the assistance of government offices:

> *January 4, 1984, Notes of a meeting with Herr Burkhardt and Herr Dr. Hantzsche, Building Academy, Dresden:* According to information in this office, it is planned to build a center for the Church of Jesus Christ on state land in Leipzig. That decision has legal consequences that could lead to a conflict with the Church. It was therefore consid-

ered useful to inform Herr Burkhardt that according to the law regarding the right to use state property, such rights can only be granted to a county. In all other cases, the buildings erected on state land are also state property. That could lead to complications, for example, in the case of a future sale or other use.

With an indefinite use permit—which is obviously intended in this instance—it could be assumed, in our opinion, that the state would never challenge the Church's right to use the building. But the Church would not be listed in the property records as the owner. Since, however, the Church expects to be recorded as the owner, it would be necessary to obtain private land elsewhere to exchange for the state property. Then there would be no obstacle to recording the Church's ownership.

Herr Burkhardt was informed that the land to be exchanged did not have to be within the city or the district of Leipzig. The purchase could take place anywhere within our republic. He was further informed that the Department of State Property would provide assistance in locating appropriate private property. He was also informed that nothing in this meeting should prevent or influence his decision to request a use permit. It was just a matter of informing him of possible consequences. The decision is solely up to the Church. Herr Burkhardt and Herr Dr. Hantzsche were of the opinion, that an exchange of land would be the cleanest solution. They are leaning in the direction of buying one large piece of land that would cover all planned building projects. (DO 4/889)

January 5, 1984, Notes of a meeting with comrade Jarchow, Department of State Property, Ministry of Finance: Comrade Jarchow confirmed that buildings erected on state-owned land become property of the state. That does not prevent the building from being used as personal property, but ownership is not recorded.... In this instance, he advised that the Church of Jesus Christ could exchange private for state-owned land in Leipzig at a later time. That has happened in other instances. Construction of the church center need not be delayed until the exchange takes place. (DO 4/889)

January 5, 1984, Notes of a telephone conversation with Herr Burkhardt: I informed him that it is possible to exchange state-owned land at a later time. He was relieved to receive this information, but asked if he could be given the information in writing. I said I would discuss it with comrade Behncke. (DO 4/889)

President Burkhardt accepted the government's offer. The groundbreaking for the Leipzig stake center took place on March 17, 1984, and the building was completed in May 1986. In 1988, the Church bought 11,500 square meters of private land in Mittweida, which was traded for the Leipzig property and other state land in Erfurt and Mittweida.

A Chapel for Zwickau

Despite the special building program, the Church's requests for new construction were hampered in some cities where local officials opposed all new churches. The Karl-Marx-Stadt district council, which had opposed the endowment house, also opposed chapels in that city and in nearby Zwickau. Correspondence between President Burkhardt, Secretary Gysi, and comrade Fichtner of the district council, found in the files of the State Secretariat, shows the arguments that the State Secretariat employed over the course of a year to overcome local opposition to a chapel for Zwickau:

> *February 16, 1983, Burkhardt to Gysi:* Permit me once again to submit an application under the special building program for a meeting house in the city of Zwickau.
>
> *April 5, 1983, Fichtner to Gysi:* We cannot support the request of this church to build a chapel in Zwickau. Construction of additional buildings for this church within this district is, in my opinion, not required by the number of its members. With permission for the temple in Freiberg, state support already has been quite generous.
>
> *September 7, 1983, Gysi to Fichtner:* My staff has confirmed the facts in the application regarding Zwickau as accurate. Therefore, I support the request, especially since this religious organization is loyal to the state. Regarding the temple in Freiberg, permit me to inform you that [the temple] is a religious center that may only be used for sacred ordinances. Regular worship services are not permitted there. From the perspective of church policy, but also because the financial status of the GDR will be enhanced by the realization of an additional two million marks in foreign currency, I ask you to re-evaluate your previous decision.
>
> *April 4, 1984, Gysi to Fichtner:* I wish to emphasize once more, dear comrade Fichtner, that I support this application for reasons of state policy, and because this religious organization is loyal toward the state in every respect.
>
> *April 30, 1984, Fichtner to Gysi:* Although there is absolutely no urgent necessity for a new building, I have decided to agree with this proposal because of church policy and economic considerations. (MS 13918)

Günther Behncke played a significant role in the Church's building program, as he did in the case of the Freiberg Temple. The above letters from Secretary Gysi to comrade Fichtner were probably written or drafted by Behncke, who also added the following comments regarding the challenges presented by some local agencies:

> The constitutional regulation of religious freedom was at the core of my work, especially the principle that every person had the right to believe what he wanted, and he needed a house of God in which to practice his faith. But construction of church buildings was very complicated. We had to struggle with two problems: first, against a certain number of functionaries, but also against part of the general population. You see, the building resources in the GDR were very limited. Many apartments were in poor condition. And suddenly come the churches and want a large meeting house. If they pay with Western currency or dollars, then it will be approved. Most people didn't understand the connection and they protested. But these protests from the people also were faked, to support opposing arguments. So we often had to be tricky, that is, we had to neutralize the negative influence of the "concrete heads" with appropriate strategies.
>
> Once I personally went and spoke with the local functionaries. We even had to find allies within the reviled state security apparatus, or at least convince them to help us. For example, there was no possibility to obtain permission to build a meeting house for the Mormons in the Karl-Marx-Stadt district [probably in Zwickau]. That went back and forth for a long time. So I called the head of security and "beat on the bush," that is, I claimed that I had heard that "the state security in Karl-Marx-Stadt district was opposed to this Mormon building. Why? The Mormons are good citizens of the GDR, they are honest and energetic workers and raise their children to be upright people." The man hung up the phone without responding, but he came to me a week later and said that the "security" in Karl-Marx-Stadt has nothing against building the meeting house, and that I should apply once more. So I prepared a letter for my state secretary, Klaus Gysi, and fourteen days later we received permission. But that only works when you are convinced that the request of the affected citizen is justified. (1991)

Other New Chapels

When the government was surprised that so many of its citizens came to visit the temple in 1985, the secretary for Church Affairs was asked to prepare a report about the Church. Excerpts from that report, relative to the building of other meeting houses, follow:

> Many reports are appearing in the Western press concerning the development of the Mormon church in the GDR that are more or less

distorted. The main reason has been the completion of the new Mormon temple in Freiberg. Therefore, the state secretary for Church Affairs was asked to review and present the facts.... That review showed that a number of construction projects for the Mormon church have been submitted and confirmed within the limits of the special building program.... The additional fact should also be noted, that these activities of the Mormons have been observed with great suspicion by the Evangelical churches, and have even run into considerable resistance.

A summary of the Mormon church's building program (confirmed projects) follows:

1982 Branch center in Leipzig

1983 Single family house for the temple president and chapels in Erfurt, Berlin, Karl-Marx-Stadt, Mittweida, Schwarzenberg, Plauen, Dresden, and Wolgast

1984 Lodging facility in Freiberg (MS 13798. No author or date)

Although these buildings were listed as "confirmed" by the GDR, the First Presidency had not yet approved the financing of the building costs in all cases. Several Church documents (CR 103 109) show the Church's plans or suggestions regarding future construction. For example, in a note dated September 21, 1987, Konrad Nagele, manager of the building department in the Frankfurt regional office, described plans for several small branches:

Plauen: Attendance 31, Membership 88.
The facility is rented. It is in very bad condition. General remodeling is urgently necessary. Difficult to heat. Chemical toilet only. Plaster is falling off the walls. Purchase of a future building lot is in progress.

Wolgast: Attendance 42, Membership 80.
The building is Church owned and built. It is of plastered wood construction. The wood is deteriorating, roof is leaking, foundation not sufficient. Water in the basement. Only one toilet. The building is not safe and needs to be demolished. Cannot be remodeled. The purchase of a future building lot is in progress.

Köthen: Attendance 36, Membership 89.
The building is Church owned and built. A small family house with two extensions in the back. About 80 years old. No insulation against cold or moisture from the ground. The condition is not too bad, it is well maintained. However, it is not representative of Church standards.

Bernburg: Attendance 27, Membership 74.
This building is rented and in good condition. It was recently renovated. It lies about 18 kilometers from Köthen. We recommend to build one building for Köthen and Bernburg on the outskirts of Köthen and to combine both branches.

Görlitz: Attendance 44, Membership 70.
The building is rented and is in poor condition. Leaking roof, mold in the roof, walls are wet, windows in poor condition, plaster falling off. Difficult to heat.

On October 14, 1987, Konrad Nagele wrote to Elder Ringger,

"Attached is the information you requested concerning the anticipated building projects in the GDR through 1995:

1. Approved projects within the government's five-year plan (for which no money has been appropriated): Plauen, Schwarzenberg, Mittweida, Erfurt, and Wolgast. Total estimated cost: DM 10,000,000 or $5,494,000.

2. Projects that are not in the government's five-year plan: Neubrandenburg, Köthen (including Bernburg), Annaberg, Cottbus, and Görlitz.

Total estimated cost: DM 11,500,000 or $6,318,020.

On November 24, 1987, the Europe Area Presidency (Carlos E. Asay, Hans B. Ringger, and John R. Lasater) wrote to Elder Russell M. Nelson:

We now have had several years of experience in dealing with GDR government agencies regarding real estate purchases, construction projects, and major maintenance on existing meeting houses. The results are well accepted. We have twenty-seven wards and branches (sixteen in rented meeting facilities, eleven in Church-owned buildings). The system used to obtain a newly constructed chapel in the GDR is as follows:

1. After the GDR government expressed a willingness to provide goods and services for a Physical Facilities program of the Church in the GDR, a five-year master plan was developed, identifying units for which new facilities were needed. The criteria for the new facilities were the location and condition of existing facilities and the control over them, which the Church had; also, but not necessarily, the current attendance of the unit. Adequate rentals in the GDR are almost nonexistent. This master plan was reviewed by the Area Presidency.... The

plan was then presented to the GDR government and a blanket agreement was reached that GDR government agencies would support the Church in realizing the plan as outlined. Whereas this five-year plan does not constitute a legal commitment or obligation on the part of the Church, it is at least a statement of intent based on which the GDR will plan material and labor force dispositions in their labor economy. With the mentality of GDR government agencies, which are used to a planned economy, short-term changes or modifications of our plan are very irritating to them. We need to be very careful to honor the plan agreed to with the GDR government.

2. After preliminary approval of an individual project by the GDR government, the Church needs to purchase land from the state. Prices for real estate transactions are very reasonable based on Western standards. Often the Church has to buy privately owned land elsewhere which can be given to the government in exchange for the land received from the government, thus enabling the government to continue to hold the same amount of land in the state.

3. After such a property purchase has been initiated, architectural planning may begin. So far, the Church has only been authorized to deal with one architectural and engineering agency, namely the Building Academy in Dresden. Dr. Hantzsche, as one of its directors, has recently been to Salt Lake City for the April 1987 General Conference at the invitation of the Church. The academy has the objective to plan and design high quality/GDR standard buildings. Several of the chapels that it has designed for the Church have been used as an exhibit at the Leipzig Fair, probably the largest industrial trade fair in the world, to show the quality of planning and design available through the academy as a representative of the GDR. It has been of significant help to us in exploring construction options and parameters in the GDR. We have been working with the academy to reduce and simplify the design of buildings, but can only do so to the point where the quality is still acceptable for the academy to justify their involvement in the projects. However, we have succeeded in reducing the LIMEX asking price significantly (up to 30 percent) on various projects. (LIMEX is the official commercial import and export agency for the GDR.)

4. After planning has been completed and necessary government permits have been obtained, a contract is negotiated with LIMEX. The prime objective of this agency is to obtain the best justifiable hard currency value for their goods and services. Since there is no free market in the GDR, and thus no competition, this company can basically dictate prices. We have attempted to negotiate a unit range (German marks per square meter), but LIMEX has been very reluctant to commit to that. It has often been a matter of diplomatic skills as well as subjective assessment to determine how low to negotiate with LIMEX.

5. When we sign a construction contract with LIMEX, we make sure that we get a certain excess quantity of major appliances and materials used for the building, which are then stored in the new Dresden Administrative Office, in order to have spare parts and repair materials for the O&M program later on. These items and materials are not readily available on the market as the need arises for their use. It is, therefore, necessary to standardize appliances and to store a number of spares anticipating future maintenance needs.

Summary Description of the GDR's Special Building Program

The Church's legal counsel in Frankfurt/Main, Jürgen Warnke, provided his personal insight into the GDR's building program of the 1980s during a 1991 interview:

> It was not legal to send West German marks into the GDR. There was an agreement between the two countries whereby the Federal Republic had helped the GDR financially for many years. It was done through an accounting process, that is, no real money was paid. The first payment we made was for the work on the temple. The accounting went through the Ministry for Foreign Trade to a subsidiary office called LIMEX. But LIMEX was very disturbed and said, "We only received accounting figures. We want hard money." We said, "OK, we'll pay in dollars." Then, as the value of the dollar fell, the GDR quickly determined that it wasn't to their advantage. They said, "We want German marks." We said, "We aren't permitted to send DM from here." They suggested that we use a LIMEX account in Switzerland. So the Church in the USA sent German marks to the Swiss account, and money went to the GDR.
>
> When we built the temple, we also attempted to build chapels, or to renovate others. . . . There were members who later said the Church's contacts with the old GDR government were too good. Our goal was to build a temple, to improve the members' situation in the GDR, to do something for the youth, and to do missionary work. We achieved those goals. I don't believe that anyone can say that we should have waited. (1991)

Beginning in 1984, Lothar Ebisch, a GDR citizen, was employed full-time by the Church as a regional building representative. His perspective regarding the special building program is taken from a 2004 interview:

> In the 1980s, I could buy land for the Church. We proceeded on two tracks. The easiest was when the property was privately owned, as in Freiberg. When private land was not available, we bought private land elsewhere and traded it. The property for the temple was paid with East marks as was the land for the other meeting houses. We also paid

for certain items with East marks, for example the inside furnishings, or when a stone base was added to the building, then we always paid East marks for the stone. The Church always required that we provide a certain percentage of the total cost. We all contributed to the temple. The state, naturally, would have preferred to be paid for everything in hard currency, but we always paid for something with our own mission funds.

I must say that once the decision was made, when the state agreed that we could build, then we received all possible support, absolutely. Then there were no further problems, no back and forth. We had a contract and when the stone once began to roll, it wasn't halted. Then they really supported us.

I once experienced an interesting case in Zwickau. We had purchased private land there. (We bought land in Zwickau several times, which we used for trades.) As we proceeded with the purchase, the owner suddenly imposed restrictions. The arrangements were already quite far advanced. I went to the city administration and explained the situation to the ladies. A few days later, I returned and the ladies said to me, very politely, "Herr Ebisch, we looked into the situation and thought about it. Then we proposed an alternative to the owner." They didn't have to do that, but did it to be helpful. One day, I recalled how nice these ladies had been and thought I should do something to show my appreciation. I bought a large box of chocolates and wanted to give it to them. They would not accept it. "We are sorry, but it was our professional duty to help. Your gift could be seen as a bribe." Everything was done correctly. It was clean.

17 The Honecker-Monson Meeting 1988[1]

> *As a person, I found Erich Honecker to be very pleasant. His political orientation and behavior, of course, were not necessarily the best. But we had to accept him, and under his leadership we had more freedom as a church than earlier under the leadership of Walter Ulbricht. Erich Honecker actually brought about a certain relaxation. Of course, he also made many mistakes, but... the contacts we had with him as a church were only positive for us. I am very thankful that President Monson worked so directly and in such a goal-oriented fashion to establish this contact with Erich Honecker. (Henry Burkhardt, 1991)*

On Thursday morning, March 30, 1989, eight missionaries from the West, together with the president of the new Dresden mission, Wolfgang Paul, drove from Hamburg to the GDR border in three vehicles. President Paul described what happened next:

> I had assumed that the entry process would take hours, until every suitcase was searched and all our material had been declared. But amazingly, we came to the border and were waved through. No one had to leave their vehicle. We were all amazed, since absolutely no control took place, no control at all. For the first time, I saw border police who were friendly and even waved as we drove through, which was never the case. After we crossed the border, our joy was so great, beyond description. President Schütze, who grew up in the GDR, who had lived through the time when the Church had to remove its name from meeting houses, etc., could hardly contain himself. He honked the horn, blinked the headlights, cheered, and cried that after fifty years, missionaries from abroad were again in his country. (1991)

Two months later, on May 26, ten young men left the GDR for the Missionary Training Center in Provo, Utah. President Burkhardt described that event:

> Brother Schulze and I personally drove these ten missionaries from Freiberg to Frankfurt/Main. We had two vehicles, an Audi and a VW-Kombi. The missionaries had never before been in a Western country. Each had their passport, not a normal one but an official government duty passport with an exit visa. As we approached the border, a long line of cars waited to cross. As we came by the first post, he saw my passport and told us to continue forward to the actual border. There they made room for us and opened the gate. We presented our passports, which they stamped, and we were allowed to continue. All the other vehicles stood and waited. It was unbelievable. (2003)

Why did the border open so easily for those two groups? The answer is found in a historic meeting in East Berlin on October 28, 1988, between Chairman Erich Honecker and President Thomas S. Monson. At its conclusion, Honecker turned to Monson and said, "The requests that you have presented will be fulfilled." In that one sentence, Honecker agreed to several requests conveyed in earlier conversations and letters. President Schütze summarized them as, "Missionaries in, missionaries out, more buildings, and more youth activities. [They] were the main four points. We didn't want much, and missionaries were the most important" (1991). Five months later, the first missionaries from the West crossed into the GDR.

This chapter details the events of 1988 that led to that meeting and its results. Frank Apel, then president of the Freiberg Stake, attended the meeting. Three years later, he commented on the significance of Honecker's approval. "Everyone waited. Will Erich Honecker say 'Ja'? And when the 'Ja' came, everyone heaved a sign of relief. Everyone thought if the other comrades who were present also heard him, everything will be okay. He said 'Ja,' and now things will get underway" (1991).

Nine months prior to the meeting, President Monson wrote in his journal on February 2, 1988:

> I am happy that a breakthrough seems to be in the offing pertaining to having a limited number of full-time young elders from the West serve as missionaries in [the GDR]. They would be located as guides at the various locations where we have buildings. This would be ideal and an answer to my real concern relative to the future growth of the Church in that nation. (*Faith Rewarded*)

Monson's journal entry did not include a reason for his optimism, and political developments within the GDR at the time could have been viewed more as a reason for pessimism than optimism. Internal resistance to the government had sharpened, and it increasingly came from groups associated with churches. Therefore, all political activities of churches were viewed with increasing suspicion.

During the night of November 24–25, 1987, the secret police entered and searched the Zionskirche, an Evangelical church in East Berlin. They confiscated papers and copying machines and imprisoned a few individuals. The Zionskirche had allowed some of its members to establish an "environmental library" in the basement, from which seminars and other activities related to "the environment and peace" were conducted with financial support from a small West German political party. The group also distributed a newspaper that criticized government policies. Following the raid, the government took action against a few lay members of church organizations and warned all churches to control their political activities (see Chapter 3).

Dr. Horst Dohle, a consultant to the state secretary for Church Affairs at the time, gave his view of the contemporary state-church relationship during a 1997 interview:

> SED church policy of 1988 was a return to the rude violence and administrative methods of the 1950s. Faced with a growing spirit of disaffection within society, which the state did not want to recognize, and a concomitant rise of small opposition groups, the party attempted to describe the situation as a church-state problem. In reality, the opposition had been pushed into the churches, but the government demanded that its functionaries responsible for church policy solve the problem. But it was not a church policy problem and therefore could not be solved. So the crisis naturally escalated.... The state secretary for Church Affairs [Klaus Gysi] was told that his only function was to control the churches. He should end all discussions and negotiations and instead instruct, forbid, and threaten them.... There was a completely new style in Party leadership and in their statements, which no longer left room for negotiation and discussion.[2]

Although the GDR's constitution proclaimed the separation of church and state, the implementation of that principle was often problematic because the state determined what was and what was not an acceptable church activity. The principle of separation was a special problem for the Evangelical churches, which had exercised significant political influence in prewar Germany and wished to maintain that influence. Their continued commentary on government policy irritated Chairman Honecker, and the activities conducted in the Zionskirche heightened the tension.

As the ramifications of the raid unfolded, Jürgen Warnke, legal counsel to the Church's Frankfurt regional office, consulted with Manfred Wünsche, an East German lawyer who had previously assisted the Church on legal matters. Warnke then wrote to President Hans B. Ringger on January 4, 1988:

> The Evangelical churches in the GDR have investigated the Zionskirche event, and the subsequent searches and arrests in November

> 1987, and came to the following conclusions, which I consider to be important for us.
>
> Recent activities of the churches have irritated the SED and caused functionaries responsible for church policy to inform them that their independence has limits. Especially during the past year, a certain degree of euphoria has been growing within the churches regarding the possibility of social reforms. The hope for future social changes has been excessively nurtured. Therefore, government leaders found it necessary to send strong signals that the limits of acceptable activity by the churches and their organizations had been breached and must be restored or even narrowed. Klaus Gysi confirmed that position by cancelling planned meetings between himself and representatives of the Ministries of Defense and Education regarding school books, kindergarten, and military defense.... While Gysi has confirmed the government's basic church policies, he has emphasized that religious institutions are expected to act within those principles to avoid serious consequences.
>
> In my opinion, this interpretation matches what Herr Wünsche has told us, that we must be more disciplined and not allow our own euphoria over accomplishments to lead to violation of the limits placed upon us by the state. (Copy in author's possession)

President Ringger's response to Jürgen Warnke's letter is not known. However, subsequent events indicate that he and President Monson quickly came to the conclusion that the crackdown against churches engaged in political activity was an opportune time for the LDS Church to emphasize and build upon its traditional policy of noninvolvement in the internal political affairs of government. This strategy was endorsed and assisted by the Church's two most important contacts within the GDR, Manfred Wünsche and Günther Behncke. The earliest known document that reveals that strategy is a summary of a meeting between President Burkhardt and Günther Behncke in the offices of the Secretariat for Church Affairs on February 11, 1988, five weeks after Warnke's letter. The agenda that day included the status of a proposed information brochure, which the Church had submitted to the secretariat several months earlier for review. President Burkhardt summarized the discussion in writing that day:

> It was emphasized that the Church of Jesus Christ of Latter-day Saints, everywhere as well as in the GDR, operates in accordance with distinct principles concerning the relationship between church and state and requires its members to do the same. Anything that is not consistent with these principles and teachings of the gospel has no place in the Church. In response, Herr Behncke said that it would be appropriate and helpful if the Church would express these principles and how the members understand their individual rights and opportuni-

> ties as citizens by adding two or three pages to the proposed brochure. He also suggested that these principles be personally conveyed to the state secretary, along with a birthday greeting. (DMO)

The three pages (previously quoted in full in Chapter 14) were written by Gottfried Richter and added to the brochure, which was published that year as *Die Kirche Jesu Christi der Heiligen der Letzten Tage Stellt Sich Vor*. The tone and substance of those three pages also influenced the text of the official declaration, which was given to Chairman Honecker prior to his meeting with President Monson later that year.

The birthday greeting, suggested by Behncke, was sent to Secretary Gysi on March 3, 1988. It began with the traditional "best wishes for health, creativity, and personal well-being" and expressed appreciation for "improvements in the relationship between the state and the Church," the liberal importation of literature, and the permission to travel to general conferences of the Church. Regarding the state-church relationship, it read:

> Our view of secular authority has been clear and distinct since the Church's restoration in 1830, namely, to respect and support that government, which secures to us the right of religious freedom and freedom of conscience. The members of the Church in this country acknowledge that they have every opportunity to practice their religion, develop their individual personality, enjoy the blessings of the gospel, and live in accordance with Christian principles. . . . We do not support a connection between church authority and political influence. Therefore, we do not routinely take positions on current political issues. Instead, the Church teaches and challenges its members in the GDR and throughout the world to become engaged in public affairs, to stand for freedom and right, and to encourage the good in every form.
>
> We see significant similarities in your and our view of the absolute separation between state and church and in the equal treatment of all churches and religious organizations. It is our wish to continue on the path of growing trust and mutual respect for different philosophies of life. (DMO)

No response from Secretary Gysi has been found. However, six weeks later, Burkhardt wrote directly to Chairman Honecker and requested an opportunity for President Monson, Elder Nelson, and local leaders to meet with him in October. The letter, dated April 18, 1988, did not include any specific requests, nor did it contain any statement concerning church-state relations, such as were included in the birthday greetings sent to Gysi. The full text of the letter to Honecker follows:

> With the generous support of the government of the German Democratic Republic, and especially through your untiring work on behalf

> of the welfare of the Christian citizens of our country, the Church of Jesus Christ of Latter-day Saints has been able to construct new meeting houses for its members in the German Democratic Republic. This has filled us with joy and thankfulness.
>
> Within the framework of the long-term church special building program, the Church's religious centers in DRESDEN and ZWICKAU will be completed and turned over to us in 1988. It is anticipated that the long-awaited dedication of both meeting houses will take place on October 26–27, 1988, by:
>
> President Thomas S. MONSON
>
> General Authority and Second Counselor in the First Presidency of the Church of Jesus Christ of Latter-day Saints.
>
> He will be accompanied by additional General Authorities of the Church:
>
> Elder Russel M. NELSON of the Council of Twelve Apostles and
> Elder Hans B. RINGGER of the Council of the Seventy;
> as well as the Presidency of the Church in the GDR
> Henry BURKHARDT as president;
> Frank APEL as president of the Freiberg Stake and
> Manfred SCHÜTZE as President of the Leipzig Stake.
>
> It is the sincere wish of these gentlemen to meet with you, Honorable Chairman, on Monday, October 24, 1988 [the meeting was later changed to October 28], to thank you for the opportunity to implement the church building program, for the freedom to practice our religion according to the principles of our faith and to discuss current problems of our time.
>
> For this reason, I wish to respectfully request, honorable Chairman, that you favorably consider this request and determine if a meeting with you could be held on October 24, 1988, at your official office.
>
> While awaiting your decision, I remain, respectively, Henry Burkhardt, Mission President (MS 13798)

The chairman responded five weeks later, on May 24, 1988. He said he welcomed the opportunity to meet with President Monson, "to have an exchange of opinions" and "to discuss citizens' requests and other current problems" (MS 13798).

While no specifics were mentioned by either party in this initial exchange of letters, Günther Behncke, in two interviews, said that both Honecker and the Church were fully aware of the issues to be discussed:

> Of course, the presidency, Manfred Wünsche, and I knew that the purpose of the meeting concerned specific issues [including] the sending and receiving of missionaries. But we couldn't jump into that immediately. We had to proceed in a political-tactical manner, and this was handled excellently by the presidency, in that they first asked to meet

> with the chairman to thank him for the fact that Mormons in this country had the same legal rights as the Catholic and Evangelical churches. And that was an honest expression of thanks, because it was not the case in all countries that the Mormons had equal rights with other churches (1991).
>
> However, Honecker had been informed about the issues in advance and had responded favorably. Were that not the case, then Manfred Wünsche would never have recommended that the Church send the letter. What would be the purpose of a meeting, when at its conclusion, Honecker had said, "and regarding your requests, unfortunately, I cannot respond favorably." That could never happen. (2006)

Horst Dohle was quoted earlier to the effect that all negotiations or discussions with the churches were to cease after the Zionskirche affair. Therefore, why was the chairman agreeable to discuss "current problems of our time" with President Monson? And given the circumstances of the time, how did the Church's request for a meeting manage to reach Erich Honecker? The second question will be addressed first.

Manfred Wünsche appears to have been a key person in reaching Erich Honecker. Although he passed away before he could be interviewed, we do have some insight into his role through Günther Behncke, who had known and worked with him previously on Church-related matters. Wünsche had provided legal advice to the Church on a variety of issues, including its building program, and he was paid by the Church for his services. Wünsche also had developed a good relationship with Jürgen Warnke, and especially with President Ringger, with whom he had discussed Church affairs directly. Therefore, Wünsche was fully aware of President Monson's interest in finding some way to bring missionaries into the GDR, and President Ringger probably was the person who asked Wünsche to help them accomplish that goal. President Burkhardt said:

> President Ringger, as well as President Monson, came up with the idea that I should attempt to make contact with Erich Honecker. I, of course, still had this inner disinclination toward that man. How could anyone talk reasonably with him? But the brethren had more faith than I had, and I am very thankful that President Monson worked so directly and in such a goal-oriented fashion to establish this contact with Erich Honecker. (1991)

Günther Behncke said that Manfred Wünsche first approached him on this matter, in confidence, in January 1988, shortly after Jürgen Warnke had written to Ringger:

> [Wünsche] said that the two of us had to meet soon, alone, to discuss an idea that was not yet fully developed, that he was trying to establish

> a meeting with Honecker. He discussed the difficulties in accomplishing that goal and said it had to do with specific wishes and requests of the Church. (2006)

Behncke said they discussed the possibility of reaching Honecker unofficially, and if that were possible, how the Church's requests could be presented in a manner that Honecker would find acceptable. Neither Behncke nor Wünsche had a direct pathway to Honecker, but Behncke said Wünsche was a very experienced man with excellent connections, who had been engaged in many serious legal issues for the government. He also had assisted high-ranking party functionaries with personal legal matters. After several days, he returned and told Behncke, "I have found a way to reach Honecker unofficially" (2006).

According to Behncke, Wünsche had spoken to a high government official who owed him a favor because of an earlier service. While Wünsche did not give Behncke the name of that official, nor did Behncke ask, he thinks that this "unofficial" route could have involved Margot (Feist) Honecker, Erich Honecker's second (or perhaps third) wife. She was the minister of Public Education at the time and had married Erich Honecker in 1953, after his divorce from a previous wife. A predivorce relationship between Erich Honecker and Margot Feist, which included the birth of a child, had concerned high party officials, and Manfred Wünsche might have been involved in arranging the divorce that enabled Honecker and Feist to marry. In any case, Wünsche had found an unofficial way to reach Erich Honecker without bringing the Church's requests to the attention of officials who most likely would have raised obstacles to a direct meeting with the chairman.

Behncke did not give Secretary Gysi, for whom he worked, advance notice of the strategy pursued by the Church and Wünsche. Gysi only learned of it when Honecker sent a copy of Burkhardt's letter to Gysi's office. Behncke explained:

> It was normal that such correspondence to Honecker would pass through the Secretariat for Church Affairs. I knew what was happening but didn't inform him, for the simple reason that I feared that other responsible people would try to shoot it down. And they did attempt to shoot it down after the fact, with the argument that there are more than thirty other small organizations, and if they all wanted to talk with Honecker, well... People in the secretariat did say, "With Honecker? That is reaching too high." They wanted the meeting to be with the third man in the government, Horst Sindermann, the president of the Parliament. But he could not decide anything in regard to the requests of the Mormons. So I had to pull on the emergency break and tell my boss, "Klaus, I plead with you, do not recommend that Honecker delegate this matter. I have accidently learned that Honecker already initialed the request—'Agreed, EH.'" Gysi briefly considered what I told him, then nodded his understanding. He didn't

> pursue the subject further, either then or during a later staff meeting. The secretary was involved with very difficult church policy issues at that time, and I think it made no difference to him whether the proposed meeting would be with Honecker or Sindermann. (2006)

President Schütze said, "We were told later that if we had sent the letter through normal channels, we would not have been successful" (1991).

In a book about Secretary Gysi's term in office, Horst Dohle raised another issue that might be relevant to Wünsche's role in this matter. Dohle wrote: "Shortly after Gysi became secretary, he had declared that he could not or would not attempt to determine church policy without the approval or knowledge of the Stasi."[3] It is not known if the Stasi was aware of the Church's effort to meet with Erich Honecker. However, Behncke indicated that Wünsche was probably, if not certainly, connected to the Stasi, and two Church leaders also have said that they always assumed that Wünsche was connected to the Stasi. One of them, who wished not to be named, said, "That man had such good connections to the state. He could cross the border at will and had so many other benefits. It was always clear to me that he was with the Stasi."

Another possible reason why the letter to Honecker was not routed through Secretary Gysi's office was the fact that signs of Gysi's political demise had appeared shortly after the Zionskirche episode. His absences from important church policy events attended by Honecker were noticed, and newspapers in West Germany had begun to speculate openly about his successor in February. On June 29, 1988, the secretariat of the party's Central Committee voted to release Gysi and designate Kurt Löffler as his successor. On July 14, the public was informed of Gysi's retirement, "for health reasons."[4]

The Official Declaration and the Church's Requests

Two important documents were written by the Church prior to the meeting between Chairman Honecker and President Monson: an official declaration, which was published in the GDR's newspapers after the meeting, and the Church's specific requests, which were never made public in the GDR. Although the Church's goals and its basic position toward the government had been informally conveyed to Honecker before Burkhardt sent the written meeting request on April 18, the official documents were composed later, between June and August 1988, as shown in the minutes of three meetings of the Church's leaders in the GDR (DMO).

On June 22, the presidency reviewed a draft declaration prepared by Manfred Wünsche, which focused on positive examples of the Church's relationship with the state. They modified Wünsche's draft to say that the present good relationship did not exclude the existence of problems that could and should be resolved, specifically in the areas of missionary and youth activities and public affairs. Care was taken to attribute any current problems to local officials who prevented Church members from enjoying the benefits of the positive relationship that existed between the Church and the central government. The presidency also drafted a supplemental list of specific requests, which could be addressed at the meeting if the opportunity arose. The list included:

> *Missionary Work:* Young GDR members should be able to go on missions abroad, and missionaries from the West should be able to enter the GDR.
>
> *Youth Activities:* Church groups should be able to hold activities anywhere, including the use of camping and sport facilities and hostels.
>
> *Public Affairs:* Examples included a visitor's center near the temple; the import and/or printing of Church literature; and use of public facilities for large Church meetings.

On June 27, the presidency reviewed additional changes to the declaration that had been suggested by Warnke and Wünsche and added more specificity to the list of requests. The declaration and the requests were then translated into English and sent to President Monson. The presidency met again on August 19, and it was reported that the declaration and personal letters to Chairman Honecker and State Secretary Kurt Löffler had been approved by the First Presidency in Salt Lake City.

The previous list of requests was no longer mentioned in minutes of the August 19 meeting, probably because those items had been incorporated into the two letters, which, together with the official declaration, were sent to Honecker and Löffler on August 22. The Church's requests were not stated identically in the two transmittal letters, and their wording was often more modest or less abrupt than in the earlier June drafts. For example, the letter to Secretary Löffler described missionary service in this manner:

> We could suppose, for example, that young members from Dresden would be assigned to Rostock or vice versa. Their time might also be served abroad. In that case, it would be based on reciprocity, so that a comparable young member from abroad would carry out his service here. Of course, there are many details to be resolved. We would be pleased, however, when a start could be made. The same could apply to older retired couples. We could see, for example, a couple from Finland active in Dresden and a couple from Dresden in Helsinki.

The description of missionary activities in the letter to Chairman Honecker began with a statement that "we fully support the church-state policy of our country and are thankful for the assistance it affords us [but] there are certainly some things that would help our members, especially our younger members, to identify themselves with our country even more strongly than in the past." That introduction is followed by a description of "missionary" activities that sounds more like humanitarian services:

> Many have, for example, assisted in projects in Latin America that strive to eliminate illiteracy, improve hygienic conditions, or increase the understanding of basic principles of proper human nutrition. In European countries, the goal is to present the teachings and principles of the gospel of Jesus Christ, and to do so especially through the contribution of the missionaries to spiritual welfare and education by: (a) strengthening the capacity of individuals for responsible service through high moral standards; (b) maintaining health and the capacity to work by observing a positive lifestyle and through proper nutrition; and (c) supporting families and thereby strengthening the foundation of a good society.... We are of the opinion that hardly any other program contributes more to understanding among countries and to peace.

Regarding youth activities, the letter to Secretary Löffler said that "it has not been easy in the past to carry out camping or sporting activities. Indeed, a reservation for a camping place, youth hostel or sports facility for activities with one hundred to two hundred participants is out of the question." The letter referred to an upcoming Church youth camp in West Germany with participants from sixteen countries. "These gatherings serve world peace and cooperation among nations through common experiences and mutual understanding. It would be a positive experience for our youth if they could participate in this church camp under the flag of our country." The letter to Chairman Honecker addressed youth activities with less detail, but emphasized that participation in youth gatherings abroad would "contribute to peace and cooperation among nations through common experiences and mutual understanding," a favorite political slogan of the government (MS 13918). Additional details about the Church's requests will be shown later in the context of the government's response.

The first draft of the declaration included examples of the good relationship between the Church and the government as well as areas where current problems could be resolved, specifically regarding missionary and youth activities and public affairs. Since all of the Church's requests had been moved into the transmittal letters, the declaration became solely a description of the Church's relationship to the state. It did not include any requests. However, it is an important statement that represents the Church's forty-year experience of learning to live with a government not of its choosing, from which it had, nevertheless, earned a degree of recognition and respect without violating its fundamental religious principles. In consideration of its significance, the entire declaration is included here:

> Declaration of the Presidency of the Church of Jesus Christ of Latter-day Saints in the GDR on the Occasion of the Requested Meeting with the Chairman of the State Council of the GDR—Erich Honecker—on October 28, 1988

Honorable Chairman of the State Council,

Allow us to thank you most sincerely for the opportunity to meet with you. It is the intention of the Church of Jesus Christ of Latter-day Saints to share with you the results of an exchange of ideas, which the Presidency of the Church in the GDR has had with the general authorities of the Church regarding basic questions of our time, the peaceful coexistence of mankind, and the preservation of God's creation.

We respect you as the representative of our homeland and our state with which we identify ourselves, in which we live and work, in which we find joy. The members of the Church have learned to appreciate that the prerequisites for the preservation of world peace and understanding among nations are being created through the policies of the GDR, and that you as the leader of this country, through your personal efforts, have made continual progress toward that goal.

We thank you and all participating officials of our country for a church policy characterized by mutual trust and understanding, which, especially since March 6, 1978, has resulted in many positive changes and improvements in the state-church relationship. The extensive building program of the Church in several cities of our land is a visible example, and the members are grateful for it, especially when they recall the history of our Church during the German Empire and under Fascism. The Church's temple in Freiberg, the recently constructed meeting houses in Freiberg, Leipzig, Dresden, and Zwickau, the meeting houses yet to be built, as well as the various church buildings that are being modernized and maintained through the love and diligence of members, all contribute to the beautification of our cities and towns. They are an expression of our joy of life.

The separation of church and state is a reality in the GDR and fulfills a longstanding goal of the Church. This has not gone unnoticed in the world. Foreign visitors to the temple grounds and meeting houses often mention it. Indeed, members of the Church in the GDR continue to attract the attention of our entire Church membership in over 130 countries. However, that attention has never caused the members here to feel that they are "unique" Mormons. They have and have had their own problems just like members anywhere else in the world. This is quite normal. However, they enjoy and support the exceptionally high social conditions and the general security of this socialist state. The support given to large families and young married couples, as well as the assurance of care for the sick and aged, are realities in the GDR.

We have experienced in many varied and positive ways the results of the church policy that was emphasized on March 6, 1978, and which has been subsequently carried out. In addition to the new meeting houses, we have been able to show our members that other generous decisions have enabled us to carry out our religious services and spiritual welfare activities at a high level in accordance with the basic principles of our Church. This has enabled local members to become even better peacemakers and to apply their faith and the principles of the gospel of Jesus Christ within their communities to serve and benefit others.

Be assured, honorable Chairman, that the members of the Church of Jesus Christ of Latter-day Saints will continue to work and apply their strength so that what has been achieved will not only be maintained but continually improved.

Sobriety, thrift, diligence, and joy in learning are characteristics of most members of our Church. Therefore, they constantly endeavor to upgrade their qualifications and to raise their children accordingly. Encouraged by the Church to give their best, we see members in the GDR being successful in their daily affairs as skilled workers, as engineers and independent craftsmen, as doctors, in agriculture, in trade, and in other occupations. Many of them have been honored by the state for their achievements. Their positive outlook on life enables them to pursue their obligations in society, the workplace, Church, and family in a responsible manner.

In that process, we have determined that there are many tasks related to the welfare of our fellow men, our neighbors, our colleagues, and quite simply all those around us where our Christian goals are in agreement with or can positively influence the state's goals.

The position of the Church of Jesus Christ of Latter-day Saints in relationship to state authority has been always clear and distinct, namely to respect and support governments that protect our right to exercise our beliefs. The members of the Church recognize that they have been given the opportunity in our country to exercise their religion, to develop themselves as individuals, and to act in accordance with Christian ideals.

Latter-day Saints are never "dropouts," but rather are positive and optimistic in thought and action. The Church's doors are opened wide for everyone of good will who comes to learn the gospel, who are seeking a solution for personal problems, or who simply are seeking information. As everyone knows, the world suffers from false information. The Church is absolutely not open to anyone seeking to use it as a platform or a cover for opposition, or to pursue "special or group goals" that cannot be brought into harmony with the mission of the Church and its stated goals.

It has been and continues to be a basic principle that we do not approve of ecclesiastical authority being used for political influence. The Church is not a political or social organization. It interacts with the surrounding society primarily through the experiences and activities of its members. Individuals act on the basis of their understanding of what is true and right.

The Church teaches and encourages its members in the GDR and everywhere in the world to be involved in public life and to stand for peace and justice. Therefore, young men in the church also accept their responsibility regarding military service.

It is our desire to continue on the path of growing trust and mutual esteem, with the goal to promote the peaceful coexistence of mankind wherever God has placed us, and especially through Christian living and in accordance with the principles of the gospel of Jesus Christ, to contribute to the strengthening of our country in order to preserve peace. The Church in general uses its extensive international connections to contribute constructively, on the basis of our Christian philosophy of life, to improve relations among all people. It therefore supports our government in its efforts toward coexistence, peace, and good relations.

This way, which we believe is the key to a happy and peaceful future for mankind, requires a continual reassessment of our own situation and that of our partners, and that is the reason for our readiness to engage in mutual conversation, to exchange ideas, and to work together. The Latter-day Saints in the GDR know that they are in a good place.

Please permit us, Mr. Chairman, to wish you health, success, joy, and the blessings of God in your responsible activities on behalf of mankind, for the preservation of peace, as well as in your personal life.

Sincerely, Henry Burkhardt, Frank Apel, Manfred Schütze (MS 13918)

Two weeks prior to the October meeting, President Monson also wrote to Chairman Honecker and said he was looking forward to the meeting and expressed his hope that Honecker would be able to come to America and visit Utah in the future. He also enclosed a short declaration from the First Presidency, which was not published in the newspapers following the meeting. It began with a reference to the many German members of the Church who had emigrated to America, from the time of the German Empire through World War II, in order to enjoy the freedom of religion that was missing in their country. The presidency noted that those immigrants later participated in the Church's welfare action that sent tons of clothing and food to postwar Germany. Referring to the present, it said, "We live in a time when men and women should stand together in peace and endeavor to protect the world around them. Our Church has learned in your country that many of these basic goals are commonly shared, which has led to trusting, constructive collaboration." The enthusiastic reception of the folk dance ensemble, the "Lamanite Generation" from BYU, was cited as a recent example of collaboration and friendship.

The First Presidency then thanked Chairman Honecker for the understanding and cooperative relationship between government offices and the

Church in the GDR. "Because of our experience in many countries of the world, we do not take that cooperation for granted, but rather consider it the result of a well-balanced church policy that looks for and builds upon mutual interests." The document ended with a principle frequently stated by the Church in the GDR: "We are not politically active as a church and refrain from exerting political influence of any kind. Instead, we encourage our members to contribute to the improvement of the country in which they live and to foster good community relations."

The declaration was signed, "Thomas S. Monson, for the Presidency of the Church of Jesus Christ of Latter-day Saints" (MS 13918).

The Government's Preparation for the Meeting

Secretary Löffler's office prepared an extensive briefing document for Honecker that reviewed and evaluated the Church's requests and the GDR presidency's declaration. (The First Presidency's shorter declaration was received too late to be included.) Löffler's briefing document (MS 13918) was intended for internal government use only and therefore provides an unvarnished view of its understanding of and attitude toward the Church at this time.

Attachment 1 contains Löffler's recommendations regarding the Church's specific missionary and youth requests. Before preparing those recommendations, Löffler sent the requests to Eberhard Aurich, secretary of the Central Council of the FDJ, and told him, "There cannot be any special rules for the youth activities of this church. However, in the interest of a reasoned application of our state-church policy, it is necessary to determine whether some of the wishes of the Mormons can be accepted within the framework of the varied activities of the FDJ."

Aurich's response was consistent with previous GDR youth policy. He stated that all activities of youth groups were the responsibility of the FDJ. Youth activities sponsored by the Church should be limited strictly to religious events and be conducted within church facilities, while the youth should join FDJ for their nonreligious activities. "Young Mormons can use youth hostels, camping places, etc.," he wrote, but "we cannot agree to reservations for group activities of a religious organization, since that would contradict the principle of the unity of the youth." He also did not support the Church's request to send a group of Mormon youth to a scouting activity in West Germany, although sending an FDJ group that included Mormons might be acceptable.

Aurich did not address the Church's request that young members from abroad be allowed to enter the GDR as missionaries. He apparently did not consider that issue to be relevant to the FDJ's mission. He did, however, address the issue of sending young members abroad as missionaries:

> Sending individual persons abroad for missionary work is acceptable. Sending an organized youth group [of Mormons] is not acceptable since that would demonstrate abroad a political-organizational division of our youth, which would harm the GDR and the FDJ polit-

ically. We recently turned down similar requests from the Evangelical churches.

Attachment 1, which contains Löffler's own recommendations to Chairman Honecker, reflects Aurich's comments but shows a greater accommodation to some of the Church's requests. Löffler addressed three specific issues:

> 1. *Hostels and Campgrounds:* Individuals can use these facilities and their programs, but church-related group activities or other religious practices such as common prayers, spiritual singing, or religious services are not allowed.
>
> 2. *Missionary Work:* Sending an organized group abroad cannot be allowed [but] sending individuals in the manner practiced by the Mormons can be allowed. Missionary activity within the GDR by retired persons, including retired persons from abroad, can be allowed, but only on condition that it take place within the church, for example in caring for the elderly. Public missionary work (e.g., from door to door) is absolutely not allowed.
>
> 3. *Participation in an international camp:* Since the participants are exclusively Mormons, the operation of the camp is considered an internal matter. The participation of a small group, including adult leaders, can be permitted.

Conspicuous by its absence in the briefing document was any reference to young missionaries being allowed to enter the GDR, although both Löffler and Behncke knew this was the Church's primary goal. When asked about that omission, Günther Behncke responded with a surprising answer and an unexpected perspective on the Church's main request:

> Allowing missionaries to enter the GDR was not the critical issue, but letting them leave was. Normal GDR citizens were not allowed to leave, so letting someone leave [as a missionary] was an issue. Who came in was not an issue, especially since they all wear similar suits. That could be managed. (2006)

Attachment 2 of the briefing document contained the government's response to the declaration submitted by the GDR presidency:

> The declaration clearly describes the political relationship of the Church and its members to the socialist society, the state, the state's policies, and the unhindered opportunity to pursue a religious life. It outstandingly demonstrates the improved relationship between state and church, especially since March 6, 1978, and clearly shows how important

> it is to implement the principle of equal respect for all churches, irrespective of their size or their peculiarities.
>
> The statement that the Church is not a political or social organization, although it interacts with its surrounding social environment, is an important statement about state-church policy. With the declaration's description of its members' attitude toward the state and the society of the GDR, it far exceeds the position taken in comparable declarations. It was preceded by other politically descriptive statements in recent years, such as its position on the basing of the MX Missile, and it reflects a continuing process in which the Church of Jesus Christ of Latter-day Saints has described its position within a socialist society. It can, therefore, be assumed that the anticipated contribution of general authority Monson to the meeting will exhibit a tendency of comparable quality. The First Presidency has approved the publication of the declaration.

Attachment 3 was entitled "Brief Evaluation of the Religious Organization of the Mormons in the GDR."

> The political and citizenship perspective of the Presidency of the Church of Jesus Christ of Latter-day Saints in the GDR, i.e., President (and Temple President) Henry Burkhardt, Stake President Manfred Schütze, and Stake President Frank Apel, is sufficiently characterized by the declaration they wrote. In addition, it can be said that they are friendly, unassuming, and open-minded in discussion. Additional characteristics are honesty and reliability.
>
> Herr Burkhardt has held his leadership position for more than thirty years.... The general authorities Monson (USA) and Ringger (Switzerland) have been repeatedly in the GDR. During each visit, they have conducted themselves in an open and respectful manner toward the socialist state. Both men are friendly, intellectually stimulating, and humorous discussion partners. Monson has a height of over 1.9 meters [6 feet 3 inches].

Attachment 4 described the Church in general, the Church in the GDR, and its relationship to the government:

> The relationship between the Mormon Church in the GDR and the state is marked by orderliness and trust. In accordance with church principles, the members are oriented toward loyalty to government, respect and obedience to socialist laws, the fulfillment of their responsibilities as citizens, and industrious and honest work. The result is that there are no relevant problems either at the central or at local levels regarding the state-church relationship.

> The leaders of the Mormon Church in the GDR have spoken out unambiguously for our socialist peace policy, including the necessity of military defense of our socialist accomplishments. The Mormons have not rejected military service or military education in school, and opposition thereto would not find support among the church's leadership.
>
> A total of twenty church buildings are planned to be built in the GDR by the mid-1990s, within the special building program.... An increase in the membership of the Mormon Church in the GDR has not been recorded in recent years and can hardly be expected in the future.

Attachment 5 consisted of recommended short statements that the chairman might make during the meeting in regard to specific portions of the declaration. For example:

> I consider your description of the policies of the socialistic state toward the churches as something that individual religious people can apply in their daily life to be a remarkable conclusion. I agree with you that real socialism fulfills not only the ideals of Communists but also reflects the goals and values of Christians.
>
> The challenges of the present and the future require that we not be thrown back into confrontation. Therefore, I appreciate the fact that you encourage, advise, and lead your members to apply the humanistic ideals of your faith to the development of human society. The responsibility for the further development of our homeland connects us more than our differences in philosophy of life or religious persuasion separates us.

The Meeting, October 28, 1988

> *President Monson:* We were ushered into a large hall where we were accorded every courtesy and amenity. As we approached the meeting rooms, Herr Honecker and his delegation came forward to meet us. Our delegation was led by me and consisted of Russell Nelson, Hans Ringger, Henry Burkhardt, Frank Apel, Manfred Schütze, and Manfred Heller. Herr Honecker had his deputies present, along with an able interpreter and his state secretary for Religious Affairs, Herr Kurt Löffler. I presented to Herr Honecker a beautiful statue entitled First Steps, wherein a mother is bending over and steadying her child as the child walks to its father. Herr Honecker seemed particularly pleased with this gift and emphasized that he advocates the strength of the family. (*Faith Rewarded*)

> *Secretary Löffler:* You should know that a few weeks before the meeting, Chairman Honecker's grandson died. So you may say, of course,

that it was like a divine coincidence, that exactly at this time of personal pain in his family, he received this sculpture. (2003)

Günther Behncke: Herr Honecker was visibly moved and touched as he accepted that sculpture, the Holy Family, from Herr Monson, and the meeting continued in that spirit. (1991)

The gift presented to Chairman Honecker was subsequently referred to by government officials and the press as the Holy Family because President Monson had said that families are holy. He then described the rest of the meeting:

Mr. Honecker began by making us feel welcome, saying that he had observed me and our Church activities for many years and that we taught our members to obey and sustain the law of the land and to be good citizens, that we emphasize the family, and that our Church members were ideal citizens of that land.

He then gave me the floor to present my matters, although the matters which I was to present had previously been submitted to him, which is their custom, so that he and his associates are never taken unawares. I pointed out that the Church had been established in the [region that now comprises the] German Democratic Republic for many, many years prior to World War II. I emphasized that this was one of the most productive areas for our Church missionary activities in all the world at that particular time. I stated that our membership base is barely holding steady and that this concerns us.... I indicated that we really needed to seek from him his permission to recommence the work of full-time proselyting missionaries in the GDR. I explained that these missionaries from other nations, when they come to his country and return to their homes, are advocates of the people and the ideals of those people with whom they have worked for two years.... By way of illustration, I commented that when the Argentine ambassador came to visit the First Presidency, we were able to take him to Brigham Young University, and there he met with about two hundred missionaries who had been in Argentina whom he could readily observe were great advocates of Argentina and her people. I then indicated that we would like to have permission for young men and women within the German Democratic Republic to receive mission calls to serve elsewhere in the world and that this would be a broadening benefit, both for the people with whom they labored and for the young missionaries themselves.

At the conclusion of my remarks, Mr. Honecker began to speak about his goals in government.... He then proceeded to acknowledge our requests and said that in the future all of our young people could meet together in youth conferences, using state facilities if necessary, for he trusted our young people and admired them. This was a great

> compliment. He then reviewed my request for missionaries and simply said, "Permission granted." (*Faith Rewarded*)

The implementation of Chairman Honecker's approval regarding missionaries will be addressed in the following chapter.

Reaction of Church Members

Since very few members knew of the meeting in advance, the news was a huge surprise. Television reports of the meeting that evening were unusually long, at least twelve minutes, and included pictures of the participants, the presentation of the gift to Honecker, and references to the declaration, which was printed in full in newspapers the next day. But the coverage within the GDR also was incomplete. There was no mention of the Church's specific requests or any indication that requests had been made or approved. Members learned about the new opportunities for missionary and youth activities gradually as details were resolved. For example, some of the young men interviewed the following February regarding possible mission calls were not only surprised to be called, but surprised that they could be sent outside the GDR. They knew that missionaries would be arriving from the West before they knew that it would be possible to fulfill identical missions abroad. Given this sparsity of information about the meeting and its achievements, it was natural that opinions about the meeting were quite varied. Representatives of the Church History Department conducted oral interviews soon thereafter, in 1991 and 1993, and asked members about their reaction to the news of the meeting:

> *Hans Schult:* We were all very enthusiastic. The news spread among the members like a wildfire. It was amazing. We actually felt like we had been recognized for our efforts over the years. We saw light ahead and said, "Yes, now there will be progress!" Of course, in the background, we knew that Herr Honecker might want to travel to the USA. (1991)

> *Klaus-Peter Kretschmar:* I was unbelievably moved. When I heard that for the first time, I fought back the tears. Yes, tears of joy. Looking back, many things actually changed for us. And that was most surprising. We immediately became better known. We were more accepted by local officials. There were also negative opinions. There were people who said, "Look at yourself, your Church is currying favor from that old Honecker." No one said, "What you did is good." Many asked, "Why did you do that?" (1993)

> *Manfred Heller:* There was a long line of members, even in our ward, that could not understand that a leader of the Church would appear that way before the chairman. We especially had problems with several young people. And there were questions and problems regard-

ing the declaration, since many interpreted it to mean that the Church was in agreement with the politics of the state. (1991)

Walter Schiele: Other Christians, who had somewhat openly fought against the Communists, said, "The Mormons are currying favor," a little like traitors. Of course, we see it differently. Our Church leaders wanted to achieve something here in this country, for example, so we could build meeting houses. When we had meeting houses that looked good, that faced the street, it had a different effect than earlier when we met in buildings not visible from the street. And of course, most importantly, that we could build the temple. Normally, a person would not sit down at a table with such a man. But I understood it. President Monson didn't do anything wrong. Quite the opposite. I say that it was right. We fully supported him. (1991)

Herbert Heidler: Yes, there were two opinions. One half said, "That finally had to happen, and the Lord determined the timing." But many said, "Now they are crawling to the Communists, that is, the Church somehow made a compromise with the Communists." Personally, however, I greeted it. I said, "Things can only get better now for the Church." And they did get better. (1993)

Ralf Bauerfeind: The next day there appeared in the newspaper a huge article on the first page. The relationship of many members with their Catholic and Evangelical neighbors and fellow citizens were very negatively affected, because the Mormons were now considered to have been given advantages, since they had yielded to the state. So we had much to explain at work the next day. (2003)

Dieter Bauerfeind: Our work colleagues said, "You are currying favor with the government." That was thrown at us on the job and probably also at school or where you studied. It was, to some degree, a negative time for us. (2003)

Walter Krause: It was a difficult chapter. One sister said to me, "No one will look at me." Can you imagine how they complained to us? "You claim to be Christians, and you talk with the government." I don't say that to accuse anyone. But I could not justify it. (1991)

Lothar Hubert: I thought, "When it reaches the point that they receive our Church leaders, then it will go well for us." However, I ran into a wall of opposition from my colleagues, who had always respected me. One colleague opened the door the next morning, threw the newspaper into my room, and said mockingly, "You, the Mormon, Ha, ha, ha," and slammed the door. Many considered it to be treason. (1993)

Jürgen Pabst: Personally, I didn't have any problem with the visit. There were, however, several discussions among members who were upset because they had been verbally attacked at work. "Your leaders are meeting with the Communist leaders. How can that be?" None of that happened to me. I had no problems with other people, who were not members of the Church. I must also say that I didn't fully understand many things. Personally, I probably would not have held such a meeting. But I attempt in my own life to be obedient. When I don't understand something in the Church, I first attempt to do it, to accept it. So it is in this case, that with hindsight, I see that it was right. (1993)

Jürgen Schiebold: The opinions of the members were very diverse. Many said, "How can anyone do something like that, to go to a state official who has brought so much disaster upon people?" That was one opinion. The other was, "We simply must establish contact with state officials or with the head of state, to win advantages for the Church." We were treated with hostility at that time. Many people came here to the temple grounds, especially from the Evangelical churches, who said, "You are Christians, but you don't do anything. You know that we are actually fighting for our freedom. Why not fight with us?" It was difficult for us to explain correctly that freedom is something different than what they were seeking. Yes, there were many different opinions among the members, and there was much that wasn't understood correctly. But I think that it was good that these discussions took place. The brethren, those who led the Church, were inspired. And when you are inspired, then you have to act. (1993)

Klaus Peter Bartsch: We were called the "Communist Church" by some, as if we wanted to join with them. That was an issue on which we were especially attacked, because it was at a time when people said, "Either there will be a big blow-up and something will happen here, or we will remain forever in this rut in which we are running." One colleague gave me a newspaper in the morning and said, "Here, look what your Church is bellowing with Honecker." I was shocked at first. We couldn't really explain it, why they were negotiating. That was often a problem for us. With hindsight, many people said, "That was a blessing from the Lord. He led and guided it." Each article filled me with pride for our Church. We cut them all out, whenever our Church was mentioned. Before, no one talked about our Church. Now we finally walked into daylight. That was tremendous. (1993)

Günter Schulze: We considered it to be a success, at least I did, which continued to grow with prayer. Even though many members today consider it to have been painful, or at least not good, I consider that, from the perspective of Church history, it was necessary. Shortly thereafter, five months later, the mission was opened. (1993)

Gottfried Richter: We were permitted to assemble. We could live in accordance with our faith and our principles. And ever so gradually, the relationship improved, as they recognized that we are orderly, energetic, and hardworking citizens. They approved the building of meeting houses and the temple. It was logical that the hour would come when they would want to speak with us. Of course they had political interests. They knew that the Church had influence, and that was important. (1993)

Hans-Jürgen Bartsch: I did not find it to be wrong that they met. But I didn't like what appeared in the newspaper accounts thereafter, which gave the impression that the Church had always been favored by the state and that the Church—that is, the members—had always been seen as respected citizens of the state. For me, personally, that was a complete reversal of the facts. Many people had significant problems with the state's apparatus. Therefore, I looked at that visit with very mixed feelings. That missionaries were allowed to enter the country or that missionaries could go abroad, that was a positive result. But everything that went with it regarding our own personal reputation with other citizens, that was not nice. I will assume that President Monson acted upon inspiration, for he would not otherwise have done it. But for us it had a completely different appearance. It had the appearance of kneeling before a socialist government. That was not good for us personally. (1991)

Eberhardt Werner: In my opinion, if the GDR had been this strong entity that it claimed to be, a meeting between President Monson and Honecker would never have taken place. As I see it, Herr Honecker absolutely wanted to be invited to the United States. If he could have accomplished that, then his system would have been recognized, and he, with his partial country, would have been a full and equal member of the society of nations. That was actually our fear, that the Church would become a means for making this unjust system respectable. That caused me to have two severely opposite feelings. On the one hand, I was, of course, thankful. We said, "Maybe it will help us, but hopefully nothing happens that enables Herr Honecker to be recognized as a gentleman and receive an invitation to Church headquarters. Then influence would be brought upon the government of the United States to actually invite him there." Therefore, I would have preferred that we had stayed in the old mode, which would have clearly shown the world that what was happening in the GDR was not right. I see that it was a very difficult situation for the Presidency of the Church, and that they must have struggled and prayed a lot about it. "Should we or shouldn't we do it?" (1993)

Anonymous: Complete and utter lack of understanding. Complete lack of understanding. The Wende came a year later, and the system was already at the tipping point. Almost everyone knew that. Nothing was working anymore. Opposition was everywhere, and the people recognized more and more that it couldn't continue. And exactly at that time, Church representatives came and sought favors from these people. That was depressing for us here. It was a miscalculation or bad advice, and it severely damaged the Church's reputation, which still has a negative impact upon the missionary work. If that had happened perhaps twenty years earlier, that would have been another matter. But it was absolutely the worst possible time. (1993)

The idea that the meeting had a negative impact on subsequent missionary activities will be addressed in the next chapter. However, there was a widespread feeling that the Church's image had been harmed to some degree. The Communist regime was widely disliked or hated, and Erich Honecker was the symbol of the state. Therefore, any meeting with him, regardless of the agenda, was seen as recognition, if not approval, of the state. In interviews conducted three years later, three Church leaders in the GDR commented on the criticism and questions that came their way, from members and nonmembers:

President Burkhardt: I often received threatening phone calls and was asked how we, as a church, could fraternize with the Communists like that. I had to put up with that for a while. I received letters that were not written with the nicest tone, because people believed that I was the one who had initiated or was desirous of this contact. But I had the inner satisfaction that President Monson wanted this connection. And it was good. There were some members among us who did not agree. But they were not the most active members. Among the active ones, there were only a few who were not convinced that such an association was good. Many took the position, "We will wait and see what comes out of this meeting, whether it was worth it." (1991)

President Apel: Some members asked us after the Wende, "Why were you with Erich? You sold yourselves." But I see it entirely differently. There were hardly any government leaders in any Western country that did not have contact with Erich Honecker, who didn't visit him, shake his hand, or sit at banquets with him. And so we said to ourselves, "We must try to obtain as much as possible without denying our faith." (1991)

> President Schütze: Naturally, there was some criticism. Some members were disturbed and asked why we should associate with the Communists now and seek their help. Many members and nonmembers also had a problem with the fact that Western money was being used to build meeting houses in East Germany, in other words, that the Church was giving money to the Communists. But we had another goal, or better said, the Lord was pursuing a different and very specific goal, namely, that people would become interested in the gospel. In the dedicatory prayer that President Monson spoke [1975] in the Dresden area, he said, in effect, "Lord, let the people develop an interest in the gospel." That is exactly what happened, and it brought a great amount of publicity. The Church leaders presented their standpoint very officially and our wishes were answered. The Church did not compromise or sell itself. There were no other agreements made, in any form. (1991)

Although Manfred Schütze said that "the Church did not compromise or sell itself," his comment reflects the fact that many people outside the Church, and a few within it, saw Monson's meeting with Honecker as having done exactly that. However, most members, including those who had some doubt about the wisdom of the meeting, expressed hope that it would result in improved conditions for the Church in the long term.

The initial interviews conducted in 1991 and 1993 did not include specific questions about the declaration that was published the day after the meeting. However, during the author's own interviews and informal conversations, beginning in 2002, members often expressed embarrassment or even anger over the text of the declaration and other Church publications of that time, including the two 1988–1989 brochures described previously.

The declaration, which was addressed to Chairman Honecker, began with the words, "We respect you as the representative of our homeland and our state with which we identify ourselves" and ended with a wish for his "health, joy, and success." It is not likely that many members of the Church "respected" Erich Honecker or prayed for his health. But more troubling to many were the tone and content throughout the document. It not only drew favorable comparisons between government programs and the Church's own priorities, such as support for large families, the aged, and the sick, but it praised GDR policies that contributed to "world peace, understanding among nations, and peaceful coexistence," phrases often found in traditional Communist propaganda and used by all Soviet-dominated countries engaged in furthering Communism worldwide. Therefore, a quick reading of the declaration led to accusations that the Church had made common cause with the Communists.

The meeting with Erich Honecker surprised and concerned members who had grown accustomed to harsh anticommunist statements by church leaders in previous decades. However, a new tone and approach to Communism emerged during President Kimball's administration, as he placed more emphasis on the development of personal and friendly relations with socialist governments. He repeatedly counseled President Burkhardt and his counselors to befriend government officials, and in 1977, after visiting Poland, he came to Dresden and spoke to 1,400 members on the subject of the 12th Article of Faith. Whereas President Reagan would later demand that the Communists tear down the Berlin Wall, President Kimball had already begun to open informal doors through the Wall.

Four years after Kimball's talk in Dresden, the First Presidency opposed the American government's MX Missile proposal and said, "We repeat our warnings against the terrifying arms race in which the nations of the earth are presently engaged. We deplore in particular the building of vast arsenals of nuclear weaponry." These statements by Church leaders emphasized the longtime principles of the Church, which opposed war and encouraged peace.

It should be noted that the declaration had been translated into English and sent to the First Presidency for approval. It is possible, but not likely, that the political significance of phrases such as "world peace, peaceful coexistence, and understanding among nations" were lost in translation. It is more likely that their inclusion was intentional or that they were not considered significantly more problematic than the rest of the declaration or the meeting itself. After the meeting, President Monson explained to the press in Salt Lake City, "Obviously, there are differences of belief that separate us, but there are many more things that unite us."[5] Those words are strikingly similar to the content of Honecker's briefing document, which said that our common goals "tie us together more than our differences in philosophy of life or religious confession separate us."

The declaration also noted members' loyalty to the state. While nonmembers cited that as evidence of being too close to the Communists, members throughout the world were taught the 12th Article of Faith, and President Kimball spoke to that topic during his 1977 visit to Dresden. This emphasis on "responsible citizenship" is found in President Monson's own correspondence. Following the meeting with Chairman Honecker, he invited Secretary Löffler to visit Utah. In two letters addressed to Löffler, he linked Church teachings with good citizenship. In one, he said he looked forward to hosting Löffler and his wife so they could see how the Church was striving to "raise our members to be good citizens." In the second letter, he again said the visit would enable the secretary to see how we encourage our members "to be good citizens" (DO 4/987).

Whether the Church compromised its principles by meeting with Chairman Honecker is ultimately a subjective judgment, based on one's own values, priorities, and willingness to "compromise" on political, as opposed to religious principles. Günther Behncke, who had been directly involved in the religious-political issues during the 1980s, had an interesting response to the question, "Did the Church compromise itself by meeting with Honecker?" He said:

> The Church truly did not sell itself. By meeting with Chairman Honecker, the Church obtained concessions without reciprocal obligations. Its leaders expressed appreciation for the opportunity to build a temple and presented requests that were fulfilled without offering anything new in return. The declaration can be seen as saying, "We fulfill our responsibilities as Christians, and in return we want our rights to be honored, specifically, the right to exercise our religion and to engage in missionary activity." The Church offered nothing in the declaration that it wasn't already doing. Concessions were obtained without reciprocal obligations. (2006)

A different perspective to the question of whether concessions were made, by either party, might be seen in the respective media coverage of the event. Newspapers within the GDR, controlled by the government, printed the entire declaration but made no mention of the government's approval of expanded missionary and youth activities. Reports in the Church-owned media in Salt Lake City detailed the government's concessions regarding missionary and youth activities but made no mention of the declaration.

Erich Honecker's Motivation

Several popular theories exist to explain why Honecker met with Church leaders and agreed to their requests. One of the most common concerns money. It is a fact that the GDR was seeking Western currency through every possible channel. The temple and the new meeting houses would not have been built without Western money. However, the earlier detailed account of events that led to the construction of the temple clearly show that Western money, while necessary, was not the GDR's prime motivation for its construction. Moreover, by 1988, every meeting house requested by the Church was already being built or planned, and no document indicates or implies that the GDR expected to gain additional money by agreeing to the Church's requests to expand its missionary and youth programs.

A second common theory concerns the members' reputation as productive and loyal citizens. Gottfried Richter has cited entries in his personal Stasi file to support that theory:

> Over the years, the attitude of state officials toward our church changed. At first, they mistrusted all churches, and especially ours. I saw this in the file the Stasi kept on me. At first, they wrote, "This church is closely tied to the USA. Leading members of the church are in the service of the American government." Then in later years, they wrote that members of the Church exhibited loyalty to their country. "Their leaders clearly restrict themselves to the principles of the church, and there is no evidence that they engage in polemics against the state." The State Secretariat for Church Affairs knew us, knew our leaders here. Over time, the relationship improved, as they recognized

> that we were orderly, industrious citizens. They knew the Church was influential. Logically, the hour would come when they would want to receive our leaders. That was very normal. (1993)

Behncke also referred to the Church's reputation. In 1991, he said, "I can fully imagine that [Honecker] remembered the assessment of the state secretary for Church Affairs during the dedication of the temple in Freiberg, that the Mormons are good and true citizens, who work honestly and industriously, who respect families and raise their children to be good citizens. I think that was a factor." But Behncke did not think it was a prime factor or a sufficient reason to receive the Church's delegation and to allow the unprecedented entry and departure of missionaries from a relatively insignificant religious organization.

A third popular theory is that Honecker was seeking an invitation to visit America and thought that the Church had enough influence with the American government to arrange an official visit, which could enhance his international stature. Gottfried Richter said, "A member of the secretariat once told me, 'We don't judge your church here based on the number of its members, but according to the influence it has in the USA and in the world.'" (1993)

It is possible that Church leaders in America thought that Honecker wanted to visit the United States and they encouraged that idea. In his letter to Honecker on October 14, 1988, President Monson wrote: "If you have the opportunity to visit the United States, we would gladly invite you to Utah. I hope that such a trip would be possible." Günther Behncke's meeting summary cited two instances where President Monson personally expressed his hope that Honecker would visit America (MS 13918).

Whether President Monson's references to a future visit accurately reflected Honecker's own personal goals is not known, but Behncke believes that the Americans were mistaken if they believed it to be the case. While he does not dispute the idea that the Church was influential in America, he does not share the theory that a visit to America was Honecker's primary or immediate goal. In 2005, he said:

> You know, many people want to hear that these events, including the building of the temple, only happened because Honecker wanted to crack open the door for an invitation to America. Of course, he had visited all of the major powers of that time, except America and England. Certainly, those countries interested him in terms of developing neighborly relations and the cause of peace. You cannot deny that. It would be almost unnatural. But that an invitation to those countries was the determining factor in this case, to that I would say with almost one hundred percent certainty, no. Hundred percent no, for then things would have proceeded differently. Then the Foreign Ministry would have been engaged and a few other ministries.

Since Behncke had participated in the planning of the meeting, his thoughts regarding Honecker's motivation deserve special attention. In his first interview in 1991, Behncke alluded to a fourth reason why Honecker received the Mormon delegation:

> Herr Honecker certainly wanted to underline the constitutional principle of the GDR, that all churches and religious organizations, regardless of their size or goals, have equal rights, that, for example, the Mormons have the same importance and the same rights as the Evangelicals, among others.

What did Behncke mean when he said that Honecker wanted to "underline" the principle that Mormons had the same rights as Evangelicals, and why would it be important to Honecker to make that point? The equality of rights among churches was a basic GDR principle, often emphasized by the State Secretariat. As a former member of that office, it would be natural for Behncke to mention that principle. But more than an academic principle was at stake in this instance. Honecker was having significant problems with the Evangelical churches at that time. The growing internal opposition to his regime, which was centered primarily in the churches, especially the Evangelicals, certainly occupied his attention more than thoughts of an invitation to visit America. However, the aftermath of the Zionskirche raid in late November 1987 showed that his church policy, which had been announced on March 6, 1978, and frequently praised by the regime thereafter, was in serious danger of collapse. Honecker could not have successfully pursued any policy initiatives abroad if he were seen as being blatantly antireligious at home. However, if he backed off from his effort to control the political activities of the churches, the Evangelical churches in particular would have declared it a victory for political activists.

Therefore, the LDS Church undertook its initiative at a politically opportune time. Honecker was able to publish the Church's declaration as an example of the success of his church policy in general, and of his regime's generous consideration of requests from a small religious organization. At the same time, and perhaps most importantly, he could send the Evangelical churches a message that a church that does not meddle in government affairs and that does not support antigovernment activity by its members, can receive significant concessions. By receiving the Church's leaders, by opening his country to missionaries and allowing its citizens to serve missions abroad, Honecker could show the world that the GDR was not antireligious.

Behncke said that "Honecker, at least in matters of foreign policy, was a realist. He knew that America and England were not at all inclined to invite him, because they viewed him and the GDR as nothing more than a satellite of the Soviet Union, with no independent voice and no influence in world affairs." However, the opportunity to receive, in East Berlin, a visiting delegation of Church leaders from America, was likely viewed by Honecker as a politically significant event. Behncke gave two examples:

> Honecker was particularly aware of the document that the Church had written regarding peace and the misuse of missiles. That document had carried a lot of weight with him, because he was in conflict with the Russians, who had stationed their new SS-20 missiles in the GDR. Honecker had said that those damn things had to be removed as soon as possible. If the Americans agreed with him, regardless for what reason, he could make use of that, so he wouldn't have to stand alone in his opposition to the missiles. (2006)

However, as important as the missile issue was for Honecker, Behncke's second point for meeting with the Church was more germane at this time:

> When the presidency of a church, whose headquarters is in America, the strongest and most powerful nation in the world, where Mormons are included in the highest levels of government, who are anticommunist, even "Kommunisten-Fresser" [people who "eat" Communists], sends a confidential letter to Honecker and requests a meeting to say thanks, that would be a reason to say "yes." Under those conditions, Honecker could show that he, personally, wasn't a "Kirchenfresser," that he actually was a person with a broad vision, and that he could conduct serious and friendly discussions with people who had opposing philosophies of life and reach an understanding that contributed to peace.(2006)

The topic of the overall church-state relations in the GDR was reviewed in Chapter 3 because of its direct relevance to many of the specific LDS-GDR issues discussed in subsequent chapters. Horst Dohle stated in that chapter that the meeting between Erich Honecker and representatives of the LDS Church signaled to other churches "the readiness of the government for discussion and negotiation about legitimate issues," which the government refused to conduct with the leaders of the Evangelical churches. The strategy employed by the Church to achieve the successful meeting with Honecker and the concessions that flowed from it, show that Church leaders were aware of the problems and opportunities of the time, especially the principles of acceptable church-state relations expressed by Honecker in his meeting with leaders of the Evangelical churches on March 6, 1978, and reemphasized in the February 19, 1988, letter composed by the Politburo and read to Bishop Leich, the leader of the Evangelical churches, after the police action at the Zionskirche in Berlin.

18 Missionaries Enter the GDR 1989

Missionaries in, missionaries out.... We didn't want much, and missionaries were the most important. (Manfred Schütze, 1991)

On November 3, 1988, six days after his meeting with Erich Honecker, President Monson wrote, "I met with Elder Russell M. Nelson, as well as with Elder L. Tom Perry, chairman of the Missionary Executive Council, to plan a strategy for the opening of missionary work in the German Democratic Republic. We will have to move with care but also without delay in taking advantage of the opening that is now before us" (*Faith Rewarded*).

The letters sent to Chairman Honecker and Secretary Löffler prior to the meeting indicated that the Church anticipated the need for post-meeting discussions to determine the number of missionaries to be allowed into the country. A government memorandum prepared shortly before the meeting suggested that only three to five missionaries should be permitted initially, until the results could be evaluated. Günther Behncke's meeting summary, prepared three days after the event, did not indicate a number, but a handwritten note on one copy said "four to six persons at first." (MS 13918) However, Behncke reported later that actual negotiations began at the number ten:

> We had agreed that ten missionaries could leave the GDR and ten could enter. However, after the meeting [with Honecker], the presidency proposed a new number. We came together in Tabarz, in Thüringen, with Herr Ringger and Henry Burkhardt, and agreed on many things. But I can tell you, that not only ten missionaries came here, but rather at least ten times that number. And all went well. (1991)

President Burkhardt also described the negotiations:

> We held our first follow-up discussion with State Secretary Löffler in early November. President Ringger and I were invited to the govern-

> ment's hotel in Thüringen, in Waltershausen/Tabarz, where we made some basic decisions. President Ringger, naturally, was a bit sly. I most likely would not have attempted it, but in that meeting with Herr Löffler, we began to talk not about ten missionaries but about ten pairs. We explained that missionaries were never allowed to be alone, but went in pairs. We remained with the number ten, which could later be increased, and Herr Löffler accepted it as quite understandable that when we spoke about ten, the ten to arrive were ten pairs (1991).
>
> When we met four weeks later with Herr Löffler, he said, yes, twenty missionaries, and Brother Ringger said, yes, twenty pairs. We agreed on that, and the number was increased from month to month thereafter. (2003)

In addition to determining how many missionaries could enter the country, it was necessary to consider the conditions under which missionary activities could be performed. These were first addressed in a plan proposed by the area presidency and sent to Elder Russell Nelson on November 23, 1988. Other than regarding the use of referrals, the plan was not implemented to any significant degree, probably because the favorable reception by the public exceeded expectations and conditions within East Germany changed rapidly within six months of the missionaries' arrival:

> Since tracting from door-to-door and public contacting is prohibited in the GDR, the proselyting program should center upon referrals obtained from Church members, at the Visitors' Center and on the temple grounds, at stake information centers, at ward or branch libraries, from public advertising, through community services, at Church open houses, firesides, cultural activities, etc.
>
> There is a great interest among the people in the GDR to know more about the Mormons. Every year we have between 25,000 and 30,000 visitors coming to the temple grounds in Freiberg. There were 29,000 visitors at the open house in Dresden and 9,000 visitors in Zwickau. This interest in the Church and the reliance upon referrals for teaching opportunities suggest a need for three referral-generating facilities: a visitors' center near the temple which should include missionary quarters, information centers in the new and larger buildings (Dresden, Leipzig, and Zwickau), and libraries in each meeting house.
>
> It is proposed that the first mission president be a North American who is an experienced Church worker with sound judgment. We recommend that the missionaries called to serve be selected from the German-language missions in Austria, West Germany, and Switzerland. Efforts would be made to achieve a balance between missionaries with U.S. citizenship and missionaries from European countries. (CR 374 16)

Except for an information center established within the Freiberg meeting house, the proposed centers were not built because the restrictions on missionary activities ended with the collapse of the GDR in late 1989. In the meantime, referrals from members provided most of the teaching opportunities for the missionaries. The chosen mission president, Wolfgang Paul, was not a "North American," but rather a West German citizen who had been serving as president of the Hamburg Mission. He described the circumstances of his calling and the preparation of the first missionaries:

> Sometime after the government permitted the Church to open a mission in the GDR, President Asay [the area president] called me and asked how my family would be affected if I were asked to lead the new mission. I told him that they had a different school system there. [Paul had three children at home, two of which were of school age.] Then on January 5, 1989, President Monson called and asked me to tell him "frank and candidly" what consequences would result if we were to move to the GDR. I will never forget his words as he said, "It took me twenty years to make this happen, we can't afford a mistake." I understood, of course, that we could not make any mistakes. (1991)

The first missionaries were selected from other missions and sent to Hamburg for training on March 26, 1989. They were Elders Yost and Powley from the Frankfurt Mission, Elders Karpowitz and Miles from the Hamburg Mission, Elders Engelke and Muir from the Munich Mission, and Elders Anderson, Smith, Tree, and Grimmer from the Zürich Mission. However, Elders Muir and Grimmer entered the GDR two weeks later than the others, after sufficient lodging had been located. President Paul described their training in Hamburg:

> We simulated every possibility, how the work should be started, what activities could be performed, and which activities were officially forbidden. We were not permitted to engage in public activities, no street meetings, and no "door-to-door contacts." We could only answer questions. We focused on avoiding mistakes. For example, how could we use our materials and what could we write home in letters, since we knew that our letters would be controlled. We were not allowed to refer to the GDR as the "zone." That was a sensitive topic, since the GDR once was the Soviet-occupied zone. We had to be careful not to mention the names of our investigators, since it could cause problems for them. We knew that the Stasi monitored the telephone, opened letters, observed us, and came into our church meetings. We practiced how to address people. We were trained about subjects we should avoid. We were not permitted to "advertise" America, and of course, all printed matter had to be approved. However, we initially brought

> with us in our baggage everything we needed, all literature, manuals, mission lessons, etc.
>
> We were told by the GDR's lawyers that we should not wear our badges. We were of the opinion that a badge is part of every missionary's attire. Therefore, we said, "We'll try it out, we'll wear the badges." I remember one meeting when Herr Behncke, the legal advisor, looked at my badge and asked, "Do all missionaries wear that?" I could tell that he didn't like my answer, but we did it anyhow (1991).
>
> Since tracting was not permitted, but we could answer questions, the badges created opportunities. When people looked at the badges, we could say, "I see you have a question about my name badge. May I briefly explain what it is?" Then we could answer their "question" and talk about the Church. (2005)

Every missionary received a copy of written instructions and were told, "It is expected of every missionary serving in the GDR to thoroughly understand these rules and carefully honor them." The instructions said:

> Always carry your passport and your missionary identity card. Follow the local laws, including traffic regulations, as well as the instructions of government officials (police, etc.). Avoid all commentary about the political situation in the GDR. Never recommend that anyone leave the country, and avoid any discussion on that subject. Never follow anyone's suggestion to exchange money illegally. Instead, use the authorized exchange offices. Never write anything about the political situation in the GDR, and never make negative statements about the country. Never photograph military or related facilities. Never distribute printed material publicly. Do not engage in "street contact" or "door-to-door" tracting. It is not permitted.
>
> Be professional and positive on the telephone, and avoid any political comment. Always be polite, helpful, and exemplary in public, and avoid groups on the street. Obey all relevant customs regulations regarding the import or export of materials. Follow strictly the speed limits on the roads, and follow traffic rules. Take care that you never take GDR money out of the country, since all currency manipulation is severely punished.
>
> Please remember that it is a great blessing for the members of the Church in the GDR for missionaries to be permitted here. You have a special responsibility to justify the trust that the Lord, the leaders of the Church, and the members have placed in you. It is a special privilege to be a missionary in the GDR. Please always remember that misconduct of an individual can result in the government withdrawing the privileges accorded to the Church. (Copy in author's possession)

The Arrival of the Missionaries

The Church planned to establish the mission office in Leipzig, but could not find living accommodations for President Paul and his family. Instead, the office was established initially in Dresden and transferred to Leipzig after the Wende. Lodging for the missionaries was also a problem. Some were temporarily placed in members' home. A letter of February 2, 1989, from President Burkhardt to Secretary Löffler shows that other options were being pursued:

> We request your support regarding lodging opportunities for the foreign missionaries that will arrive in the coming months. We will attempt to lodge missionaries in Leipzig in the homes of members, but that can only be a short-term solution. By chance, we have discovered across the street from our stake center in Leipzig, a large apartment occupied by a very weak women, more than seventy years of age, who can barely maintain her apartment, which is in a very desolate condition. Our specific question is whether you can make available for this lady, who knows nothing of this request, an appropriate apartment so her apartment can be made available for the expected missionaries. (DMO)

The first eight missionaries arrived on Thursday, March 30, 1989. Two were placed in East Berlin, two in Leipzig, two in Dresden, and two in Zwickau. They were the first of twenty that entered the GDR within the next month. Günter Schulze described the arrival of the two in Dresden:

> There was an element of uncertainty about the state's reception of the missionaries. We knew that the people would accept them very well, because they were Americans and other foreigners. But we constantly remembered that open "missionary" activities were forbidden. When Americans come and speak with the people, how will the state react? That was my concern. When the missionaries arrived, we drove to the Hechtstraße in Dresden-Neustadt. Our ward had prepared lodging there. The missionaries stepped out onto the side street. These were full-blooded missionaries, the best, and before I knew it, they had engaged two citizens of Dresden. In the evening at eight o'clock, two people were walking on the sidewalk, and the missionaries spoke to them. I thought, "Oh my goodness! They have no idea who those people were. It could be a couple of Communists." (1993)

Elders Miles and Tree were lodged with Hans and Ruth Schult in East Berlin. Hans Schult described their arrival:

> I said, "Elders, I must register you." That was for my own security. We went immediately to the police, and they were shown into a room. A police officer came by, looked in to see who was there, and closed

> the door. The two missionaries began to be a little nervous. I understood the tactics of our police. Then they were asked, "Where is your residency permit?" I said, they have their passport and an entry permit for the GDR and for Berlin. There is an agreement between President Monson and the government of the GDR, and that is why they are here. Otherwise, they would not have been permitted to enter. The officer asked again, "Where is your residency permit for Berlin?" Well, there wasn't one. "Well, then they must leave the GDR by tomorrow afternoon at 3:00 p.m. They must have a residency permit for Berlin, or they must exit." He took the two passports and stamped them with the notation, "expelled." The missionaries were quite upset. The next day I went with them to the State Secretariat for Church Affairs. They were very friendly. I explained the situation, and someone said, "Relax. Go to Alexanderplatz to the office for foreigners and everything will be taken care of." We went there. They were waiting for us, opened the door, and invited us in. Then they placed another stamp in the passports and everything was okay. Some people were totally confused. They never had experienced such a thing, and so they didn't know what they should do, because there was only one office that could say "yes" to such a situation. (2003)

Elder Miles said, "We were aware that a problem existed but saw it more as a misunderstanding or inadequate communication. To be honest, I don't think I was ever worried about being thrown out of the country. Maybe I was just naive" (2005).

State Secretary Löffler helped to solve several similar issues regarding the presence of the missionaries and their activities. He said:

> When it started in March, all the rules of the GDR stood suddenly in the way of the missionaries. There was no law that allowed citizens of foreign countries, who might be temporarily here, to conduct missionary activities. So I said, we will prepare a document on my letterhead, include their names, where they came from, and where they were born. Then I'll request that they receive all necessary support of state offices in their activity as missionaries for the Church of Jesus Christ of Latter-day Saints. That was followed with my stamp and my signature, and it was accepted, although it was fully illegal. The GDR was a state of very precise and obdurate laws, which could, however, be interpreted in useful ways, even including visa laws. (2003)

Since missionaries were not allowed to go from door-to-door, or to initiate discussion on the street, they often pretended to ask people on the street for directions. President Paul gave an example:

> It happened in Schwerin, that the missionaries asked people on the street for directions, such as "Where is the Post Office?" to initiate discussion. One lady heard their American accent and answered in English, since she taught English. The missionaries made an appointment and taught her and her husband. A short time after they had left, the branch president received a phone call from the city's legal advisor for church affairs. He was told, "Your missionaries are engaging people on the street and asking for directions. That is missionary work, which is not allowed." So we knew that this family immediately went and reported the incident. (1991)

Elder Miles explained how the missionaries operated:

> We originally traveled by street car and train. This had its advantages—it allowed us to sit next to and talk with a number of people. We believed our room was bugged and we were followed constantly. From the very first day we were able to pick out who was following us and when they would make the switch. We even approached one and asked him for directions. He answered but could not get away from us fast enough. (2005)

Upon arrival, the missionaries began immediately to meet with friends of members. These people were already well informed about the Church. The missionaries only had to teach and invite them to be baptized:

> *President Paul:* The missionaries began immediately to meet with the ward and branch missionary leaders to determine where they should begin. I was personally in Dresden, and our first discussion took place on Friday [one day after their arrival]. That family had become interested in the Church because of the Freiberg Temple, had already attended church meetings frequently, and was very friendly. The feeling was very strong that they were ready. So we presented the challenge, "Will you follow the example of Christ and be baptized on Sunday?" The ward mission leader was present, and as he heard that they agreed to be baptized two days later, he almost fell off his chair.
>
> You must remember that the members had already made many contacts, that they had acquaintances. They had already provided much information, but had never properly challenged individuals to be baptized. At first, the members could not understand that we could sometimes issue the invitation for baptism during the first discussion. But as the members saw how the Holy Ghost really worked, that it didn't matter how long they had known the Church or if they knew everything, but rather had a testimony through the spirit, then the members began to understand and then they led us to the investigators and

> their friends and many relatives, etc. In this way, many already existing connections were used to bring people to the Church. (1991)
>
> We had several wards where we baptized weekly. Since the people in the GDR had almost no opportunities to have spiritual experiences, the missionaries provided these opportunities for them. That contributed to the fact that many investigators received a testimony within seven or ten days and could be baptized. But it was still necessary to attend church meetings and get to know the bishop. (2005)

In May 1989, two months after the arrival of the first eight missionaries, a total of twenty-four were active in the GDR. Alfred Bastian described how the members in Annaberg-Buchholz made preparations for some of the missionaries in this second group:

> I was given the assignment of finding an apartment for two missionaries in Annaberg. A sister in our ward had died, and I went to the housing administration and obtained an apartment with three rooms for the missionaries. We renovated the apartment and added a shower. Within a week, we had prepared very nice quarters. We even painted the building's stairwell as well as the bathroom in the stairwell that was used by other tenants of the building. The first missionaries we received were very tall, over 2 meters [6 feet 6 inches], and we had the problem that they didn't fit in the beds. I spoke with the mission leadership in Dresden and within two weeks we received new beds from Sweden that were 2.2 meters [7 feet 2 inches] long.
>
> We had over forty convert baptisms [in Annaberg-Buchholz]. The mission president recognized that two missionaries were not enough, and the bishop was asked to prepare for a second pair. With fear in my heart, I went once more to the housing administration. The official said, "I hope you are not coming for another apartment." I said, "Yes, two more missionaries are on their way. We also have a brother from Walthersdorf, who went on a mission to Canada, and he writes that he has wonderful lodging there." She promised to help me, but she couldn't make the decision herself, because it had to go through the commissioners. They all said that the missionaries could not be given one of the newer apartments and wanted to assign us to an old building. A week later, the office person called me and said, "Come here immediately. I have an apartment in a newer building, but this time I'm not taking the matter to the commission." Within two weeks, without having to renovate anything, we could provide the new missionaries with an apartment. Although this woman was a strong SED comrade, she always supported me and helped the Church. The state in general did not have a good reputation, but there were always individuals who supported us as a church. (1991)

The fact that the missionaries came from America or from other Western countries was certainly an important factor in their success. Most GDR citizens had never met or spoken with an American, and many took the opportunity to find out what they were doing in the country. Marco Engelhardt, a young man from Leipzig, said that the opportunity to speak with Americans, who could speak excellent German, was a great attraction. "That was one reason why I listened to them. It was something new in the GDR, the Wende was not anticipated, but suddenly Americans were present. I had had no other contact with an American, and that awakened my interest. I would never have been baptized only because of an American, never, but it was the main reason why I listened to them" (2006).

While most of the first conversions came out of the members' circle of friends, who had some familiarity with the Church's teachings and were ready to accept the baptismal challenge, other investigators were not at all familiar with the Church or its teachings. The following two accounts describe the reaction of some members to the speed with which many baptisms took place. The first is taken from the minutes of a meeting of the GDR Presidency on September 20, 1989:

> The work of the full-time missionaries was discussed in detail. Despite the exceedingly great and welcome progress, the priesthood leaders have been repeatedly irritated by the methods used sometimes in the conversion process. Therefore, the brothers wish to meet with President Ringger as soon as possible. (DMO)

A member who wished to remain anonymous remembered his response to some of the baptisms:

> In the first years, things happened in the Church that displeased me, and I simply had to protest. The first mission president had told his missionaries that couples who were not married could be baptized if they promised to be married soon. Three such couples were baptized here, based on that promise, but only one of those couples married. I complained to the stake president and said, "You can't do that. If the people get married today, then as far as I'm concerned, they can be baptized tomorrow, but not the reverse." And children were baptized when only the mother gave her permission. The father didn't know anything about it, and we had problems afterwards. In order to baptize people on Saturday evening, some were given three or four lessons in a row that morning. I said, "That can be done with friends who have already attended meetings for two years, who already know everything, but not with people who were raised as atheists and now should be baptized within a few hours." We had many problems of that type. The area presidency and the regional representative apparently became involved, and those practices were soon ended. Perhaps we no

> longer had as many baptisms, but I must say those who were baptized were stronger. (1993)

The experiences of one family reveal some of the differences in the approach to missionary opportunities before and after the arrival of the missionaries from the West. In October 1988, Waltraud Haid and her two daughters visited the new Dresden Stake building during its open house. They liked what they heard about the Church's activities and asked if children of nonmembers could participate. They filled out a visitor's card and requested a Book of Mormon. The book never arrived, and no one made contact with the family. Sister Haid assumed that the members were simply too busy to visit all the people who attended the open house. One of her daughters and a friend later visited the chapel a second time, after the open house. They were greeted by a friendly member who showed them around the building, but there was no follow-up. In the spring of 1990, however, one year after the arrival of the new missionaries, Sister Haid happened to meet two young men in the stairwell of her apartment house. They had come to visit a recently baptized family. She did not associate the name of the church on their badges with the "Mormon building" they had visited eighteen months earlier, but she agreed to meet with them later, with her family. She, her husband, and two daughters were baptized shortly thereafter. One of her daughters, Daniela Bauerfeind, later served a full-time mission and then married a member in Leipzig (2006).

Mission records show that an average of seven convert baptisms had taken place annually in the GDR between 1975 and 1984. In contrast, convert baptisms in 1989 took place at the following rate: April, 29; May, 56; June, 66; July, 62; August, 44; September, 90; October, 78; November, 65; and December, 69 (LR 2012570 3).

A similar rate of baptisms continued in 1990. However, with the opening of the border on November 9, 1989, changing social and employment conditions soon led to a decline in the number of baptisms:

> *President Paul:* We noticed that the people no longer had much interest in the missionaries or the Book of Mormon, since other things became available to which they could turn. Earlier, the few things that they encountered from the West were desirable and interesting. But now those opportunities were much greater. Moreover, after 1990, people began to concentrate on retaining or finding a job, because the flood of goods and services from the West forced the factories and businesses within the GDR to close. The number of baptisms declined under those conditions. (1991)

> *Herbert Heidler:* Before the Wende, all the people were dissatisfied. When the missionaries from America arrived, the people said, "Perhaps they can help us. They have something new to offer." So they listened and some said, "Yes, I'll accept what you are telling us." But that

> changed when the Wende didn't bring what they had hoped it would. Most of the people became unemployed, and that was a huge disappointment. So no one was willing to listen to missionaries anymore. When missionaries came, the people said, "Leave me alone," and hardly anyone was being baptized. (1993)

In 1991, the Leipzig Mission was split and a new Berlin Mission was established. Its president, Manfred Schütze, recounted some of the reasons why the number of baptisms declined shortly after the borders were opened:

> We have so many social problems, problems with unemployment, new laws, lack of day care for children. Many people are disoriented. They tell the missionaries, "What you are doing is great. But please excuse me, I have no time now to read the Book of Mormon. I must focus on retaining employment. I must learn how to fill out a tax return. I must establish my own business or strengthen my company." The changes bring new challenges. There are many problems now, including drugs, pornography, and unemployment. There are many foreigners here and many, many distractions, different movies, even sex movies. All these things play a big role in people's lives, so they are not so open for missionary activities. (1991)

In the previous chapter, a member was quoted anonymously, who said that the meeting between President Monson and Chairman Honecker "had severely damaged the Church's reputation, which still has a negative impact upon the missionary work." That statement cannot be supported by the available data. Convert baptisms were remarkably high immediately after the arrival of missionaries from the West in 1989 and through 1990, and there is no documented evidence that the Monson-Honecker meeting had a negative effect at that time. The decline in conversions began later, as a result of the changing social and economic conditions.

If the Monson-Honecker meeting had not taken place, it would have required several months of preparation to transfer a significant number of missionaries into that region, because the downfall of the regime and the opening of the border came as a surprise to even the most astute observers of East Germany. Whether more people would have joined the Church if they had first met the missionaries months or years after the borders were opened cannot be known, but it is highly unlikely, given the adverse social and economic changes that took place very quickly. Moreover, many of the existing members left for the West as soon as the borders were opened. Therefore, the net effect of theoretically deleting the Monson-Honecker meeting from history would most likely have been smaller wards and branches throughout the former GDR region.

Fortunately, that didn't happen and the East benefited from the extraordinary number of convert baptisms that took place in the window of opportunity between the Monson-Honecker meeting and the collapse of the existing social structure in the GDR.

GDR Members Called to Full-Time Missions Abroad

The first ten young men who left on missions from the GDR were interviewed by their bishops, stake presidents, and Elder Ringger in February 1989. They were Ralf Bauerfeind, Leipzig; Tobias Burkhardt, Karl-Marx-Stadt; Steffen Dzierzon, Plauen; Jörg Küchler, Walthersdorf; Jörg Klaus Neumann, Leipzig; Luka Ortlieb, Dresden; Robby Sven-Axel Schulz, Neubrandenburg; Andre Johannes Schumann, Erfurt; Tom Gottfried Teubner, Freiberg; and Daniel Werner, Leipzig.

Elder Ringger wrote to Elder Nelson in March 1989, "All of them have good family relations and a strong desire to return to their home country after their mission. It is understood by the GDR government that these young men will serve abroad and that they will receive thorough training before they enter the mission field in order to be good representatives of their country." Each prospective missionary was asked about his willingness to return to the GDR after his mission, and they were all told that the future of this unusual missionary opportunity was dependent upon their return. They did return, not to the GDR they expected, but to a reunified Germany.

Two of the first ten missionaries who departed in May 1989 later described their missionary interviews and first experiences:

> *Luka Ortlieb, Dresden:* It was a total surprise. My father said that the bishop was coming to our house on Monday evening to talk with me. I could not imagine what he would have wanted. He interviewed me and then said that I should go to Freiberg on that evening to talk with the stake president. He only indicated that it may be possible in the future for young men to serve a mission. We then went to see the stake president. He said that on the basis of the meeting with Erich Honecker, young people would be able to leave the GDR to serve missions abroad. We were told not to discuss this with anyone, other than our parents at home. We then met with President Ringger. He primarily wanted to determine our worthiness, if we had a testimony and how we had lived in the GDR, whether we were opposed to the government or had always lived as good members in accordance with the gospel. He also asked how we would feel if we were sent abroad and if we were prepared to return to the GDR. We had to promise that we definitely would return to the GDR, so that the Church wouldn't suffer any negative consequences.
>
> I was very happy that I could go on a mission, but I knew absolutely nothing about a missionary's life, since there had never been missionaries in our country. I knew nothing about how a missionary worked or what it really meant to be a missionary. I only learned that later when the first missionaries entered the GDR. For that reason, I

had never thought much about going on a mission because I simply didn't have a strong belief that it could happen. It was really a surprise. (1993)

Ralf Bauerfeind, Leipzig: I was called by the bishop and asked to come to our meeting house. I asked why. He said it would be a great surprise, so just come. It was absolutely unbelievable, since I had never met a young man of my age who had ever left the GDR for the West, except this small group of ten people. We went to our meeting house and were kept a little separate from each other. I had the impression that we shouldn't say much to each other. Then we went into the office and the first question was, "If you could go on a mission, would you return to the GDR?" When I said yes, I was interviewed and asked if I was prepared to go on a mission. I also had an interview with Brother Ringger. The questions and instructions were always the same. We must return to the GDR, so others could have the same opportunity, and to protect the Church. I think the interviews took place in February, and we left in May.

Our Church leaders instructed us to be careful what we said about the GDR, to avoid consequences for the Church and other youth. We were also told to be careful what we wrote our parents, for it was assumed that every letter would be read before it reached our parents. The letters from my parents always had the famous slit on the back where the camera had been inserted.

Of course, the main difference between us and other missionaries was not what we were told but how we were handled. Even our trip to Salt Lake City was unusual. We were taken to Frankfurt/Main and spent three days learning about missionary work. Then we were accompanied on flights to Chicago and Salt Lake City, where we were met by many people, reporters, cameras, and former GDR members. I saw Elders Monson and Nelson. We later met President Benson. We had special teachers in the Missionary Training Center who took care of all our needs. We received new suits and other clothing and didn't have to buy our books. We didn't have any money. Every day we were given cookies and cake, and even balloons. Later, we received love letters from girls we had never seen before. It was quite an experience. We certainly were a unique phenomenon. We were the first that had ever arrived from an East Block country.

None of us had ever considered going on a mission. The wish to serve the Lord was certainly there, but we knew that we would never see anything other than the GDR. It was just like with the temple. When we were told to live worthy of going to a temple, we were also told to be prepared to serve a mission. Whether you could ever go, that was a totally different question. But prepare yourself. Of course, we thought that someday we might be sent to Russia, or to Hungary,

> etc., since we all had to learn Russian in school. But such events as we experienced were never considered possible. (2003)

Shortly after the first baptisms took place in the GDR, some of the young converts also had the opportunity to serve full-time missions. Günter Schulze was a bishop in Dresden when interviewed in 1993. He talked about the number of young converts in his ward who also were called as full-time missionaries shortly after the first ten had departed:

> Among the new converts in the Dresden Ward, six have already returned from full-time missions. I have four more who are still serving, all from among the newest members. Of course, they had not saved money for a mission. They also didn't have parents who were members. They had essentially been integrated into the ward as individuals, so I have had problems finding money to support them on missions. So far, I have managed, but always with fear and trembling that they might go hungry or not be able to pay their rent. But I am very thankful that these young people had the desire to serve a mission. (1993)

Why Did So Many GDR Citizens Join the Church in 1989–1990?

The Freiberg Temple attracted about ninety thousand GDR citizens to the two-week open house held in 1985. Gottfried Richter said, "Some just came out of curiosity. But I could read their faces. Even though they didn't know it themselves, many came out of a longing for something better, something more beautiful, something more noble than they had." He described an encounter with one young couple who asked him, "What is eternity?" After his response, he said, "they walked away in deep thought" (1993).

Many visitors were impressed by what they saw, heard, and felt during their visit to the temple, but accounts of conversions following the open house are difficult to find. Four years after the temple's dedication, and shortly before missionaries from the West entered the GDR, Dr. Helmut Obst, then professor of ecumenical theology at the Martin Luther University at Halle-Wittenberg in the GDR, published an article about the small churches in that country. Regarding the LDS Church, he wrote:

> The fact that almost one hundred thousand people visited the temple [during the open house] was one of the most noteworthy religious events of recent years and cannot be attributed only to curiosity. It signaled a new religious awakening. However, the people's interest was diffuse. They sought information, were kindly disposed, but avoided commitment. Some Evangelical churches feared that the large public relations impact of the temple's construction and the resultant visits by their members could lead to an exit from their churches, but that did not happen. Despite intensive missionary efforts, the ranks of the Mormons were not increased. The impediments associated with Mor-

> mon doctrine, and especially the required lifestyle (tithing, renunciation of coffee and tobacco, etc.), proved to be too high.[1]

Since the doctrinal and lifestyle impediments that Dr. Obst identified did not change between 1985 and 1989, it would be interesting to know how he would have explained the dramatic rate of conversions that took place in the GDR, within that narrow window of time after the arrival of the missionaries from the West and before the fall of the government. What was the difference between 1985 and the early months of 1989? The subject is certainly worthy of additional research.

19 The Wende—End of the GDR 1990

We lost some things after the Wende, for example, the feeling of unity. Now that people can travel everywhere, we are no longer as dependent upon others. The concern for fellow members was always stronger in the East than in the West. There are many examples, but the communal spirit that we had, where we met together for friendly discussions on a Sunday afternoon, we no longer have. Unfortunately, we've already lost something. (Hans-Jürgen Bartsch, 1991)

The members in the East were a solid community. One needed the other. The Church was always the middle point, because we lived in a diaspora, very isolated. Everything has two sides, but much has been lost. It will depend on the individual member, but I hope that the next generation will not become too rich or too comfortable. I have a little fear about that. But fear doesn't mean that we are not optimistic. We must simply be aware of and fight against it. (Manfred Schütze, 1991)

This chapter does not attempt to describe the political and social developments of 1989–1990, but focuses instead on the reaction of Church members to those developments, especially in relationship to their religious life.

Involvement in the Political Demonstrations

Frank Apel: The demonstrations began in Leipzig in 1989 at the Nikolai Church and became larger and larger, and they extended to other cities. As Church leaders, we said that we should remain detached as much as possible, simply to protect the Church. That was only said as a recommendation, not as a command. Everyone had to decide for himself what to do. Many of our members participated in the demonstrations. (1991)

Manfred Schütze: The Church had good relations with the government and was not necessarily interested in destroying it. When the members asked us if they should participate, we naturally said, "If you participate in this freedom movement, then do it as citizens, as private persons, but not as the Church." Many churches opened their buildings to such meetings. We said, "That is not our function." At that time, and still today, many churches are more social or citizens' rights institutions and lose their real function, namely, to proclaim and to live the gospel of Jesus Christ. We strongly emphasized that it is not our function as a church to become involved in political affairs, not only in the GDR, but also not in other countries.

Of course, not everyone understood that, and emotions ran quite high. We were strongly criticized on one occasion, and I went to Leipzig where we discussed the subject with the members for two hours. I'm sure that not even half of them agreed with our position, but we had to be led by inspiration, and I can say in all humility that we were responsible for the Church. Of course, I had my own personal opinion on that matter.

Many of our members were immediately involved, joined citizens' committees, joined political parties, and stood for election to political offices. Some members still do the same today. But they do it as private individuals, not as representatives of the Church. As Church leaders, we could not take a stand. (1991)

Hans Schult: No preaching was done, for or against. It was left to the individual member. In Leipzig, I told my children, "I'm an old man." My daughter said, "You are not too old to go into the street. Our entire apartment, retired people, children, parents are going into the street to demonstrate in Leipzig. We are there every Monday." Whether they went every Monday, I don't know, but that was the reaction of my children. (1991)

Frank Apel: Some of our members thought, "We must leave, we must go to the West." Things here were spiraling downward, economically and all. The youth especially didn't see much of a future. They said, "We want to leave." As stake president, I said at a conference, "It is our job to stay here." That did not make me popular with some, but I had no choice. I said, "The Lord placed us here. We were born here to establish his kingdom, and not somewhere else." I later received a very bitter letter from a brother who had intended to leave. He was a branch president. I first slept on the matter and then met with him and told him again that, as stake president, I think we should remain here, to fulfill our purpose. I said we would not be disadvantaged by staying. That brother is still here and is still a branch president. His life is going well, and he is happy that he remained here. I really had the feeling then that I should tell the members what I did, and I did it. (1991)

Unity and a Communal Spirit

Günter Schulze: We have baptized about 250 members in Dresden since the opening of the mission. At the same time, about 150 to 200 members left for the West to find employment. (1993)

Manfred Heller: Some members said, "Earlier, when we met in the Dr. Kurt Fischer Allee [the old meeting house in Dresden] we were a close group. Rarely did a friend attend our meetings. We hardly ever had convert baptisms. We knew each other. And that was much nicer, more comfortable." Now in our ward, we don't know this and that person. There are so many new brothers and sisters, and to establish and nurture friendships, to grow closer together, is certainly a bit of a problem. But the young people all feel very comfortable here with us. That is also important for the Church, that we have a refreshing from outside. For that reason, I say that the freedom and the new members will greatly contribute to the growth and progress of the Church. And despite all other issues, that will eventually be an advantage for us. (1991)

Gerwin Baasch: Before the Wende, the members had a very strong feeling of togetherness. Because of the political pressure of past years, we became a very close community, some of which has been lost. With the opening of the border, not only have some of the new members moved away, but also some of the older members have moved to West Germany. And some of the new members also use the weekend to travel somewhere. Of course, we are happy to be able to visit relatives now and then on weekends, but the cohesion among members has loosened to some degree. However, the changes have also brought much good. (1991)

Freedom vs. Insecurity

Klaus Peter Bartsch: The advantage of freedom is that man is totally free and can express his opinions without thinking, "Should I say that, or will I somehow have my legs cut off?" That is freedom. It is beautiful. It is wonderful. (1991)

Manfred Heller: Earlier, many things, including aspects of our personal life, were spelled out for us. We didn't have as much to think about, money for children, applications for housing assistance, etc. Now everyone has to worry more about himself. If you don't, you are left out.

And this change from being spoon-fed, from having someone acting on your behalf, to self-initiative is very, very difficult for many, especially for older people. Younger people adapt, are more flexible. (1991)

Luka Ortlieb: As a result of my mission, I have come to understand that freedom is something totally beautiful, but that it depends on how individuals use it. Naturally, every freedom brings danger with it. Many think only materialistically, and they become hard of heart, proud, or follow the wrong path. Freedom itself is wonderful, and I have no wish to return to the GDR. I'm happy that we have become one country, and I'm happy that we are free. However, life has become more difficult in many ways. (1993)

Ralf Bauerfeind: The "absolute security" that ruled then, whereby we knew (or thought we knew) what to expect in fifty years, absolutely does not exist today. No one knows what will happen next year. You don't know if you'll have employment, or perhaps you will lose the house you built, which had to be financed. Or you don't know how your children will develop or be allowed to develop. All that used to be known. At least, in my opinion, it could be anticipated better then than now. Everyone in the GDR had predictable, similar experiences. You could talk with every young person at a youth conference and know they had the same problems as you. But what everyone experiences today is not the same. And the time that is available to speak about these things with others has been reduced. There is less time in the family, because more of the parents work longer hours. So the certainty of your designated pathway through life no longer exists, and that is one reason why many people, I think, are unsatisfied today. (2003)

Freedom to Travel

Manfred Heller: After people's freedom to travel had been restricted for so many years, there was a natural and strong urge to travel. For that reason, some members drove here and there on the weekend and sometimes neglected their church callings by not being in their wards and branches. I have the feeling that this practice is becoming less severe, that such things are being stabilized again, after the initial urge or curiosity had been fulfilled. (1991)

Frank Apel: My impression is that the freedom, which we now have, is not understood correctly by many. For example, everyone now thinks they have to travel. We have to see what we haven't yet seen. We have to go to Italy, Spain, or wherever. To do that, we need money. Earlier, our money wasn't worth much, because there wasn't much to buy. Now people think, "There is so much to buy, but we don't have enough money, so we have to work more." In that process, we've lost a little of that which we earlier had in the GDR. (1991)

Jürgen Pabst: When the border opened, everyone thought they had to look on the other side, and many things were ignored for a while. Perhaps it wasn't as bad in church as on the job, but it seemed to me as if everyone wanted to leave. That played itself out eventually and is no longer the case. (1993)

Günter Schulze: We have many activities here in the ward, and they are of high quality. We have activities every week, whether for the elderly or for the younger, and not just soccer, etc., but also theater plays, crafts, and everything imaginable. There are numerous offerings, missionary work, home evenings, lectures, and discussion groups. Everything is offered and is well attended. But the urge to travel, that is my problem. And that hasn't yet settled down. I always thought that after four years, people wouldn't have any money left with which to travel. But so far they always have enough money. I'm anticipating that it will eventually level off, that people will use their money for more valuable things than just for travel. But that lies in the nature of the former GDR citizens—to finally explore everything, to see what for decades we couldn't see or hear. (1993)

Time for Church vs. Work

Herbert Heidler: The difference between the Church in the GDR and the Church today is that church life in the GDR was considerably more peaceful and balanced. Before the Wende, members had more time. That had an impact on the temple. Many were able to leave work at noon on Fridays and travel to the temple, or to take another day in the week. That was possible. I could go to the cemetery during the day, when necessary, to conduct a funeral. That was tolerated. But no longer today. People have to work longer and harder to earn money. That naturally has an effect on church work.

I personally believe that people are more challenged on the job, and that more things can be bought with money. Many work extra hours to earn more money, because they say, "I want to buy this and that." That attraction didn't exist in the GDR in the past. Everyone had his work, but couldn't earn more. Now it is different. Must a person learn to use freedom? Oh yes, I believe that. (1993)

Jürgen Pabst: I don't think that members are necessarily less willing to do church work or to accept assignments, but the entire amount of available time is measured differently now. In the GDR, we had the opportunity to conduct private activities during our official work time. Our job was more secure and our professional activities were not so strictly organized as today. Many people today have to work longer hours than before and thus have less free time. I have also determined that there are some people who work longer to earn more money, and perhaps give church work a little lower priority, simply because the desire to do something with that money is stronger than before. Earlier, you had to wait fifteen or twenty years for a car. So you had twenty years to save for it. Today, you can buy a car immediately, so you have to earn the money quicker. The opportunities and the offered goods are much greater now, so that the amount of time allocated to church work is reduced. I am confident, however, that people can and must learn to master those changes. When much is now offered, people must think it through and make priorities. "What is actually most important for me? Is it important to travel abroad often, or is it important to be active in church?" I must say, it is perhaps no longer as bad as it was in the beginning. (1993)

Gerhard Müller: People now have a greater fear of losing employment. That adversely affects church activities. On the other hand, the growth of the Church increased the work for the core members, since those who constitute the core were expected to take on new responsibilities for the new converts. In fact, we sometimes were told that some of them became inactive because we were not caring enough for them. Sometimes, large numbers of people joined the Church in the belief that their problems would somehow be solved, that we would provide a social support system for them that we could not actually provide. (1993)

Eberhard Werner: I notice that many members now concentrate more on their jobs. It remains to be seen if that is a temporary phenomenon or a permanent tendency. But it means that more stress has entered into our lives. (1993)

Michael Schult: In the GDR, the amount of income that was directly received by a worker was only a part of that which a person actually earned. For example, child care services, kindergarten, school expenses cost absolutely nothing for the individual. Public transportation was very cheap and vacations for the entire family could be obtained for two hundred marks. Now that has been changed because people must pay individually for all those aspects of life, and people need to be concerned about things that were automatically provided earlier. (1993)

Unemployment and Social Fears

Frank Apel: We were all about on the same level. Now there are more economic and social distinctions. Some have very little, not even a job. Life for others is average, while for some, conditions are considerably better. Unemployment is a sudden phenomenon that we never experienced earlier. It brings new worries, new problems. We once had a priesthood manual with lessons where a quorum president worked with his members to help another brother find employment. We always laughed and said, "What a strange lesson. Everyone is employed here." Suddenly, we now have new conditions here. (1991)

Klaus Peter Bartsch: Social fear has entered. Earlier, life was predetermined—education, professional training. Everyone could learn a skill, follow a career. Whether it was your desired career was another matter, but you were given a career, a profession. Those who so desired could pursue some type of further training, to improve your qualifications. There was little unemployment, practically none. And everyone was insured, that is, we had health insurance. (1993)

Herbert Heidler: At the moment, all the fast offerings we receive are given out to members. Before the Wende, we always transferred at least part of the contributions to the stake every month. We had old people who had only a small pension, and we helped them with a winter supply of potatoes, or once in a while we bought new shoes for a sister. But those weren't problems of the magnitude that we have today because of unemployment. We now rarely are able to help someone find a job. Now we have the unemployed who seek money through crooked ways. A bishop has to say something now and then, to teach members not to engage in shady activities in order to obtain money. (1993)

Drugs, Addiction, Pornography, and Criminality

Herbert Heidler: We have more criminality in our communities than earlier. Then, police knew every individual, and no one could escape. Today, the borders are open, the police don't know the people, and criminals appear and disappear and no one knows where they are. Criminality has greatly increased. And there are more things that attract the youth. Most of that only appeared after the Wende. There is certainly a difference between then and today. (1993)

Dieter Bauerfeind: Drugs and pornography didn't exist in the GDR. Criminality, a burglary, that was a sensation. You could leave your doors open, and you let your children play in the street, all without fear. The state had the criminality well in hand. And the temptations were, I would say, almost zero. (2003)

Frank Apel: You now see newspapers with naked women at every newsstand. That didn't used to be. Now you have to talk with the youth, teach them that we live in a world that is becoming more and more evil, but that we cannot participate in what the world is doing. Earlier, the youth were strong in a different way, they knew how to defend their opinions, maintain their standards against the world around them. Now, it is no longer a problem to be a Christian or a member of the Church. But to avoid following the crowd, the world, that is suddenly a problem. (1991)

Klaus Peter Bartsch: Earlier, we were isolated. Few people could enter the country, and they were controlled, and we couldn't leave. There were more controls on addictive products, drugs, and criminal elements trying to enter the country. That was a protection for our children, and actually a nice thing. We didn't need to have concerns for our children in that regard, that they might be offered drugs or other addictive products in school, as it is today. (1993)

Jürgen Pabst: I don't believe that it is more difficult today to retain the youth in the Church. The youth want to get together, to be active together. There certainly are more opportunities now for them to travel and to do other activities that might be dangerous. But despite the changes, I have concluded that they are holding to the Church, that they are not lowering their sights or standards. (1993)

East-West Relations

Klaus Peter Bartsch: After the fall of the Wall, psychological walls have been built that are difficult to explain. During the GDR years, people were often dependent on support from relatives in the West and were happy to receive a bar of soap that smelled good, because we didn't have that here. Yes, a bar of soap! That brought pleasure. Of course, we had soap here. We were not so bad off as other East Block states, but it was still a joy to receive such a thing, or a stick of gum, which always pleased the children.

After the Wende, the West Germans lost that feeling of our dependence on them, while simultaneously we had more of the feeling, "Now we can do it ourselves." That led somehow to a conflict, in that we turned more and more away from each other. Such things as "Besserwessi" and "dumme Ossi" [better Westerners and dumb Easterners] arose, because some of the West Germans thought that we were emerging out of caves and only now learning about life. Unfortunately, that also existed in the Church. That wasn't always the case, but we had to hear such things, perhaps in the heat of a soccer tournament. Those barriers are still there, and whether they will disappear will be seen in the future. (1993)

20 President Henry Burkhardt

> *Despite all the problems that we had during those years, that experience did not harm us. Of course, there were certain sacrifices, but they were not so great that they were life threatening. We lived and we had good spiritual experiences. Those were the best times for me. (Henry Burkhardt, 1991)*

Henry Burkhardt was born in Chemnitz in 1930. His parents and grandparents were members of the Church. Between 1952 and 1990, he was the recognized leader of the Church in the GDR, first as a counselor to mission presidents who lived in West Berlin or in Hamburg, then after 1969 as the president of the Dresden Mission, president of the Freiberg Temple, and finally president of the Church of Jesus Christ of Latter-day Saints in the GDR. The latter role was basically a political position, done to satisfy the government's wish to have just one responsible Church representative.

He spoke about his youth in a 1991 interview:

> I began an apprenticeship with the German railroad in the spring of 1945, shortly before the war ended. I was on the career path to become a railroad official, but there were no "officials" under the new regime, so I became an "employee."...I was slated to study at the Arbeiter-und-Bauern-Fakultät ["Workers and Farmers" technical high school] in 1949, on the condition that I join the FDJ. Since I had previously been required to join the Hitler Youth and knew that kind of system, I had promised myself that I would never join a political party after the war. I would gladly have attended that school, but not if I had to join a party. So someone decided to transfer me into an office of the FDJ, where a former colleague had been given a supervisory position....I could not prevent that transfer....On my first day on the job, my boss said, "You won't be here very long, you will soon be sent to advanced schooling. But first you will join the FDJ."

On that same evening, my district president called me to an interview and asked if I was prepared to go on a mission. That was an answer to my prayers.... I gave a three-month notice and was free in May to go on a mission. (1991)

Milestones in His Life

May 23, 1950: Called as a missionary, he served in Bernburg, later as branch president in Gotha and as president of the Thuringia District.

June 24, 1952: Became a counselor to the mission president, with responsibility for the mission's activities in the GDR. His responsibility increased after the Berlin Wall was built.

June 14, 1969: Appointed president of the new Dresden Mission.

March/April 1972: Attended General Conference in Utah for the first time.

June 3, 1984: Called as president of the Freiberg Temple and released as mission president, after all members were organized into two stakes; served simultaneously as president of the Church in the GDR until 1990.

August 31, 1991: Honorably released as temple president.

Personal Descriptions of President Burkhardt

The following statements from President Thomas S. Monson are quoted from his book, *Faith Rewarded*:

June 14, 1969: At the chapel [in Dresden], we met with Henry Burkhardt, one of the most faithful Latter-day Saints I have ever met. Truly the Lord has raised him up to help provide for the Saints in East Germany.

October 24, 1970: We met with Henry Burkhardt, our president of the Dresden Mission. The meeting was held in our automobile so that no listening devices could record our conversation. It was a privilege to meet with this giant of the Lord who goes forward in directing our affairs behind the Iron Curtain without regard to any consequence to himself or his family.... As Brother Burkhardt walked from our car out into the rainy night, I could not help but realize that the day of sacrifice is not over and that there serve in the Church today men equally as dynamic and spiritually powerful as in any dispensation.

April 27, 1975: We know of no man of greater faith in Thy kingdom. And for a man to serve as he has served has required the support of a devoted companion. (Prayer at the dedication of the land of East Germany)

November 27, 1984: Henry and Inge Burkhardt...are truly persons without guile and totally dedicated to the work of the Lord.

Joel Tate, president of the Berlin Mission, described Henry Burkhardt after meeting with him for the first time on May 12, 1963, in East Berlin:

> As we sat and talked to President Burkhardt, we felt as if we had gone back into the New Testament times. We were reminded of Paul as President Burkhardt told us of his travels among the Saints to help and strengthen them and to hold them together. We feel that the Lord has raised up a man in President Burkhardt who is willing and ready to sacrifice greatly for the building up of the Church and Kingdom.
>
> The following incident will indicate President Burkhardt's sensitivity to the affairs of the Church in East Germany. [A district leader] played some music on a record player during the service. The music was not exactly fitted to a sacrament meeting. After the meeting, President Burkhardt spoke to me and said that he didn't like that type of music during a sacrament meeting. He asked me what I thought about it, and I replied that I didn't like it. He said he would mention it to the brethren. (LR 691 2)

Descriptions of Henry Burkhardt as a young mission counselor by then Elder Spencer W. Kimball are found in Chapter 5.

Gottfried Richter, a convert to the Church, served under President Burkhardt in several capacities, including as a counselor in the mission presidency. He and his wife, Gertraude, provided the following description of Henry Burkhardt:

> Brother Burkhardt attracted my attention in one of the first meetings of the Church that I attended. This twenty-year-old spoke in a sacrament meeting in Chemnitz upon his departure as a full-time missionary. He preached earnestly, just as I heard him do in the following decades. A sense of responsibility and seriousness were his basic characteristics, but they did not exclude humor. He enjoyed a laugh and could also react mischievously or with a wink. The cause of his laughter, however, was never inappropriate.
>
> I think that the main reason for his growth in responsibility was his faith, for him a very significant type of learning, which he availed himself of regularly. He also had to make many decisions "alone," early in life, despite many good colleagues. He was the designated leader of the Church in the former GDR, often under dangerous circumstances.

There were serious, unique experiences for the Church in a state in which atheism had been elevated to official doctrine. Especially noteworthy was his reserved, polite style, with which he gradually won the confidence of others and became known among the political decision makers of the land as being trustworthy.

He often was confronted by the restrictions of this system, but he always tried to avoid turning restrictions into battle lines. All with whom he associated knew him to be extremely controlled. He knew to "wait for his hour." That was especially valuable in his dealings with the power centers of the state. And in so doing, he was careful to remain in accord with the teachings of the Church. There was no apostasy. The unity of the members of the Church in the GDR is the reason for the good condition of the wards and branches at the time of the 1990 Wende.

When one speaks of Henry Burkhardt, one must also speak of his wife, Inge. She always stood true, responsible, reliable, and caring by her husband's side in all situations of life. He received from her all possible support and help, thus fulfilling the expectations that the leaders of the Church had of her. He received much strength from his family. She often waited long and with concern for his return from constant travel throughout the GDR and from the mission office in Dresden.

A common highpoint of their life and service in the Lord's work was the calling of Henry Burkhardt as temple president and of his wife as temple matron. The return home of his beloved Inge in the spring of 2005 was a deep loss in his life. With her, despite problems and difficulties of that time, he had experienced much joy and the great and marvelous blessings of the Lord for this country. The work of Henry Burkhardt will not be forgotten. (2006)

Andreas Ortlieb is a member of the "younger" generation in the GDR, those who were born around the time that the Berlin Wall was built. Their teenage years were significantly influenced by the youth programs that Henry Burkhardt and his associates managed to organize despite the restrictions of the state. Ortlieb wrote the following description of President Burkhardt in 2004:

For me personally, Brother Henry Burkhardt is one of the best and most valuable men that the German people and the GDR ever had. He was an outstanding Church leader and negotiator with public officials, and he always kept the welfare of the Church in the GDR foremost in all he did. He was an approachable mission president for anyone, never distant, but open to personal communication. He is a very admirable, very just man. As a shepherd, he knew his sheep well. He always knew which sheep were troubled, why they were having problems, and where he needed to help. He was a great spiritual leader. His instructions and his interpretation of the scriptures were well worth hearing. We were always happy to hear him.

He preferred to handle differences of opinion in person, with one-on-one discussions. He was determined to make fair decisions and treated all people equally. A regular branch member, a young man or a young girl had, in his eyes, the same right to be recognized, to be protected, to be helped, and to receive the attention of the Church as every other. He was very consistent in that regard. Many branches in the GDR were very small, often consisting primarily of one or two close families and a few members who were not in one of those families. Problems arose under those conditions, and he was the one who always resolved them. It was difficult, and I give him much credit for that. It required much courage and strength, and he always had that.

He always said, "Brother, what we need is faith. Do you believe that the Church is led by God and Jesus Christ? Do you have faith in the appointed priesthood leaders? Do you believe that I could do anything contrary to the Lord's will or anything that the leadership of the Church doesn't want? I would never do that. Therefore, everything I do, even when I cannot tell you why, I do because I love God, because I love the Church, and because I carry a special responsibility for you. I think about you often, how it is going with you. And what I need from you is your trust, your support, and your love. I cannot give you reasons for everything, but I plead that you will follow my counsel and have trust. I do nothing that has not been discussed with and approved by the president of the Church." That was enough for me. I could live with that. I knew that he would never do anything that would damage the Church or that was against the will of the Church. It was clear to me, of course, that he operated under certain requirements. But he protected the branches, and we always had a life in which we could live and exercise our faith within the Church. (2004)

Appendix A Travels of the Mission Leaders 1945

After the war ended, the acting mission leaders traveled almost constantly from mid-June through mid-September 1945, finding, visiting, organizing, and helping members throughout the mission. The travelers on the first two trips were noted as Richard Ranglack, Paul Langheinrich, and Gottfried Neumann. Participants on the third trip were not named. The following reports, written by one of the travelers, unnamed, were sent to President Thomas McKay by Col. Richard Barnes, along with an English translation (CR 271 40). Langheinrich wrote later that the first trip began on bicycles because the trains were not running in the Berlin area. He said, "When you have not ridden a bike for years, that's a bit much for old bones."

The First Trip, June 16–July 6, 1945

> June 16: The brethren began with a short bicycle trip to visit members close to Berlin. We rode to Wannsee, Potsdam, and Leest and held a meeting in Leest that evening, which was attended by nine members and eleven friends. We returned to Berlin the next day and prepared for a longer trip.
>
> June 20: Riding on bicycles, we arrived late afternoon in Cottbus, after being stopped sixteen times by Russian patrols and repairing two flat tires. Held a meeting that evening in Cottbus attended by ninety-three members.
>
> June 21: Left Cottbus. Robbers stole our bikes, and a truck took us to Riesa.
>
> June 22: Traveled by train through Chemnitz to Annaberg-Buchholz.

June 23: Regained control of the meeting house that had been confiscated by the Nazi government. Held a meeting in Annaberg-Buchholz with thirty-one priesthood members.

June 24: Sunday School was held in the Jungs' home [relatives of Paul Langheinrich] in Walthersdorf. The afternoon sacrament service was held in a Methodist church.

June 25: Met in the Schaarschmidts' home in Geyersdorf with thirty-eight persons, including nine friends.

June 26: Visited in Schlettau; later in the Jungs' home with eighteen members and six friends.

June 27: Left for Zwickau, which was occupied by American troops. Managed to cross the Russian lines on foot, on the third attempt, after numerous detours in the rain.

June 28: Brother Fassmann arranged an evening meeting attended by two hundred members.

June 29: Took the bus to Planitz and then by foot twenty-four kilometers over the border again, without difficulty. From Hartenstein to Annaberg by train. Overnight in Geyersdorf.

June 30: To Chemnitz by train. Met with thirty-three priesthood holders.

July 1: Could not find a large meeting room and held Sunday School in two locations. In the afternoon, held a worship service with 318 attendees in a larger facility.

July 2: Traveled by train to Dresden. Met with ninety-seven people that evening.

July 3: Left for Cottbus. Spent the night in a refugee facility en route.

July 4: Walked ten of the last thirty-eight kilometers to Cottbus. Met with eighty-four people.

July 5: Obtained bicycles and rode to Neu Zauche.

July 6: Rode bicycles the last ninety-seven kilometers to Berlin. Had one flat tire.

The Second Trip, July 11–August 5, 1945

July 11: Traveled by train to Wittenberg. Spent the night in an air raid shelter.

July 12: Traveled by train to Falkenberg. Due to destroyed tracks, rode in trucks to Riesa and Döbeln. Spent the night on the floor of the train station.

July 13: Traveled by train to Chemnitz and visited members. Gottried Neumann was sent on assignment to Zwickau; Ranglack and Langheinrich traveled to Geyersdorf.

July 14: We discussed the food situation with Bro. & Sis. Seifert, who own a large farm, and received a report from Fritz Lehnig and Walter Krause, who had been sent from Cottbus to consider setting up another refugee facility in Walthersdorf.

July 15: Met in a Methodist church in Walthersdorf with 205 members and 27 friends. The evening service was attended by 184. Later, Ranglack and Langheinrich instructed 38 priesthood members and met with Fassmann, Lehnig, and Krause.

July 16: Preparations were made to transfer thirty-one refugees (who had no ration cards) to Cottbus where more food was available. They were divided into groups of ten, with a leader for each group. Sister Ruth Birth was in charge of the transportation. They all left early the next morning.

July 18: Returned to Walthersdorf to explore options to establish a refugee camp there and to locate more food. Later, traveled to Zwickau and met with Gottfried Neumann.

July 19: Went to Steinpleis to open a branch there. Had a meeting with fifty-three members and twenty-nine friends.

July 20: We tried to cross the border again to meet with the American army. We had identification papers and arm bands, which showed that we belonged to the Church of Jesus Christ with headquarters in the U.S.A., and were able to get through the first three lines. At the fourth line we were turned back to get permission from the commandant of Plauen. Instead, we bypassed that line and reached the last post just before dark. There, we slept on straw in a barn.

July 21: We hoped to clear the last post in the morning but were stopped, searched for weapons, robbed, sent to the local commander, and turned back. Our return trip was very difficult. We arrived in Plauen late and spent the night with a member.

July 22: Attended Sunday meetings in Plauen. Then we traveled to Ruppertsgrün where we met several members for the first time and talked until late in the night.

July 23: We traveled to Zwickau, bought a hundred pounds of salt, and took it to Annaberg.

July 25: In Geyersdorf, we learned that the property of the Seiferts had been recognized by the commandant as American property. Its produce, above that which had to be turned over to the government by law, could be given to our members. The slaughter of an ox and a pig was authorized.

July 26: Ranglack and Langheinrich traveled to Döbeln, where the branch president was the chief dairy man on a farm, to discuss available food sources. Held a meeting that evening in an open field with twenty-three members and three friends.

July 27: It took twelve hours to travel from Döbeln back to Annaberg, where we learned about trouble in Drehbach.

July 28: The Evangelical minister in Drehbach threatened the inhabitants against visiting the LDS Church. Nevertheless, we had a small meeting with seven persons.

July 29: Held meetings for the first time in the newly renovated rooms in the Willertstr. building that had been confiscated during the war, which we had regained in June.

July 30: Documents were presented to the Evangelical superintendent of the church in Drehbach in an effort to resolve the hostility there. We received no promises and will write to the Russian commander. We decided to send two missionaries to Drehbach and made preparations to slaughter an ox, a pig, and a calf.

July 31: An ox of sixteen and a half hundredweight [1,650 pounds] was slaughtered, but the council prevented us from taking it. We immediately contacted the Russians, and they allowed us to take it. That evening, the Geyersdorf mayor claimed to have authority from the Russians to seize the meat, and he confiscated it. We protested, and the next day, the mayor and council were reprimanded by the Russian commandant. Every member received two pounds of meat from the ox and some bones. Children and the sick received some calf meat.

Alice Wagner Flade: The meat came to our house, and the word spread throughout the members. They came to pick up their portion. . . . That night, my mother and I were in our kitchen when the mayor came with two policemen. They said, "We were told there was an ox butchered." I said that was true, but with the okay of the Russian commandant. He said, "No, no, no. I have to speak to those men." I looked outside and there were more police out there. They talked to my dad and to the mission president and our branch president. My dad said, "I have the papers." They said, "We can't go by that. This is our village and I'm the mayor. I can't let you get meat and our people have nothing." They took the remaining meat. It was all taken back to the slaughterhouse. The next morning, my father went to the Russian commander and told him about it. He was upset and gave my father another paper and said, "Go and show the mayor. Get that meat back for your people." Two days later they had to release the meat. It all came back to our house. But the news went through the village like wildfire. Everyone said, "Do you know what the Mormons did?" My father's own brother and sister, who were not members, didn't even want to talk to him because he helped the members. (1991)

August 1: The distribution of the meat continued. All members received a portion.

August 5: We left Annaberg early in the morning and arrived in Dresden the following afternoon. During the next stage from Dresden to Berlin, the train was attacked by bands of robbers who stole baggage and violated women. Our trip of twenty-five days, in which the Lord helped us, was successful. With the work of the brethren, the inadequate food supply in Annaberg was partially resolved.

The Third Trip, September 18–24, 1945

September 18: We left on Tuesday in a small truck, carrying a large cooking kettle for camp "Waldfrieden" in Wolfsgrün/Erzgebirge. Two hours later we had a flat tire, followed by four more. When darkness came, we were forced to overnight on straw at a farm in Kemberg, not far past Wittenberg. The next morning, we proceeded with hope for better luck than yesterday. Unfortunately, the necessary repairs took so much time that we decided in late morning to continue via train through Leipzig to Zwickau, where we stayed overnight with a member.

September 20: Arrived at nine a.m. in Wolfsgrün/Erzgebirge. As we saw Waldfrieden from a distance, its appearance promised more pleasant surprises. We viewed all the rooms with great enthusiasm, from the basement to the attic, as well as the smaller building, the beautiful park, and the meadow. Our joy and thankfulness were indescribably great. The Lord's blessings had been poured out upon the brothers who had been able to obtain this home for the members. After a good meal and discussions with various leaders, we traveled on to Annaberg, where we held meetings with the leaders.

September 21: We traveled back to Zwickau, where we met with local officials responsible for the welfare assistance needed by the members.

September 22: We arrived in Dresden early Saturday morning and make preparations for a district conference. The brethren had reserved a good meeting room in the Evangelical church at Martin Luther Platz 5. Long before the first meeting, enthusiastic members arrived from outlying branches with great expectations and joy and greeted each other with tear-filled eyes.

September 23: All Sunday meetings went well and we traveled overnight via Cottbus to Berlin. The trip and the conference showed us again that the members need assistance to protect them under miserable conditions. We were often able to see the hand of the Lord and his guidance and are extraordinarily thankful to be engaged in the work of the Lord at this time. The mission MIA leaders were able to meet with the youth and inspired them to set new goals and plans for the coming year.

A Trip to Schwerin, January 1946

January 26: Mission leader Richard Ranglack and missionaries Helga Birth and Walter Böhme traveled to Schwerin. Seats were hard to find, the train was not heated, all window glass was missing, and the temperature was between three and nine degrees Centigrade [thirty-seven to forty-eight degrees Fahrenheit]. We reached our goal, traveling 208 kilometers [129 miles] in ten and a half hours.

January 27: The organization of the branch took place at ten a.m. in the music room of the Volkszeitung [newspaper]. The branch has twenty-three recorded members: three Elders, one male member without the priesthood, seventeen female members, and two children. Missionary Gustav Pollesche was called as branch president. Twenty-four persons attended. A special meeting was held at two p.m., attended by twelve members and twenty-six friends. Four copies of the

Book of Mormon and one copy of the Pearl of Great Price were sold, and tracts were distributed.

January 28: We traveled back to Berlin with the same train under the same conditions. (Copy from Klaus-Peter Kretzschmar)

Appendix B Two Refugee Centers 1945–1947

Manfred Henkel: I lived in both facilities, Cottbus and Wolfsgrün, between my eleventh and thirteenth years. They were a tremendous accomplishment of self-initiative and inspiration. They provided protection and support for members in that unstable time, were a refuge for widows and orphans, and gave the younger generation direction and goals for the future. Many members who had been separated during the war found one another again and made common plans for their life after the camp. The total number of people who lived there was far greater than the maximum occupancy at any specific time. (2006)

August 7, 1945: About 150 members are living together in the meeting house in Cottbus, because they cannot return to their homeland and cannot receive ration cards elsewhere. (Paul Langheinrich, CR 271 40)

September 8–9, 1945: A total of 136 members were living in the meeting house in Cottbus at the time of the district conference, including ten elders, two priests, one teacher, seven deacons, one male member, 60 female members, 27 male children under age eight, and 28 female children under eight. Of the 136 members, 67 had no ration cards and were supported with food obtained through other means. (Paul Langheinrich, CR 271 40)

Arnold Schmidt: We had 68 members in the Wolfsgrün home during Christmas 1945, and the most at any one time was 99 members. (MS 14466)

December 13, 1945: You are hereby forbidden to remove the 85 occupants living in the home in Wolfsgrün. (SMAD to local officials in Schwarzenberg, MS 5382 1)

The Cottbus Refugee Center

Joachim Lehnig: The building was once a restaurant with the well-known name of "Zum grauen Affen" [At the Gray Monkey]. Later, it was used as a storage facility for old rags, paper, bones, etc., that people collected, so you can imagine that its appearance was not especially nice. Fortunately, Brother Fritz Lehnig could see beyond the present. The mission president who visited the building and smelled it said, "No, Brother Lehnig, we cannot use that for the Church." That must have been about 1936. But Brother Lehnig held firm to his vision. He called a young carpenter in Frankfurt/Oder, Brother Walter Krause, who came and looked over the building. He also must have been inspired, for he saw how the building could be renovated. And it was renovated by the brothers from Cottbus, Forst, and other branches and occupied in 1937. Since the Church wouldn't take it over, my father leased the entire property and used the upper floor for the Church. It consisted of a large room, a smaller room with a stage, and some classrooms. The lower floor was our apartment, i.e., for Fritz Lehnig and his family. I grew up in that house.

That house was important for the Spreewald District, because all district conferences were held there, as well as activities such as the Gold and Green Ball. On the front of the meeting house was a balustrade on which a very large wooden sign was mounted. It said, "The Church of Jesus Christ of Latter-day Saints." It was very visible. I know that in the Nazi period, Brother Lehnig had trouble because of the sign. The police or the political party wanted him to take it down. But Father Lehnig had said that he would rather go to prison than take it down. I understand that he told the police, "You know, we had just been considering whether to light the sign so it could be seen at night."

Wartime was, of course, very bad. All the young men, as well as those of middle age, were drafted. In the branch, we only had just a couple of older brothers or very young boys who were not yet old enough for the army. In 1945, the front came closer and closer. Forst was evacuated. The huge air raid on Dresden took place on February 13, 1945, and the same on Cottbus two days later. That event and the approaching front caused Brother Lehnig to consider what should be done. What would happen to the families, the women and children, when the Russian Army arrived? Earlier, he had said that it would be important for the members to come together, to survive those times together. At the end of April, the members of the branches in Forst, Guben, and Frankfurt/Oder were asked to come to Cottbus. Not all the members followed that instruction, but many did. Sister Czerny had connections to a farm in the village of Stradow by Vetschau. Brother Lehnig first gathered all the members in Cottbus and drove them to Stradow with a small truck, with two seats in the front and a flatbed in the rear. We experienced the arrival of the Russians from that location. Of course, they immediately confiscated our vehicle.

The question later was, where should we go? We had no information at that time, no radio, no telephone connection, but we knew that the Americans were to our west. It was Brother Lehnig's goal to take the group to the Americans. But where were they? No one knew. And how should we transport the members and their baggage? Brother Lehnig went to the commander of the Russians in the village and requested horses and wagons. Can you imagine what that meant at that time? The Russians themselves had come with horses and wagons. Of course they had trucks, too, but they would not give up any of them. Brother Lehnig had a missionary certificate, issued on December 10, 1929, signed by Heber J. Grant, Anthony W. Ivins, and Charles W. Nibley. He went to the Russians with that document. He certainly was not dumb about such things. He was a salesman and very experienced in dealing with people, but I think he was inspired to do what he did. He made it very clear to those people that we belonged to a church headquartered in America. He was given horses and two wagons, which was unheard of at that time.

We left the village of Stradow very heavily loaded. I estimate there were fifty to eighty people, including children. All young women and all young girls were made to appear old. Many smeared dirt on their face. All wore headscarves, so they couldn't be easily recognized. We arrived at a crossroads at Vetschau. From Vetschau you could go toward Cottbus, toward Lübbenau and Berlin, or toward Calau and westward. Our goal was to go westward, to meet the American troops somewhere. A Russian woman controlled the traffic at that crossroads. We wanted to go straight ahead toward Calau, but she didn't permit that. She constantly directed us toward Cottbus. I don't know how often Brother Lehnig tried to change her mind, without success. She pointed toward Cottbus, and allowed no alternative. We had no choice. I sat up front, next to Brother Lehnig. I was ten years old and very interested in what was happening.

We arrived in Cottbus late at night and couldn't enter the city itself. We stopped at Sister Annemarie Grünewald's house. An incident took place there because Russian soldiers came.... Afterward, we all left immediately and went to a nearby cemetery where we stayed overnight. The next day, most of the group went to the meeting house in the Lausitzer Straße.

All of the members were able to stay in the meeting house. How was that possible? It was the result of the war. It was obvious that the Germans would have to leave the eastern provinces, East and West Prussia, Pomerania, and Silesia. The government had sought out available sites in many cities, including Cottbus, where temporary facilities could be erected, where people could stay overnight before being transported elsewhere. So the large meeting room had been confiscated, without opposition by the Church, because it was necessary. Wooden beds with blankets and straw mattresses were set up in the room. Additional toilets as well as washing and cooking facilities were also built in. Previously, the building had only one toilet. Two windows were also placed in the wall of the large room, which earlier would not have been permitted. That happened in early 1945. With those changes, the large room now had daylight, and all of the members who came out of Stradow could live in the meeting house. That was very important, because so many apartments had been destroyed, and many members had nowhere else to live. Downstairs in our apartment, my brother and I gave up our room to another family, and we slept above with the youth. Other rooms below were also given to families, except for one that Brother Lehnig kept for his family.

We in the meeting house had little contact with the Russians. Once in a while they came by to inspect. Plans were made for those instances. Someone kept watch and signaled if they were coming. The sisters would once again make themselves look old and went into the cellar, which was very deep and separated from the other basement rooms. You could only enter if you bent over. The young boys would then move a closet in front of the opening. The sisters went there often.

But the people had to be fed. How was that possible? That had to be considered by the leaders who had assembled the members, then where could food be found in 1945? There was nothing. Of course, Brother Lehnig's 1929 missionary certificate again played a significant role. He went to the commanding officer and was given an ox! And milk for the children. You cannot imagine today what that meant then. A great woman, Sister Annemarie Grünewald, was the chief cook. She organized everything, and it was not easy. But there were plenty of women and everyone helped. The washroom in the basement was converted into a large kitchen. Food was cooked for everyone in what used to be the wash kettle. The meals actually tasted very good. My mother had preserved fruit and vegetables and set aside oil and butterfat during the war. We had often asked her to give us some, but no, she had always set it aside, and in the end, it benefited everyone.

The meeting house had not been plundered, neither from the Russians nor from other Germans, because after the fall of the city, no one went out on the street. So that was the inspiration of the Russian woman at the crossroads in Vetschau who wouldn't allow us to proceed toward Calau. If we had gone to Calau, we would not have known where to go next. What would have happened then? So we actually had this center, where the people could find each other and live together. Nothing had been destroyed or plundered. The only things missing were my father's accordion and a leather coat.

When my father moved to Cottbus in 1937, he had been a textile salesman, but he also took over a small business in a village. It was a wholesale vegetable concern, actually an unfamiliar business for him. But he said that a German salesman ought to be able to sell anything. He built up a good business with a rather high level of sales. But more important, he developed a good relationship with the farmers in the villages of the Spreewald region, because he bought all their produce and sold it in cities throughout Germany. After 1945, he also established a weaving facility so that he could produce something. He traded knitted goods for fruit and vegetables and maintained his relationships with the farmers.

Of course, there had to be strict rules when more than a hundred people, at times 150 to 200, lived in one house. Rules were necessary. Naturally, that didn't please everyone, but Brother Lehnig was tough enough to pull it off, since it benefited everyone. We began every morning with a devotional meeting and prayer. Then everyone received work assignments. Some went out to regular jobs, while others sought out work in the city. After work, everyone assembled in the house for a common evening meal. I will never forget the indescribably fine home evenings, which we held once each week. All the families gathered together to sing songs and have fun. The wonderful Sunday Schools and other meetings were impressive. They were enlivened by the brothers and sisters who came from different regions, from Königsberg, Silesia, Breslau, Liegnitz, Landsberg, and elsewhere. Many moved on after a short stay, but many remained, so that the branch became rather large.

There were many illnesses after the war, and typhoid broke out in our group. No doctor could be called because that would result in the entire building being quarantined. What should be done? I'll never forget it. The elders went from bed to bed and gave each sick person a blessing. They were not immediately healed, but all became healthy and none died. Unfortunately, some members who lived outside the building did die from typhus, but not many. For me, as a young man, that was a testimony. I experienced it, I saw it.

Brother Lehnig's experience with his missionary authorization gave him other ideas. He knew that it impressed the Russians. Documents with many signatures and stamps always impressed them, even if they couldn't read. In the first weeks after the war, he also mounted a sign above the door that said "American Property," and he raised an American flag. Naturally, everyone in the neighborhood was amazed, and they wondered what it meant. It kept the Russians from bothering us. (2004)

Herbert Grünewald: An active, intensive branch life began to develop. In fact, the entire life of the members, whether they lived inside or outside the meeting house, was filled by the Church. In addition to the Sunday meetings (teacher training or leadership meetings at nine o'clock, Sunday School at ten, followed by children's choir practice, interviews and lunch, six o'clock choir practice and sacrament meeting at seven), Primary, Relief Society, Mutual, and priesthood meetings were held during the week.

Work assignments within the building took up much of the remaining free time. Construction, reconstruction, and the cleaning and heating of the meeting house were constant and time-consuming responsibilities of the priesthood. It was understood that each person devoted their talents and abilities to the needs of the branch. Craftsman skills were especially important and masons, painters, carpenters, glaziers, locksmiths, shoemakers, upholsterers, and tailors were represented. The sisters focused on food, nutrition, and clothing. They cooked under the expert direction of Sister Grünewald and created tasty or at least enjoyable meals with simple ingredients. The meeting house was simply the center of life. Even medical care and immunizations were carried out there and not in the city's facilities.

But life was more than just prayer and work. Free time activities were within the domain of the branch. To seek fun outside the Church was not only frowned upon, but it was also not necessary. Dances were held frequently, in addition to theatrical performances, ballad, operetta, and folk song evenings, and also sport activities. Special events included spring, fall, Christmas and New Year festivals, Pioneer celebrations, and bazaars. Erwin Gröschke and his orchestra often played at dances. With his help, the musical life of the branch blossomed. The musical group that he formed and led was known through the East German Mission. All in all, an extensive and varied cultural life was nurtured.

The Mormon Pioneers served as the great example for this type of community life. People spoke often about them, and the effort to follow them and to incorporate their ideals gave meaning and significance to life at that time. Pioneer celebrations were, therefore, always special events. What held the members strongly together was a common expectation that, following the terrible catastrophe of World War II, the time must be soon at hand when the call would come to gather to Zion.

The refugee facility was gradually dissolved between 1946 and 1948, and life slowly returned to normal. Hard times remained, and everyone still had to struggle to survive. Nevertheless, the willingness to take in others as guests, to share with them the little they had, went without saying among most members, even when the small amount of food that could be obtained with ration cards was further reduced. Members who were driven out of the eastern regions were always willingly received, fed, and housed.

Was this to some degree a paradisiacal condition? At the end, had this become the "good old times"? No. This period had its special requirements, its ideals, but also its unique problems. The talks given in the sacrament meetings of that time not only encouraged members to remain active and enthusiastic, to work to strengthen the community, but also warned against gossiping, resentment, jealousy, and envy. Those themes were also evident in the songs that were often sung in those days. "Come, come ye Saints" was a staple of the time. Songs like "Put your shoulder to the wheel," "We are all enlisted 'til the conflict is o'er," and "School thy feelings, brother" were also sung often. The intense, often too familiar atmosphere, against a background of unresolved war losses, led to a life filled with conflicts that became especially evident when the Church's first welfare shipments arrived and had to be distributed. In addition to sincere thankfulness for the food and clothing, there appeared, mostly among the weakest members of the branch, a feeling of being discriminated against. The unique circumstance of that time required significant work, willingness to sacrifice, satisfaction with a simple life, patience, understanding, and forgiveness, which were not always forthcoming. It was the same as in normal life. Happiness and sorrow, love and hate, plus conflicts that occur whenever people live and work together in tight circumstances, were present and added spice to community life.

The first welfare shipment was received in 1947. This alleviated hunger and allowed the members of the Church to be among the best clothed people of that time. While many still continued to see their meals as monotonously one-sided, many tasty items were nevertheless received, for example, the peach preserves, which some still remember with pleasure. The clothing, in fact, even led to a little vanity, accompanied at times with envy and resentment. Many joined the Church at this time, some known as "Büchsenmormonen" [literally "Can Mormons"], because many turned their backs on the Church as soon as the welfare shipments ended. The branch grew significantly, although Cottbus was just a transfer station for many who moved on further westward. Brother Fritz Lehnig held everything together with a strong hand. There were rules and a strictness that cannot be imagined under today's circumstances.

Humor and time for conversation were important. It had to be part of every activity. The semiannual conferences, which usually lasted three days, always included a fun social activity. The members simply took time for that. The life of the individual members was determined by the rhythms of the Church, which provided a strong separation from the rest of the world. That was the uniqueness of that time. (Excerpts from Herbert Grünewald, "Cottbus, eine Zeit intensiven Gemeindelebens" 2000)

Walter Krause: In early July 1945, I was called to lead the Cottbus branch. [Fritz Lehnig had become the district president.] One day, two Soviet officers asked me to accompany them. I was taken to a glass factory near Peitz and given glass to install in windows in a building they controlled. Brother Werner Birth and I soon completed the job and received food in return. When we didn't return, the Russians asked us why. I said that we had enough work to do for our members. They accepted that, but said we should instead install glass in the roof of a mill, which extracted oil from linseed.

A funny story happened at that mill. A Soviet guard was stationed there to protect against theft. Oil (fat) was especially valuable, along with bread and potatoes. Many people gave away their wedding rings and other valuables for such things. As we replaced the windows on the roof, we could look down into the mill, and the smell of the oil rose up to us. We considered how we could obtain some of it. We had security ropes, and when we noticed that the guard left for lunch, Brother Birth lowered himself down with the rope, filled a container with oil, and quickly returned. With pure greed, we drank the entire warm oil. The result was sweeping. Everyone can imagine what I mean. On the next day, we worked again on the roof. This time we brought a large empty bottle. We waited again until the guard left and quickly filled the bottle. This time, however, we took our prize home to the camp. It was a great help for the sisters who cooked for everyone. Turnips, carrots, cabbage, peas, and everything else we found thereafter tasted much better with the oil and was more nutritious. (Copy from Edith Krause to Joachim Lehnig, 2002)

The Wolfsgrün Refugee Camp

Paul Langheinrich: I needed a house for our refugees and knew where to find one. The Nazis had renovated the villa of a deceased millionaire into a home for new mothers. Every room had beds and wash basins. I knew that because my sister-in-law had been employed by that millionaire. (MS 5382 1, ca. 1953)

Arnold Schmidt: Toward the end of August 1945, I and my wife were called by the mission leaders to lead the Mormon home in Wolfsgrün. [Schmidt had been the branch president in Kreuz and district president of Schneidemühl in West Prussia before fleeing from the Russian army at the end of January 1945.] The calling was totally unexpected, and we considered ourselves too weak to carry out this assignment. But we accepted, since we believed that when God gives his servants a calling, he also gives the wisdom and ability to accomplish that calling, when we are humble. The purpose of the Mormon home was to provide a home and food for members who had become homeless due to the war and couldn't find accommodations elsewhere, until they could find housing elsewhere. The leader of the mission welfare program was Brother Paul Langheinrich.

I wish to describe how the Church came to this beautiful villa. Brother Langheinrich, Max Jeske of the mission leadership, and I went together in late August 1945 to the mayor of Wolfsgrün, in order to obtain an empty former Nazi home for mothers. The mayor was not opposed to the plan, if the Russian commander in Eibenstock gave his written permission. As we went through the forest to Eibenstock, we joined in prayer to ask for the Lord's blessing. The Lord was merciful and heard our prayer. Brother Langheinrich gave the Russian commander a petition to use the villa for the homeless refugees of the Church of Jesus Christ of Latter-day Saints, and he soon had the written permission in his hand. On the afternoon of the same day, all formalities were completed with the local representatives. The villa was now available for the homeless refugees of the Church.

The villa itself was like a small palace built on a rise with a large park and a pond. It was surrounded by hills and forest. Upon entering the main door, you came into a large reception room with several adjacent large rooms, which we used as workrooms, plus a very large dining hall. The bedrooms on the next two floors accommodated ninety-nine people. The area known as Wolfsgrün belonged to the town of Blauenthal, about fifteen kilometers from the county seat of Aue. It lay in a beautiful valley in the middle of the Erzgebirge and included a railroad station. We named the villa "Waldfrieden" [peaceful forest] since it was actually a place of peace for the homeless members.

My wife and I entered that home on September 3, 1945, and began immediately to clean and prepare it for occupancy. Sister Fassmann and another sister from Zwickau assisted us. We purchased bunk beds and straw mattresses from the town of Wolfsgrün. Since some feather beds were also in the home, we could provide one to every elderly and sick member. The first members arrived within a few days, followed by one group after another. There was an active coming and going. Some members remained only a short time before moving on to relatives. Others, without relatives, remained in the home until they found other accommodations. At Christmas 1945, we had sixty-eight members and the highest count at one time was ninety-nine.

What was the condition of the members when they arrived? Almost all of them were completely exhausted, worn out, and sick, having a long flight and terrible experiences behind them. They came out of the provinces of East and West Prussia, Pomerania, and Silesia and had often traveled long distances by foot to reach a train. They were often robbed of all they had along the way. Whoever had a good coat or dress or boots were stripped of such items. How thankful and happy they were to reach this home in Wolfsgrün, where they could finally wash and bathe themselves, receive food and drink, and be relieved of many of their worries. Their thankfulness was often expressed in the monthly testimony meetings.

After a few weeks in the home, during the fall district conference in Chemnitz, I was called by the mission president, Richard Ranglack, to be the president of the new Erzgebirge district. I remained in that calling until I fled from the Soviet Zone on July 20, 1952.

The feeding of the members was a special problem in Wolfsgrün. Although we had permission from the Russian commander to live in this beautiful home, German officials, especially Saxony's provincial magistrate, opposed us. They refused to issue ration cards, in order to starve us, in the belief that we would then be forced to leave. So we had to support ourselves with purchases on the free market. That was especially difficult in the winter of 1945–1946, since the German economy had completely collapsed. Most farmers who had something to sell held onto it because the money had no value. It was very difficult to obtain anything, and it was difficult for my wife to prepare daily meals for the many members. At first, she traveled once or twice a week to Meerane (seventy kilometers to the north), to obtain food [that the Schmidts had grown and stored there during the summer before being sent to Wolfsgrün]. We don't know what would have happened in those first weeks, when we had nothing, if we had not [followed the impressions we had received earlier] to store what we produced. We see that the ways of the Lord are wonderful. Although we had not anticipated our later calling, the Lord had blessed us with a large harvest, which we could use later. We used our stored wheat in soups, and traded some for bread. Brother Martin Wagner from Annaberg provided a large part of our food. He went daily from house to house to buy potatoes, meat, and vegetables. We have him to thank that we had many carrots, which enabled us to survive during the winter of 1945–1946.

Once, his wife bought two pigs under difficult circumstances, and we were all delighted to obtain some meat. But when the pigs were slaughtered, the criminal police came from Zwickau and confiscated the meat. My wife managed to quickly put aside a large pot of rendered fat, which we were able to use in preparing our meals for many weeks. Although we had the right to purchase meat on the open market, we still had great difficulty with the local offices. It remains a wonder for us today, how it was possible for a cup of quark [a soft curd or yogurt-type cheese] to be used by forty people for such a long time.

In order to still our hunger, we went into the woods to collect mushrooms and berries. We collected stinging nettle for our soup. . . . In the winter of 1945–1946, carrots were our main dish, prepared in different ways. Although we grew tired of them, they saved us from starvation. Our meals that winter were unvaried and without much fat.

When our supply of meat and fat was totally exhausted, and we didn't know what we should cook the next day, a wonder took place. We were awakened from sleep at night, and the mission leadership arrived with a car and brought us what we needed. We were all very delighted over this rare, high-ranking visit and very thankful for the help. We saw once more that when the need is the greatest, God is the nearest. Since the purchase of food with the worthless money had become very difficult, we made slippers and house shoes from leftover material, which my wife exchanged with farmers for food. We were able, in that way, to obtain vegetables and fruit, which my wife and Sister Hedwig Wolf carried back home long distances in hundred-pound sacks on their backs. Sister Wolf was a great help. She was always willing and ready.

It appeared that Christmas 1945 would be cheerless for us. We only had some rye bran with which to bake cookies. A few days before Christmas, my wife again went shopping to Meerane. Her sister, Magdalena, worked in a store and had often helped us. This time she had obtained sixty pounds of spoiled wheat flour, which was not useable for cooking and should be sold as animal feed. My wife bought it and was able to bake a nice Christmas cake for everyone. The smell of the flour had totally disappeared as a result of the baking process, so it was possible to set a nice Christmas table.

Special recognition for their help should be given to Brother and Sister Surmann, who had a food store in Steinpleis by Zwickau. They often brought us sugar, cookies, noodles, artificial honey, candy for the children, candles, and many other things. Brothers E. Eichler, W. Horn, and W. Jonischus also distinguished themselves by finding food for us.

Beginning in February 1946, we received ration cards and our nutritional status improved thereafter. Later, when the Church's welfare shipments arrived, our greatest needs were met. That spring we dug up the large grassy area of the park with great effort, since we had almost no shovels and the ground was rocky. We planted potatoes and vegetables. The Lord blessed our efforts, and we achieved a good harvest. Brother Wilhelm Lawrence and his wife took charge of that project.

Obtaining food was made more difficult because the Russians made most of the Erzgebirge into a restricted zone, due to their search for uranium ore. No one and no vehicle could enter that zone without a special permit from the Russian headquarters over that area. Everyone who traveled by train into this area was controlled, all roads were blocked, and every vehicle was searched. When I mentioned earlier that the mission leadership came unexpectedly during the night and brought us food, they had put themselves at risk of arrest because they took many detours in the darkness to avoid the control points. I mention that to show how difficult the food situation was.

Once, in the spring of 1946, my wife told me that we had no more potatoes and she didn't know what to do. I told her that the Lord knows and will help us at the right time. We had tried, without success, to buy potatoes. The next morning at eight o'clock, we had an unusual visit. The mayor came and said, "I have heard that you must be starving." I told him, "Herr Mayor, we are not starving here but we have no potatoes at the moment." He replied, "Send someone to me and I will sell you five hundred pounds of potatoes." I must say again, when the need is the greatest, God is the closest. At that time, we were able to obtain potatoes from several sources. Who caused the mayor to come to us, since he was not otherwise friendly to us? The Lord heard our prayers, and it was he who caused the mayor to help us.

Since I, as district president, had to visit all of the branches every month and took my reports to the mission office in Berlin each month, I had many dealings with the criminal police. Because the mission office was in the American sector of Berlin, I was suspected of spying for America. I was often searched by the criminal police during my train travel to and from Berlin. They also came into and searched my living quarters. Once, upon my return from Berlin, I was questioned by the criminal police at the train station for hours.

The provincial magistrate tried every possible action to force us out of the villa, which we had received from the Russians. Since I did not follow his personal orders, he sent the head of Saxony's criminal police from Dresden between Christmas and New Year 1945. He asked me when we planned on leaving the villa. I told him that the Russians had given us this house and we had no intention of leaving it. He then told me in an excited voice, "You will see that you will leave here in five days." I just responded by saying that we had the right to live here. In that moment, someone knocked at the door and in walked Paul Langheinrich. He continued the debate with the criminal police. We did not leave in five days, but remained for almost eighteen months longer. We were there until all the members found accommodations elsewhere.

In January 1946, at a time of extreme cold, the mayor, accompanied by four policemen, came at the request of the provincial magistrate and demanded that I and all the occupants leave the house immediately, otherwise he would forcibly evict us. I told the mayor that we would not leave willingly, that he would have to remove each individual by force. When the mayor saw that he would not be successful with threats, he and the policemen left. Later, I received a written order from the provincial government in Dresden. It said, "All occupants of the Mormon refugee camp in Wolfsgrün will be taken immediately via Ölsnitz to the western zones. The mayor is authorized to provide train cars and provisions for three days." When the mayor asked when we would leave, I again told him that we would not leave the home, since we had permission to live here. On February 8, 1946, I visited the mayor and requested ration cards. He told me that we would not receive any because the provincial magistrate would not allow it, and he has the authority regarding that matter. I said, "Herr Mayor, there is 'One' who stands above you and the provincial magistrate and when 'He' wills, then we will receive the ration cards." Two days later, on February 10, 1946, the mayor asked me to meet with him, at which time he said that the provincial magistrate had called and that we were to receive ration cards immediately. There were eighty-nine members in the home at that time. Our nutritional status was greatly improved as a result of receiving ration cards. [See Chapter 2 regarding communications between Paul Langheinrich and the SMAD in Berlin-Karlshort that led to this decision.]

Wolfsgrün was a constant battle for me. I was in constant close contact with the mission leadership and had their complete support. When we were strongly pressured by the local officials and were in danger of being evicted from the home, I informed the mission leadership, and they contacted the Soviet Military Administration in Berlin. In those days, we always had the Russians on our side, although that changed later. When the provincial magistrate allowed us to receive ration cards on February 10, 1946, he did so only because he was ordered by the SMAD. In February, the Russian commander in Eibenstock, at the request of the SMAD, went to the mayor in Wolfsgrün at eleven o'clock p.m. and told him that the Mormon refugees were not to be evicted.

I dealt frequently with the local officials, especially with the commander in Eibenstock, the county commander in Aue, and with the provincial magistrate. I remember one week in particular when I traveled to those offices every day regarding the villa or the branch in Wolfsgrün. The magistrate knew the commander in Eibenstock was aware of our written permission regarding the villa, but he attempted to influence the commander to take the document from us. Long after we had occupied the villa, I was asked to see the commander, and he demanded the document from me and wouldn't return it. [It was only a copy.] I was often visited by the Russian officers, who wanted to be informed about the Church, and they were always polite toward us.

I wish to describe an event that showed that the Lord was with us. One morning I lay in my bed and thought about our very difficult circumstances. I must have closed my eyes for a moment and I saw a man sitting at my table in front of my bed. I thought it was a missionary. He said to me, "You can relax, for all will be well again." I opened my eyes and saw no one sitting at the table. It wasn't a dream, since I had not fallen back to sleep. I described this experience during our morning service, and all the members were reassured. That afternoon I received a telegram from the mission office in Berlin, which said we could remain in the home.

Now I wish to describe a little of our life in the home. In the summer, we awakened at 6:00, in the winter at 6:30. Everyone arose, made their personal preparations, and put their room in order, because one hour later we came together for our common morning service. It began with heartfelt greetings and a song, followed by a reading from the scriptures and a short talk. Then a story or a poem was presented, and when someone had a birthday, then that happy occasion was remembered and we sang the birthday child's favorite song. The service was closed with prayer. Then the day's work assignments were discussed, who had kitchen service, who was responsible for cleaning the house, for garden work, for gathering of mushrooms and berries, for hauling of firewood, etc. Then we had breakfast together before each went to his or her workplace. Work time was from 8 until 12 and 2 until 6. We ate together again at noon and again in the evening at 6:30. Our head cook at first was Sister Jonischus, and when she left us, Sister Frieda Möser took over that assignment.

The washing and ironing was done once a week, electrically. Sister Frieda Titze led that task very conscientiously. The sewing work was led by Sister Duschl. To allow all the sisters to conduct their work in peace, all the children who didn't go to school were cared for during the working hours by Sisters Hedwig Wolf and Elli Naujoks. My wife, who had been trained as a Red Cross sister, took care of first aid. Sisters who could crochet, were assigned to that work. Brother Martin Wagner from Annaberg provided us with yarn. Tablecloths were crocheted, which Brother Wagner took to sell. A nearby cardboard factory stamped out shoe insoles, which we sorted, bundled, and prepared for shipment, for pay. Our financial accounts were kept by Sister Freimann, then by Sister Marquardt, and finally by Sister Wolf. All members, except the aged and sick, were employed in some manner.

We also organized the Church. The branch president in Wolfsgrün was Brother Wilhelm Jonischus. When he left the home, I assumed that assignment. Sister Auguste Höppner was the Relief Society president. We also organized the Sunday School, Mutual, genealogy classes, and priesthood classes. The average attendance in the sacrament meetings was 90 to 95 percent. Those meeting always had a good spirit and the testimony meetings were very spiritual. . . . During my time in Wolfsgrün, we had eleven convert baptisms from the surrounding community of less than four hundred inhabitants.

While I have reported on our difficulties in our home, no one should think that we were without light and sunshine. We lived almost cut off from the world and had to stand on our own feet. We were like a large family and had many youth. It was, therefore, our assignment to help everyone rise above our sad situation through games and good discussions. In our weekly discussion evenings we engaged in wonderful fun and intellectually challenging games, common trips, sports, and theatrical plays.

There was almost always something to practice or to learn. At first we had two sister missionaries, Renate Berger and Ingrid Bendler. They contributed much to our activities during their short sojourn with us. Then my wife and Sisters Wolf, Naujoks, and Titze took the lead in planning and organizing activities. Sister Wolf had a good voice and pleased us all with beautiful songs. She was our nightingale. Even when you couldn't see her, she could be heard throughout the home. Our winter sports were wonderful. Since we didn't have any skis, we satisfied ourselves with three large sleds, which Brother Langheinrich provided. Sledding provided a lot of fun, and we laughed a lot in the process. Sister Duschl sprained her thumbs so badly that she remembered that sport for months thereafter whenever she wanted to sew. Brother Reinhard Lawrenze found a new sled run, which was so steep that the sled flew so far and so fast that it landed in a small creek. That is just one of many experiences that brought joy and hearty laughter. When then the sporting persons came into the home, they naturally were hungry and sang out in unison, "We are hungry, we are hungry, we are hungry." They cried out so long that my wife, somewhat fearfully, gave each one a slice of dry bread. That was not so simple, to give out extra bread outside of mealtimes, since every person received only one three-pound loaf of bread per week, and it was divided precisely for each meal. Each evening we received the most bread, two dry slices, and a portion of carrots, red beets, or sugar beet salad.

On one activity evening, seven fairy tales were presented. The best thereof, but also the most difficult, was the snow queen, for she had to descend about eighteen feet. We didn't have appropriate costume material. It all had to be created with great effort. As the curtain was raised, which in this case was the large sliding door, the snow queen was slowly lowered eighteen feet onto a snow-white bed on the floor, singing a bewitching song. We recognized our nightingale, Sister Hedchen Wolf, by her voice. The effect was enhanced because the audience's room was dark and the stage room was brightly lit. That was followed by the fairy tales "Hans im Glück," "Puss 'n Boots," Red Riding Hood and the Wolf," "Die Sterntaler," and "Sleeping Beauty." These had been practiced every night for four weeks. The fairy tale "The Seven Dwarfs" was not presented, rather it was implemented, because just as the seven dwarfs worked untiringly, our youth worked to prepare all these presentations. Some brought small trees out of the words, while others sawed and hammered. They built and painted everything and worked as enthusiastically as the seven dwarfs. These preparations filled the youths' free time so none were bored. These presentations were especially successful and made a good impression on the spectators. We invited friends from the town to the presentations. The deputy mayor also attended once. The friends were enthusiastic and praised the presenters. The village residents also were amazed at the harmonious life among so many people in one house. We appeared to them to be very special people.

Another wonderful celebration was a large garden festival, held in the evening, to which we invited friends. People took a walk in the dark through the large park and encountered surprises, prepared by the youth, that sprang into action when approached. The result was great fun and laughter. We also took interesting stories out of the *Stern* and reworked them into plays that we presented. Through such engaging activities, we didn't have time to complain and put up easier with the tough time, especially the winter of 1945–1946. Even the eating of much dry bread and the limited menu of available foods was not as noticeable with these diversions.

As described above, we held regular services in the home. However, we didn't have any musical instruments as Christmas 1945 approached. Through the mission office, I learned that the branch in Zwickau had an extra harmonium that we could have. But how could we bring it to Wolfsgrün? Zwickau was more than thirty kilometers away. Without a car, we had no choice but to transport the harmonium with a hand wagon, which we had. My wife walked to Zwickau with four young members and the wagon, leaving at 5:00 in the morning with good spirits and song. They intended to return by midnight. The spirit is willing, but the flesh is weak. After arriving in Zwickau, they immediately loaded the harmonium, and without stopping to eat or rest, they began the return trip. But the return was more difficult, for the loaded wagon had to be pulled uphill to Wolfsgrün. Their strength gave out, their courage sank, weariness set in, and after covering half of the return route, they could hardly proceed any further. After a joint prayer, they gained new courage to at least reach Schneeberg, where Brother and Sister Braun lived. Late in the evening, they arrived in Schneeberg and knocked on their door. The harmonium was taken inside and the five tired travelers could spend the night. First, Sister Braun kindly gave everyone something to eat and then prepared simple sleeping arrangements. Early the next morning, she also made sandwiches for everyone, and after a common morning prayer, the last ten kilometers from Schneeberg to Wolfsgrün was accomplished with new strength. The joy in the home was great, for we now had music in our services and for the approaching Christmas.

The Mormon home was only a temporary arrangement to bring together and care for those who had become homeless as a result of the terrible war. This goal was actually achieved. With this facility, the mission leadership did create a temporary home for those who had been evicted from their homeland and had saved them from want and misery. The occupants of the home were very thankful. The next important goal of the mission leadership was to find new individual living quarters for these Saints. Through these efforts, most of the members found accommodations in West Germany. The rest were accommodated within East Germany. About thirty members found living quarters in Wolfsgrün and the surrounding communities. Therefore, the Wolfsgrün branch continued after the refugee home was closed in July 1947.

Finally, we who led the home from beginning to the end wish to give our testimony. We know that the home in Wolfsgrün was a facility that provided rich blessings and assistance for many members. We know that the blessings of God were always with us, and that he inspired us in our actions. We are thankful, that God called us to fulfill this mission, and he knows that we also attempted to follow the directions of the mission leadership and to do our best. At the same time, we learned the truthfulness of the saying, "To please all people is impossible." We wrote this report according to our best ability and understanding. Should someone find a mistake therein, it was not intentional and we ask for God's forgiveness. This report was compiled and written by Brother Arnold and Sister Gertrude Schmidt. (MS 14466, Wolfsgrün: Die Geschichte eines Teiles der vertriebenen Heiligen der deutschen Ostgebiete 1945 im Mormonenheim in Erzgebirge, ca. 1955)

Appendix C Recovery of Genealogical Records 1946

Paul Langheinrich and Rudolf Pöcker wrote detailed descriptions of their activities associated with the recovery of genealogical records, which the Nazi government had stored in several remote locations during the war. Their reports were sent to Thomas E. McKay (CR 271 40). Erich Sellner also participated in that activity, and related portions of his journal (MS 9471) have been inserted into the report:

> *Langheinrich:* I had gained insight into the operation of the government's genealogical department through my own research activities and had become acquainted with some of the officials of that agency. Therefore, I knew that films had been made, [and] from 1939 to 1942, I had conducted negotiations to purchase the films for the Church. But since the films were not perforated, they couldn't be copied.... I had often told the sister missionaries that it was my goal after the war to gain possession of those films for the Church.
>
> After the collapse in 1945, my thoughts often turned to these genealogical records. On August 9, 1945, I wrote to the Soviet commanding general, Marshall Shukov, regarding the needs of the members in the East German Mission. I was driven by the Spirit to include a request for all church books, films, and photocopies and said that I wanted the film for the Genealogical Society in Utah. I wrote that these items had no value for the Soviets but were very important for us, and that the Genealogical Society was a neutral body that would preserve and make them available to everyone. On August 16, 1945, we received an answer from a Soviet officer, signed by General of the Army Sokolovsky, in which we were informed that we could search for the church books, films, and photocopies and, if found, we could treat them as our property.
>
> Because of the extremely difficult conditions, it was hard to find clues to their location. Everything was destroyed and there was no

means of transportation, etc. Although our most important assignment was to care for our members, to visit and build up the branches, and to find lodging for the refugees, it was nonetheless possible to pursue clues regarding the location of the documents. A missionary, Erich Sellner, was called to pursue these clues in Berlin. The first hints pointed toward the basement of the Jewish synagogue in Berlin, Oranienburger Straße 29. However, there was nothing at that location. We then followed other clues. Brother Sellner went to Potsdam and visited with a man who had been involved with the former genealogy agency.

Sellner: On Monday, January 28, I went to Potsdam because of the documents. While there, I had the opportunity to bear my testimony, and I learned where some of the documents were located.

Langheinrich: This man said he knew that some had been stored in a mineshaft by the Elbe and some in the Kyffhäuser region. With this information, we called a second missionary, Rudolf Pöcker, who spoke Russian. Brothers Sellner and Pöcker then traveled to the Kyffhäuser on this genealogical assignment.

Pöcker: Brother Sellner and I departed on Monday, February 4, for the Kyffhäuser and found there a woman who had previously worked for the government's genealogy agency. She informed us that many items from that agency had been stored in the Rathsfeld Castle.

Sellner: We also had a gospel discussion and left several tracts.

Pöcker: We went to the Rathsfeld Castle, which had been converted into a Soviet military hospital. To our regret, we determined that a large portion of the Jewish records had been sent to a paper factory, and others had been stored in the basement. The commanding officer of the hospital accepted the letter from General of the Army Sokolovsky as proof that these items belonged to us and said he would not permit any more records to be destroyed if we removed them within five days. In the meantime we had learned that a former major in Bad Frankenhausen likely knew more about the church books.

Sellner: It was a long way to Bad Frankenhausen. Despite the rain, we sang and prayed in the woods. We were thoroughly soaked. Then a car came by and picked us up. We thanked God in our hearts, and we were dry when we arrived in Bad Frankenhausen.

Pöcker: When we arrived there, we first found lodging in a hotel where we had opportunity to proclaim the gospel to other hotel guests. We determined that these people were very hungry for the gospel and were happy to hear such a good and simple message. We also determined that the major for whom we were searching lived in Steinthaleben, and we went there. Through these efforts and through conversation with the local pastor, we finally obtained the information we sought about the location of the church books. Everything pointed to Rothenburg Castle, and we found thousands of books when we arrived there. Unfortunately, much to our grief, we had to admit that some of those books had been used by local people as heating material. Furthermore, we determined another large portion of the books had been left exposed to snow and ice. After we took measures to prevent further destruction, we returned to Berlin to make preparations for the recovery of these books.

Langheinrich: In the meantime, I had personally learned that documents had been stored in salt mines in Stassfurt, as well as in Schönebeck on the Elbe. Since my authority only extended to taking possession of photocopies and films of the church books and the Jewish card file, whereas the above books were the original church registers, I met with the leaders of the Evangelical and Catholic churches. I informed them that the original church registers of East Prussia had been found and that I was in the process of bringing them to Berlin. After I described the entire contents of what had been found, they were all agreed that I should retain them for the present time....

I also met with the city administration to obtain space for a large genealogical library in which we could store all of the books, including those we might find in the future. Space was set aside in the former Museum of Ethnology in Berlin-Dahlem. After all this had been agreed to, and we had obtained permission to use railroad cars to transport these books, we traveled to Berga-Kelbra and directed all missionaries who were active in that region to go there.

Sellner: We were engaged in the above work of recovering these records between February 18 and 22, 1946. We also had many opportunities to bear our testimony and to sell copies of the Book of Mormon.... On Monday, February 25, we all went to Kelbra and met the other missionaries there.

Langheinrich: We were a total of eleven brothers. Although we didn't arrive until the afternoon, I took two brothers to Rothenburg, to gain a precise view of the situation.... On the following morning, Brother Sellner and Brother Kupitz were assigned to bring the vehicle we had reserved to the castle, while the rest of the brethren went there on foot to make preparations. The work proceeded well, but we waited for hours for the vehicle, which did not arrive. After a long time, Brother

Sellner came on foot and said that the vehicle was stuck on the mountain and couldn't go forward or backward because the mountain, which was fairly steep, with thirty-six sharp curves, was so icy that this method of transportation wouldn't work. I took three brothers, and we went a short distance down the mountain into the woods and prayed. Exactly in that moment when we said amen, we heard the vehicle coming up the mountain. However, the driver had left the trailer behind. He intended to turn around at the top and to go home. I succeeded in convincing him to use his vehicle, a tractor, which had a box that could carry 30 hundredweight. On this day we brought over 150 hundredweight of original church books to the valley, where we had reserved a waiting room at the train station to accommodate these books.

As four of us then discussed the situation, Brother Sellner said: "If we wish to drive up the other mountain, we will first need a warm rain." Our railroad car was due to arrive the next day, but it came two days late. We could not determine the reason for the delay, but are convinced that the Lord, once again, had intervened, for we would not have been ready at the agreed time, due to the difficult circumstances.

On the next day we actually had a warm rain, in fact during the entire day, and the mountain road was completely free of ice and snow. We worked only in the morning and rested in the afternoon. In the morning, I went with Brother Pöcker and my son Armin to the Rathsfeld Castle and agreed with the Soviet commander concerning the transport of the things stored there. On the next day we came up the mountain with one vehicle and two trailers. We placed one trailer at Rothenburg to load the remaining items and took the other to Rathsfeld Castle. We determined that we had made an extraordinarily important and valuable catch there, since we had found the Jewish church books from many countries, especially from Holland, and many things from the Jewish card file. Unfortunately, we could only load several hundred, since the vehicle was almost filled. When we reached Berga-Kelbra in the afternoon, the weather became worse as we had freezing temperatures and strong snowfall, which was so strong during the night that the mountain road was completely impassable the following morning. But no matter, we had achieved our goal! By late evening we had loaded the railroad car and the next morning at seven a.m., it left for Berlin with Brother Kupitz aboard. The missionaries returned to their branches and we returned to Berlin. Two days later, Brother Kupitz was there with the railroad car and we brought the books to our new mission home in Berlin-Dahlem. We estimate that we transported about eight to ten thousand books in this first effort.

Brother Sellner and Brother Pöcker departed for Strassfurt on Monday. They had learned that 140 cases of films of church books,

1,500 packages of photocopies of church books, 1,500 original church books, 60 cases of original books, and 30 cases of card files had been stored in the Perlebach shaft of the salt mine in Stassfurt. After confirming that information, they traveled to Schönebeck and found in the Moltke shaft 66 cases of church books. These have since been brought with great effort, with a railroad car, to Berlin. In the course of negotiations, Brother Kupitz and I were taken to a hearing in Magdeburg, where we had a discussion with high ranking Soviet officers until 1:30 a.m. and were able to inform them of the gospel. I believe we were only taken there so we could obtain something to eat on that day, for we did receive a very good meal. After we had loaded the wagon, we prayed and said, "Now, dear God, you must bring this train car to us in Berlin, because we have done our part," and we went home. The train arrived almost as soon as we did.

We then obtained the above-mentioned items from Stassfurt: 135 cases of church books from Helmershausen, 450 cases of church books from Bad Salzdetfurth, all the church books of Springen in the Rhine Province, and the church books and valuable library of Naumburg a.d. Queis. The latter is in the Polish-occupied territory and taking that material was only possible with the help of our brothers in the U.S. through the Polish ambassador in New York. Included in these church books are 7,200 films of church books from Breslau and the entire region of Silesia.

Throughout this entire project we have strongly felt the presence of the Lord with us, and that we have been tools in his hand. Although our faith was not weak earlier, it is gigantic now, and we have experienced so many wonderful events, that we now know that this is the work of the Lord!

In a letter to Major Donald Corbett, dated November 14, 1952, Paul Langheinrich added this detail to his earlier report:

When Brother Benson and Brother Bennett were here, it was decided to return the documents to their previous owners and to have microfilm copies made for the Church. Today, there are about 5,000 books in the main archive in Dahlem. In East Berlin, the German Archive for Genealogy, of which I am the founder and manager, has been established with the agreement of the occupation forces and German officials. We have 15,000 church books and 30,000 genealogical books in the former state library in East Berlin.

Appendix D Conferences 1946–1948

Despite very difficult economic and social conditions, the mission leadership organized outstanding conferences and other activities in the immediate postwar years, to which members and the public were invited via public announcements carried out with the approval and support of the Soviet occupation forces. The following descriptions are quoted directly from original sources.

District Conference in Leipzig, March 1946

The morning service was attended by 518 people, the afternoon by 800. Posters and handbills were printed with permission of the Soviet authorities to advertise the conference and distributed throughout the city by the missionaries:

> Invitation to the Spring Conference,
> Church of Jesus Christ of Latter-day Saints
> Sunday, March 10, 1946
> Morning Service at 10:00 a.m.; Main Service at 4:00 p.m.
>
> Topics to be Addressed:
> What is Mormonism?
> The Eternal Nature of Man
> The Coming of Christ
> God's Calendar
> The Abode of God and Angels
> (MS 8242)

District Conference in Dresden, May 1946

The conference was held in a renovated former German army officers' casino in the Dr. Kurt Fischer Allee, which had been a partially destroyed building just eight weeks earlier. An account of the restoration of the building is found in Chapter 11. The following undated conference report was written by Walter Kindt, a full-time missionary who assisted in the renovation of the building.

On Monday, April 29, 1946, 420 placards advertising the district conference were posted throughout the city. They announced the conference themes, "The Purpose of Man's Existence on Earth," "A God that Speaks," and "The Second Coming of Christ." In addition, the city's residents found handbills in all the streetcars, which invited them to the conference. That was the beginning of a program to present a distinct message of the true gospel to Dresden's residents. As proof that our placards and handbills were not prepared in vain, 750 people attended the Sunday School and 780 were present at the main service.

Indeed, the message found on the placards and handbills—just fourteen months after the devastating bombing of Dresden—must have appeared as a miracle to the city's inhabitants. Our members and investigators were overjoyed. You could see the joy in their eyes, that Mormonism's message for the city and the world could finally be openly presented again. Our motto was, "You shall know the truth and the truth will make you free." It was a real symbol for the members in those days and months, because we had just one wish, to be allowed to proclaim the truth of the gospel to everyone.

Officials of the city and many investigators attended Sunday's morning meeting, and prior to the start of the main meeting, the newly restored hall was filled to overflowing. The choir on the balcony could not be seen by those seated below, and Brother Krause said that during the singing, it sounded to those seated below as if angels of God were singing with them.

Those who had lost much and experienced deprivation and poverty, presented messages of hope. They spoke to members and visitors who had little to eat and who lived under unbelievable circumstances. The people of Dresden were still occupied with the removal of all the debris from the once-beautiful city on the banks of the Elbe. Here they were sitting in the casino that until recently had been used by Nazi soldiers and just eight weeks earlier had been nothing more than a bombed-out ruin. When you now looked around, you saw a hall that had been restored by a small handful of people and brought to a condition that few, if any, buildings in Dresden could match. Above them a choir sang songs full of hope and joy. Little wonder that Brother Krause later remembered the enthusiasm of the visitors with these words:

The missionaries made many appointments with people who desired to meet with them, and many wanted to read the Book of Mormon. Unfortunately, we didn't have enough copies and could have used a thousand. The desire of many investigators for Church literature was so strong that the possession of your own copy of the Book of Mormon clearly would have brought the greatest joy on that day.

The conference ended [on Monday] with a district missionary conference, which, due to the enthusiasm of the missionaries, began at eight a.m. and continued until two p.m. No one wanted to leave this conference place of peace and protection to return to the chaos of every day. On Monday evening, the Mutual organization offered entertainment that ended with a dance. The members were reminded of the spiritual and social joys of earlier times, while the visitors must have noticed the crass difference between what Brother Krause called the dignified and virtuous atmosphere of that evening and the dancing and games of chance previously conducted in the casino.

The conference brought strength and courage to weakened members. As we sang the last song, we all had the feeling that it was not the end of the conference, but rather that the conference would continue with us in our hearts and prayers. That feeling remained with us, and we took leave of each other with more songs at the train station. I believe that the Dresden train station had never before experienced such wonderful singing, as we joyfully sent off the last members on trains to Cottbus, Leipzig, and Naumburg. People standing nearby were amazed and asked who these people were. Our missionaries answered, "We are Mormons, people who have the same food stamps as you, but who are happy, very happy." At that train station, we sang with joy the song, "A Mormon boy, a Mormon boy, I am a Mormon boy; I might be envied by a king, for I am a Mormon boy." For the members of the Dresden branch, this was a wonderful experience and a great compensation for all their problems and their hard work.

Mission Conference in Leipzig, June 1946

Elder Ezra T. Benson: We received details concerning the recent mission-wide conference held in the city of Leipzig, one of the most amazing chapters yet written in the history of any mission in Europe. The Russian government permitted extensive advertising—the radio carried announcements three times each day for two weeks in advance, posters were on every billboard in the city and in every streetcar, so by the time the conference began, nearly every person in the entire area knew of it. The amazing attendance of 11,985 persons at the various sessions was the result, and the Sunday evening meeting alone attracted 2,082 persons—by far the greatest attendance ever to be present at a meeting of the Latter-day Saints in Europe.

At a special concert held June 10, featuring a mission-wide chorus of 250 voices and an orchestra of eighty-five pieces, 1,021 were in attendance, and at the Gold and Green Ball that evening 1,251 participated. The beautiful Congress Hall at the Leipzig Zoo, which is being rebuilt, afforded excellent accommodations, and hundreds of people became sincerely interested in the program of the Church.

We feel with all our heart that events such as these testify stronger than words of the faith and devotion of our Saints in these war-devastated areas. Railroad officials scheduled two special trains which went from city to city to pick up our members and take them to this great conference. This has been without a doubt one of the outstanding events ever to take place among the LDS people in this land. The spirit of faith and courage it has engendered will do much to strengthen them during this very critical period which they now face. (CR 271 5)

Alfred Paul Schulz: I located a print shop that would prepare a poster for every advertisement pillar, smaller posters for the street cars, six thousand handbills, one thousand conference invitations, three thousand conference programs, and two thousand food stamps. The city posted our announcement on every pillar, posters were hung in every streetcar, and the radio station advertised the event. The Church members arrived in special trains. Three microphones transmitted the messages in each room, and the choir, which looked wonderful, presented a concert that brought joy and satisfaction to everyone. The ball at the end of the conference confirmed the beauty of the conference. The food will never be forgotten, and music was played during the meals. Many of the visitors indicated a desire to be baptized. (MS 8242 and MS 2002)

Walter Krause: What impressed me most were the repeated scenes of joyous reunions. Many refugees from the eastern provinces were reunited with relatives and members of branches that no longer existed. Many sought specific people or news about the location of family members who had been separated. News was exchanged about soldiers who had returned home, were still prisoners of war, or were missing. (Edith Krause, *Walter Krause in Seiner Zeit*)

Conference Program:
June 5–7: Training for genealogists
June 7: District, branch, and Relief Society presidencies
June 8: Auxiliary leaders and teachers; Opening program
June 9: 8:00 a.m. Adult meeting; 10:00 a.m. Morning service; 1:00 p.m. Lunch and concert; 6:00 p.m. Main service
June 10: 7:00 a.m. Youth outing; 10:00 Musical service; 1:00 Lunch; 3:00 p.m. Genealogy and Relief Society displays
June 11: Missionary meeting

Musical Program for Monday Morning, June 10:
Serenade from "Eine kleine Nachtmusik," W. A. Mozart
Romance in G major, L. V. Beethoven (Violin Solo)
Overture from "Die Entführung aus dem Serail," W. A. Mozart

Fantasy from "Lohengrin," R. Wagner
"Peer Gynt Suite," E. Grieg
Overture from "Oberon," C. M. v. Weber

One Hundredth Pioneer Anniversary Conference in Dresden, July 1947

Joachim Lehnig: I was only twelve years old when we held the huge one-hundredth anniversary celebration in Dresden. People came from throughout the entire mission, but often with great effort. They brought their own food, in addition to their bedding. Straw had been placed in the former horse stalls of the military barracks, where all the youth slept. (2003)

Joachim Albrecht: President Stover arranged for a special train from the Mecklenburg area, which picked up members from various branches along the way. I was twelve years old and traveled with my mother. The train was filled. It was wonderful. We sang as we traveled, because everyone was traveling to the pioneer celebration. (2004)

Eberhard Gäbler: I was set apart as a missionary by President Walter Stover on June 9, 1947. On June 17, I reported to my first assignment in Erfurt, where I was charged by district president Anton Larisch to visit refugee families who had sought temporary asylum in the region of Thuringia. Later, I was asked to travel a specified route to the big pioneer conference in Dresden. It was our assignment to encourage members and friends along the way, under the motto, "All things are possible to those who have faith." Our assignment took us to branches or smaller groups of members in Gotha, Erfurt, Weimar, Großschwabhausen, Jena, Gera, Weida, Kleinaga, Meerane, Altenburg, Glauchau, Chemnitz, Freiberg, and Dresden, where we arrived on July 20. We traveled by train or on foot to the smaller locations and stayed overnight with the members. Special meetings were held in each branch to encourage attendance at the conference. We also bore our testimony about the restored gospel and how we could follow the example of the pioneers. We held smaller cottage meetings with the members, to which friends and acquaintances were invited.

All of the other full-time missionaries in the Soviet zone of occupation traveled similar routes toward Dresden and preached the gospel along their way. We were filled with enthusiasm and devoted our full strength toward the success of that great conference. All the members and friends who attended were equally enthusiastic and looked forward to that gathering.

The Dresden meeting house had been destroyed in the war and the Church had been assigned to a portion of the former army officers' casino in the Dr. Kurt Fischer Allee, which included a large park that provided space for all the conference attendees. A Pioneer service was held outside in good weather, in which the spirit was very strong. Five thousand people attended the main service on Sunday.

The "feeding of the five thousand" took place on Sunday, when lunch was served in stages, by district. The boat trip on Monday, which was financed by President Stover, was followed by a program held on the open-air stage in Rathen. The conference ended with a Pioneer celebration on Monday. Following the conference, the missionaries cleaned up the facility. The many chairs that had been borrowed throughout the city were returned by truck, and the same truck later transported us to Berlin for a meeting with President Stover. (2005)

Francis R. Gasser, civilian army employee: President Stover made application to the Religious and Propaganda Department of the Soviet Military Government for Occupied Germany, in which he requested that the Church be permitted to stage the intended celebration. After considerable negotiation, the SMAD granted the necessary written permission. Of course, this did not solve all the problems connected with the successful presentation of such a festival. There were problems such as transportation, food, lodgings, etc. In order to satisfactorily dispose of transportation matters, the central Administration for Rail Service was visited. Here again it became necessary to explain the Church's purpose in Germany and other nations, its beliefs and doctrines, and the general intention of our proposed centennial celebration.

Although interzonal travel in Germany is rigidly restricted and each would-be traveler must obtain permission, the authorities attached special coaches to their trains and reserved them for the Church members journeying between Berlin and Dresden. They also scheduled two special twelve-coach trains to make the Erfurt-Leipzig-Zwickau-Dresden run, and reserved the same for the members. Thus they journeyed to and from the centennial in what one in present-day Germany would term "comparative luxury." All enjoyed seat space, and none were forced to ride on top, between, or on the steps of the coaches as so many thousands are forced to do. The forty local German missionaries trekked to Dresden from their various fields of labor. On their way they distributed tracts, made possible by reason of the recent understanding allowing the exchange of literature between the various zones, and held meetings in the branches along their route.

It became necessary to raise funds that would enable everyone, regardless of their present economic station in life, to attend. A special mission-wide fast day was proclaimed on the fifteenth of June. These fast offerings, augmented by generous voluntary contributions on the part of the more fortunate German Saints, and funds raised through musicals in each of the branches, were sufficient to insure each and every member a round-trip rail or bus ticket to Dresden.

Food during the journey and stopover in Dresden posed the next obstacle. Members were required to bring with them all the food they would consume, as food ration cards are good only within the community or district of issue.... Once again the more fortunate, those from farms and semirural regions and those who have gardens, aided their less-fortunate fellow men. At Dresden, an inn was leased for the centennial and made possible the serving of one good substantial hot meal per day to each of the assembled. The Church donated canned meats, grease, powdered milk, etc., from the residue of the church welfare supplies at the mission home.

The question of lodging still remained [since the city had been destroyed in 1945]. As the suburbs of the city have but limited lodging facilities, which were already overtaxed, the members in Dresden conducted a house-to-house canvas to acquire lodging for the visitors. However, even then many were obliged to sleep on the straw out beneath the star-studded blue blanket of heaven.

As Dresden did not have an auditorium large enough to contain the anticipated throng, the branch chapel was enlarged sufficiently to hold approximately two thousand people. The brethren felled trees, filled in an old air-raid water reservoir, landscaped the chapel grounds, and installed a public address system with conveniently located loudspeakers. The chapel is situated on a nice wooded plot of ground surrounded by a high stone wall that reminds one of Temple Square. Chairs, stools, boxes, and planks were collected from the inhabitants of the suburbs who were willing to part with them temporarily and employed to seat the assemblage.

Saturday afternoon, July 26, 1947, the children enjoyed donkey rides, races, and games. At six p.m., the MIA held its mission-wide contest for public speaking, poetry, etc., and the individual district choirs competed in song. On Sunday morning, Sunday School featured the white-clad children's choir, and children of the mission recited poems and gave brief remarks. In the evening assembly, a choir of three hundred and fifty voices, the German counterpart of the famous Tabernacle Choir, sang the songs of Zion, and speakers recalled the faith of the Mormon pioneers engendered through the gospel. The morning of the twenty-eighth found everyone assembled aboard steamers on the Elbe River. They were enjoying a stretch of the river scenery between Dresden and Rathen known as the "Sächische Schweiz." At Rathen, a small city near the Czechoslovakian border, an hour's program was staged at the "Felsenbühne," an amphitheater carved out of the rocks and cooled by the luxuriant growth of pine. Thereafter they returned to Dresden. That evening the pioneer dances were demonstrated, pioneer scenes such as the hand cart company, etc., were portrayed, and pioneer songs, including "Come, Come Ye Saints" were sung.

The meetings were attended by approximately five thousand members and visitors. An actual count disclosed four thousand nine hundred and eight-six persons present at one of the meetings. Numerous Russian military authorities and representatives of the German and Russian press, including the Russian news agency TASS (Telegraph Agency Soviet Union), also attended. Many were the tears as persons presumed dead or in other countries met and greeted each other, their friends and relatives having been separated and incommunicado for so many years. However, paradoxically, he who had worked the hardest to realize a successful gathering was unable to attend. President Stover's permit to enter the zone failed to come through in time.

Tuesday the forty local male missionaries aided by the five local female missionaries and the members of Dresden returned the chairs, stools, boxes, planks, etc., borrowed from the inhabitants and raked and cleaned the chapel grounds. Wednesday morning at four a.m., they left Dresden by truck and arrived in Berlin at eight a.m., where they attended a day-long missionary meeting. President Stover at this time gave them instructions and praised them for their work. (LR 2428 2; published in the *Church News,* August 30, 1947)

Freud-Echo [Echo of Joy] in Berlin, June 1948, by Mission Secretary Heinz Hinkel

As the first of three expected special trains arrived on time at the "Reichssportfeld" train station in the early morning hours of June 26, 1948, the desire of many Saints to participate in the 1948 "Freud-Echo" in Berlin was fulfilled. It was the fulfillment and simultaneously the reward for month-long preparations for the largest Mutual conference that, despite many problems, became one of the finest experiences because of the steadfastness and firm faith of all participants and the help of the Lord. Because of the experience of past years, the preparations were begun very early. In fact, at the conclusion of the fall 1947 conference, leadership of the activity was assigned to the Mutual Improvement Association.

"Freud-Echo"! What an exalted goal, to give the members the opportunity to come together in these eventful days, in these difficult times, to praise and honor the Lord. It gave many the opportunity to shake the hands of friends and acquaintances, whom they had not seen for many years because of recent events.

At first, an appropriate location had to be found, which would enable everyone to participate. Therefore, the former capital city of Berlin and its Reichssportfeld were chosen. Who cannot remember the wonderful days of the Olympiad of 1936 at the Reichssportfeld? Yes, it was to be an Olympiad for us, a spiritual Olympiad, built upon the principles of our magnificent gospel. No other location could be better suited for this purpose: the "Waldbühne" for the public religious services, the clean and well-designed tournament and playgrounds for the sporting competitions of the youth, and the nearby "Seeschloss Pichelsberge" for the entertainment and the dance on Monday to conclude the conference. It was not surprising that in these days of planning and preparation, one could often spot President Stover and his associates, who despite their many mission responsibilities, took time to personally review and evaluate many details of the plans directly at the Reichssportfeld.

Far greater problems arose concerning the necessary arrangements for the lodging of the expected five thousand participants. Knowing that good lodging and well-rested bodies would significantly influence the joy and satisfaction associated with such a conference, the highest priority was given to these preparations. Since enough lodging opportunities could not be found solely among the local members, everyone understood that another course must be pursued. One approach involved the conference theme, "I am not ashamed of the Gospel of Jesus Christ." Those assigned to seek lodging opportunities among their friends and neighbors were asked to allow the light of the gospel to shine through themselves. Could there be a better opportunity to proclaim the gospel? Who would not participate in this magnificent and necessary assignment? Who would want to hide his light under a basket? The result was that fourteen days before the start of the conference, the required number of quarters had been fully met. What was achieved here was a testimony to the strength, the faith, and the steadfastness of the members of the Berlin district.

Still, not all problems had been solved. How should the participants come to Berlin from the various districts? Whoever knew Germany's travel situation after the war could imagine what challenges had to be overcome. Our goal to travel to Berlin in special trains was considered by the responsible people in the Reichbahn's leadership for many months. Finally, it was favorably decided that three special trains would be used, specifically:

Special train "Fritz": Dresden-Cottbus-Berlin
Special train "Herbert": Erfurt-Leipzig-Berlin
Special train "Walter": Zwickau-Chemnitz-Berlin

The joy over this success and our thankfulness toward our Heavenly Father can hardly be described with words. Again, the phrase was confirmed: "All's well that ends well." However, we soon learned that an upcoming currency reform would take place before our conference date, which would threaten all our planning. [The currency reform took effect on June 21, 1948, and was followed by the blockade of West Berlin by the Soviet occupation forces.] What to do? After further negotiations with responsible offices of the Reichsbahn, we were permitted to pay the expenses of the reserved trains in advance. Two days before the currency reform, we paid for the trains and had a written receipt. The conference was thereby assured! What a huge testimony that was for us, what an additional reason to be thankful to our Father in Heaven for all he provided!

We still faced the major and important task of caring for the welfare of the individual participants. Everyone recognized their living conditions. Everyone recognized the physical demands that such a conference would place on everyone. We had to provide assistance, but how? Because of the welfare plan of our Church, and with tireless work of the members, contributed food was distributed to every district. What we couldn't achieve through our own effort was provided by our Father in Heaven through the love of members in Zion. We also were able to provide two meals for every participant. We did everything necessary to make the visit of every participant as pleasant as possible.

The excitement over the coming conference was very great. The youth especially undertook all tasks assigned to them with great enthusiasm. The spring conferences had already demonstrated that the youth were prepared and capable of worthily representing the Church. Competitions were held in advance in the areas of free speech, recitation of history, music and song, etc.... In advance of the conference, posters and handbills with the exalted figure of Angel Moroni welcomed all to hear the messages of the servants of God. Preparations were also made to present the word of God through music and song, utilizing the talents available within our mission. We anticipated that the conference would proceed as planned. But as experience had taught us, it would not be entirely so.

As a result of the currency reform and the measures taken by the various governments, the borders between the zones were closed. It is difficult to describe what that meant for the mission, to care for and administer to members who lived on both sides of the border. The news could not have been worse. So many members in the West had looked forward to and had worked untiringly to prepare for and participate in this gathering. So many had planned to join again with dear friends who had remained in the East. All that was prevented by these political activities. However, we later learned that the members in the Hannover District planned and held a Junior Freud-Echo in their region.

The morning worship service on June 27, 1948, was a special experience for all participants. Still filled with the joy and events of the previous day, about six thousand members and friends of truth gathered on a beautiful Sunday morning to gain strength and courage for the future. How indescribably thankful we could be, to have the opportunity in this world of hate and envy, in this land of want and misery, in this city, characterized by the ruins of the past war, to gather and hear the word of the Lord.

In warm, lively words, the secretary of the European Mission, Wallace G. Bennett, expressed his joy of being among us in Berlin. Then the eyes of all present turned to the two-hundred-voice mission choir, which under the able leadership of the choir leader, Brother Friedrich Wernick of Berlin, presented the oratorio "The Vision," by Evan Stephens. The special mission of our prophet Joseph Smith was masterfully presented in song by Brother Hans Karl Schade of Gera. There could have been no more appropriate place to present these events through music than in the environment in which we found ourselves. In the middle of a thin stand of pine trees, with the blue sky above us—exactly as in those days when the prophet Joseph Smith went into the woods on a spring morning in the year 1820, to receive knowledge of the true gospel from God the Father and the Son—it was written in everyone's heart, through music, what words could not have expressed any better. A solemn stillness engulfed the attendees. Who was not focused on the events of 1820, on the great mission of our prophet Joseph Smith? We especially felt the influence of the Holy Ghost during those hours and gained strength for the coming days.

The concluding words at this spiritual feast on that wonderful morning were given by President Jean Wunderlich of the West German Mission who captivated all listeners with his logical and detailed presentation, which presented the principles of the gospel—faith, repentance, and baptism—to the assembled members and friends.

As the listeners were still captured by the music of the oratorio and the inspiring words of the speakers, another important event was being prepared, the "feeding of the five thousand," which took care of the physical needs of the attendees.

Promptly before the start of the evening meeting on Sunday, six thousand people were once more assembled, the largest meeting of the Church ever held on the European continent. In contrast to the wonderful sunshine of Sunday morning, darkening clouds appeared and thunder could be heard in the distance, warning that the good weather would not last much longer. However, the attendees were not deterred in the least from attending this solemn hour. It was to be the reward of all the planning, preparation, and work for this huge event. Still filled from the events of the previous hours, the enthusiastic members joined their thousands of voices into a choir that praised the Lord and opened the main worship service.

In the meantime, it began to rain, but all the assembled remained in their seats. Thousands of umbrellas suddenly changed the picture, and right at that time, the first speaker, the best in the previous "free speech" competition, was given the challenge of proving his ability to capture the assemblage with his words. The short-lived rain did not hinder the meeting at all, which was evident in the words of Archibald F. Bennett, the general secretary of the Genealogical Society of Utah, who managed to bring a little humor into the meeting by stating that we would no longer have to listen to a "dry" speaker.

It was then a joy for all to hear a message from Brother Francis R. Gasser, especially for many members among whom he had earlier fulfilled a mission here in Germany. He encouraged the Saints to remain true and to endure to the end. Thereafter, everyone was pleased to be able to hear from their dear mission president, Walter Stover, something which had seldom been possible up to that time. With simple words, but in a loving manner and with friendly smiles for everyone, he knew how to present a clear and unambiguous message for everyone that went from heart to heart.

President Alma Sonne then took the opportunity to speak again. His words became a memorial for everyone. He carried us back to the time when our prophet, Joseph Smith, and his brother Hyrum sealed their testimony with their blood, which caused us all to ask ourselves, are we as strong? Yet he also knew how to share words of praise and recognition.

Then, with great enthusiasm, the choir and assembled members brought forth with song what could no longer be expressed with words. How powerful was the power of God among us! Who could think at that moment on the difficulties of the time? Everyone was filled with praise and thankfulness to our Heavenly Father for this wonderful experience, for the strength that we had received once more.

How often were the words spoken, "Man is that he might have joy." That was to become fact on the following morning. Although the weather was not so good, about four thousand participants gathered to join in the programs offered by the various districts under the motto, "The East German Mission freut sich!" Sports, gymnastics, dance, and humor were given priority and showed the uniqueness of the attendees who, just like the pioneers of old, maintained a positive attitude and a joyful heart even in the worst days.

Unfortunately, President Sonne and his associates could not remain with us longer, since Church members in Scandinavia awaited their arrival also. We wished them all a safe trip and were thankful that we had been able to greet these servants of God who had come to visit us here in Berlin. We hope to be able to see them again soon.

Some of the activities planned for the afternoon were limited by strong rains, but not the soccer games, which were carried out by the youthful sports enthusiasts from various districts and by the missionaries. The final results were that Mecklenburg defeated Thuringia and Leipzig defeated Chemnitz.

Finally, nice weather returned, the dark clouds moved away, and the evening sun sent its last greetings. It was time for the several special trains to depart. We will never forget the feelings we received at the Reichssportfeld train station, the heartfelt goodbyes, the eyes that shown with joy and satisfaction, and the strength that everyone had received and could take with them. President Stover was there to wish every member and friend a personal farewell and encouragement to be strong regardless of future challenges. Shortly before the departure of the trains, we sang together the song, "God Be with You 'til We Meet Again." We felt a deep connection with each other and knew that the conference had been a success. At that time, outsiders who happened to pass by us must have thought, "What unique people," for our appearance, our philosophy of life, our every action and thinking must have seemed odd to them. However, those who experienced these past days, who attended this conference, understood completely and fully the words, "For the preaching of the cross is to them that perish foolishness; but unto us which are saved, it is the power of God." 1 Cor. 1:18. (This report was printed in 1948 and distributed throughout the mission.)

Appendix E Mission Choir Tour 1949

Justus Ernst: The East German Mission Choir, with 170 members, conducted a week-long tour of the major cities in the Soviet occupation zone. They traveled with a special reserved train and gave six performances that included two works by Evan Stephens, "The Vision" and "The Martyrs," to a total audience of 6,000 listeners: Dresden 700, Chemnitz 1,000, Zwickau 950, Leipzig 650, Weimar 850, and Berlin 1,850. (MS 1359)

Joachim Lehnig: It was really quite unique. Choir members came from all of the branches, and do you know what they sang? "The Vision" and "The Martyrs." Of course those are oratorios and very difficult musical works, but that is what the choir sang. Brother Wernick was the choir director, and we had excellent singers. Brother Hans Karl Schade was an operatic tenor, and he sang the solos in the oratorios. They were outstanding events. (2003)

Author unknown: The Berlin members of the choir met at our reserved special train at 7:30 a.m. on July 23 at the Anhalter train station in Berlin. All were present except our soloist, Brother Hans Karl Schade, and the violinist, Miss Galster. President Stover wished us well, and the train left on time in wonderful weather. Everyone was given a can of fat and a can of marmalade, which were received with great enthusiasm. We traveled to Dresden, where we were to join with other choir members and present our first concert.... We arrived in Dresden about 11:45 a.m. and were welcomed by several members, including Brother Lehnig. Our extensive baggage had already been placed on baggage carts.

We took the streetcar to the Nordallee, where the Dresden meeting house was located. There we sat at tables decorated with flowers and ate "Grütze" [grits] with milk, peaches, and generous amounts of sugar.... The orchestra's practice began at 3:00 p.m., followed at 5:00 p.m. by the combined practice of the choir with the orchestra. Many errors were corrected, but we finally had to quit at 7:30 p.m. In the meantime, Brother Schade und Miss Galster had arrived.

On Sunday at 10:00 a.m., the morning service was held in the park of the Dresden meeting house. The first song was "The Morning Breaks." After the prayer, a double quartet from Chemnitz sang a song from the choir book, followed by a cello solo by Erwin Radtke, a talk by Paul Radeke, a men's double quartet, and talks by Paul Schmidt and Heinz Hinkel. Brother Schade and Sister Wolf sang the closing song, "Jesus, Lover of My Soul."

We gave our first concert at 3:00 p.m., seated on the terrace that led from the meeting house to the park. After the prayer, Walter Pöcker presented an introduction to the oratorio "The Vision." Following the presentation of the oratorio, Paul Vielstich presented an introduction to the second oratorio, "The Martyrs." There was a reverent stillness among the approximately seven hundred attendees.

The next morning, the choir members met at the main train station. The train stood ready for a 7:30 a.m. departure. Everyone had a reserved seat during the entire trip, arranged by district. We arrived at 10:00 a.m. in Chemnitz and went to the meeting house, which was located close to the train station, where we held a choir practice. Lunch was provided at noon. Sister Klein, the Relief Society leader, had a huge task, but she had a group of young sisters who untiringly cared for us. They stood nearby to fill our plates. All of the members in Chemnitz, despite their limited monthly rations, had sacrificed to feed us. We had noodles with meat, followed by peaches for dessert. The choir practice continued after the meal. Then each retired to assigned quarters.

At 7:00 p.m., the room at the restaurant "Zweininger" was filled to capacity with about 1,100 people. The heat at that time was oppressive. However, we were aware of our assignment, and despite a few errors, we made a very good impression.

On Tuesday, our reserved train departed at 7:57 a.m. for Zwickau, past fields and woods in bright sunshine. Poppies were blooming in the fields. The grain had already been partially cut and stood upright in sheaves like so many puppets. But our travel leader, Paul Schmidt, appeared not to notice. He hurried about, conducting his business with a file under his arm in which our lodging was recorded. It was not so simple to assign the right people to the right quarters. It was to be expected, that he also carried with him a number of notes with complaints. It required great effort to satisfy everyone, but he managed to accomplish it.

We met together that afternoon in a beautifully arranged meeting house, which had been prepared with great effort and sacrifice by all members of the branch. Colorful glass windows in the large meeting room showed events in Church history. The room shone in the bright light of electrical ceiling and wall fixtures. To honor the choir, a short program about the origin and significance of the city of Zwickau was presented by Brother Voigt in a humorous manner. Brother Voigt also greeted the choir and orchestra members with a self-composed poem. Then followed a choir practice, in which the choir had to correct several problems that concerned the choir director.... At the conclusion of the practice, Brother Fassmann presented every choir member with a coupon for two desserts in the restaurant "Schwanenschloss," where the concert would also be held. The choir was then divided into groups that were taken on a tour of the city on their way to the Schwanenschloss. After enjoying dessert, the choir was photographed. Following the choir practice, the guests filled the room, and we had for the first time the feeling that they expected a concert in the truest sense of the word. The festively lit room and the festive mood of the visitors elevated our mood, and our performance was far better. Hugh applause followed our presentation, and we were pleased when Brother Wernick and Brother Schade were presented with flowers, then we felt we had also received a gift. 950 persons attended here in Zwickau.

On Wednesday, we left early at 8:25 a.m. for Leipzig. We made a stop in Werdau, where a few additional choir members joined us. Here, we heard again that our concert in Zwickau had been applauded. We arrived at 10:30 a.m. and were greeted by Brother Kindt and Brother Winter. We were taken to the meeting house, where we were given important announcements. Then we met for lunch in the Zoo restaurants. The members in Leipzig took great effort to care for us. At 2:00 p.m., special streetcars took us to the Völkerschlachtdenkmal [Battle of the Nations Memorial]. For many, it was their first visit to this famous and huge memorial. In the evening, the Mutual program was held. The opening activity gave the visitors and the Leipzig members the opportunity to put their knowledge to the test in order to win a prize.

The day was open to use as we wished—we should relax. Some members visited the zoo, others toured the city. We met again for a common lunch. Choir practice was held at 7:00 p.m. in the White Room of the Zoo Restaurant. The concert began at 8:00 p.m. However, Brother Schade had caught a cold that affected his voice and brought Brother Wernick great concern. The two joined in a prayer before the concert, which then proceeded relatively well. Whenever possible, Brother Schade did not sing. It was almost unbearably hot in the room, which made singing very difficult. However, everyone felt the importance of the event and did their best, although the condition of the stage left much to be desired regarding the coordination of the choir and the orchestra. Six hundred fifty persons attended the concert.

We received a hearty goodbye Friday morning at the train station and traveled to Weimar. . . . As we arrived there, what did we see? Certainly it was not for us. A musical group awaited us, to welcome us. We were all touched, and many shed tears. We then found our lodging and assembled again for a common lunch in the FDGB [trade union] hall. We were actually surprised by the good meal. How could this small district prepare such a meal? We had a fruit soup, roast beef, cabbage, tomato sauce, and peaches for dessert. Then we went on a tour of Weimar in smaller groups. We visited the memorials of our two greatest poets [Goethe and Schiller]. Our school learning was renewed and even augmented because now we could see and not just be told. The tour took us through the Goethe Park and permitted a view of the Goethe Garden House, covered in green. Then a surprise awaited us in a small restaurant at the end of our tour, wonderful coffee and cake, including ice cream. Although Brother Wernick warned us against eating the cold ice cream, we could not resist. As we returned by bus, we saw everywhere on bulletin pillars and house corners huge posters that announced our concert. Some had anticipated a poor turnout for the concert, since Weimar is very spoiled. So we were surprised when the room was filled to the last seat by 850 people.

The next morning, we saw other sights in Weimar, including the new meeting house. Then after an excellent meal, we went to the train station where we were again greeted by the musical group, which played for us, "God be with you till we meet again," "Muss i denn, muss i denn zum Städtele hinaus" [German folksong], etc. No one wanted to leave, but Berlin was waiting for us.

We arrived in Berlin at 6:30 p.m. Here again we were greeted by a musical group, and a large banner welcomed us. President Stover and Brother Larisch also were present to greet us warmly. . . . We had lunch together on Sunday morning at 11:00 a.m. in the Sophienstraße. In that regard, the Berliners were not behind the other districts. The meal, which consisted of vegetables, meat, and gravy, tasted very good. Every choir member also received a package of cake for later. Then we went to the Korso Theater where the concert was held at 2:00 p.m. The theater held almost 2,000 people and about 1,850 seats were occupied. We were happy to see President Sonne and his wife and secretary among those present. Here we gave our best performance, and Brother Schade was also well again. As the two oratorios faded away, the listeners were greatly moved. Brother Larisch came on the stage and praised Brother Wernick, the choir, and the orchestra. All choir members probably had a silent prayer in their heart, thanking God for the help, protection, and success that we had on this trip. (Copy from Walter Kindt)

Appendix F Youth Pioneer Trek 1962, by Herbert Goliasch

It is hard to rationally describe a great joy that even overwhelms one's emotions. But the Youth Pioneer Trek of the Berlin Mission was such a great joy for all who followed the call of the mission's two Mutual committees to travel on bicycles to several branches in order to proclaim the gospel through music. To be honest, many discussions, pro and con, had preceded the decision. Not everyone was excited about sacrificing one's vacation for such a "strenuous, unpeaceful, and hardly relaxing enterprise." And not only were some of the youth unwilling to follow the call and place a Church activity ahead of their comfort, but many older "experienced" brothers and sisters doubted the feasibility of the plan.

So it happened that the announcement was delayed and then eventually sent out late, and the closer the scheduled departure date came, the more concerns arose among the responsible persons. However, once again, the truthfulness of the testimony of Nephi was confirmed, who also stood before an apparently hopeless situation and declared with certainty, "I know that the Lord giveth no commandments, save he shall prepare a way for them that they may accomplish the thing which he commandeth them!"

Despite all prophecies of doom, the trip was a wonderful event. The experiences and impressions during the trip were so overwhelming, that no one can really describe with words our enthusiasm and joy. Even excessively flowery words cannot reflect the happiness that the youth felt, who came and gave their best effort. At the happy ending of the Pioneer Youth Tour, they were richly blessed and had to admit, "It was the nicest vacation that we ever had!"

Let's follow the trip in its chronological order, whereby it must be stated, at the outset, that the following descriptions are only a tiny piece of the great experience and joy.

Saturday, July 7: The point of department was the Leipzig meeting house. The participants pedaled into the city with mixed feelings. Despite the continuing rain clouds, everyone was convinced the trip would have good weather. After all, it can't rain forever. In that certainty, participants turned their attention to the nice surprise that our hosts had prepared for the evening. Herr Vit, a member of the Leipzig Orchestra, gave a slide presentation about the trip to Japan that he had made with the orchestra. The wonderful pictures of the strange Far East captivated everyone,... especially when one realized that the Church was making progress even in that country.

Sunday, July 8: The Leipzig members prepared well for their young guests and organized and made their short stay in Leipzig very pleasant. The weather appears to be improving. The youth are bubbling over with anticipation. Brother Rudi Sommer, who gave the Sunday School lesson in the youth class, received a small taste of it, because his lesson was so enthusiastically discussed that he wasn't able to finish it. That was unfortunate, but there will certainly be many opportunities during the trip to continue the discussion.

After lunch, however, the first serious work of a choir was begun. Only a few members had been able to practice the songs in advance in their branches, quite aside from the fact that the choir had never sung together. But the choir directors, Gerwin Baasch from Leipzig and Klaus Schröder from Cottbus, showed no mercy. The choir practice ended only thirty minutes before the start of the special worship service, and all of the songs had not yet been mastered. However the weariness is forgotten, as the trip became serious for the first time. The enthusiasm of the singers covered up all of the rough edges of the musical presentations, which were supplemented with messages from Bernd Schröder, Berlin, Rolf Schumann, Erfurt, and Walter Krause, who was the senior member of this trip. Although the song "Oh my Father" was only practiced once together, it was sung a capella at the end of the 90-minute service, attended by 151 persons. The singing had many problems, but the members, who allowed themselves to be led by the enthusiasm and not from technical musical considerations, were deeply impressed.

The common evening meal ended this successful day. On the way to their lodging, thoughts about the prospects for the rest of the trip whirled through everyone's head.

Monday, July 9: The first bicycling day has arrived, accompanied by good weather. This Monday brought the first rays of sun in several weeks. Together with the excellent breakfast provided by the Leipzig Relief Society, it was another reason to be in good spirits. Before departure, a short request program was held as a thank you for the good care by the branch members.

The group departed for the next goal, the Erfurt branch, in two groups. Naturally, this was not a competitive race; rather it was adapted to the weakest of the weak. The plan was to bicycle to Weißenfels and to take the train from there to Erfurt. "Father Krause" took his car and trailer, with all the baggage, so the trip could begin unburdened.

The first group, under the direction of Wolfgang Zwirner from Dresden, arrived in Weißenfels without any damage despite a flat tire and a light crash—while still in Leipzig. From there, they went by train as planned. However, the second group wasn't as fortunate. Barely outside of Leipzig, Ralf Schröder had a flat and that happened again before Markkleeberg. In both instances, some stayed behind to help him while the rest proceeded under the care of Harald Henkel and Rudi Sommer. Ralf's brother Arndt became the "chief mechanic" and resolved the flat tires in very short order, and they were able to catch the others before Weißenfels.

Beyond Weißenfels, the sisters of the second group, except for Dagmar Hachenberger, took the train. Since the weather was so beautiful, the rest wanted to bike farther, at least to Naumburg. However, not only was there much sun, but also more flats. Everyone was happy to reach Naumburg.

The advance propaganda for the trip did not simply present it as a new form of a common vacation, but rather as a missionary assignment for the youth of the mission. Therefore, at every stage, the participants could learn the truthfulness of the saying, "Obedience is better than sacrifice." They had obediently accepted the request to participate, which the Lord blessed, and the testimonies of all the participants were thereby strengthened. Alone, the fact that there were no serious injuries on such a trip with about sixty youth was not taken for granted. For example, Brigitte Ullmann from Annaberg was one who made the trip in the group of motorized participants on a motorbike. When she stopped to obtain gas in Leipzig, her passenger, Margit König from the Döbeln branch, climbed off the bike. Then Brigitte made a turn without yielding to an oncoming Wartburg car. The car struck the bike at a speed of 60 to 70 km/h. Brigitte flew into the air, fell on her back onto the hood of the car, slid off the hood, and stood up without any noticeable injury and without significant pain. The eyewitnesses thought they would not see her among the living again. The motorbike sustained considerable damage and was taken to a repair shop. However, the group continued their trip with thankful hearts.

The many doubters did not think it was possible that the logistical arrangements for the group could be taken care of smoothly, but that was not the case. Everything had been well arranged in Erfurt as in Leipzig. The enthusiastic sisters constantly took care of every need. After the evening meal, a short choir practice was held before everyone went to their lodging at members' homes. A big outing was planned for the next day.

Tuesday, July 10: Beautiful weather accompanied the group on this tremendous day. First, everyone had an opportunity to become better acquainted with each other during the train trip to the Wartburg. The visit to the Wartburg and the Bach house, as well as the wandering through the Drachenschlucht [dragon's ravine], followed by a stop in the forest, steadily elevated the mood of the group. The Erfurt sisters had also prepared so much food for our Wartburg outing that we could hardly eat it all. Some of the brothers had obtained terrycloth shirts in Eisenach, which were expertly evaluated by the others. The conclusion was that the shirts could replace hand towels and washcloths, but that soap would still be required.

As the only occupants of an entire train car, one song followed another during the return trip, and to overcome the noise of the train, the singing became louder and louder. While it didn't become raucous bawling, since church songs were also sung, the end result was that most singers became hoarse. Brother

Joachim Lehnig, therefore, had to issue an order against further singing and shouting. In consideration of our strained voices, the choir practice was cancelled, and our generous evening meal ended the day, which had been greatly enjoyed by everyone.

Wednesday, July 11: All of the sportsmen, and those who once were or wanted to be, had their opportunity in the morning. There were opportunities to play ball and to swim. After breakfast, the brothers were immediately involved in a vigorous soccer match. It was fought out with great energy and spirit, during which time the rules were liberally interpreted. The referee, Joachim Lehnig, who was most intent on enforcement of the singing and shouting prohibition, soon left the battlefield and sought out more peaceful pastures. As the organizer of a Völkerball [dodge ball] game for the non-soccer players and the sisters, he shameless took a defensive position among those watching the game. Fortunately, there was some water in the area so that everyone, not only the heated players, could quickly cool off with a swim.

A choir practice was held after lunch. Although the practice was not too long, Gerold Schröder had more than he could bear. He sent a note to the choir leader, Gerwin Baasch, which said, "Let us sing the second verse of number 96 three times." ["Let us sleep in peace, make our souls pure; let us and all people be hidden in thee. Then all voices will sound clearly as choirs of angels, which will let us sleep in peace and our wish will become reality."] As usual, Gerwin showed no mercy, but everyone had enough time in the afternoon to get dressed for the worship service.

However, as we came to the second performance of the trip, no one felt the exertions of the day. The musical presentation by Brother Baasch on the bassoon, the messages by the three brothers, and the enthusiasm of the choir resulted in a service that was a great experience for the participants. The brothers sang the closing song, "Oh my Father," and the 105 attendees, including five friends, felt that it was a worthy ending to a successful evening, for the singing had improved significantly over the first evening.

As previously in Leipzig, the choir thanked the energetic, sacrificing sisters of the branch with several requested songs. It was in part through the service of the members of the several branches that the youth developed into such a close group that it was difficult to part at the end of the trip.

Thursday, July 12: The group traveled by train in two groups from Erfurt to Gera. The second group was very lucky. Their train was filled with vacation groups. Only three cars were left for other travelers, and they were completely packed. However, one of the vacation groups did not show up, so everyone had a comfortable seat. The trip continued on bicycles from Gera, through the Märchenwald, to Werdau. However, the first flat tire occurred upon leaving Gera. Herbert Grünewald had to patch his tire. Again, Arndt sprang into action and repaired the damage. Rudi Sommer, who remained behind, recorded this historical moment with his camera.

The sun was missing on this stage of the trip, and it even began to rain in the Märchenwald. But they were only short showers that didn't cause much damage. We stopped, ate another breakfast, and offered expert advice about the crash experienced by Eberhard Werner from Leipzig, who suffered a few scratches on his legs. Soon the trip continued in pleasantly cool weather toward Werdau. Small showers contributed to an increased tempo. The hills on this stretch provided a small taste of the challenge in the Erzgebirge.

It didn't go so well with Brigitte Ullmann, who had bravely continued on a bicycle after her crash in Leipzig. She had to be taken by car from Werdau to her home in Jöhstadt by Annaberg. An examination by a doctor revealed that her illness, a case of shingles, had nothing to do with her accident, from which she had escaped uninjured.

In the Werdau branch, the members had prepared a unique reception. Facilities for washing had been set up, tables covered, and the warm meal tasted wonderful after our ride. But that was not all. It was evident that they were pleased to have the youth of the mission visit their branch. They quickly formed a small choir, and under the direction of Brother Sellner, presented to the surprised singers a welcoming song that earned unending applause. Everyone was greatly enthused. No wonder that we parted unwillingly to our lodging. But that was necessary, for the next day presented its challenges.

Friday, July 13: It had been planned to go bathing in the Koberbachtalsperre [reservoir] in the morning. However the weather was too uncertain, the sky was cloudy, and it began to rain lightly on and off. But the youth don't lose their enthusiasm easily. Dancing with tape-recorder music, table tennis, and group games quickly occupied the hours. When the weather cleared, a soccer match was organized. Once again, lunch tasted wonderful. It is hard to describe how the enthusiasm increased hourly. Since the worship service was to be held in the evening, part of the afternoon belonged to the choir director, who strove to eliminate unevenness with persistence and patience.

That evening became an unforgettable experience for the travelers. Among the approximately 180 guests were 30 friends, and the youth choir sang with an enthusiasm that brought out all the joy of the previous days. Everyone was carried away. The speakers completed the musical presentations. It was amazing that the youth heard the messages of the three brothers in every branch, yet they were always enthusiastic and impressed. They closely followed the talks.

The day had yet other high points. Before everyone went to their quarters again, all sat down to a common meal, which, as always, was excellent. Suddenly, Brother Sellner appeared with flowers, which he presented to Brother Lehnig with kind words of praise and appreciation for the choir. Again, the sisters of the Relief Society asked that the choir sing several songs, and their wishes were met with enthusiasm. At the conclusion, the members of the Werdau branch sang "God be with you 'til we meet again." It is completely impossible to describe the wonderful spirit and joy that was present at that time. Someone who didn't participate in this trip could not comprehend why these bland-sounding events became some of the finest experiences of these youth, and why the Werdau branch will never be forgotten.

Saturday, July 14: The youth have been on the road for a week, which has brought unforgettable experiences. Further travel from Werdau will be done only by bicycle. Today's goal is Karl-Marx-Stadt. Divided into four groups, the route went through Zwickau into the mountains. Two flat tires, two light crashes, and a completely irrational detour stole some strength but none of the enthusiasm. There seemed to be no end to the hills and valleys, and the goal seemed to come no closer. But even the most tiring streets finally have an end. Although it rained heavily in Karl-Marx-Stadt, we arrived dry. After a common meal, we outsmarted the cool weather and went swimming, not outside, but rather in the city's large indoor swimming pool. The fine fifty-meter pool and the diving boards provided opportunity for everyone to swim as much as they desired. In the evening, the youth enjoyed several hours of Mutual activities with the members of the branch, which included, naturally, an opportunity to dance. Everyone was highly enthusiastic and equally as tired, when it was time to find our lodging with the members.

Sunday, July 15: It rained heavily the entire day, and most of the brothers had sore throats. Gottfried Bock, with his small supply of lozenges, was a much-sought-after man. But bad weather and a frog in the throat is no reason to not participate in the Sunday School. Gottfried Richter, district president of Karl-Marx-Stadt, presented the lesson in the youth class on the subject "The Price of Sin."

Lunch was eaten at members' homes, which permitted the youth to become better acquainted with them. The afternoon was again spent in choir practice. Lothar Radke's operatic tenor gave new spirit to the practice and new work for our Gerwin. Despite bad weather, 201 people attended the evening performance. Although the circumstances (cold and tiredness) were not the best, the performance went well, perhaps our best concert to date. Although the description of the performances in the several branches may appear identical, the meetings themselves were not at all uniform, although they each contained similar elements. They were the high points of a tour that had no lack of highlights.

Monday, July 16: Already before the groups set off for Annaberg, the bikers learned that cars also could have breakdowns. The group had asked the branch president to express their thanks to all the members for their hospitality and were standing next to the cars parked by the meeting house. Lothar Radke's car had unmistakable signs of old age and motor asthma, which could only be solved by an urgent course of treatment. Bicycling is cheaper after all. However, as the route went into the mountains, the first rain showers hit all the bikers. Fortunately, it was a warm rain, which didn't cause any particular discomfort, even when the ever-present flat tires reappeared. As fast as one became wet to the skin, one became quickly dry again. As earlier, some of the sisters preferred the quicker alternative of traveling by truck instead of the tiring pedaling, but they were soaked just the same.

The mountainous stretches became the subject of detailed discussion during the following excellent lunch in the beautiful meeting house in Annaberg.

Despite universal weariness, a thorough choir practice was held in the afternoon. Gerold Schröder viewed the unmerciful strictness of the choir director to be particularly unappreciated on this rainy afternoon. He quietly slipped away without undue attention to a quieter room to indulge in some sleep on an air mattress. After all, what do bikers know about the effort it takes to control the strength of a motorbike? But there can be a disadvantage to being such a muscleman. The absence of his deep bass was missed by Gerwin, the sweet slumber ended quickly, and the choir practice continued.

After a generous evening meal, everyone assembled for a small social evening. Poor Brother Krause! With great skill, he had managed to overcome all problems with his auto, only to have Rudi Sommer lead him onto slippery ice in the evening. Brother Krause, an amateur astrologer, was the right person to be presented with a tricky astrological question, "Was time is the most important time for an astrologer?" His frown, throat clearing, and similar signs of energetic thinking filled the room. It was a difficult question. One thought of light years, seasons—hmm, very difficult. Fortunately, he also had a son who could help. Helaman knew, "meal time"! Further explanation was not necessary.

Tuesday, July 17: The days flew by. The program today included an outing to Oberwiesenthal. It becomes constantly more difficult to find new adjectives to describe the hike from the train station to the Fichtelberg. One could say, very strenuous and very warm, great drudgery with terrific sweating. But no one considered it as such, and it wouldn't be accurate, for everything strenuous is not necessarily drudgery, and everything wonderful requires some effort now and then. To describe the event correctly, one must say, it all ended too soon.

After a short pause on the highest mountain in the GDR, the route went down to Oberwiesenthal where our lunch awaited us. A squirrel that preferred being fed by hand more than exerting the effort to feed himself was an occasion to use the camera, as was the tall ski jump. After eating, the swimming pool, despite a cooler temperature, offered unending possibilities for some, while the others enjoyed the meadow and benches for warm and relaxing observation. Some children's seesaws offered sporting activity of another sort and were taken over by the sisters. A visit to the Czech border provided the last impressions of Oberwiesenthal, before the express train quickly transported everyone to Annaberg.

This day brought still other unforgettable experiences, although the special worship service began with a shock. In the full meeting house (198 present, including 70 friends!), the acoustics are totally different than during practice in an empty room. The sounds are dampened and flatter. But all were full of healthy ambition, and it was possible to elevate the musical presentation to its full height. The concluding song by the young men's choir, "Oh my Father," sounded beautiful.

After the service, all of the traveling members had one of the most wonderful experiences of the entire trip. Horst Tschirschke of Annaberg, a member of the touring choir, was one of three people baptized in the font in the meeting house. The small room could not contain all who wanted to witness this moment. The youth choir planned to sing two songs, but the second one was literally drowned in tears. The joy was simply too great. The confirmation took place thereafter in the meeting room, and Brother Tschirschke was immediately ordained a deacon, according to the order of the Church. Thereafter, at the wish of the branch members, the brothers again sang the song, "Oh my Father." As we separated that evening, the weariness of the strenuous hike and other activities of the day could not dampen the joy that all carried in their hearts.

Wednesday, July 18: The heavens seemed to open all its gates and appeared to consist only of rain. In this refreshing shower, the brothers traveled the sixty kilometers by bicycle to Freiberg. The sisters, accompanied by a few brothers, took the train as far as Flöha, but as they mounted their bikes there, it poured again. Fortunately, a tractor with a trailer shorted the trip for them. One should consider that the total trip covered more than three hundred kilometers.

The travelers didn't miss anything on this day. They learned that one can quickly become used to rain, and the view is not particularly different. As the required flats failed to appear, there was much happy laughter (at first). The rain actually penetrated only to the skin. Briefcases, etc., with all their contents, were also softened. By the next generous flats, the memories of better days were comforting. Everyone said it was good fortune that not all days were as wet. One became used to the rain, but still preferred the sunshine of earlier days. Two accidents took place on this stretch, fortunately neither too serious. The first who made contact with the ground was Klaus Schröder, the second was Helaman Krause. On a steep decline, he ran into Ralf Schröder, who had to quickly brake. Helaman flew high over the handlebars, but he only received a few scratches. His bike suffered more.

Finally, everyone arrived completely soaked and also tired, but still in good spirits, and most important, healthy, in Freiberg. Although the youth only remained one day in that branch, the members had prepared everything for them. However, there was little time to relax, since the service would be held that evening.

Despite the rainy effort of the day, the presentation of the choir and the musical pieces by Gerwin Baasch on the bassoon were not hampered. Everyone gave their best effort, as had been the case in all of the branches. The 110 attendees included three friends. As in Annaberg and Werdau, the brothers were also requested in Freiberg to repeat "Oh my Father." The youth did not forget, either, to thank the sisters of the Relief Society with songs for their efforts. Then everyone separated to their lodgings, for the last leg of the trip would take place tomorrow, to Dresden.

Thursday, July 19: The rain clouds were blown away, the sun again shone out of a blue sky, and it promised to be a pleasant ride to Dresden. The slower tempo of this stretch was not only the result of the obligatory flats, but the wild berries shone temptingly red on the edge of the road, and the cool shade of the forest contributed to a restful stroll on bicycles, which compensated for the efforts of the previous day.

It was a good feeling to know that the branch had prepared well for our arrival. Papa Krause had already placed himself behind the wheel of his vehicle the previous evening and drove to Dresden. With his own energy, he helped to complete the preparations to feed his large "band of children." Since he was not only a master organizer, but also a great expert with cooking utensils, the praise and honor, which he had certainly more than earned, knew no bounds.

Because local circumstances prevented an afternoon choir practice, the time was devoted to extensive sunbathing in the garden, playing of badminton and volleyball, and sorrow that the wonderful time would soon be over. Following a massive evening meal, during which the epicurean talents of the choir's new chief cook were appropriately honored, the choir practice was held, at which time the participants of this unique tour could again learn that is not advisable to get on the nerves of the choir director. An energetic closing of the music stand ended the practice, and the baffled singers then had the belated opportunity to be more understanding.

Friday, July 20: Pleasant weather and a wonderful boat trip on the Elbe to Königstein allowed the problems of yesterday to be forgotten. Everyone enjoyed the beautiful Elbe landscape, the Sächsischer Schweiz, and the mighty fortress of Königstein. . . . Another choir practice followed lunch, in preparation for the final special presentation of this "Youth Pioneer Tour" that evening, which was attended by 128 guests, including 17 friends. In this beautifully acoustic meeting house, the choir exceeded itself. Already after the second song, many friends began to cry. The enthusiasm was really indescribable, and the tears of joy were very close for the choir members also. A wonderful spirit was present, and when the brothers sang the closing song, "Oh my Father," the choir sat still for a moment, for the spirit was simply overpowering. It was said by all that it was unfortunate to only have one more day on this tour.

Saturday, July 21: The participants in the Youth Pioneer Tour were somewhat melancholy on this last day. The time flew by too quickly, and everyone was sad to think that it was finished. At least we would see each other again soon, at the special worship service in Leipzig and whenever a youth conference was held. That was the only comfort. On this morning, few wanted to go into the city but preferred to spend the last hours together. Table tennis, badminton, and volleyball ruled the morning. (Copy from Gerwin Baasch)

Appendix G The Rededication of the Land 1975, by President Monson

The setting was as beautiful a spot as could be imagined. We walked through the woods for about twenty minutes into a clearing overlooking the Elbe River, with Meissen on the right and Dresden on the left.... The day had been overcast, but during the prayer the sun shone brilliantly upon us, warming our bodies and giving us the assurance that our Heavenly Father was pleased with the prayer which was being offered.

> Our beloved Heavenly Father, under the inspiration of Thy Holy Spirit, which we acknowledge freely and appreciate greatly, we assemble on this mountainside on this, Thy holy day, to dedicate and rededicate this land for the advancement of the work of the Church of Jesus Christ of Latter-day Saints.
>
> Thou knowest the faith of the people of this land—the many tens of thousands who have embraced Thy gospel and have served to build up Thy church wherever they have been. Thou knowest the sermons which they have preached in song, for they sing with their hearts and echo the feelings of their souls. Thou knowest, Heavenly Father, the sufferings of this people, and Thou hast been near to them in times of trouble and in times of joy.
>
> We express our gratitude unto Thee for the privilege we have of holding meetings here, for bringing to the membership of the Dresden Mission the entire program of the Church. These blessings were scarcely imaginable a few years ago. We confess before Thee that it has been through Thy intervention that this blessing has been brought to pass. We acknowledge Thy hand in every aspect of our lives and pledge our lives to Thy service.
>
> In the authority of the holy apostleship which I bear, and in the name of Thy Beloved Son, Jesus Christ, the Savior and Redeemer of the world, I dedicate and rededicate this land for the advancement of Thy work. I invoke, Heavenly Father, upon this people Thy divine

blessings. Wilt Thou bless the membership of the Church. Grant that every member may have a desire to serve Thee and keep Thy commandments. Father, we ask Thee to cause that each one who is called to serve may serve with all of his heart and all of his strength. Grant unto Thy membership here a significant blessing, the blessing mentioned in the book of Third John: "I have no greater joy than to hear that my children walk in truth." Grant that the children of the membership of the Church in the Dresden Mission may be loyal to Thy cause, and the grandchildren, even unto the last generation before the second coming of Thy Beloved Son. Grant, Heavenly Father, that the membership here may receive their patriarchal blessings and live in such a way as to bring the promises to fulfillment.

Heavenly Father, wilt Thou open up the way that the faithful may be accorded the privilege of going to Thy holy temple, there to receive their holy endowments and to be sealed as families for time and all eternity.

Heavenly Father, we invoke a blessing upon the nonmembers of this land, that they may be touched in their hearts, that they may respond to the examples which the members set before them. Arouse within them a curiosity concerning the Church, and then cause that this curiosity may turn to a desire to know more, and then that this desire to know more will result in conversion to the gospel and that the membership of the Church may stabilize and indeed grow. Heavenly Father, wilt Thou intervene in the governmental affairs. Cause that Thy Holy Spirit may dwell with those who preside, that their hearts may be touched and that they may make those decisions which would help in the advancement of Thy work.

We seek a blessing of peace upon this people, the peace promised by Thy Beloved Son. We look forward to the day when Thy missionaries may again be permitted to preach the everlasting gospel in this area, for we know there is much of the blood of Israel here. May today mark the dawning of a new beginning of Thy work in this land. Amidst the ringing of church bells this morning and the singing of birds in this, the forest which Thou hast created, music fills our souls and gratitude fills our hearts as we humbly acknowledge before Thee that Thou art our Father, that with Thee all things are possible, and that Thy gospel has been restored upon the earth.

Let the word go forth from this place, Heavenly Father. In Thy due time grant that many hundreds may seek membership in Thy church, and that Thy children whom Thou hast preserved may indeed be saved in the celestial kingdom of God.

Our Heavenly Father, wilt Thou bless the president of the Dresden Mission. We know of no man of greater faith in Thy kingdom. And for a man to serve as he has served has required the support of a devoted companion. Bless the counselors in the mission presidency who stand by the side of the president and perform a marvelous work and a wonder among this people. Bless their companions and the families of each member of the presidency. Grant unto these men Thy power, for they are men who are righteous in the use of power and who are resolute and true in defending Thy word.

Shower down upon us, Heavenly Father, Thy bounteous blessings. Bring to this land Zion in all of its glory. Bring to the heart of each member a firm testimony of the gospel and grant that from this day forth, the way may be opened for Thy word to go forward in greater power. Grant that the way may be cleared for the program of the Church in its fullness to come to this people, for they, through their faith, have merited such blessings.

As Thy humble servant, acknowledging the divine revelation and inspiration of this day, I therefore invoke Thy holy blessings upon Thy work and upon Thy people in the Dresden Mission of the Church of Jesus Christ of Latter-day Saints. We as a group acknowledge before Thee our indebtedness to Thee and place in Thee our trust, knowing that Thou issued a holy promise. Thou hast said, "I, the Lord, am merciful and gracious unto those who fear me, and delight to honor those who serve me in righteousness and in truth unto the end. Great shall be their reward and eternal shall be their glory." With these divine words from the seventy-sixth section of the Doctrine and Covenants ringing in our ears, we offer up unto Thee this dedication and rededication prayer, in the name of Thy Beloved Son, Jesus Christ, amen. (*Faith Rewarded*, April 27, 1975)

Appendix H Origin of the Freiberg Temple 1983

"Wie es zum Bau des Tempels kam," by Henry Burkhardt

Note: The original manuscript was dated October 1, 1983. After the Wende, Burkhardt added a few sentences and deleted the attachments. The added text is italicized. The attachments have been incorporated into Chapter 15.

It was common for Latter-day Saints to speak about the temple and desire to enter into covenants with the Lord therein. They had learned to value temple ordinances and had been taught by former and present prophets of God to prepare themselves and their children to receive these ordinances by living an honorable and clean life, for they knew that only Church members who could demonstrate their worthiness would have that opportunity. They knew that not everyone had access to a temple, and hardly anyone had the expectation of attending a temple during their lifetime, despite their faithfulness to the commandments of God. However, the commandment to attend the temple remained an unfulfilled part of the gospel plan for everyone in Europe and other parts of the world where no temple existed.

In past decades, the members in this part of the world had listened wistfully as modern prophets, apostles, and other General Authorities of the Church taught that no one would be denied blessing in the eternities that they had earned in this life through their faithfulness to God's commandments. Many left this earth with the firm conviction that these blessings were certain. The Latter-day Saints carried these promises in their hearts and strengthened their faith in God. Yet they never lost the wish to personally go to the temple of the Lord and there solemnly enter into these covenants.

How great was the joy of the members when it was made known during the administration of President David O. McKay, that additional temples would be built. Two of them were to be constructed in Europe, including one in Switzerland. Suddenly, the possibility of reaching a temple became greater and nearer. After the temple in Zollikofen was dedicated in 1955, the wish burned within many Saints to go there. Many left their homeland to live in a place from which they could visit the temple. But most had to remain where they were, and only a few of them had the opportunity to see their wish fulfilled. Therefore, many quiet prayers were directed to heaven, that ways might be found for them to visit the temple.

Nothing was more important to the priesthood leaders of our country than to find opportunities to fulfill our members' wish. The temple in Zollikofen—so near and yet so far away for the members of the GDR—was the most sought-after goal. *The existing laws of the land did not allow the average person to travel to the West.*

If not myself, then it would have fallen to another, to earnestly be engaged in the pursuit of this wish. However, I became directly involved in this problem as a result of being called into the mission presidency on June 24, 1952. One of my assignments was to develop and maintain contact with state offices, in order to improve the lot of members of the Church, i.e., to find ways whereby all branches could hold their worship services, obtain Church literature, and travel to the temple in Switzerland. With approval of the various mission presidents, I pursued every opportunity to emphasize to responsible state offices the importance of temple visits. However, I always received the same answer, that the necessary conditions for travel to Switzerland do not yet exist and that this request must be set aside. So, almost two decades passed before we could move forward on this matter. It seemed that our requests would never be accepted, and even I did not anticipate what eventually happened. But looking back, I must say today that the Lord was working on our behalf.

In the second half of the 1960s [actually on October 24, 1970], I met with Elder Thomas S. Monson in *the Thuringian city of* Erfurt. It was a short meeting in my car—*the risk of being overheard inside the Erfurt meeting house was too great*—where we discussed mission issues. Suddenly, Elder Monson asked if I could imagine attending the General Conference in Salt Lake City. On the basis of my experiences in the GDR, I told him that there was no chance of that happening. But Elder Monson responded with a prophetic statement, "When the Lord considers the time to be right, you will attend a conference in Salt Lake City!"

In June 1969, Elder Monson organized the eighty-second mission of the Church in the eastern part of Germany, the present GDR. I was called to be the mission president. I had seldom been so surprised by a calling in the Church as at that time. *For seventeen years, I had served as a counselor to various mission presidents.* There were so many other worthy priesthood holders in the country, so I had only one goal, namely, to devote my entire strength to the building of the kingdom of God. I felt such a strong responsibility for the more than 4,300 members of that Dresden Mission, that I wanted to work with all my strength on their behalf. And what would be more important than to prepare a way to the temple?

I was invited by the First Presidency to attend the spring 1972 General Conference and therefore I visited the responsible office of the Dresden District Council to request permission to travel. However, turning the invitation into reality appeared hopeless at first. The Dresden District Council sent me to the

State Secretariat for Church Affairs in Berlin, so the invitation led to my direct contact with the highest government office responsible for church issues. Permission was not easily granted—for example, I had to travel more than three thousand kilometers by car in order to obtain a travel visa [the nearest U.S. embassy was in Prague]—but permission was granted. Elder Monson's prophetic words were fulfilled.

From that time forward, I was constantly in contact with the highest government office, especially in regard to the yearly travel of members of the mission presidency and their wives, to General Conference. During each of those meetings, I mentioned the wishes and needs of the Church members in our country regarding the temple.

In [1978], our mission was visited by Bishop H. Burke Peterson. We visited various branches and came to one [Groitzsch, on May 10, 1978] that had built a small meeting house through their own efforts. Bishop Peterson was interested in the needs of the members. We had spoken during our entire trip about the faithfulness of our brothers and sisters and, naturally, about their wish to travel to the temple in Zollikofen. Here, in this small branch, while visiting that meeting house, Bishop Peterson initiated a subject that I had never before considered. He said, "Why wouldn't it be possible to dedicate one or more newly renovated rooms in such a building in which members could receive their personal endowment?" He was remembering the former Endowment House in Salt Lake City, which was used before the temple was built. Bishop Peterson returned and gave this report to the First Presidency. Although I never saw that report myself, he certainly reported that the possibility existed to create an endowment room in a selected meeting house.

On May 31, 1978, during a discussion at the State Secretariat for Church Affairs in Berlin, when I again raised the issue of members traveling to the temple, it was suggested that we should build a temple in the GDR. That suggestion was entirely unexpected, and I attempted to present all the reasons why that would not be possible. I mentioned that we did not have the required number of members for a temple district. I especially mentioned the sanctity ["Unantastbarkeit"] of such a building once it has been dedicated. Also, that only the First Presidency could decide such a question. Despite all my reasons for declining the suggestion, I was politely asked to discuss the idea with the First Presidency. I brought the subject to the First Presidency through our regional representative, Dan C. Jorgensen.

In a letter dated February 2, 1979, the First Presidency informed me that I should undertake further discussions with the responsible government offices regarding an endowment house. A provisional sketch of the exterior of such a building was enclosed. I, therefore, had another meeting in Berlin in March 1979, where I was asked to discuss the matter further with the First Presidency during my visit to Salt Lake City for the spring General Conference, because such a project could only be undertaken within the so-called Special Building Program, that is, the required construction funds must be provided in freely convertible currency.

After I discussed this subject with Elder Monson and the First Presidency during General Conference, these brethren authorized me to seek a building permit for an endowment house in Karl-Marx-Stadt. I, therefore, met again with representatives of the Secretariat for Church Affairs on April 25, 1979, and was asked to submit a written application, which I sent to that office on May 17. [The full text is quoted in Chapter 15.]

In August 1979, I was summoned to a meeting in Berlin with Frau Dr. Schumann-Fitzner, the secretariat's legal counsel, and her colleagues. They informed me that our application had been received and that several questions needed to be clarified before proceeding further. We spoke about the organization of the Church, the purpose of temple ordinances for the members and our intent, as stated in my letter of May 17, to simultaneously use specific areas of the building as a meeting house for the Karl-Marx-Stadt branch, in order to simultaneously resolve two problems. Frau Dr. Schumann-Fitzner promised to support the application and to coordinate associated preparations with government offices. She noted that these preparatory activities would take about one year.

During a subsequent visit to the secretariat on March 7, 1980, I again called on Frau Dr. Schumann-Fitzner to ascertain the current status of the preparatory work. I wanted to know the project's status before I left for General Conference. Frau Dr. Schumann-Fitzner promised to give me an answer the following week, so that I could share that information during my stay in Salt Lake City. When she didn't contact me, I called her office again on March 17, 1980. She informed me that she would go to Karl-Marx-Stadt before the end of March, to negotiate with district officials regarding a building site.

Frau Dr. Schumann-Fitzner called me on April 29, 1980, and asked me to come to Berlin on May 9. I informed her that Elder Hans B. Ringger, our regional representative—and in this instance our architect—would also be present. His participation had been approved by the First Presidency, at my request, and he had been briefed on the project by the brethren during the past General Conference. At the meeting on May 9, Frau Dr. Schumann-Fitzner stated that the district council for Karl-Marx-Stadt would resolve the building site question by June 24 and that we should meet again on June 30. [However], I was also told, for the first time, that the district council planned to recommend a building site in a county seat within the district. When I asked if I had heard correctly, she confirmed that a building site within the city of Karl-Marx-Stadt would not be approved, but rather in another county within the district.

Following the meeting, Elder Ringger and I discussed the current situation and agreed that such a location would not help us resolve our two problems—a meeting house for the branch in Karl-Marx-Stadt and an endowment house. We agreed that I should undertake a personal visit to the Karl-Marx-Stadt district council, to discuss our problem directly with those people.

On May 13, 1980, I went to the Karl-Marx-Stadt district council to discuss our proposed building with the responsible persons. I explained our proposal and they confirmed that permission to build a church within the city would not be granted, because the city already had enough such buildings. After I presented my justification for building within the city's boundaries, even if on the edge of the city, and explained that the construction of an endowment house at a county seat would not resolve the need for a meeting house for the local branch, they requested more details about the organization of the Church and agreed to reconsider their previous decision and seek a building lot that met our needs.

On June 25, 1980, Frau Dr. Schumann-Fitzner called to say that her meeting with the Karl-Marx-Stadt district council did not take place as planned on the previous day and, therefore, we could not meet on June 30. She promised to provide further information as soon as possible.

I called Frau Dr. Schumann-Fitzner again on June 30, 1980, to schedule a meeting. She said it would have to wait until late July or early August, and she hoped to have a decision from the Karl-Marx-Stadt district council by then. I described my own meeting with the district council on May 13 and emphasized that the endowment house had to be in Karl-Marx-Stadt and that a county seat was unacceptable because the operation of an endowment house would require a certain number of members, which could only be found in Karl-Marx-Stadt and in no other branch in the district. She promised to thoroughly evaluate my reasoning. Therefore, I understood that she could not yet give me an answer when I called her again on July 31. She said she would let me know when she knew something.

On August 25, 1980, my first counselor, President Richter, met with a pastor of an Evangelical church in Karl-Marx-Stadt, who indicated that his church had previously asked the Karl-Marx-Stadt city council to buy the church's property in the center of the city, on which a large church had stood until 1945. However, the city had declined the offer. The pastor told President Richter that we could obtain the property immediately. So I called Frau Dr. Schumann-Fitzner the next day to discuss this property with her. However, her secretary informed me that she was on vacation until September 15 and could not meet with me until then.

On September 3, 1980, President Richter and I went to the Nicolai parsonage in Karl-Marx-Stadt to speak with the lead pastor about purchasing the property. He said he would favor our purchase of the property because the cost of its maintenance exceeded their budget. However, he could not approve the sale without the agreement of the church council, which would not meet again until October. Moreover, he explained that the property actually belonged to the state church of Saxony. I explained that we would discuss this matter with the district council in a few days, and he approved that action. *President Richter's involvement with this property was carried out only with the thought of building a meeting house for the Karl-Marx-Stadt branch. He was not aware of the plan to build an endowment house, and I had not been given authority by the First Presidency to inform him of the plan.* [When Richter was informed of the endowment house plan is not clear. However, he was present when Burkhardt told the district council of the manpower needs of an endowment house, and he participated in the subsequent consideration of the Freiberg option, as shown below.]

On September 5, 1980, President Richter and I went to the district council, where we were received by a division leader and another colleague. The division leader greeted us and thought we would be pleased to learn that they had decided to approve the building of an endowment house. However, he was surprised that we objected to building in Freiberg (or close to Freiberg, as a specific location was not stated), because we were seeking approval for a location within the city borders of Karl-Marx-Stadt. To support our objections [to the Freiberg location], I explained that

(a) an endowment house required a large number of workers, which could only be provided by the Karl-Marx-Stadt branch, and
(b) this building would be used simultaneously, in part, as the meeting house for the Karl-Marx-Stadt branch, in order to resolve the long-time problem of that branch.

The division leader indicated that the council understood the branch's problem and would try to resolve it by providing another old building, although they didn't yet know where to find such a building. But new construction would absolutely not be authorized.

I then explained to these two men that the Evangelical church had offered to sell a building lot, which would resolve the property issue. They promised to consider the matter, but offered little hope that we would be given permission to build an endowment house within the city's borders, since there were enough church buildings that were not fully utilized. They would instead attempt to identify property in one of the smaller communities surrounding Karl-Marx-Stadt that could be suggested to us. *At that time, Karl-Marx-Stadt was a major socialist city, whose leaders thought that atheism was marching triumphantly forward. It would have been a blow against the ruling ideology of the day if they had permitted a single new church building.*

Following the meeting, the mission presidency discussed the current situation and the council's offer to locate the endowment house in the Freiberg area. To avoid a possible offer of a building site in a small town outside the city limits of Karl-Marx-Stadt, which could require us to accept unfavorable commuting conditions for branch members, we accepted the necessity of earnestly fasting about the Freiberg offer and objectively considering the pros and cons of that offer.

The better we became familiar with the available facts, and as a result of our fasting *and prayer,* we found that Freiberg should not be immediately dismissed. We objectively evaluated the Freiberg area and determined the following: This city is halfway between Karl-Marx-Stadt and Dresden. The branch in Annaberg-Buchholz is also just fifty-six kilometers from Freiberg. An autobahn was recently completed from Leipzig to Dresden, which passes close by Freiberg, so that members from Leipzig only have to travel one hundred kilometers on the autobahn to reach Freiberg. In addition, there are several smaller branches in the neighborhood of Freiberg, so that we could not escape the feeling that we should not reject Freiberg. *Subsequent days of fasting strengthened these feelings, which I shared in writing with the area president [Elder Robert D. Hales] and the First Presidency.*

On January 15, 1981, I was informed by the Karl-Marx-Stadt district council, by telephone, that the county council of Freiberg needed a floor plan and an external sketch of the building in order to identify a building site. I sent those documents to Freiberg on the same day. I still felt that Freiberg was a good central location. On March 3, 1981, I received a letter from the Freiberg county council, in which I was invited to a meeting in Freiberg on March 24. I was agreeable to that date, since I was scheduled to travel to General Conference in Salt Lake City on the next day.

I took my first counselor, President Richter, to the meeting. The well-organized meeting was led by Herr Hoffmann, deputy chairman of the Freiberg county council. After greeting me as the mission president of the Church of Jesus Christ of Latter-day Saints in the GDR, he introduced the other meeting participants:

Frau Engler, Church Affairs representative to the Freiberg county council,
Herr Dr. Runge, mayor of Freiberg, and
Herr Dr. Benedix, city building architect.

Herr Hoffmann explained the purpose of the meeting and said that Freiberg County had been directed by the State Secretariat for Church Affairs in Berlin to find solutions for our project intended for the district of Karl-Marx-Stadt. Since this building project was to be implemented in the city of Freiberg, he, as the responsible representative of the county council, had invited the mayor and the city building architect to clarify related issues.

Herr Dr. Runge then explained that Freiberg had been specifically identified by the Karl-Marx-Stadt county council as the location where the project should be accomplished. Freiberg would be celebrating its eight hundredth anniversary in 1986 and would have to complete major projects before that time to improve the appearance of the city. The historic old inner city must be preserved, specifically in accordance with relevant guidelines of the United Nations, and it was not possible to change the outward appearance of that portion of the city by erecting therein a building such as we had proposed. In order to suggest an appropriate building site, more details from our architect would need to be submitted. The city architect then requested additional information in order to make further decisions.

Further questions were then posed to facilitate subsequent steps. The meeting was conducted in a very open and forthcoming manner, and we—President Richter and I—could not escape the feeling that these representatives of the county and city were proud that such a building was to be constructed in their city. I mentioned that I would be traveling to Salt Lake City the next day to discuss these matters with the General Authorities of the Church.

Herr Hoffmann stated his understanding that this house was intended for use not only by members of the Church in the GDR, but also by members in other socialistic countries and the Scandinavian countries. (That was in accordance with discussions that I had conducted earlier with the secretariat in Berlin.) He said that Freiberg officials, therefore, anticipated the arrival of many visitors from other countries and suggested that parking and overnight lodging for visitors and support staff be included in the plan at the outset. *His suggestions were consistent with issues that had already been discussed with the General Authorities and left me with a very positive feeling at that time.* After the conclusion of the meeting, President Richter and I, once again, had a strong feeling that Freiberg could actually be a good location for the endowment house.

On April 5, 1981, I attended a meeting in Salt Lake City with Elders Robert D. Hales and Hans B. Ringger, Emil Fetzer, Marvin VanDam, and Bishop H. Burke Peterson, which followed a meeting a few days earlier with Elders Monson and Hales. I was authorized at that time to pursue the Freiberg location further. Therefore, upon my return from Salt Lake City, I wrote to the Freiberg county council on April 29 that

(a) we have definitely decided on the city of Freiberg as the location for our temple, and
(b) our architects, in accordance with the suggestions and thoughts of the mayor and the city architect, are preparing detailed project plans.

On June 20, 1981, I received from our regional representative the project plans and supporting documents for further review. In addition to the temple *(and no one spoke any longer about an endowment house)* a meeting house for the Freiberg branch was included, which should simultaneously provide overnight lodging for temple visitors. In accordance with the suggestions of the General Authorities in the meeting on April 5, I sent these materials to the State Secretariat in Berlin.

No action took place in any of the government offices during the summer period. On September 22, 1981, I again visited the State Secretariat for Church Affairs in Berlin. There I was told by the newly appointed legal counsel [Günther Behncke] that the government had given a "green light" for the building in Freiberg, and I was asked to immediately submit a written application for the building, so it could be included in the Five-Year Plan 1981–1985 as a "Valuta-Sonderbau" [special building program with Western currency]. The size of the building lot and the endorsement of the project by the city of Freiberg should be mentioned therein.

[Behncke] immediately arranged for a meeting on October 1, 1981, with Herr General Director Seidel from the Ministry for Foreign Trade in Berlin. I asked Elder Monson to authorize our regional representative, Hans B. Ringger, and the Church architect [in Frankfurt], Konrad Nagele, to attend. *The time had come when the project had to be done properly, when nails with heads were required ["wo Nägel mit Köpfen gemacht werden müssten," a play on Nagele's surname, i.e., Nägel = nails]. Since it was a project costing millions, I no longer wanted to be solely responsible. The First Presidency gave both men the assignment to accompany me to this meeting. We encountered a receptive, folksy general director and had a very constructive meeting. Since both brothers, as architects, were completely familiar with the material, they had a healthy ability to evaluate the suggestions of Herr Seidel. The meeting was conducted to our complete satisfaction.*

On November 3, 1981, I sent to the Freiberg county council the details that I had promised in my letter of April 29, 1981. Regarding the selection of a building lot, I thought that the majority of our members would travel to the temple by train. Therefore, the building lot should have a good connection to the train station in Freiberg.

On November 4, I submitted written applications for construction in Freiberg to the State Secretariat for Church Affairs and the Ministry for Foreign Trade in Berlin and enclosed a file containing the details of the project.

In the meantime, I received indications that Elder Monson was having second thoughts as to whether Freiberg was really a favorable location in which to build a temple. Therefore, on November 5, I wrote to him [*and explained again our experiences and the answers to our repeated prayers*].

I had made an appointment to meet with Herr Hoffmann, the representative of the Freiberg county council, on January 19, 1982, to discuss any possible issues. Upon my arrival, I found Herr Rossow, the city building director, present. We greeted each other warmly and exchanged best wishes for the new year. I was immediately informed by Herr Hoffmann that two building lots were available for our consideration and was presented with a map of the city marked with the two locations. Herr Rossow added that each location, naturally, had advantages and disadvantages. The property near the center of the city, immediately outside the old city wall, contained the remains of an old building that would have to be removed and possibly rebuilt on another location, while the property at the edge of the city would entail a greater expense to bring in the necessary utilities. The choice would be left to me. I stated that the Church architect would visit me on January 28, and I arranged for a meeting between him and the city architect. I then visited the two sites with Brother Frank Apel, the mission's executive secretary. *The centrally located lot was indeed downtown, but next to and slightly below a heavily traveled road. Everyone traveling on that road would only have a view of the roof of the temple. The lot was also rather small, and it was above an old mine shaft that already showed signs of collapse. We both felt a stronger attraction to the property at the edge of the city. It really was at the city's end, and the public transportation to it was not very favorable. However, the lot was on a slight hill. The land had been used for agricultural production, and the lot was capable of being extended. We received a distinct impression in our hearts, that this was the place where a worthy house should be erected to the Lord.*

On February 9, Elder Hales visited the two building sites for the first time. He also chose the lot on the edge of town.

In the previously mentioned meeting of January 19, 1982, I had already received the government's approval to build not just one but two buildings. I was told that after we chose the specific location, we would need to request approval from the county council in Karl-Marx-Stadt. Herr Rossow, however, indicated that their decision could be expedited if submitted via the Foreign Trade Ministry's company, LIMEX. That approach would first need to be discussed with the appropriate authorities.

I was invited to meet with LIMEX in Berlin on February 10, 1982, where I met with the director, Frau Schiefelbein, concerning further necessary procedures. On February 26, I attended a meeting between LIMEX and the county council in Karl-Marx-Stadt where I was asked to submit further detailed information about the project. During the month of March, LIMEX informed me that a construction company and a project leader had been found, with whom I should meet on March 22 or 23. Elder Ringger and Konrad Nagele also were invited as Church architects.

On March 19, Frau Schiefelbein of LIMEX called to inform me that the Building Academy of the GDR in Dresden would oversee the project. I also spoke with the leader of the project planning department of the academy, Herr Dr. Hantzsche. Schiefelbein and Hantzsche had met at the Leipzig Fair that day and jointly contacted me. We agreed to meet on March 22 at the academy in Dresden with our Church architects. I set up a meeting with the city architect in Freiberg for the same afternoon and informed Brothers Ringger and Nagele of these appointments. Those short meetings led to the first real working sessions held later from April 21 to 23, 1982. From that time forward, each meeting agenda was determined by Brother Nagele and/or the Building Academy.

Many smaller events that I have not mentioned here were conducted by myself. In each instance, I felt the direction of our Heavenly Father. Later, for example, regarding the purchase of the property or the question of the source of power to heat the building, I experienced actual miracles. The Lord always held these matters tightly in his hand and inspired all involved so that the decisions regarding this project were always favorable to its success.

May the temple be a real blessing for everyone who will visit it, and may this holy house also be a blessing for this country and for the city of Freiberg, which has supported us so well.

Appendix I Freiberg Temple Open House and Dedication 1985

from a letter by Karlheinz Leonhardt, Temple Recorder, to friends in Utah

Today [July 7, 1985] is the first Sunday following the temple's first week of operation. . . . The doors of the open house opened promptly at 10:00 a.m. on June 1, 1985. We had about 3,600 visitors on that Saturday and almost twice that number on Sunday, for a total of 10,500 on the first weekend. It was an entirely new experience for us, that people literally came to us in masses. Even more people came to visit the temple on the following days. The normal hours of the open house were from 10:00 a.m. to 8:00 p.m. On Tuesday, June 11, about 2,000 people were still waiting to enter at closing time. They were all given an opportunity, and the last visitor left the temple at 1:16 a.m. the next morning. Earlier that afternoon, at about 6:00 p.m., we had placed two young men at the end of the several-hundred-meter-long line of waiting visitors, where people were standing four abreast, to tell those still arriving that there was no sense in joining the long line. That was no easy assignment, for the people wanted to stand in line anyhow.

People stood in those lines for hours. The longest reported waiting time during the two weeks was about seven (7) hours! On Thursday of the last week, the weather was terrible. It was cold, and it rained heavily, but hundreds waited anyhow. We asked how long they had waited in that weather and learned that some had stood in line for four hours. They arrived in the temple thoroughly soaked and frozen, for the outside temperature that day only reached forty-six degrees Fahrenheit. Nevertheless, we had more visitors that day than we had in the sunshine on the first day. When we added up the numbers at the end of the last day, about ninety thousand had gone through the temple.

We received about nine thousand addresses from people who requested personal visits or more information, and the guest books available at the exit contained many moving entries, which we had not expected. We, who organized the open house, often asked ourselves if we would have chosen to stand for several hours in the rain and wind, late into the night. But the many visitors who came thought it was worth their time. We think the spirit of God had influenced those people to come and see.

Our missionaries performed exceptionally well in those days, and they grew through these experiences, which were new to them. There were many incidents that should be recorded. Especially interesting were the disputes that our visitors conducted among themselves. One history professor responded to an Evangelical minister, who had attempted to attack the Church. He told the minister, "You should be aware that there are only two alternatives in the world, namely Mormonism or atheism. The doctrine of the Evangelical church is outdated and obsolete!" Our missionary, a very young elder who had just been ordained a few weeks earlier, didn't need to add a single word to that, because the minister left without further discussion with the professor.

We had guests from government and scientific institutions who came to see the House of the Lord, including theological and philosophical faculty from the universities in Berlin, Leipzig, Halle-Wittenberg, Rostock, etc. They all engaged in very interesting discussions and sought information about the Church, its goals and teachings. So the open house was a unique event, an opportunity to make the Church better known.

It also should be emphasized that we worked together very well with local city officials. Because of the great flood of visitors, the streets approaching the temple were hopelessly clogged. We controlled the streams of cars and the parking of hundreds of vehicles in cooperation with the police. It was an event for the city of Freiberg, whose significance extended far beyond this region. In all businesses and institutions, the only conversation that took place at free moments concerned the temple of the Mormons. We distributed about a hundred thousand leaflets to people, which generated yet more requests for information. There were many requests for the Book of Mormon, which, unfortunately, were not available for purchase, since none had been printed in the GDR in more than thirty years.

After the open house ended, we had to take care of some minor repairs. The carpeting had suffered hardly any damage, since we had provided all visitors with "shoe service," i.e., a fabric shoe cover. The young ladies of the stake had taken on this challenging assignment, which all the visitors thought was very nice and considerate. Our young ladies performed in an outstanding manner. Every evening, they fell dead asleep in their beds, anticipating the shoeing of thousands of feet again the next day. Yet they did it gladly for the holy temple. Other "services" should be mentioned also. Attendants, in addition to our missionaries, were present in and around the temple to ensure order and calm. Everyone wore a badge so the people could recognize them. We also organized people for kitchen, cleaning, transportation and other services, as well as a medical team (with a doctor, nurse, and even an examining room). We had information and directional signs on the grounds to guide the visitors. Since they stood four abreast in lines that stretched for several hundred meters, we had blocked off portions of the temple grounds and the parking areas, to prevent any mass confusion. All in all, our organization was excellent and everything functioned smoothly. City officials said, in fact, that we should help them prepare for Freiberg's eight hundredth anniversary celebration in 1986. For us, that was a confirmation that we had prepared correctly and well. The Freiberg brethren performed in an outstanding manner, regarding both their dedication of time and means.

As stated earlier, and this should be emphasized, only minor repairs needed to be made at the end of the open house. Some of the wallpaper needed to be replaced where it had been soiled at the corners. In the meeting house, some walls needed repair, because they had been too narrow for the flood of visitors. Our hand workers undertook these tasks in an exceptionally careful manner, to remove every speck of damage. Areas were painted, varnished, glued, and cleaned, so that everything would be ready for the dedication in a manner befitting a temple, with everything spotlessly clean and organized.

Then came the preparations for the dedication itself, and the closer the time came, the more hectic became the effort. Every visitor (especially those from the headquarters of the Church) wanted to be informed of the status of the preparations, and requested changes that were agreed to, and then changed again.

The cornerstone ceremony began at ten a.m. on Friday. The ninety invited guests were first assembled in the temple for an opening meeting, which representatives from the government attended. Congratulatory messages and greetings were exchanged, including messages to and from the chairman of the State Council of the GDR [Erich Honecker]. Short talks were given by President Hinckley, President Burkhardt, and guests. Afterward, the cornerstone was placed at the northeast corner of the temple by President Hinckley, and the temple president, the stake presidents in the GDR, Elder Monson, and other general authorities all participated in sealing it. A combined choir of the Leipzig and Freiberg stakes sang at this ceremony, and closing remarks by President Hinckley ended the small outside ceremony, which was recorded by the state's television personnel. A forty-second report was carried by the GDR's television network.

Thereafter, ninety-six invited guests went to the restaurant "Schützenhaus" to a festive meal. At that time, the mayor of Freiberg was presented with a gift from the Church, which was very symbolic: seated on a rock, a pioneer mother was teaching her small girl to play a violin. The mayor, himself an optimist in his philosophy of life, was evidently very impressed with the almost sixteen-inch bronze sculpture, which was quite heavy.

The Church's guests were bid farewell at the restaurant. Thereafter, a leadership meeting for the GDR region was held in the new chapel of the "Freiberg 1st Ward" or the "Templeview Ward," at which President Hinckley presided. Many of our members had their first opportunity to see the Church leaders up close and to sit directly in front of them. We were very impressed by the meeting and felt the Spirit in our midst. Then the Church leaders returned to the Hotel "Bellevue" in Dresden.

Early on Saturday, promptly at eight a.m., the dedication of the temple began with the first session, which was followed by six additional sessions, concluding with the last dedication session on Sunday at two p.m. It was a unique experience for us to attend the dedication of a temple. The Church leaders and associates all had an opportunity to speak at a session. Present were President Hinckley, Elder Monson, President Bangerter, Elder Wirthlin, Elder Sonnenberg, Elder Peterson, Elder Ringger, and Bishop Hales, all with their wives. Further attendees were President Kimball's secretary, Brother Haycock, the temple architect, Brother Fetzer, the special representative of the Church, and Brother Kennedy, as well as the head of the Church's public relations office, Brother Lindsay. Additional representatives of the temple department, video technicians, etc., attended. The dedication sessions held in the endowment room were shown in the celestial room, the two sealing rooms, in the baptistry, and in the foyer, enabling about three hundred persons to attend each session. While these sessions were not shown in the meeting house, the cornerstone ceremony on Friday was shown there, on four television sets.

The dedication sessions were conducted by various members of the General Authorities. The testimonies and thoughts that we heard from President Hinckley and Elder Monson were impressive. Elder Monson, who has such a great love for the members in our country, saw in these days the fulfillment of one of the prophecies he had expressed in his dedicatory prayer of April 27, 1975, where he said, "Heavenly Father, wilt Thou open up the way that the faithful may be accorded the privilege of going to Thy holy temple, there to receive their holy endowments and to be sealed as families for time and all eternity?" Tears came in his eyes as he remembered this prayer, which had been spoken ten years earlier on the Lößnitzberg. We all recognized that nothing is impossible with God! In those hours, I, as a member of the temple committee, was reminded of what was said by Elder Hales, presently the presiding bishop, when the temple committee was organized in Freiberg on February 8, 1982. President Spencer W. Kimball had sent us his greeting via Elder Hales, wherein he said that he would remain on this earth until the temple in Freiberg was dedicated. We all looked at one another and only comprehended it when we recorded it in our journals that evening. That statement by President Kimball, when he was almost eighty-seven years old, was made when his health was very poor. Today, after almost three and a half years, President Kimball still lives among us, and that prophetic statement has also been fulfilled. I remembered that when Bishop Hales stood at the pulpit. We were able to hear and experience many teachings and testimonies at that time, especially since I and my wife were able to attend all seven sessions in the endowment room and to experience it all firsthand. Those were strenuous days for us, but they will remain with us always.

On July 1, the temple had been prepared for its actual purpose, and the work for our ancestors began at three p.m. Ten youths from the Freiberg Ward, five boys and five girls, came to participate in the first holy ordinances. That afternoon, 643 proxy baptisms were conducted, and we all had the impression that the building had become a proper House of the Lord, because the first functions for which it was built had been conducted. In the following days, the first endowments and sealings were performed, whereby the Freiberg Ward had the privilege of coming to the temple first. The members of the Freiberg Ward had, indeed, accomplished most of the work and had earned that right.

The first week was a most difficult start for all who participated in the temple work, whether for the new temple workers, the president and his wife, his two counselors, the building caretaker, or, last but not least, the temple recorder. Everyone had to learn so much and master their assignments. But this last week showed that they can master it, even if there were many bumps and jerks along the way! (MS 15837, July 7, 1985)

Appendix J Freiberg Temple Dedicatory Prayer

President Gordon B. Hinckley gave the prayer in English in the first session on June 29, 1985, followed immediately by a German translation. Only the German version was used in the following six sessions.

> Almighty God, Thou great Elohim, in the name of Thy Beloved Son, Jesus Christ, we bow before Thee in prayer and thanksgiving. On this day of dedication our hearts turn to Thee. We thank Thee for this holy temple in this land and nation. We thank Thee for all who have made possible its building—the officers of the government who have given encouragement and made available land and materials, the architects and the builders, and all who have made possible this glorious day of dedication. We are grateful unto Thee that it is now complete and that we may present it to Thee, our beloved Father, and to Thine Only Begotten Son, the Savior of the world. Wilt Thou accept it as the offering of Thy grateful sons and daughters.
>
> Thou knowest we have long prayed that we might have a temple in our midst. Thou knowest that we love Thee, and that we love the ordinances and blessings of Thy house. We thank Thee that we are able to worship Thee in spirit and in truth. We thank Thee that we may now come to this sanctuary and feel of the hallowed influence here to be found.
>
> We are grateful that prior to this dedication tens of thousands of the people of this land visited this sacred edifice. They partook of its beauty and its influence. We humbly pray that their coming may have brought them to greater appreciation for the good and the beautiful elements of Thine everlasting truth. We are met here today as people of various nations bound by a common love for Thee our Father and Thy Son, the Redeemer of all mankind. We thank Thee for the peace which makes this possible and for the hospitality of this nation in permitting us to join together in this house of sacred worship. Our hearts

are touched by the bond of fellowship we feel one with another. Strengthen that bond, and may we reach out in a spirit of love and appreciation and respect for one another. This gospel, which so deeply touches our lives, is the gospel of peace. May we grow in knowledge and understanding of Thine everlasting plan for Thy children, Thy sons and daughters of all nations.

We thank Thee for the consecrations of Thy people which have supplied the means for the building of this sacred house. Bless them each one. Smile with favor upon them and may they feel of Thy divine love. We pray that all who have contributed to this sacred undertaking shall be blessed of Thee with the good things of the earth and the divine things of heaven, and that all shall live with gratitude unto Thee and thanksgiving for Thy great beneficence.

Father, we thank Thee for the measure of peace to be found in the world, and pray that it may continue and grow that men and women everywhere may use their time, their talents, and their means for good. May understanding and respect increase between the nations of the earth.

Comfort and sustain the widow and her children. Soften the loneliness of the bereaved husband who has lost his companion. May each know that through Thy divine providence the sacred bonds of marriage may be made eternal and everlasting. Thou hast restored the priesthood which will be exercised in this house, binding in the heavens as it binds upon the earth, sealing together husbands and wives, parents and children, in generations of families united eternally.

Now, beloved Father, in the authority of the Holy Priesthood in us vested and in the name of Jesus Christ, we dedicate unto Thee and unto Thy Son this the Freiberg DDR Temple of the Church of Jesus Christ of Latter-day Saints. We dedicate it as Thy holy habitation. Wilt Thou accept of it, dear Father, and wilt Thou sanctify it that all who come here may feel the presence of Thy Holy Spirit. We consecrate it for the great and holy work which will be performed herein. May it be as a bright and shining star to Thy faithful sons and daughters. May the truths herein taught and the ordinances herein performed be accepted with thankful hearts by those who love Thee as our Father and our God.

Bless this house, we pray Thee. May Thy watchcare be over it. May it be preserved from the storms of nature and from any defiling hand or act of man. May it be a place of holiness, a house of peace, a sanctuary of righteousness. May those who enter its doors come with clean hands and pure thoughts. May they leave with joy and peace in their hearts, and sing songs of thanksgiving and worship unto Thee.

Bless the fathers and the mothers among Thy saints that they may be examples to their children, and nurture them with love and truth. Bless the children that they shall honor and respect and love their parents. May Thy peace abide in the homes of Thy people. Smile with favor upon them and grant unto them Thy rich and cherished blessings. May none go hungry or naked or without shelter from storms that blow about them. May knowledge of Thee and Thy ways grow in their hearts and minds. May their love for Thee strengthen. May they reach out with love to their fellowmen, walking in righteousness and faith as becomes the saints of God.

To Thee we lift our voices in anthems of praise. To Thee we pledge our love. To Thee we pray with faith and gratitude. May this day long be remembered in the annals of Thy Church. May it be recalled with gratitude and appreciation. May it mark the beginning of a new day of gladness for Thy people. May their tears turn to smiles. May their burdens be lightened. May their cares be lifted. May the assurance that Thou art near strengthen every heart.

Eternal Father, accept of our thanks. Hear our prayer. Smile with favor upon us. Forgive our sins and shortcomings. Shelter and protect us from evil. Accept of our offering of this house. Bless it from the footings to the top of the tower, its walls, its roof, its halls and rooms and altars, and all the furnishings and fixtures thereof.

As we dedicate this house we dedicate ourselves anew to Thee and to Thine eternal purposes. O God, Thou great everlasting Father, for these things we pray as Thy thankful children and bear testimony of Thee and Thy Beloved Son, in His Holy Name, even the name of the Redeemer of the world, the Lord Jesus Christ, amen. (*Church News*, June 30, 1985; online at www.ldschurchtemples.com/freiberg/prayer)

Note: The temple was renovated, expanded, and rededicated by President Hinckley on September 7, 2002.

Appendix K Membership Statistics

When the East German Mission was organized in 1938, it included eastern German provinces that were taken from Germany after the war. Statistics for 1939–1942 include those provinces but do not include Thuringia, which was in the West German Mission at that time. Thuringia was added to the East German Mission after the war, since it was under Soviet control. In September 1947, the West German districts of Schleswig-Holstein and Hannover were added to the East German Mission, as were the districts of Bremen and Hamburg in July 1954. However, the western districts are not included in the membership statistics for 1948–1961.

In 1957, the East German Mission was renamed the North German Mission. In June 1961, that mission office moved to Hamburg, and a new Berlin Mission became responsible for the GDR districts. The Berlin Mission was closed in 1965, and the GDR was again placed in the North German Mission. Total mission membership at that time was about 7,100, including 4,750 members in the GDR. In 1969, a new Dresden Mission became responsible for the members in the GDR. Anecdotal reports indicate that between 3,500 to 4,500 members lived in the GDR thereafter.

1939–1942

Table K.1. Statistics for the years 1939–1942 are from the *Sonntagstern* and the *Sonntagsgruß*. The number of branches in 1940 and 1942 are shown in parentheses.

District	1939		1940	1941		1942
Berlin	1270	(10)	1274	1186	(9)	1291
Breslau	808	(7)	824	830	(7)	840
Chemnitz	1051	(6)	1062	1058	(6)	1022
Danzig	200	(3)	194	201	(3)	212
Dresden	775	(8)	781	775	(8)	766
Hindenburg	72	(3)	75	79	(3)	79
Königsberg	781	(5)	805	800	(5)	798
Leipzig	606	(7)	562	564	(6)	562
Rostock	248	(4)	251	249	(4)	242
Schneidemühl	277	(6)	282	272	(5)	269
Spreewald	351	(4)	346	347	(4)	344
Stettin	479	(4)	477	478	(4)	469
Zwickau	690	(8)	686	675	(8)	666
Total	7608	(75)	7619	7514	(72)	7560

Membership 1948–1961

Table K.2. Total Members and Elders

District/Branch	1948	Elders	1959	Elders	1961	Elders
Chemnitz/K-M-S	992	62	793	73	688	83
Chemnitz/K-M-S	553	41	446	33	422	47
Freiberg	204	8	204	27	142	22
Gr. Hartmannsdorf	52	3	39	5	32	5
Mittweida	58	3	50	5	54	8
Döbeln	84	5	54	3	38	1
Nössige	41	2	(a)			
Dresden	949	46	861	67	806	68
Dresden	351	9	353	27	332	26
Cottbus	216	16	193	18	164	18
Görlitz	141	6	106	7	102	8
Forst	88	7	90	6	82	6
Bischofswerda	89	7	66	6	73	7
Bautzen	64	1	53	3	53	3

District/Branch	1948	Elders	1959	Elders	1961	Elders
Leipzig	932	32	765	54		
Leipzig	432	16	378	30		
Halle	85	4	58	4		
Magdeburg	75	2	64	4		
Naumburg	58	2	37	1		
Dessau	42	1	30	1		
Bernburg	50	1	51	5		
Halberstadt	35	1	43	2		
Köthen	23	1	23	5		
Groitzsch	29	3	27	2		
Delitzsch	35	1	54			
Aschersleben	68	0				
Zwickau	925	49	790	59	729	60
Zwickau	270	12	200	16	180	13
Plauen	146	9	128	8	118	8
Werdau	148	6	147	8	133	12
Hohenstein-Ernsthal	153	6	126	7	83	6
Wilkau	63	5	58	5	60	6
Planitz	84	8	83	8	70	8
Meerane	61	3	48	7	53	7
Auerbach					32	0
Thuringia	580	27	437	22	401	20
Erfurt	216	12	138	7	205	8
Gotha	52	0	40	1	(b)	
Gera	124	8	128	9	107	8
Weimar	109	4	87	4	89	4
Nordhausen	58	2	44	1	(b)	
Pössneck	21	1				
Erzgebirge	478	42	377	47	364	48
Annaberg-Buchholz	353	33	299	39	290	40
Schwarzenberg	62	7	63	8	59	8
Auerbach	35	0	—	—	(c)	
Wolfsgrün/Blauenthal	28	2	15	0	15	0
Mecklenburg	506	22	420	27	397	29
Rostock	115	8	91	6	91	7
Neubrandenburg	93	3	78	2	77	2
Schwerin	78	4	65	4	54	6
Demmin	58	4	43	3	43	2
Prenzlau	48	3	35	4	33	5
Wolgast	52	0	108	8	99	7
Greifswald	36	0	(d)			
Barth	26	0	(d)			

District/Branch	1948	Elders	1959	Elders	1961	Elders
East Berlin	674	36				
East	249	18				
Central	200	8				
Potsdam	52	1				
Rathenow	54	3				
Eberswalde	37	1				
Brandenburg	47	4				
Leest	35	1				
Total	6036	316	5043	381	4585	392
West Berlin	841	58				
West	203	18				
Neukölln	199	8				
North	163	12				
Charlottenburg	145	15				
Spandau	131	5				

(a) to Dresden District; (b) to Erfurt Branch; (c) to Zwickau District; (d) to Wolgast Branch (LR 2428 29, LR 2428 30)

Notes

Introduction

1. When capitalized, "Church" refers to the Church of Jesus Christ of Latter-day Saints, as do the terms "LDS Church" and "Mormons."
2. Henry Burkhardt to Dr. Helmut Obst, February 28, 1974, DMO.
3. Raymond Kuehne, "The Freiberg Temple: An Unexpected Legacy of a Communist State and a Faithful People," *Dialogue: A Journal of Mormon Thought* 37, no. 2 (Summer 2004): 95–131.
4. "The Wende" (meaning "a turn or change") is the common German word to identify the political and social events associated with the end of the GDR regime.

Chapter 1, Germany before 1945

1. Andrew Jenson, *Encyclopedic History of the Church*, 281.
2. Gilbert Scharffs, *Mormonism in Germany*, 58–59.
3. Daniel H. Ludlow, ed., *Encyclopedia of Mormonism*, 471.
4. Jenson, 282.
5. Ludlow, 472.
6. Klopfer was initially addressed in letters from Utah as Mission Supervisor, later as Acting Mission President and also as President. His successor, Richard Ranglack, did not typically use the title of president, but it does appear on some documents. When Elder Benson came to Berlin in March 1946, he officially designated Ranglack as the "mission president," and he served in that capacity until the arrival of Walter Stover in November 1946.
7. Preston R. Nibley, "The East German Mission," *Relief Society Magazine*, August 1956.
8. The mission's monthly newsletter, *Sonntagstern* (Sunday Star), was changed to *Sonntagsgruß* (Sunday Greeting) after the name *stern* was prohibited by the Nazi government.

Chapter 2, Soviet Military Administration 1945–1949

1. Donald C. Corbett, "Records from the Ruins," 20.
2. Melani Schiele, *In Deutschland auf Mission*, 190–191.
3. Walter Fassmann, "A History of Walter Fassmann," 33-34.

4. Horst Dohle, ed., *SED und Kirche: Eine Dokumentation ihrer Beziehungen* (cited hereafter as *SED und Kirche*), vol. 1, ix.
5. Ibid, 4.
6. Edith Krause, *Walter Krause in Seiner Zeit*, 110.
7. Corbett, "Records from the Ruins," 5–9.

Chapter 3, The Church-State Relationship in the GDR

1. Hans-Hinrich Jenssen and Herbert Trebs, eds., *Theologisches Lexikon*, 321–323.
2. Ibid., 110.
3. The SED was generally called the Communist Party, both in conversation and in documents cited herein. However, the SED's literature distinguished the current socialist society from communism. The Party's goal was to create a socialist society that served as the foundation for a gradual transition to communism in the future.
4. *SED und Kirche*, vol. 1, 10.
5. Ibid., 4.
6. Ibid., 54.
7. Ibid., 66.
8. Ibid., 98.
9. Ibid., 106.
10. Ibid., 153.
11. Ibid.
12. *Joachim Heise, SED und Kirche*, vol. 2, 281–282.
13. Ibid., 284–291.
14. Ibid., 306–307.
15. Horst Dohle, "Der 6. März 1978," *Berliner Dialog-Hefte*, 2/1988, 28.
16. Ibid., 21.
17. Ibid., 30–33.
18. *SED und Kirche*, vol. 2, 413–430.
19. Ibid., 552–556.
20. Ibid., 505.

Chapter 5, Life Prior to the Berlin Wall 1949–1961

1. David O. McKay journal, June 7, 1957.

Chapter 6, Living with the Wall 1961–1989

1. David O. McKay journal, August 24, 1961.
2. Ibid., September 6, 1961.
3. Ibid., September 21, 1961.
4. Henry Burkhardt, "Wie es zum Bau des Freiberger Tempels kam" [How the Freiberg Temple Came to Be].
5. "Profit und Prophet," *Wochenpost*, 1974.

Chapter 7, How Mormons Defined Citizenship

1. Karlheinz Leonhardt, "Freiberg, die ersten hundert Jahre."

Chapter 9, Church Youth Programs

1. *Theologisches Lexikon*, 112.

Chapter 11, The Old Meeting Houses

1. Manfred Schütze, "Was Du Ererbt von Deinen Vätern."

Chapter 12, Importing Church Literature

1. Edith Krause, *Walter Krause in Seiner Zeit*, 201.

Chapter 13, Financial Administration

1. Walter Fassmann, "A History of Walter Fassman," 37.
2. Ibid., 39.
3. Ibid., 42.

Chapter 14, Improved Relations in the 1970s and 1980s

1. *Neues Deutschland*, July 4, 1986.
2. Gottfried Richter, "Man nennt sie Mormonen: Die Kirche Jesu Christi der Heiligen der Letzten Tage."
3. "Ein Indianer auf Besuch im Karl-May-Museum," June 5, 1987.

Chapter 15, The Origins of the Freiberg Temple

1. This chapter is a revision and extension of the author's article, "The Freiberg Temple: An Unexpected Legacy of a Communist State and a Faithful People," *Dialogue: A Journal of Mormon Thought* 37, no. 2 (Summer 2004): 95–131.
2. Henry Burkhardt, "Wie es zum Bau des Freiberger Tempels kam."
3. Ibid.
4. Ibid.
5. *Stern*, April 1995, 27–33.
6. Burkhardt, "Wie es zum Bau des Freiberger Tempels kam."
7. Ibid.
8. Ibid.
9. Ibid.
10. Ibid.
11. Ibid.
12. Personal communication from Karlheinz Leonhardt, Temple Recorder, February 2004.
13. Viewed at www.ldschurchtemples.com, February 2004. Until recently, that website also included a common belief that the GDR did not allow a statue of Moroni to be placed on the temple. However, President Burkhardt said that the Church never requested the statue, but, in his opinion, it would have been approved if requested.
14. Regional Council minutes, July 14, 1990, copy in author's possession.
15. Floor plan in author's possession.
16. Henry Burkhardt to Melani Schiele, July 2002, in Melani Schiele, *In Deutschland auf Mission*.
17. Freiberg postcards from 1987, in the author's possession.

Chapter 17, The Honecker-Monson Meeting 1988

1. This chapter is an extension of the author's article, "How Missionaries Entered East Germany: The 1988 Monson-Honecker Meeting," *Dialogue: A Journal of Mormon Thought* 39, no. 2 (Winter 2006): 107–137.

2. Hans-Joachim Beeskow, interview with Horst Dohle, June 1997.
3. Horst Dohle, *Klaus Gysi*, 56.
4. Ibid., 61.
5. "German Democratic Republic grants rights for missionary service," *Church News*, November 12, 1988.

Chapter 18, Missionaries Enter the GDR 1989

1. Helmut Obst, "Das Verhältnis zu den Religionsgemeinschaften in der DDR," 52–53.

Bibliography

The bibliography begins with the three main categories of records that became the foundation of this book: LDS mission records, GDR government records, and oral interviews with Church members who lived in the GDR. These three categories are followed by other published records and manuscript sources.

LDS Mission Records

The following mission files were viewed at the LDS Church Archives in Salt Lake City and are listed by their call number. These same call numbers also are cited in the text instead of in the endnotes. Most mission files are composed of a variety of documents, which are not paginated or are paginated only within subsections of the file. Therefore, most documents quoted in the book must be located in the files by date rather than by page:

LR 691 2 Berlin Mission, Manuscript history and historical reports.
LR 691 25 Berlin Mission, Mission president's correspondence 1959–1966.
LR 694 23 Berlin Stake, 25 Years 1961–1986.
LR 2428 2 East German Mission, Manuscript history.
LR 2428 25 North German Mission, President's files 1959–1973.
LR 2428 29 North German Mission, Maps and Statistics 1948.
LR 2428 30 North German Mission, Membership lists 1945–1961.
LR 2428 38 East German Mission, Officer lists 1946–1949.
LR 2428 39 East German Mission, General policy file 1947–1955.
LR 2428 40 North German Mission, District conference reports 1961.
LR 2428 48 North German Mission, Office files 1945–1969.
LR 2428 51 East German Mission, Freud-Echo conference 1948.
LR 2428 54 East German Mission, Lesson manuals 1941–1949, 1987.
LR 2428 56 North German Mission, Missionary files 1952–1962.
LR 2428 57 North German Mission, Auxiliary training meeting minutes 1961–1969.
LR 3457 22 Groitzsch Branch, Dresden Mission 1963–1984.
LR 5392 24 Mecklenburg District, Dresden Mission, General minutes 1945–1977.
LR 10260 21 Wolfsgrün Branch, East German Mission, General minutes 1945–1950.
LR 2012570 3 Leipzig Mission, Annual historical reports 1989–1990.
* CR 103 109 Proposed GDR physical facilities 1987.

* CR 271 40	European Mission, Thomas E. McKay Correspondence 1939–1946.
* CR 271 5	European Mission, Historical reports, 1946–1950.
* CR 374 16	Material for a Compiled History, 1988–1989.

* Files viewed with permission.

The records of the Dresden Mission (1969–1984), as well as other records kept in the Dresden office prior to and after these years, are cited in the text with the notation "DMO." They were viewed at the Freiberg Temple Annex in Germany. Photo copies and/or typescripts of documents from that source are in the author's possession.

Records of the German Democratic Republic

GDR government records in the LDS Church Archives also are cited in the text by their call numbers, which begin with the letters MS. These records were extracted from the files of the Stiftung Archiv der Parteien und Massenorganisationen der DDR (SAPMO), a German foundation established to preserve and make available information related to the political parties and mass organizations of the GDR.

MS 13216	Socialist Unity Party, Files related to Mormonism 1947–1959.
MS 13798	SAPMO, Selected documents 1954–1988.
MS 13918	SAPMO, Documents from the Secretary for Church Affairs 1950–1990.
MS 15346	Erich Honecker, Letter May 24, 1988.

The author has copies of additional GDR records from the SAPMO files. They are cited in the text by their SAPMO file numbers, which begin with the letters DO or DY.

Oral Interviews

The third major category of records used in this book consists of approximately forty oral interviews conducted by Church archivists between 1989 and 1993 plus thirty interviews conducted by the author between 2003 and 2007. Each interview excerpt begins with the interviewee's name and ends with the year. Typescripts of interviews between 1989 and 1991 may be accessed in the LDS Church Archives by the individual's name. They are in the original language, usually German. Interviews conducted by myself from 2003 to 2006 are in my possession.

Published Sources

Dähn, Horst and Helga Gotschlich, eds. *Und führe uns nicht in Versuchung: Jugend im Spannungsfeld von Staat und Kirche in der SBZ/DDR 1945 bis 1989*. Berlin: Metropol Verlag, 1998.

Dohle, Horst. "Der 6. März 1978." *Berliner Dialog-Hefte, Zeitschrift für den christlich-marxistischen Dialog*, vol. 2, 1998.

———. *SED und Kirche: Eine Dokumentation ihrer Beziehungen*, vol. 2, 1968–1989. Edited by Frédéric Hartweg. Neukirchen/Vluyn: Neukirchen Verlag, 1995.

Dohle, Horst, and Joachim Heise, eds. *Klaus Gysi: Staatssekretär für Kirchenfragen 1979–1988*. Berlin: Eulenspiegel-Verlagsgruppe, 2002.

Gaunt, LaRene. "Elder Robert D. Hales vom Kollegium der Zwölf - Eine Ehrenvolle Rückkerhr." *Der Stern*, April 1995, 27–33.

Heise, Joachim. *SED und Kirche. Eine Dokumentation ihrer Beziehungen*, vol. 1, 1946–1967. Edited by Frédéric Hartweg. Neukirchen/Vluyn: Neukirchen Verlag, 1995.

Jenson, Andrew. *Encyclopedic History of The Church of Jesus Christ of Latter-day Saints.* Salt Lake City: Deseret News Publishing Company, 1945.

Jenssen, Hans–Hinrich, and Herbert Trebs, eds. *Theologisches Lexikon*. Berlin: Union Verlag, 1981.

Die Kirche Jesu Christi der Heiligen der Letzten Tage: Die Gemeinde in Leipzig. 1989.

Die Kirche Jesu Christi der Heiligen der Letzten Tage Stellt Sich Vor. 1988.

Krause, Edith. *Walter Krause in Seiner Zeit*. Hamburg: Mein Buch, 2005.

Ludlow, Daniel H., ed. *Encyclopedia of Mormonism*, 4 vols. New York: Macmillan Publishing, 1992.

Monson, Thomas S. *Faith Rewarded: A Personal Account of Prophetic Promises to the East German Saints*. Salt Lake City: Deseret Book Company, 1996.

Nibley, Preston R. "The East German Mission." *Relief Society Magazine*, August 1956.

Obst, Helmut. "Das Verhältnis zu den Religionsgemeinschaften in der DDR." In *Kirchen, Freikirchen und Religionsgemeinschaften in der DDR*. Edited by Hubert Kirchner, 46–61. Berlin: Kirchener, 1989.

Richter, Gottfried. "Man nennt sie Mormonen: Die Kirche Jesu Christi der Heiligen der Letzten Tage." *Begegnung: Zeitschrift für Katholiken in Kirche und Gesellschaft*, October 1985.

Scharffs, Gilbert. *Mormonism in Germany: A History of the Church of Jesus Christ of Latter-day Saints in Germany between 1840 and 1970*. Salt Lake City: Deseret Book Company, 1970.

Newspaper Articles (in chronological order)

"Verschleppte Kirchenbücher aufgefunden," *Neue Zeit*, June 9, 1946.

"Die Heiligen der letzten Tage, Hauptbrüder der getauften Schieber/Blinde 'Schäfchen' lernen sehen." *Berliner Zeitung*, June 8, 1956.

"Prophet und Profit." *Wochenpost*, Nr. 51, 1974.

"Konstruktives, freimütiges Gespräch beim Vorsitzenden des Staatsrates." *Neues Deutschland*, March 7, 1978.

"Unsere Väter verkündten Frieden: Mormonen protestieren gegen Bau der USA Interkontinentalrakete MX." *Neue Zeit*, July 16, 1981.

"Kirchenpräsident Burkhardt an Erich Honecker." *Neues Deutschland*, July 4, 1986.

"Ein Mormone hat den Segen der Staatspartei: Frank Apel genießt Religionsfreiheit und ist Privatunternehmer." *Münchner Abendzeitung*, October 25, 1986.

"Ein Indianer auf Besuch im Karl-May-Museum." *Sächsischen Zeitung*, June 5, 1987.

"Religion ist eine Norm des sozialistischen Alltags." *Hamburger Abendblatt*, August 28, 1987.

"Erklärung der Präsidentschaft der Kirche Jesu Christi der Heiligen der Letzten Tage in der DDR anläßlich der Begegnung mit dem Vorsitzenden des Staatsrates der DDR, Erich Honecker, am 28. Oktober 1988." *Neues Deutschland*, October 29, 1988.

"Begegnung Erich Honeckers mit kirchlichen Repräsenten." *Neues Deutschland*, October, 29, 1988.

"Sozialismus entspricht christlichen Zielen und Wertvorstellungen, Repräsentanten der Kirche Jesu Christi der Heiligen der Letzten Tage bei Erich Honecker." *Tagezeitung der CDU in den Bezirken Dresden und Karl-Marx-Stadt*, October 29/30, 1988.

"German Democratic Republic grants rights for missionary service." *Church News*, November 12, 1988.

"Opportunities unfold in 'week of wonder.'" *Church News*, November 12, 1988.

"Unsere Ziele, Stärkung der Republik und Friedenserhalt: Präsidentschaft der Kirche Jesu Christi der Heiligen der Letzten Tage in der DDR an Erich Honecker." *Neues Deutschland*, November 24, 1988.

"German Democratic Republic to Welcome Missionary Work." *Ensign*, January 1989.

"Altes muß Neuem weichen: Schweriner Kirchengemeinde baut neu." *Schweriner Blitz*, May 7, 1995.

Manuscript Sources

Amtsgericht, Berlin. Registration of "Verein der Deutschen Mission der Kirche Jesu Christi der Heiligen der Letzten Tage," Number 6779, April 1, 1943. Photocopy in author's possession.

Beeskow, Hans-Joachim. Interview with Dr. Horst Dohle, Berliner LeseZeichen, June 1997. Copied June 3, 2006, at www.luise-berlin.de/lesezei/Blz97_06/text03.htm.

Behncke, Günther. "Bescheinigung," May 2, 1985. Confirmation of state recognition of the legal capacity of the LDS Church. Photocopy in author's possession.

Burkhardt, Henry, Frank Apel, and Manfred Schütze to Staatssekretär Gysi, March 3, 1988. Copy in author's possession. Birthday greetings.

Burkhardt, Henry, Frank Apel, and Manfred Schütze to Staatssekretär Löffler, August 25, 1989. Copy in author's possession. Birthday greetings.

Burkhardt, Henry J. "Wie es zum Bau des Freiberger Tempels kam." 1983. Unpublished typescript in author's possession.

Corbett, Donald C. "Visit of Elder Ezra Taft Benson to Berlin, Germany, 1946." Unpublished typescript in author's possession. Corbett arrived in Berlin with occupation forces in August 1945. He was LDS servicemen's group leader in Berlin.

———. "Records from the Ruins." Unpublished typescript in author's possession.

Fassmann, Walter. "A History of Walter Fassmann." Unpublished manuscript in author's possession. District president and counselor to President Walter Stover.

Gäbler, Eberhard, and Elfriede Gäbler. Unpublished typescript of branch history and photocopies of government documents regarding the transfer of ownership of the Forst meeting house to the Church, 1972–1981, in author's possession.

Gäbler, Elfriede. Unpublished typescripts of ballad evenings and theatrical programs performed in the Leipzig district by the Leipzig branch MIA 1949–1952, in author's possession.

Goliasch, Herbert. "Pionierfahrt der Jugend der Berliner Mission 1962." Unpublished typescript in author's possession. Member of Leipzig branch.

Grünewald, Herbert. "Cottbus, eine Zeit intensiven Gemeindelebens." 2000. Unpublished typescript in author's possession. Grünewald lived in Cottbus.

Hinckley, Gordon B. "Freiberg Temple, Dedicatory Prayer," *Church News*, June 30, 1985. www.ldschurchtemples.com/freiberg/prayer

Kimball, Spencer W. Typescript notes of visits to Berlin, August 1955 and January 1962, in author's possession.

Kommission zur Verteilung der ausländischen Spenden. "Mormonen-Spende." October 22, 1948. Photocopy in author's possession.

"Konferenz-Führer." Photocopy of an eight-page printed program of the mission conference in Leipzig, June 5–11, 1946. Photocopy in author's possession.

Krause, Walter, and Joachim Lehnig. "Lager Cottbus." Unpublished typescript in author's possession. Krause was branch president, Lehnig lived in Cottbus meeting house.

Langheinrich, Paul, to Henry Burkhardt, June 9, 1953. Registration of LDS Church with SMAD. Photocopy in author's possession.

Lehnig, Fritz, to Walter Kindt, February 18, 1947. Photocopy in author's possession. Conditions in the Cottbus meeting house.

McKay, David Oman. "David Oman McKay Papers," MS 688, Manuscript Division, J. Willard Marriott Library, University of Utah.

Leonhardt, Karlheinz. "Anmeldung einer Veranstaltung." June 28, 1985. Request for permission to hold a luncheon in a restaurant for invited guests at the Freiberg Temple dedication. Photocopy in author's possession.

———. *Die ersten hundert Jahre: Eine Geschichte der Gemeinde Freiberg.* Privately published, 2000. Freiberg Temple Recorder. Copy in author's possession.

Paul, Wolfgang. "Richtlinien für Missionare in der DDR." February 23, 1989. Photocopy in the author's possession. He entered the GDR in 1989 as mission president.

"Protokoll über die Organisierung des Tempelkomitees der Dresdener Mission." Unpublished typescript in author's possession.

Schiele, Melani. *In Deutschland auf Mission: Erinnerungen, Tagebuchaufzeichnungen und Zeugnisse ehemaliger Missionare.* Privately published, 2003. In author's possession.

Schütze, Manfred. "Was Du Ererbt von Deinen Vätern," 1988. Photocopy of excerpts from an unpublished typescript in author's possession.

"Spatenstichfeierlichkeit Freiberg." The Freiberg Temple Committee's account of the groundbreaking ceremony and the dedicatory prayer by Elder Thomas S. Monson. Unpublished typescript in the author's possession.

[Unknown]. "Unsere Chorreise: Ein Bericht über die Reise des Chores der Ostdeutschen Mission, 1949." Unpublished typescript in author's possession.

Warnke, Jürgen, to Günther Behncke, March 15, 1990. Photocopy in author's possession. Warnke was legal counsel to the Church in Frankfurt.

———. to Hans. B. Ringger, January 4, 1988. Photocopy in author's possession.

Werner, Eberhard. Leipzig Branch history. Excerpts from the typescript in author's possession.

Additional Manuscript Sources

The following additional manuscript sources are located in the LDS Church Archives and are cited directly in the text with their archive file number:

MS 1359	Justus Ernst, History of the German-speaking missions.
MS 2002	Alfred Schulz, Autobiography.
MS 5382 1	Paul Langheinrich, Papers 1946–1970.
MS 5382 2	Paul Langheinrich, Scrapbook 1935–1953.
MS 7648	Paul Langheinrich, Papers 1945–1950.
MS 8242	Alfred Paul Schulz, Papers 1921–1950.
MS 9471	Erich Sellner, Journal 1945–1950.
MS 13797	Thomas Manfred Heller, Newspaper clippings 1955–1991.
MS 14071	Kasmira Würscher, Autobiographical Writings.
MS 14466	Arnold Schmidt, The History of Wolfsgrün.
MS 15837	Karlheinz Leonhart, Letter, July 7, 1985. Temple Open House.

MS 16395	Alma Sonne, Correspondence 1946–1950.
MS 16593	Walter Schiele, Papers 1968–1969.
MS 16594	Gottfried Richter, Papers 1983, 1989, 1993.
MS 17696	Paul Langheinrich, Interview 1976.
MS 17716	Eberhard Werner, Leipzig Branch Documents 1968–1969.
MS 18389	Wolfgang Kelm, Mission Journal 1949–1952.